The Public Speaking Playbook

Fourth Edition

We dedicate the fourth edition of this book to our grandchildren, Beckham Myles and Mackenzie Naya, both of whom since learning to speak have been informing and persuading us; our parents, Nan and Wesley Gamble, and Martha and Marcel Kwal; our children, Lindsay and Matthew, and their respective loves, Dan and Tong; and all our students. Together, they represent our circle of life, love, and learning.

Sara Miller McCune founded SAGE Publishing in 1965 to support the dissemination of usable knowledge and educate a global community. SAGE publishes more than 1,000 journals and over 800 new books each year, spanning a wide range of subject areas. Our growing selection of library products includes archives, data, case studies, and video. SAGE remains majority owned by our founder and after her lifetime will become owned by a charitable trust that secures the company's continued independence.

Los Angeles | London | New Delhi | Singapore | Washington DC | Melbourne

The Public Speaking Playbook

Fourth Edition

Teri Kwal Gamble

College of New Rochelle

Michael W. Gamble

New York Institute of Technology

Los Angeles | London | New Delhi
Singapore | Washington DC | Melbourne

FOR INFORMATION:

SAGE Publications, Inc.
2455 Teller Road
Thousand Oaks, California 91320
E-mail: order@sagepub.com

SAGE Publications Ltd.
1 Oliver's Yard
55 City Road
London, EC1Y 1SP
United Kingdom

SAGE Publications India Pvt. Ltd.
B 1/I 1 Mohan Cooperative Industrial Area
Mathura Road, New Delhi 110 044
India

SAGE Publications Asia-Pacific Pte. Ltd.
18 Cross Street #10–10/11/12
China Square Central
Singapore 048423

Acquisitions Editor: Charles Lee

Content Development Editor: Megan O'Heffernan

Marketing Manager: Victoria Velasquez

Production Editor: Veronica Stapleton Hooper

Copy Editor: Talia Greenberg

Typesetter: diacriTech

Cover Designer: Lysa Becker

Printed in Canada

Library of Congress Cataloging-in-Publication Data
Number: 2022033826

Names: Gamble, Teri Kwal, author. | Gamble, Michael W., author.
Title: The public speaking playbook / Teri Kwal Gamble, College of New Rochelle, Michael W. Gamble, New York Institute of Technology.
Description: Fourth Edition. | Thousand Oaks, California : SAGE Publications, Inc, [2024] | Includes bibliographical references and index.
Identifiers: LCCN 2022033826 | ISBN 9781071854488 (spiral bound) | ISBN 9781071854532 (epub)
Classification: LCC PN4129.15. G36 2024 | DDC 808.5/1--dc23 LC record available at https://lccn.loc.gov/2022033826

This book is printed on acid-free paper.

23 24 25 26 27 10 9 8 7 6 5 4 3 2 1

BRIEF CONTENTS

PART VI   INFORMATIVE PRESENTATIONS

PART VII   SPEAKING TO PERSUADE

PART VIII   SPECIALIZED SPEAKING CONTEXTS

CONTENTS

PREFACE

Writing the fourth edition of *The Public Speaking Playbook* was energizing for us and especially meaningful, as we accomplished it during the COVID-19 pandemic. With the realization that college campuses in the time of COVID are likely to be a mix of virtual and face-to-face classes, we wrote to this reality. We hope you find that the attention we give to recent events improves the *Playbook,* making it even more relevant, readable, and engaging than the text's prior editions. As with each of the previous editions, our goal in preparing the fourth edition was faithful to our original objective—to provide a resource that coaches students on how to prepare, practice, and present speeches for diverse and differently sized audiences who gather in an array of forums—from classrooms to community centers, from organizational to public venues, from face-to-face to virtual settings.

Playbooks continue to serve multiple audiences—athletes, actors, musicians, dancers, politicians, community organizers, leaders, and speakers—who rely on them to master their craft, improve their skills, and accomplish their goals. All work under pressure, achieve individually or as part of a team or ensemble, and regularly plan and practice and evaluate in order to grow and improve performance outcomes. We continue to weave the *Playbook* analogy throughout the pages of this text, repeatedly demonstrating how plans of action get results. Reviewing, practicing, and executing the right plays takes the fear out of public speaking and frees students to share their interests and knowledge, passions, and concerns with others.

By design, the fourth edition contents reflect the times in which we now live, with more coverage devoted to developing skill in presenting virtually in addition to before live audiences. The COVID-19 generation of students will continue to be shaped by their pandemic experiences. This fourth edition represents our desire to respond to their interaction expectations and needs. To this end, the *Playbook* retains its interactive focus, coaching students in building skills and training them actively in presentation fundamentals. Each *Playbook* section contains brief learning modules that let students get to the "how-to" quickly, offering the essentials needed to work both independently and collaboratively in preparing, rehearsing, and presenting a speech. The *Playbook's* eight main parts are divided into a series of "plays" that facilitate students working play by play to deliver winning presentations at increasingly higher levels. Embedded in every section are objectives, coaching tips, new self-assessment activities, exercises to build skills and reinforce key competencies, and a game plan designed to precipitate positive outcomes.

Also woven through the *Playbook* and remaining central to our goals is the concern for diversity, ethics, and civic engagement, which we so wish students to share. Neither bigotry, personal attacks, nor divisiveness have a positive role to play in public speaking. Even more committed to this precept, this new edition continues to provide students with tools to build bridges of understanding between themselves and the audiences they address.

We think *The Public Speaking Playbook* is a resource not only worth using but also worth keeping. We hope you do, too, as you sharpen your skills to public speaking success!

NEW IN THE FOURTH EDITION

The fourth edition of *The Public Speaking Playbook* incorporates many changes informed by feedback from instructors and students.

- **Objectives have been streamlined for clarity and focus.** We painstakingly edited each chapter, combining sections that work better together in order to highlight the most important content and skills, allowing students to get to the information they need more quickly and efficiently. We retained our focus on all of the key components to effective speechmaking, while giving students more guidance on how to build their success.

- **Updated for currency and relevance.** We have updated examples extensively throughout the text to provide students with an array of contemporary and relatable models for effective speeches.

- **Refreshed "storytelling" focus.** Emphasis is given not only to the text's chapter on storytelling, but also to how students have life-stories to share that can improve the speaker–audience connection.

- **Increased attention on the power of words and the validity of information.** Contemporary examples speak to the differences between information, misinformation, and disinformation, and the ability of a speaker to stir up emotions of audience members or reason logically with them.

- **New self-assessment activities.** Every chapter offers students the opportunity to assess different aspects of public speaking, from their attitudes toward public speaking, to their readiness to present, to specific public presentation skills.

- **Fresh look at the role of empathy in public speaking.** Whether performing the role of speaker, audience member, or evaluator, the ability to empathize increases effectiveness.

- **New annotated speeches for deeper analysis.** We have provided many new annotated speech examples to promote deeper understanding of effective speech construction through review and critique. Among the new examples are a new sample commencement address, and keeping with our civic engagement focus, a new informative speech on women and the vote, and a new persuasive student speech on the Electoral College. Other speech examples have been contemporized with new supporting materials and updated references.

- **Expanded and updated coverage.** Where needed, chapters have been revised and updated to include new attention-getting openings, fresh real-world examples, and additional instructional content reflecting reviewer requests. For example, Chapter 23, "Presenting Online," contains a wealth of fresh information on how to use Zoom and how to avoid Zoom fatigue, how to create podcasts, and how to ensure that transitioning between formats, from face-to-face to virtual, goes smoothly.

TEACHING RESOURCES

This text includes an array of instructor teaching materials designed to save you time and to help you keep students engaged. To learn more, visit sagepub.com or contact your SAGE representative at sagepub.com/findmyrep.

ACKNOWLEDGMENTS

We want to thank all our partners at SAGE for working so diligently and energetically with us through the years of the pandemic. Working with this team continues not only to be fun but also inspiring. We again thank Brenda Carter for her unflinching support; Charisse Kiino for continuing to champion the text; associate director of SAGE Publishing Matthew Byrnie for his unflinching belief in and firm commitment to the *Playbook*'s success; Lily Norton, Lauren Gobell, and Charles Lee for continuing to add their excitement, creative touches, and fresh insights to this project; and Megan O'Heffernan and Jen Jovin-Bernstein, our developmental editors, whose careful reading and thoughtful insights have been inspirational, and who have guided us so skillfully in revising and improving every edition of the text; and copy editor Talia Greenberg for asking us all the right questions and working painstakingly to maintain the book's accurateness and readability. We also offer a special thank you to production editor Veronica Stapleton Hooper for gently keeping us all on track, marketing manager Victoria Velasquez for seeing the promise in possibilities, and diacriTech and Lysa Becker, the book's designers, for the inviting look and visual appeal of this edition.

It is to the book's reviewers, adopters, and student users that we owe our most heartfelt thank you. The individuals listed here gave so generously of their time and talents, contributing ideas and recommendations that were invaluable in helping us shape the fourth edition, preserving its strengths while making it even more accessible, practical, and useful!

FOURTH EDITION REVIEWERS

Rebecca Carlton, *Indiana University Southeast*
Natalie Dudchock, *Jefferson State Community College*
Vanessa C. Ferguson, *Mott Community College*
Amy L. Keller, *Cuyahoga Community College*
Jennifer A. Likeum, *Northern Illinois University*
James Rowland, *Broward College*
Susan Sheridan Smith, *Radford University*
Ibrahim Yoldash, *Indiana University Northwest*

THIRD EDITION REVIEWERS

Jennifer Bieselin, *State College of Florida*
Bill Boozang, *Boston College*

Daniel B. Johnson, *Southwestern Michigan College*
Merrie E. Meyers, *Nova Southeastern University*
Hilary Parmentier, *Florida Keys Community College*
Keira J. Wade, *The University of Texas at Tyler*

SECOND EDITION REVIEWERS AND FOCUS GROUP PARTICIPANTS

Traci E. Alexander, Harrisburg Area Community College; **Nicole Allaire,** Iowa State University and Des Moines Community College; **Suzanne J. Atkin**, Portland State University; **Diane M. Badzinski,** Colorado Christian University; **Kristyn Hunt Cathey**, Lamar University; **Becky DeGreef,** Kansas State University Polytechnic Campus; **Jeff Drury,** Wabash College; **Benjamin M. Han**, Concordia University; **Paul T. M. Hemenway**, Lamar University; **Christina M. Knopf**, SUNY Potsdam; **Satish Kolluri**, Pace University, New York City; **Douglas J. Marshall**, Southern University at New Orleans; **Richard Maxson,** Drury University; **Christy Mesaros-Winckles**, Adrian College; **Elizabeth A. Nelson**, North Carolina State University; **Anthony Ongyod**, MiraCosta College; **Emily Berg Paup**, College of St. Benedict and St. John's University; **Sandy Pensoneau-Conway,** Southern Illinois University–Carbondale; **Rheanna Rutledge**, NOVA Southeastern University; **Chris Smejkal**, St. Louis Community College; **Brigit K. Talkington**, Midland University; **Ty Williams**, St. Philip's College

FIRST EDITION REVIEWERS

Sandra Wheeler Abeyta, Cosumnes River Community College; **John E. Anglin**, East Central College; **Derek Arnold**, Villanova University; **Robert L. Arnold**, Richland College; **Diane M. Badzinski**, Colorado Christian University; **Kay B. Barefoot**, College of The Albemarle-Dare; **Cameron Basquiat**, College of Southern Nevada; **Valerie C. Bello**, Genesee Community College; **Mary D. Best**, Christopher Newport University; **Annette Bever**, Vernon College; **Kenneth W. Bohl**, Westmoreland County Community College; **Jennifer Emerling Bone**, Colorado State University; **Michael T. Braun,** Milliken College; **Deborah Cunningham Breede**, Coastal Carolina University; **Anna Maria Ruffino Broussard**, Nicholls State University; **Barbara Ruth Burke**, University of Minnesota, Morris; **Megan Burnett**, Alice Lloyd College; **Rebecca Carlton**, Indiana University Southeast; **Gregory S. Carr**, HarrisStowe University; **Rod Carveth,** Charter Oak State College; **M. Chislom Jr.**, University of Wisconsin–Platteville; **Scott Christen**, Tennessee Technological University; **Jeanne Marie Christie**, Western Connecticut State University; **James D. Cianciola**, Truman State University; **Marcia J. Clinkscales**, Howard University; **Erica F. Cooper**, Roanoke College; **Jennifer Dahlen**, Northland Community and Technical College; **Thomas Damp**, Central New Mexico Community College; **Lissa D'Aquanni**, University at Albany; **Dale Davis**, University of Texas at San Antonio; **John R. Deitrick**, Becker College; **Norman F. Earls Jr.**, Valdosta State University; **Belle A. Edson**, Arizona State University; **Karen L.**

Eichler, Niagara University; **Dana Emerson,** Linn Benton Community College; **Jerry M. Engel**, State University of New York, College at Geneseo; **Mary M. Ertel**, Erie Community College; **Rebecca J. Franko**, California State Polytechnic University, Pomona; **Kathleen M. Golden**, Edinboro University of Pennsylvania; **Ronald P. Grapsy Jr.**, Kutztown University; **Stacy Gresell,** Lone Star College–CyFair; **Neva K. Gronert**, Arapahoe Community College; **Howard Grower**, The University of Tennessee; **Donna L. Halper**, Lesley University; **Edward Hatch**, Thomas College; **Gillie Haynes**, American University; **Keith Hearit**, Western Michigan University; **Ronald W. Hochstatter**, Northland Community and Technical College; **Tracey Quigley Holden**, University of Delaware; **Lisa Holderman**, Arcadia University; **Tracey Holley**, Tarleton State University; **Samuel Holton**, Southeastern Technical College; **Jason Wayne Hough**, Hartnell College; **Mary E. Hurley**, St. Louis Community College at Forest Park; **Jacqueline A. Irwin**, California State University, Sacramento; **Kathleen Jacquette**, Farmingdale State College; **John Jarvis**, Bay Path College; **Rebecca Kamm**, Northeast Iowa Community College; **Pamela A. Kaylor**, Ohio University Lancaster; **Chris Kennedy**, Western Wyoming Community College; **Dave Kosloski**, Clark College; **Reeze LaLonde Hanson**, Haskell Indian Nations University; **Kimberly A. Laux**, University of Michigan–Flint; **Amy K. Lenoce**, Naugatuck Valley Community College; **Tammy Swenson Lepper**, Winona State University; **Linda Levitt**, Stephen F. Austin State University; **Sandra Lieberg**, Lake Michigan College; **Andrew Lovato**, Santa Fe Community College; **Tobi Mackler**, Montgomery County Community College; **Matthew Thomas Malloy**, Caldwell Community College and Technical Institute; **Jeanette Martin**, United Tribes Technical College; **Chandra K. Massner**, University of Pikeville; **Janet Rice McCoy,** Morehead State University; **Susi McFarland**, Modesto Junior College and San Joaquin Delta College; **Shellie Michael**, Volunteer State Community College; **Nicki L. Michalski,** Lamar University; **Thomas P. Morra**, The Catholic University of America; **Laura D. Morrison**, College of The Albemarle; **Katie Kavanagh O'Neill**, University of Pittsburgh; **Lynne Orr**, William Paterson University; **Lisa Pavia-Higel**, East Central College; **John H. Prellwitz**, University of Pittsburgh at Greensburg; **Brandi Quesenberry**, Virginia Tech University; **Rasha I. Ramzy**, Georgia State University; **Ramesh N. Rao**, Longwood University; **Renton Rathbun**, Owens Community College; **Christina L. Reynolds**, Otterbein University; **Emily Richardson**, University of Pikeville; **Jeanette Ruiz,** University of California, Davis; **Ann B. Russell**, Bladen Community College; **Stephanie Shimotsu-Dariol**, Western Governors University; **John Spinda**, Murray State University; **Roberta G. Steinberg**, Mount Ida College; **Lesa A. Stern**, Westmont College; **Karen Stewart,** Arizona State University; **Chelsea A. H. Stow**, Front Range Community College; **William Swanger**, Susquehanna University; **Brigit K. Talkington,** Midland University; **Belinda Collings Thomson**, Brescia University; **Debbi Vavra**, Blinn College; **Mark "Dog" Wallace**, Thomas College; **R. Lester Walsh**, Valley City State University; **Kathleen Watters**, University of Dayton; **Susan M. Wieczorek**, University of Pittsburgh at Johnstown; **Jonna Reule Ziniel**, Valley City State University

We also want to thank the following students and faculty for providing us with a treasure chest of speeches that added to the richness of this text's contents: Austin J. Beattie, Eric Mishne, Tanika L. Smith, Cathy Frisinger, Alicia Croshal, Denalie Silha, Jim Eae, Camdyn Anders, and Dolores Bandow.

ABOUT THE AUTHORS

Teri Kwal Gamble enjoyed a career as a full professor of communication at the College of New Rochelle in New Rochelle, New York (PhD, New York University; MA and BA, Lehman College, CUNY), and **Michael W. Gamble** is a full professor of communication at the New York Institute of Technology in New York City (PhD, New York University; BA and MFA, University of Oklahoma). The Gambles are partners in life and work. Professional writers of education and training materials, the Gambles are the coauthors of numerous textbooks and trade books. Their most recent publication is the 2nd edition of *The Communication Playbook*. Teri and Mike  also are the coauthors of *The Interpersonal Communication Playbook* (2020). Among other books the Gambles have written together are *Nonverbal Messages Tell More: A Practical Guide to Nonverbal Communication* (2017), *Leading with Communication* (2013), and *The Gender Communication Connection* (3rd ed., 2021).

Previously, Michael served as an officer and taught leadership skills for the U.S. Army Infantry School during the Vietnam War. The Gambles also are the founders of Interact Training Systems, a consulting firm that conducts seminars, workshops, and short courses for business and professional organizations. Teri and Mike also produce training and marketing materials for sales organizations and are the coauthors of the trade book *Sales Scripts That Sell*.

istockphoto.com/monkeybusinessimages

YOU CAN SPEAK CONFIDENTLY

UPON COMPLETING THIS CHAPTER, YOU WILL BE ABLE TO

1.1   Demonstrate the personal, professional, and societal benefits of public speaking.

1.2   Explain the face-to-face and digital contexts of public speaking, also identifying the essential elements of communication.

1.3   Assess and build your speechmaking confidence.

1.4   Use a step-by-step approach to prepare for your first speech.

Welcome to the fourth edition of *The Public Speaking Playbook*. **Public speaking** is the act of preparing, staging, and delivering a presentation to an audience. A **playbook** is a game plan for continuous improvement—a plan of action designed to help you become a peak performer.[1] The purpose of this playbook is to provide every public speaking student with a game plan—a set of easy to follow, practical steps to success. Accomplished speakers prepare, practice, and present speeches that others judge to be of high quality. To rise to this level, you first need to master and then apply skills. And just like elite athletes, actors, and others who appear in public, you need to be able to perform under pressure, either individually or as members of a team. Proficient speakers also practice consistently and assess their performances so that every one of their presentations is as good as or better than their last. With a game plan and practice, you can join their ranks. You can become comfortable with the idea of stepping up to speak in public. You can become a more capable communicator. In this chapter, we introduce you to the nature of public speaking today, the many venues available to speakers, the means you can use to build your speechmaking confidence, and the "know-how" to deliver your first presentation.

While it may not seem fair, people judge us, at least in part, on our public speaking skillfulness. We place a high value on public speaking ability because it is a vital means of communicating and connecting with others. Today, people give speeches live, as they have been for centuries. But they also present them as TED Talks,[2] upload them to YouTube, or deliver them via podcasts, which we then experience using our smartphones or other digital devices. No matter the forum or mode of delivery, the ability to speak in and to the public is a powerful skill to develop. Audiences are drawn to the words of renowned speakers such as paralympic champ Amy Purdy, Nobel laureate Malala Yousafzai, talk show host and interviewer Oprah Winfrey, self-help expert Deepak Chopra, motivational speakers Tony Robbins and Chris Gardner, and climate activist Greta Thunburg, because they inspire, reassure, and interest them.

Being able to speak in public without injecting vitriol is similarly powerful. What will you do? You can be the smartest person in the room, but if deficient speaking skills keep others from understanding your ideas, being smart isn't enough. A class in public speaking gives you and your peers the opportunity to work together on improving your public speaking skills.

COACHING TIP

"Through my education, I didn't just develop skills, I didn't just develop the ability to learn, but I developed confidence."

—Michelle Obama, former first lady of the United States

Merely reading and talking about public speaking won't make you a better speaker. Only involving yourself in the process and doing it will help you improve. The more you speak in public, the easier it will become and the more you will improve. Doing it builds confidence.

SPEECHMAKING'S BENEFITS

> **1.1**   *Demonstrate the personal, professional, and societal benefits of public speaking.*

Becoming a skilled public speaker benefits us personally and professionally; it also delivers benefits to society as a whole.

Personal Benefits

Speaking in public builds self-confidence and even can trigger self-discovery and creative self-expression. For instance, as a result of researching a topic, such as the problems faced by soldiers returning from a war zone, you might discover that you have the desire to engage in service learning by volunteering at a veteran's facility.

As a public speaker, you are expected to reflect on your interests, to explore where you stand on controversial issues, and to consider the needs and concerns of others. You would need to consider your position and how to best make your argument so that even those who disagreed with your stance initially would listen to and understand it. Becoming a more confident speaker will also make you a more confident student. By developing the ability to speak in public, you develop your ability to speak up in class—any class (see Chapter 22).

At the same time, as you build speaking confidence, you might find yourself wanting to become more civically engaged, speaking up and sharing ideas beyond the classroom.

Whether your major is business, computer programming, nursing, engineering, media and journalism, social work, or any other subject— unless you also can present information clearly and effectively, others may question your credibility and knowledge. By mastering the ability to communicate your ideas in public, you harness the power of speech. By being better able to control yourself and your ideas, you enhance your ability to control your environment. From corporate meetings to trade shows, from educational conferences to political rallies, from town halls to your classroom, from YouTube to Facebook, from Ted.com to Twitter and Instagram, public speakers—individuals with stories to tell—play key roles. Public speaking is like a form of personal currency, only instead of providing entrance to the marketplace of goods and services, it provides access to the marketplace of ideas. We share the responsibility to make our voices heard—to tell our stories. Every one of us has stories to tell that others can benefit from hearing.

Career Benefits

In the United States, there are more than 20,000 different ways of earning a living, with effective speech essential to every one of them.[3] This helps explain why public speaking is a core 21st-century skill.[4] Most of the jobs of today and tomorrow will require us to speak up. We may present to a team, need to get a point across in a meeting, or answer questions posed by a panel. Success in public speaking helps us grow professionally. Our ability to attain professional success is related to our ability to communicate effectively both in writing and orally, online and in the same physical space, what we think, know, and can do. This is especially helpful in a job interview, since prospective employers favor candidates who have communication skills, including working in a team and in speaking in public.[5]

How far you advance in your career may well depend on how capable you are in addressing, impressing, and influencing others and in communicating your ideas clearly, creatively, and effectively.[6] The executives and entrepreneurs of tomorrow need to be skilled public speakers— masters of the art of speaking before groups of all sizes, including the news media and online audiences.

Societal Benefits

Words we speak in public matter. The stories we tell, whether true or hypothetical, make a difference in others' lives. For these two reasons alone, public speaking is more consequential than ever. As we realized during the Trump administration and in the leadup to the 2021 inauguration of President Joseph Biden and Vice President Kamala Harris, public speeches can have both positive and uplifting and negative and harmful outcomes. A public speaker's words can instill information and motivate prosocial behavior, but they also can incite, serve as disinformation, and stir up a mob. With our words, we let others know what we care about and what we want them to care about, too. Public speaking lets us exercise effective personhood and effective citizenship.

Speaking of effective citizenship, freedom of speech has always been viewed as an essential ingredient in a democracy. What does freedom of speech mean? It means

1. We can speak freely without fear of being punished for expressing our ideas.

2. We can expose ourselves freely to all sides of a controversial issue.

3. We can debate freely all disputable questions of fact, value, or policy.

4. We can make decisions freely based on our evaluation of the choices confronting us.

Our political system depends on a commitment by citizens to speak openly and honestly free of government censorship and to listen freely and carefully to all sides of an issue—even those with which we vehemently disagree. It depends on our ability to think critically about what we listen to so that we are able to evaluate the speaker's goal and make informed decisions about our future.

Democracy depends on our willingness to understand and respond to expressions of opinion, belief, and value that are different from our own, and to do so with civility, without becoming disagreeable, and without being cancelled or wanting to cancel those who take issue with our message.

PUBLIC SPEAKING CONTEXTS: FACE-TO-FACE AND DIGITAL

> **1.2** *Explain the face-to-face and digital contexts of public speaking, also identifying the essential elements of communication.*

Skilled public speakers have unique powers to influence. But like other forms of communication, public speaking is a circle of give-and-take between presenter and audience, whether the speaker and/or the audience is physically present or online. The better we understand how communication works, the better our ability to make it work for us. The following elements are an integral part of the process:

- The source
- The receiver
- The message
- The channel
- Noise
- Feedback
- Situational and cultural contexts

One way to study the interactions of these elements is with a model of the communication process in action (see Figure 1.1).

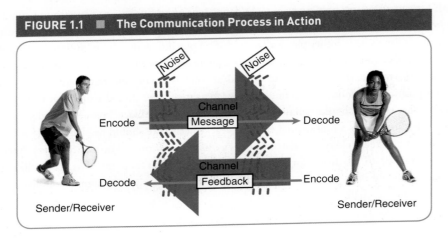

FIGURE 1.1 ■ The Communication Process in Action

Look closely at the variables depicted in Figure 1.1 to identify how they relate to each other dynamically during public speaking. Both the speaker, or source, and the listener, or receiver, participate in communication. Each party simultaneously and continually performs both sending functions (giving out messages) and receiving functions (taking in messages). Neither sending nor receiving is the exclusive job of any person.

Between the source and receiver, messages—both verbal and nonverbal—are sent and received. The words and visuals we use to express our ideas and feelings, the sounds of our voices, and our body language (or nonverbal communication) make up the content of our communication and convey information. Everything we do as senders and receivers has potential message value for those observing us. If a speaker's voice quivers or a receiver checks their watch, it conveys a message.

Channels are pathways or media through which messages are carried. The auditory channel carries our spoken words; the visual channel carries our gestures, facial expressions, and postural cues; and the vocal channel carries cues such as rate, quality, volume, and pitch of speech. Communication is usually a multichannel event.

Noise is anything that interferes with our ability to send or receive a message. Noise need not be sound. Physical discomfort, a psychological state, intellectual ability, or the environment also can create noise. As the model in Figure 1.1 shows, noise can enter the communication event at any point. It can come from the context, the channel, the message, or the persons themselves. Different languages, translators, generational terms, jargon, and technical terms play a role in the day-to-day noise of communication in our diverse world.

The situational/cultural context is the setting or environment for communication. Because every message occurs in a situation with cultural and social meanings, conditions of place and time influence both behavior and the outcome of the communication event. The after-dinner speaker addressing a large number of people who have just eaten and are feeling full will need to give a different kind of speech than the person whose task is to address the members of a union protesting a layoff. Similarly, the online speaker faces different challenges than does the speaker addressing a live audience. Especially in our age of abundant digital connections, public speakers are in demand with the number of platforms open to them increasing. During the many months of the COVID-19 pandemic, both our use of and reliance on digital media increased.[7] With little warning, we became even more dependent on technology to connect and communicate with those with whom we shared both personal and professional relationships. Because of our inability to be together physically, we shifted our interactions to common digital video chat spaces. We not only ventured into these digital zones to preserve the social fabric of our lives, but also to impart our stories—to share ideas about issues of concern to us, and to advocate for our positions on controversial questions, such as if colleges should reopen for face-to-face classes; whether bars should remain closed; whether to join a Black Lives Matter demonstration; or because it was a presidential election year, whether we should be able to vote by mail. Fundamentally, technology became the means we used to inform and influence others. Internet sites became "go-to" platforms for millions of us. It's likely that for many of us, Zoom-like apps will carry into our post–COVID-19 future as well. We will continue to augment our live speaking experiences with digital ones.

Feedback is information we receive in response to a message we have sent. Feedback tells us how we are doing. Positive feedback, like applause, serves a reinforcing function and causes us to continue behaving as we are, whereas negative feedback, such as silent stares, serves a corrective function and leads us to eliminate any ineffective behaviors. Internal feedback is that which you give yourself (you laugh at a joke you tell); external feedback comes from others who are party to the communicative event (receivers laugh at your joke, too).

Picture the Parts Working Together

All parts of the communicative model continuously interact with and affect each other—they are interconnected and interdependent. When something happens to one variable, all the other variables in the process are affected. Communication is also cumulative; the communicative experiences we have add up and have the potential to alter our perceptions and behaviors. The effects of communication cannot be erased; they become part of the total field of experience we bring to the next communication event. Ultimately, our accumulative experiences—the sum of all our experiences—influence our attitudes toward the speech event and our receivers, affecting both our desire to communicate and the way we do it.

Know your parts. As you put your presentation together, keep your eyes on your goal to create a more dynamic and influential speech.

iStock.com/RawpixelLtd

Your success as a source ultimately depends on your ability to

● Establish common ground with your receivers

● Encode or formulate a message effectively

- Adapt to cultural and situational differences
- Alleviate the effects of noise
- Understand and respond to the reactions of those with whom you are interacting

Your effectiveness depends not only on what you intend to communicate, but also on the meanings your receivers give to your message. A self-centered communicator is insensitive to the needs of receivers, which limits their effectiveness. It is better to be audience-centered and keep your eyes on your receivers and speaking goals, instead of focusing solely on yourself.

Consider Audience Expectations

Although being able to (1) organize ideas logically, (2) encode or express ideas clearly, and (3) analyze and adapt to receivers readily are skills every communicator needs, they are particularly important for public speakers.

> **COACHING TIP**
>
> "We live in an era where the best way to make a dent on the world may no longer be to write a letter to the editor or publish a book. It may be simply to stand up and say something . . . because both the words and the passion with which they are delivered can now spread across the world at warp speed."
>
> —Chris Anderson, *TED Talks: The Official TED Guide to Public Speaking*
>
> Picture the model in Figure 1.1. Communication and understanding are key. Focus on your audience. Make it easy for those in it to understand you. You just might significantly affect their lives.

Receivers usually have higher expectations for public speakers than for other communicators. For example, we expect public speakers to use more formal standards of grammar and usage, pay more attention to their presentation style and appearance, fit what they say into a specific time limit, and anticipate and then respond to questions their receivers will ask.

So, when speaking in public, you will need to polish, formalize, and build on your basic conversational skills in order to reach your goal—whether you're live or online.

BUILD SPEECHMAKING CONFIDENCE

| 1.3 | *Assess and build your speechmaking confidence.* |

You are in good company if the thought of speaking in public causes you some concern. When on the campaign trail, President Joseph Biden spoke about his fear of stuttering when speaking in front of others and how he overcame his anxieties. Biden also used his experiences to encourage other stutterers, including 13-year-old Brayden Harrington, who demonstrated the confidence to address the Democratic National Convention in 2020.[8] Speakers are not alone in experiencing fear or feeling stressed at the thought of performing in public. Athletes, dancers, actors, and musicians also have to handle their fear and emotional stress, which, if not channeled effectively, can interfere with their ability to perform.[9] When they control their fear, however, the stress becomes useful, helping them gain a competitive edge, boosting their energy, and readying them to deliver a peak performance. How does this happen? Quite simply, athletes and others who perform in public focus, face their fears, and train to handle pressure. And they do this gradually, over time—not once, but regularly.[10] You can, too. Start by confronting your feelings about giving a speech.

SELF-ASSESSMENT 1.1: HOW CONFIDENT ARE YOU ABOUT PUBLIC SPEAKING?

Directions

Use the following scales to evaluate your speechmaking anxiety by indicating where on the scale you fall for each statement.

Statement	Not at all concerned 1	Not very concerned 2	Somewhat concerned 3	Very concerned 4	Extremely concerned 5
1. I will forget what I plan to say.					
2. My words will confuse the audience.					
3. My words will offend the audience.					
4. Audience members will laugh at me when I don't mean to be funny.					
5. I'm going to embarrass myself.					

Statement	Not at all concerned 1	Not very concerned 2	Somewhat concerned 3	Very concerned 4	Extremely concerned 5
6. My ideas will have no impact.					
7. I will look foolish in front of the audience.					
8. My voice and body will shake uncontrollably.					
9. I will bore the audience.					
10. Audience members will stare at me unresponsively					

Apprehension Analysis	Implication
Add together the numbers you chose on each scale: _____ Total To determine your level of apprehension, refer to the range below: 41–50 You have speech anxiety. 31–40 You are very apprehensive. 21–30 You are concerned to a normal extent. 10–20 You are very confident.	What does your score reveal? Although this evaluation is not a scientific instrument, it should give you some indication of your level of concern. Note that it is normal to display some level of anxiety. If you had no apprehension about speaking in public, you would not be typical; what's more, you probably would not make a very effective speaker, either.

Understand Public Speaking Anxiety

According to public speaking coach Viv Groskop, when it comes to giving a speech, "Feeling anxious is just a sign that you're human."[11] Under ordinary circumstances, we rarely give our speaking skills a second thought—that is, until we are asked to stand up and speak in front of others. Once we know this is what we're going to have to do, if we're like most adults, we complain about it, because we fear it more than we fear bee stings, accidents, or heights (see Figure 1.2).[12]

FIGURE 1.2 ■ Activities Adults Say They Dread	
Public speaking	46%
Thoroughly cleaning their home	43%
Visiting the dentist	41%
Visiting the DMV	36%
Doing taxes	28%
Waiting in line at post office	25%

Source: USA Today, May 14–16, 2010, p. 1A.

Fear of public speaking, also known as public speaking anxiety (or in medical terminology, *glossophobia*), affects a significant percentage of the public, and is capable of undoing the best of us.[13] In fact, when asked how they feel about speaking before others, many jokingly answer that they'd rather be in the casket than be delivering the eulogy. **Public speaking anxiety**, also known as PSA, is a variant of communication anxiety that affects some 40 to 80 percent of all speakers.[14] PSA has two dimensions: process anxiety and performance anxiety.

- **Process anxiety** is fear of preparing a speech. For example, when you experience process anxiety, you doubt your ability to select a topic, research it, and organize your ideas.

- **Performance anxiety** is fear of presenting a speech. It finds you stressful about delivering the speech, fearful that you'll tremble, forget what you want to say, do something embarrassing, be unable to complete the speech, not make sense to receivers, or simply be assessed as a poor speaker.[15]

Why are some of us afraid to speak before a group? What makes public speaking an activity that many dread?[16] Consider this: We all talk to ourselves. We call these internal conversations **self-talk**. It's how we talk to ourselves that matters, though. For example, what do you say to yourself about having to give a speech? Is your self-talk facilitating or debilitating? We can talk to ourselves in ways that turn our apprehensiveness into positive energy—a means of acknowledging "We have this. We can do this." Such self-talk is facilitative. Self-talk, however, also has a more debilitative side. Excessive concern creates a host of worrisome "what if" questions. These questions harbor negative thoughts that if we're not careful can turn into self-fulfilling prophecies born out of irrational thinking.[17] Let's consider the kind of "what if" self-talk questions that increase our anxiety about giving a speech.

What if I fail?

While we all fear failure at one time or another, it's irrational to assume failure or think your speech will be a disaster.[18] If we choose not to take risks because we visualize ourselves failing rather than succeeding, if we disagree with what we hear or read but choose to keep our thoughts to ourselves, then we are probably letting our feelings of inferiority limit us. Keep in mind that the nervousness you feel likely is not apparent to the audience.

What if I haven't had enough experience?

Some of us fear that we may not know enough or have not had enough experience with the topic. The unknown leaves much to the imagination, and far too frequently, we irrationally choose to imagine the worst thing that could happen when making a speech. Instead, harness the nervousness you feel so you can use it to your advantage.

What if others don't like my speech?

Some of us also worry excessively about others judging our ideas, how we sound or look, or what we represent. When given a choice, we prefer not to be judged. It is rare that any of us can please everybody in our audience. So, don't waste time worrying about it.

What if everyone stares at me?

We also may fear being conspicuous or singled out. Audience members usually focus directly on the speaker. Some of us interpret receivers' gazes as scrutinizing and hostile rather than as revealing a genuine interest in us. By keeping a receiver orientation, you can shift your focus from yourself to those in your audience.

What if we have nothing in common?

Ethnocentricity—the belief that one's own group or culture is better than others—makes some of us think that we share nothing in common with the members of our audience. Feelings of difference make it more difficult to find common ground, which in turn, increases anxiety about making a speech. Instead, acknowledge we're all different, but we can find common ground.

What if other presenters aren't as apprehensive as I am?

Our culture may influence our attitudes toward speaking in public. For example, research suggests that Filipinos, Israelis, and other Middle Eastern peoples are typically less apprehensive about public speaking than are Americans.[19] In these cultures, children are rewarded for effort, making judgment and communication anxiety a less intrusive force.[20] With this in mind, accept your nervousness as normal, but refocus it by keeping your outlook positive. You have the chance to make a difference as you add to your experience and develop your confidence.

One of the best ways to cope with the apprehension we have about giving a speech is to design and rehearse your speech carefully. Being prepared is a confidence builder. While you still might feel anxious, there are steps you can take to control both the physical and mental effects that you may experience.

Address the Physical Effects of Speech Anxiety

The first thing to do is to recognize the bodily sensations that accompany and support feelings of nervousness. Make a list of the physical symptoms you experience. Then compare your list with the symptoms and thoughts that others in the class identified. Do the lists include any of these physical symptoms?

- Rapid or irregular heartbeat
- Stiff neck
- Stomach knots
- Lump in the throat
- Shaking hands, arms, or legs
- Nausea
- Dry mouth
- Dizziness

When we experience the physical effects of anxiety, adrenaline is released into our systems and our respiration rate and heart rate increase. When our anxiety levels get too high, we need to manage the physical effects of speech fright. For example, if we're runners, we could go for a run. If not, we could take a moment to stretch our limbs.

Another technique is systematic desensitization, a way to reduce the physical responses of apprehension.[21] The principle behind systematic desensitization is that after being tensed, a muscle relaxes. Following are several methods you can try.

Tense/Relax

Tense your neck and shoulders. Count to 10. Relax. Continue by tensing and relaxing other parts of your body, including your hands, arms, legs, and feet. As you continue this process, you will find yourself growing calmer.

Strike a Powerful Pose

How we stand can affect our speaking success. Merely practicing a "power pose" in private before presenting a speech lowers speaker stress levels, thereby reducing outward signs of stress and enhancing confidence:[22]

- Stand tall.
- Stand tall and lean slightly forward.
- Stand tall and open your limbs expansively.
- Leaning slightly forward, stake out a broad surface with your hands.

Leaning slightly forward engages an audience. Opening the limbs expresses power. Staking out a broad surface conveys a sense of control. In contrast to power poses, low-power cues increase stress and decrease confidence. Adopting a close-bodied posture conveys powerlessness, touching your neck or face is a symptom of anxiety, and folding your arms comes off as defensive. Use power poses that convey authority instead. Doing so will boost confidence at the same time.

Address the Mental Effects of Speech Anxiety

Debilitating self-talk fans the flames of our fears instead of extinguishing them.[23] We create a self-fulfilling prophecy, meaning that we form an expectation and adjust our behavior to match. In the end, the expectation we created becomes true. Negative thoughts can cause unnecessary problems.

Do you ever find yourself uttering statements like the following to yourself?

"I just can't cope."

"I'm under too much pressure."

"This is my worst nightmare."

"I know something terrible is going to happen."

The solution is to use **thought stopping** to make self-talk work in your favor. Every time you find yourself thinking an upsetting or anxiety-producing thought, every time you visualize yourself experiencing failure instead of success, say to yourself, "Stop!" and tell yourself, "Calm." Thought stopping is an example of **cognitive restructuring**, a technique that focuses attention on our thoughts rather than on our bodily reactions. Cognitive restructuring works by altering the beliefs people have about themselves and their abilities.

A second technique is **centering**.[24] When centering, we direct our thoughts internally, and we feel an inner calm. Instead of being consumed by negative self-talk, we learn to trust ourselves. Key in this procedure is the **centering breath**, designed to help us breathe like it matters so that we may focus on the task mentally. Try it. Take a deep breath. Follow it with a strong exhalation and muscle relaxation. This done, you'll be better able to narrow your focus on the external task.

Using thought stopping and centering together allows you to gain control by diverting attention from thoughts that threaten your success to positive ones. They also aid you in developing a growth mindset—the idea that if you change your thinking and behavior and persist, you can succeed.[25]

COACHING TIP

"The mind is everything. What you think you become."

—Buddha

Nerves are not your enemy. Face them, control them, and you transform normal anxiety into a positive. Harnessing the excess energy that accompanies any apprehension you feel energizes you and enhances your development as a speaker.

Use Skills Training

We can combat both the physical and the mental effects of speech anxiety by making an effort to

- Speak on a topic about which we truly care
- Prepare thoroughly for the speechmaking event
- Keep in mind that our listeners are unlikely to perceive our signs of anxiety

Because you are just beginning your training to become a better speaker, it is reasonable to expect you may still feel anxious about speaking in public. As you increase your skill level by learning how to prepare and deliver speeches, you become consciously competent and aware of your competence. The idea of public speaking becomes less threatening.[26] By making your anxiety work for you, by converting it into positive energy, you learn to fear anxiety less, and you learn to like public speaking more.

Anxiety Can Be Transformative

Contrary to what you may think, as a speaker, you neither can nor should rid yourself of all speech anxiety. Rather, using your anxiety to perform more effectively is better than experiencing none at all.

In the book *Face of Emotion,* author Eric Finzi suggests that "putting on a happy face" not only erases a frown, it actually can lift your mood.[27] Nonverbal communication expert Paul Ekman agrees, acknowledging the possibility that facial expressions can affect our moods.[28] It follows, then, that changing any negative thoughts you have about giving a speech to positive ones can similarly influence your performance. With that in mind, prepare thoroughly and rehearse and visualize a positive experience.

Prepare Thoroughly and Rehearse

Preparation helps instill confidence. It includes everything you do between thinking up a topic and speech delivery. Prepared speakers are competent speakers.

Visualize a Positive Experience

Instead of focusing on your negative thoughts and fears, focus on the potential positives of your performance. Visualize yourself being successful from start to finish.

Remind Yourself That Receivers Usually Cannot See or Hear Your Fear

Although you may feel the flutters that speech anxiety causes, the audience generally cannot detect these in your performance. In fact, observers usually underestimate the amount of anxiety they believe a speaker is experiencing.[29]

Use an Array of Supportive Techniques

Speakers report that other techniques also can help reduce speech apprehension. Some try to include a bit of humor early in the speech in order to elicit a favorable response from the audience right away. They say that such a reaction helps them calm their nerves for the remainder of the presentation. Others look for a friendly face and talk to that person for a moment or two early in the speech. Others use visuals aids, like PowerPoint, to help them organize the material. The visual shows the next major point to be covered, eliminating the necessity for the speaker to remember it or refer to notes. Still others rehearse a speech aloud, standing in front of an imaginary audience and "talking through" the material again and again. Some even deliver their speech to their pets, while others look to their smart speaker or AI to help them modify negative thinking. What other techniques have you found helpful?

Remember, experiencing some apprehension is normal. Although you probably never can eliminate it totally, by preparing, practicing, and giving yourself time to polish your presentation, you can counter your list of "what ifs" and be successful.

If we take the time to analyze and practice successful behaviors, we can learn to handle ourselves more effectively as speakers. With practice, we can develop the understanding and master the skills that will turn us into articulate presenters who are organized, confident, competent, and able to communicate in such a way that others are interested in us, energized by our ideas, and persuaded by us.

We can prepare you to present your first speech by putting the entire speechmaking process into a logical, step-by-step sequence that you can follow. The process serves as a road map that you can use to prepare every public presentation you'll ever make.

USE THIS SYSTEM TO READY YOUR FIRST SPEECH

> **1.4**   *Use a step-by-step approach to prepare for your first speech.*

Before delivering your first speech, you need to complete three plays: (1) topic selection; (2) speech development, support, and organization; and (3) practice and delivery. A fourth play, the post-presentation analysis, is completed immediately after you give the speech. The staircase-like chart in Figure 1.3 illustrates this systematic, step-by-step, play-by-play approach to public speaking. As you make your way up the staircase, you move from one speechmaking phase into another (see Figure 1.3).

Select Your Topic

The first step in topic selection is to analyze your interests and use this information to select a general subject area—one you are knowledgeable about and comfortable with. In fact, one of the best means of controlling your fear and laying the groundwork for a successful speech is to choose a topic that is important to you, that you have some familiarity with, and about which you want to find out even more. Doing this helps in controlling your fear and laying the groundwork for a successful speech. Such an analysis also can aid you in calling up personal narratives or anecdotes to integrate into your speech. Highly anxious speakers rarely do this. As a result, they spend far too much preparation time trying to interest themselves in or master a subject and far too little time rehearsing the presentation itself.[30] Use the topic selection techniques discussed here to find an appropriate subject.

FIGURE 1.3 ■ **Systematic Speaking Process**

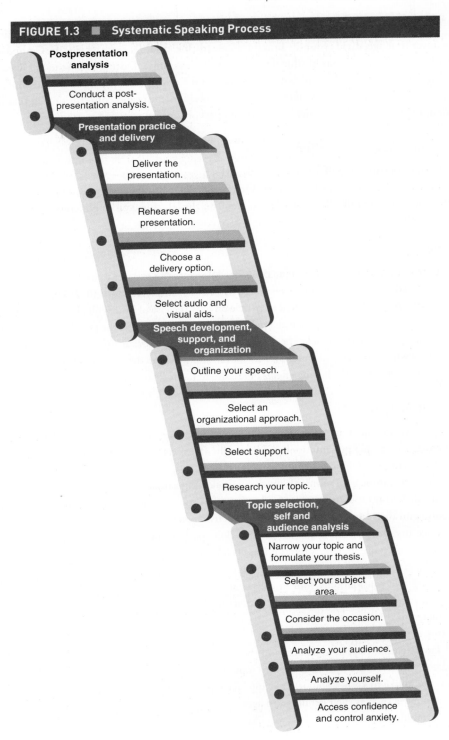

Postpresentation analysis

Conduct a post-presentation analysis.

Presentation practice and delivery

Deliver the presentation.

Rehearse the presentation.

Choose a delivery option.

Select audio and visual aids.

Speech development, support, and organization

Outline your speech.

Select an organizational approach.

Select support.

Research your topic.

Topic selection, self and audience analysis

Narrow your topic and formulate your thesis.

Select your subject area.

Consider the occasion.

Analyze your audience.

Analyze yourself.

Access confidence and control anxiety.

Conduct a Life Overview

Whatever your age, divide your life into thirds—early life, midlife, more recent life. Compose a sentence to summarize your life during each stage; for example, "During high school, I lived in Norman, Oklahoma, where my dad worked for an oil company, and I went to Sooner football games." Under each summary statement list your main interests and concerns during that life period. Examine your list. Which topics still interest or concern you?

Focus on This Moment in Time

Fold a sheet of paper in half. On the left side, list sensory experiences—whatever you are able to see, hear, taste, smell, or touch right now. On the right side, list topics suggested by each sensory experience. For example, if you wrote "balloon" on the left side, you might enter "party planning" on the right side.

Be Newsy

1. Peruse a newspaper, newsmagazine, or online news aggregator to find potential topics. Read a story and list topics suggested by it. For example, the July 30, 2020, issue of the *New York Times* featured an article on how the city of Louisville, Kentucky was considering declaring racism a public health crisis.[31] Imagine the possible speech topics suggested by this article: the dangers of racism, how to be an antiracist, the meaning of white privilege, disputes over memorials to the Confederacy, the Black Lives Matter movement, or the lasting effects of racism, to name just a few.

Use Technology

Explore websites such as About.com, eHow.com, Ted.com, Pinterest.com, or YouTube.com, searching for sample presentations. Additionally, the speech topic resources at edge.sagepub.com/gamblepsp4e can prove helpful.

▶ See **Chapter 5** for more information on selecting a topic.

While highly anxious speakers tend to be self-obsessed, more effective speakers focus their attention on their listeners. When you avoid focusing on your anxiety and concentrate on your audience instead, you shine the communication spotlight on those you are speaking to and you minimize your anxiety. Thus, an important move in topic selection is to adapt your general subject area to your audience and the occasion by conducting an audience analysis. Why? Because if you consider only your interests and don't take the needs and interests of your audience into account, audience members are more likely to experience boredom and become easily distracted. If this happens, you lose the attention of receivers, which prevents your message from getting through.

Pay attention to your audience, and they will pay attention to you. Consider how familiar audience members are with your selected topic area, what their attitudes toward it are, and what they would like to know about it. Take into account some of the demographic characteristics of the audience, such as their genders and ages, the cultures represented, and their socioeconomic backgrounds. Think about how factors like these could influence how members of the audience feel about your topic and, consequently, how you should frame it. For example, if you decide to speak about student services for on-campus residents but your class is made up primarily of students who commute to campus, a substantial number of students could find your talk irrelevant.

Take the time needed to get to know your receivers. Talk to them, asking about their interests and concerns. For your first speaking assignment, chatting with three to five students should be sufficient. Ask them what they already know about your topic, whether it appeals to them, and what else they would be interested in finding out about it. Their answers will help you narrow your subject and relate it more directly to them.

▶ **Chapter 4** will help you analyze your audience and adapt your presentation to them.

There are a number of other criteria aside from speaker and audience interests to consider when selecting a topic for your initial speech:

1. Avoid overused topics, unless you will be taking an unusual slant or offering a fresh perspective. Thus, rather than speaking on the legalization of marijuana in your state, speak on how it helps deter the ill-effects of chemotherapy.

2. Select an appropriate topic—not one that will be alienating or that you or your receivers have no interest in learning more about. Make the effort to meet their needs and expectations.

3. Limit the scope of your topic so that it fits the time allotted for your speech. For example, speaking on The Story of My Life or The History of the Computer could be too broad, making it impossible for you to cover the topic in the time available.

4. Make sure you have access to the material you will need to prepare the speech.

It is of paramount importance that your selected topic speaks to your audience. Among the topics students have used for a first speech are

- My Favorite Ancestor
- The Significance of My Name
- What I Learned While Studying Abroad
- My Greatest Fear
- A Difficult Choice I Had to Make
- Why You Need a Mentor
- How Discrimination Affects Me
- How to Avoid Boredom
- The Dangers of Disinformation
- How to Get the Most Out of College

Which of these, if any, interests you? What topics would you like to hear about?

▶ **Chapters 4** and **5** will give you more strategies for selecting a topic that is appropriate for your audience.

Develop, Support, and Organize Your Speech

Once you have selected a topic, you need to

- Formulate your speech's purpose

- State your thesis

- Identify the main points of the speech

- Research and select materials to support the main points

- Outline your speech, integrating transitions and signposts

and

- Consider presentation aids

Let us move through these in turn.

The Speech's Purpose

Your speech should have a **general purpose** (to inform, persuade, or entertain an audience) and a **specific purpose**—a statement specifying your goal, giving your speech direction beyond its general purpose. For example, if your goal were to inform receivers about self-driving cars, your specific purpose might be "to inform my audience about three ways self-driving cars will impact society." You then use the specific purpose to develop your central idea or thesis.

▶ **Chapter 5** will show you in more detail how to develop the general and specific purpose of your speech.

The Thesis Statement

Your speech should also contain a **thesis statement**. The thesis statement expresses the central idea or theme of your speech in just one sentence. Here are three examples of thesis statements:

- Self-driving cars will change the way we live and get around in three ways: (1) by reducing accidents, (2) by permitting overnight travel, and (3) by fundamentally changing the taxicab and ride-sharing industries.

- Excessive personal debt is burdensome, inhibits a person's quality of life, and also results in financial instability.

- We fear the COVID-19 virus because of the number of deaths and serious illnesses it causes, as well as the long-term effects many victims experience.

The thesis statement, along with the specific purpose, acts as a road map for building your speech. Your next move is to develop the main points that flesh out the thesis.

▶ **Chapter 5** will show you in more detail how to create an effective thesis statement.

The Main Points

If your specific purpose and thesis are clearly formulated, it will be easy for you to identify your speech's **main points**—the blueprint for your speech containing those major ideas your speech will relay to receivers. Most of your speeches will contain two or three main points, with each main point supporting your expressed thesis. For example, let's look at the last thesis statement identified in the previous section. Its three main points might read:

I.   There is fear of a surge in deaths due to the COVID-19 virus.

II. Members of the general population can contract an array of serious illnesses attributed to the COVID-19 virus.

III. Responses to protect some members of the general population from suffering lasting effects from COVID-19 have thus far been only partially effective.

We see the speaker plans to first confront the fears about COVID-19 and then discuss the serious illnesses related to the disease and efforts to control the effects long-haulers experience. Once you formulate the main points, your next move is to locate and select supporting materials.

▶ **Chapter 9** will help you to establish your main points.

Conduct Research to Gather Supporting Materials

At this point, your attention turns to conducting research and gathering supporting materials for your speech. To develop your speech, for example, you will use personal experiences, examples and illustrations, definitions, expert testimony, statistics, and analogies. The better your research and selection of support, the more credible receivers will find your speech.

We can divide every speech into three major parts: the introduction, the body, and the conclusion. Develop the **body of the speech**, the part that elaborates on the main points, first. When it is done, you then bring it together with an **introduction** and a **conclusion**. In the introduction, orient the audience to your topic, pique their attention and interest, state your thesis, and preview your main points. In the conclusion, restate your thesis in a memorable way, remind receivers of how your main points supported it, and motivate them—leaving them thinking and/or ready to act.

Develop an Outline

An **outline** provides the skeleton upon which you hang your main ideas and support. Two principles guide its creation: **coordination** (the main points should be relatively equal in importance) and **subordination** (the support underlying your main points). The outline of your speech's body will look something like the following example.

Introduction

Body

Main Point I

A. First level of subordination

1. Second level of subordination

2. Second level of subordination

Main Point 2

A. First level of subordination

1. Second level of subordination

2. Second level of subordination

Main Point 3

A. First level of subordination

1. Second level of subordination

2. Second level of subordination

Conclusion

When outlining your speech, you'll want to keep each of the speech's main sections in mind—paying careful attention to the components contained in the introduction, body, and conclusion. The first component in your introduction should be an attention-getter, followed by your thesis statement, then a statement of what's in it for the audience (why they should care), a credibility enhancer for yourself (why they should listen to you), and a preview of your main points. Similarly, the outline of your conclusion should contain a summary of your main points and your "home run"—a move that clinches audience support for and belief in your message.

▶ **Chapters 8** and **9** will demonstrate how to organize and outline your speech.

Once the outline is complete, you'll want to create transitions that connect the parts. You can use signposts, such as "first," "next," and "finally," to let receivers know where you are in your speech, and brief statements, such as "most important," to help focus the audience's attention.

Then it's time to consider whether visual or audio aids, such as physical objects, drawings, charts, graphs, photographs, or sound recordings, will enhance the understanding and interest of receivers. Be sure to indicate in the outline when you will use such aids, if you choose to do so.

▶ **Chapter 14** will offer you tips on using presentation aids effectively.

Practice Delivery

How well you do in your first speech depends in part on how effectively you have prepared, practiced, and overcome any anxiety. Instead of reading a speech word for word or, worse, choosing to wing it, practice speaking in front of a mirror or before family members or friends. Make it a habit to plan and prepare the structure of your speech and all content, including supporting materials and visuals. Then rehearse extensively so that on the day you present your speech, you are comfortable using your notes to remind yourself of its content.

You will want to become so familiar with the contents of your speech that you can deliver it seemingly effortlessly. Focus on the word *seemingly* for a moment. Preparing and presenting a speech requires real effort on your part. But if you work diligently and conscientiously, your audience will see only the end results—to them it will seem as if you are a natural.

When it comes to vocal cues, for example, you'll want to regulate your volume, rate, pitch, and vocal variety, being especially careful not to speak in a monotone, and being certain to use correct pronunciation and clear articulation, so you convey ideas accurately and clearly. Beyond words, you'll also want to use appropriate facial expressions, sustain the right amount of eye contact, and use gestures and movement in support of your message

Practice giving the speech at least four to six times, and as we noted, deliver it initially to a mirror, and then to a small audience of family and friends. Stand when you practice. Always say your speech aloud. Use a timer. Revise your words or presentation as needed. Replicate the same conditions you will have when delivering it for real. Practice from the speech's beginning to its end without stopping. You might even record a rehearsal to assess how you're doing.

▶ See **Chapters 12** and **13** for more help with the delivery of your speech.

When you've finished speaking, audience members may have questions to ask you. When prepping for your presentation, think about what you would ask if you were a member of the audience. Also solicit questions from the rehearsal audiences made up of family and friends.

▶**Chapter 24** will prepare you for questions that the audience may ask about your speech.

You've prepared. You have rehearsed and revised, and now it's time to have fun! Harness any nervous energy and remember to use the confidence-building techniques you learned earlier in this chapter. Visualize yourself succeeding!

Conduct a Post-Presentation Analysis

Like any athlete or performer, you'll want to review and critique your own performance, comparing and contrasting your expectations with your actual experience. Try to learn as much as possible from the first speech so you can apply these lessons to your next one. Complete a self-assessment scorecard or checklist that you can compare to the one your professor and/or peers offer.

▶ **Chapter 3** will help you listen effectively in order to analyze your fellow students' speeches and assess your own presentation.

Use the accompanying preliminary scorecard (located after the Game Plan) to assess your performance.

GAME PLAN

My First Speech

- I have addressed my own feelings and fears about speechmaking.
- I have chosen a topic that I and my audience care about.
- I have researched my topic, integrating the best supporting materials into it.
- I created my outline using the most appropriate organizational framework for my speech.
- I rehearsed delivering my speech.
- The night prior to my speech, I practiced a powerful pose—I stood tall, leaned forward, and opened my arms to the audience, staking out a broad surface with my hands.
- Right before I started delivering my speech, I took a moment to center my breathing and thoughts.
- I delivered my speech confidently.

Use this scorecard to track your progress and assess your performance. Needing or seeking to improve isn't a negative; it's a step on the road to mastery. It's time to measure up! Score yourself on each item using a scale of 1 to 5, with 1 meaning not at all effective and 5 meaning extremely effective.

Post-Presentation Scorecard

Introduction: How Well Did I Do?

- Capturing attention_____
- Conveying my thesis_____
- Previewing my main points_____
- Relating the topic to my audience_____

Body: How Well Did I Do?

- Communicating each main point_____
- Transitioning between main points_____
- Integrating support for each main point_____

Conclusion: How Well Did I Do?

- Restating the thesis_____
- Summarizing my main points_____
- Motivating receivers to think and/or act_____

Delivery: How Well Did I Do?

- Using vocal cues to create interest and convey meaning_____
- Using eye contact to connect with receivers_____
- Using gestures and movement that were natural and appropriate_____
Overall, I would give myself _____ points out of 5.
I believe my strong points were

_____
_____
_____
_____
_____

I believe I need to improve when it comes to

_____
_____
_____
_____
_____

Based on this scorecard, I set the following goals for my next speech:

_____
_____
_____
_____
_____

EXERCISES

Get a Strong Start

Becoming proficient at public speaking, like any other skill, is accomplished with practice. With introspection comes insight; with practice comes mastery. Take advantage of every opportunity to build your confidence and speaking skills.

1. Deliver a Tip on How to Enhance Confidence

For practice, customize a topic related to speech apprehension, such as "Taking the Fear Out of Public Speaking," "The Uses of Hypnosis," or "How to De-stress." Once you select a topic, research it, and explain the guidelines given to reduce apprehension.

2. TED on Body Language

Watch either the TED Talk "Body Language Is in the Palm of Your Hands," by Allan Pease, available on YouTube, or Amy Cuddy's TED Talk about power poses, "Your Body Language May Shape Who You Are," available at ted.com. Each presentation reveals how body language shapes assessments of a person. Based on what you learn, identify what you can do to help others judge you to be a "powerful" presenter.

3. The Opening

View the opening monologue of an afternoon or late-night TV show such as *The Late Show* with Stephen Colbert, *The Tonight Show* with Jimmy Fallon, or *The Daily Show With Trevor Noah*. Assess the host's confidence delivering the opening monologue. What was the host's topic? Did it appeal to the audience? Why? Did the host come across as knowledgeable? Why? Did they come across as confident? Why? What signs of anxiety, if any, did you see the host exhibit? Was the host's focus on the audience or on themselves? How do you know? What three adjectives would you use to describe the host's performance? What aspects of your analysis can you apply to your performance as a speaker?

4. Warm Up to Public Speaking

First, prepare a list of "do and don't" suggestions for preparing a first speech. Include the speaker's role in selecting a topic, formulating a goal, researching, thinking about their relationship to the audience, organizing ideas, preparing to present, and assessing the extent to which the speaker and the speech succeeded. Next, choose one of the following assignments and share your thoughts with your peers in a two-to-three-minute presentation. Structure your presentation so it has a clear introduction, definite body, and strong conclusion.

   a. Interview another member of the class to identify a number of interesting facts about that person. Be as creative as possible in organizing and sharing what you discovered about your partner and what it has taught you.

   b. Describe a significant personal experience that challenged your sense of ethics.

   c. Based on a review of recent news stories, share a concern you have regarding the ability of members of society to respect one another and get along.

   d. Bring to class a picture, object, or brief literary or nonfiction selection that helps you express your feelings about a subject of importance to you. Share the selection with the class, discuss why you selected it, and explain how it helps you better understand yourself, others, or your relation to the subject.

   e. We often identify with our name. What does your name mean to you? Share your name's story with the class. Research your name by interviewing family members regarding how your name was chosen; exploring its meaning on name-related sites, such as Americannamesociety.org, Names.org, or Ancestry.com; and revealing any relevant facts, statistics, or interesting details/images connected with your name.

Finally, offer advice to a student whose task it is to critique this speech. What should they look for? How should they offer feedback?

5. Analyze This: A First Speech

Let's look at one student's first speech. (Comments or annotations on the speech are presented as side notes, or SN.) The topic was "My Hometown." As you read the speech, imagine it being delivered. Here are some questions for you to consider when evaluating it:

a. How do you think students in your class would respond to the speech? Would they, for example, find the topic as relevant and appealing as did the speaker? Why or why not?

b. Is the speech organized effectively? What do you believe is its purpose? Can you identify the thesis? Does the speech have an introduction that captures your attention, a clear body, and a sound conclusion? Are there transitions to link ideas? Is there sufficient support for each of the speaker's points?

c. What changes, if any, would you suggest making to improve the speech? For example, would you add presentation aids?

d. What questions would you like to ask the speaker?

My Hometown

Good afternoon. I have learned a lot from all of you about your hometowns in the United States by listening to your speeches over the last few weeks. You've shared fascinating details that have helped me form mental pictures of many places I have never seen. Now I would like to take you to my hometown, the city of Shanghai, China.

SN 1

> *In the opening, the speaker relates the present speech to preceding ones. The use of the active verb* take *positions receivers to travel along imaginatively with the speaker. The speaker's use of a question is involving.*

Have you ever been to New York City? Did you know that Shanghai has almost twice as many skyscrapers as New York City and will soon have 1,000 more? It is one of the biggest and most modern cities in China, and 18 million people live there. Shanghai already has many elevated highways and a subway, and the government is building a new ship terminal. The city even has a high-speed train line, the fastest in the world, that brings visitors from Shanghai's international airport into the city. And there are thousands of cars, many of them taxicabs in bright gold, red, and blue.

SN 2

> *The speaker builds rapport by comparing what receivers know about New York City with his own city of Shanghai.*

There are big changes taking place in Shanghai today, and they are happening very fast, but first I want to tell you about the city the way I remember it. Try to picture it with me.

Over the past hundred years, many Chinese people were able to improve their lives by moving into "the city about the sea"—that's what the name Shanghai means, the city about the sea. Leaving the undeveloped countryside behind, they came to the city to work and live, and they made their homes in small apartment buildings near the Huangpu riverfront or at the northern and southern edges of the city. My parents came to the city when they were young, leaving their families behind in the countryside. They worked hard, riding bicycles to their jobs and saving as much as they could. For a long time, they didn't have very much.

SN 3

> *The speaker demonstrates a deep emotional connection to the topic. The sense of change is in the air. The speaker's use of narrative draws receivers into the body of the presentation.*

I grew up in our two-room apartment on the third floor and knew everyone in our neighborhood. Everyone knew everyone, in fact! We lived on the western riverbank, near the famous Shanghai Bund, which is a thoroughfare about a mile long of historic old buildings in the Western style. Our own neighborhood was also old but crowded and full of busy apartment buildings. Our building was separated from the others by narrow lanes filled with bicycles and motorbikes, and there was laundry hanging everywhere to dry. I could often hear our neighbors laughing, arguing, or playing the radio, and the smell of food cooking was always in the air.

SN 4

> *The speaker's use of description and sensory images resonate.*

I walked or rode my bicycle to school, and my route took me past the open-air markets and street vendors selling all kinds of food. Sometimes, it was hard not to stop and buy something or to linger by the park where there was always a little crowd of people performing their morning tai chi exercises, but I would never want to shame my parents by being late for school.

Sometimes, when we had a school holiday, my friends and I would go to Nanjing Donglu. That is the big shopping area in the middle of Shanghai, where there are all kinds of stores. There are places to buy food of all kinds, like duck, sausages, fish, oysters, and shrimp, and of course tea, and you can also find tools, hardware, art, clothes, and even pets. My friends at home have told me that, because one part of it is now closed to cars, Nanjing Donglu has even more tourists than ever before. These are mostly Chinese tourists, from other parts of the country, who enjoy coming to Shanghai to see the sights.

SN 5

> *The speaker changes tone to make clear the downside of modernization.*

There were still cars allowed in Nanjing Donglu when I was growing up in Shanghai, but as I said, there are many changes happening there. One of the biggest is the change in old neighborhoods like mine, which are being torn down to make way for the new skyscrapers I told you about, and other developments like new ports, factories, shipyards, and parks and pavilions. The World Expo took place in Shanghai some years back, and the government was very anxious and worked really hard to make the city as modern and as developed as possible, and it did this very quickly at great cost. There are many people who worked to preserve as much of old, historic Shanghai as they could, but hundreds of people lost their homes in the old town and moved away into the suburbs.

SN 6

> *In the conclusion, the speaker prompts continued interest by leaving the audience wondering what will happen when the speaker returns to Shanghai.*

Next time I return to the city, my neighborhood near the Bund will be the first place I visit. I want to see whether my old home and my neighbors are still there.[32]

6. Approach the Speaker's Stand: Give Your First Speech

Use what you have learned about topic selection; speech development, support, and organization; presentation, practice, and delivery; and harnessing positive energy to prepare and give your first speech on a topic such as your hometown or another topic selected by your instructor. After delivering the speech, offer a self-assessment of your performance.

RECAP AND REVIEW

1.1   Demonstrate the personal, professional, and societal benefits of public speaking.

Public speaking precipitates self-discovery and the art of creative self-expression. It enhances self-confidence and the ability to influence or control one's environment. In addition, prospective employers favor people with public speaking abilities. And society benefits from people who are able to function as responsible citizens and participate in the exchange of ideas.

1.2   Explain the face-to-face and digital contexts of public speaking, also identifying the essential elements of communication.

The following elements are integral to communicating: the source formulates and delivers a message; the receiver interprets the source's message; the message is the content of the speech; the channel is the pathway that carries the message; noise is anything that interferes with the sending or receiving of a message; the cultural context, including whether the speaker and audience are physically present or online, is the environment in which communication occurs; feedback is information received in response to a sent message; effect is the outcome or exchange of influences occurring during communication; and the field of experience is the sum of all the experiences that a person carries with them when communicating.

1.3   Assess and build your speechmaking confidence.

Public speaking anxiety is composed of process anxiety (the fear of preparing a speech) and performance anxiety (the fear of presenting a speech). It is important to acknowledge and face whatever fear you have so that you are able to harness the excess energy that accompanies it. Among the common sources of speechmaking anxiety are fear of failure, fear of the unknown, fear of evaluation, fear of being the center of attention, fear of difference, and fear imposed by culture. A variety of strategies can help you address both the physical and mental effects of speech anxiety. Practice tensing and relaxing your muscles, strike a powerful pose, focus on changing your own negative thoughts, and take comfort in honing your own competence by practicing and delivering speeches.

1.4   Use a step-by-step approach to deliver your first speech.

There are four basic plays in speechmaking: (1) topic selection; (2) speech development, support, and organization; (3) practice and delivery; and (4) post-presentation analysis. By working your way through all the plays step by step, you approach speechmaking systematically. Only by preparing and delivering a speech can you tell how well you understand and how effectively you are able to execute the plays involved. Like athletes, actors, and musicians, speakers review and critique their own performances, attempting to learn as much as possible from each experience so they can apply the lessons to future events.

KEY TERMS

Accumulative experiences (p. 7)

Body of the speech (p. 21)

Centering (p. 14)

Centering breath (p. 14)

Channel (p. 8)

Cognitive restructuring (p. 14)

Communication (p. 6)

Conclusion (p. 21)

Coordination (p. 21)

Effects of communication (p. 7)

Ethnocentricity (p. 12)

Feedback (p. 7)

Field of experience (p. 29)

General purpose (p. 20)

Introduction (p. 21)

Main points (p. 21)

Message (p. 8)

Noise (p. 6)

Outline (p. 21)

Performance anxiety (p. 11)

Playbook (p. 4)

Process anxiety (p. 11)

Public speaking (p. 4)

Public speaking anxiety (p. 11)

Receiver (p. 6)

Self-talk (p. 11)

Situational/cultural context (p. 6)

Source (p. 6)

Specific purpose (p. 20)

Subordination (p. 21)

Thesis statement (p. 20)

Thought stopping (p. 14)

2 PUBLIC SPEAKING IN A CONNECTED WORLD

Inclusion, Ethics, and Critical Thinking

UPON COMPLETING THIS CHAPTER, YOU WILL BE ABLE TO

2.1   Explain why cultural understanding enhances the effectiveness of speakers and audiences.

2.2   Discuss the importance of ethics, identifying ethical principles and guidelines relevant to public speaking.

2.3   Demonstrate the role critical thinking plays in public speaking, explaining its significance for speakers and audiences.

We've all been there. Speaking before members of other cultures, we inadvertently make a messaging mistake and end up miscommunicating. For example, what if you didn't know that in Brazil, raising your fist means a person's spouse is cheating, while putting your fist to your forehead indicates you think someone is stupid? In the United States, we interpret a raised fist as a power sign, while putting our fist to our forehead means we're thinking or have a headache. In the United States, raising two fingers and giving the V sign means victory or peace. In Australia, however, it is the equivalent of raising the middle finger in the United States, while in the United Kingdom, it's basically an invitation to fight. In the United States, the thumbs-up gesture signals "good job," but in Iran and Iraq it's one of the worst nonverbal insults you can make.[1] When cues like these cross cultures, they can be misinterpreted, becoming intercultural faux-pas. Should this happen to you, it's best to transform your miscommunication into a cultural lesson and learning opportunity.[2] For one thing, ask yourself what you erroneously assumed or failed to understand. Make the effort to discover what to say and/or how to gesture differently next time.

What do *cultural diversity* and *inclusion*, and *ethics* and *critical thinking* have to do with public speaking? Winning public speakers practice certain skills to reach diverse groups of receivers and to make each speaking engagement meaningful and respectful. Speakers who take cultural differences into account, demonstrating inclusivity and respect for diversity, develop messages with broad appeal. But it doesn't stop there. Ethics and critical thinking matter, too. Just as we expect athletes to play by certain rules and game referees to make fair calls, we expect speakers to make sound ethical choices—and to present their ideas, arguments, and information in a fair and balanced way. If a speaker is being unfair, we, the audience, then need to rely on our critical thinking skills to keep from being unknowingly manipulated. In this chapter, our goal is to help you become a culturally aware, ethical, and sound thinker—equipped with assets you can use not only on your campus but also well beyond it, including at work and in your community.

RESPECT DIFFERENT CULTURES

2.1   *Explain why cultural understanding enhances the effectiveness of speakers and audiences.*

Public speakers need to prepare to speak before diverse audiences.[3] **Cultural diversity** is the recognition and valuing of difference. It encompasses such factors as age, gender, race, ethnicity, ability, religion, education, marital status, sexual orientation, and income. **Inclusion** is the opposite of exclusion and marginalization, ensuring that everyone has an equal opportunity to belong, influence, and be heard.

Speeches and our responses to them demonstrate our understanding of difference and our tolerance for dissent. Beyond mutual respect, however, lies our own self-interest. When we demonstrate respect for cultural diversity and inclusivity, we reduce the chances of alienating members of the audience and increase the chances of eliciting the audience response we seek. By recognizing, for instance, that receivers from different cultures may be offended by different things, and that speakers from other cultures may display more or less expressiveness than their receivers, we become more culturally attuned and less culturally tone-deaf (see Table 2.1).

TABLE 2.1 ■ Focus on Cultural Diversity	
A Speaker Who Respects Diversity	**A Speaker Who Neglects Diversity**
Develops a complex view of issues	Develops a simplistic view of issues
Does not stereotype, avoiding its consequences	Frequently stereotypes, having to face the consequences
Sees things from others' viewpoints—empathizing with them	Sees things only from their own perspective; assumes others share their values
Is comfortable speaking before a culturally diverse audience	Becomes anxious when speaking before a culturally diverse audience
Does not alienate receivers by trying to impose their views on them	Tries to impose their views on others, risking open hostility from receivers

Attune Yourself to Difference

Why should attuning yourself to cultural differences be part of your public speaking training? For one thing, according to demographers, diversity is reshaping the future of the United States and transforming our person-to-person ties even more quickly than was originally predicted. While the 2020 U.S. Census Bureau reported that 191.7 million people identified as non-Hispanic white people, the number of white people is declining. Nearly 4 in 10 people now identify themselves as other than white.[4] For the first time, the percentage of white people dropped below 60 percent. Some 57.8 percent of the U.S. population identify as non-Hispanic white people or white alone; 12.1 percent as Black or African American alone; 6.1 percent as Asian alone; and 1.1 percent as American-Indian and Alaska Native alone. 2.8 percent identified as two or more races. Native Hawaiians and Pacific Islanders comprise .2 percent of the population. At 18.7 percent, Hispanics and Latinos are now the largest minority group. The under 18 population is now majority people of color at 52.7 percent. Within one generation, underrepresented groups are forecast to become the majority.[5]

More than half the children in the United States currently are of a minority race or ethnic group.[6] Given such statistics, there is a good chance you will find yourself speaking before audiences whose cultural backgrounds and perspectives differ from your own. Your success depends on your ability to face up to cultural diversity and speak freely and listen critically across cultures.

SELF-ASSESSMENT 2.1: HOW PREPARED ARE YOU TO ADDRESS AND LISTEN TO PEOPLE OF DIVERSE CULTURES?

Directions

Use the following scales to evaluate your feelings about multiculturalism by indicating where on the scale you fall relative to each statement.

Statement	Totally Disagree 1	Disagree 2	Neutral 3	Agree 4	Totally Agree 5
1. I am equally as comfortable speaking before people who are like me as I am speaking before people who are different from me.					
2. It is important to me to consider the concerns and respect the values, beliefs, and customs of all groups in society equally.					
3. Public speakers always should take into account the differences between themselves and their audiences.					
4. I am equally comfortable listening to people from other cultures and listening to people from my own culture.					

Statement	Totally Disagree 1	Disagree 2	Neutral 3	Agree 4	Totally Agree 5
5. I believe in respecting the communication rules and preferences of people from other cultures, just as I would want people from other cultures to respect the communication rules and preferences of my culture.					
6. I support the right of people from other cultures to disagree with my values and beliefs.					
7. I accept that people from other cultures may choose not to participate in a dialogue or debate because of their culture's rules.					
8. I understand that expressiveness, including facial expressions, gestures, and nonverbal signals, vary from culture to culture.					
9. I respect that a culture provides its members with a continuum of appropriate and inappropriate communication behaviors.					
10. I do not believe that my culture is superior to all other cultures.					

Analysis	Implication
Add together the numbers you chose on each scale: _____ Total To determine your level of comfort with multiculturalism, refer to the range below: 41–50 You are accepting of diversity 31–40 You are ambivalent towards diversity 21–30 You are somewhat unaccepting of diversity 10–20 You are very unaccepting of diversity.	What does your score reveal? The higher your score, the better equipped you are to enrich the public speaking arena by welcoming people from diverse cultures into it. Although this evaluation is not a scientific instrument, it should give you some indication of your general feelings toward and acceptance of diversity.

Assess Your Understanding of Cultural Diversity

When speaking before audiences small or large, if we want to share ideas successfully, we need to take cultural differences into account. Speechmakers and their audiences need to consider how the language, norms and rules of their culture impact them and others. In addition to sensitizing themselves to the differences in the meanings attached to the nonverbal cues used, which as we see is necessary to avoid misinterpreting messages sent and received, they cannot overlook the importance that members of diverse cultures place on cultural customs. Too frequently, ethnocentrism—the belief that one's own culture is superior to all other cultures—impedes communication by arousing feelings of prejudice and hostility toward those different from us. Overcoming the negative effects of ethnocentrism does not require agreement with another culture's practices. What it does require is respect for the different cultures present and a willingness to adjust both messages sent and expectations. Rather than judge one another on the basis of appearance or delivery, listen like you would want a person from another culture to listen to you.

Reflect Cultural Values

Culture is the system of knowledge, beliefs, values, attitudes, behaviors, and artifacts (objects made or used by humans) that we learn, accept, and use in daily life. Typically, cultural norms and assumptions are passed from the senior to the newer members of a group. Adept speakers use these cues to adapt to different audiences.

Co-cultures

Within a culture as a whole are co-cultures. Co-cultures are composed of members of the same general culture who differ in some ethnic or sociological way from the dominant culture. In American society, for example, African Americans, Hispanic Americans, Japanese Americans, Arab Americans, disabled, LGBTQ+, and older Americans are just some of the co-cultures belonging to the same general culture[7] (see Figure 2.1).

People belonging to a **marginalized group**—a group whose members feel like outsiders—may passively, assertively, or aggressively/confrontationally seek to reach their goals relative to the dominant culture.

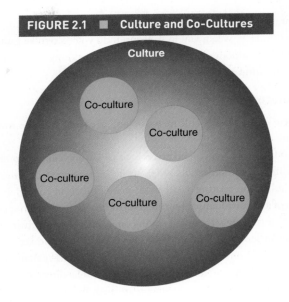

FIGURE 2.1 ■ Culture and Co-Cultures

A Culture and Its Co-cultures. The term *co-culture* is preferred over sub-culture because the prefix *sub* denotes inferior status. A co-culture is a culture within a culture.

- Co-culture members who practice a *passive approach* usually avoid the limelight or the lectern, accepting their position in the cultural hierarchy. They embrace the cultural beliefs and practices of the dominant culture. Recent immigrants to the United States who desire to attain citizenship may choose this path, hoping to blend in.

- Co-culture members who employ an *assertive approach* want members of the dominant group to accommodate their diversity. At the same time, they are receptive to rethinking their ideas, giving up or modifying some, but holding strong with regard to others. For example, many Chinese Americans spoke openly of their support for America while also expressing their desire to live free from racism's reach during the COVID-19 pandemic. Similarly, years earlier Muslim Americans spoke openly of their support for the War on Terror while also expressing their desire to live according to their religious values and beliefs, which were falsely conflated with those of the terrorists behind the attacks of September 11, 2001.

- Co-culture members who take an *aggressive/confrontational approach* more intensely defend their beliefs and traditions, leading to their being perceived by members of the dominant culture as "hurtfully expressive" or "self-promoting." They make it difficult for members of the dominant culture to ignore their presence or pretend they do not exist.[8] Co-culture members adopt this strategy in an effort to de-marginalize themselves and actively participate in the world of the dominant culture. In their early years, the members of ACT UP, a gay rights organization, employed such an approach, much like members of the Black Lives Matter movement do now.

Within the context of cultural diversity, how would you identify yourself? Consider your own classroom or workplace. When you look around, do you recognize groups that constitute co-cultures? When taking a podium, remember to avoid speaking solely to one group. Public speaking is about communicating to as many listeners as possible.

Different Communication Styles

We need to recognize both how the culture we belong to affects our communication and how other people's cultures affect theirs.

Individualistic cultures like the United States tend to use **low-context communication** (members favor a more direct communication style), while **high-context communication** (members are very polite and indirect in relating to others) is predominant in collectivistic cultures such as China. As members of an individualistic culture, North Americans tend to speak in a low-context way, addressing an issue directly rather than relying on innuendo to get their point across. Persons from Asian countries including Japan and South Korea, usually avoid confrontation, relying on a high-context communication style that is based on inference rather than direct statements and allows others to save face.[9] Thus, a North American speaker may directly contradict what another person has said, while an Asian speaker's comments are likely to be more indirect and subtle.

In some cultures, dissent and disagreement with friends and relatives is considered normal—it is possible to separate a speaker from her words—while in other cultures, speakers and their words are perceived as one. In the latter case, when you dispute someone's words, you also cast aspersions on their character. As a result, rarely will one Saudi Arabian publicly criticize or chastise another because doing so would label that speaker as disloyal and disrespectful.[10] It is important that speakers and audience members not interpret each other's behavior based on their own frames of reference or cultural norms, but work to understand the cultural dynamics of persons from their own as well as other cultures.

COACHING TIP

"Diversity is the mix. Inclusion is making the mix work."

Andres Tapia, Global Diversity and Inclusion Solutions leader and author

Creating community out of diversity depends on keeping the "isms" at bay. Because they exclude rather than include, ethnocentrism, racism, sexism, and ageism have no place in your speaker's toolbox. Maya Angelou observed, "We should all know that diversity makes for a rich tapestry, and we must understand that the threads of the tapestry are equal in value no matter what their color." Diversity is not divisive. Its recognition is inclusive.

Understand Cultural Identity

We also need insight into **cultural identity**, the internalization of culturally appropriate beliefs, values, and roles acquired through interacting with members of our cultural group. Cultural identity also is a product of our group memberships. We all belong to a number of different groups and form identities based on these group memberships, with cultural notions influencing what it means to be a group member.

- *Gender* affects the way males and females present themselves, socialize, work, perceive their futures, and communicate. Men tend to adopt a problem-solving orientation and prefer to use a linear approach to storytelling and presentations, while women typically offer more details and fill in tangential information.[11]

- *Age* influences our beliefs about how persons our age should look and behave. An older person may be perceived as wiser. Age can also influence judgments of credibility and precipitate disagreements about values and priorities. For this reason, persons belonging to different age groups are likely to perceive issues such as Social Security reform, transgender rights, and the value of rap music differently.

- *Racial and ethnic identities*, in addition to being based on physical characteristics, are also socially constructed. Some racial and ethnic groups share experiences of oppression; their attitudes and behaviors may reflect their struggles. Thus, race influences attitudes toward controversial issues such as affirmative action, welfare reform, interracial marriage and adoption, and racism. What does race mean to you? Can you boil your thoughts down to to a six-word micro-speech that sums up your thoughts, observations, and experiences about race? For example, Susan Goldberg, the editor of *National Geographic,* came up with: "White, privileged, with much to learn."[12]

- *Religious identity* is at the root of countless contemporary conflicts occurring around the world, including in the Middle East, Northern Ireland, India and Pakistan, and Bosnia-Herzegovina, and it sometimes influences receiver and speaker responses to issues and world events. In the United States, for example, evangelical Christians may have a different view of the relationship between church and state than do members of other religious groups.

- *Socioeconomic identity* frames our responses to issues, influencing our attitudes and experiences as well as the way we communicate. The widening gap between the ultra-wealthy and the middle and lower classes in this country contributes to different attitudes on a host of issues, including tax cuts.

- *National identity* refers to our legal status or citizenship. People whose ancestors immigrated to the United States generations ago may still be perceived as foreigners by some Americans.

A speaker should be aware that the culture, economic and social class, and gender of receivers might influence the way audience members will process the examples the speaker employs. For example, based on their personal experience, audiences of mostly women, mostly men, or mixed gender likely would react differently to the examples used in this excerpt from a speech on "Why Girls Matter" by Anna Maria Chavez, CEO of Girl Scouts of the United States of America. How do you react to it, and why?

> Our alumnae have made huge impacts on all sectors of our communities. In the world of entertainment, for example, Taylor Swift is a Girl Scout. In the world of athletics, so is tennis star Venus Williams. Media great Robin Roberts is a Girl Scout alumna. Virtually every female astronaut who has flown into space was a Girl Scout. And one successful businesswoman who was a Girl Scout is Ginny Rometty, CEO of IBM. All the former female U.S. secretaries of state were Girl Scouts: Madeline Albright, Condoleezza Rice, and Hillary Clinton. Fifteen of the 20 women in the U.S. Senate are Girl Scout alumnae. So are more than half of the 88 women in the House of Representatives. And of the five women who currently serve as governors across our nation, four were Girl Scouts.

> Embracing the values of tolerance and civility is not a hindrance to success, it is clear, but an asset because it instills the values of character, confidence and courage. That is more than a matter of opinion. According to a recent survey, nearly two-thirds of Girl Scouts view themselves as leaders, compared with 44 percent of other girls, and 52 percent of boys.[13]

Speakers also need to be aware of how different cultures process humor. When integrating humorous stories, keep in mind that humor does not always translate. For example, topics such as sex and dating could be distasteful to Muslims, and "your mama" jokes could be unacceptable to Zambians, because Zambian parents are revered like gods.[14]

By considering ethnic and cultural identity, respecting diversity, and developing our understanding of people who are unlike us, we improve our ability to use public speaking to create community.

Consider Preferred Learning Styles

Speakers need to be sensitive to how receivers prefer to learn and process information. Some of us are aural learners, others are visual learners, and some of us need to be approached at an abstract level. If a speaker offers a variety of support that appeals to more than one learning style, that speaker will succeed in reaching the audience.

Understand Difference to Build Bridges and Confidence

Acknowledging that all cultures do not share the same communication rules benefits us both as citizens and as public speakers. The more we know about those from other cultures, the more confident we become speaking or listening to others. Use the following two tips as guides.

We are unique. Take into account that diversity means audience members may learn differently.

istockphoto.com/hispanolistic

Avoid Formulating Expectations Based Solely on Your Own Culture

When those you speak to have diverse communication preferences, acknowledge them and accept their validity. By not isolating yourself within your own group or culture, you become a more effective speaker.

Make a Commitment to Develop Speechmaking and Listening Skills Appropriate to Life in the Age of Multiculturalism and Globalization

By talking openly about controversial topics, listening to different viewpoints, and understanding how policies may inequitably affect people belonging to different cultural groups, you take a giant step toward understanding why diversity matters.

Although culture is a tie that binds, the global world grows smaller and smaller each day through technological advancement and ease of travel. Respecting difference, speaking and listening responsibly, and ethics go hand in hand. With this in mind, make it a priority to

- Be a respectful and patient listener.

- Engage and ask questions—rephrase if confusion persists.

- Have empathy and imagine yourself in another's shoes.

SPEAK ETHICALLY

> **2.2**   *Discuss the importance of ethics, identifying ethical principles and guidelines relevant to public speaking.*

Ethics express society's notions about the rightness or wrongness of an act, the distinctions between virtue and vice, and where to draw the line between what we should and should not do.[15] For example, what ethical code do we expect college athletes to follow? We expect them to follow the rules and avoid performance-enhancing drugs; to play fair, not cheat. Is it any different in public speaking? The kinds of cheating that speakers and audience members engage in involve breaches in trust similar to those committed by athletes and other performers. Would you cheat to impress an audience? Or would you sacrifice your goals if they turned out not to contribute to the overall well-being of others?

Here are some more ethical quandaries to resolve:

- Is it an ethical breach to speak on a subject about which you personally don't care?

- Is it ethical to use a fabricated story to increase personal persuasiveness but not tell the audience the story is made up?

- Is it right to convince others to believe what you do not yourself believe?

- Is it ethical to refuse to listen to a speaker you find offensive?

When facing ethical dilemmas or potentially compromising situations, our personal code of conduct guides us in making ethical choices.[16] Ethical speakers treat receivers as they would want a speaker to treat them; they do not intentionally deceive listeners just to attain their objectives. You should reveal everything your listeners need to know to be able to assess both you and your message, and not cover up, lie, distort, or exaggerate to win their approval and support. A functioning society depends on our behaving ethically.

Ethical communication is honest and accurate and reflective, not only of your best interests but also the best interests of others. **Ethical speechmaking** has its basis in trust in and respect for the speaker and receivers. It involves the responsible handling of information as well as an awareness of and concern for speechmaking's outcomes or consequences.

Ethical Behavior Audiences Expect of Speakers

When receivers judge a speaker to be of good character, they are more likely to trust the speaker's motives, concluding that the speaker will neither take nor suggest they take any action that would bring them harm. When receivers discover that speakers have been less than candid or truthful, they lose faith in the speaker's trustworthiness, integrity, credibility, and sincerity. Once receivers doubt a speaker, their words soon lose their impact, and trust, once lost, is extremely difficult to restore.

To be perceived as ethical in the eyes of audience members, adhere to the following tips.

Play fair. As in sports, being honest and ethical in public speaking is essential for success.

Stockbyte/Thinkstock

Share Only What You Know to Be True

Receivers expect you to be honest. That said,

- Do not misrepresent your purpose for speaking.
- Do not distort information to make it appear more useful.
- Never deceive receivers regarding the credentials of a source.

Avoid committing an **overt lie** (deliberately saying something that you know to be false) or a **covert lie** (knowingly allowing others to believe something that isn't true). Whenever you hope to convey a false impression or convince another to believe something that you yourself do not believe, you are lying.[17] Such deceptive behavior is a violation of the unspoken bond between speaker and receivers.

Respect the Audience

Your audience doesn't want you to exploit their wants and needs, manipulate their emotions, or trick them into believing a fabrication to fuel your own desire for power or profit. Instead, they expect you to be honest and open—to engage them in dialogue and critical inquiry. Audience members have the right to be treated as your equals. Consider their opinions, try to understand their perspective on issues, respect their right to hold opinions that differ from yours, and acknowledge that you do not know it all.

COACHING TIP

"I'm telling you a lie in a vicious effort that you will repeat my lie over and over until it becomes true."

Lady Gaga, singer and songwriter

Repeating what you want others to believe doesn't make what you are saying any truer! Personal biases can affect the impact messages have. Step back and examine yours. Then add logic and reason to the mix. Be sure to "tell the truth, the whole truth, and nothing but the truth." If others don't view you as trustworthy, your words won't matter. Truth telling is not necessarily easy. In fact, telling others the truth is often more difficult than lying. But audiences deserve the truth. Telling them lies undermines their best interests. Make truth telling part of your personal code.

Prepare Fully

Receivers expect you to be thoroughly informed and knowledgeable about your topic. They should be confident that you will present them with correct information, more than one side of an issue, and not knowingly mislead them by shaping, slicing, and selectively using data. You need to explore all sides of an issue (not just the ones you favor) and "tell it like it is" (not like you want your receivers to think it is).

Put the Audience First

Audience members have a right to expect that you will attempt to understand and empathize with them and the situations they face. A person who speaks on the importance of tax cuts for the rich without exploring the impact of such a policy on working families fails in their duty. Receivers also have a right to know that you will not ask them to commit an illegal act or do anything that is destructive of their welfare. For this reason, it would not be ethical to speak on a topic like the virtues of underage drinking or getting out of speeding tickets.

Be Easy to Understand

Audience members have a right to expect that you will talk at their level of understanding, rather than below or above it. The audience should come away feeling they have sufficient grasp of your content to make an informed decision. If you use language unfamiliar to receivers, they will fail to grasp your message. And if you talk down to receivers, failing to recognize the knowledge base they have, they will feel insulted or belittled.

Don't Weaponize Words

Although your words may not literally wound others, they can do psychological damage. Willfully making false statements about another, engaging in name-calling or other personal attacks, or using inflammatory language to incite panic is unethical. Speak civilly.

Don't Spin

The audience has a right to expect that you will not manipulate their reactions by providing half-truths or failing to share information that proves you wrong. A speaker who knowingly suppresses information that contradicts their position destroys whatever bond of trust existed between speaker and audience.

Don't Spread Disinformation

Disinformation, the 2019 word of the year, is the deliberate spread of false or inaccurate information with the intention of influencing public opinion. It is deceptive and manipulative. Composed of lies and conspiracy theories, disinformation is insidious, infecting the minds of receivers with false information that is then repeated and shared.[18] The dangers disinformation presents for a democracy are evident in what happened on January 6, 2021, when a mob breached the U.S. Capitol after being fed disinformation about the validity of the 2020 presidential election results. To avoid passing on disinformation use reliable news sources, fact-check websites, and double-check your own confirmation biases (the tendency to accept that information that confirms held beliefs).

Number one. Putting the audience's needs first will help you deliver a speech that is ethical and has greater impact.

iStockPhoto.com/Propicture

Respect Difference

Audience members may have different ideas about what constitutes an interesting topic, proper language, appropriate structure, or effective delivery. In order to meet their expectations, speakers need to look at the contents of a speech through the eyes of the members of different cultures rather than assume that all audience members see things the same way. By acknowledging the differences among receivers, speakers can accomplish their goals. For example, members of some cultural groups—African Americans, for example—expect to participate overtly in a speech event, even to the point of helping to co-create it, while members of other cultural groups consider such participation to be disrespectful of the speaker.[19] Similarly, U.S. audience members may judge a presentation that is blunt and opinionated acceptable and even preferable, while Chinese audience members may judge it to be rude or insensitive.[20] Whatever their cultural backgrounds, receivers have a right to their attitudes and beliefs. They have a right to expect that you will acknowledge and respect their right to disagree with you.

TABLE 2.2 ■ Focus on Ethics	
An Ethical Speaker	**An Unethical Speaker**
Is intent on enhancing the well-being of receivers	Is intent on achieving their own goal, whatever the cost
Treats audience members as they would like to be treated by a speaker	Treats audience members strictly in terms of their own needs, ignoring audience member needs
Reveals everything receivers need to know to assess both speaker and message fairly	Conceals, lies, distorts, or exaggerates information to win the approval and support of receivers
Relies on valid evidence	Juices evidence, deliberately overwhelming receivers with appeals to emotion
Informs receivers whom, if anyone, they represent	Conceals from receivers the person or interest groups they represent
Documents all sources	Plagiarizes others' ideas, exhibiting a reckless disregard for the sources of ideas or information

Hold Yourself Accountable for Plagiarism

Listeners expect you to be morally accountable for your speech's content and to distinguish your personal opinions from factual information. You are not merely a messenger; you bear responsibility for the message.

Receivers also have a right to believe that, when uncredited, the words are yours. If you present the ideas and words of others as if they were your own, then you are committing plagiarism. The word itself is derived from the Latin word *plagiarius*, meaning "kidnapper." Thus, when you plagiarize, you kidnap or steal the ideas and words of another and claim them as your own (see Table 2.2). Whether you steal a little or a lot, it's stealing. Whether you plagiarize a lot (pass another person's speech off as your own), filch a few lines verbatim from different sources that you fail to credit, or take a small section of another person's speech to integrate into your own speech, it's plagiarism.

Here are four simple steps to follow to avoid passing off someone else's ideas or words as your own:

1. Attribute the source of every piece of evidence you cite. Never borrow the words or thoughts of someone else without acknowledging that you have done so.

2. Indicate whether you are quoting or paraphrasing a statement.

3. Use and credit a variety of sources.

When students fail to adhere to these guidelines, they expose themselves to serious personal consequences, such as academic probation or expulsion.

Credit where credit's due. Citing sources for all your research and anything you borrow is an essential task of ethical behavior.

iStockPhoto.com/blackred

Ethical Behavior Speakers Expect of Audiences

Civility, the act of showing regard for others, should be the watchword of receivers. Even if receivers disagree with a speaker, they should not heckle or shout down the speaker. Instead of cutting off speech, receivers need to hear the speaker out, work to understand the speaker's ideas, and in time, respond with speech of their own.

Give All Ideas a Fair Hearing

Do not prejudge speakers. Evaluate what they have to say, see it from their perspective, and honestly assess their speech's content based on what they share and not on any preconceptions you may have.

To act ethically, listen to the whole speech and process the speaker's words before deciding whether to accept or reject the speaker's ideas. Do not jump to conclusions and blindly accept or reject the speaker's ideas on the basis of the speaker's reputation, appearance, opening statements, or manner of delivery. Be a patient receiver.

Be Courteous, Attentive, and React Honestly

Speakers have a right to expect that you will listen and respond honestly and critically, not merely politely or blindly, to a presentation. To do this, you need to focus fully on the ideas being presented. Although you need not agree with everything a speaker says, you do need to provide speakers with accurate and thoughtful feedback that indicates what you have understood and how you feel about the message.

When questions are permitted after a speech, effective questioners first paraphrase the speaker's remarks to be sure they accurately understand the speaker's intentions, and then go on to ask a question or offer an opinion.

Speakers have a right to expect that you will listen to them regardless of any differences in age, culture, religion, nationality, class, sexual orientation, or educational background. An ethical listener recognizes that not all speakers share their perspective. But above all else, the behavior of ethical listeners does nothing to undermine a speaker's right to be heard.

THINK CRITICALLY

> **2.3**   *Demonstrate the role critical thinking plays in public speaking, explaining its significance for speakers and audiences.*

Critical thinking is the ability to explore an issue or situation, integrate all the available information about it, arrive at a conclusion, and validate a position. A form of information literacy, it plays a key role in public speaking.[21] Both speakers and their audiences need to be critical thinkers, arriving at a judgment about the plausibility of information only after an honest evaluation of alternatives based on available evidence and arguments.[22] Critical thinkers are honest inquirers who do not accept information without weighing its value.[23]

It is up to you as both public speaker and listener to take an active role in the speechmaking and speech evaluation process so that you practice critical thinking rather than subvert its use. When a speaker makes an emotional appeal for your support, be diligent in determining whether information exists that justifies responding as the speaker requests. Examine the evidence on which conclusions are based to ensure they are valid and sound, to spot weaknesses in arguments, and to judge the credibility of statements.

It is important, however, also to think creatively. Play with existing ideas so they yield new and fresh insights. Work to see the interconnectedness among ideas. It is also up to you to avoid accepting stale or faulty arguments. Look for differences or inconsistencies in various parts of a message. Ask questions about unsupported content. Decide whether conclusions are convincing or unconvincing and whether an argument makes sense. Base your opinion about the message on the evidence.

Critically thinking speakers expand receivers' knowledge, introducing them to new ideas and challenging them to reexamine their beliefs, values, and behaviors. Similarly, the listener who is a critical thinker does not judge a speaker or the speaker's remarks prematurely, is willing to reexamine ideas and beliefs, and refuses to use shoddy thinking habits to substantiate invalid conclusions. Speakers and listeners must hold each other accountable for both truth and accuracy. To accomplish this, follow the guidelines outlined in Table 2.3.

Set Goals

Prior to attending a speech, consider the speaker's and/or the listener's motivations for being there. Think about the degree to which the speaker is speaking to serve their own interests or the interests of others. Reflect on the degree to which your mind is open to receive the speaker's ideas.

The thinker. As a speaker, try to see ideas from fresh perspectives, and as an audience member, don't take all pieces of information at face value.

iStock.com/Siphotography

TABLE 2.3 ■ Focus on Critical Thinking	
A Speaker Who Thinks Critically	**A Speaker Who Thinks Uncritically**
Recognizes the limitations of their knowledge	Thinks they know everything
Is open-minded, taking time to reflect	Is closed-minded and impulsive, jumping to unwarranted conclusions
Pays attention to those with whom they agree and disagree	Pays attention only to those with whom they agree
Looks for good reasons to accept or reject others' opinions	Disregards opinions others offer, even if valid
Insists on getting the best information	Picks and chooses information to suit their own purpose
Explores what is stated and unstated, investigating all assumptions	Focuses only on what is stated, ignoring unstated assumptions
Reflects on how well conclusions fit premises and vice versa	Disregards a lack of connection between evidence and conclusions

Analyze Consequences

After a speech, speaker and receivers evaluate one another's behavior, their own behavior, and the likely consequences of their behavior.

For every speech event, seek to determine

- If honesty prevailed
- If language was used ethically
- If convictions were clearly expressed
- If logical evidence was used
- If emotional appeals added interest, but did not conceal the truth, and
- If selfish interests were disclosed

Assess Outcomes and Their Effects

Was the speech a success or a failure, and why do you think so? Think in terms of how effective the speechmaker was rather than whether the speaker was *entirely* effective or ineffective.

Personal record? Which goals did you achieve, fall short of, or easily surpass?

iStock.com/vgajic

For example, seek to

1. Identify what the speaker did to demonstrate respect for difference.
2. Explain what the speaker did to earn your trust.

3. Assess the effectiveness of both the words and support the speaker used. What sources did the speaker use? Were they credible?

4. Recognize the kinds of information the speaker used to support claims. Were they unbiased? Were perspectives other than those held by the speaker addressed?

5. Identify which of the speaker's ideas you accept, which you question, and which you disagree with.

6. Determine the extent to which the speech changed you.

7. Evaluate the extent to which the speech enhanced consideration of an important topic.

8. Identify any questions you would like to ask the speaker and any information you need the speaker to clarify.

GAME PLAN

Inclusivity, Ethics, and Critical Thinking

- I have reviewed my speech for derogatory words or statements that might alienate members of the audience.
- The main ideas of my speech are supported by truthful evidence.
- All evidence, ideas, quotes, and statistics from other sources are properly cited with full credits.
- In writing my speech, I accounted for differences of opinion.
- I have reviewed my speech for instances of "spin."
- I stand behind the words and ideas in my speech—I am accountable for my presentation.

EXERCISES

Cultural Diversity, Ethics, and Critical Thinking

Participating in the following exercises will broaden your understanding of what it means to value cultural diversity, live up to high ethical standards, and think critically.

1. The Danger of Overgeneralizing

Sometimes, when faced with people and situations we don't know, we resort to stereotyping—a thinking shortcut that organizes our perceptions into oversimplified categories. Stereotypes exist for short people, blondes, Asians, Black people, Millennials, and older adults, just to name a few. Though many of us have been the unwilling target of others seeking to stereotype us, we likely have done the same. List assumptions you have made about others, what you did to pigeonhole and classify them, and why you now believe the assumptions you made are true or flawed.

Facing up to your assumptions about others should help prepare you to speak before them. Whenever you speak, it is important to treat the members of your audience respectfully and as individuals rather than as members of a category. Doing so demonstrates not only cultural awareness but also sound critical thinking and ethical judgment skills.

2. How We Learn Matters

If you were delivering a speech to college students on "The Effects of Grade Inflation," what kinds of materials would you use to ensure your speech appealed to each style of learner? To facilitate this task, imagine yourself as each type of learner as you consider possible materials.

Similarly, ask yourself how persons from cultures other than your own would respond to the kinds of material you selected. To what extent, if any, do you imagine their responses would differ from your own?

By stepping outside of who you are and considering your speech from the perspective of others who differ from you, you gain fresh insights and facilitate the establishment of common ground.

3. Analyze This Speech: Thinking Critically About Diversity and Inclusion

Holger Kluge was president of the Canadian Imperial Bank of Commerce. He delivered the following remarks during a speech made to the Diversity Network Calgary, Alberta, Canada. As you read his words, consider these questions:

- What assumptions did the branch manager make?

- What did Holger Kluge learn about diversity? What have you learned?

- What ethical issues are exposed in this excerpt?

- How might critical thinking skills have avoided the problem altogether?

I'd like to begin my remarks with a story. A number of years ago we hired an employee as a teller in one of our branches. A few weeks after this individual began work, he was called into the branch manager's office for a discussion.

SN 1

> *Kluge uses a story to involve the audience.*

The manager was a good boss and a good mentor, and he wanted to tell the employee the facts of life about working for the bank.

He told him not to expect to rise too far in the organization.

SN 2

> *Kluge uses the manager's words verbatim before paraphrasing the remainder of the manager's comments.*

When the young man asked why, the manager replied:

"You've got an accent. You weren't born in Canada. And you're not Anglo Saxon. Basically, you've got the wrong name and the wrong background for advancement."

He went on to say that the best the employee could hope for was to someday become a branch manager.

I was that employee.

SN 3

> *The speaker identifies himself as the subject, surprising the audience.*

The irony is, that at the time I was considered an example of the bank's progressive hiring practices.

SN 4

> *The speaker explains why he is sensitive to diversity, providing receivers with an important lesson.*

Somehow, the significance of this honor eluded me. In the space of a few moments, I had been banished to a wilderness of diminished expectations all because of my name, the way I spoke, and my country of origin.

That's one experience that shaped my views on diversity, knowing what it's like to be on the outside, having to overcome obstacles which others don't, simply because you're different.[24]

4. Approach the Speaker's Stand

Speakers need to educate receivers, not merely tell them what they want to hear or serve their personal self-interests; but politicians, public relations practitioners, advertisers, talk show hosts, and other public figures often seem to violate this advice. Indeed, the use of deception by those in the public arena is not new. Keeping this in mind, choose one of the following three- to four-minute speaking assignments or one of your instructor's choosing.

a. Identify a public figure who you believe deliberately deceived the public. Describe the alleged deception for the audience, and offer your opinion of the public figure's behavior, specifying how you believe the person ought to have behaved.

b. Describe an ethical choice that you had to make, how you decided what to do, and why you believe your decision was right.

c. Prepare an ethical analysis of a recent speech, commercial, tabloid news report, or infomercial.

RECAP AND REVIEW

2.1   Explain why cultural understanding enhances the effectiveness of speakers and audiences.

It is likely you will speak before audiences whose cultural backgrounds and values differ from your own. By respecting and adapting to difference, speakers and audiences are inclusive, bridging their diversity.

2.2   Discuss the importance of ethics, identifying ethical principles and guidelines relevant to public speaking.

Ethics reflect a society's feelings about right and wrong. Questions of ethics arise whenever speakers and audiences interact. Receivers expect speakers to share only what they know to be true, to be fully prepared to present a speech, to consider what is in the best interests of receivers, to make it easy for others to understand them, to refrain from using words inappropriately, to refrain from putting either a positive or a negative spin on information just to win a point, to respect cultural diversity, and to be accountable for the message. Plagiarism includes both misrepresentation and lying. A plagiarist steals the ideas and words of another and claims them as their own. Speakers expect receivers to give them a fair hearing and to be courteous, attentive, and honest about their responses.

2.3   Demonstrate the role critical thinking plays in public speaking, explaining its significance for speakers and audiences.

Critical thinking is the ability to explore an issue or situation by integrating all available information, arriving at a conclusion, and being able to validate the position taken. Both speakers and receivers need to arrive at judgments only after honestly evaluating alternatives rather than on the basis of faulty assumptions. By broadening the lens through which we process people and experience and working to ensure that emotion does not overcome rationality, we demonstrate our ethical commitment to and respect for the speechmaking process.

KEY TERMS

Co-culture (p. 36)

Covert lie (p. 43)

Critical thinking (p. 48)

Cultural diversity (p. 33)

Cultural identity (p. 39)

Culture (p. 36)

Disinformation (p. 45)

Ethical communication (p. 42)

Ethical speechmaking (p. 42)

Ethics (p. 42)

Ethnocentrism (p. 36)

High-context communication (p. 38)

Inclusion (p. 33)

Low-context communication (p. 38)

Marginalized group (p. 37)

Overt lie (p. 43)

Plagiarism (p. 46)

istockphoto.com/Brothers91

3 MINDFUL LISTENING

UPON COMPLETING THIS CHAPTER, YOU WILL BE ABLE TO
3.1   Define listening and its role in public speaking, explaining its six stages and culture's impact on them.
3.2   Identify the benefits of listening mindfully.
3.3   Distinguish among four types and four styles of listening.
3.4   Apply critical thinking and listening skills at live and online speaking events.

How often do you walk around wearing headphones or earbuds? Yet, when you have something to share, you want others to remove their devices, and open their ears so that they can respond to what you have to say? Ours has been described as a "talking head, Twitter-finger culture."[1] Too often, we don't respond to or acknowledge what others say. We fail to give our undivided attention. Even when we think we've listened, we talk *at* each other, invalidate the other person and their statements, make assumptions, and rush to react to what we *think* was said without actually thinking critically about it. Missed and misheard messages have consequences, especially for speakers and their audiences. To combat such behavior, we need to work on developing our listening and evaluating skills—which are more important now than ever.

Do others listen to you? Do you listen to them? Do you care about one another's stories? When you understand a person's stories, you understand the person. Whose responsibility is it to listen when a speech is delivered and stories are told? If your answer is "It's the audience's responsibility," you are correct, but you are only half correct. The actual answer may surprise you. The speaker *and* audience members need to listen to each other during speechmaking. Speaker and receivers share an ethical responsibility for listening.

OPEN EARS, OPEN MINDS, AND THE SIX STAGES OF LISTENING

3.1   *Define listening and its role in public speaking, explaining its six stages and culture's impact on them.*

For speakers to make sound decisions about their topic and speech content, they have to listen to and understand the members of the audience. For audience members to assess the quality, appropriateness, and value of the presenters' spoken words, they also need to listen. Both speakers and receivers need to develop two key skills: (1) the ability to listen ethically, and (2) the ability to think critically. Both skills have their basis in making valid judgments about the audience and about a speaker's claims and conclusions, including evaluating the speaker's information and arguments. In fact, research reveals that listening and the ability to relate to and influence others are positively related.[2] We tend to think more positively about and accept the words of those who listen to us.

Are Your Ears and Mind Open?

Speakers and listeners put trust in one another, sharing ethical responsibilities and caring about the consequences of their behavior. When we put ethical listening and critical thinking to work, we distinguish facts from inferences, valid from invalid evidence, and logical from flawed reasoning. We resist taking the easy way out by questioning flimsy or unsupported claims and arguments. We refuse to accept a speaker's words at face value. Rather, we work actively to get the most out of a speech by setting listening goals to support our listening efforts.[3]

What do we listen for? We listen for facts, examples, testimony, and statistics that support a speaker's position. We assess whether or not the evidence the speaker offers is accurate or faulty, provided by a credible or biased source, and if it strengthens or weakens the speaker's position. We make a concerted effort to resist false assumptions, overgeneralizations, and other reasoning errors.

SELF-ASSESSMENT 3.1: HOW OPEN ARE YOUR EARS AND MIND?

Directions

Use the following questions to evaluate behaviors that facilitate and impede listening. Simply respond to each query.

Questions	Never 1	Rarely 2	Sometimes 3	Usually 4	Always 5
1. Do you ever find yourself thinking that you know better than a speaker and tuning out?					
2. Do you ever daydream when you should be listening to a speaker?					
3. Do you ever jump ahead of a speaker?					
4. Do you ever fake paying attention to a speaker?					
5. Do you ever try to avoid listening to difficult material?					
6. Do you ever stop listening to a speech because the topic doesn't interest you?					

Questions	Never 1	Rarely 2	Sometimes 3	Usually 4	Always 5
7. Do you ever try to process every word a speaker says?					
8. Do you ever let the speaker's delivery or mannerisms interfere with your reception of his or her remarks?					
9. Do you ever let the environment or personal factors distract you from paying attention to the speaker?					
10. Are there some topics to which you refuse to listen?					

Listening Analysis	Implication
The higher your total score, the more you need to work to improve your listening skills.	What have you discovered about how you listen?
Pay special attention to columns 3, 4, and 5, as these represent your problematic listening behaviors.	Although this evaluation is not a scientific instrument, it should give you some indication of behaviors you need to work on.

COACHING TIP

"Tell me to what you pay attention and I will tell you who you are."

—José Ortega y Gasset, Spanish philosopher

If you are like most people, you pay attention to what interests you. It is equally important, however, to pay attention to what might not interest you but could be beneficial to you.

A speaker and their listeners need to exhibit active and mindful listening. **Active listening** involves engaging cooperatively in a three-prong process: (1) speaker and listener need to express verbal and nonverbal interest in what the other says; (2) they need to interpret and paraphrase the message received; and when confused, (3) they need to ask for clarification or elaboration.[4] **Mindful listening** also involves staying attentive, maintaining focus by not letting electronic devices serve as distractions, and displaying sufficient mental energy to engage fully in the speechmaking moment, including thinking of good questions and providing feedback. Mindful listening is focused and purposeful. Mindful listeners set goals, identify main ideas and key points, pick-up on nonverbal messages, perceive the organizational pattern in use, evaluate the speech and the speaker, and respond appropriately.

Do You Know the Six Stages of Listening?

Hearing and listening are very different processes. Hearing is an involuntary physiological process, while listening is a voluntary mental process involving selecting, attending, sense-making, recalling, and responding to verbal and nonverbal messages. In other words, just as we do not need to think to breathe, so we do not need to think to hear. But listening is a system of interrelated components, inclusive of both mental processes and observable verbal and nonverbal behaviors, and occurring in six stages: hearing/receiving, understanding, remembering, interpreting, evaluating, and responding (see Figure 3.1).[5]

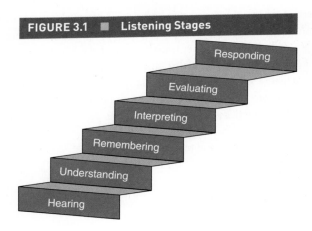

FIGURE 3.1 ■ Listening Stages

Responding

Evaluating

Interpreting

Remembering

Understanding

Hearing

Stage 1: Hearing/Receiving

During the hearing stage, we receive aural stimuli—or sounds. We may choose to ignore some stimuli, like advertisements, while we choose to focus on others, such as instructions for an assignment in class.

We all attend to some sounds but block out others. Attending involves our willingness to focus on and organize particular stimuli. Unless our attention is engaged and held, however, we soon refocus on something else. Attention is highly selective. Speakers quickly learn that it is not enough to capture the attention of listeners; they also have to work to retain it. To do this, speakers may

- Focus on subjects of particular interest to receivers

- Use words and images that evoke pictures in the minds of receivers

- Incorporate activity and movement into presentations

- Tell stories that create suspense, describe conflict, or evoke humor

Stage 2: Understanding

During the **understanding** stage, we focus on meaning, using our own reservoir of information to decode a message. Refrain from judging a message and tweeting about it or responding to it until you are certain you comprehend it and can summarize the key ideas and evidence. To promote understanding, follow these guidelines:

- Use your eyes and ears to process the speaker's verbal and nonverbal messages.
- Refrain from judging. Rather, work on seeing things from the speaker's perspective—as the speaker intends for you for to understand the speech.

Stage 3: Remembering

During **remembering**, we mentally save what we've gained from the speaker's message for further use. Here again, we make choices as we decide what is worth remembering and what we can discard. A good speaker builds redundancy into their message to increase the audience's chances of remembering it. Sometimes, we may also take notes, or if permitted, record the speaker's remarks. If you anticipate a speech will be particularly important, ask the instructor or speaker if you can make an audio or video recording of the presentation to be sure you are able to retrieve it for future reference. During this stage

- Identify the speaker's thesis and main points
- Identify supporting materials
- Identify the organizational pattern
- Sum-up the speaker's message

Stage 4: Interpreting

Just as we may see different colors depending on how our brains and eyes perceive them, so we may hear different words. A few years back, there was a great social media debate over whether a speaker had uttered the word *Laurel* or *Yanny* in a three-second clip. The Internet was divided in its response. We experience information in different ways because our brains rush to fill in gaps or ambiguities.[6] We bring a lot of ourselves to what we hear affecting our interpretations. When listening to a speech, during the **interpreting** stage, we seek to understand the message from the speaker's perspective. Doing this keeps us from imposing our meaning onto the speaker's ideas. To interpret a speaker's message accurately, we may

- Relate what the speaker says to what we already know
- Compile questions to ask to clarify things
- Paraphrase the speaker's thoughts in our own words

By adopting these behaviors, we ensure our listening is focused as well as purposeful.

Stage 5: Evaluating

In the **evaluating** stage, we use critical thinking skills to weigh the worth of the speaker's message, evaluating what we have heard and understood. We decide whether we accept the speaker's point of view, whether the message has relevance for us, and whether we find it to be valid and well intentioned, based on what we know. Whether we find the speaker's position valid or well intentioned should depend on the kind of evidence and reasoning a speaker offers and our understanding of the issues involved. For this to happen

- Separate facts from inferences
- Determine if self-interest or bias affected the speaker's message
- Ask yourself if any personal biases you hold interfere with your giving the speaker's message a fair hearing

Stage 6: Responding

During the **responding** stage, we react and provide feedback. We communicate our thoughts and feelings about the message we've received verbally and nonverbally. Both during and after a speech, we let the speaker know whether we thought the message was successful or flawed.

The last time you applauded a speaker or failed to laugh at a joke or told your friend how much you appreciated the toast he made at your party, you were responding and providing feedback. To improve responding:

- Respond honestly while making comments constructive and supportive.
- Use "I" messages, demonstrating that you take personal responsibility for both your positive remarks and suggestions regarding how the speaker could have made the speech more effective.

Instant replay. We can get feedback during the speech based on audience response and afterward by talking with others.

iStockPhoto.com/SteveDebenport

Are You Aware of Culture's Impact?

Each of the preceding six stages of listening is influenced by emotional and intellectual biases that can prevent us from processing a speaker's message in an impartial way. For each of us, culture, lifestyle, attitudes, and values influence and help determine

- what we attend to,

- what we comprehend,

- how we evaluate communication, and ultimately,

- what we retain.

Culture affects willingness to listen. As we've noted, **ethnocentrism**, the tendency to assess the values, beliefs, and behaviors of our own culture as superior to those of others, can impede our ability to be receptive to the words of a speaker from a culture other than our own. Effective listeners need to recognize and adapt to potential biases brought on by ethnocentrism. They also need to pay attention to the other ways culture may intervene. Because culture affects speaking style, it also can impede listeners from fairly processing a speaker's words. For instance, whereas some cultures advocate for succinctness and directness, others practice elaboration and exaggeration. The Arab proverb "A man's tongue is his sword" gives us insight into the Arab perception that words can be a punishing weapon. The speech of members of Arab cultures, for example, often contains forceful assertions and significant repetition, causing many who do not understand their culture well enough to conclude that they are being aggressive or threatening.[7] Attuning ourselves to differences between cultures can help diminish the impact of the prejudices, biases, and misconceptions we have developed over the years.[8]

We all wear glasses. Culture, lifestyle, and other biases shape the lenses through which you view the world, so be aware of how they impact your perception.

iStockPhoto.com/peshkov

LISTENING HAS ITS REWARDS

> **3.2**   *Identify the benefits of listening mindfully.*

Effective audience members listen to gain knowledge, think critically about the message's meaning, and evaluate a message's validity and worth. They distinguish between main and minor points, differentiate facts from opinions, assess evidence, and identify errors or weaknesses in reasoning. When listening mindfully, receivers do much more than simply "hear" the speech, and their efforts are rewarded with a host of benefits.

Reduced Stress

As information is communicated, complex data are simplified, objectives are clarified, and the stress levels of listeners drop. The stress level of speakers also goes down as they are provided a forum to speak their minds, fulfilling their communicative needs.

More Learning

Listeners learn more about the speaker and the subject. Speakers learn more about what audience members respond to and how they react to the speaker's ideas. As a college student, you spend approximately 60 percent of each class day listening.[9] Becoming a better receiver will increase both your personal confidence and your grades. Because you understand what has been said, you gain confidence in your ability to participate and express your opinions, whether sharing ideas with friends, when at work, or in a public forum.

Improved Speaker–Audience Relationship

We all need someone to engage with and respond to us. We appreciate those who listen to us much more than those who ignore us. We also tend to tune in to those people who listen to us. Listening can create bonds between people from diverse backgrounds.

Improved Decision Making

Exposure to a wide range of information, attitudes, and beliefs provides you with a bigger picture and the kind of input you need to develop better judgment.

Improved Speaking

When speakers perceive themselves to have the rapt attention of their listeners and when they perceive their listeners to be open, alert, and active, then they are more comfortable in the speaking role and able to do an even better job of communicating their ideas.

A Better Society

People who listen critically to the messages of others and do not just accept what is presented to them can spot faulty reasoning, invalid arguments, and gross appeals to prejudice that encourage the believing of lies and half-truths and undermine democracy. Only if citizens become less vulnerable to disinformation can society avoid its consequences.[10]

WHAT'S YOUR LISTENING TYPE AND STYLE?

3.3	*Distinguish among four types and four styles of listening.*

Listening theorists identify four different types and four different styles of listening.

Listening Types

The four types of listening are appreciative listening, empathic listening, comprehensive listening, and critical/deliberative listening (see Table 3.1).

Type 1: Appreciative: Listening for Pleasure

You recently may have attended a live concert, taken in a movie or play, or spent an evening at the local comedy club. Why? You probably wanted to have a good time. Often, we listen simply because doing so enables us to unwind, relax, or escape. The appreciative listener's purpose is to enjoy the power and impact of words that are well chosen. Studies have shown that listening appreciatively can help buoy mood by lowering stress.[11]

Type 2: Empathic: Listening to Provide Emotional Support

Empathic listening serves a therapeutic function. It helps speakers come to terms with problems and develop clearer perspectives on the situations they face and aids them in restoring emotional balance to their lives. Used most in interpersonal relationships, empathic listening also occurs during public presentations, such as when a speaker who lived through genocide describes their experiences for us.[12]

Type 3: Comprehensive: Listening to Get Information

When you are lost and ask another person for directions, when you attend a presentation and seek to comprehend the speaker's message, when you sit in class and listen to a lecture, you are listening with the objective of gaining knowledge. Similarly, when we listen to news reports or to a physician delivering a diagnosis, we are listening comprehensively. Being able to listen comprehensively requires us to be able to recall facts, distinguish main and supporting points, and summarize what we have learned.

TABLE 3.1 ■ Types of Listening		
Type	**Example**	**Goal**
Appreciative	Listening to music	Be entertained
Empathetic	Listening to a friend talk about a breakup	Therapeutic—to be a sounding board
Comprehensive	Listening to a lecture	Acquire information
Critical/deliberative	Listening to a political debate	Make an evaluation

Type 4: Critical/Deliberative: Listening to Make an Evaluation

Frequently, in addition to working to understand the content of a message, we must also make judgments about its worth and validity and, ultimately, whether we accept or reject it. Critical or deliberative listening goes a step beyond comprehensive listening, requiring us to separate fact and opinion, point out weaknesses in reasoning, and assess whether evidence is sound.

Listening Styles

Adherents of each of the following listening styles display different attitudes and beliefs about listening (see Table 3.2). Which one of the following styles is your personal favorite?

People-Oriented Listening

Those who like to focus on the emotions and interests of others prefer the people-oriented style. When you take your time, and work to understand what others think and feel, you improve your chances of getting to know them well. Thus, the people-oriented style fosters relating to others in more meaningful ways.

Action-Oriented Listening

If you value clarity and preciseness above all else, you are apt to use the action-oriented style often. Action-oriented listeners don't like to feel frustrated by others' indirect messages. They want the persons they speak with to be direct and straightforward.

Content-Oriented Listening

Those who enjoy being intellectually challenged and having to work ideas through practice the content-oriented style. Comfortable listening to messages that are ambiguous and spark debate, content-oriented listeners commonly relate what they are listening to with their own views.

Time-Oriented Listening

Time-oriented listeners expect the speaker to get to the point. Impatient and efficient, they like others to impart messages that are quick and brief, allowing the listeners to work through them efficiently.

TABLE 3.2 ■ Styles of Listening	
Style	**Focus**
People-oriented	Emotions and interests
Action-oriented	Clarity, precision, and assumptions
Content-oriented	Facts, details, and ambiguities
Time-oriented	Efficiency and succinctness

IMPROVING LISTENING BEHAVIOR LIVE AND ONLINE

> **3.4**   *Apply critical thinking and listening skills at live and online speaking events.*

Consider the very best listeners you know. What words would you use to describe their behavior whether they are sitting in the same room as you, listening to you deliver a speech virtually, or participating with you in a meeting held online? Most people choose words like *concerned, open-minded, intelligent, attentive, interested,* and *respectful.* Now do the same for the worst listeners you know. Probably among the words you've chosen to describe them are *inattentive, closed-minded, bored, impatient, nonresponsive,* and *rude.* Which list of words would you prefer to have others apply to you? Which would you prefer to use when describing the members of your listening audience whether they're physically present or in cyberspace?

   Far too often, problem behaviors interfere with listening. To become more effective at both speaking and listening, you need to recognize those internal and external factors that contribute to deficient listening and then act to eliminate them. The kinds of listening problems that violate the mutual trust that should exist between speakers and listeners are identified in Table 3.3. Which, if any, of them have you been guilty of?

TABLE 3.3 ■ Problem Listening Behaviors	
Behavior	**Consequences**
Tuning out	Loss of focus decreases understanding.
Faking attention	Pseudo-listening is deceptive.
Prejudging	Prematurely evaluating can contribute to missing most of a message.
Becoming overly emotional	The message's meaning can be distorted.
Being lazy	Avoiding difficult material and taking the easy way out decrease comprehension.

Behavior	Consequences
Being egocentric	Placing the focus on the self, not the speaker, makes it more difficult to understand others, positions, and points of view.
Being easily distracted	Oversensitivity to setting or context, personal appearance, or delivery decreases understanding, as does multitasking.
Wasting time	Failure to use the thought–speech differential to advantage increases daydreaming.
Offering a critique that is vague or attacking	Not offering feedback that is specific and constructive is counterproductive.

Stay Tuned In

Poor listeners do not pay the speaker sufficient respect or attention. It seems as if their ears and minds are "out to lunch." Words bounce off them. Nothing penetrates. We have all at one time or another been guilty of preferring to pursue our private thoughts, reminisce, worry about a personal problem, or make silent plans for an event rather than concentrate on a speaker. To guard against tuning out, expend energy from the outset of a speech to its conclusion. Adopt an attentive posture, keep your eyes focused on the speaker, and work to remain alert. By looking at the speaker, you help your mind follow the lead set by your body.

React Honestly

Persons who don't value listening only pretend to listen. They look at the speaker, smile or frown appropriately, nod their heads approvingly or disapprovingly, and even utter remarks like "ah" or "uh-huh." All the external cues tell the speaker they are listening, but they really are not.

Stop faking attention during a speech; instead, take notes. Note-taking prevents you from becoming distracted and helps you listen for main ideas, transitions, and supporting materials. It also increases the probability that you will retain the speech's content.

Give a Fair Hearing

Before even giving the speaker a fair hearing, people who have not learned to listen effectively decide that the speaker looks uninteresting, sounds boring, or does not merit their attention because they do not represent their views. Such prejudgments contribute to their missing the real value in the speaker's remarks.

For example, a progressive Democrat more than likely supported wearing masks and getting vaccinated against the COVID-19 virus, telling stories about those who died because they had not been vaccinated. A conservative Republican would have been more likely to argue that having to wear a mask violated their personal freedom, and that the COVID-19 vaccine posed too many dangers, telling stories about those who suffered adverse side effects after taking the vaccine. Were those who supported and opposed the wearing of masks and taking the vaccine reacting to the same stimuli? It's possible, but erroneous prejudgments may have limited their ability to open their minds, identify reliable sources, and critically process relevant information.

To avoid prejudging speakers on the basis of their reputation, appearance, or manner, allow them to complete their presentations before you even begin to evaluate their effectiveness. Keep an open mind and hear the speaker out.

Bye bipartisanship. The major political divide in the United States means that it's less likely that party members will give fair hearings to those outside the party.

iStockphoto.com/WildLivingArts

COACHING TIP

"The success of your presentation will be judged not by the knowledge you send but by what the listener receives."

—Lilly Walters, professional speaker

We learn by listening. Audience members learn from listening to speeches, and speakers learn from listening to audience members. How you listen facilitates or debilitates the speaker's performance and/or the audience's response to and evaluation of your speech. What kinds of questions should listeners ask themselves when preparing to listen to a speaker? What kinds of questions should speakers ask themselves about how to encourage a receptive audience?

Control Emotional Reactions

Sometimes individuals let their disagreement with the speaker's position get in the way of listening. They avoid anything with which they do not agree, that they believe has little relevance to their lives, or that they feel will be too difficult for them to comprehend. Feeling personally threatened by a speaker's position, they do not really listen to it.

Ineffective listeners also allow particular words spoken by a speaker to interfere with their ability to listen. These words, referred to by listening pioneer Ralph Nichols as "red-flag words," trigger an emotional deafness, causing listening efficiency to drop to zero. Among such words are *taxes, fake news, Nazi, fascist, COVID-19,* and *welfare.* Are you aware of any specific words or phrases that cause you to erupt emotionally, thereby disrupting your ability to process a speaker's remarks accurately?[13]

To avoid reacting too emotionally and jumping to conclusions, don't mentally argue with a speaker during a presentation. If you listen first to what the speaker has to say rather than assuming you know what's coming next, and if you refrain from focusing on something the speaker does or says that sets you off, then you will be better able to fairly evaluate the speaker's presentation.

GAME PLAN

Preparing to Listen

- I have turned off my phone and eliminated other distractions so I may actively listen.
- I have a sheet of paper or will use a laptop or tablet to take notes.
- I will not multitask while listening.
- I am ready to listen with an open mind. I am prepared to learn something new.
- I am prepared to critically evaluate the speaker's message.

Challenge Yourself

Deficient listeners often avoid material that is challenging. Believing they won't comprehend it anyway, they pass up the chance to exercise their minds. Would you willingly attend a speech on thermonuclear engineering, molecular biology, or the privatization of industry, or would you tune out because you would have to work too hard? Oliver Wendell Holmes once noted, "The mind, once expanded to the dimension of larger ideas, never returns to its original size." Poor listeners, however, refuse to stretch their minds; they won't work at listening.

Because listening is not easy, you need to commit to making the effort to do it. In other words, prepare yourself to listen by mentally clearing your mind of extraneous thoughts, reading up on the speaker's subject prior to the presentation, or researching the speaker.

Focus on the Value in the Speech

Those who don't value listening to others tend to be egocentric. They view themselves as the center of the universe, and they dismiss speeches that might be relevant to society but not to them personally. Seeking only self-satisfaction, they are so wrapped up in themselves that they fail to realize the interconnectedness of all human beings.

Instead of focusing on yourself, focus on the value to be found in every speech.

Control the Physical Environment

If we let them, whether we're in our own homes or another setting, physical factors can function as distractions. Physical discomfort, whether hunger, cold, or pain, have real effects on listening ability. Someone whose stomach is rumbling or who is rubbing their arms in a struggle to stay warm distracts others' focus as well. When preoccupied by the room's temperature, the arrangement of seats, or a room's acoustics, attention and productivity drop off.[14] Individuals sometimes also find themselves obsessed with a speaker's accent, mannerisms, or appearance. Once they succumb to such distractions, their attention is dispersed, and they fail to concentrate on the speaker's message.

Even if the environment for the presentation is less than optimal, do whatever you can to maintain your focus. Resist multitasking while listening, which similarly distracts your focus.[15] Put away other books and papers and turn off your phone.

No free time. How can you use the speech–thought differential to your advantage in a speech?

iStockPhoto.com/ferrantraite

Use Time Wisely

The average person speaks at a rate of 150 to 175 words per minute. The average listener, however, comprehends at about 400 to 500 words per minute. The difference between the two is referred to as the **speech–thought differential**. Too many of us waste this extra time by daydreaming instead of focusing on, summarizing, and asking ourselves questions about the substance of a speaker's remarks.

Make good use of your "spare" mental lag time. Interact with the speech's content by producing your own examples or relating what the speaker is saying to your own experiences.

Give Constructive Feedback

When critiquing a speech, you offer your evaluation, providing feedback related to the speech's content, organization, and delivery. The purpose of a critique is to be constructive, not destructive; to offer guidance for improvement, not destroy a speaker's motivation to improve. Effective feedback is specific ("I found the introductory story about X really moving. It pulled me into the speech," not vague ("Nice use of stories"). If suggesting what the speaker could do to improve, again aim for specificity. For example, rather than saying, "Your supporting materials were weak," say, "I was impressed with the statistics you gave regarding diversity on campus. I think your speech would have benefited from more personal examples describing the experiences that students from diverse cultures have on campus as well as your own experiences working to build a culture of inclusiveness." Thus, specific feedback statements are based on observations of what worked or did not work, describe how behavior and messaging affected the listener, and are phrased from the audience member's perspective.

Daydreamer. While not always easy, focusing on the value in every speech is an excellent skill to develop.

iStockPeople.com/PeopleImages

EXERCISES

Listening Mindfully

Active listening is hard work. When you listen actively, your body temperature rises, your palms become moist, and your adrenaline flow increases. Your body prepares itself to focus. Let's look at what you can do to improve your skills as listener and thinker.

1. Seven Points

Provide an example of how following each of the seven points below can help you become a better listener:

- **Point 1.** Listening is a conscious process. It requires your full attention. You can't half-listen; the half you miss could be critical.

- **Point 2.** Evaluation should follow, not precede, reception. Effective listeners withhold evaluation until they are certain they have understood the entire message. Never allow what the speaker says or how they say it to close your mind.

- **Point 3.** Every speech presents you with the opportunity to learn something new. Use—don't abuse—that opportunity. At times, you might need to overlook a speaker's monotone or lack of eye contact. Instead, try to concentrate on the message.

- **Point 4.** Both negative and positive prejudices toward a speaker or a topic can cause you to judge quickly. Either you will be too busy arguing against the speaker or too quickly impressed by what they are saying to listen accurately to the message.

- **Point 5.** Effective listeners focus their listening efforts; rather than working to absorb every isolated fact, they concentrate on identifying the main points and the evidence used to support them.

- **Point 6.** Your job is to look for relationships among a speaker's ideas, not to jot down or retain every word the speaker says.[16] Learning to take notes effectively, whether on paper or alternately, electronically, will help you listen effectively, and vice versa.[17]

- **Point 7.** If you seek opportunities to practice skillful listening, you will become a more skillful listener. Work to increase your attention span, and you'll find quite a lot worthy of attending to. By challenging yourself to listen to difficult material, you will also prepare yourself to meet the speaker's challenge.

2. Take Notes

Active listening requires you to take an active role in setting listening goals and listening for main ideas and supporting information. The following suggestions will help you improve both your note-taking, whether initially live or electronic, and your listening abilities.

a. Divide a page in half. At the top of the left column write "Facts and Evidence." At the top of the right column write "My Questions and Reactions."

b. Jot down key words but not a verbatim transcript of the speaker's ideas. You are attempting to summarize and then evaluate the speaker's message, not reproduce it.

c. Use your extra thinking time to analyze whether the speaker answers the questions you noted in the right column and determine whether your responses to the message are favorable, unfavorable, or mixed.

d. Finally, decide on the extent to which you agree with the ideas and point of view expressed by the speaker and evaluate the speaker's presentation.

3. Respond With Constructive Criticism

When using "I-messages," you directly attribute what you found right and wrong to yourself and not someone else. After noting a negative in the speech or weak behavior in the speaker, be sure to suggest how it might be improved. Try, "I couldn't determine the support for your second main point. It would have been helpful to me if you had offered examples and statistics to reinforce your position," instead of, "You failed to provide evidence for the second main point of the speech."[18] Following this advice, respond with constructive criticism to the following speaker weaknesses:

1. The introduction failed to arouse your interest.

2. The lack of transitions made the speech hard for you to follow.

3. You couldn't tell the speech was ending.

4. Approach the Speaker's Stand

Find a partner and pick a topic from the list provided in this activity, or select another controversial topic of your choosing. Each of you will represent an opposing side of the argument.

Discuss the following as you craft your speeches:

● What core messages do each of you want to convey?

● What buzzwords might turn others off from listening to the topic?

● How might you craft a message to ensure listeners give you a fair hearing?

● Do certain facets of the argument elicit particularly emotional responses?

	Agree	Disagree
1. Cell phones should be inaccessible during class.	☐	☐
2. Capital punishment should be abolished.	☐	☐
3. Condoms should be distributed in all public schools.	☐	☐
4. Increasing cognitive diversity in organizations is less important than efforts to increase race and gender diversity.	☐	☐
5. School teachers should be armed.	☐	☐
6. All Americans should pay the same income tax rate.	☐	☐
7. College should be free for all students.	☐	☐
8. Colleges should consider economic diversity when making admissions decisions.	☐	☐
9. The federal government should legalize recreational marijuana.	☐	☐
10. Prayer should be permitted in public schools.	☐	☐

RECAP AND REVIEW

3.1   Define listening and its role in public speaking, explaining its six stages and culture's impact on them.

Both speakers and receivers need to develop two key skills: (1) the ability to listen ethically and (2) the ability to think critically. Listening is a voluntary psychological process composed of the following six stages: sensing, attending, understanding and interpreting, evaluating, responding, and remembering. Critical listening and critical thinking skills are necessary to distinguish facts from inferences, valid from invalid evidence, and logical from flawed reasoning. These skills enable people to make informed choices and help preserve democracy.

Both our culture and our values affect our listening ability. In order to become better listeners, we need to work to eliminate the prejudices, biases, and misconceptions we have erected. Members of different cultures exhibit different listening styles. Those who do not understand a culture may misinterpret the communication of the culture's members.

3.2   Identify the benefits of listening mindfully.

Effective listeners experience less stress, learn more, develop better relationships, make better decisions, and are able to contribute more to society.

3.3   Distinguish among four types and four styles of listening.

There are four different types of listening. They are (1) appreciative: listening for pleasure; (2) empathic: listening to provide emotional support; (3) comprehensive: listening to derive information; and (4) critical: listening to make an evaluation.

There are four listening styles. They are (1) people-oriented listening; (2) action-oriented listening; (3) content-oriented listening; and (4) time-oriented listening.

3.4   Apply critical thinking and listening skills at live and online speaking events.

By taking the time to understand the listening process and practicing effective listening habits, we can eliminate listening deficiencies. Among facilitating behaviors are staying tuned in, reacting honestly, giving all ideas a fair hearing, keeping emotions in check, challenging yourself, focusing on a speech's value, controlling the physical environment, using time wisely, and offering constructive feedback.

KEY TERMS

Active listening (p. 58)

Attending (p. 59)

Ethnocentrism (p. 62)

Evaluating (p. 61)

Hearing (p. 59)

Interpreting (p. 60)

Listening (p. 59)

Mindful listening (p. 58)

Remembering (p. 60)

Responding (p. 61)

Speech–thought differential (p. 70)

Understanding (p. 60)

istockphoto.com/dx312

4 ANALYZING AND ADAPTING TO THE AUDIENCE

UPON COMPLETING THIS CHAPTER, YOU WILL BE ABLE TO

4.1   Analyze your audience, using formal and informal tools to tailor your message to them.

4.2   Plan your speech to reflect audience demographics.

4.3   Make use of audience psychographics to increase receiver interest.

4.4   Take the nature of the speechmaking situation into account.

4.5   Use creative means to find out more about the audience.

Who ultimately decides if a speech succeeds? The audience! Thus, you need to create your speech with the audience in mind. Answer this question: Would it be smart of you or strategic to deliver the exact same speech to two or more different audiences? The answer: "probably not." Consider this: how a political candidate such as Bernie Sanders or Kamala Harris rallies an audience in Boston, Massachusetts, likely will differ from how they appeal to one in Mobile, Alabama. While the issues covered in their political stump speech may remain constant, being able to mobilize support depends on their being able to understand what's important to voters locally.

The speaker and the audience are in this together. The public speaker's audience is composed of individuals who come together to listen to and respond to a speech. Every speech is designed to be shared with a specific audience. In fact, successful speakers view the audience as central to their speech. They use the audience as they would a compass—for direction. After all, no speaker should speak to inform, convince, motivate, or entertain themselves. They should speak to inform, convince, motivate, or entertain their audience. Thus, in many ways, speaker and audience create a speech together. How? The speaker turns the audience into their partner—taking the time needed to empathize with and learn all they can about them—particularly about their backgrounds, cultural values, and social characteristics as these help the speaker match the speech's approach to the audience's personal interests and concerns.

Your success depends on your ability to reach out to and partner with your audience—building your relationship and sharing your message. That's why we focus on **audience analysis**, the process of gathering and interpreting information about receivers. Part of your task is to put yourself in their shoes, so you can understand them, empathize with them, and adapt your message to meet and reflect their needs and interests. Are you ready to do this?

COACHING TIP

"People will forget what you said, people will forget what you did, but people will never forget how you made them feel."

—Maya Angelou, poet

Actors are a lot like speakers. Actors who are in tune with audience members reach them on a level that those who perform only to hear themselves speak cannot hope to attain. If you consider only your words without considering the needs and wants of audience members, you risk having the words that are so important to you miss their mark. To accomplish your goals, take time to customize your speeches for the people you are trying to reach—whether your purpose is to inform, persuade, or entertain them.

FOCUS ON YOUR AUDIENCE

4.1   *Analyze your audience using formal and informal tools to tailor your message to them.*

Imagine the potential audiences you might speak before in the near future. Perhaps you'll speak to a student group; the members of a temple, church, or mosque; a teachers' organization; coworkers; a sales force; a community group; or an alumni group. Would you know each of these audiences equally well? Would you speak to each group about your topic in the same way? It is likely you would not. Your knowledge of each audience would influence your approach.

To decide how best to reach, influence, motivate, or entertain an audience, you need to figure out its members. This is not a new notion. More than two millennia ago, in his *Rhetoric*, Aristotle noted, "Of the three elements in speechmaking—speaker, subject, and person addressed—it is the last one, the listener, that determines the speech's end and object."[1]

Consider the Audience's Makeup—Explore and Celebrate Its Diversity

When you partner with the audience, you adapt your speech to reflect their makeup and perspective. While not everyone in the audience may like what you have to say, if you adapt your speech to reflect areas of common concern, you increase the likelihood that they will give your ideas a fair hearing. Focus on areas of agreement. Divisive rhetoric, including appeals to racism, sexism, anti-Semitism, Islamophobia, homophobia, xenophobia, and bigotry diminish us and have no place in a public speaker's tool box.

Not only do audiences differ, individual members also differ. Not all white people, 20-year-old women, or college students, for example, think alike. You will be well served to discover just how much you and the receivers have in common and tailor your message to reflect their interests.[2] Infusing your presentation with knowledge gained from audience research will help you learn who the members of your audience really are instead of your relying on inaccurate assumptions and stereotypes about who you merely *think* they are.

Be Audience Centered—Use Empathy

If you center your attention on audience members, they will center their attention on you. When your words resonate, audiences are more likely to be more attentive and respond as you hope. The more you find out, the more adept you become at adapting and tailoring your presentation.

Effective speakers select topics based on both their expertise and their knowledge of what audience members need or want to listen to. The **audience-centered** speaker is not self-centered but is motivated by an understanding of receivers. Speakers who are audience-centered seek to empathize with their receivers. The word **empathy** is derived from the Greek word *empatheia,* meaning "feeling into." It involves the ability to suspend one's own point of view, and internalize or feel into the cultural values, beliefs, and perspectives of others—in this case, the audience. If you can empathize with audience members, taking the perspective of your receivers and exhibiting emotional responsiveness to their wants and needs, then it becomes more likely that they will listen to and respond to your message as you hope they will. When demonstrating empathy, a speaker reveals the moral obligation they feel toward others, building bridges of meaningful connection. Speakers exhibiting empathy are "other-oriented," understanding the needs and goals of audience members as opposed to being egocentric, self-oriented, and focused primarily on their own needs and goals.

Empathy is composed of a triad of components that work collaboratively: it has a *cognitive* or thinking component during which the speaker socially decenters and takes the perspective of another person, an *affective* or feeling component during which the speaker feels the emotions of receivers, and a *communication* component during which the speaker relies on verbal and nonverbal cues to express their understanding and concern for their receivers. Effectively, empathy allows a speaker temporarily to become "an audience member." We enact empathy by listening carefully, deciphering others' feelings, demonstrating interest in what others say, being sensitive to others' needs, and understanding others' points of view.

Journalist and political consultant Peggy Noonan served as a speechwriter for Presidents Ronald Reagan and George H. W. Bush. In her book *What I Saw at the Revolution,* Noonan advises speechmakers to find inspiration from unlikely public venues—one place being a shopping mall—that are filled with people from all walks of life, like the audiences whom speakers seek to reach. She counsels, "Show [your audience] respect and be honest and logical in your approach and they will understand every word you say and hear—and know—that you thought of them."[3] As a speaker, how do you know when you are able to connect and empathize with those in your audience despite any differences? Is it making the effort to understand that's important, or should the speaker truly feel and understand as if an audience member?

SELF-ASSESSMENT 4.1: HOW EMPATHETIC AND AUDIENCE-CENTERTED AM I?

Directions

Responding to the following statements will help you evaluate your empathic abilities and audience centeredness. Indicate the degree to which you believe each statement below is true or false as follows: Score the statement "1" if you think it is always false, "2" if you think it is usually false, "3" if you think the statement is sometimes true and sometimes false, "4" if you think the statement is usually true, and "5" if you think the statement is always true.

Statement	1	2	3	4	5
1. I use the receivers' perspective to understand their experience rather than relying solely on my perspective.					
2. I can decipher the emotions that members of the audience experience.					
3. I treat receivers as they would like me to treat them.					
4. I try to imagine how audience members feel, rather than how I would feel were I in their situation.					
5. I can tell how audience members feel without their having to tell me.					
6. I understand the emotions receivers are experiencing.					
7. I can imagine how others feel when they have problems.					
8. I do my best to see the audience the way they want me to even if that calls on me to adapt to a different communicative norm.					
9. The audience and I may face similar situations but experience very different feelings.					
10. I'm pretty accurate at reading what others are thinking when we communicate.					

Scoring Method	Scoring Analysis
Add your scores together. The highest score you can receive is 50. The higher your score, the more you believe that you are able to empathize with others and the more audience-centered you are likely to be.	Identify the reasons for your feelings on each question and the ramifications of each of your scores and your total score.

Answer Preliminary Questions

Audience members pay closest attention to messages they perceive to be meaningful. To penetrate the invisible shield that receivers use to protect themselves from information irrelevance, relate your ideas to their specific values, beliefs, needs, and wants.

Posing questions like these early in your analysis of the audience can help you get a jump start in designing a speech to which your audience will tune in:

- To whom am I speaking?

- How do they feel about my topic?

- What would they like me to share with them?

- What kind of presentation do they expect me to deliver?

- What do I hope to accomplish?

- How important is my presentation to them?

- What do they know, want to know, and need to know about my subject?

- How do they feel about me?

- What problems or goals do the members of the audience have?

- What should I do to gain and maintain their interest and attention?

Finding Ellen. Commencement speakers often try to relate their life experiences and values with those of the graduating class.

AP Photo/Bill Haber

Drawing on her knowledge of what new college graduates expect to hear from her, in an address given some years back to the graduating class of Tulane University, comedian Ellen DeGeneres told them: "Follow your passion. Stay true to yourself. Never follow someone else's path unless you're in the woods and you're lost and you see a path. Then by all means, you follow that."[4] Because she knew her audience well, she drew a big laugh. On a more serious note, responding to the continuing COVID-19 pandemic, Stanford speaker and surgeon, Dr. Atul Gawande, told an audience composed of advanced degree graduates: "This plague forced us all to see our lives anew. Under crisis, we had to pare our lives down, decide what could be jettisoned and what truly mattered. We had to try living in new ways. We had to figure out how to endure."[5]

COMPOSE A DEMOGRAPHIC SNAPSHOT

4.2 *Plan your speech to reflect audience demographics.*

Developing an understanding of an audience starts with drawing its demographic profile. A **demographic profile** is a composite of characteristics including age; gender; sexual orientation; educational level; racial, ethnic, or cultural ties; group affiliations; and socioeconomic background.

For example, imagine that you are asked to speak to two different audiences on the value of taking socioeconomic diversity into consideration in college admissions. Your first audience is composed primarily of middle-aged, well-educated, wealthy people employed in professional or executive jobs. Your second audience is composed primarily of middle-aged, high school–educated Americans who live in the inner city, work in service or trade jobs, and occupy the lower or lower-middle rungs on the socioeconomic ladder. Which group do you believe would be more sympathetic to your position? Why? Would a successful speaker give the same speech to both groups? Without sacrificing your own stand on the issue, how could you adapt your message to these and other groups?

A **homogeneous audience**—one whose members are similar in age, have similar characteristics, attitudes, values, and knowledge—is rare. More often than not, you will speak before a **heterogeneous audience**—one composed of persons of diverse ages with different characteristics, attitudes, values, and knowledge. When this is the situation, be sure you include all groups, paying attention to the kinds of demographic data you can use to help enhance communication with them.

Consider Age

How old are the members of your audience? One of your key goals is to diminish the age difference between you and those you hope to reach. To accomplish this, you need to be sensitive to the references you employ and the word choices you make. Ask yourself questions like the following:

- Will they give the same meanings to the words I use?
- Will they be able to identify with my examples and illustrations?
- Are they old or young enough to be familiar with persons and events I refer to?

The age of audience members affects their views about subjects and issues. Speakers would be wise to understand how generational differences influence their receivers. According to Lynne Lancaster and David Stillman's *When Generations Collide,* age is a key determiner of audience attitudes.[6] They note, for example, that those born before 1945 are more apt to lean

Cultural diversity. How can you make yourself more cognizant of the diverse experiences your audiences bring to your speeches?

iStock.com/LeonardoPatriz

toward the conservative end of the spectrum, respect both authority and symbols such as "the flag," and be less easily persuaded. Their guide word is *loyal*. Baby Boomers, born between 1946 and 1964, tend to be belongers, competitive, more cynical, and less likely to bow to authority. Their guide word is *optimism*. Generation X members, born between the mid-1960s and 1980, are more apt to have grown up in blended or single-parent households and tend to be more independent and media savvy. Their watchword is *skeptical*. Millennials, born between 1981 and 2000, have grown up with technology and are both friendship and safety focused.[7] Their watchword is *reality*. A newer generation, known as iGen or Gen Z, were born between the late-1990s and the end of the first decade of the 21st century. They are the first generation to have spent their teen years completely in the smartphone age.[8] They are safety obsessed and value equality. The generation's guidewords are *security* and *interaction*.[9] The most current generation, Generation Alpha, is a moniker that signals a transition to the Greek alphabet and the start of something new. This generation's members born in or after 2011 are for the most part preteens or about to be teenagers. Forecast to be the most technologically immersed generation ever, they also are the most likely to spend most of their childhood in living arrangements that don't involve both of their biological parents. This cohort's members also are said to care more about issues and display an impatience to get things done.[10] Speakers are wise to use the events and trends that serve as generational markers to guide them in appealing to different audience segments.

Of course, age is more relevant to the development of some topics than others. For example, the age of listeners is crucial if you are speaking about life after retirement, but it would be less important if your topic were taking care of planet Earth. Considering the age of audience members can help you choose an appropriate topic and support for your speech.

Consider Gender

Another key variable to consider when analyzing your audience is the gender ratio. According to sociolinguist Deborah Tannen, whereas "women speak and hear a language of connection and intimacy . . . men speak and hear a language of status and independence."[11] Whether you are a male, female, or gender-fluid speaker addressing a predominantly male, female, mixed-sex, or gender-fluid audience, this finding should affect the amount of time you spend building rapport with your listeners and could alter the approach you select to deliver your information and ideas to them. For example, if you were speaking about national security to an audience of mostly cisgender men, you might focus on the importance of strengthening defenses and the necessity for surveillance. On the other hand, if you were speaking on the same topic to an audience composed of mostly mothers of school-aged children, you might focus instead on what needs to be done to ensure that children learn in environments that are safe and secure.

Respect Sexual Orientation

Although sexual orientation is often an invisible variable, it is important to recognize that not everyone in your audience will have the same orientation as you. Just as using racially insensitive remarks or demeaning the race or ethnicity of receivers is inappropriate, so is speaking disparagingly of or displaying a bias against someone's sexual orientation. By making the effort to include supporting materials that feature not only heterosexuals but also members of the LGBTQIA (Lesbian, Gay, Bisexual, Transgender, Queer and/or Questioning, Intersex, Asexual and/or Allied people) community, you ensure that you include all types of receivers. For example, if you were to speak about adoption, you may include in your speech information about local and state resources for both heterosexual couples and same-sex or transgender couples who seek to adopt.

Gauge Knowledge Level

Knowing the average level of education of receivers will help you make choices regarding vocabulary, language style, and supporting materials. Your goal is to adapt your words to your listeners' knowledge. If you miss your mark and speak above their knowledge level, they will not understand you. If you speak below their knowledge level, you will insult and bore them.

When speaking before a more knowledgeable audience, you will want to deliver a **two-sided presentation**—that is, a presentation that considers alternative perspectives rather than the more simplistic **one-sided presentation**.[12] For example, if you were speaking on the trade policies of the United States to a well-informed audience, you would want to show receivers how familiar you were with the variety of viewpoints on this issue and explain why, after reviewing existing trade stances, you chose the position you now want them to adopt. Because individuals who are knowledgeable are used to processing complex communication and distinguishing among a variety of options, they will be more accepting of your ideas if you present them with strong evidence to back them up and include arguments that are logically sound.[13]

What's their expertise? Speaking on a new type of medicine would lead to two very different speeches for an audience of doctors and an audience of nondoctors.

iStock.com/ChristopherFutcher

Understand Racial, Ethnic, Religious, and Cultural Ties

As you prepare your speech, keep in the front of your mind any potential misunderstandings that racial, ethnic, religious, and cultural differences could foster. For example, a predominantly

Catholic or Orthodox Jewish audience is likely to support the abolition of abortion. If you have an audience of diverse listeners, it is helpful to acknowledge that some of your listeners may disagree with your stance or point. However, it is also up to you to find ways to encourage them to consider different ideas.

Identify Affiliations

Memberships in occupational, political, civic, and social groups also provide speakers with a pretty accurate prediction of the way audience members will react to a topic. Group affiliations serve as a bond. Workers who belong to the same union, citizens who support a political candidate, or parents who are active in the PTA (Parent Teacher Association) probably share a number of key interests, attitudes, and values with others in the group.

Whenever you function as a speaker, you need to consider how the various affiliations of audience members could influence both your topic and your approach. Remember, your goal is to identify clues regarding how listeners will respond to your presentation.

Consider Socioeconomics

Socioeconomic status encompasses the incomes, educational background, and occupations of a group of people. People from different socioeconomic backgrounds naturally look at situations, events, and issues from very different perspectives. A highly educated wealthy audience who never had difficulty finding work might not appreciate what it means to grow up in poverty. It is up to you to increase audience understanding of and identification with your subject.

Writing about this issue some years ago, journalist Anthony Lewis noted, "Upper-income Americans generally, whether in public or private employment, live not just a better life but one quite removed from that of ordinary families. They hardly experience the problems that weigh so heavily today on American society." How can you as a speaker close the perceptual gap created by this disparity? How can you encourage empathy?

Speakers need to develop insight into how socioeconomic factors affect life experiences. For example, a more privileged and well-off audience member listening to a speech exploring whether the teaching of Critical Race Theory has a place in today's schools might approach the issue differently than would a member of a marginalized group who likely is less resistant to change and more progressive in their thinking. It is necessary to locate examples and appeals that relate your topic to the varied experiences of your audience and make direct references to them during your speech.

Consider Physical Ability

In 2019, Ali Stroker made history becoming the first person who uses a wheelchair ever to win a Tony Award. She won it for her performance as Ado Annie in the Broadway play *Oklahoma*.[14] Individuals without disabilities are prone to viewing disability as an unfortunate condition, but according to many who have disabilities, it can be rewarding to belong to the community of individuals with disabilities. Speaking before people with disabilities may require speakers to make adaptations—including using sign language to communicate with members of the Deaf culture, identifying yourself when speaking before someone who is visually impaired, placing yourself at eye level when communicating with a person in a wheelchair, or being certain not to ask audience members to stand and move around when some members of the audience have limited mobility. Keep in mind that disability is but one feature of an audience member, not their only identifying characteristic.

Although each member of your audience is a unique individual, they also are a composite of a set of demographic factors. Rather than functioning as a means for stereotyping receivers, demographic variables should guide you in knowing your audience.

COMPOSE A PSYCHOGRAPHIC SNAPSHOT

> **4.3** *Make use of audience psychographics to increase receiver interest.*

Learning about your audience members' **psychographics**—how they see themselves; their attitudes toward various issues; their motives for being in the audience; and how they feel about your topic, you, and the speaking occasion—provides additional clues to their likely reactions. To draw this kind of audience picture, you need to understand the beliefs and values that underlie audience members' attitudes.

Understand Values, Beliefs, and Attitudes

Values are the principles important to us; they guide what we judge to be good or bad, ethical or unethical, worthwhile or worthless. They represent our conception of morality and are the standards against which we measure right and wrong. Knowing that respect for elders is among the core values shared by Chinese people; machismo and saving face are important to many Mexicans; devoutness and hospitality are valued by Iraqis; and family, responsibility to future generations, and a healthy environment are valued by many in the United States, can facilitate your reaching the audience. How, for example, might you adapt a speech on texting and driving to appeal to members of each group?[15]

Beliefs are what we hold to be true and false. They are also the building blocks that help to explain our attitudes. For example, those who believe that individuals will make better decisions with their money than the government often favor lower taxes. Because our belief systems are composites of everything we hold to be true and untrue, they influence the way we process messages. Some beliefs are more important to us than others. The more important our beliefs, the harder we work to keep them alive and the less willing we are to alter them.

Our values and beliefs feed into our **attitudes**, the favorable or unfavorable predispositions that we carry with us everywhere we go. The attitudes we hold help direct our responses to everything, including a speech. Attitudes are evaluative in nature and are measured on a continuum that ranges from favorable to unfavorable. For example, some hold favorable attitudes toward school voucher programs; others do not. Our attitudes reflect our likes and dislikes and are shaped by myriad influences, including family, education, culture, and the media.

What this kind of analysis suggests is that a speaker needs to appeal to audience member feelings, not merely their logic, and then to use it to build connection.

Know your audience. What's your audience's perception of you, and how will that impact your credibility and their listening?

iStockPeople.com/PeopleImages

Understand How the Audience Perceives Your Topic

Before class starts or right after it finishes are good times to make small talk with your peers in an effort to discover what they think about certain topics. Even just listening to what's on their minds as they chat with others can provide you with clues about their mindset. Knowing your audience's attitudes toward your topic can help you determine how to handle your material. It can aid you in your search for common ground. If you can gauge your audience's predisposition to respond favorably or unfavorably, you can adapt your approach so that you address their beliefs and reflect their values and more readily identify the kind of information you need to add or the misconceptions you need to correct. And if you can demonstrate for them how your message supports the values they already hold dear, you are much more likely to succeed.

Understand How the Audience Perceives You

No matter how audience members feel about your topic, if they believe you to be a credible source, they are much more apt to listen to what you have to say. But what if you know audience members don't look favorably on you? Ask yourself whether they lack information, have received misinformation, or have a legitimate reason for holding the judgment. Then identify what you can do to influence them to view you more favorably. For example, if they don't believe you are an authority on your subject, you can work into your presentation experiences you've had that qualify you to speak on the topic. One student who asked their audience to accept that the U.S. government should significantly increase social services to the homeless made their message stronger by relating their own experiences as a homeless person some years earlier.

What your audience thinks of you could change the way they respond to your message. Your credentials and your reputation accompany you to the podium.

CONSIDER THE SPEAKING SITUATION

> **4.4**   *Take the nature of the speechmaking situation into account.*

An important component of your audience analysis is considering the reason the audience is attending the speech as well as the occasion, location, and time at which the speech will take place.

Analyze the Occasion

Is your audience attending the speech voluntarily or are they required to attend? If you know in advance why people are present for your speech, you can adjust your remarks accordingly.

When thinking about the occasion, you also need to consider the kind of speech audience members are expecting you to deliver. If you are speaking to commemorate someone who has passed away, they expect you to deliver a eulogy. If you are speaking at a rally to encourage fund-raisers, listeners might well anticipate a motivational speech.

Whenever possible, it is wise for you to fulfill audience expectations. Be sure you can answer these questions:

- What is the nature of the group you are to address?

- What is your reason for speaking?

- What is the length of time allotted for your presentation?

Environmental variables like place, time, and audience size similarly affect the audience, influencing their reaction to you and your presentation. Consider how these factors could affect your style, language, and manner of delivery, and take steps to ensure that "little things" like the room being too small or the presentation running overtime don't stand in the way of communication.

Consider the Location

Consider some of the ways that the physical setting could affect the receptivity of listeners by answering these questions:

- Why do we find it difficult to concentrate when we're too hot or too cold?

- Why do we find it tough to focus on or pay attention to a speaker when a room is poorly lit or noisy?

- Why might an environment that is unattractive or too attractive adversely affect audience response?

- Why might the location and space affect use of technology?

Adapt your presentation to reduce listener discomfort and promote understanding and acceptance. That could mean talking louder or more softly, turning a thermostat down or up, bringing extra lights, or working extra hard to attract and maintain audience interest. The location and its space also could influence the nature of the technology used. Some rooms, for example, have smart boards and are digitally enabled, while others are not.

Consider the Time

If you are giving a speech early in the morning, right after lunch, later in the evening, or late in the week, you probably will have to wake up members of your audience by doing something unusual or by including some intriguing or startling example or illustration that compels their attention. You might, for example, ask a question or relate an experience that reveals your understanding of the situation.

Also consider the length of time you are given to speak. If you go over the time allotted, don't expect audience members necessarily to listen. If you speak for much less time than expected, don't expect that audience members will necessarily be pleased. Instead, find out the amount of time you are given, and work to fill that time with as stimulating and as informative a presentation as you possibly can.

Another consideration is the number of speakers sharing the program with you. Will you speak first, last, or somewhere in-between? Will you be flexible enough to tie your remarks to the remarks of those who precede you? Will you be sensitive to the lethargy that could affect your audience after a long evening of virtually uninterrupted listening?

Speakers need to empathize with what the audience is feeling and decide how best to communicate that empathy. Accurate perception can prevent audience rejection.

Gauge Audience Size

How many people will be in your audience: five, ten, fifty, a hundred, five hundred, a thousand, tens of thousands, or millions? Audience size and formality are directly related. As audience size increases, speaker formality increases. Audience size also directly influences the amount of interaction you are able to have with members of your audience, the kinds of visual aids you use, and whether you will use an amplification system and a podium. Adept speakers are ready to vary their manner and means of presentation to meet the requirements of different audience sizes. In fact, audience size is one of those variables that help make every speech situation different. When you are sensitive to it, you increase your chances for success.

REACH OUT TO ACQUIRE EVEN MORE AUDIENCE INFORMATION

> **4.5**   *Use creative means to find out more about the audience.*

By now you should understand the kinds of information it would benefit you to have about your audience. How can you collect it? What do you ask, where do you go, and what kinds of tools can you use to gain insight into the audience? What creative means can you use?

Ask Your Contacts

Earlier, you posed and thought about some preliminary questions about your audience. It's now time to reach out for more thorough answers. A sensible person to contact is the person inviting you to speak. Ask that individual about the group they represent. Questions such as the following will yield valuable information:

- Why does the group exist?
- What goals does the group have?
- What is the nature of the occasion at which I will speak?
- How many people do you anticipate will be in attendance?
- Can you share any insights about the composition of the audience?
- How much time will be allotted for the presentation?
- What expectations do you believe audience members will bring with them to the presentation?
- Are you aware of any attitudes held by audience members on the whole that could positively or negatively affect how they receive my presentation?
- Will any other speakers be sharing the program with me?
- At what point in the program will I speak?
- What will the physical setting be like?
- Will I be introduced?

Of course, your sponsor is not the only person you might query. If you know anyone who has spoken to the group before, or if you know members of the group, you might also ask them similar questions.

Observe and report. Make observations of your audience members beforehand to make educated guesses about their characteristics.

iStock.com/Yuri_Arcurs

Use Personal Knowledge and Observations

If you'll be speaking before a group to which you belong, such as a class, club, or civic organization, you can make decisions regarding your presentation based on prior conversations you have had with audience members, your perceptions of their opinions of you, and insights you have gained from hearing many of them voice personal opinions. Don't be afraid to watch people in action prior to the speech and to make educated guesses regarding ages, education and income levels, and cultural backgrounds. Think of the audience as a potential date—what information do you need to know about them to gauge if there's a match between you, your topic, the information you're sharing, and their concerns and interests? What will it take to engage them?

Research Audience Attitudes

The library and the Internet hold clues to the attitudes of audience members. By researching what local, regional, and national opinion polls reveal about the attitudes of various groups on a variety of social and political issues, you might be able to make a number of assumptions regarding the attitudes of those before whom you will speak.

To increase specificity and add to the knowledge you are gathering about the group you will address, you can also use a questionnaire.

The Questionnaire

Your instructor may allow you to distribute questionnaires in class or online, especially if your class is set up as a listserv and you have access to a platform such as Blackboard or Canvas. Twitter and online survey sites such as SurveyMonkey also can be used. A well-thought-out questionnaire helps you estimate the amount of knowledge your listeners already possess about your subject and their attitudes toward it. Questionnaires generally contain three different kinds of questions: closed-ended questions, scaled questions, and open-ended questions.

Closed-ended questions are highly structured, requiring only that the respondent indicate which of the provided responses most accurately reflects their opinion and so generate clear, unambiguous answers. The following are examples of closed-ended questions:

Do you think the open carry of guns should be banned in the United States?

☐ Yes   ☐ No   ☐ Undecided

Will a sugar tax help reduce obesity?

☐ Yes   ☐ No   ☐ Undecided

In contrast, **scaled questions** make it possible for a respondent to indicate his or her view along a continuum or scale that ranges by degree from polar extremes, such as *strongly agree* to *strongly disagree, extremely important* to *extremely unimportant,* and *extremely committed* to *extremely uncommitted,* thereby allowing the respondent to indicate the strength of their feeling. The following are scaled questions:

How important is it for Congress to raise the minimum wage?

_____ Extremely Important _____ Important _____ Neutral _____ Unimportant _____ Extremely Unimportant

To what extent do you agree or disagree with the following statement? "Colleges should consider socioeconomic background when making admissions decisions."

_____ Strongly _____ Agree _____ Neutral _____ Disagree _____ Strongly

Open-ended questions invite participants to answer in their own words and so produce more detailed and personal responses; however, they are also harder to interpret and may not provide the desired information. For example,

How do you feel about schools that require students to wear uniforms?

Respond to this statement: "No one is above the law, not even the President of the United States."

Because each kind of question can aid you in drawing a profile of your audience, use a mix in any questionnaire you design. (See the sample questionnaire in Figure 4.1.)

Developing a comprehensive understanding of your audience will have profound effects on your speechmaking. Your challenge as a speaker is to find ways to make your message inclusive

---

FIGURE 4.1 ■ Sample Questionnaire on the Open Carry of Firearms

1. Age:

2. Sex: □ Male   □ Female   □ Transgender
                                                                       □ Gender non-conforming

3. Race: □ White   □ African American   □ Hispanic
                 □ Asian   □ Native American   □ Other

4. Religion: □ Catholic   □ Protestant   □ Jewish
                 □ Buddhist   □ Muslim   □ Atheist
                                                                       □ Other

5. Highest education
        Level attained:
                 □ High school   □ College   □ Graduate school

6. Occupation:

7. Organizational memberships

8. Income: □ Under $25,000   □ $25,000–$49,999
                 □ $50,000–74,999   □ $75,000–$99,999
                 □ $100,000–$149,999   □ More than $150,000

9. Marital status: □ Single   □ Married   □ Widowed
                    □ Divorced   □ Separated

10. Political affiliation:
                 □ Democrat   □ Republican   □ Independent

11. Do you or a member of your family own a gun?   □ Yes   □ No

12. Have you or a significant other ever fired a gun?   □ Yes   □ No

13. Have you or a significant other ever been the victim of gun violence?   □ Yes   □ No

14. Have you or a significant other ever taken a gun-safety course?   □ Yes   □ No

15. On a scale of 1–10, with 1 representing not at all knowledgeable and 10 representing extremely knowledgeable, how knowledgeable do you feel you are about the open carry of firearms in the United States?

16. How important is the issue of open carry of firearms to you?
    □ Very important   □ Important   □ Neutral   □ Unimportant   □ Very unimportant

17. Which answer best reflects your opinion of the following statement: "The open carrying of a firearm should be prohibited."
    □ Strongly agree   □ Agree   □ Neutral   □ Disagree   □ Strongly disagree

18. Explain your response to question 17.

of the different ages, religions, educational levels, gender identities, races, cultures, group memberships, and psychographic profiles represented among the receivers. As you prepare and plan your speech, keep in mind everything you have learned about your audience as well as the specifics of the speaking situation. You need to

- Phrase your topic in such a way that audience members will not be turned off by it or tune it out.

- Resist the urge to concentrate exclusively on what you want to say; spend more time understanding what the audience wants to hear.

- Convince audience members early in your presentation that what you are communicating will solve a problem they have, help them reach their goals, or otherwise enrich their lives.

- Use your creative powers to encourage your listeners to care about your subject.

- Build on whatever common ground exists between you and your audience; make a personal connection with them.

- Always refer first to areas of agreement before speaking about areas of disagreement.

- Demonstrate that you respect your listeners; if they sense that you think you're superior to them, chances are they won't listen to you. If you communicate to them in words they don't comprehend, your speech won't matter even if they listen to it.

- Hear and see yourself and the speaking environment through the ears and eyes of the members of your audience. Put yourself in their place and they will more readily give you their attention.

GAME PLAN

Analyze Your Audience

- I have considered the demographic factors of my audience and strategized the best approach for my speech.

- I have a good understanding of my audience's values, beliefs, and attitudes toward my topic.

- I understand the purpose of my speech, and I know what my audience expects of me.

- I have queried my contact about the physical setting and order of speeches, and I've adjusted my speech to suit the occasion.

EXERCISES

Audience Analysis

Participating in the following activities will enhance your audience adaptation abilities.

1. What Do You Know?

Use what you know about demographics and psychographics to analyze the members of this class and another class. Explain how you will apply the information in your next speech or presentation in each class.

2. Adapt This

Imagine that you were asked to deliver a speech on the contributions of the women's movement twice—first to an audience composed of primarily feminist receivers and then to an audience composed of predominantly antifeminist receivers. Describe how you might prepare your speech to appeal to members of these diametrically opposed audiences without sacrificing your personal principles.

3. Analyze the Audience: Do Audience Members Want to Be Present?

Some audiences attend speeches voluntarily, while others have to be present, which affects how you go about presenting your message. Explain what you will do to try and win over audience members who don't want to be there. What will you do to make your speech relevant and interesting to them? What will you do to create a relationship with them that draws them into your speech and invites them to shift the way they think of themselves?

4. Approach the Speaker's Stand

Develop an audience survey to analyze an issue of your choice; your survey should contain closed-ended, scaled, and open-ended questions. Once you are sure your survey's questions are clear and unambiguous, have class members complete it. Then explain how you would take that information and your personal knowledge about your audience into account when planning a presentation.

Specifically, in a two- to three-page paper, explain how conducting such an analysis helps in addressing both the needs and interests of receivers and describe how you could use the insights you gained from surveying receivers to guide you in

- Formulating your objective
- Creating an introduction and a conclusion
- Organizing your main points
- Wording a speech

Once this is done, develop a presentation that puts your plan into action.

Finally, after delivering your presentation, ask your classmates to rate your speech on a five-point scale indicating

- How relevant it was to them

- How interesting it was to them

If the outcome is not what you anticipated, discuss steps you might have taken to increase receptivity and interest.

RECAP AND REVIEW

4.1 Analyze your audience, using formal and informal tools to tailor your message to them.

Speakers need to adapt their speech to account for the makeup of the audience they address. Speakers should seek to be audience-centered, using empathy to understand and think like an audience member. In addition to acknowledging differences, speakers need to discover how much they and their audience members have in common.

4.2 Plan your speech to reflect audience demographics.

By developing an understanding of audience characteristics, including the age, gender, or educational level; sexual orientation; racial, ethnic, or cultural ties; group affiliations; socioeconomic status of audience members; and physical ability, public speakers are better able to customize and adapt their messages to reflect the specific needs and interests of receivers.

4.3 Make use of audience psychographics to increase receiver interest.

By learning about audience member psychographics—what's going on in the minds of receivers and their attitudes, beliefs, and values—speakers are better able to fine-tune their speeches and develop presentations that speak to the lifestyle choices and preferences of receivers.

4.4 Take the nature of the speechmaking situation into account.

By conducting environmental or situational profiles, speakers develop a fuller understanding of how the "where and when" of presentations affect speech content, delivery, and audience reaction.

4.5 Use creative means to find out more about the audience.

In addition to drawing three key audience analysis profiles—a demographic profile, a psychographic profile, and an environmental situational profile—speakers need to query contacts, use their personal knowledge and observations, and when possible, also research the attitudes of their audience using a questionnaire.

KEY TERMS

Attitude (p. 86)
Audience analysis (p. 76)
Audience-centered (p. 78)
Belief (p. 86)
Closed-ended questions (p. 92)
Demographic profile (p. 81)
Empathy (p. 78)

Heterogeneous audience (p. 81)
One-sided presentation (p. 84)
Open-ended questions (p. 92)
Psychographics (p. 86)
Scaled questions (p. 92)
Two-sided presentation (p. 84)
Values (p. 86)

iStockPhoto.com/Prostock-Studio

SELECTING A TOPIC AND PURPOSE

UPON COMPLETING THIS CHAPTER, YOU WILL BE ABLE TO

5.1   Use creative techniques to choose a topic appropriate for you, your audience, and the occasion.

5.2   Develop effective general and specific purpose statements together with an audience-focused behavioral objective.

5.3   Formulate an effective thesis (central idea).

What does it feel like to stare at a blank page? All of us have done it. Some even argue that when we're born, the mind is formless, a *tabula rasa,* meaning that at birth it too is pretty empty—like a blank slate, but ready to receive sensory impressions. With time, we become the products of our experiences, defined by life events, and free to achieve our goals and pursue our interests.[1] Whether you accept this premise or not (and many do not), consider these examples. Before this book was written, this page was blank. Before a film is shown, the screen is blank. Before the set and actors appear, the a theater's stage is bare. Before a play in sports is planned, the coach's chalkboard or tablet is empty. Well, you're going to give a speech. Has your mind suddenly reverted to its blank state? Let's fix that. Most speech topics yield endless variations. Thus, a speaker has infinite possibilities to choose from.[2] Mastering these pages of the *Playbook* calls on you to approach your speech both systematically and creatively. It asks you to work within a format but think creatively every step of the way. Once you combine a reliable system with a spirit of innovation, no speaking hurdle will be insurmountable. Becoming an elite speaker is closer than you imagine.

FORMULATE A TOPIC

> **5.1**   *Use creative techniques to choose a topic appropriate for you, your audience, and the occasion.*

As the saying goes, "Necessity is the mother of invention," with **invention**—the rhetorical process of discovering what you're going to say and speak about—also happening to be an integral part of speech development.[3] Get ready to participate in a series of invention experiences that will spur you to transform the blank page that currently is your speech into an effective presentation!

Fill in the Blank Page: Find a Topic That Links Self, Audience, and Occasion

When delivering a speech in a professional or civic situation, the speaker's choice of topic tends to be somewhat limited, and typically is based on perceptions of their expertise, audience expectations, and the nature of the occasion. But even if the topic of their speech is set, a speaker still has the opportunity to give it a slant that is uniquely their own. This also is true of the presentations you will give in this class, where you likely also will experience more freedom in choosing and/or customizing your speech topic.

When your instructor does not pre-assign you a topic, the choice of what to speak about is yours. And even if your instructor does pre-assign you a topic, like a professional speaker, you will want to adapt it to reflect your unique audience and speaking situation. If you know what to talk about with your friends, you already hold the key to discovering a good topic for a class speech. When given the option, choose a topic that you are familiar with or would like to know more about—one that suits the speaking situation, reflects your personal concerns or convictions, and, you believe, will interest listeners and allow them to gain knowledge and insight.

What's at stake? Choose the right topic—one that is appropriate for you, your audience, and the occasion—and you enhance your chances of delivering a "total quality speech." Choose the wrong topic—one that you and your audience care nothing about or that is inappropriate to the speaking situation—and you'll probably find yourself unable to maintain your own interest, let alone that of the audience. Whatever your topic, find a creative way to make it your own.

SELF-ASSESSMENT 5.1: FILL IN THE BLANK

Directions

Responding to the following statements will help you evaluate your readiness to choose and narrow a topic, one that will interest you and your audience. Indicate the degree to which you believe each statement below is true.

Statement	1 Absolutely True	2 Mostly True	3 Sometimes True; Sometimes False	4 Mostly False	5 Absolutely False
1. I can use creative techniques to identify at least 10 possible speech topics (ones I know about and would like to know more about) that interest me and that I believe also will interest my audience.					
2. I can narrow the topic I choose so that I can manage it in the time allotted for my presentation.					

Statement	1 Absolutely True	2 Mostly True	3 Sometimes True; Sometimes False	4 Mostly False	5 Absolutely False
3. I can phrase my purpose for speaking so that it is absolutely clear to me and the audience.					
4. I can formulate a statement that summarizes the central idea for my speech.					
5. I can specify what I hope my speech will enable the audience to know, believe, or do.					

Scoring Method	Scoring Analysis
Award yourself 20 points for each statement you labeled "Absolutely True"; 15 points for each statement you labeled "Mostly True"; 10 points for each statement you labeled "Sometimes True and Sometimes False"; 5 points for each statement you labeled "Mostly False"; and 0 points for each statement you labeled "Absolutely False." Add your scores together. The highest score you can receive is 100. The higher your score, the readier you are to select a terrific topic for your speech.	Identify the reasons for answering each question as you did. Explain how your answers affect the nature of the work you have ahead of you.

Use Brainstorming Techniques

A key step in topic selection is to compile a list of possible subjects that interest you and appeal to your audience. **Brainstorming** is a process of free association in which your goal is to generate as many ideas as possible without fear of critique. Give each of the following idea-generation techniques a try:

- **Brainstorm.** Get every possible idea down on paper.[4] Don't rule out any topic until you have had a chance to evaluate it.

- **Piggyback ideas.** Mix and match ideas you've generated to form interesting combinations. You might combine interests in the environment and in transportation for a speech on why people should drive environmentally friendly cars.

- **Don't censor.** Go idea-wild. You'll have ample opportunity to tame an idea once you evaluate it for usefulness and appropriateness to the speaking situation. During a brainstorming session, one student suggested a wild idea—implanting human stem cells in animal brains to produce animals that think like humans—only to discover that such research was actually being considered in scientific circles.

Brainstorm. It's best to write down anything that comes to mind and refine and discard topics that don't work later.

iStock.com/alvarez

Technique 1: Brainstorm to Develop a Personal Inventory of Interesting Subjects

Think about subjects you either have some knowledge of or would like to learn more about. They may relate to something you have experienced personally, like a hobby, or something you would like to explore, like a tsunami.

Another possibility is to take an "on looking" walk with your smartphone or other recording device as your companion. As you walk, notice potential topics hidden in plain sight. Record examples that come to mind from architecture, street signs, passersby, dog walkers, and anything else you see.[5]

A variation of the same exercise is to focus on *the here and now* for a source of potential topics. On the left side of a sheet of paper list everything you are able to see, hear, taste, smell, or touch from your present location. Once you have identified 10 to 15 items, note on the right side of your paper topics that might naturally evolve from each observation or experience (see Table 5.1). Don't censor your ideas; write down everything that comes to mind. A general subject area may surface that you can then develop into a more specific speech topic. Later in this chapter, we will see that topics are modified to meet the needs of each specific speech genre. For example, a speech on How Airplanes Fly would be appropriate for an informative speech while a speech on The Dangers Drones Pose would be appropriate for a persuasive speech.

TABLE 5.1 ■ Topic Inventory	
The Here and Now	**Possible Topics**
A passing airplane	Mass Transportation, Flight Safety, The History of Flight, How Airplanes Fly, The Future of Air Transport, Flying Cars, The Dangers Drones Pose
The hum of the air conditioner	Brutal Heat and the Least Air-Conditioned Cities in the United States, How a New Variation on the Color White Will Affect the Environment, The Invention of the Air Conditioner, How People Kept Cool Before Air Conditioning, The Energy Impact of Air Conditioning, Alternative Energy Sources
A smartphone	Texting, The History of Facebook, How Instagram Works, Smartphone Addiction, Big Tech Is Watching, Phone Hacking Spyware
A stuffed bear	Toy Manufacturing, Consumer Safety Regulations, The History of the Teddy Bear, Child Development
A dog	The Life of a Seeing Eye Dog, The Importance of Supporting the ASPCA, The Domestication of Dogs, Dogs and COVID-19, All Dogs Are Comfort Dogs
A food store	The Safety of the Food Supply, Sugar and Obesity, Effects of Meat Eating on Climate, The New Food Pyramid

Technique 2: Brainstorm Using Categories as a Stimulus

Divide a page into six columns. At the top of each column, list one of the following words: *people, processes, phenomena, possessions, products,* and *programs.*[6] Then devote the next 30 minutes (5 minutes per category) to writing down every word you associate with each category, in turn (see Table 5.2). Review your lists of responses and see which, if any, of the general subject areas you might develop into a specific topic that reflects your interests and also will interest your audience.

TABLE 5.2 ■ Brainstorming Using Categories					
People	**Processes**	**Phenomena**	**Possessions**	**Products**	**Programs**
the mayor	recycling	meteor shower	sunglasses	chocolate	literacy
Michelle Obama	digestion	earthquake	gold necklace	smartwatch	orientation

People	Processes	Phenomena	Possessions	Products	Programs
Mom	rusting	sinkhole	Treasury note	lawnmower	Peace Corps
novelist	baking a cake	tornado	jade statue	handbag	Medicaid
Albert Einstein	making origami	lightning	car	stereo	Boy/Girl Scouts

Get creative. You never know which ideas will spark your **interest**!

iStock.com/solidcolours

Technique 3: Brainstorm Using the A-B-C Approach

The A-B-C approach uses the alphabet to help find a potential topic. This technique is particularly useful in helping prevent "idea paralysis." We provide you with one potential topic idea for each alphabet letter; generate at least one more on your own.

	Topic 1	Topic 2
A	Artificial intelligence	_____
B	Black holes	_____
C	Coffee	_____
D	Date rape	_____
E	Echolocation	_____

(Continued)

	Topic 1	Topic 2
F	Fly fishing	_____
G	Gun control	_____
H	Hair loss	_____
I	Irritants	_____
J	Justice system	_____
K	Kentucky Derby	_____
L	Lupus	_____
M	Mindfulness	_____
N	Nobel Prizes	_____
O	Organ donation	_____
P	Procrastination	_____
Q	Quantum physics	_____
R	Radiation	_____
S	Social networking	_____
T	Ticklishness	_____
U	UFOs	_____
V	Voting Rights	_____
W	Wilderness	_____
X	Xenophobia	_____
Y	Yeti	_____
Z	Zoom revolution	_____

Use Other Topic Selection Techniques

These idea-generation exercises will help you develop areas of interest into a topic for presentation.

Technique 4: Scan the Media

Newspapers, magazines, books, advertisements, films, broadcast news, sitcoms, or the Internet might just provide the spark that lights our fire on a particular subject. For example, the July 23, 2021, issue of the *New York Times* featured an article on the Summer Olympics being held in Tokyo, Japan. Imagine the possible speech topics suggested by the article: how to train like an athlete, protests at the Olympics, Olympic scandals, nationalism and the Olympics, terrorism and the Olympics, Olympic boycotts, the meaning of the Olympic rings, just to name a few.[7]

Browsing through news, entertainment, and Internet sites, as well as listening to or watching specialized programs, could result in a list of possible topics like the following:

Increases in Food Recalls

Social Media Monopolies

Right to Privacy

The Death Penalty

Fertility Clinics

The Electoral College

Human Mission to Mars

Space Tourism

Diversity and the Corporation

Depression and Holidays

Volunteerism

Trans Rights

24/7 news. The Internet and the world are at your fingertips, so just browsing your phone can spark an idea.

iStockPhoto.com/Tero Vesalainen

Immigration

Virtual Reality

Chronic Distraction

Robotic Surgery

Sustainable Fishing

Sexual Harassment

Cuba–U.S. Relations

Prison Privatization

Airline Safety

Job Hunting

Technique 5: What's Taboo to Whom?

Consult resources such as David Livermore's *Leading With Cultural Intelligence,* or conduct an online search of "cultural mistakes" or "cultural taboos" around the world to identify speech topics that specific groups of people might find offensive or inappropriate for public discussion.[8] For example, in many Arab, Asian, and African cultures, talking about sex to audiences made up of both men and women is likely to be judged offensive.[9] Of course, some U.S. audiences might find it offensive as well. That said, not every potentially sensitive topic is taboo or off-limits. We need to remain open and process ideas we find disagreeable fairly.

On a smaller scale, be careful not to assume that because you are interested in a topic, others in your class will automatically be interested in that topic as well.

Technique 6: Draw a Mind Map

A mind map is a visual means of showing relationships among brainstormed ideas (see Figure 5.1). To create a mind map, begin by writing a word or phrase smack in the middle of a blank piece of paper. For example, in Figure 5.1 the word *lightning* triggered a number of surrounding related ideas/images associated with the term. We see that as ideas about the center word came to mind, the surrounding words relied on arrows to indicate linkages between ideas, and colors to make the different ideas stand out.[10] This process, while similar to word association, helps you focus on the relationships between ideas and concepts. As your ideas get clearer, feel free to redraw the map.

After completing these exercises and compiling an extensive list of possible topics, you are ready to assess each topic's viability. As you review the possibilities, remember that you should be passionate about the topic you ultimately select. Your topic should be adaptable to the diverse interests and concerns of receivers, have significance for you and them, and allow you to add to or acquire information.

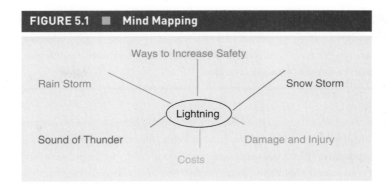

FIGURE 5.1   ■   Mind Mapping

Ways to Increase Safety

Rain Storm

Snow Storm

Lightning

Sound of Thunder

Damage and Injury

Costs

Technique 7: Draw a Topic Cone

There is a strategy you can use to avoid biting off more than you can chew—or talk about. Select a topic and place it at the top of a topic cone. Then subdivide it into constituent parts; that is, break it down into smaller and smaller units, as shown in Figure 5.2 (a topic cone on poverty). The smallest unit should appear on the lowest level of the cone. This process is like whittling or carving a stick of wood. The more you shave off, the narrower the topic becomes. Like the carver, you decide what shape to give your topic and when to stop shaving.

Here's another example. Let's say that you want to speak on the need to save the rain forest. One way to narrow your topic would be to focus on how Indigenous people can save the rain forest. Your topic could be focused even further. You might explore how their harvesting of native plants can stop deforestation or, more specifically, how their harvesting of fruit can help preserve the ecological balance.

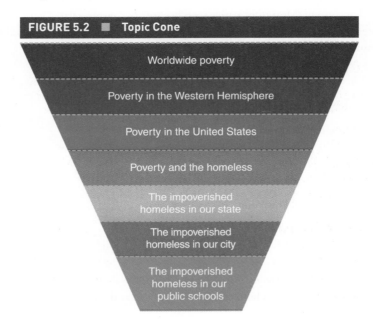

FIGURE 5.2   ■   Topic Cone

Worldwide poverty

Poverty in the Western Hemisphere

Poverty in the United States

Poverty and the homeless

The impoverished homeless in our state

The impoverished homeless in our city

The impoverished homeless in our public schools

FORMULATE GENERAL AND SPECIFIC PURPOSES

> **5.2**   *Develop effective general and specific purpose statements, together with an audience-focused behavioral objective.*

In this section, we explore the plays involved in linking your selected topic with both the general and specific purpose of your speech. Once you have picked a general topic, be sure to connect it first to the general purpose that reflects your assignment, and then to the specific purpose that facilitates the attainment of your primary objective. To accomplish this, you will need to answer two questions:

1. What general purpose do I want to fulfill by speaking on this topic?

2. What is my specific topic and goal?

Formulate the General Purpose

The **general purpose** is the overall effect you hope to have on your audience. Virtually all speeches fulfill one of three general rhetorical purposes: to inform, to persuade, or to entertain.

Speaking to Inform

An informative speech is designed to teach. Thus, an informative speaker resembles a teacher whose primary goal is to communicate and share knowledge with an audience—to give listeners new information. Speakers deliver informative speeches when they want to explain a process, procedure, organization, or function; when they describe a person, place, or thing; or when they define a word or concept. Most informative speeches are not controversial. They occur in virtually all classes you take and are equally common in work and community settings. The following are examples of informative speech topics:

- The Effects of Sleep Deprivation on the Body

- How mRNA Vaccines Work

- How 9/11 Changed Music

- How to Save Money

- How to Dress for a Job Interview

- The Effects of Lead Poisoning

- The Role of Water in Our Lives

Speaking to Persuade

The speech to persuade is designed primarily to change the thoughts and/or the behaviors of receivers. The persuasive speaker hopes to alter not only what the audience members know, but also how they feel and/or act.

Persuasive speech topics are more controversial than informative speech topics because others may oppose what the speaker advocates. Thus, while a speaker may deliver a speech supporting abortion rights, a number of audience members may hold very different opinions about the subject. The following are examples of persuasive topics:

- The Dangers of Conspiracy Theories
- The Right to Offend
- Monuments to the Confederacy
- The Worsening Homeless Crisis
- Alcohol Consumption During Pregnancy
- The Anti-Vaxxers
- Opt-Out Organ Donation

Speaking to Entertain

The speech to entertain is designed to amuse an audience. If, as a result of the speaker's efforts, audience members smile, laugh, and generally feel good or have a good time, the speech is a success.

You might be called on to deliver a speech to entertain when serving as an after-breakfast, luncheon, or dinner speaker, or when delivering a comic monologue at a comedy club, for example. Humor is usually an essential ingredient in the speech to entertain; skill in using it is necessary. The following are examples of topics of speeches to entertain:

- How to Fail a Course
- Least Effective College Essays
- The Part of the City I Wouldn't Show a Tourist
- How to Lie
- Text Messaging Mistakes
- Handshakes I Have Experienced
- The Best Ways to Waste Time

After you have chosen a general purpose, the next step is to fill in the details.

Formulate the Specific Purpose

The **specific purpose** of a speech is your statement of the speech's main objective. It is an infinitive phrase that identifies what you want your speech to accomplish or what you hope to do with your speech.

The specific purpose statement of an informative speech often contains such words as *show, explain, report, instruct, describe,* and (not surprisingly) *inform.* The following are examples of specific purpose statements for various kinds of informative speeches:

- To *describe* for audience members how decreases in state funding to colleges will affect them

- To *inform* my audience about the effects of sickle cell anemia

- To *explain* to my audience the signs of a stroke

- To *report* on efforts to raise college graduation rates

- To *instruct* class members on how to interview for a job

Words like *persuade, motivate, convince,* and *act* are characteristic of specific purposes for persuasive speeches, as in the following examples:

- To *motivate* listeners to buy organic food

- To *persuade* listeners to register as organ donors

- To *convince* audience members to maintain a financial "rainy day" fund

What do you notice about each of the preceding specific purposes? Though formulated for very different topics, they share at least five characteristics:

1. The specific purpose is stated as an infinitive phrase, for example, *to explain* or *to convince.*

2. The specific purpose is for your personal use and is written from your perspective; it identifies your concrete goal and can guide your research and the direction of your speech.

3. The specific purpose focuses on a single, distinct idea.

4. The specific purpose relates your topic to your audience by specifying what you want the audience to know, think, or do as a result of your speech.

5. The specific purpose is clear and concise, not muddled or unfocused.

COACHING TIP

"Communication is 'purpose driven.'"

—Larry A. Samovar and Edwin R. McDaniel, intercultural communication pioneers

The purpose of a speech is the driver of the speech. Make that purpose crystal clear. There should be no doubt in the audience's mind regarding what you hope to accomplish.

While a good specific purpose is ambitious rather than trivial, it does not overreach. If you're unable to develop a speech that reflects your specific purpose in the time available, then you need to narrow your specific purpose even more.

The sharper your specific purpose, the easier you will find it to develop your speech. So while formulating your specific purpose, complete this checklist:

- Does my specific purpose reflect the assignment or speech situation?
- Will I be able to obtain my specific goal in the speaking time allotted me?
- Will I be able to prepare a speech that fulfills my specific purpose in a manner my listeners will be able to understand and respond to?
- Will my audience assess my goal to be relevant to their needs and reflective of their interests?
- Will my audience judge my purpose to be significant and worthy of their attention?

Be sure you answer each of these questions with a "yes" and with a reason before you proceed.

Consider the Audience's Perspective

In addition to formulating a specific purpose written from your own perspective, it is helpful to assess the speech from the audience's perspective. You might find it useful to compose a desired **behavioral objective**. Complete the sentence, "After experiencing my speech, audience members will . . ." in order to describe the response you expect from audience members.

Sample Behavioral Objectives for Informative Speeches

After experiencing my speech, audience members will be able to

- List three reasons why pedestrian death rates are rising
- Name four effects of climate change
- Explain how the U.S. deficit will affect them

Sample Behavioral Objectives for Persuasive Speeches

After experiencing my speech, audience members will

- Contribute money to support art museums
- Register to vote
- Sign a petition advocating for a cashless society

Writing a behavioral objective will help you focus the content of your speech on those aspects that audience members will find most interesting or appropriate. By identifying what audience members should know, think, or do after listening to your speech, you position the audience and its behavior in the forefront of your mind.

Activate your audience. What do you want people to *do* after hearing your speech?

Jupiterimages/Creatas/Thinkstock

The next task facing you is to formulate a central idea or thesis.

GAME PLAN

Choosing a Topic

- Am I genuinely interested in my topic?
- Am I willing to research the topic to enhance my knowledge of it? Will an exploration of this topic benefit my listeners?
- Is my topic suitable for this particular situation?
- Will my listeners find a discussion of my topic worthwhile, important, and interesting?
- Have I narrowed my topic sufficiently to fit the speaking time allotted me?
- Have I identified a general speech purpose appropriate to the assignment or speaking situation?
- Have I formulated a clear, specific purpose?
- Have I composed a behavioral objective that identifies the specific response I desire from audience members?
- Have I phrased my thesis/central idea so that it helps me control the development of my speech?
- By making careful choices, you focus your content and communicate more clearly, concisely, and confidently. Narrowing your focus will better enable you to get your message across.

FORMULATE THE THESIS STATEMENT OR CENTRAL IDEA

5.3   *Formulate an effective thesis (central idea).*

Speakers are often encouraged to develop theses, also referred to as **central ideas,** for their speeches, just as writers do for papers. A **thesis** is limited to one and only one central idea that is expressed as a declarative sentence and divides a topic into its major components, effectively summarizing the main points of your speech.

Thesis Statements for Informative Speeches

When your speech is an informative one and not intended to be primarily persuasive, the thesis statement (which, as we noted, some practitioners prefer to call the central idea) is phrased in a relatively objective and neutral manner. Its focus is on what you want audience members to understand or learn—for example, "Nuclear power plants have three major parts: the reactor core, vessel, and control rods."

Thesis Statements for Persuasive Speeches

When your speech is persuasive, the thesis is sometimes called a claim. It expresses an arguable opinion or point of view; for example, a thesis for a persuasive speech against the use of nuclear energy plants might be, "Nuclear power plants should be decommissioned."

Whether the speech is informative or persuasive, the thesis statement is your speech "in a nutshell." It is a statement of the key concept of your speech that all the facts, quotations, and ideas in the speech are designed to support.

COACHING TIP

"Education is the most powerful weapon which you can use to change the world."

—Nelson Mandela, first Black president of South Africa

A speaker is an educator. Formulating an effective thesis provides receivers with an understanding of the speech's major components, paving the road to learning.

Evaluating the Thesis Statement or Central Idea

An effective thesis statement or central idea fulfills five criteria. Use this checklist of criteria to evaluate yours:

1. It is a single sentence that conveys the essence of the speech.

2. It focuses the attention of audience members on what they should know, do, or feel after experiencing the speech.

3. It forecasts the development or organization of the speech.

4. It is phrased diplomatically, avoiding figurative language that is apt to inflame.

5. It supports the specific purpose.

When listeners are asked what your speech was about, they should be able to respond by offering your thesis. Even if they remember nothing else, it is the thesis you hope they retain. To show how this works, let us examine one of the examples we used earlier and develop it into a usable thesis.

Specific purpose: To explain to my audience the signs of a stroke

Thesis: There are three symptoms of a stroke that require immediate medical attention.

From this thesis, we can say that the speaker will explore three main points in their speech, each point corresponding to one of the three symptoms of a stroke that are face drooping, arm weakness, and difficulty speaking.

Unlike the specific purpose, the thesis is usually delivered directly to the audience. Thus, a well-phrased thesis not only helps you divide your presentation into its major components, it helps your listeners follow the speech's progression. The following are examples of effectively phrased theses:

Thesis: Universal health care would improve the lives of Americans by bolstering the economy.

Thesis: Practicing yoga will enhance your personal and professional life in four key ways.

Phrasing your thesis brings you a step closer to developing the structure of the speech itself.

EXERCISES

Topic and Purpose

Participating in the following activities will let you apply what you know, putting your skills into action.

1. Top 10 Topics

Alone or in a group, create a list of 10 topics you believe worthy of both your and an audience's time. For each topic on your list, develop a thesis or central idea and explain what makes the topic meaningful and worthwhile. Then identify which topic you consider to be the most interesting, and why.

2. Purposeful Purposes

Using the 10 topics in Exercise 1, demonstrate how each topic can be adapted to reflect the general purpose of an informative speech as well as the general purpose of a persuasive speech.

3. Analyze This: Is It Clear?

Read the following student speech on Planned Parenthood. Focus on how well the speech clarifies the following for receivers: (a) its general purpose, (b) its specific purpose, (c) its behavioral objectives, and (d) the thesis. After reading the speech, phrase each of the preceding speech components in your own words. Then, using the criteria discussed in the text for each component, assess the extent to which each component fulfills its function.

Planned Parenthood: Service Provider

SN 1

The speaker begins the speech with a question designed to arouse the audience's curiosity.

How many of you are familiar with the terms chancroid or granuloma? If you've never heard of these diseases before, you've likely never been tested for them before. Here's the good news. Planned Parenthood provides free STD testing every day at facilities all across the United

States, even during the Covid-19 pandemic. Planned Parenthood focuses on both male and female reproductive health and therefore is crucial for college students. After working with politicians in my area, I realized that too many people are unfamiliar with the services provided at Planned Parenthood outside of abortions. Today I will address the care offered at Planned Parenthood, as well as inform you of the continuing need for it in our society.

SN 2

The speaker uses facts to destigmatize Planned Parenthood.

To understand what Planned Parenthood is, it is important to first address the stigmas that surround the organization. Planned Parenthood is beneficial to everyone, even if you're pro-life or pro-choice. Whether or not you support a woman's right to abortion should not be the deciding factor in whether you think Planned Parenthood merits government funding. In its 2020 annual report, published in the midst of the Pandemic, it was noted that across 50 states, 491 counties, and 650 clinics, Planned Parenthood provides comprehensive, quality health care to 2.5 million women and men in the United States.

I'd like to clarify that abortions are not considered health care and therefore are not funded by the government. This was made clear by the Hyde Amendment, which passed in 1976, which specifies that government funds cannot legally go toward abortions. This is from an article titled "Why Hyde Matters" that was written in 2016.

SN 3

The speaker provides an overview of Planned Parenthood services and the groups that benefit, including underserved populations.

In an interview titled "116 Minutes," conducted a little over a decade ago, Daniel Fromson spoke with Cecile Richards, the president of Planned Parenthood at the time. Cecile Richards clarified that Planned Parenthood is about pap smears, not abortions, routine women's health care, not ideological crusading. Essentially what Richards revealed was that Planned Parenthood does not need to be a polarizing institution.

Regardless of where you stand on abortion, you're likely benefiting from Planned Parenthood services. For example, Planned Parenthood is for women of all ages. They do things like breast exams, cervical cancer screenings, pap smears, and UTI tests every single day. It's also for women expecting children. Planned Parenthood has adoption services, child birth classes, and prenatal services, such as ultrasounds, all at little or no cost to the patient. Planned Parenthood also offers free birth control and affordable emergency contraceptive pills.

What's more, Planned Parenthood isn't just for women. It's for men as well. Erectile dysfunction and prostate cancer screening and treatment are provided everyday across the nation. Free condoms are also given at Planned Parenthood facilities, which is very beneficial to men who either can't afford to buy this product or don't have a good resource to ask questions about this product.

Other people who benefit immensely from Planned Parenthood are the members of the LGBTQAI community. Hormone therapy is a costly procedure. It is offered at Planned Parenthood at a very low cost for the patient; Planned Parenthood also offers counseling to go along with that service. Planned Parenthood offers members of this community sexual education which cannot be found elsewhere to the extent that it's offered at Planned Parenthood, particularly because there is a lack of openness and a lack of understanding toward the members of this group.

SN 4

The speaker transitions, using a variety of support to build credibility for the position the speaker is taking.

Now that you are aware of the services provided by Planned Parenthood, let's explore both the need for them in today's society today and why Planned Parenthood deserves government funding. According to reporter Paige Winfield writing in the October 21, 2020 *Washington Post*, even former President Donald Trump during his term in office did not defund Planned Parenthood. Despite this, in 2021, Congressperson Vickie Hartzler introduced a bill in Congress to defund the organization. Here's why defunding Planned Parenthood is not a good idea.

Defunding Planned Parenthood would result in a loss of services that would disproportionately affect low income women of color and women living in rural and other medically under-served areas. According to Michael Hiltzk's April 16, 2021 *Los Angeles Times* article, it would decimate their access to affordable birth control and screening for cancer and sexually transmitted diseases. Basically, we see that while Planned Parenthood is convenient for some, it is crucial for others. Taking away government funding would take away Planned Parenthood from both poor women and women in rural areas, hurting them significantly more than others.

Reproductive health services are crucial, and Planned Parenthood may be the only source that some people have for obtaining these services. Items distributed by Planned Parenthood actually prevent the need for abortions, but these items, such as condoms, emergency contraceptive pills, and IUDs, are not free for Planned Parenthood. But they're offered free or at little cost for the patient, which means government funding is needed to bridge that gap to keep costs low.

SN 5

The speaker cites specific examples to underscore the needs being met by Planned Parenthood.

Contraceptive services provided by Planned Parenthood prevent approximately 579,000 unintended pregnancies annually. That means that women have the power to decide when they want to have their families. In his 2017 work titled "Double Trouble," political scientist Rob Boston explains how nonprofit institutions can cite religious objections to deny insurance coverage for contraception to its employees and students. This is a money issue that's being disguised as a religious issue. Big corporations don't want to pay for contraceptive services and are citing religious reasons for that.

But birth control can cost over $100 every time a woman goes to fill her prescription, meaning that this hurts women much more than it hurts men. And if women aren't receiving these products through their medical insurer, they're going to need to find it elsewhere at a low cost, which is offered at Planned Parenthood. Also, if people don't have cheap access to STD screening, they're likely going to go without it. In a 2017 article for AIDS care, psychologist V. Ganta explains how rates for pap smear screening in Nevada are below the national rate. And, of the pap smear screening results taken, 29.4 percent were abnormal. Frequent screening, which does happen at Planned Parenthood, can help us prevent the spread of cancer in the United States; this is especially important during the current pandemic.

A lack of education on certain diseases and services absolutely results in an unprotected public. Pharmacist Marie Bernard wrote in 2017 of a questionnaire she gave to college students reporting that only 28 percent of females and 20.8 percent of males were aware that there was an HPV test for men. Like I said before, not knowing that this test exists likely means you've never had it done. And HPV is a very serious STD. It can cause cancer for you and all of your sexual partners. Bernard continues, saying that most people with HPV have no visible signs or symptoms, which means that this disease could be spreading all across America and the only way we know if we have it is if we get tested for it.

Finally, in her 2017 work titled "If There's One Benefit, You're Not Going to Get Pregnant," psychiatrist Michelle Estes explains that today's current sex education curriculum in schools and families is still centered around heterosexuality, meaning that gay students are less informed on sexual encounters and reproductive health than their heterosexual counterparts. Excluding these topics also perpetuates the invisibility of lesbian, gay, and bisexual students, and that's also from Estes's 2017 work. The LGBTQAI community is marginalized in every sector of health care, but as I noted before and will stress again now, Planned Parenthood helps prevent that from happening in reproductive health.

SN 6

The speaker summarizes the points made in the speech and issues a call to action.

With the data I've provided today, I hope you understand that Planned Parenthood is an organization that should not be scrapped by the federal government. It is helpful to everybody, especially college students. If you believe that Americans are entitled to reproductive health screening, or if you believe that contraception should be accessible by all, or if you believe that people need a resource for sexual education, you should support government funding of Planned Parenthood. I hope you are inclined to call your local representative and voice your support today.

Source: The original speech on Planned Parenthood by an unnamed Missouri State student was updated in 2021 by students at New York Institute of Technology.

4. Approach the Speaker's Stand

On your own or in a team, tackle the following scenario: You have been invited to speak at First Year Student Orientation. You are asked to select a topic that will help first-year students complete the year successfully. Understanding and sharing the steps you take when moving from a general topic to a specific purpose to behavioral objectives and finally to a thesis can help others. In a presentation, not to exceed two minutes, provide an example for your peers that illustrates your progression of thought as you move from a broad subject to a much more specific and focused thesis or central idea for the speech you will deliver to those attending orientation.

RECAP AND REVIEW

5.1   Use creative techniques to choose a topic appropriate for you, your audience, and the occasion.

A good topic is one that is appropriate for the speaker, the audience, and the occasion. Speakers use a variety of idea-generation exercises to help examine their personal behaviors and interests, they scan the media, and they survey reference books and indexes.

5.2   Develop effective general and specific purpose statements together with an audience-focused behavioral objective.

The general purpose statement describes the overall effect a speaker hopes to have on an audience. The specific purpose statement is the speaker's personal statement of the speech's main objective. It describes what the speaker wants the audience to know, think, or do as a result of the speech. A behavioral objective is a specific outcome, an observable, measurable audience response that begins with seven words—"After experiencing my speech, audience members will"—and then describes the response the speaker expects from audience members.

5.3   Formulate an effective thesis (central idea).

A thesis (or central idea) divides a speech into its major components and makes a clear point about the topic. A declarative sentence, it summarizes the speech's main points. Speakers must answer "yes" to 10 key questions to determine whether they can move forward with the speech; otherwise, they have more thinking and refining ahead of them.

KEY TERMS

Behavioral objective (p. 113)
Brainstorming (p. 102)
Central idea (p. 115)
Claim (p. 116)

General purpose (p. 110)
Invention (p. 100)
Specific purpose (p. 111)
Thesis (p. 115)

6 FINDING AND EVALUATING RESEARCH FOR YOUR SPEECH

UPON COMPLETING THIS CHAPTER, YOU WILL BE ABLE TO
6.1 Draw on primary research from your personal knowledge and experience, including interviewing persons possessing special knowledge related to your topic.
6.2 Locate and use secondary research sources.
6.3 Critically evaluate all research, documenting and citing all sources.

You have chosen a speech topic. Now, how do you go about researching it, and why does the thoroughness of your research matter? For one thing, an accurately researched speech will help to increase your presentation's effectiveness by enabling you to integrate an array of relevant facts and other materials in support of your speech's thesis. In this chapter, we offer you a research plan to use in order to discover, evaluate, and cite research. Doing this will document your speech's content and build your credibility.

When done carefully, and fact-checked, research adds substance, believability, and impact to a presentation. In the effort to be truthful and avoid communicating misinformation to the audience, researchers carefully assess what they find. Ask yourself, "Who says?" "How do they know?" "Are they biased?" Think about the self-talk that audience members will engage in when listening to your speech. Conscientious receivers listen critically, looking for concrete support for the speech's thesis. When you engage in fact-checking you show your audience that you know what you're talking about, helping them to trust in you.

What's the best way to gather research? If you want to try a new restaurant, you might ask your friends for recommendations, peruse a restaurant guide such as Zagat or Yelp, or review various restaurant home pages on the Internet. What does this have to do with public speaking? The research we do when preparing to speak in public is very much like the personal research we conduct daily. However, because a speech is shared with others in a more formal setting, we rely on a plan and use more formal approaches when gathering research materials. Researching a speech is a kind of investigation, and it is your job to take nothing for granted in investigating your topic. Work the plan by first asking yourself what you already know and what you need to find out. Then think about how to acquire the information you're missing, and how much time you have to do so. Research sources available to you include both primary and secondary ones. *Primary sources* are other people you consult or interview directly (and can include yourself). *Secondary sources* are composed of already published works, including, but not limited to, statistics, texts and articles by experts, and media documents.

COACHING TIP

"If something comes from your heart, it will reach the heart of your audience."

—(یفوک هیزوف) (Fawzia Koofi), Afghan women's rights activist

Your speech is only as strong as the research and personal experiences upon which it is based. If you want audience members to accept what you say, then you have to impress them with how much you know.

USE PRIMARY RESEARCH

> **6.1**   *Draw on primary research from your personal knowledge and experience, including interviewing persons possessing special knowledge related to your topic.*

Public speaking students frequently overlook **primary research**. Primary research is original research involving the collecting of firsthand data, including using your knowledge and experiences, conducting surveys, and interviewing credible sources.

Use Personal Knowledge and Experience

By the time you enrolled in this class, you probably have had some job experience to your credit and while in school been studying a wide variety of subjects. In your lifetime, you have probably read a vast number of newspaper and magazine articles, watched countless hours of video, written papers, listened to podcasts, and talked with an array of individuals—many of whom are more knowledgeable than you. Just going about the business of living provides you with many experiences from which to draw raw material for a speech. Yet many college students often discount the value of their own lives when they begin to research a topic.

Once we write down our experiences, they serve as a form of personal research and enhance our credibility. This is not to suggest that you can't speak about a topic unless you have lived it. By researching the subject, you can talk about poverty without actually having been impoverished. However, if you have experience with a topic that is important to you, that experience—when supplemented with additional outside research—will greatly increase your credibility with your audience. Thus, you can capitalize on your own experience to provide effective explanations, examples, or definitions.

For instance, one student, a survivor of Hodgkin's lymphoma, explained to his class how he coped with the impact of the illness. He described first discovering that he had Hodgkin's, its symptoms, his treatment, and survival rates. He buttressed his message by revealing his personal fears in depth. The speaker's simple words conveyed his message more meaningfully and eloquently than if he had quoted another source. Even if your experiences are not as dramatic or as emotionally powerful as surviving cancer, you can still use them to your advantage. Think over your life and consider how you could integrate one or more experiences into a speech to add a sense of freshness and authenticity to your message.

Interview Others With Specialized Knowledge

Although personal experience is often a starting point for speech research, rarely will it be sufficient, if only because few—if any—student speakers have enough material from their own lives on which to base an entire speech. Thus, you need to consult other sources, too.

Interviewing those with special knowledge is a key means of acquiring both information about and insight into a topic. One possibility is to talk to individuals who others will find credible because they possess special knowledge or are experts on the subject. For example, if your goal is to speak about the dangers of nuclear power plants, a call or email to a nuclear physicist at the Nuclear Regulatory Agency in Washington, D.C., could bring you up to date on the issues you plan to discuss in your speech.[1]

Conducting interviews with specialists will not eliminate your need to conduct other research, such as examining newspaper and magazine articles or reading relevant books on the subject. But questioning experts can help you structure your research and provide you with ideas and information to bring your speech alive. However, you must begin by doing some preliminary research that will enable you to formulate the particular questions for which you need an expert's answers.

Prepare for the Interview

The first task is to determine why you are interviewing someone. What qualifies the individual as an expert? For example, one student decided to talk about controversial road construction near his campus that would likely disrupt access to the college and its nearby business district. He began his research by reading news reports on the topic and discovered one particular shopkeeper had surfaced as the voice of opposition to the project and was often quoted in local articles. A phone call produced specific insights about the building project that the student was able to use in his speech. Because he wanted to be sure to inform his audience about multiple perspectives, the student also interviewed a government official as well as an engineer familiar with the project and incorporated the results of those interviews into his speech.

To set up an interview, all you need to do is pick up the phone and ask permission. You might use the following template:

> Hello, (Mr., Ms., Dr., Professor) _____. My name is _____, from _____ College/University. I am researching a presentation for my public speaking class on the subject of _____. I understand that you are well versed in this field, and I wondered whether it would be possible for us to talk about it now or in the near future.

If you fail to reach the person you want to interview by phone, and if time allows, you could send a letter or email to the desired source. You might begin such a letter as follows:

> Dear (Mr., Ms., Dr., Professor) _____: I am a student at _____ and am currently working on a speech on the topic of _____. It is my understanding that you are an expert in this field, and I was wondering whether it would be possible for us to get together either in person or over the phone to discuss it.

I would only need a few minutes of your time to answer some basic questions about
_____. My peers would really enjoy hearing your views.

Please contact me at _____, so we can work out the details of such a
meeting. Thank you for your help. I look forward to meeting you.

Sincerely,

_____

Before you conduct an interview, be certain that you have a series of questions to ask your
interviewee that display a sense of purpose, direction, and familiarity with the subject. Here are
sample questions you might ask if your topic was lie detector tests and you were interviewing a
source from the American Polygraph Association about their usefulness and reliability.

PRELIMINARY QUESTIONS FOR THE AMERICAN POLYGRAPH ASSOCIATION REPRESENTATIVE

1. What is the scientific basis of the polygraph?
2. How do people train to administer lie detector tests?
3. How and when was the test developed?
4. How many tests are administered each year?
5. What are polygraph tests used for?
6. Is it possible to cheat on a polygraph test? How?
7. How does an administrator prepare to give a polygraph test?
8. How should a person prepare to take a polygraph test?
9. What ethical guidelines do polygraph administrators follow?
10. Why did you decide to become a polygraph administrator?

Whenever you conduct an interview, preserve its results. Take detailed notes or, if the interviewee grants you permission, record your conversation. You might use the following template
for documenting that you have the interviewee's permission to record the interview:

This is _____, and today's date is _____. I am
with _____, who has consented to this interview being recorded. Is
that correct _____ [insert interviewee's name]?

If the interviewee answers "Yes," then you can proceed with the interview, safe in the knowledge that not only your interview, but also the permission to record it will be captured on tape.

Let's say you plan to speak on an issue that especially concerns you—perhaps racism or climate change. Though some people are unlikely to consent to an interview, for the purposes of
this exercise, assume that you can reach any public figure. Identify the desired interviewee and

their position and explain why you consider them an expert on your chosen issue. Then compile a list of at least 10 specific questions you would like to ask the expert either in person, via email, or by phone.

Conduct the Interview

You now have an interviewee lined up and have prepared your questions. How do you proceed?

First, arrive on time. It is better to find yourself waiting for the interviewee and using the extra time to strategize than it is to make the interviewee wait for you.

Second, explain your reasons for the interview right away. *You* know why it was important to interview the subject, but your interviewee may not be sure why you're there. If you need to prepare to record, you can use that time to establish some common ground with the interviewee and give them a few extra seconds to focus on your topic.

Once you begin, the person you are interviewing may take your discussion into other areas. If the tangents are adding material to the interview that is relevant to your objectives, by all means let the interviewee pursue the area. If the detour is irrelevant, gently guide the interviewee back by returning to your prepared list of questions.

During the interview, ask questions designed to elicit needed information. Don't waste time asking questions you can get answered elsewhere. Ask open questions that require more than one-word answers. Follow up with **probing questions** that seek more information, such as, "Why did you make that decision?"

Also remember to give the interviewee feedback. For example, you may want to say, "So, what you are saying is . . ." or "What I hear you telling me is. . .". Asking mirroring questions—such as, "You said attitude is more important than aptitude?"—encourages discussion while also verifying the interviewee's meaning. An even more effective approach is to combine a mirroring response with a probing question: "So you are suggesting that emotional intelligence is as important as IQ. Are you implying that schools should be teaching this as well?"

Techniques like these help ensure that you have accurately processed and understood the information that the

Investigative journalism. Interviewing someone knowledgeable on your topic is a great way to conduct research.

Stockbyte/Stockbyte/Thinkstock

interviewee is giving you and also show the interviewee that you really care about what they are sharing.

Conduct a Post-Interview Review

You should review your notes or recording immediately after the interview to clarify what you've written and so that you do not misquote your expert. Concentrate on isolating the main points from the conversation. Be alert for specific examples and information that you can incorporate into your presentation.

Compile a list of key ideas covered during the interview. Having such a list will make it easier to determine which pieces of information are relevant to your speech and which can be discarded. Transcribe or rewrite your notes, focusing on the most relevant material. You may want to write each piece of information on an individual index card so it will be easier to organize your presentation. For example, you might record information resulting from an interview about damage caused by a recent hurricane, as shown in Figure 6.1.

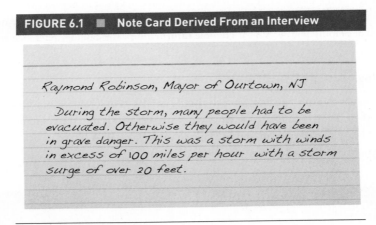

FIGURE 6.1 ■ Note Card Derived From an Interview

Raymond Robinson, Major of Ourtown, NJ

During the storm, many people had to be evacuated. Otherwise they would have been in grave danger. This was a storm with winds in excess of 100 miles per hour with a storm surge of over 20 feet.

iStock.com/petermccue

GATHER SECONDARY RESEARCH

> **6.2**   *Locate and use secondary research sources.*

Secondary research includes published statistics, texts and articles by experts, and media and personal documents. Suppose, for example, that you have decided to speak on the dangers that the transmission of misinformation poses to a democratic society, and as part of your speech you want to explore the role misinformation played in causing the siege of the U.S. Capitol on January 6, 2021. Where would you go to get your information? To what resources would you turn in order to give context for misinformation, including what it is, how it functions, why people use it, and what are its effects? For instance, both those who supported and opposed the certification of the 2020 presidential election electoral college results framed their respective positions by telling stories of either election irregularities or steps taken to ensure the election's integrity. Might a comparison of such framed stories serve as good examples for your speech? As you conduct your research, and familiarize yourself with the research resources available, you become better able to answer such questions. Since the library is a repository for a wide variety of such research materials, consider it your ally. If you are familiar with your college's library, this section will simply be a quick review. If your library is still a mystery (perhaps because you do your research online), this is your opportunity to get to know it better. Even with the ease of researching online, the library has resources such as librarians, reference works, and the catalog that you may find useful to consult.

Library Resources

The library is a prime source for research materials. You can visit it in person (which we advise) and access it from afar. When you go to the library, you have ready access to research librarians (skilled at helping you search for credible information), the catalog, reference works, and databases.

The Catalog

Using the library's online catalog, you can find resources even if you do not know a specific author or title. All you need to do is enter two or three key words into the computer, and it will search the library's collection for you to find relevant material. A librarian can guide you in searching your school's catalog most effectively.

COACHING TIP

"We live for self-expression and the opportunity to share what we believe is important."

—Garr Reynolds, communication consultant

You have a speech in you. You think it's important and want receivers to think so too. For this to happen, you need to give the audience good information. Choose wisely! If your audience remembers only one piece of research, what do you want that to be?

Reference Collections and Other Resources

The catalog is only one stop along your investigatory road. Visit the reference section of the library, where you will find encyclopedias, yearbooks, dictionaries, biographical aids, atlases, and an array of indexes. (Keep in mind that these also are available online; in fact, when in the library, you likely will use a computer to conduct your search since printed reference works have corresponding online sites.)

- The *Statistical Abstract of the United States* is a U.S. Census Bureau– produced reference that includes an incredible array of facts about U.S. birth rates, death rates, family income, employment data, and hundreds of other topics.

- *The World Almanac and Book of Facts* lists award recipients, sports record holders, natural resources in various countries, and much more.

- *Facts on File* collects news articles on major topics like science, sports, medicine, crime, economics, and the arts in weekly issues bound in a yearbook annually.

- Monthly magazine *Current Biography* provides complete articles about newsworthy people from around the world.

- *Who's Who* references, including *Who's Who in America* and a number of volumes for specific fields, including business, science, math, and engineering, are valuable biographical resources.

- The *Biography Index* collects biographical information from magazines and newspapers.

- Subject-specific dictionaries—*Black's Law Dictionary,* for example—can help you define technical terms or jargon.

- The *Oxford English Dictionary* provides detailed history of a specific word.

- *Bartlett's Familiar Quotations* contains more than 20,000 quotations.

Ask an expert. Focus your interview questions on gaining new insights into your speech topic.

AP Photo/Phil Sears

- *Merriam-Webster's Geographical Dictionary* is a gazetteer that gives facts about nearly 50,000 locations around the world.

- *The Readers' Guide to Periodical Literature* is a general index of periodicals that is also available online. Articles that appeared in more than 450 major magazines are cited by author, title, and subject. Each listing gives you all the information you need to locate a particular issue.

- Major U.S. newspapers are indexed, with back issues available on microfilm and online. (Most local newspapers in the United States are not indexed, but are online. If you see an article in a local paper that would be appropriate for your speech, clip it out or save it digitally.)

Online Sources—Ask Questions

We have already seen that a variety of sources are available for you to research online using your smartphone, a tablet, or a computer. For example, most college libraries pay to subscribe to the *Encyclopedia of Associations* through GALENet, LexisNexis, or another online directory resource. All the major associations listed within it—the National Rifle Association, the American Civil Liberties Union, the Children's Defense Fund, and many more—have their own websites that are full of helpful information.

Other online resources include

- The *Catalog of U.S. Government Publications* searches current and historical federal publications (http://catalog.gpo.gov/).

Business Index ASAP provides bibliographic references, abstracts, and full articles from more than 800 business, management, and trade organizations.

- The *Consumer Information Catalog* lists free and low-cost publications available from various federal agencies on a wide range of topics (http:// www.pueblo.gsa.gov/).

- The site https://www.usa.gov/statistics pulls together data and statistics about the United States including census data and federal government data and statistics.

Infotrac covers general publications and government documents (see Figure 6.2).

- *The World Factbook,* published by the CIA (Central Intelligence Agency), contains maps and detailed information on every country, dependency, and geographic entity in the world (https://www.cia.gov/library/ publications/the-world-factbook/).

- Various search engines, such as Google, also function as online databases (see Figure 6.3). Since they are not as reliable as are the research databases maintained by EBSCO, Gale Research, the U.S. government, or academic institutions, you'll want to be sure to distinguish more trustworthy search results from those that are less reliable.

FIGURE 6.2 ■ Infotrac

U.S. and World Newspapers & Media

This innovative full-text newspaper resource allows users to search articles instantly by title, headline, date, author, newspaper section, or other fields. *InfoTrac Newsstand* provides access to more than 2,300 major U.S. regional, national, and local newspapers, as well as leading titles from around the world. It also includes thousands of images, radio and TV broadcasts and transcripts. Exclusive features, including Topic Finder, *InterLink*, and a mobile-optimized interface, support and enhance the search experience. SHOW MORE ›

Infotrac, https://www.gale.com/databases/infotrac

A variety of sophisticated databases containing journal articles written by scholars on virtually any subject are available for you to consult.

- ASI (https://library.truman.edu/microforms/american_statistics_index.asp)
- Academic Search Premier (www.ebscohost.com)
- LexisNexis (www.lexisnexis.com/)
- Infotrac (https://www.gale.com/databases/infotrac)
- JSTOR (www.jstor.org)
- GoogleScholar (scholar.google.com)

When consulting some academic databases, you may want to seek help from a research librarian. Because some of these resources require the payment of a fee, if your library does not subscribe, be certain of the specific information you need before using them.

In many ways, the Internet now functions as a well-equipped international library of information resources. Among the most used search engines are Google (www.google.com), Bing (www.bing.com), and Yahoo! (www.yahoo.com). Video search engines also are becoming commonplace. Search online for relevant videos on YouTube, Google, Blinkx, and Bing Videos.

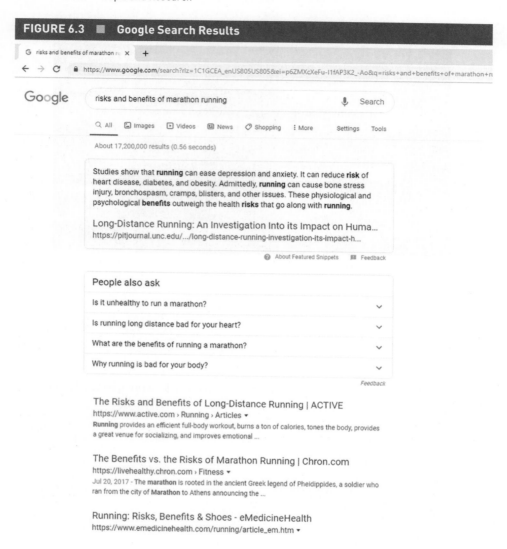

FIGURE 6.3 ■ **Google Search Results**

Websites—Consider Trustworthiness

As of 2022, there were approximately 2 billion websites in the world but only about 400 million of them active.[2] Given the huge numbers, how do you decide which sites are worthwhile? Very careful searching can lead you to websites that provide relevant information for a speech. Again, be sure to evaluate each site's objectivity together with the credentials of its author(s) and its sponsor(s). Websites maintained by universities, think tanks, or nonprofit and governmental organizations tend to be more valid sources of information than many commercial websites designed for promotional purposes. Some websites present one-sided perspectives rather than multisided consideration of issues, so you'll need to balance the information provided. It also helps to verify information found with other sources.

Blogs—Be Cautious

When blogs engage qualified academics or other professionals in conversation, they can contain credible information and be enlightening, but you need to exercise caution. There is a difference between postings by credible sources and those offered by random members of the public who may not be well informed about the subject. Therefore, unless you can determine the expertise of the blogger and responders, it is better to view them skeptically. Another reason to be wary is that blogs often represent the point of view of the blogger and may be biased. Among popular blogs are the Huffington Post, National Review, Politico, and Slate—each of which has a particular political slant. Therefore, pay careful attention to the evidence put forth and make an effort to assess the blogger's accuracy. On the other hand, blogs can be helpful in gauging public opinion and in determining the amount of controversy that exists on a subject. In addition, many blogs contain detailed posts by reputable authors and links to other sources.

Wikis—Be Wary

A **wiki** is a website whose content is composed and edited by members of the public. It is a user-created site. Though potentially useful in introducing a subject and identifying potential sources, wikis' use should be limited for these reasons: anyone can post and edit material, the expertise of the person posting is not necessarily considered, and the information provided is sometimes inaccurate or outdated.

Thus, other than as a starting point or source of basic information, do not rely on wikis such as Wikipedia for information. Never rely on them as your only source of information. In fact, citing Wikipedia as a source may damage your credibility. It is important to take the time to locate more reliable source material.

SELF-ASSESSMENT 6.1: QUESTIONING RESEARCH

Directions

Use the following questions and evaluation scales to measure the effectiveness of your research.

Criteria	1 Fully	2 Mostly	3 Somewhat	4 Not Really	5 Not at All
1. Did I develop an effective research plan?					
2. Did I identify primary research possibilities?					

Criteria	1 Fully	2 Mostly	3 Somewhat	4 Not Really	5 Not at All
3. Did I carefully consider which, if any, source(s) to interview?					
4. Did I take full advantage of library resources?					
5. Did I consult credible online sources?					
6. Did I avoid using biased information?					
7. Did I rely on information that was timely?					
8. Did I avoid the inclusion of misinformation?					
9. Did I carefully weigh the value of every source?					
10. In general, did I give myself the time needed to consult sufficient research?					

Scoring Method	Analysis
Identify the questions to which you responded "somewhat," "not really," or "not at all." These represent your weaker behaviors.	Explain specifically what you need to change about how you research to be able to respond "fully" or "mostly" to each question.

CRITICALLY ASSESS RESEARCH, KEEPING A RESEARCH RECORD

> **6.3**   *Critically evaluate all research, documenting and citing all sources.*

As we noted above, it's wise to ask questions and be wary and cautious about the research you use in your speech. In addition, when assessing the credibility of information, determine whether the sources you consulted not only are qualified but also are unbiased. Specifying the names, positions, and affiliations of your sources as well as their expertise enhances credibility. Referring to a source generally, such as "Researchers have found ... " tends to detract from credibility.[3] Verifying and thinking critically about the quality of the information, whether you find it in traditional print research sources or online, is a serious responsibility.

Assess Traditional Research Sources

Sources that have an economic self-interest in the subject are less credible than sources that have nothing to gain. Financial incentives can skew the presentation of information. For example, a little over a decade ago, a study in the American Heart Association journal, *Circulation,* precipitated a call for the lowering of cholesterol limits. The government panel issuing the new recommendations failed to disclose its members' links to pharmaceutical companies, many of which manufactured cholesterol-lowering drugs. This omission called the impartiality of the research and the validity of the conclusion into question.[4]

Evaluate Online Sources

Although the information contained in traditional research sources, including books, magazines, and journal articles, is typically reviewed and checked by several people before being published, virtually anyone can post information on a website or through social media. As you decide what to include in your speech from your Web search, carefully weigh the credibility, accuracy, reliability, and timeliness of each source, asking yourself the following questions about information you find on websites and on social media:

- Who is the site's sponsor? Was it found through a search engine or a library database? (Generally, library databases direct you to more reliable and higher-quality information.)
- To what sites, if any, is the site linked?
- What is the connection between the site and the links? Are the links from reputable sites?
- What clues does the Internet address of the site provide? Is it, for example, an advocacy organization (.org), a business (.com), the government (.gov), a network or Internet service provider (.net), an educational institution (.edu), or someone's personal site? The origination of the site offers clues to its mission or function.
- Who wrote the material that appears on the site?
- Is the author a qualified and reliable source?
- How recent is the webpage?
- How often is information on it updated?
- Why is the site on the Web?
- Is its primary purpose to provide information or to sell a product or idea?

By attempting to determine whether the source or site sponsor has any apparent or hidden bias, whether claims made are justifiable, and whether postings are specific or general and up-to-date, you demonstrate your commitment not to trust information simply because it is published on the Internet. Always seek confirming sources for what you discover.

Assess reliability. Even sources you find traditionally, such as in a library, should be checked for their objectiveness and credibility.

iStockPhoto.com/valentinrussanov

Websites such as FactCheck.org, a nonpartisan arm of the Annenberg Public Policy Center of the University of Pennsylvania, researches the factual accuracy of news releases, statements by political figures, comments made in interviews, and political ads in the effort to expose misleading claims.

GAME PLAN

Reviewing Your Research

- I have explored and included information from a variety of sources, including my own personal experience, library resources, as well as online resources such as websites.

- I have kept a clear record of research notes with roughly enough sources to fit the "rule of one to three."

- I have reviewed my sources with a critical eye to make sure they are independent and reliable.

- I have incorporated my sources into my speech to acknowledge the words and work of others.

- I have compiled a list of works cited as well as a list of works consulted to show that I did not misuse or plagiarize the work of others.

As you work your way through your research materials, you'll find yourself adjusting and editing the information that you actually plan to present to your audience. Keep your mind open: New and exciting roads for inquiry will surface only if you are willing to explore them. If your explorations are to be meaningful, you will need to record the information you hope to use.

Take Good Notes

Many researchers use a notebook, laptop, or tablet to keep track of information, allocating a new page or entry for every source they use; this makes it easier for you to organize and document your work when it is time to construct your speech. Others prefer using 4-by-6-inch index cards, which allow you literally to shuffle the cards into the order in which you will use the information in your presentation. Try this approach:

- Use a unique card for each article you reference.
- Record the title, author, and subject on the top of each card.
- Record one piece of information per card.

Write it down. Take careful notes as you conduct your research.
iStock.com/Ammentorp Photography

For examples of what note cards look like, see Figure 6.4. Notice how each card contains either a direct quotation from the material or paraphrased information. Using a computer to take notes allows you to move information around wherever you need it or want to use it in the speech itself. You will want to treat each page of your document as you would a note card.

Cite Source Materials Carefully

As you take notes, be sure to give each source correct attribution to avoid plagiarism. Giving sources the credit due them not only protects you but also increases your credibility. Let your research show. Do not ever cover it up or try to claim someone else's ideas as your own.

Audiences do not expect you to have developed all the ideas contained in your speech. During the presentation, you will need to provide **oral citations, verbal references** that reveal the sources of your information to the audience. Such citations are not difficult to include as long as you have done your research and recorded your information carefully. What do you say in an oral citation? Here are some samples.

FIGURE 6.4 ■ Sample Bibliography Cards

Joe Peta, <u>Trading Bases: A Story About Wall Street, Gambling and Baseball</u>. New York: Dutton, 2013.

Direct Quotation:

From Peta, <u>Trading Bases: A Story About Wall Street, Gambling and Baseball</u>, p. 203.

"Baseball researchers get ridiculed by traditionalists for the alphabet soup of newfangled statistics they create. WAR, VORP are harder to grasp than basic counting statistics like RBIs and wins but that's because they measure skills and evaluate talent more accurately."

Paraphrase Card:

From Peta, <u>Trading Bases: A Story About Wall Street, Gambling and Baseball</u>, p. 203.

Author Joe Peta points out that baseball researchers are ridiculed for the statistics they create. Runs batted in and wins are easier to count, but modern researchers who use Wins Above Replacement or WAR for short to determine how many wins would change if a particular player was changed, together with a calculation that demonstrates how much a hitter contributes offensively to the team also known as VORP or the player's Value Over a Replacement Player, are able to measure a player's skills more accurately.

istockphoto.com/petermccue

If you are citing a speech or article, you might say,

In his inaugural address, given at the U.S. Capital on January 20, 2021, President Joseph R. Biden told the world, "This is democracy's day."[5]

If you are using a direct quotation, state the name of the author and the source:

"*In his 2019 book,* Nervous States: Democracy and the Decline of Reason, *author William Davies states..."*

If you are paraphrasing a book or article, you might tell your audience,

"Howard Gardner, author of the best-seller Changing Minds, *feels that most of us change our minds gradually. The notion that mind change happens suddenly is wrong."*

Use a specificity progression in your oral citation of a source. The first time you cite a particular source, you want to be fairly specific. For example, in a speech on the impact of fake news, one speaker told his audience, "As Gordon Pennycook and David Rand note in their article for the January 20, 2019, *New York Times*, "These questions have become more urgent in recent years, not least because of revelations about the Russian campaign to influence the 2016 United States presidential election by disseminating propaganda through social media platforms." The speaker's second reference to the Pennycook and Rand article was briefer, with him saying, "In their article for the *New York Times*, Pennycook and Rand note that "social scientists are working hard to understand what prevents people from seeing through propaganda." The speaker's third reference to the Pennycook and Rand article contains even less source specificity, with the speaker saying, Pennycook and Rand demonstrate that to combat misinformation, we need to devote resources "to the spread of accurate information and to training or encouraging people to think more critically."[6]

As you build your speech, you bring experts onto your team in order to gain credibility and give your message the maximum impact. A Works Cited page lists the sources you mention during your speech. A list of all the sources you referenced when conducting your research is known as a Works Consulted page. Your instructor will probably ask you to turn in your Works Consulted when you submit the formal outline of your speech. When preparing either one, be sure to a use a consistent referencing style. The MLA (Modern Language Association) or APA (American Psychological Association) formats are the most popular.[7] (See Figures 6.5 through 6.7 for information on using these formats.) When using either format, arrange the list alphabetically—either by the last name of the author, by the title if no author is mentioned, or by the last name of the person interviewed. For examples, see the Works Consulted sections of the sample speech outlines included in the chapters on informative (Chapter 15) and persuasive speaking (Chapter 16 and 17).

FIGURE 6.5 ■ What to Include When Citing a Work
Name of author(s) or editor(s)
Title of the source
Title of specific article
Publisher or website sponsor
Date of publication
Date of retrieval of electronic source(s)
Web address (URL)
The issue or volume of the journal
The name of the database used
Page numbers

FIGURE 6.6 ■ Guide for APA-Style Citations

Book—One Author

Last name, First Initial. Middle Initial. (date). *Title of book*. Publisher.
King, S. (2021). *Billy Summers*. Scribner.

Book—Two Authors

Last name, Initial. Initial., & Last name, Initial. Initial. (date). *Title of book*. Publisher.
Perry, B. D., & Winfrey, O. (2021). *What happened to you*? Flatiron Books.

Journal Article

Last name, Initial. (date). Title of article. *Journal Name, volume*(issue), page numbers. URL
Nothias, T. (2020, April 22). Postcolonial reflexivity in the news industry. *Journal of Communication, 70*(2), 245–273. https://doi.org/10.1093/joc/jqaa004

Magazine

Last name, Initial. (date). Title of article. *Magazine Name, volume*(issue), page numbers.
Sabar, A. (2021, December). The antiquities cop. *The Atlantic, 328*(5), 32–39.

Newspaper

Last name, Initial. Initial. (date). Title of article. *Newspaper Name, volume*(issue), page numbers.
Fritze, J. (2021, December 2). Court signals support for Miss. abortion ban. USA *Today, 40*(56), 1A, 6A.

Internet

Organization. (date). Title. URL
St. Jude Research Hospital. (2021, July 15). *Send a free card to St Jude patients*. https://www.stjude.org/get-involved/other-ways/online-card-message-patients.html

Video

Name of person or group uploading the video. (date). *Title of video* [Video]. YouTube. URL
Smith, S. (2021, July 4). *Asteroids doomsday or payday* [Video]. https://www.pbs.org/wgbh/nova/video/asteroid-doomsday-or-payday/

Blog Post

Last name, Initial. (date). Title of post. *Name of blog*. URL
Baker, C. (2021, May 6). Too many places. *Nomadic matt*. https://www.nomadicmatt.com

TED Talk

Speaker Last Name, First Initial. (date). *Title* [Video]. TED Conferences. URL
Jaouad, S. (2019, April 15). *What almost dying taught me about living* [Video]. TED Conferences.
https://www.ted.com/talks/suleika_jaouad_what_almost_dying_taught_me_about_living?language=en

FIGURE 6.7 ■ Guide for MLA-Style Citations

Book—One Author

Last name, First name. *Title of Book*. Publisher, Date.
King, Stephen. *Billy Summers*. Scribner, 2021.

Book—Two Authors

Last name, First name and First name, Last name. *Title of Book*. Publisher, date.
Patterson, James and Bill Clinton. *The President's* Daughter. Little, Brown, 2021.

Journal Article

Last name, First name. "Title of Article." *Journal Name,* vol. #, issue #, date, page numbers.
Nothias, Toussiant. "Reflexivity in the News Industry." *Journal of Communication,* vol. 70,
no. 2, 2020, pp. 245-73.

Magazine

Last name, First name. "Title of Article." *Magazine Name,* vol. #, date, page numbers.
Sabar, Ariel. "The Antiquities Cop." *The Atlantic,* 328, Dec. 2021, 32–39.

Newspaper

Last name, First name. "Title of Article." *Newspaper Name,* vol. #, date, page numbers.
Fritze, John. (2021, December 2). "Court Signals Support for Miss. Abortion Ban. *USA Today*,
vol. 40, 2 Dec. 2021, 1A, 6A.

Internet

Organization Name. "Title." Website, date, URL.
St. Jude Research Hospital. "Send a Free Card to St. Jude Patients." St. Jude Children's
Research Hospital website, 15 July 2021,
www.stjude.org/get-involved/other-ways/online-card-message-patients.html.

E-mail

Last name, First name (of sender). "Title of Message." Received by First Name Last Name.
Day Month Year.
Jamison, Jon. "Classes starting soon." Received by Michael Gamble. 3 Feb. 2020.

Interview

Last name, First name (of interviewee). Personal interview by First Name Last Name. Day
Month Year.
Jackson, Joyce. Personal interview by Michael Gamble. 23 Mar. 2019.

Blog Post

Last name, First name. "Title of Post." Blog Name, date, URL.
Baker, Carson. "Too Many Places." *Nomadic Matt,* 6 May 2020, www.nomadicmatt.com.

TED Talk

Speaker Last name, First name. "TED Talk Title." *TED*, date, URL.
Jaouad, Suleika. "What Almost Dying Taught Me about Living." *TED*, 15 Apr. 2019, www.ted.com/
talks/suleika_jaouad_what_almost_dying_taught_me_about_living?language=en.

EXERCISES

Research

Becoming an adept researcher is a serious responsibility. Let's look at other research-based activities to get you in quality researcher shape.

1. Use a Checklist

Select a topic of interest to you. Go to the library and online and locate as much information as possible on your topic. Classify the material you find using categories such as *scholarly, professional,* or *popular.* Also decide whom you might interview on the subject and the extent to which you personally can contribute.

Use the following checklist to guide your search:

- The library's catalog

- Periodical indexes

- Newspaper indexes

- Research room
  - General encyclopedias
  - Specialized encyclopedias
  - Yearbooks
  - Biographical references
  - Dictionaries
  - Quotation books
  - Atlases and gazetteers

- Computerized sources and databases
  - Email and Listservs
  - Websites
  - Blogs

- Potential interviewees identified

- Any other research

2. Analyze Research Cited

In the following speech on *Bitcoin,* the speaker draws on research to educate receivers regarding this form of cryptocurrency. After reading the speech, and considering the accompanying comments, answer these questions:

- Who, if anyone, was the speaker able to interview?

- Were you the person researching a speech on this topic, who might you have interviewed?

- How many different sources and forms of support did the speaker use? Were they equally effective? Explain.

- What additional kinds of research materials, if any, might the speaker have benefited from using?

- Do you think that the speaker used the Internet to their advantage?

- Did any research errors impede the speaker's effectiveness? If so, identify and explain them.
- Based on this speech, to what degree do you believe the speaker realized their speaking goal?

Bitcoin

SN 1

The speaker uses the introduction to announce the topic, relying on the popularity of a sports figure to involve the audience.

In 2021, famed Quarterback Tom Brady and his wife Gisele Bundchin starred in a twenty-million-dollar campaign for cryptocurrency. In the ad, Brady says to Bundchin, "It's time to get involved in crypto." The aim of the campaign featuring the duo was to bring crypto to the masses. We're part of the masses. I've spoken to my friends, some of their parents, and even our peers. Though Gary Gensler, the Chair of the Security and Exchange Commission was quoted in the September 14, 2021 *New York Times* as saying, "It's a highly speculative asset class," people like us are getting involved in investing in and using a cryptocurrency like Bitcoin.

SN 2

The speaker clearly defines the subject of the speech and the key points the speech will cover.

According to *Statistica,* the most well-known cryptocurrency is Bitcoin. Let's explore what a Bitcoin is, how you buy it, and the upsides and downsides of investing in Bitcoin.

SN 3

The speaker introduces the first main point. The speaker integrates research to enhance content credibility. The speaker also employs analogies to give the audience points of reference and comparison.

In 2009, an unknown person using the alias Satoshi Nakamoto invented the crypto peer-to-peer monetary system called Bitcoin. Bitcoin was created to facilitate person-to-person monetary transactions on the internet. Bitcoin is virtual money or digital tokens used to invest, store value, or transfer value. According to Nathaniel Popper writing in the October 1, 2017 issue of *The New York Times*, Bitcoin, which has no physical backing, operates free of any central control. In other words, transactions occurring over bitcoin exchanges are made without the involvement of governments or financial institutions such as banks and credit card companies.

However, every bitcoin transaction is tracked methodically on an electronic public ledger called a blockchain. The blockchain, similar to a bank ledger, keeps a record of every bitcoin transaction and is shared with the entire bitcoin network. You and I can purchase an entire bitcoin or a small fraction of a bitcoin through a coin exchange like Coinbase which is the nation's largest cryptocurrency exchange. When a purchase is made, bitcoin transactions are mined by a vast network of individually owned, decentralized computers that constantly work to verify the system's accuracy by tracking all trades, sales and purchases. The system is open sourced, a Wikipedia of finance—in that the system is maintained by a group of volunteers. Bitcoin is not connected with any country or regulatory system. The documentary "Rise, Rise Bitcoin," focused on a group of young people creating the computer network large enough to do this. The number of bitcoin is capped at 21 million. That number cannot be manipulated.

SN 4

The speaker segues to the second main point. Can you come up with a better transition? Do you think there ought to have been more information and research cited in this section of the speech? How would you have developed this main point? Might some examples or interviews have helped?

Buying Bitcoin is easy. Before purchasing the crypto, the first thing you do is join bitcoin. When you sign up you are given a Public Key number which will unlock your personal vault or electronic wallet. Then using a mobile app or computer, buyers and sellers send Bitcoin to each other.

SN 5

The speaker elaborates on the third main point, integrating a variety of research.

Bitcoin has a number of advantages. Bitcoin is private. The names of buyers and sellers remain secret. What you buy and sell can't be traced back to you. But anyone who wants to send you Bitcoin can deposit it in your vault. You alone have sole access to your digital wallet which is located either in the cloud or a computer. Bitcoin is flexible. You can use it to make online purchases and trades. For example, Richard Branson accepts Bitcoin from people wishing to fly in space on his Virgin Galactic Rocketship. You can use it globally any day of the week. The Bitcoin exchange does not close at a particular time or on a specific day as do many banks and investment firms. Bitcoin is based on equality. People belonging to marginalized communities are now able to build wealth outside those institutions that once excluded them. Referring to two recent surveys, *USA Today* reporters Charise Jones and Jessica Menton noted on August 16, 2021 that more Black and Hispanic Americans own Bitcoin than do whites.

Bitcoin, however, has a number of disadvantages. It is irreversible. Once you spend it, it's gone. Like any investment, the price of Bitcoin rises and falls. For example, in 2017, Laslo Hanyecz, a Florida resident, offered 10,000 bitcoins to anyone who would deliver two pizzas to his home. Today, the 10,000 bitcoin he offered would be worth over a million dollars. In early 2010, a bitcoin was worth a fraction of a penny. During the first quarter of 2011, it was worth over one dollar. In late 2017, it was worth about $20,000. According to Coinbase, one bitcoin is now worth $43,710.

Unlike money deposited in a bank, bitcoin is not insured by the FDIC. Bitcoins worth tens of thousands of dollars have been hacked from accounts with no way of recovering them. Because buyers and sellers of bitcoin are unknown, it's become the currency of choice of drug dealers and those engaging in illicit transactions. On August 4, 2021, *Wall Street Journal* reporter Paul Kiernan wrote that investing in bitcoin is like being in the Wild West. Because of the real risks, we should not be investing our life savings, college tuition, or car down payment in bitcoin. Bitcoin investors currently have no protection. If you choose to invest, begin by budgeting an amount you can afford to lose. Dave Michaels, Caitlin Ostroff and Elaine Yu writing in the August 24, 2021 issue of *The Wall Street Journal*, agree, observing that governments around the globe are taking notice.

According to *CNN Money*, a number of countries including China, Australia and Japan are concerned about their inability to control bitcoin or collect taxes. They have begun weighing how to regulate the currency. Currently, the world economy relies on the dollar. If and when it changes to bitcoin, no one can predict what will happen.

SN 6

The speaker concludes the speech by referring back to the introduction. Do you think the conclusion was sufficient? Did you know it was coming?

Remember the Tom Brady ad I referred to at the start of my speech? Imagine I'm Tom Brady. If I said to you, "It's time to invest in crypto," how would you respond?

3. Do You Know What They Know?

As Ralph Waldo Emerson said, "Every fact depends for its value on how much we already know." Conduct research to figure out what your audience already knows about the health dangers of a sedentary lifestyle or another topic of your choosing.

4. Approach the Speaker's Stand

Your instructor has asked for examples of the primary and secondary research you plan to incorporate into your next speech. In preparation for this, develop a list of sources you intend to consult. Then, prepare note cards showing proper citation for the following: a direct quotation and a paraphrase of a quotation from one primary and two secondary research sources, one of which is a Web source.

RECAP AND REVIEW

6.1   Draw on primary research from your personal knowledge and experience, including interviewing persons possessing special knowledge related to your topic.

By using personal experience, a speaker enhances their credibility and adds believability to the presentation. By conducting interviews with authorities on a subject, the speaker comes into direct contact with recognized experts and invests the presentation with even greater validity and relevance.

6.2   **Locate and use secondary research sources.**

Library and computer-assisted research enable the speaker to discover and integrate the latest in credible, authoritative information into the speech. The Internet has a wealth of resources you can consult to find material for your speech, including databases of scholarly journals, professional websites, news and magazine indexes, and image and video repositories.

As with all research, evaluating the trustworthiness of sources is essential.

6.3   **Critically evaluate all research, documenting and citing all sources.**

Since trustworthiness is important, evaluating the credibility, authoritativeness, currency, and relevance of the sources and information you intend to use is integral to an effective presentation.

Using note cards featuring facts, quotes, and complete source information facilitates the organization and documentation of materials you integrate into your speech.

KEY TERMS

Oral citations (p. 141)
Primary research (p. 125)
Probing question (p. 128)

Secondary research (p. 129)
Verbal references (p. 141)
Wiki (p. 135)

7 INTEGRATING SUPPORT

	UPON COMPLETING THIS CHAPTER, YOU WILL BE ABLE TO
7.1	Deploy effective examples in your speech.
7.2	Use explanations and descriptions that clarify and evoke sensory responses.
7.3	Include definitions that enhance understanding.
7.4	Integrate analogies that provide helpful comparisons and contrasts.
7.5	Provide facts and statistics that strengthen claims.
7.6	Include testimony that increases credibility.
7.7	Properly cite support in a speech.

It was July 2021. Despite the resurgence of the COVID-19 pandemic, the Summer Olympics were held in Tokyo as scheduled, with viewers around the world watching. Providing context, sports reporters narrated an extensive array of video features highlighting the careers of different athletes. They had at their fingertips a wealth of supporting materials to integrate into the segments they aired. Among the kinds of support used were *definitions* explaining the nature of a sport; statistics documenting the athlete's wins, losses, and records set; *examples* revealing the athlete's personal stories and challenges; *descriptions* of the athlete's training regimens; *comparisons and contrasts* with other athletes; the use of *repetition and restatement* to solidify the athlete's stature; and *testimony* provided by eyewitnesses and experts familiar with the athlete's career. The feature presentations that ran during the Olympics shared much in common with the features that reporters such as Norah O'Donnell, Sean Hannity, or George Stephanopoulos used to tell the stories of the candidates who ran for president in 2020. Here, too, a team of researchers supported the interviewer in developing features on the candidates. Information about the candidate's past wins and losses, strengths and weaknesses, and personal dramas were available for the interviewer to consult, refer to, or air during an interview. Video profiles detailing the struggles and successes of the candidate were pre-recorded and cued up. The same holds true for all the features aired about those who died from COVID-19. Virus variants were defined. Statistics of deaths and hospitalizations were reported. Face-time videos were shared. Testimony of experts was used to try to convince the unvaccinated to get their shots. Comparisons and contrasts between the United States and other countries around the world were in abundance. Were it not for the varied nature of support used in covering the Olympics, presidential campaigns, and the COVID-19 pandemic, the reports might have come off as dry and viewers might have tuned out. The same holds true for your speech and its audience. There is significant overlap with the kinds of support reporters rely on and the kinds of support that speakers like yourself can integrate into your speech.

An effective speech is infused with support that amplifies, clarifies, and vivifies its ideas. In addition to building audience interest and understanding, the right supporting materials help arouse emotion and enhance audience memory. Use effective support that speaks to the audience and reflects the speaking context or situation, and you win speech supporters. To avoid having your speech fall flat, it is essential to search diligently for supporting materials to elaborate on, prove, or enliven the main points in your speech. Supporting materials bolster facts. In this chapter, we offer some tried and true ways to use different kinds of support to make research come alive and speak to the audience (see Table 7.1).

TABLE 7.1 ■ Support	
Type of Support	**Primary Use(s)**
Examples	To support specific points; to engage the audience
Explanations and descriptions	To clarify; to evoke a sensory response
Definitions	To explain words and concepts
Analogies	To promote understanding via comparisons and contrasts
Facts and statistics	To identify a verifiable truth; to strengthen claims and reinforce facts
Testimony	To increase believability and credibility

EXAMPLES

7.1   *Deploy effective examples in your speech.*

The right kind of examples can breathe life into a dull or uninteresting speech. Listeners are more likely to believe speakers who include and cite factual information, and they are more likely to engage in a story. As Nancy Duarte, the author of *Resonate,* notes, "Personal stories are the emotional glue that connects your audience to your message."[1]

Short Examples

Short examples are used to support a specific point. Although most short examples are typically no longer than a sentence or two, when used in a series, they gain power. In a speech on why we lie in job interviews, a speaker used a series of brief examples to explain the kinds of lies to which job interviewees admit: "One interviewee admitted to researching the interviewer's views and incorporating them into her answers to the questions the interviewer asked her. Another interviewee admitted to covering up some 'skeletons in his closet.' Yet another reported telling the interviewer that the salary they made at their last job was a lot higher than it actually was."[2]

COACHING TIP

"Personal example carries more weight than preaching."

—Chinese proverb

Don't go it alone when speaking in public. You have a support team to take to the podium with you. Use examples, definitions, analogies, statistics, and testimony appropriately and creatively, and you will increase the likelihood that your audience engages with and responds favorably to your ideas.

Narrative Examples

Extended examples are also called illustrations, narratives, stories, or anecdotes. More detailed and vivid than brief examples, extended examples are built very much like a story: they open, reveal a complication, contain a climax, and describe a resolution. Though narrative examples are longer and thus take up more time, when well planned and placed they are also more emotionally compelling and add a real sense of drama to the speech. Storytellers at heart, human beings love to tell and listen to stories. In many ways, each of our lives is the sum of our stories. The most effective speakers understand this. (See Chapter 21 for more information on storytelling.)

In a keynote speech given at the Democratic National Convention well before his run for the presidency, back when he was a candidate for the U.S. Senate, Barack Obama used a personal illustration to demonstrate that his life story was typical of the American dream:

> My father was a foreign student, born and raised in a small village in Kenya. He grew up herding goats, went to school in a tin-roof shack. His father—my grandfather—was a cook, a domestic servant to the British. But my grandfather had larger dreams for his son. Through hard work and perseverance my father got a scholarship to study in a magical place, America, that stood as a beacon of freedom and opportunity to so many who had come before. . . .
>
> My parents shared not only an improbable love; they shared an abiding faith in the possibilities of this nation. They would give me an African name, Barack, or "blessed," believing that in a tolerant America your name is no barrier to success.
>
> They imagined me going to the best schools in the land, even though they weren't rich because in a generous America you don't have to be rich to achieve your potential. . . .
>
> I stand here knowing that my story is part of the larger American story, that I owe a debt to all of those who came before me, and that, in no other country on Earth, is my story even possible.[3]

By touching audience members in a way that a generalization never could, an illustration helps the speaker pull listeners into the speech and focuses their attention on the issue at hand.

Hypothetical Examples

The examples cited in the preceding sections were factual. They did happen. Sometimes, however, you will find it useful to refer to examples that describe imaginary situations. When you integrate brief or extended examples that have not actually occurred but could happen into your speeches, you are using **hypothetical examples**. Speakers are ethically bound to let audiences know whenever they use one.

In order for hypothetical examples to fulfill their purpose, audiences must accept that the fictional scenarios you create could really happen. The function of hypothetical examples is not to trick your listeners into believing something that is not true. Rather, you use hypothetical examples when you are unable to find a factual example that suits your purpose, you want to exaggerate your point, or you want to encourage your audience members to imagine facing a particular scenario. Sometimes, rather than being totally contrived, the hypothetical situations you cite will be a synthesis of actual situations, people, or events. But be careful. If you use a hypothetical example that is too far-fetched, audience members won't judge it credible.

Ron Reagan, the son of former president of the United States Ronald Reagan, used the following hypothetical example in an effort to convince receivers to support the funding of stem cell research:

> Let's say that 10 or so years from now you are diagnosed with Parkinson's disease. There is currently no cure, and drug therapy, with its attendant side effects, can only temporarily relieve the symptoms.
>
> Now, imagine going to a doctor who, instead of prescribing drugs, takes a few skin cells from your arm. The nucleus of one of your cells is placed into a donor egg whose own nucleus has been removed. A hit of chemical or electrical stimulation will encourage your cell's nucleus to begin dividing, creating new cells which will then be placed into a tissue culture. Those cells will generate embryonic stem cells containing only your DNA, thereby eliminating the risk of tissue rejection. These stem cells are then driven to become the very neural cells that are defective in Parkinson's patients. And finally, those cells—with your DNA—are injected into your brain where they will replace the faulty cells whose failure to produce adequate dopamine led to the Parkinson's disease in the first place.
>
> In other words, you're cured.[4]

Hypothetical examples are especially useful when someone's privacy is at stake. Persons whose work involves confidentiality—physicians, lawyers, clergypersons, and therapists—often choose to use hypothetical rather than real examples when discussing cases. Still, when faced with the option of whether to use a real or hypothetical example, consider whether your receivers will be influenced more by something that did take place or by something that might take place.

Assess the Power of Your Examples

Whether you use real or hypothetical, brief or extended examples, what matters most is that they reinforce, clarify, and personalize your ideas, as well as relate directly to your listeners.

If you think of yourself as a storyteller and each example as a key part of your story, then you'll be better able to use your words, your voice, and your body to paint mental pictures that engage, touch, and bring your listeners into the center of your story's plot. To do this successfully, you need to search for and/or create examples that your listeners can get excited about and identify with. Use the following checklist to gauge the power of each example:

- Is the example universal?

- Does the example involve people?

- Does the example make an abstract idea more concrete?

- Does the example clarify your message?

- Is the example directly relevant to your message?

- Is the example vivid—that is, is it filled with detail?

- Can you relate the example to your audience without relying excessively on your notes?

- Can you use speaking rate and volume to increase the impact of the example?

- Will your listeners readily identify with the example?

- Will your listeners accept the example as credible?

As the checklist suggests, it is important that any examples you use are suitable for your audience, topic, and occasion.

EXPLANATIONS AND DESCRIPTIONS

> **7.2** *Use explanations and descriptions that clarify and evoke sensory responses.*

Explanations and descriptions are important tools in public speech. We use explanations to clarify what we have said, and we use descriptions to help our audience imagine they can see, hear, smell, touch, taste, or feel what we do. Both types of support help to engage our listeners in our topic.

Explanations

One speaker who anticipated a lack of subject familiarity on the part of her audience used an **explanation** to clarify the nature of Tourette syndrome:

> Put your hands in your lap. Now keep them there and don't scratch that itch on your head. Don't scratch it. It itches so badly, but keep your hands in your lap. That's what

it feels like to have Tourette syndrome and to try to control it. Tourette's is a medical condition characterized by involuntary movements or sounds known as tics. People like me who have Tourette's are unable to control our actions.[5]

Because the speaker believed that most people lacked knowledge on the subject, the explanation was designed not to be overtechnical but to facilitate their understanding.

Descriptions

While speakers use explanations to clarify the unfamiliar for their receivers, they use **descriptions** to produce fresh and striking word pictures designed to provoke sensory reactions. Senator Bernie Sanders, a Democrat from Vermont, crossed party lines when he selected a quote from former president Dwight D. Eisenhower, a Republican, to use in a speech delivered at Westminster College. The Eisenhower quote that Sanders used relied heavily on description:

> Every gun that is made, every warship launched, every rocket fired signifies, in the final sense, a theft from those who hunger and are not fed, those who are cold and are not clothed. This world in arms is not spending money alone. It is spending the sweat of its laborers, the genius of its scientists, the hopes of its children. The cost of one modern heavy bomber is this: a modern brick school in more than 30 cities. It is two electric power plants, each serving a town of 60,000 population. It is two fine fully equipped hospitals. It is some 50 miles of concrete highway.[6]

Notice how the speaker's description transports you to an alternative choice, helping you feel and see what's described.

Assess the Power of Your Explanations and Descriptions

Consider how your audience will respond to each explanation or description. Use the following checklist to gauge the power of each explanation and/or description you use:

- Am I using the explanation to deliver information the audience clearly does not know?
- Have I avoided over- or underexplaining?
- Is the description rich in specific detail?
- As a result of the description, will the subject of my description come more alive for listeners?
- Have I been appropriately selective in choosing what I explain and/or describe?

Move your audience. Vivid descriptions should elicit reactions from your audience.

Caiaimage/Martin Barraud/Getty Images

DEFINITIONS

> **7.3** *Include definitions that enhance understanding.*

Definitions help bridge cultural divides, enhance audience understanding, and facilitate audience acceptance of a speaker's ideas. Definitions are especially useful when your audience members are unfamiliar with the way you are using key terms or when they might have associations for words or concepts that differ from your own.

Which Words Should You Define?

When speaking, you need to define words that are technical in nature, that have specialized meanings, that are rarely used and with which the audience may be unfamiliar, that you are using in unique or unusual ways, or that have two or more meanings. If the context fails to make the meaning of the word immediately apparent to your listeners, then it is up to you to define it. In a speech on the destructive force of derechos, a student defined a derecho as "a widespread, long-lived windstorm that is associated with a band of rapidly moving showers or thunderstorms."[7] She then went on to flesh out this definition with more specifics, saying: "To be classified as a derecho, a storm must traverse at least 240 miles and attain a wind speed of at least 58 miles per hour, though the wind's power often is much stronger than that. In fact, one of the most destructive derechos to hit the U.S. traveled across the mid-west, covered over 700 miles, killed 22 people and caused serious damage."

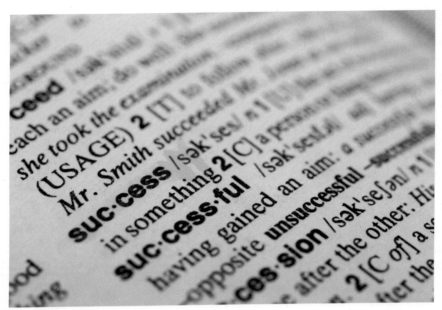

Define the unfamiliar. If a definition cannot be grasped from the speech's context, you should define it.

iStock.com/Aslan Alphan

How Do You Define a Word?

When you take your definition from a dictionary, you invest the meaning you cite with a degree of authority and credibility. At the same time, using an original definition could help audience members share your personal meaning for a word and could help make the speaker–audience connection more intense. Of course, using definitions supplied by experts also could help precipitate audience understanding and acceptance.

In a speech debunking the idea that the purpose of college was to train students for a job, one speaker used a definition from dictionary.com to explain why this is impossible:

> To train is to develop or form the habits, thoughts, or behavior by discipline and instruction, such as—to train an unruly boy; to make proficient by instruction and practice, as in some art, profession, or work: to train soldiers; to make fit by proper exercise, diet, practice, as for an athletic performance; to discipline and instruct (an animal), as in the performance of tasks or tricks; to treat or manipulate so as to bring into some desired form, position, direction: to train one's hair to stay down.

> We can't be in the business of "training" you for specific jobs because those jobs won't even exist in the future.[8]

In this way, the speaker made it clear that change is a constant and as a result the educating that colleges accomplish cannot be job-specific.

Assess the Power of Your Definitions

Definitions are intended to increase listener understanding or acceptance of your ideas. By helping you explain the nature of a term or situation to your audience members, a definition may help you inform and persuade them. You can use the following checklist to gauge the power of each definition you employ:

- Does my definition contribute to the overall goal and purpose of my speech?

- Is my definition easily understood?

- Am I consistent in the way I define or explain a term or problem?

- Will audience members readily accept my definition?

ANALOGIES

> **7.4**   *Integrate analogies that provide helpful comparisons and contrasts.*

Sometimes the most effective kind of support available to a speaker is an analogy. An analogy aims to explain one thing by comparing it to another. Like the definition, the analogy functions to increase understanding, but unlike the definition, it does so through comparison and contrast. There are two main types of analogies: *literal* and *figurative.*

Literal Analogies

A **literal analogy** compares two things from similar classes, for example, two viruses, two novels, or two crises. When delivering a speech on why we love horror movies, a student used a literal analogy, noting, "If you loved the film *Saw,* you'll also love *The Grudge.* Both films are cut from the same cloth." Another student used a literal analogy to compare the Dodge Intrepid to a NASCAR vehicle, noting that when accelerating in her Intrepid she felt like she was beginning a NASCAR race. She then went on to describe the engine characteristics of NASCAR race cars that share much in common with the engine in the Intrepid.

As long as the things being compared are close enough to one another, the speaker will benefit from using a literal analogy. Because literal analogies tend to come off as more logical than emotional, the audience is likely to accept them as true.

Figurative Analogies

A **figurative analogy** compares two things that at first appear to have little in common with each other—a war and a dragon, or mad cow disease and an alien. A student giving a speech on horror movies made use of a figurative analogy in his speech, noting, "A horror move is like a fairy tale on steroids."

Early in the COVID-19 pandemic, then–New York governor Andrew Cuomo used a figurative analogy when speaking to the public about the virulence of the COVID-19 virus: "It's these large gatherings where you can expose a number of people in a very short period of time and then it's like dominoes, right, then the tree continues to expand with branches."[9]

Speakers use figurative analogies to awaken the collective imagination of the audience—to prod them into accepting that two things that appear to have little, if anything, in common, actually share one or more vital similarities.

Your primary purpose in using an analogy is to explain the unfamiliar by relating it to something with which the audience is more familiar. The essential similarities inherent in your analogies should be readily apparent. If you strain to create them, audience members may conclude that your analogies are far-fetched, inappropriate, unbelievable, or unpersuasive.

Now, try this. Create a literal and figurative analogy for each of the following: a course in public speaking, your job, and your love life.

Assess the Power of Your Analogies

Analogies enhance audience understanding and acceptance of a message by making the unfamiliar familiar or prompting audience members to use their imagination to consider the point being made. You can use the following checklist to gauge the power of the analogies you use:

- Does the analogy have a clear purpose within the context of the speech?
- Is the analogy easily understood?
- Is the analogy easily visualized?
- Is the analogy original?
- Is the analogy apt and descriptive?

Drive audience understanding. Use analogies to compare and contrast.

iStockPhoto.com/SerhiyDivin

FACTS AND STATISTICS

> **7.5** *Provide facts and statistics that strengthen claims.*

Facts are verifiably true. That's what distinguishes them from opinions. Opinions may be based on facts, but they are not facts—they are beliefs or judgments. Facts, in contrast, are provable and reliable. "The circumference of a circle is 360 degrees" is a fact. "A circle is the most perfect shape" is an opinion or belief. Be careful not to confuse facts with opinions. While we may think the beliefs we hold are true, only facts can be confirmed empirically. Both facts and beliefs have their place in speeches, as we will see when we discuss testimony below.

There is something comforting in the fact that we can express what we know with numbers. We use statistics, quantifiable measures, to clarify and strengthen our ideas and claims and to express the seriousness of a situation and/or the magnitude of a problem.[10] We also use them to help the audience gain perspective.

Understand What Statistics Mean

Statistics are efficient ways to convey factual observations. We need to be able to distinguish among common statistical measures such as *range, mean, median, mode,* and *percentage.* The *range* measures the dispersion of values; it is computed by determining the difference between the highest and lowest number in a list of numbers. The *mean* is the arithmetic average; it is computed by adding together all the data points in a population and dividing by the total number of data points. The *median* is the center point or middle number in a sequence of numbers. The *mode* is the number that occurs most frequently in a list of values. Though all three may be referred to by the term *average,* the mean, median, and mode are different measures and potentially could be used to mislead those who fail to understand the difference between each measure. A *percentage* is a part of the whole expressed in hundredths.

Figure 7.1 clarifies each of these concepts by comparing the monthly commissions received by the members of a sales team. Understanding such statistical measures strengthens your ability to highlight their importance, difference, and significance for receivers.

FIGURE 7.1 ■ Making Sense of Numbers

GIVEN THE MONTHLY SALARIES LISTED BELOW, WE CAN DETERMINE THE FOLLOWING:

$12,000 This salary is **21.09%** of all salaries combined: 12,000 / 56,900 =.2108963.

$10,000

$8,400

$7,000

$5,000 This is the **median salary**: 50% of salaries fall above and below it.

$4,000

$4,000 This is **the mode**: the number that occurs most frequently in the number group.

$4,000

$2,500

The mean salary is the total of all salaries divided by the number of salaries:

$56,900 / 9 salaries = $6,322.22.

The range is 9,500, the difference between 12,000 and 2,500.

Put Statistics to Use Ethically

Speaking on the topic of gun violence in the United States, a speaker reported that gun violence in the United States was killing more children more frequently. Then, to drive home the seriousness of the situation, the speaker added that since the year 1963, no less than 186,239 children and teens had been killed on American soil, four times the number of U.S. soldiers killed in action in the Vietnam, Persian Gulf, Iraq, Afghanistan, and Iraq wars combined.[11] Notice how the statistics cited help to establish the problem's magnitude by adding context.

It's easy for unethical speakers to use numbers to fool the public. Factual information offered by biased sources may contain distortions or omissions.[12] In contrast, objectivity and reporting the facts accurately enhance credibility.

Examine the following two groups of numbers. Each list contains the monthly commission of sales teams at different corporations.

GROUP 1 Sales Commissions	GROUP 2 Sales Commissions
12,000	16,000
10,000	15,000
8,400	9,500
7,000	8,400

(Continued)

GROUP 1 Sales Commissions	GROUP 2 Sales Commissions
5,000	5,000
4,000	4,200
4,000	4,000
4,000	3,000
2,500	3,000

Relying on your understanding of statistical measures, determine the range, mean, median, and mode for each group and a percentage measure for the first number in each group. Check your answers by comparing them with these:

- The range is 9,500 for Group 1 and 13,000 for Group 2.

- The mean for Group 1 is 6,322. The mean for Group 2 is 7,567.

- The median is the same for both groups; it is 5,000.

- The mode is 4,000 for Group 1 and 3,000 for Group 2.

- The number in the top row is 21 percent of the Group 1 total and 23 percent of Group 2.

Imagine that these figures were the monthly commissions earned by sales executives with the Triple X Corporation (Group 1) and the Triple Y Corporation (Group 2). Now imagine yourself to be an aspiring sales representative who has just been offered a job by both companies. How might the recruiters at Triple X and Triple Y use these figures to convince you to take the job?

How would you feel if you were the applicant, and the recruiter for Triple X cited the median salary ($5,000) to show that the "average" earnings of sales representatives in both corporations were identical, while the recruiter for Triple Y cited the mean salary of her sales representatives ($7,567) and the mean salary at Triple X ($6,322) to demonstrate that Triple Y employees earned on the "average" $1,200 more a month?

Although both recruiters would technically be telling the truth, unless when considering the job offer you understood how each recruiter was selecting their statistics, you could be misled. Manipulating statistics to support an agenda is unethical. We trust those supplying statistical information not to mislead us but to present "the facts" in a straightforward, fair, and unbiased way.

Because the results obtained depend on the measure used, it is important that you fully explain your statistics to your audience. It is equally important that you not engage in numerical exaggeration.

Present Statistics Visually

A visual aid can save time and make it easier for the audience to understand the significance of the statistical evidence you cite. Suppose, for example, you chose to speak on the prevalence of certain kinds of cancer in women and men. In the course of your presentation, you might well include a number of these findings: in women, breast, lung, and colorectal are the three types of cancer most expected to be diagnosed, while in men it's prostate, lung, and colorectal cancer.[13] These are interesting findings, but they probably would be even more effective if displayed on a simple graphic, like Figure 7.2.

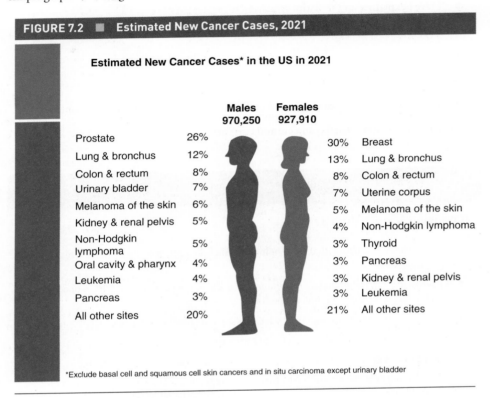

FIGURE 7.2 ■ Estimated New Cancer Cases, 2021

Estimated New Cancer Cases* in the US in 2021

	Males 970,250	**Females** 927,910	
Prostate	26%		
Lung & bronchus	12%	30%	Breast
Colon & rectum	8%	13%	Lung & bronchus
Urinary bladder	7%	8%	Colon & rectum
Melanoma of the skin	6%	7%	Uterine corpus
Kidney & renal pelvis	5%	5%	Melanoma of the skin
Non-Hodgkin lymphoma	5%	4%	Non-Hodgkin lymphoma
Oral cavity & pharynx	4%	3%	Thyroid
Leukemia	4%	3%	Pancreas
Pancreas	3%	3%	Kidney & renal pelvis
All other sites	20%	3%	Leukemia
		21%	All other sites

*Exclude basal cell and squamous cell skin cancers and in situ carcinoma except urinary bladder

Source: American Cancer Society, 2021.

It is your responsibility to ensure that the statistics you use represent what you claim to be measuring, that you obtain them from a reliable source, that you use them correctly, and that you interpret them accurately. If you follow these precepts, then your statistical support will help you make your speech both more understandable and more memorable.

Assess Your Use of Statistics

The impact of examples is strengthened when they are followed by statistics that demonstrate their representativeness. But before you integrate any statistics into your speech, you need to use your critical thinking skills to evaluate their usefulness. Use the following checklist to gauge the effectiveness of your statistics:

- Are the statistics representative of what I claim they measure?

- Am I being totally honest in my use of these statistics?

- Have I obtained my statistics from a reliable source that has no vested interest in the figures?

- Have I interpreted the statistics correctly?

- Have I used statistics sparingly?

- Have I explained my statistics creatively?

- Have I rounded off my statistics to facilitate understanding?

- Have I used a visual aid to increase the memorability of my statistics?

- Have I provided context for the statistics?

- Have I used statistics to clarify and enlighten rather than confound and confuse?

- Are the statistics I used complete and current?

GAME PLAN

Choosing Speech Support

- I have chosen support that will help me communicate my ideas more clearly and creatively.

- I have found examples that are useful and representative of my topic. I have used statistics that are relevant, reliable, and solid.

- I have incorporated testimonials from qualified and unbiased sources.

- My audience will find each piece of support relevant and appropriate.

- Each piece of support I have used increases the memorability of my speech.

- I am offering receivers a sufficient variety of supporting materials.

TESTIMONY

7.6   *Include testimony that increases credibility.*

When speakers use the beliefs and opinions of others to reinforce claims they are making, they are using **testimony**. Though, of course, your own beliefs and opinions do count, you will find that audiences, in general, are more influenced when you supplement your personal beliefs and opinions with the beliefs and opinions experts express.

Expert Testimony

Expert testimony is provided by sources recognized as authorities on your topic; when you cite an authority, and establish their reputation, you enhance your credibility and that of your speech as well. One student used expert testimony to try to convince receivers that campus fraternities should be abolished:

> John Hechinger, a journalist, is the author of *True Gentlemen: The Broken Pledge of America's Fraternities*. He devoted two years to researching and writing the book, speaking to students, and investigating both disciplinary and court records. According to Hechinger, "Universities tend not to be regulators until someone dies." Since 2000, 70 deaths have been attributed to hazing. Like Hechinger, I believe we need to see the dangers and damage of hazing especially when it involves hard liquor consumption. Pledges are drinking themselves to death.[14]

Because the student's topic was controversial and the audience may have hesitated to accept her stance, relying on an expert on the subject makes sense. Speakers integrate expert testimony into their speeches by using a source's direct quotations or by paraphrasing the source's words. Notice how in the preceding example the student used both when speaking of Hechinger's findings.

Supporting materials are evaluated twice: initially by the speaker and subsequently by receivers. Speakers and receivers who are well trained to think critically are able to spot the strengths and the weaknesses in the messages they deliver to others and that others deliver to them. Critical thinkers assess the credibility of the speaker's statements and the validity of the evidence supplied by the speaker.

Peer or Lay Testimony

In contrast to expert testimony, **peer** or **lay testimony** comes from people who are not necessarily recognized authorities but "ordinary people" who have firsthand experience with the subject. Peer or lay testimony provides audience members with greater personal insight; such a speaker shares the feelings, the reactions, and the knowledge of individuals who have "been there." During the COVID-19 pandemic, for example, peer or lay testimony was prominently featured in the Public Service Announcements (PSAs) that the U.S. government used to counter misinformation and convince the unvaccinated to get vaccinated.[15]

In a speech called "Homeless Children: A National Crisis," the speaker used the testimony of Sherry, a homeless girl who had a written a poem about her experiences. By asking the audience to listen to Sherry's own words, the speaker was able to convey the girl's innermost feelings to the audience.

I Want to Live in a House
I saw them at their house today.
They had new coats and mittens.
I don't have a house like that,
I don't have a coat or mittens.
Things will change; Mommy said they will
As she buttoned my cotton blouse.
I sure hope it's true, you know,
'Cause I really want to live in a house![16]

What determines whether you paraphrase an opinion or quote it directly? You should paraphrase testimony—that is, restate it in your own words—if doing so would increase audience members' understanding of or response to it. If the quotation is not too long or too difficult for audience members to comprehend and if you believe it has sufficient force and clarity the way it is, a direct quotation is generally preferred.

Assess the Power of Your Testimony

Testimony works because it lets you borrow someone else's credibility. In effect, testimony enables you to associate your ideas with the knowledge, experience, qualifications, and reputation of another. It will do you no good to associate yourself with someone who is not an authority on your topic, is not highly regarded by others, or does not have firsthand experience with your subject. Use the following checklist to gauge the effectiveness of the testimony you cite:

- Have I clearly identified the source of the testimony?
- Is the source I cite recognizable, objective, and credible?
- Is the testimony I am using absolutely relevant to my presentation?
- Have I quoted or paraphrased the source accurately and used his or her words in proper context?
- Have I used verbatim quotations whenever possible?
- Have I used lay or peer testimony to enhance the audience's ability to identify with my topic?
- Did I use the most up-to-date testimony available?
- Have I stressed the source's qualifications so audience members will not have to strain to find his or her statement credible?

SELF-ASSESSMENT 7.1: IDENTIFYING SUPPORT

Directions

Evaluate the extent to which you have identified sufficient and varied kinds of support for your speech.

Criteria	5 Totally	4 Usually	3 Sometimes	2 Rarely	1 Not at All
1. Have I identified a sufficient number of short examples?					

Criteria	5 Totally	4 Usually	3 Sometimes	2 Rarely	1 Not at All
2. Have I identified engaging narrative examples?					
3. Have I identified effective explanations?					
4. Am I making good use of descriptions?					
5. Do I provide definitions where needed?					
6. Have I identified helpful analogies?					
7. Am I using meaningful statistics?					
8. Have I identified credible testimony?					
9. Have I weighed the usefulness of every piece of support I intend to use?					
10. In general, did I give myself the time needed to select the best support possible?					

Scoring Method

Identify the questions to which you responded to some extent or not at all. Consider what you need to do to turn your answer to each of these questions into "absolutely."

CITING SOURCES IN YOUR SPEECH

> **7.7** *Properly cite support in a speech.*

It's one thing to find support, another to integrate it into your speech, and a third to cite it correctly during your speech's delivery and in its bibliography. Keep in mind that your audience members will have access only to the sources you identify orally, known as oral citation. It is unlikely the audience will see the bibliography you submit to your instructor. Thus, to enhance your credibility, you need to tell audience members where you got your information and what makes it credible. This requires orally referencing your sources—that is, sharing with receivers the name and author of a book, article, newspaper, or Web document; explaining what makes the author a qualified source; and revealing the date the material was published or posted. The goal is to integrate such oral citations into your speech seamlessly (see Table 7.2).

TABLE 7.2 ■ Commonly Used Oral Citations	
Source Cited	**Information to Share**
Book	The book's title, author, some information on the author's qualifications, and the publication date
Journal or magazine article	The name of the journal or magazine, the article title, the author's qualifications, the publication date
Newspaper	The name of the newspaper, the article title, the author of the article and his or her qualifications, the date the article appeared
Government document	Agency name or branch of government that produced the document, publication name, and date
Brochure/ pamphlet	Title, publisher, date of publication
Weblog	Blog site, name of blogger, qualifications, date of posting
Interview conducted by you	Cite yourself as the interviewer, identify the person interviewed and the date and place of the interview

The following excerpt from a speech fulfills requirements for oral citation. Notice how it differs from the bibliographic citation:

Oral Citation: The website of the United Network for Organ Sharing, unos. org, reports that as of July 27, 2021, there were 106,759 people in need of a life-saving organ transplant. Of those individuals, only 64,792 are active waiting list candidates. Even with a 38 percent increase in donations over the last five years, the need for organ donors remains immense.

Bibliographic Citation: "Transplant Trends." United Network for Organ Sharing (UNOS). https://unos.org/data/transplant-trends/ (accessed July 27, 2021).

The speaker gave the name of the organization and its Web address, adding the needed credibility to the statistics being offered. Notice how the speaker also established the information's timeliness.

In another speech on the benefits of doing an internship before graduating, a student included this oral reference to a source:

Oral Citation: In an article appearing last June in the *Wall Street Journal,* recruiters said that the Covid-19 pandemic made interning even more important for us in landing a job.

Bibliographic Citation: Dill, Kathryn. "Do You Need to Do an Internship Before You Graduate from College?" *Wall Street Journal,* June 6, 2021, https://www.wsj.com/articles/ do-you-need-to-do-an-internship-before-you-graduate-from-college-11622983500

Although the audience might have been better served if the speaker had given the date of the article and its author when citing it, it isn't always necessary for you to include the exact date in your presentation, but it should appear in your bibliography as a complete citation. Written citations contain more detail.

In another speech on the safety of our food supply, a student included this more specific oral reference to a news article:

Oral Citation: As journalist Sean Rossman reported in his article "Recalls Rise: Food Is Fatal to 3,000 a Year," which appeared in the January 18–20, 2019, issue of *USA Today,* between 2013 and 2018, meat and poultry recalls have increased by two-thirds.

Bibliographic Citation: Sean Rossman, "Recalls Rise: Food Is Fatal to 3,000 a Year," *USA Today,* January 18–20, 2019, p. 1A, 4A.

On-air reporters may not orally cite the source of their information if it is being provided to the audience in a graphic accompanying their report. On the other hand, podcasters and radio journalists do rely on oral citations.

Use the following checklist for citing oral sources:

- Did I share the name of the author or origin of the source?

- Did I include the title or description of the source?

- Did I set the source in context by providing a date?

- Did I establish any relevant credentials or affiliations of the source?

- Did I establish the source's credibility?

- Did I cite the source without interrupting the flow of my presentation?

- Could an audience member locate the source I cited if they wanted to?

EXERCISES

Support

You can apply what you have learned by participating in the following activities:

1. Finding Facts, Statistics, and Examples

Locate an interesting fact, statistic, and example to use in a speech on one of the following subjects. Explain the value of each and properly identify its source:

- UFOs
- Benefits and Risks of Using Robots
- Introverts

2. Reliable Sources

Identify a reliable source whose testimony you could cite in a speech on each of the topics listed in the preceding exercise.

3. Assess the Speech: Identifying Support

Read or view a speech given by the current president of the United States. The president's inaugural or State of the Union addresses should be readily available online. Identify the kinds of support the president used to support the goals of the speech.

4. Approach the Speaker's Stand

Using the right support and citing sources appropriately takes practice:

1. Select a topic that concerns or interests you.
2. Formulate a statement related to the topic that you are prepared to support. Your statement should begin, "I think that . . ." or "I believe that. . .".
3. Locate two types of support from two different research sources that you can use to make your point.
4. Develop a 60-second presentation.

Once you select your issue, ask yourself these questions:

- Have I selected an issue that I can support?
- What types of support should I use?
- Does each potential piece of support back up my claim?
- How can I use other forms of support to further enhance the impact of my remarks?

RECAP AND REVIEW

7.1 Deploy effective examples in your speech.

When examples are useful and representative, they help you develop ideas. Although short examples support specific points, lengthier narrative examples deeply influence receivers. Hypothetical examples encourage audience members to imagine what it would be like to face the situation described.

7.2 Use explanations and descriptions that clarify and evoke sensory responses.

Explanations help clarify content. Descriptions rely on sensory appeals to engage receivers.

7.3 Include definitions to enhance understanding.

Definitions are needed when audience members are unfamiliar with terms used or might have different associations for them.

7.4 Integrate analogies that provide helpful comparisons and contrasts.

Analogies rely on comparison to enhance understanding. When used appropriately, they help make the unfamiliar more familiar.

7.5 Provide facts and statistics that strengthen claims.

Facts are the verifiable information in your speech. Statistics are quantifiable measures. If fully explained and used ethically, statistics clarify and strengthen ideas and claims.

7.6 Include testimony that increases credibility.

Use both expert and lay opinion to borrow credibility and supplement your use of personal opinion.

7.7 Properly cite support in a speech.

Orally identify sources in your speech and provide complete information in your bibliography. Doing this correctly enhances both your and the speech's credibility.

KEY TERMS

Definitions (p. 156)
Descriptions (p. 155)
Expert testimony (p. 164)
Explanations (p. 154)
Facts (p. 160)
Figurative analogy (p. 158)
Hypothetical examples (p. 153)

Lay testimony (p. 165)
Literal analogy (p. 158)
Narrative (p. 152)
Peer testimony (p. 165)
Statistics (p. 160)
Testimony (p. 164)

8 ORGANIZING THE MAIN POINTS OF YOUR SPEECH

UPON COMPLETING THIS CHAPTER, YOU WILL BE ABLE TO
8.1   Explain why speech organization matters, including how it affects understanding and memory.
8.2   Describe linear organization, providing examples and illustrating the different patterns.
8.3   Identify culture's influence on organization preference, explaining the configural approach and the use of narration.

Have you ever sent or received flowers? When it comes to floral arrangements, are you a fan of formality or informality? Either approach gives organization to a flower display; however, their feel is different. It's the same thing with arranging furniture in a room. Some rooms are more or less formal, with each room display sending a different message. Now, what if the arrangement of flowers or furniture was chaotic, instead? What message would that send?

How do you visualize chaos? Can you, for example, imagine trying to follow a ballet troupe, a theatrical ensemble, or a sports team if the performers or players involved had no idea where they were supposed to be positioned or what they were supposed to do when performing for the public? The dancers would bump into one another. The actors would stumble about the stage. The athletes would be in disarray. What is more, there would be no pattern for those watching to follow, so they wouldn't know where to look to make sense of the performance or game they were attending. The ability to organize a game's plays is critical for most sporting events. The same principle holds true for public speakers and audiences.

When the right pattern is used to give order to the main ideas in a speech, it becomes easier for speakers and receivers to function as critical and effective communicators. Whether we're speaking of giving and following lectures, delivering or processing complex information, and/or making or weighing persuasive appeals, the arrangement of ideas into an effective pattern is an integral part of the message.[1]

COACHING TIP

"Organize, don't agonize."

—Nancy Pelosi, Speaker of the House of Representatives

Never let your ideas wander about aimlessly. Give them order. Strategize when selecting an organizational pattern. Choose the organizational strategy that will work best for your speech's purpose, content, and audience. Select wisely, and your main and supporting points will flow, virtually effortlessly, from the strategy.

UNDERSTAND SPEECH PATTERNS: ORGANIZATION

> **8.1** *Explain why speech organization matters, including how it affects understanding and memory.*

What's a pattern for? A pattern is a model or guide. Patterns repeat in predictable ways. They help provide the assemblage of order to a seemingly chaotic world. Our brains aid in providing order by patterning the information we receive. Speeches, too, have patterns—logical groupings of the most important ideas or what will be the speech's main points, eventually to be fleshed out with supporting subpoints. Organization empowers a speech. In fact, the arrangement of ideas and content are equal partners in speech development. If a speech is poorly organized, even if the information presented is first rate, audience comprehension suffers.[2] Unless audience members are able to follow and understand a speech, they might as well not listen to it. Research supports what we know intuitively—we learn more from a speech that is well organized.[3] For this reason alone, it is important to learn to craft a speech that doesn't ramble but instead is coherent and balanced—whether formally or informally.

Creating a speech has been compared to writing an essay. Yet in some ways, creating a speech and an essay are very different experiences (see Table 8.1). Whereas audience members usually listen only once to a speaker delivering a speech, readers are able to visit and then revisit written passages in their search for meaning. In order to facilitate comprehension of a spoken message, speakers normally use shorter sentences than do writers, and they also repeat the main ideas of their work more frequently. Writers may use clearly visible headings and subheadings. When presenting, however, we must find ways to let the organization of our speech reveal itself naturally to the members of our audience.

TABLE 8.1 ■ The Speech Versus the Essay

Speech	Essay
Is heard once	May be read many times
Contains short sentences	Contains complex sentences
Contains repetition	Contains less repetition
Organization revealed naturally	Organization revealed by heads and subheads

Just like an essay, a speech benefits from having a clear beginning, middle, and end. In writing a speech, think of the often-repeated adage: "Tell them what you are going to tell them. Tell them. Tell them what you told them." We begin by introducing the topic, offering a preview of what's to come. This done, we go on to discuss the topic, developing it fully. Then we wrap up with a concluding statement that summarizes the main points and ties the presentation together. This formula acknowledges the principle of *redundancy*—the use of repetition to reduce the uncertainty of receivers—and is especially important because not every audience member is adept at listening skillfully. By building a certain amount of repetition into a speech, a speaker improves receiver comprehension.

In addition, because many receivers don't take notes during a speech, the audience needs to be able to remember what the speaker says. For the audience to remember, the speaker needs to make the message memorable. Short-term memory can be fleeting; it is erased by what comes after. Long-term memory is more enduring; we carry it with us. Strategically organizing ideas facilitates both short- and long-term memory. Thus, hanging two to five main points of a speech on the right organizational pattern enables speakers to help their audiences recall their message in both the short term and hopefully long term, too. Only when the audience is able to follow the progression of the key ideas in the body of a speech can they be expected to remember what the speaker shares.

ARRANGING A SPEECH'S MAIN POINTS USING LINEAR ORGANIZATION

> **8.2**   *Describe linear organization, providing examples, and illustrating the different patterns.*

Traditional organizational formats use a linear logic that is representative of the way many North American speakers organize their thoughts. A speech has a **linear format** if its main points develop and relate directly to the thesis or central idea—that is, the topic sentence that comes early in the presentation. Since main points are key points, they are relatively equal in importance, and should be accorded similar emphasis in the speech. It is best when how you word the main points makes them easy to remember. Additionally, it is important to develop and support each main point independently. When exhibiting linear logic, a speaker develops ideas step by step, relying on facts and data to support each main point. Then, the speaker links each main point to other main ideas via a series of bridges or transitions.

Members of low-context cultures, such as the United States, often use a linear format. They characteristically relay information explicitly. Why? Because they expect receivers will have difficulty understanding what is not said overtly. Rather than rely primarily on emotional appeals and stories to make their points, they offer relevant supporting facts—that is, hard evidence and proof in defense of positions taken.

We will look at five traditional or linear approaches to ordering material: (1) chronological order; (2) spatial order; (3) cause-and-effect order; (4) problem–solution order; and (5) topical order (see Table 8.2).

TABLE 8.2 ■ Linear Formats

Format	Purpose	Especially Useful In
Chronological	To explain to audience members the order in which events happened; to describe a series of sequential developments	Informative speaking
Spatial	To describe the physical arrangement of objects in space	Informative speaking
Cause-and-Effect	To categorize a topic and relevant materials into those related to the causes and consequences of a problem	Informative and persuasive speaking
Problem– Solution	To identify a significant problem that needs a resolution and then a solution to alleviate the problem; to demonstrate a problem's nature and significance, then solution(s)	Persuasive speaking
Topical	To highlight the natural divisions of a topic; to identify the natural clusters or subtopics of a speech	Informative, persuasive, and special-occasion speaking

Time Order: It's Chronological

When you use time or chronological order to organize the body of your speech, you explain to your audience members the order in which events happened. For example, you may develop your topic by taking a historical approach.

Chronological organization can move from the past forward to the present.

Purpose: To inform the audience about the evolution of marijuana laws

Thesis: Laws about marijuana have changed dramatically since the early 1900s.

  I. Marijuana was a common ingredient in 19th-century medicines.

 II. The government began to regulate marijuana starting around 1910.

III. In 1996, California legalized medical marijuana.

 IV. In 2012, Colorado became the first state to legalize recreational marijuana use.

  V. By 2021, recreational marijuana use was legal in18 states and the District of Columbia.

Time warp. A time pattern can be either earliest to latest or vice versa in order to convey a point.
iStockPhoto.com/Viliam Simko

A time pattern can also be used in a subsection of a speech where the overarching organization is of another style. For example, a speaker delivering a speech on the problem of institutionalizing the mentally ill might first chronologically explain how mental institutions developed in this country. Such an organizational tactic would offer receivers a context against which to process those points the speaker will explore during the remainder of the presentation.

Especially useful in informative speaking, a chronological structure helps when you organize your main points from earliest to latest (forward in time) or vice versa (backward in time) in order to illustrate a particular progression of thought. The next example relies on a chronological approach to move forward in time:

Purpose: To inform the audience about the history of the Havana Syndrome

Thesis: The Havana Syndrome, dating back to 2014, is a set of unexplained medical phenomena, possibly initiated by a hostile foreign power using a mysterious weapon targeted at the brain or nervous system, that causes the people targeted to experience mysterious, debilitating symptoms.

I. The first known incident of the Havana Syndrome occurred in Havana, Cuba, when a U.S. businessperson, Chris Allen, became ill with mysterious symptoms in 2014.

II. In 2016 and 2017, CIA agents working out of the American embassy in Havana, Cuba, reported experiencing similarly mysterious medical issues.

III. From 2017 to 2021, cases of the syndrome were reported outside of Cuba, in Russia, China, Washington, D.C., Austria, and Vietnam.

In some speeches, it's more productive for the speaker to use a chronological organization that moves from the present backward to the past.

Purpose: To inform the audience about the development of the Internet

Thesis: The Internet has changed dramatically since its invention.

I. More than 4.66 billion people have access to the Internet today.

II. The World Wide Web was invented in 1989, making the Internet accessible to non-experts.

III. The first computer networks were developed in the late 1960s and early 1970s.

Chronological organization can be used to describe the sequence of any event, even childbirth.

Purpose: To inform the audience about the three stages of labor and childbirth

Thesis: There are three stages of labor.

I. The first stage of labor has two phases.
  A. Early labor is the first phase, which begins with very mild contractions.
  B. Active labor is the second phase, when contractions become more intense.

II. The second stage of labor is birth.

III. The third stage of labor is the delivery of the placenta.

Spatial Order: It's Directional

If you can observe your subject in space, it may be a candidate for spatial order. For example, we can discuss the planets in order of their proximity to the sun or describe the street plan of Washington, D.C. In spatial order, main points proceed from top to bottom, left to right, front to back, north to south, and so forth—or vice versa. Here is an example of how a speaker used a spatial pattern in talking about the White House:

Purpose: To inform the audience about the layout of the White House

Thesis: The White House includes 67,000 square feet of offices, reception and meeting rooms, and living space in three distinct areas.

In this example, main points move from east to west.

I.   The East Wing houses the offices of the First Lady and the social secretary.

II. The Residence is the site of public events like state dinners and receptions and is the home of the first family.

III. The West Wing contains the Oval Office and the offices of other key executive staff.

Like chronological order, spatial order is used most frequently in informative speeches.

Cause-and-Effect Order: It's Relational

Cause-and-effect order requires you to categorize your materials into those related to the causes of a problem and those related to its effects. You then decide which aspect to explore first.

Cause-and-effect order and effect-and-cause order are quite versatile. They are used in both informative and persuasive speeches. Here's an example from a speech about distracted driving:

The first main point focuses on causes.

The second main point discusses the effects.

I.   Drivers use their cell phones on 88 percent of their journeys.

II. Just a two-second distraction increases the risk of crashing by 20 percent.

Context. With a cause-and-effect argument, you can establish why something happens so you can talk about changing it.

iStock.com/imaginima

Problem–Solution Order: It's Workable

Speakers seeking to influence often select a **problem–solution order** whereby the speaker first reveals a significant problem that needs a resolution and then offers a solution to alleviate the problem. Notice in the following example how the emphasis is on how the problem can best be resolved:

Purpose: To convince my audience that having to provide one year of national service will help unite our divided country.

Thesis: Divisions are ripping our country apart.

The problem

I.   Our democracy is being ripped apart because we no longer know how to listen to each other.

The solution

II. Compulsory national service for young people is the solution to reuniting the country, saving our democracy.

When using a problem–solution format, a speaker may discuss the advantages of the solution as well. When this occurs, the speaker's organization includes a third main point: the advantages of adopting the solution. The next example also presents a pragmatic solution to a problem.

Purpose: To convince my audience that we need to revise the reporting of poverty statistics

Thesis: We should act now to solve the problem caused by the way poverty statistics are currently reported.

The problem

I.   The poverty level is currently understated in order to keep people off welfare rolls.
  A.   The income level defined as poverty for families of four is absurdly low.
  B.   Poverty thresholds for single-parent families are even more outrageous.

The solution

II. Minimally acceptable income levels must be raised.
  A.   Government levels of aid must be raised for families.
  B.   Additional help must be given for single parents.

The advantages of adopting the solution

III. These increases will solve some of the problems of the poor.
  A.   They will make life easier for families.
  B.   Additional aid to single parents will help them help themselves and their children.

Problem–solution order is most frequently employed in persuasive presentations.

Topical Order: It's Part of the Whole

When your speech does not fit into any of the patterns just described, you may arrange your material into a series of appropriate topics. This is topical order. For example, you use a topical order to speak about the pros and cons of a particular issue..

> **Purpose**: To inform audience members of the advantages and disadvantages of a vegetarian diet
>
> **Thesis:** Eliminating meat from your diet presents both advantages and disadvantages.
>
> I.   There are two advantages to a vegetarian diet.
>   A.   It does not support inhumane factory farming or require the death of any animal.
>   B.   A vegetarian diet is linked to better overall health.
>
> II.   There are two disadvantages to a vegetarian diet.
>   A.   Some people are unable to get the nutrients they need without eating meat.
>   B.   It can be difficult to eat out at restaurants or at friends' homes and maintain the diet.

Other examples of topical order also may include categorical arrangements that look at the social, political, and economic factors that contribute to a problem; the perceptions of upper-class, middle-class, and lower-class people on an issue; or any other divisional structure that breaks the material into units such as the following:

> **Purpose**: To inform the audience about online job applications
>
> **Thesis**: Making sure an online application stands out from others is tricky.
>
> I.   For your application to stand out, use the right keywords when preparing it for submission.
>
> II.   For your application to stand out, understand how online tracking systems work.
>
> III.   For your application to stand out, use industry connections.
>
> IV.   For your application to stand out, follow up.

When employing topical order, you may find that you can intermingle time, spatial, cause-and-effect, or problem–solution order within the topical order. In addition, although the subdivisions of a topical-ordered speech typically correspond to different aspects of the topic, subdivisions may also serve as a *mnemonic* (a device that is used to trigger memory). For example, in a speech on speechwriting, one speaker used the word *BRIEF* as follows to organize the body of the presentation:

Brainstorm ideas

Research ideas

Interpret ideas

Energize ideas

Finalize ideas

Because it lends itself to almost any subject, topical organization is a very popular organizational format.

SELF-ASSESSMENT 8.1: ORGANIZATION MATTERS

Directions

Indicate the extent to which you can do the following where 1 represents not at all, 2 represents, with difficulty, 3 represents sometimes, 4 represents usually, and 5 represents fully.

Statements	1	2	3	4	5
1. I can explain why organization matters.					
2. I can illustrate the differences between a speech and an essay.					
3. I know when there's too much or too little information.					
4. I can distinguish the introduction and conclusion of a speech from the body of the speech.					
5. I can use redundancy to increase comprehension.					
6. I can match each linear format with its purpose.					
7. I can get the main points of a speech across directly as well as indirectly.					
8. I understand the purposes patterns serve.					
9. I avoid confusing others.					
10. I capitalize on the relationship between organization and memory.					

Listening Analysis	**Implication**
Pay special attention to columns 1, 2, and 3. These are indicative of organizational factors that merit significantly more attention on your part.	What have you discovered about organizational matters? Although this evaluation is not a scientific instrument, it should give you some indication of your readiness to organize a speech.

NARRATION (STORIES): THE LESS DIRECT CONFIGURAL FORMAT

> **8.3** *Identify culture's influence on organization preference, explaining the configural approach and the use of narration.*

Although English is primarily perceived to be a "speaker-responsible" language, other languages, including Japanese, Chinese, and Arabic, are perceived to be more "listener responsible."[4] Native users of speaker-responsible languages typically believe it is up to the speaker to be explicit about what they want the listener to know. Speech strategies organized by linear logic present support and evidence in a very direct, speaker-responsible way. In contrast, native speakers of listener-responsible languages typically believe that speakers need indicate only indirectly what they are speaking about. They believe it is up to the listener, not the speaker, to construct the speech's meaning.[5] Nonlinear formats, also known as configural, are less explicit in offering hard evidence in defense of a position. Instead of previewing and discussing main points one a time, configural thinkers approach their subject from a variety of perspectives, using examples and stories to carry the crux of their message. Because configural speakers believe the explicit stating of a message is unnecessary, those who use

Think it out. What types of speeches would work best with configural formats, and what types should follow more traditional formats?

iStockPhoto.com/kupicoo

this style expect receivers to understand more of the subtleties in their presentation. Instead of directly stating the conclusion, the speakers lead receivers to their goal indirectly and by implication.

Speakers who prefer the configural pattern devise a series of "stepping stones" that circle their topic; they do not hit it head on. Three distinguishing features are characteristic of configural organization:

1. The speech gradually builds up to the speaker's thesis, which the speaker likely does not reveal or delays until the speech is nearly over.

2. Threads of thought refer back to the speaker's purpose. Although to Western ears the speaker may seem to be rambling or off topic at points, to receivers in other cultures the tangents the speaker explores are connected to the speaker's topic and make it more meaningful.

3. Speakers often rely on a **narrative pattern**, which has the speaker telling a story or series of stories without stating a thesis or developing it with main points. When using this pattern, the speaker may only "discover" the main point via a series of illustrations and parables.[6]

In a configural organization, the speaker implies rather than explicitly states the main points. Because the speaker does not explicitly state the speech's main points, the audience will need to participate actively in interpreting what the speaker only implies. The following speech outline is organized configurally:

Purpose: To persuade my audience that biological weapons research is a problem

    I. A hypothetical worker, Alan, who works in a lab funded by the Defense Department, inadvertently infects himself with the biological weapon he is studying.

    II. Alan suffers the kind of death that our enemies would suffer were biological weapons used during episodes of warfare.

    III. Alan's family suffers with him.

    IV. Today, members of Alan's family address Congress, asking, "How can America be involved in something like this?"

Looking at the preceding example, you can see that first the speaker sets the scene for receivers, introducing the subject and the situation. The speaker then reveals the consequences of what has occurred, describing the situation's effects. Finally, the narrator points to a solution. If you choose narration, tell a solid story, use descriptive language, intersperse dialogue when possible, build interest or suspense, and help your audience identify with the people involved. When serving as a narrator, either you can place yourself in the situation and tell the story in the first person, use the second person and help audience members imagine themselves in such a situation, or use the third person (as the speaker in the provided example did) and describe what happened. As a speaker embellishes each of the ideas identified in their outline during their presentation, it is up to the receivers to interpret the meaning of the speaker's narrative from the stories, examples, and testimony offered. The speaker will not state directly what receivers should think or do but will rely on them to draw their own conclusions and come up with their own solutions.

In this next excerpt from a speech on sports betting, the speaker uses the stories of two people who engage in sports betting to spur the audience to draw their own conclusions about the dangers involved:

> Two people I know actively bet on sports. The first, Len, lives in Las Vegas and has been a professional sports bettor for 34 years. Len is doing quite well. He rises at ten every morning and goes to bed at two a.m. the next day. Much of Len's time in between getting up in the morning and going to sleep at night is spent researching sports teams and players. Len never drinks. He combs sports data and relies on psychology to decide his wagers. Many of Len's bets are on the underdog. The second person, Alex, is a college student and thinks of sports betting as a hobby. Alex spends an hour every week deciding which teams to bet on. Having a few beers makes the decision easier for Alex. Almost all of Alex's bets are on the teams he favors personally—especially if the professionals favor them too. Alex has been spending a lot of time talking to his dad recently. He's $70,000 in debt to an offshore sports book.

For more on how to tell a story, see Chapter 21, Storytelling.

According to Richard Nisbett, there is a *geography of thought* when it comes to both the development of a worldview and the frameworks of thinking that support it.[7] In the West, speakers summarize and offer a conclusion. In the East, speakers tend to cycle back into the same topic from different directions.[8] The following example—offered by a professor—addresses the difference in approach:

> I was surprised when one of my students who had been a teacher in China before coming here told me that she didn't understand the requirements of essay structure. I told her to write a thesis statement and then prove its three points in the following paragraphs. She told me if she wrote this way in China she would be considered stupid. "In China," she said, "essays were written in a more circular fashion moving associated ideas closer and closer to the center."[9]

While we need to be cautious about overgeneralizing—especially because people from one culture who spend time in another culture tend to adjust their thinking styles—when speaking to an audience composed of people from diverse cultures, speakers may consider adjusting their organizational preference. Exhibit flexibility in deciding which organizational strategy to use. Pick that strategy that best serves your speech and audience.

> **GAME PLAN**
>
> **Organizing Your Speech**
>
> - I have reviewed all of my options for organization, and I understand their similarities and differences.
> - I have chosen an organizational format that best suits my topic and goal.
> - I have taken culture into account and used the organizational format that best conveys my message while adhering to speaker-responsible and/or listener-responsible strategies.
> - I have considered my audience and plan to present my topic in a way that is accessible to them.

EXERCISES

Organization

Use the following chapter exercises to think strategically about speech organization.

1. Organization Matters

Create a PowerPoint storyboard of a recent event or sports game at your college. Be sure to take photos of the performers or players warming up, key moments, the crowd reacting, and the performers walking off the stage or field at the end. Post the photos in random order. Ask a student who has not yet taken a course in public speaking to tell you a story about the event or game based on your PowerPoint presentation. Next, rearrange the photos in the correct sequence. Have the student describe how their understanding of how the event changed when the sequence of events was properly ordered.

2. Pick a Pattern

a. Take a speech topic such as "the search for alien life" or "student debt." How could you develop a speech on the subject using chronological, spatial, cause-and-effect, problem–solution, topical order, or any linear format of your choice?

b. Using the same topic, how could you develop a speech on the subject using an alternative configural pattern?

3. Analyze the Speech: Contemplate Cultural Perspectives

According to cultural anthropologist Edward T. Hall, culture guides attention, helping us decide those stimuli to which we will pay attention and those we will ignore.

With this in mind, what steps should a speaker take to ensure that audience members who prefer an organizational pattern other than the one the speaker has chosen pay attention to the right things in the presentation? For example, let's say a speaker from a low-context culture such as the United States were asked to give a speech on how globalization affects the U.S. middle class to an audience composed of economists from Saudi Arabia or Mexico. How might the speaker adapt the speech's organizational format to appeal to members of a high-context culture? In your opinion, does changing the organizational structure also change the speech's content, so that a speaker who makes such adaptations is no longer being true to their beliefs? Explain your position.

4. Approach the Speaker's Stand

a. Select a topic such as organ donation, the danger of asteroids, Native American rights, women in combat, human trafficking, or the opioid crisis. Research your choice, identifying main points for the topic that would be appropriate if you were to use a chronological, spatial, cause-and-effect, problem–solution, topical, or alternative organizational pattern. Consider how each of these organizational formats affects the speech. Then, identify the organizational pattern you believe works best and why.

b. Visit AmericanRhetoric.com or Gifts of Speech: Women's Speeches from Around the World (http://gos.sbc.edu). Working in groups, select three speeches from either or both sites that relied on different organizational patterns, explaining the strengths and weaknesses of each of the patterns used.

RECAP AND REVIEW

8.1 Explain why speech organization matters, including how it affects understanding and memory.

When ideas are unorganized, they are disorienting to receivers, making it difficult for them to make sense of your speech. A speech is listened to—usually once. By summarizing main points we reduce the uncertainty of receivers and increase their comprehension.

8.2 Describe linear organization, providing examples and illustrating the different patterns.

Linear formats are more commonly used in the West to convey information in a direct and straightforward manner. Key linear formats include (a) chronological, (b) spatial, (c) cause-and-effect, (d) problem–solution, and (e) topical.

8.3 Identify culture's influence on organization preference, explaining the configural approach and the use of narration.

Configural formats are nonlinear and built using subtleties, intuitive thinking, and informal logic that cycles back to the same topic from different directions. Key configural formats include the deferred-thesis pattern, (b) the web pattern, and

(c) the narrative pattern. Culture attunes us to different ways of thinking and processing information. We adhere to the "geography of thought" in both the development of a worldview and the frameworks of thinking that support it.

KEY TERMS

Cause-and-effect order (p. 180)

Chronological order (p. 177)

Configural formats (p. 184)

Deferred-thesis pattern (p. 188)

Linear formats (p. 176)

Narrative pattern (p. 185)

Problem–solution order (p. 181)

Spatial order (p. 179)

Topical order (p. 182)

Web pattern (p. 188)

istockphoto.com/fizkes

9 OUTLINING YOUR SPEECH

UPON COMPLETING THIS CHAPTER, YOU WILL BE ABLE TO

9.1   Identify the parts of a speech outline, developing preliminary and full-sentence outlines that adhere to appropriate form and structure.

9.2   Link the parts of the outline together.

9.3   Prepare an extemporaneous or presentation outline, also known as speaker's notes, from a formal outline.

Once you have thought through how to organize a speech, it's time to complete the outline. "I know the organizational pattern I'm going to use," you say. "Why do I need to create an outline?" Were it not for an outline, a speech could end up a chaotic composite of ideas. An outline gives order to ideas. It details the speech's organizational plan. Thus, after selecting the organizational pattern you believe will best support the subject matter and main points of your speech, you need to continue building the outline. Demonstrating the relationship among ideas, the outline reveals your speech's structure. It organizes and clarifies your ideas. It guides you in distinguishing important material from that which is irrelevant by forcing you to test and assess how ideas fit together. By making relationships clearer, you help the audience to process and think critically about your speech's content.

An outline also functions as a presentation road map. It lets you visualize how the parts of your speech fit together. An outline ensures that each part of your speech has unity and coherence and that your main and subpoints are well developed and supported. Use your outline to determine if your speech holds together before delivering it to an audience.[1] By using an outline you can

- Confirm clarity of both the purpose statement and thesis

- Critique construction of both main and subpoints, ensuring the main points relate to the thesis and subpoints relate to the appropriate main point

- Identify placement of transitions or idea connectors

In other words, the outline helps to control both the development of your material and the flow of your speech.

COACHING TIP

"The more work you put in your outline and getting the skeleton of your story right, the easier the process is later."

—Drew Goddard, screenwriter

Outlining works. As we have shown, begin the outline as soon as you start preparing your speech. Use it to double-check the underlying logic of your ideas. Fix any flaws you discover.

The outline is your visual depiction of your speech. It will show you if the parts fit together well. If something doesn't belong, take it out. If something is missing, add it. Put the effort in up front and your audience will thank you by following your road map and maintaining their focus and direction.

CREATE AN OUTLINE THAT WORKS FOR YOU

9.1   *Identify the parts of a speech outline, developing preliminary and full-sentence outlines that adhere to appropriate form and structure.*

In many ways, an outline resembles a building constructed using a modular design. Instead of working with building blocks, however, a speechwriter works with idea blocks and structures the outline in stages.

- During the first stage, create a preliminary *working outline* composed of a few words to identify what likely will become the key points of your speech. Also create a mind or concept map to visualize the relationship between ideas (see Figure 9.1, from a speech about bees).

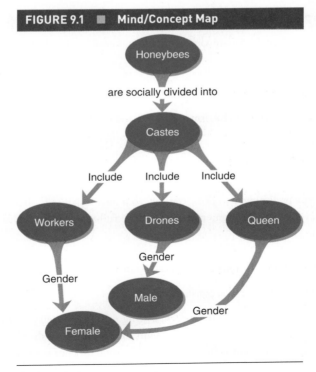

FIGURE 9.1 ■ Mind/Concept Map

iStock.com/petermccue

- Once you research and fully flesh out the ideas contained in the working outline, rework it, developing it into a more detailed *full-sentence outline.*

- Finally, as you become more familiar with your full-sentence outline, transform it into an *extemporaneous or presentation outline*, also known as *speaker's notes*. This becomes the outline you will use to guide your delivery of the speech (see Table 9.1).

TABLE 9.1 ■ Three Stages of Outline Development		
Stage	**Outline Type**	**Description**
One	Preliminary working outline	Words or phrases identifying a speech's points
Two	Full-sentence outline	Elaborates main and subpoints
Three	Extemporaneous/ presentation outline	Speaker's notes, used when delivering a speech

On the HBO program *Last Week Tonight*, John Oliver made a compelling case for paying reparations to Black Americans because of the history of housing discrimination in the United States.[2] Let's imagine that you were one of the program's writers, and involved in devising a preliminary working outline for Oliver's speech. It might have looked something like this:

Specific Purpose: To explain why reparations should be paid to African Americans

Thesis: African Americans are due reparations because of a long history of housing discrimination.

    I. Definition of Reparations.

    II. Connection Between Racism and U.S. Land Ownership.

    III. The Fair Housing Act.

    IV. Reparations and the Wealth Gap.

Once you have a preliminary working outline, your next task is to flesh it out by integrating more content, developing a full-sentence outline. The full-sentence outline should fulfill the following criteria:

1. It identifies the specific purpose and thesis statement or central idea.

2. It exhibits coordination and consistency.

3. It presents a visualization of the speech, distinguishing between your main points, your speech's subtopics that directly support your thesis, and your subordinate points—those ideas that function as support or amplification for your main ideas or subtopics.

4. It reveals a division of the whole.

5. It exhibits parallelism.

6. It labels as well as indicates transitions between your introduction, the main points of the body, and the conclusion.

7. It identifies the works you consulted.

Though we later discuss and provide examples of these criteria in action, a few deserve special attention now.

Identify Your Main Points

As we noted in Chapter 8, the basic structure of an outline begins with its **main points**. Like a skeleton that gives our body shape and purpose, these ideas serve as the framework of the outline that makes a successful speech. You want your receivers to retain the main ideas of your speech; otherwise, there would be little reason to have an audience listen to you. For example, if you were speaking on the safety of drinking water, you might structure your outline as one student did with two main ideas:

Purpose: To inform audience members about the fears concerning the safety of drinking water in the United States

I. Fears about the safety of drinking water are prevalent in the United States today.

II. Questions about efforts to protect against unsafe water remain unanswered.

Map it out. Not every speech has to follow one format, but no matter how you deliver it, you should always plan and outline it first.

istockphoto.com/Imagesines

The ordering of points should flow logically so receivers can follow the presentation easily. In the above example, the speaker chose first to confront existing fears about the safety of our drinking water and then to discuss the questions revolving around how best to protect us from unsafe water. It would have made less sense for the speaker to start with how researchers plan to protect our water and end with existing fears. However, sometimes the main points of a presentation can be attacked in any order. For example, suppose you were presenting a speech on popular hobbies. Your speech might focus on

I   Hobbies conducted with a group.

II   Hobbies conducted alone.

No particular reason exists to put main point I before point II or vice versa. The order depends only on how you choose to approach the subject.

Support Main Points With Subordinate Points

Subordinate points, or subpoints, are the foundation on which larger ideas are constructed. Continue the organizational process by arranging your materials into clusters of main and subordinate ideas. As you proceed, identify which evidence supports which idea, keeping in mind all the kinds of support identified in Chapter 7.

When you take the time to prepare an easy-to-follow structure for your speech, your main points alert receivers to listen for supporting information. Because receivers are not struggling to give order to a disordered array of information, they are able to focus instead on the thesis of your speech and the support you offer to build your presentation. Since your ideas are carefully laid out, you can focus on establishing a good relationship with audience members instead of concentrating on what to say next.

A developed outline indicates the relative importance of each item included in it. The main points (indicated with Roman numerals I, II, III, and so on) are the most important items you want your audience to remember. Your subpoints (capital letters A, B, C, and so on) are supportive of but less important than the main points. Likewise, sub-subpoints (Arabic numerals 1, 2, 3, and so on) are supportive of but less important than subpoints. Remember to line up the entries in your outline correctly. Locate the main ideas closest to the left margin. The subpoints should begin directly underneath the first letter of each main point. Generally, at least two subpoints must support every main point.

Items that support the subpoints begin directly underneath the first letter of each subpoint. If needed, indicate the supporting materials for the sub-subpoints with lowercase letters (a, b, c, and so on). In this way, the full-sentence outline functions as a visual representation of the supportive underpinnings for ideas. In general, there should be at least a 3-to-1 ratio between the total words in your speech and the number of words in your outline.

Format for Main and Subpoints in Your Outline

SN 1

Make your main points the most prominent part of the outline by using Roman numerals and aligning them with the left margin of your page.

I. Here is where you put your first main point.

SN 2

Use capital letters for subpoints, and indent them evenly below the first word of each main idea they support.

    A. Your first subpoint includes evidence that supports the main point.

SN 3

Use Arabic numerals for sub-subpoints and indent them evenly below the subpoints they support.

        1. The first sub-subpoint gives additional information about subpoint A.
        2. The second sub-subpoint gives additional information about subpoint A.

SN 4

Include at least two sub points for each main point.

    B. Your second subpoint includes evidence that supports the main point
        1. The first sub-subpoint gives additional information about subpoint B.
        2. The scond sub-supoint gives additional information about subpoint B.

SN 5

All main points should be of equal importance.

II. Here is where you put your second main point.

SN 6

Repeat the process shown above for the second and any additional main points.

Using symbols and indentations, the body of a full-sentence outline for a speech covering the lasting effects of COVID-19 might look like the following.

Full-Sentence Outline

Specific purpose: To inform audience members about fears and questions concerning how the COVID-19 virus will affect our future.

Thesis: Acknowledging the fears and questions concerning the COVID-19 virus can help us confront the challenges that this disease and other viruses present.

Rock solid. Even with strong main points, a speech will fall apart without meaningful sub-points and sub-subpoints to support it.

istockphoto.com/AlSimonov

I.   Several fears concerning the COVID-19 virus persist in society today.
  A.   People like us fear that the COVID-19 pandemic will remain a global problem.
    1.   There is concern that COVID-19 cases will continue to occur as the virus mutates.
    2.   There is concern that the COVID-19 virus will remain uncontrollable unless nations are prepared to issue vaccine mandates.
    3.   There is concern that travel, especially by air, will continue to accelerate transmission of the disease around the world.
  B.   Scientists fear that the COVID-19 virus may never be eradicated.
    1.   The elderly and people with suppressed immune systems will remain at risk.
    2.   Persons who engage in risky behavior will remain at risk.
    3.   Children returning to school will remain at risk.
    4.   Every person exposed poses a potential risk to others.

II.   Questions are being asked regarding future efforts to protect society against this and other virus strains capable of causing a pandemic.
  A.   There is the question of any vaccine's long-term effectiveness.
    1.   Whether the vaccine developed for COVID-19 will prove to be effective against other similar viruses is unknown.
    2.   Because scientists do not know what the next pandemic virus will look like, it is difficult to make an effective vaccine in advance.
  B.   There is the question regarding the state of international cooperation.
    1.   We need to increase awareness of continued pandemic threats.
    2.   We need to improve new virus surveillance and diagnosis.

      C. There is the question regarding the effectiveness of biosecurity.

          1. The biosafety of laboratory research must be maintained.

          2. The N95 mask provides some protection from the droplets that spread the virus.

          3. Discouraging personal stockpiling, the government must focus on pandemic planning and maintaining national and regional supplies.

Use Coordinate Points

The best outlines consist of **coordinate points**. This simply means that all the main points you discuss are of equal weight or substance. For example, if you were to speak about Mexican customs, you might organize them topically according to social, business, and religious customs as follows:

    I. Understanding the social customs of Mexico can improve Mexican–American relations.

    II. Understanding the business customs of Mexico can improve Mexican–American relations.

   III. Understanding the religious customs of Mexico can improve Mexican–American relations.

The outline reveals that the speaker plans to spend about the same amount of time discussing the three divisions of Mexican customs. What if the speaker were unable to find much material on religious customs? One solution would be to limit the speech to business and social customs. If there were some religious customs that were essentially social in nature, those elements might be subordinated under the social category.

Exhibit Parallelism

A good outline must be devised in such a way that the concepts in it exhibit **parallelism**—that is, words, phrases, or sentences are parallel or balance with one another. Similar in construction, they mirror each other. This approach also helps the audience to process and retain your speech's points. For example, in the preceding outline, each main point mirrored the main point preceding it.

Also note that in the preceding outline about COVID-19, every entry is subdivided into two or more points. The entries all rely on the same grammatical pattern and are complete full, simple sentences. This technique also lets you think through your ideas without writing a complete manuscript.

Label All Parts

Effective outlines clearly label all parts, which eventually will include the body, on which we have focused in this chapter, together with the introduction, the conclusion, transitional tools (see the next section), and the works cited list. By handling each of the parts of your speech separately and labeling them clearly, you take the steps necessary to ensure that you

1. Develop an adequate body of material to share.

2. Prepare an effective introduction and conclusion.

3. Anticipate how you will get from section to section and point to point.

4. Highlight the sources (books, magazines, newspapers, government documents, television programs, interviews, and Internet sites) you consulted during the speech preparation process.

You thereby improve the chances that you will realize your essential speechmaking objectives.

FACILITATE SPEECH FLOW

> **9.2**   *Link the parts of the outline together.*

Audience members who rely on linear logic will expect you to transmit your ideas with clarity and fluidity. They will count on you using transitional tools—transitions, internal previews, and internal summaries—as you move from one idea to the next to create a sense of coherence and unity.

Use Transitions

Moving from one main point to the next is very much like getting from one side of a river to the other. In the world, a bridge serves that purpose very nicely. In public speaking, **transitions** work as bridges from idea to idea. A transition also serves as the glue that binds your ideas into a completed presentation rather than an array of unrelated concepts.

As you work with transitions, remember that they fall into one of the four Cs:

● **Chronological transitions** help the listener understand the time relationship between the first main point and the one that follows. Words and phrases such as *before, after, later, at the same time, while,* and *finally* show what is happening in time order.

● **Contrasting transitions** include terms such as *but, on the one hand/on the other hand, in contrast,* and *in spite of.* These words show how the idea that follows differs from the ones that precede it.

● **Causal transitions** are words like *because, therefore,* and *consequently;* they help show the cause-and-effect relationships between the ideas.

● **Complementary transitions** help the speaker add one idea to the next. *Also, next, in addition to,* and *likewise* are examples.

See Table 9.2 for some examples of transitions in action.

TABLE 9.2 ■ Transitions	
Type	**Examples**
Chronological	After we completed the first phase of the project . . . At the same time that we were exploring cultural values . . .
Contrasting	Although the money was available to build the senior center . . . On the contrary, we should also consider . . .
Causal	As a result of the ways the members of different cultures define what is "real," "good," and "correct," their interpretations of . . . Because the maintenance needed on the bridge was ignored . . .
Complementary	Likewise, our experiment was designed to demonstrate that . . . It is just as important to examine the ways in which animals . . .

You also may use more than words to bridge ideas. Visuals, for example, can help you transition, as can physical movement. Walking from one side of the podium to the other as you move to the next main point can serve to show your audience that you are literally changing direction from one idea to the next in your presentation.

Use Internal Previews

An **internal preview** also helps hold your speech together but is generally longer than a simple transition. It prepares audience members for the information that will follow. Let's examine how previews can work for you.

In a presentation on genetic engineering, a speaker told the audience the following:

> We will next consider a technique that allows biologists to transfer a gene from one species to another. It is called recombinant DNA technology.

Pass the baton. The audience should know when you're transitioning to a new point, no matter how you accomplish it.

istockphoto.com/IPGGutenbergUKLtd

More than just a transition, this speaker's statement gives the listener a specific indication of what to look for as the speech progresses.

Use Internal Summaries

The internal preview precedes the information you are discussing; the **internal summary** follows it. Summaries help speakers clarify or emphasize what they have said. For example, here the speaker provides a mini-conclusion by noting what she just covered before introducing her next point:

> It should now be clear why violent video games can desensitize young people and make them meaner. We next need to turn our attention to what we can do about it.

In this case, the internal summary is combined with an internal preview, creating a bridge to the next section of the speech.

Use Signposts

Speakers use **signposts** to make receivers aware that they are about to explain something, share an important idea, or let the audience know where they are in the progression of a speech. Signposts are indicated by an array of signaling cues such as

- Numbers ("first," "second," and "third")

- Phrases designed to focus receiver attention ("You'll especially want to keep this in mind," or "Above all else, remember this")

- Phrases that indicate an explanation is forthcoming ("For example" or "To illustrate what I mean")

- Rhetorical questions ("What steps can we take to make things better?" or "Why is this important?")

In addition to facilitating the speaker's movement from idea to idea, signposts serve as a guide for receivers, focusing the spotlight on what the speaker believes is most important. When giving a speech on the challenges posed by violence in schools, a speaker used the following signposts to mark or signal each of the speech's main points:

I. The first challenge I'll discuss is the one students face.

II. The second challenge I'll discuss is the one teachers face.

III. The last challenge I'll discuss is the one communities face.

Signposts also signal the end of a speech. When a speaker says something like "Finally," or "To sum up," the speaker is signaling the receiver that the speech is about to end. So, in addition to moving a speech forward, signposts draw it to a close.

Now it's time to put all of the elements together. The following is an example of one student's outline. As you read it, note the student's use of attention-getting material at the outset, how the introduction provides a preview of the speech, which ideas the student chose to emphasize, the relationship of main points to the thesis, how subordinate ideas are used to support the main ideas, how transitional tools link ideas, and how the conclusion reinforces the speech's purpose and makes it memorable. Consider where in the outline the student might add references to sources the student used.

Read the signs. Help your audience out by signaling important information and guiding them through the speech.

istockphoto.com/gguy44

Sample Full-Sentence Outline

Elder Abuse and Abandonment

Specific Purpose: To explain the growing abuse and abandonment problem that thousands of older adults are experiencing.

Thesis: Increased family stresses and a lack of sufficient government assistance are causing families both in the United States and abroad to mistreat and abandon their older relatives.

Introduction

SN 1

See Chapter 10 to learn how to introduce your speech.

Introduction

    I. Just about a half-century ago, the late playwright Edward Albee wrote *The Sandbox*, a drama telling the story of a family who bring their grandmother to a playground and dump her in a sandbox.

    II. Back then, people called Albee's play absurd.

    III. Now that this has been happening worldwide for decades, with older people subject to physical, psychological, and financial abuse, it is all too real.

    IV. Today, we're going to look at the elder abuse and abandonment problem that people aged 60 and over face.

        (*Transition:* Let's begin by examining the story of one elderly person.)

SN 2

Signposts signal the progress of the speech.

Body

I. Years before the COVID-19 pandemic, thousands of families in the United States were already abusing and abandoning their aging parents.

    A. John Kingery, 82, was abandoned outside a men's room in Post Falls, Idaho.

        1. His clothes were stripped of their labels.

        2. An Alzheimer's sufferer, Kingery was not able to remember his name.

    B. Thousands of older Americans have faced similar situations, too often being left in hospitals.

        1. The American College of Emergency Physicians estimates that 70,000 older adults are abandoned each year in hospital emergency rooms.

        2. Most of the families who abandon relatives do so because they cannot pay for the necessary care.

        3. The COVID-19 pandemic produced an economic downturn, and many who suffered financially became vulnerable to predators who too often turned out to be family members.

            (Transition: This is not only an American problem. In 2021, the abuse of people over age 60 affects one in six globally. In South Korea, China, and India, older people face similarly uncertain futures.)

SN 3

Transitions bridge one idea to the next.

II. In South Korea, the breaching of the Confucian social contract has left many older people to fend for themselves.

    A. Denied welfare, thousands of South Koreans age 65 and older commit suicide.

        1. One 78-year-old widow staged her death as a final act of public protest against a society she said had abandoned her by drinking pesticide in front of her city hall.

        2. South Koreans are denied welfare because their children are capable of supporting them.

    B. Thousands of older Chinese people face equally horrific fates.

        1. Chinese parents invest heavily in their children's education, thinking the children will repay the debt to them later in life.

        2. The children do not live up to their responsibilities.

        3. Their older parents find themselves with no financial reserves.

    C. Older people in India also are being abandoned.

        1. Every year, thousands of grown Indian children abandon their parents.

        2. With society no longer parent-oriented, older adults in India are left to fend for themselves.

            (Transition: Why are family members and governments not living up to their responsibilities?)

III. Responsibilities are overwhelming those in the United States and in other countries who in the past would have cared for older relatives.
   A. The social fabric of societies continues to fray.
   B. The COVID-19 pandemic by isolating older adults and increasing ageism toward them eroded the family structure, also increasing the risk that they would be abused and abandoned.
   C. Caregivers suffer physical and mental stress.
      1. Exhausted caregivers become susceptible to high blood pressure and strokes.
      2. Caregivers suffer from depression.
      3. Caregivers experience guilt.
         (Transition: So much for the reality of elder abuse and abandonment; what about the future?)

IV. There are a number of ways to ensure that elder abuse and abandonment ends.
   A. Families can do more.
      1. They can avoid placing all the responsibilities on one person.
      2. Relatives can help out with the never-ending stack of paperwork required by government agencies.
   B. Governments can do more.
      1. Programs need to be added so that patients can be cared for outside the home at least part of the time.
         a. This would provide variety for older parents.
         b. Such programs would also give a much-needed rest to the family so they could avoid burnout.
      2. Suicide prevention centers need to be established.
         a. The government needs to protect its people.
         b. Older adults need to feel there is hope.
      3. A holistic approach to elder care needs to be adopted.
         Conclusion

SN 4

See Chapter 10 for guidance on concluding your speech.

   I. Though some 50+ years ago, Albee's *The Sandbox* was labeled as an example of absurdism, the abuse and abandonment of our older adults has become an all too real and all too tragic way of life for tens of thousands of people around the world.
   II. It is time to treat our aging and older relatives with the respect and dignity they deserve.

Works Consulted

Ron Acierno, et al., "The National Elder Mistreatment Study: An 8-Year Longitudinal Study of Outcomes," *Journal of Elder Abuse & Neglect,* 2017.
   Edward Albee, *The Sandbox.* New York: New American Library, 1961.

Keith Bradsher, "In China, Families Bet It All on College for Their Children," *New York Times*, February 16, 2013, https://www.nytimes.com/2013/02/17/business/in-china-families-bet-it-all-on-a-child-in-college.html.

"Elder Abuse: A Hidden Tragedy," *Biotech Week*, October 20, 2004, p. 195.

"Granny-Dumping by the Thousands," *New York Times*, March 29, 1992, https://www.nytimes.com/1992/03/29/opinion/granny-dumping-by-the-thousands.html.

Homewatch CareGivers, https://www.homewatchcaregivers.com. A support group of caregivers for people who suffer from Alzheimer's disease.

Rebecca Ley, "Why Do So Many Children Abandon Parents in Their Darkest Hour?" *Daily Mail*, May 28, 2014, http://www.dailymail.co.uk/femail/article-2642006/Why-DO-children-abandon-parents-darkest-hour-Im-stunned-Ian-Botham-didnt-visit-dementia-stricken-father.html.

Judy Lin, "Honor or Abandon: Societies' Treatment of Elderly Intrigues Scholar," *UCLA Today*, January 7, 2010, http://newsroom.ucla.edu/stories/jared-diamond-on-aging-150571.

Lena K. Makaroun, Rachel L. Bacrach, and Anne-Marie Rosland, "Elder Abuse in the Time of COVID-19—Increased Risks for Older Adults and their Caregivers," *The American Journal of Geriatric Psychiatry,* May 2020.

Choe Sang-Hun, "As Families Change, Korea's Elderly Are Turning to Suicide," *New York Times*, February 17, 2013, https://www.nytimes.com/2013/02/17/world/asia/in-korea-changes-in-society-and-family-dynamics-drive-rise-in-elderly-suicides.html.

Stacy Singer, "Lawyers Warn of Granny Dumping," *Palm Beach Post*, June 14, 2011.

Jennifer E. Story, "Risk Factors for Elder Abuse and Neglect: A Review of the Literature," *Aggression and Violent Behavior,* January–February, 2020.

Yongie Yon, et al. "Elder Abuse Prevalence in Community Settings: A Systematic Review and Meta-Analysis," *The Lancet Global Health,* February 2017.

SELF ASSESSMENT 9.1: CAN I DEVELOP AN EFFECTIVE FULL-SENTENCE OUTLINE?

Directions

Use the following questions and evaluation scales to rate your ability to complete a full-sentence outline.

Criteria	Absolutely	Usually	Somewhat	A Little	Not at All
1. I understand the logic behind outlining.					
2. I can format a standard outline.					

Criteria	Absolutely	Usually	Somewhat	A Little	Not at All
3. Give me a topic, and I can divide it into an appropriate number of segments.					
4. I can use symbols to demarcate the main and subpoints of an outline.					
5. I can use spacing to visually distinguish the main and subpoints of an outline.					
6. I can divide main points into a minimum of two subpoints.					
7. I can formulate main points that flow directly from the purpose statement and thesis.					
8. I am able to balance the time allotted to cover the main points.					
9. I am able to label the parts of the outline correctly.					
10. I can use transitional tools to achieve coherence and unity between sections of the outline and main and subpoints.					

Scoring Method	Analysis
Scoring Calculation Identify the questions to which you responded somewhat, a little, or not at all.	Explain specifically what you need to do regarding your mastery of outlining in order to be able to respond "fully" or "usually" to each question.

USE A FORMAL OUTLINE TO PREPARE SPEAKER'S NOTES

> **9.3**   *Prepare an extemporaneous or presentation outline, also known as speaker's notes, from a formal outline.*

Once you have researched your topic, identified your supporting materials, and developed a full-sentence outline of your presentation, you're ready to become your own audience.

Explore the Sound of Your Speech

You now need to explore the sound and feel of your speech by holding a first tryout. The essential ingredients at this point are (a) your full-sentence outline, and (b) a smartphone to time and video or audio record your speech so that you can review the exact words you used to express your ideas. Before starting, turn on the timer and recorder. Then begin speaking. In effect, what you are doing is preparing an oral rough draft of your presentation.

Look for the following elements:

1. Does your presentation consume too much or too little time?

2. Are any ideas not expressed as clearly as you would like?

3. Have you expressed the same thoughts again and again?

4. Is the structure confusing because of missing or inappropriate transitions?

5. Did you remember to include an effective attention-getter?

6. Is the information in the body of your presentation too detailed or technical for receivers?

7. Does your conclusion satisfy the psychological requirements you established for it?

If you discover that your main attention-getter is not as effective as it could be, this is when you improve it. If the supporting material under, say, the second main point sounds confusing, rewrite it. Refine your speech until it is as close as possible to what you want to present. Once you reach that point, it is time to prepare notes enabling you to give your speech extemporaneously.

Prepare Speaker's Notes

After practicing delivering the speech a few times using the full-sentence outline, your next step is to adapt your detailed outline into an **extemporaneous or presentation outline,** also known as **speaker's notes** (see Figure 9.2). The purpose of an extemporaneous outline or speaker's notes is to remind you of the key parts of your speech and the support you will use to develop each point when delivering your speech. Only when you are comfortable and familiar with your speech are you ready to rely exclusively on speaker's notes.

Your primary goal when preparing speaker's notes is to keep them as brief as possible so you won't be tempted to read them aloud instead of maintaining eye contact with the members of your audience. It is okay, however, to include a number of delivery cues in the margins of note cards, such as "emphasize," "cite this source," or "hold up the visual aid," much as an actor marks up a script to help facilitate speaking smoothness. Following this advice and using the preceding outline on elderly abandonment, try your hand at creating speaker's notes.

When creating your speaker's notes, print or type in large block letters and use just a key word or two in place of the complete sentences in your outline to remind you of your main and subpoints.

For all practical purposes, speaker's notes are much like a key-word outline together with information, such as sources, statistical data, or direct quotations that you may have trouble remembering. Speaker's notes also contain delivery cues, including when to show a visual, and what words to stress.

FIGURE 9.2 ■ Sample Speaker's Notes

I. Researchers have demonstrated how harmful smoking is.
   A. Animal studies (show visual of animal tests)
   B. Human studies (show visual of human lungs)
II. Smoking must be banned totally.
   (the surgeon general says. . .)
   A. Current laws
   B. New laws needed

iStock.com/wdstock

EXERCISES

Outlining

Use the following activities to help you refine your outlining skills.

1. Develop an Outline of a Speech

In addition to helping you prepare your own presentation, a speech outline helps you prepare to analyze others' presentations. If, as you listen to a speaker's ideas, you can also picture the structure of their ideas, you will be better able both to recall the main points of the speech and to determine whether the support the speaker supplies is adequate. After you develop a clear image of the visual framework of a speech, you are also better equipped to critique the speech and ask the speaker relevant questions.

For practice, read a speech of your choice, perhaps the transcript of a TED Talk, or one assigned by your instructor. Working alone or in a group, develop a sentence outline of the main points of the speech's body. Once your outline is complete, answer these questions:

- Is the body of the speech well organized?

- Does the speech exhibit structural integrity?

- How does making an outline of the speech help you answer the two preceding questions?

2. Take the Transitional Challenge

In your next class, keep track of the transitions, internal previews, and summaries and signposts that your professor uses in class. Describe how their use promotes understanding and learning.

3. Assess the Speech: YouTube and TED

June 15 is World Elder Abuse Awareness Day. Log on to the Internet to review the fact sheet that the World Health Organization (WHO) put out about the elder abuse problem on June 15, 2021. Then find two speeches in addition to the one contained in this chapter on the subject, perhaps from TED Talks, YouTube, Vital Speeches, or another source. Develop an outline of each speaker's introduction, body, and conclusion, comparing and contrasting main and subpoints. Based on your examination of the outlines, which speech do you believe exhibits more structural integrity, and why? Based on your review of the WHO fact sheet, which speech addresses more of the issue's key points?

4. Approach the Speaker's Stand

Based on the information in this chapter as well as research you conduct independently, prepare a podcast or YouTube video on the tenets of outlining, being certain to discuss each of the outline's parts along with your guidelines for creating one that is effective.

RECAP AND REVIEW

9.1 Identify the parts of a speech outline, developing a preliminary and full-sentence outline that adheres to appropriate form and structure.

An outline is a speech road map. It contains the following parts: the specific purpose, the thesis, the main ideas, the introduction, the body (composed of key main and supporting points), transitions, and the conclusion. Developing an outline helps the speaker organize their thoughts into a meaningful framework. An effective outline exhibits (a) coordination and consistency, (b) subordination, (c) a division of the whole, and (d) parallel structure.

9.2 Link the parts of the outline together.

Speakers rely on transitional tools—transitions, internal previews, and internal summaries—to facilitate the move from one idea to the next. The use of transitional tools creates a sense of coherence and unity.

9.3 Use a formal outline to prepare speaker's notes.

Once an outline is completed, the speaker then develops a shortened version of the outline containing key words and sources to use when delivering the presentation.

KEY TERMS

Causal transitions (p. 200)

Chronological transitions (p. 200)

Complementary transitions (p. 200)

Contrasting transitions (p. 200)

Coordinate points (p. 199)

Extemporaneous (or presentation) outline (p. 209)

Internal preview (p. 201)

Internal summary (p. 201)

Main points (p. 195)

Parallelism (p. 199)

Signposts (p. 202)

Speaker's notes (p. 209)

Subordinate points (p. 196)

Transitions (p. 200)

istockphoto.com/master1305

10 BEGINNING AND ENDING YOUR SPEECH

UPON COMPLETING THIS CHAPTER, YOU WILL BE ABLE TO

10.1   Identify at least six ways to introduce a speech, illustrating the purpose and function of the introduction.

10.2   Describe the conclusion's purpose, demonstrating how to end a speech strong.

10.3   Explain how to avoid introduction and conclusion pitfalls.

Making a positive impression in both the opening and closing segments of a speech are vital to speechmaking success. The very first words you speak should capture the audience's attention. The last words you speak are equally crucial. To understand why, picture this. You're at a soccer game. The game is almost over. The score is tied. All the fans are on edge. The star striker, taken down in the box just as she is about to shoot, is given a free kick. The striker lines up, fakes to the right, then drives the ball past the goalie into the net! A thrilling finish means everyone will remember the game's outcome. That's the kind of reaction you want to create in the audience as you deliver your speech's conclusion. During a presentation's final few moments, the audience listens and observes as the speaker does their best to drive home the message of the speech while leaving the audience with a favorable impression. Like the introduction, an appropriate ending can make or break the entire speech. The conclusion should compel the audience to continue thinking about your speech—even after you have stopped speaking. Together, the introduction and conclusion demonstrate a **primacy-recency effect**: Receivers are likely to remember that which they listen to first and last.[1] Thus, for the audience to understand and recall the main points of your speech, you need to draw them in at the beginning and summarize and motivate them to remember what you shared with them in the conclusion.

COACHING TIP

"You've got to be very careful if you don't know where you are going, because you might not get there."

—Yogi Berra, renowned baseball player and coach

A speaker has one chance to make a good first impression. The first words you speak to an audience should both command attention and establish a connection. Involve the audience. Build your esteem in their eyes. Add momentum to your speech. By crafting a winning attention-getter, you give your speech a running start. Also end your speech with flair. The conclusion is a significant moment in your speech's life. It is when you "get there." Take advantage of your last few moments speaking to remind the audience why your ideas are important and why they should care. You have one final chance to be sure you reach your goal and connect with the audience. Make it memorable!

THE HOW AND WHY OF THE SPEECH INTRODUCTION

> **10.1**   *Identify at least six ways to introduce a speech, illustrating the purposes and functions of the introduction.*

When we speak, we hope others will pay close attention to our words. But how do we capture their attention? While late-night talk show host Stephen Colbert starts his show with these words: "I'm your host Stephen Colbert," unless you're Stephen Colbert, beginning by introducing yourself is not sufficient; nor is it appropriate. Instead, think about the opening song at a rock concert and its effect on fans. The introduction of your speech works the same way. Though it often is written after the body of the speech is written and usually takes only about 10 percent of total speaking time, an effective introduction captures attention and interest, builds your credibility and goodwill, and orients receivers to the organizational pattern your speech will follow. The better you are at accomplishing these objectives, the more likely it is that your audience will listen. During the first few moments of a presentation, audience members form their initial impression of both the speaker and the speech. How you begin affects the audience's motivation to listen.

How to Capture the Audience's Attention

Audience members quickly form impressions of you. Unless your speech attracts attention and builds interest from the get-go, you may fail to communicate your point simply because the audience isn't listening. Let's look at several effective attention-getting techniques you can use to arouse interest (see Table 10.1):

- Startle or shock the audience

- Directly involve the audience

- Arouse curiosity and build suspense

- Use an interesting quote from a relevant source

- Use humor

- Use a story to arouse emotion

Startle or Shock the Audience

The goal of an introduction is to compel attention. The speaker's initial words make such an impact that it becomes virtually impossible for the thoughts of audience members to stray. Consider the opening of this speech, titled "The Story of the Lost Corpse":

> I've spent my career as a hospital administrator talking about the need for values, but it's not always easy to walk the walk, especially when a crisis erupts and the

TABLE 10.1 ■ Attention-Getting Techniques	
Technique	**Examples**
Startle or shock the audience	Emma Gonzalez began her speech at the 2018 March for Our Lives rally with six minutes and 20 seconds of silence—the time it took the shooter at Marjory Stillman High School to kill 17 victims.
Involve the audience	One student began a speech on student loans with these words: "If you, a relative, or a friend of yours has a student loan, please stand up."
Arouse curiosity and build suspense	An art student asked this question at the outset of her speech on art therapy: "Can simply drawing a picture improve mental health?"
Quote a relevant source	Speaking about the importance of creating a video résumé to land a job, job applicant Taylor Haywood noted, "I felt so seen, because I felt this really did represent me as a person, as a worker, and as a content creator."
Use humor	Comedy Central's Hissan Minhaj relied on humor throughout his presentation to attendees at the White House Correspondents' Dinner starting with the introduction: "I would say it's an honor to be here, but that would be an alternative fact."
Arouse emotion	In the introduction to a speech given in Beijing to draw attention to a worldwide dearth of toilets, Microsoft founder Bill Gates held up a jar of human feces, telling the audience: "This small amount of feces could contain as many as 200 trillion rotavirus cells, 20 billion shigella bacteria and 100,000 parasitic worm eggs. So, in places without sanitation, you have lots more than that, and that's what kids when they're out playing are exposed to all the time."

most expedient response is often the unethical one—I learned that the day we lost a corpse. We had two bodies in the morgue of a hospital I previously led; one was going to be taken to a mortuary for a traditional funeral and the other was going to a university as a donation to science. As it turned out, the wrong body went to the university. . . . My risk manager gave me the news. I asked him what he thought we should do, and he promptly responded, "No harm, no foul. No one knows, so let's leave it that way. . . ."

That didn't seem the appropriate response, and it was contrary to the values of the hospital. I told him, "If it was your loved one, you wouldn't have wanted the body to be taking a ride across the state to the university?" I decided to inform the family.[2]

Storytime. Opening with a story, whether it's a personal anecdote, about someone's life, or a fictional plot, can grab your audience's attention.

iStockPhoto.com/CharlieAJA

Startling or shocking statements are effective and easy to use. However, you need to weigh carefully how much shock effect is consistent with an honest treatment of the topic. With that in mind, evaluate your attention-getter:

- Will audience members perceive it as relevant to the topic?

- Will they follow it without difficulty?

- Will it ignite their interest?

Using an introduction only because of its shock value but failing to connect it to your remarks can lead audience members to become confused or irritated rather than interested. Startling statements must be both true and supportable.

Involve the Audience

When audience members believe your topic directly affects them or is something for which they share personal responsibility, they will pay closer attention.[3] Notice how in the very first sentence of a speech on the career skills gained from playing video games, the speaker immediately draws you in:

> Raise your hand if you're an experienced video game player. Have you included that fact on your resume? You should. Across a range of industries, employers are embracing resumes in which applicants highlight their videogame playing backgrounds. Why? Because they believe the hobby fosters online collaboration, problem solving, and teambuilding.[4]

Arouse Curiosity and Build Suspense

Rhetorical questions, questions requiring no overt answer or response, arouse curiosity and build suspense. As your listeners mull over how to respond to your question(s), their participation is ensured. In a speech on why we procrastinate, one student asked the audience,

> Have you ever put off an important task by doing something like watching a Netflix film or giving yourself a manicure instead? If you have, then you've procrastinated. What if you knew that putting off that important task in the end would cause you harm? According to Dr. Piers Steel, the author of *The Procrastination Equation: How to Stop Putting Things Off and Start Getting Things Done,* procrastinating, which is caused by negative thinking, has negative consequences for the procrastinator.

Imagine being in that audience. How would you respond if asked that same question? You'd probably start thinking about something you put off doing that you should have tackled but didn't due to the negative associations you had for the tasks and your fear of failure. With a single question, a speaker paves a path for you to join them.

Quote a Relevant Source

Sometimes a quotation is the most effective technique you can use both to impress your audience and to capture their attention. The words of a well-known figure, a passage from a work of literature, or a familiar phrase may help you communicate information in a more persuasive or comprehensible manner than your words alone otherwise could accomplish.

Delivering a speech at the Israeli embassy in Washington, D.C., then-president Barack Obama enhanced his credibility by quoting from the Talmud:

> The Talmud teaches that if a person destroys one life, it is as if they've destroyed an entire world, and if a person saves one life, it is as if they've saved an entire world.[5]

The words of ordinary people can also be used when appropriate to arouse greater interest. Speaking about past racial and economic injustices, one student began their speech with these words:

> Have you ever wondered how your world differs from the world your grandparents grew up in? When I was in high school, I asked my great grandma what it was like growing up when she was young. Her words stung: "When I was your age, the high school was all white. No Blacks were allowed to attend it. I played sports on an all-white team because no Blacks were allowed to play on our teams. I rode in the front of the bus. They could not. They also couldn't drink out of the fountain I drank from. And they couldn't sit next to me in the luncheonette. I never even met a Black person until I left our town and went off to college." My grandmother's world lacked diversity. It was colorless rather than color-full.

Use Humor

When used wisely, appropriately, and with discretion, humor encourages audience attention and portrays the speaker as a likeable, friendly person.[6] In many ways, humor acts as a bridge to goodwill.

Humor works best when it is directly related to the content of a speech and not merely "stuck on" for effect or as an afterthought. Addressing Dartmouth's graduating class, talk show host Conan O'Brien began with these words:

> Before I begin, I must point out that behind me sits a highly admired president of the United States and decorated war hero while I, a cable television talk show host, have been chosen to stand here and impart wisdom. I pray I never witness a more damning example of what is wrong with America today.[7]

If you think audience members might find the humor you are considering using offensive or in any way inappropriate, don't use it. While humor that pokes fun at the speaker or the human condition usually is effective, at no time are racist, sexist, or ethnic jokes or stories appropriate.

Arouse Emotion

When integrated effectively into introductions, stories also capture listener attention and hold listener interest. We all enjoy a good story, and if that story is filled with the drama of human interest and is amusing or suspenseful, we enjoy it even more. Of course, the story you use should not only involve the audience, it also should be clearly relevant to the issues you discuss in your speech.

A student used the following story in the introduction of his speech on the world that "ghost parents" live in, describing for the audience, in an empathic way, the all-consuming grief that parents who suffer the loss of a child experience:

> A baby orca died over half a month ago. For 17 days, the orca mother carried her dead baby around with her just off the coast. Covered extensively by the news media, we were able to watch as the mommy whale just would not let her calf disappear into the sea, even as its body slowly deteriorated. If it fell beneath the water as the mama orca swam, she would dive, scoop it up, and bring it back to the surface. When grief exhausted her, other whales in the pod carried the dead calf for her. A child's death is a parent's greatest fear.

In addition, if the story involves you or someone you know personally, it can help establish your experience with the topic. The student who recounted the orca's story was also the parent of a child who passed away unexpectedly soon after birth. Aside from capturing the attention of receivers, stories add color to a speech and also help the speaker make the ideas in the speech less abstract and more concrete.

Why to Build Credibility

While capturing your audience's attention and engaging them , your introduction also should build your credibility. Part of your job is to convince receivers that you are a knowledgeable and believable source.

See Yourself Through Their Eyes

Credibility is based on a receiver's judgment of a source's expertise on a particular topic. Once a speaker convinces you that they are qualified, sincere, and someone with whom you can identify, you likely will perceive them as trustworthy and believable. Whether the speaker actually possesses those qualities is not the issue; in your eyes, the speaker is someone who you believe is competent to offer you advice, has your best interests at heart, and is a person of goodwill.

You may, of course, respect the speaker's competence when it comes to some subject areas but not others. You may, for example, be ready to listen to the advice of television personality Dr. Phil on psychological matters but not on financial issues. Thus, you need to help your receivers understand why you are qualified to speak on your chosen topic. You might show them that you know what you are talking about by sharing experiences, interests, and research findings related to your topic.

Your audience members' initial impressions of you will be based on how you look, what you say, and how you communicate during your opening remarks. Speakers who are well dressed, passionate about the importance of their topics, speak clearly, use inclusive language, make eye contact, and stand with an open body position are seen as more credible than speakers who lack these qualities. If at the end of your introduction audience members believe you are qualified to speak on your chosen topic, if they identify with you and respond to you because they like and trust you, then in their eyes you will be a credible source.

In the mirror. Be aware of how you will come across to others in the introduction of your speech.

istockphoto.com/DaniloAndjus

Demonstrate Your Credibility

To hone your own level of credibility, answer these five questions as you draft your speech:

1. Why should audience members listen to *me*?
2. What have I done or experienced that qualifies me to speak on the topic?
3. How personally committed am I to the ideas I am about to share with my audience?
4. What steps can I take to communicate my concerns and enthusiasm to the audience?
5. How can I use my appearance, attitude, and delivery to help establish my goodwill and make my case?

If you are mindful of the ways listeners perceive you, then you will find that you can use attitude, demeanor, and content to build your credibility in their eyes. Notice how one student uses her abilities as well as research to build credibility with receivers in a speech on the need for Americans to speak a foreign language. As you read this excerpt, consider how effectively the speaker communicates her thesis to receivers:

America is facing a crisis of ignorance. *Es muy probable que ustedes no están entendiendo lo que yo digo ahora.* If you are like the majority of Americans, you have no idea what I just said. Which is essentially what I said, only I said it in Spanish, and therein lies the problem. Since you are all "speechies" of one sort or another, I certainly do not need to impress upon you the importance of communication. However, most Americans are currently depriving themselves of a tremendous tool that could open up whole new worlds— the ability to communicate in a foreign language.[8]

Your ability to show your audience members your concern for them will encourage them to listen to you. Both the sincerity of your voice and the commitment portrayed by your facial expressions, eye contact, and gestures can enhance your audience's opinion of you and do much to cement the feeling of goodwill that is so integral to their assessments

Believable. How can you effectively use your tone, demeanor, eye contact, and stance to convey passion and genuineness in your speech?

istockphoto.com/NicolasMcComber

of your credibility. When your listeners understand how you personally relate to the subject, they are better able to relate to it and to you.

Establish Topic Credibility and Relevance

The audience needs to understand how your topic affects them. They need to be provided with a credible reason to listen—an answer to the question: What's in it for me? Would these words from a student speech about the cost of a college degree have relevance for you? Do you find them credible?

> Here we are at college. Many of us have taken loans to finance our educations. According to the U.S. Student Loan Center, the average debt of a college student now is $37,172, a $20,000 increase from 13 years ago. That's a lot when you consider that according to the National Association of Colleges and Employers, as a new college grad, we many earn only about $50,000 a year. How much will you owe when you complete your education?

> Since many students have loans that will take years to repay, the speaker enhanced her credibility by establishing a problem she and her audience shared in common.

Connect Credibility and Culture

In some cultures, speakers are emotional and passionate, while in others they are restrained and unexpressive. If you are of the same sex, ethnic background, and age as the majority of your audience members, you have an obvious advantage. But most speakers cannot count on having such a uniform audience. Again, it is up to you to think critically and plan your opening not only to excite and motivate listeners but also to establish **common ground** with them.

Then-president Bill Clinton accomplished this in a speech given to African American leaders on the site in Memphis, Tennessee, where the Reverend Martin Luther King Jr. delivered what turned out to be the last speech of his life. The president began his remarks with phrases that reflected the words King had used nearly three decades earlier. Clinton internalized King's tone, words, and style in an effort to establish his own credibility and win over his audience.[9]

Clinton began his address:

> I am glad to be here. You have touched my heart. You have brought tears to my eyes and joy to my spirit.[10]

He then continued by referring to the Bible:

> The proverb says, "A happy heart doeth good like medicine, but a broken spirit dryeth the bone."[11]

By paying homage to King's style, Clinton sounded a lot like a preacher. However, he was careful not to mimic, appropriate, or pander to King's cultural heritage or legacy,

Clinton established himself as a concerned member of the community, one who shared the same interests as his receivers and whom they now viewed as more credible. By identifying and sharing the concerns of your receivers, you can enhance your cultural credibility as well.

The Importance of Previewing the Big Ideas

In addition to attracting attention and building your credibility, a good introduction sets the scene for your presentation, preparing audience members for what is to come. If you focus on your goal, your listeners' eyes, ears, and hearts will follow. A preview

1. introduces the audience to your speech's subject and purpose, and

2. identifies the main ideas that will constitute the body of your speech.

From the very beginning, your audience should have a pretty clear understanding of your intended topic (unless you are using a configural format; see Chapter 9). If your introduction fails to introduce the subject of your speech, the audience's attention will remain unfocused. Your introduction should clarify and not confuse receivers. Notice how one student used this brief but effective introduction to prepare the audience for the body of the speech:

> Gossip has a bad reputation. It hasn't always had, and it doesn't always deserve it. Allow me to give you the real scoop. First, I will give you a brief overview of the history of gossip. Then, I'll explain how it fulfills psychological needs, how it functions anthropologically, and finally, how gossip is real news.[12]

While following the preceding advice will enable you to build a strong introduction for your speech, as we noted, it's equally important to end your speech strong.

Coming attractions. Your introduction should set the scene of your argument to pique the interest of your audience.

istockphoto.com/magical_light

END THE SPEECH AS STRONGLY AS YOU BEGAN IT

> **10.2**   *Describe the conclusion's purpose, demonstrating how to end a speech strong.*

A well-designed conclusion, one that ends strong, fulfills these functions:

1. It lets the audience know a presentation is drawing to a close.

2. It summarizes key ideas the speaker shared.

3. It "wows" receivers, reenergizing them and reminding them of the response the speaker seeks.

4. It provides the speech with a sense of closure.

The final minutes you and your audience are together is your last opportunity to plant your ideas firmly in their minds. It takes great skill to end a game in a way that brings fans to their feet. The same is true for a speech. Although you might be tempted to take the easy way out and bring your speech to a close with a "That's all folks," "I'll stop now," or "And so it goes," ending like that could ruin an otherwise fine presentation. Instead, put audience members in a mood conducive to achieving your goals by concluding your speech in as memorable a way as you began it. If you do this, you'll add additional "wow" power to your words and achieve closure, much like early colonial patriot Patrick Henry did when he delivered these closing lines to his speech: "I know not what course others may take, but as for me, give me liberty or give me death!" His ending is part of the national heritage of the United States, and an example of how a great ending to a speech is constructed.[13] Although the conclusions you create may not become part of U.S. national heritage, you can design ones in which you use a clear vocal shift and transitional word or phrase to clue receivers that the speech is coming to an end, summarize main points, and rouse your audience so your speech becomes memorable (see Table 10.2).

TABLE 10.2 ■ How to End Your Speech Strong	
The Do's	**The Don'ts**
Keep it short—but not too short	End abruptly or with a "that's all"
Forecast the finish line—use a transitional word or phrase and/or a vocal shift to cue the audience	Take the audience by surprise
Restate the thesis or central idea—drive your message home	Introduce something new
Motivate the audience—again	Reduce emotion, energy, and effort
Achieve closure—come full circle tying the pieces together and achieving presentation wholeness	Leave ideas hanging

Keep It Short

A conclusion should be brief. The average conclusion comprises about 5 percent of a speech. However, just as with your introduction, the materials in your speech's conclusion must be relevant to your topic, appropriate to the audience and occasion, interesting, and involving. They also need to provide audience members with a sense of completion. The conclusion is your last chance to put the spotlight exactly where you want it to shine.

At the close of one student's speech on the dangers of overconfidence, for example, in about 60 seconds, he reminded the audience of the differences between healthy self-confidence and cockiness, reviewed the risks of overconfidence, and then ended with these words: "The bottom line is that to instill confidence in others we need to model confidence. But as we now know, there's a fine line between being confident and overconfident, between having self-confidence and being arrogant."[14]

Forecast the Finish Line

A conclusion should not take the audience by surprise. Instead, cue the audience that you are about to stop speaking. You might pause, decrease or increase your speaking rate, build momentum, alter your voice tone, or use a transitional phrase to cue receivers. For example, you might say, "In conclusion," "To review," or "Let me end by noting." Such techniques help your audience adjust to the fact that you are approaching the speech's end.

Here is how Romaine Seguin, president of UPS Americas Region, signaled the end of a speech on the lessons for working women, specifically Black working women, contained in the film *Hidden Figures:*

> So, in closing, I'm going to ask you to do three things: One, estimate the collective power of all the knowledge and ability in this room. Two, envision the potential of that power, defiant in the face of obstacles—those we share, and those we choose to. And then, three: entertain the impossible. As the character Al Harrison—Katherine's boss—said: "We get to the peak together, or we don't get there at all." Ready? Let's climb.[15]

Restate the Thesis or Central Idea and Main Points

New ideas have no place in the conclusion to a speech. Instead, use the conclusion to reinforce the main points you want audience members to remember. Think of it this way: you are putting your presentation on "rewind" for a moment. In order to accomplish this, you can

- Recap your thesis or central idea and your main points one last time so your audience enjoys an instant replay of your position and your rationale

- Use a quotation that summarizes or highlights your point of view

- Make a dramatic statement that drives home why audience members should be motivated and committed to respond as you desire

- Take the audience full circle by referring to your introduction

Ronald Berenbeim, an instructor at New York University's Stern School of Business Administration, used the conclusion of a talk entitled "Ethical Leadership—Winning With Integrity" to reemphasize the core message of his speech:

> The requirements for ethical leadership are easier to state than to exercise because we cannot teach the character that moral reasoning requires. Character in the broadest sense is the ability to understand the connection between our experience which is what we see and know and the rules by which we live and act towards others. In sum, it is empathy—which is the essential quality for the ethical leader who seeks to win with integrity.[16]

Motivate the Audience (Again)

Just as an effective introduction motivates audience members to listen to a speech, an effective conclusion motivates receivers to respond appropriately. Your conclusion is no place for you to let up on effort or energy. It certainly is no place for you to let down your audience. Instead, take the time you need to create a striking ending that supports and sustains your speech's theme.

Many of the same kinds of materials you used to develop your introduction can help you set a proper concluding mood. Reminding receivers of a startling fact, using a quotation, integrating humor, asking a rhetorical question, or using an effective story can pump up a conclusion.

Don't let up. Maintain your energy at the conclusion of your speech to motivate and inspire your audience.

istockphoto.com/FatCamera

For example, one speaker used a humorous quotation to set the mood for continued contemplation and action by audience members. In a speech titled "Rediscovering a Lost Resource: Rethinking Retirement," the speaker closed with this anecdote:

> Listen to Warren Buffet, who has built an investment empire. When asked a few years ago about leaving a woman in charge of one of his companies after celebrating her 94th birthday, he replied, "She is clearly gathering speed and may well reach her full potential in another five or ten years. Therefore, I've persuaded the board to scrap our mandatory-retirement-at-100 policy. My God, good managers are so scarce I can't afford the luxury of letting them go just because they've added a year to their age."[17]

Achieve Closure

An effective means of giving a speech balance is to refer in the conclusion to ideas explored in the introduction, achieving closure. You might reuse a theme you introduced at the beginning of your speech, ask or answer the rhetorical question you used at its outset, refer to an opening story, or restate an initial quotation. Integrating any one of these strategies helps to provide audience members with a desired sense of logical and emotional closure. Because such strategies help your speech sound finished, audience members are not left wondering whether your speech is actually over. Leave your audience hanging and you leave your ideas hanging. If your conclusion convinces audience members that you have delivered what you promised in your introduction, they are more likely to accept your thesis and take the action you advocate.

In the closing minutes of a speech on the importance of citizen journalism for the Black Lives Matter movement, the speaker reviewed the roles that citizen and police videos play in documenting events. The speaker directly referenced the video that 17-year-old Darnella Frazier had made of the murder of George Floyd, a Black man whose death was attributed to the callousness of white police officer Derek Chauvin. Chauvin had knelt on Floyd's neck for nine minutes and 29 seconds while Floyd gasped for air until he died. Ultimately, Chauvin was tried and convicted of the crime. The speaker concluded with these words: "By bearing witness and hitting record on her smartphone, and then posting the video clip on Facebook, 17-year-old Darnella Frazier's video became a key witness for the prosecution. It may have changed the world. Might your work as citizen journalists change the world too?"[18]

By referring back to ideas explored earlier in their speeches, speakers help audience members acknowledge the wholeness and completeness of their presentations.

SELF-ASSESSMENT 10.1: SPEECH BEGINNINGS AND ENDINGS

Directions:

Use the following questions to evaluate speaker behaviors that can enhance the effectiveness of speech introductions and conclusions. Simply respond to each statement.

Statements	Never	Rarely	Sometimes	Usually	Always
1. I use the introduction to startle or wake up the audience.	1	2	3	4	5
2. I use the introduction to involve the audience.	1	2	3	4	5

Statements	Never	Rarely	Sometimes	Usually	Always
3. I use the introduction to arouse the audience's curiosity.	1	2	3	4	5
4. I include a quote from a relevant source in the introduction.	1	2	3	4	5
5. I use humor in the introduction when it's appropriate.	1	2	3	4	5
6. I cue the audience that the speech will soon conclude.	1	2	3	4	5
7. I restate the thesis in the speech's conclusion to drive home the speech's message for the audience.	1	2	3	4	5
8. I use the conclusion to remotivate the audience.	1	2	3	4	5
9. I keep the conclusion short—without ending abruptly.	1	2	3	4	5
10. I use the conclusion to achieve closure.	1	2	3	4	5

Scoring Method	Add together your scores for questions 1–5 focusing on introductions: _____ Add together your scores for questions 6–10 focusing on conclusions: _____ Add together the numbers you chose on each scale: _____ Total
Scoring Calculation	The higher your total score, the better your understanding of ways to begin and end a speech.
Feedback	What have you discovered about speech introductions and conclusions? Although this evaluation is not a scientific instrument, it should give you some indication of what to include in speech introductions and conclusions.

OVERCOME COMMON PITFALLS

> **10.3** *Explain how to avoid introduction and conclusion pitfalls.*

It all comes down to two things: (1) the first impression you make, and (2) your ability to motivate the audience to remember your speech. The beginning: What will the audience think of you? And the ending: What will they do about it? When it comes to speech beginnings and endings, there are a number of pitfalls speakers have the power to avoid.

A common error speakers make is not being sufficiently audience-focused. Successful speakers are audience-centered and take the audience's interests to heart every step of the way. A second trap is for the speaker to take their credibility as a source for granted. Speakers need to share with the audience what their qualifications are to speak on their topic and why the audience should view them as a person of good will in whom they feel comfortable placing their trust. A third mistake speakers make is to neglect explaining their reason for speaking to the audience. If a speaker doesn't share their goal or purpose, the audience will find it difficult to follow the speech. The same holds true if the speaker forgets to transition from the introduction to the body of the speech and from the body of the speech to the conclusion.

While a good introduction does not guarantee that your speech will be successful, if you don't invest time and effort in preparing it, working on potential beginnings until you determine the best beginning possible, you are almost certain to build an impenetrable wall between you and the audience. To ensure all goes smoothly and avoid committing an introductory foul, follow these guidelines:

- *Prepare.* Lack of preparation is not something audience members readily forgive. Lack of preparation demonstrates a lack of commitment on your part. Simply be prepared.

- *Be true to yourself.* Don't pretend to be what you are not. Audience members want to know you; they want to know what you think, what you feel, and why. If you pretend to know something when you don't or pretend to feel something when you don't care, then in time—usually sooner rather than later—you will be exposed as a fraud.

- *Keep your speech gimmick-free.* Gimmicks have no place in a speech. Treat the audience fairly. If you trick them into paying attention, in the end, they won't. If an introduction doesn't suit your topic, don't use it.

- *No need to pad the speech.* Under ordinary circumstances, your introduction should use about 10 percent of your speech. If you persist in introducing your ideas, you'll find that by the time you get to the body of your speech, your audience will be short on patience and endurance.

- *Write the introduction after you write the body of the speech.* Don't create the introduction before you create the body of the speech. It's a lot easier to make a good decision about how to begin your speech after you have prepared the speech's body and thought about how you want to endthepresentation.

At the end of a theatrical performance, actors take a bow. It represents their thank you to the audience for acknowledging the effectiveness of their craft. Creating an effective conclusion will help ensure an effective presentation because it leaves the audience fulfilled and in the mood to think about or do what you recommend. Your closing comments are your last chance to make a good impression and fulfill the purpose of your speech. Because it comes last, the conclusion is the part of the speech your audience will remember most clearly. Make sure to leave a positive final impression by avoiding these pitfalls:

- **Don't end abruptly.** A conclusion needs to be built carefully, or the ideas you've worked so hard to develop will topple like a house of cards. Let your audience know you are wrapping up so they aren't caught by surprise.

- **Don't be long-winded.** When you end a speech, you cross the finish line. Hang around that finish line too long without crossing it, and your audience could lose interest in you and your ideas at a very critical juncture. Build your conclusion, but keep it tight.

- **Don't introduce new ideas.** Though it's appropriate to restate in a fresh way the ideas you've covered in your speech, it's not appropriate to introduce new ideas in the conclusion. The conclusion is your last opportunity to drive home important points, not the time to start making new ones.

- **Don't end with a thud.** Devise a conclusion that will stick in the minds of your listeners, not one that may have little, if any, impact on what they retain. If you create an ending that has real emotional appeal, you will inspire rather than let down your audience. Your ending should be striking, not count as a strike against you.

You have the knowledge and ability to create an introduction or conclusion that "wows" receivers. Are you ready to captivate and wow your audience?

GAME PLAN

Creating Captivating Introductions and Conclusions

- Based on my topic and personality, I am using curiosity and suspense/humor/emotion/a relevant quotation to capture the attention of my audience members.
- I've considered our shared experiences and built upon our common ground to develop an introduction that establishes a positive relationship with my audience.

- I've made sure that my introduction includes the necessary information to orient receivers to the thesis of my speech by previewing its main ideas.

- I have established my own credibility and relevance to the topic to satisfy audience members' skepticism.

- I know how much time is allotted for my speech, and I've made sure that the introduction is no more than 10 percent of the total time and the conclusion is no more than 5 percent of the total time.

- I have included transition words such as *in closing* to forecast the speech's end for my audience.

- After I transition into my conclusion, I don't introduce new ideas but rather focus on recapping my thesis and key ideas.

- I've used the techniques discussed in this chapter to elicit an appropriate reaction from audience members so my words will linger in their minds.

EXERCISES

The Introduction and the Conclusion

Creating effective introductions and conclusions takes practice and skill. To hone your ability, use these training camp drills to get your introduction and conclusion in shape.

1. Captivate and Wow Me

First, prepare hypothetical, startling statements you could use to introduce a speech on one of the following topics:

- Gun Safety

- Transgender Rights

- Preparing for a Robot-Filled World

- Hazards of the Electric Scooter as a Means of Transportation

Next, create a conclusion that achieves closure for the same selected topic.

Finally, create an introduction designed to arouse the audience's curiosity or emotion and a conclusion designed to wow receivers and leave them thinking about what you've shared with them on one of these topics:

- Service Learning

- Dog Adoption

- Gluten

- Misinformation

2. Learn From TV

Spend time carefully watching television advertisements. Describe examples of ads that use startling or shocking openers, rhetorical examples, humor, or emotion to capture audience attention and encourage involvement. Then, find examples of openers that are used in the monologue of a late-night talk show host and a local or national news program and do the same.

3. Analyze This Introduction and Conclusion

Select a recent speech from *Vital Speeches of the Day* or TED Talks. Evaluate the extent to which the speaker used the introduction to capture attention, build credibility, and preview the content of the speech. Also, assess the degree to which the speaker ended the speech effectively.

4. Approach the Speaker's Stand

Develop three possible introductions and conclusions for a speech on any one of the following subjects, or a subject of your choice:

Artificial Intelligence	Suicide	Free Speech
A Conspiracy	Gerrymandering	Eleanor Roosevelt
Asteroids	#MeToo	Reparations

Present them to the class. Then, ask your classmates to tell you whether they found them effective and which they found most effective.

In a one- to two-page paper explain the techniques you relied on in each introduction and conclusion.

RECAP AND REVIEW

10.1 Identify at least six ways to introduce a speech, illustrating the purpose and function of the introduction.

Effective introductions serve these key functions: (a) they capture attention, (b) they build credibility, and (c) they orient receivers to the organizational development and tone of the speech. To fulfill the functions of introductions, rely on a number of techniques: startle or shock receivers, directly involve receivers, arouse curiosity or build suspense, employ an arresting quote, make your listeners smile or laugh with them, or move them with stories. In order to build credibility, the speaker first must understand how receivers perceive them and then help the audience view them as qualified. To accomplish this, they relate personal experiences, identify credentials, use reputable sources, establish topic relevance, and build common ground. Effective introductions also communicate the subject of a speech and its purpose, as well as preview what's to come.

10.2 Describe the conclusion's purpose, demonstrating how to end a speech strong.

To achieve the functions of conclusions, keep the closing words short, use cues to help receivers adjust to the fact that a speech is ending, review key points covered, use a dramatic statement or quotation to reinforce a speech's central idea(s), and take the audience full circle by referring to the speech's introduction, thereby creating a sense of closure. A strong conclusion forecasts the finish line, provides receivers with a sense of completion, restates the thesis, and motivates receivers to continue thinking about the speaker's message.

10.3 Explain how to avoid introduction and conclusion pitfalls.

During introductions, speakers should not apologize for lack of preparation, pretend to be what they are not, rely on irrelevant gimmicks, or be long-winded. The introduction also should not be created before the speech's body . When concluding, speakers should not end too abruptly, be long-winded, introduce new ideas, or end with a thud.

KEY TERMS

Closure (p. 227)
Common ground (p. 222)

Primacy-recency effect (p. 214)
Rhetorical questions (p. 218)

iStockPhoto.com/simonkr

11 WORDING THE SPEECH

UPON COMPLETING THIS CHAPTER, YOU WILL BE ABLE TO

11.1   Explain the nature of language, choosing words for your speech that will share meaning and resonate with the audience.

11.2   Strategically select your words based on understandability, contextual suitability, and tone.

11.3   Adopt an oral style.

While you may or may not be a fan of ice hockey, think about the following analogies between it and public speaking. The object of the game of ice hockey is to propel a puck past the goal line and into the net that a goal-tender is guarding. In public speaking, the speaker's objective is to propel the words they are speaking into the minds of receivers. In ice hockey, when a player commits a dangerous foul, the referee orders the player into the penalty box. As long as that player is off the ice, the team remains a player short. This gives the opposing team the advantage—called a power play—during which they have a good opportunity to score. The power play is the situation that advantages one team over the other. Public speakers score during power plays, too. In public speaking, the person who has a way with words has the advantage over the person whose failure to choose the right words puts them in a figurative penalty box. For example, way back in 1863, Abraham Lincoln scored a power play when he delivered his now historic speech, the Gettysburg Address. Given at an event to mark the dedication of a battlefield cemetery, Lincoln was not even the event's main speaker. The event's primary orator was a former governor and senator, Edward Everett, who spoke for about two hours delivering a speech complete with Greek and Latin phrases. Soon afterward, Lincoln stepped to the podium to speak. In contrast to Everett's lengthy speech, Lincoln's address contained just 272 words and lasted less than two minutes. It became, however, one of the most important and most quoted speeches in U.S. history. It is not how many words you speak, but whether you speak the *right* words. That's what is key in scoring a speechmaking power play. In large part, the message you communicate to the audience and the meaning receivers extract depend on your word choices.

Your words can cause ideas to live in the minds of your receivers long after you finish speaking. But only if you select words with audience appeal—words that succeed in moving others emotionally and intellectually—are you likely to create the audience connection you seek. Choose the wrong words—those that lack vividness, are difficult to understand, or fail to capture the imagination—and you might well contribute to the audience's boredom or confusion. Communicating simply, accurately, and effectively increases your chances of delivering a memorable speech.

In this chapter, we will explore your role as a creator of word power plays. We'll look at how language works and how your word choices can spell the difference between speechmaking success and failure.

CHOOSE WORDS THAT SHARE MEANING

> **11.1** *Explain the nature of language, choosing words for your speech that will share meaning and resonate with the audience.*

Do you think about the meaning of your words? While we may think the meaning of our words is obvious, the meaning others attribute to them may be more complicated than then we realize. How exactly do words evoke meaning? Language is a unified system of symbols that permits us to share meaning.[1] A *symbol* stands for or represents something else. Words, as symbols, represent things or ideas. For example, the word *homeless* is not the thing "homeless." Because words can convey different meanings to different listeners, good speakers must understand the relationship that exists among words, thoughts, and human behavior.

The Triangle of Meaning, devised by communication theorists C. K. Ogden and I. A. Richards, provides a model of the tenuous relationships among words, thoughts, and things (see Figure 11.1). The dotted line connecting a word and a thing indicates that there is no direct connection between the two. The only connection between the word *coat*, for example, and a physical coat is in people's thoughts. It is feasible that a number of us could look at the same object, think entirely different thoughts about it, and thus give it entirely different meanings based on our experiences. One person might hear the word and think of a winter jacket, another a suit coat, and a third a coat of paint.

It is dangerous to assume everyone understands what you mean. Once communication is the goal, we can no longer consider only one meaning for a word. We must also focus on what our words mean to those with whom we are communicating.

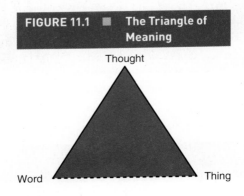

FIGURE 11.1 ■ The Triangle of Meaning

Use Words to Connect With Receivers

For words to work, there must be a common understanding about what the words we are using mean to others. Only then can we share meaning and experience.

Different words that describe the same event can evoke very different responses. For example, how do you react to each of the following words or phrases? What kinds of thoughts do the terms in each column below generate? What image(s) do you visualize for each term?

war	*fired*
defensive response	*let go*
massacre	*dismissed*

Though the event being described could be the same, the words used to describe it express our perception. If we use the word *massacre*, we suggest disapproval, while a *defensive response* might be a justified reaction to an attack. Similarly, being fired suggests more disapproval than either of the other words. And this influences how our audience responds, as well. Our words can help listeners perceive our ideas as we want, influencing their attitudes, values, and actions. Used well, words can cause an audience to feel intensely, overcoming their apathy.

Words matter. Words should not be easily thrown away, so be precise and considerate in your word choices.

Istockphoto.com/bowie15

COACHING TIP

"Words. . . . They're innocent, neutral, precise, standing for this, describing that, meaning the other, so if you look after them you can build bridges across incomprehension and chaos."

—Tom Stoppard, playwright

Words help you connect. Select the right words and they convey your ideas with clarity and power. Remember to use simple words. Speech is for the ear, not the eye. Speak in short units. Eliminate jargon. Keep it personal. With their words, speakers soften hardened hearts, helping them to win over the hearts of audience members. Reason reaches receivers on a logical level. Figurative language, rich in sensory appeals, reaches them on an emotional level. Choose your words with care. Make the audience feel, and you make your message real!

Meaning exists not in words, but in the minds of those using the words. Your goal in communicating with your audience is to create meaning overlap. Only if the audience gives similar meanings to your words will they be able to make sense of your message and respond as you desire. Accordingly, one of your prime objectives is to translate your ideas into language your listeners will understand and to which they will respond. This requires you to be culturally sensitive.

Overcome Communication Obstacles

Words have both denotative and connotative meanings. The **denotative meaning** is the word's dictionary definition, precise and objective. Audience members are not dictionaries; when you use a word, they should not have to consult a dictionary to find meaning number four for that word. What audience members do carry with them in their heads is the connotative meaning of words. **Connotative meaning** is variable and subjective. It includes all the feelings and personal associations that a word stimulates. For example, the feelings and personal associations people have for words and phrases such as *home, immigrant, gun control,* or *celebrity* differ depending on whether the experiences they associate with each word are good or bad.

If you fail to consider the possible connotative meanings a word could evoke among audience members, you increase your chances of being misunderstood. Search for words that seem likely to elicit the meanings and responses you desire from as many audience members as possible. Focus on the audience instead of simply speaking the first words that pop into your mind. Take time to identify the best way and the best words to use to evoke a desired reaction.[2]

Consider Time and Place

Every generation evolves new meanings from old words. It's as if we recycle language. This fact becomes important when you are speaking to audiences composed primarily of persons not your own age. Consider, for example, how an audience of your peers, an audience of people in their 70s, and an audience of elementary school–aged children might interpret any of the following words: *radical, net, sandbox, rap, poke, cloud, ghost, chill, hook-up, bad, tag, shade, awesome.* Because time can affect a word's meaning, speakers must be aware of the meaning any given audience member could attach to a word.[3]

The meanings of words change not only through time. Words also change meaning from one section of the country to another. Pop, soda, and Coke are all the same drink, depending on where you live. Public speakers need to be sensitive to how regional differences affect word meanings, or they could find themselves facing a widening communication gap.

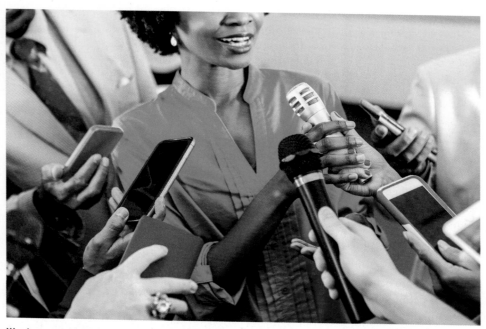

Words are worlds. Be considerate of your audience, know what words have value to them, and be thoughtful in how you employ them.

iStockPhoto.com/SDI Productions

Observe Reasoning and Thinking Preferences

Our words provide clues to our worldviews, interests and concerns, and what we believe to be important. They also reveal how we think.[4]

People in Western cultures tend to rely on both inductive and deductive reasoning to make points and to understand those points others make. Inductive reasoning relies on observation and specific instances or examples to build a case or argument. Deductive reasoning takes a known idea or general principle and applies it to a situation.

Contrastingly, people from non-Western cultures likely rely on other ways of presenting their messages in lieu of making objective observations. Rather than limiting themselves to inductive and deductive reasoning when speaking before others, for instance, people in the Arab world tend to express their emotions and religious faith, personalizing their reasons.[5] As a result, Westerners who aren't attuned to Arabs' preferences may struggle to locate the main ideas in speeches given by Arabs, and vice versa.[6] Arab speakers, for example, sometimes change course mid-speech. To Westerners, it may seem as if they have gone off on a tangent as they personalize and emote. Consequently, Western audiences often find themselves working harder to identify an Arab speaker's purpose than they do when listening to a speaker of their own background. Arab speeches also may contain exaggerations and repetitions. Additionally, Western receivers often interpret the stress patterns of the Arabic language incorrectly, perceiving them as aggressive or disinterested when that likely was not the speaker's intent.[7]

Members of Asian cultures also differ from Westerners in their language use and preferences. Whereas North Americans tend to exhibit a frank, direct speechmaking style that is sometimes confrontational, Asians tend to place a high value on politeness and are more likely to use hints and euphemisms to convey their meaning.[8] They typically neither preview nor identify their speech's purpose or main points for receivers. Instead, these are suggested through stories and personal testimonies.[9] In contrast, members of Spanish and Latin American cultures eagerly engage in conversation and are willing to share their feelings with others.

Clearly, there is more than one way to express ideas verbally. In our diverse world, it is counterproductive to consider the expression preferences favored by the members of one culture superior to another's. We run into problems when we allow feelings of ethnocentrism to interfere with our ability and willingness to process others' thoughts as accurately as possible and without bias. While culture influences language use, the goal should be to shrink the language divide, not widen it.

Hero, hoagie, sub, or wedge? Consider whether the language of your presentation is attuned to regional differences.

iStockPhoto.com/LauriPatterson

Use Plain, Unbiased Language

It is important to respect all members of the audience, acknowledging their cultural beliefs, norms, or preferences, and taking their perspectives into account when selecting your words.

- Eliminate idioms and jargon that persons unfamiliar with your topic would find confusing or frustrating.

- Speak in short units that facilitate the processing of your words, while making certain that you do not "dumb down" your content or talk down to the members of your audience.

- Avoid using overly technical language as well as overblown or bloated language that overwhelms rather than speaks to listeners.

- Keep in mind that big ideas don't require the using of big words. Words with one and two syllables can be very effective.

- Use plain talk, choosing words that clearly convey meaning

For example, generally the words *gay* and *lesbian* are preferred to refer to men and women, respectively, who have a sexual preference for persons of their same sex. The term *older adult* is preferred to *old adult* because it is perceived as less offensive. The word *Hispanic* is appropriate when referring to persons who identify themselves as belonging to a Spanish-speaking culture. While some Hispanics say that they prefer *Latinx*, most rather being called Latino or Hispanic. Most African Americans refer to themselves as *African American* or *Black*.[10] When referring to American Indians, *Native American* is the preferred term, not *Indian*, which is best reserved for referencing to persons from India. The correct means of identifying persons from Asia is *Asian*, not *Oriental*, which is suggestive of a European bias.

Be respectful. Word choice is always important in avoiding showing disrespect or prejudice toward any one culture, gender, religion, sexual orientation, and so on.

iStock.com/Alessandro Biasconi

BE STRATEGIC

> **11.2**   *Strategically select your words based on understandability, contextual suitability, and tone.*

Only if your audience shares your meaning will they truly perceive your message accurately. To achieve this, you need to make strategic word choices that favor the simple over the complex, the concrete over the abstract, the appropriate over the inappropriate, and the vivid over the vague. Let us explore each of these language options in turn.

Keep It Simple

Whenever you have the choice, select the simplest, most familiar word available to you. Never use a technical word like *cephalalgia* when a simpler one like *headache* will do—the latter is usually clearer to your listeners (see Table 11.1). Far too often, speakers who spout unfamiliar words and **jargon and technospeak** (specialized language) to uninitiated audiences succeed only in communicating their stuffiness and pretentiousness. No real sharing of meaning can occur between such a speaker and their audience because the audience has no idea what the speaker is talking about.

TABLE 11.1 ■ Using Simple Language	
Instead Of	**Use**
endeavor	try
commence	begin
altercation	fight
vista	view
eschew	avoid
edifice	building
remunerate	pay
precipitation	rain

The following story illustrates how poorly chosen language can obscure meaning:

A plumber who had only a limited command of English knew that hydrochloric acid opened clogged drainpipes quickly and effectively. What he didn't know, however, was whether it was the right thing to use. So, the plumber decided to check with the National Bureau of Standards in Washington, D.C. Seeking confirmation that hydrochloric acid was safe to use in pipes, he wrote the bureau a letter. After processing his letter, a scientist at the bureau wrote back this response: "The efficacy of hydrochloric acid is indisputable, but the corrosive residue is incompatible with metallic surfaces."

The plumber interpreted the scientist's response as a confirmation and wrote a second letter to the bureau thanking the scientist for the quick reply and for giving him the go-ahead to use hydrochloric acid.

The plumber's thank you note really bothered the scientist who showed it to a superior. His superior decided to write the plumber a second letter. This letter read, "We cannot assume responsibility for the production of toxic and noxious residue which hydrochloric acid can produce; we suggest that you use an alternative procedure."

Though this response left the plumber a bit baffled, he hurriedly sent the bureau a third letter telling them that he was pleased they agreed with him. "The acid was working just fine."

When this letter arrived, the scientist's superior sent it to the head administrator at the bureau. The head administrator ended the confusion by writing a short, simple note to the plumber: "Don't use hydrochloric acid. It eats the hell out of pipes."

The more difficult your language, the more likely your audience—particularly if unspecialized—will have difficulty understanding it. For this reason, before using the jargon of a field, always check whether audience members share the specialized vocabulary.

Keep It Concrete

Concrete words are specific when compared with abstract words, which tend to be general. Using concrete rather than abstract wording helps your audience members picture what you want them to. It leaves no doubt about your meaning, and it will help prevent possible misinterpretation of your message.

Remember, the more abstract the word, the more meanings people will have for it. Concrete words evoke more precise and vivid meanings. If you make a conscious effort to be more specific and less general, the speeches you deliver will become clearer, more interesting, and easier to remember. To reduce ambiguity, be concrete (see Table 11.2).

TABLE 11.2 ■ Using Concrete Language	
Instead Of	**Use**
expensive car	Mercedes-Benz
help the manufacturer	help the U.S. car manufacturer
livestock	cattle
dog	Bichon Frisé

Instead Of	Use
sound business principles	employee participation
a bundle	$1,000,000
be fair	use the same standard for all
help the homeless	volunteer at a soup kitchen
physical activity	aerobics

Indirect expressions, called **euphemisms**, make it easier for speakers to handle unpleasant subjects, but often they also make it harder for audiences to develop a clear and accurate perception of what the speaker is saying. Notice how your reactions are changed by the words used in the trios in Table 11.3.

TABLE 11.3 ■ Word Choice And Audience Perception		
put to sleep	euthanized	killed
loved one	dead body	corpse
slumber chamber	coffin	casket
misstatement	fabrication	lie
executive car	pre-owned car	used car
public school	free, nonprivate school	state-run school
sanitation engineer	refuse collector	garbage person

Pre-owned or used car? Choose your words carefully.

Istockphoto.com/tomeng

Receivers generally find the words in the first column less harsh and more pleasing, but do they convey the clearest meaning? How do the pictures they create in your mind differ from the pictures created by the words listed in the second and third columns?

A speaker's word choices play a role in our reaction to their speech. For example, the words *janitor* and *sanitary engineer* both mean *custodian*. Yet the terms have very different connotations. We frequently react to the words the speaker uses instead of to what the words actually refer. Receivers need to work hard to prevent a speaker's words from blinding them to what those words represent.

Keep It Appropriate

Phrase your speech with words that you understand and are comfortable using and that your audience will understand, accept, and respond to positively. Obscene, racist, ageist, or sexist remarks are usually judged offensive by audiences, reducing your credibility. Thus, common sense must prevail. Although we may use certain terms when conversing with our close friends, such expressions may be inappropriate in a speech. For example, in 2019, Tom Brokaw, a former NBC news anchor speaking on the news show *Meet the Press,* nonchalantly said, "Hispanics should work harder at assimilation." His belief that Hispanics needed to try harder to blend into American culture struck some as xenophobic since the word *assimilation* can be interpreted to mean denying one culture for another.[11]

Confront the Issue of Political Correctness

For some, **political correctness** means using words that convey respect for and sensitivity to the needs and interests of different groups. Thus, when we find ourselves speaking about various issues to audiences composed of persons who are culturally different from us, we may also find ourselves adapting our language so that it demonstrates our sensitivity to their perspectives and interests. For others, however, political correctness means that we feel compelled by societal pressures *not* to use some words for fear that doing so would cause members of our audience to perceive us as either racist or sexist. For example, some years back, David Howard, an aide to the then mayor of Washington, D.C., when referring to the budget, used the word *niggardly*. Howard's use of the word, meaning "stingy," caused a stir. The aide was compelled to resign even though the word used was unrelated to the N-word. (Using the term *N-word* in place of the actual word is also a form of political correctness.) Some try to do whatever is necessary to avoid offending anyone. Others, however, view political correctness as a very real danger to free speech. Which of these viewpoints comes closest to representing your own?

Use Unbiased Language

We can show our respect with words, but we can also use words to signal our lack of respect or contempt. Effective speakers seek to be inclusive, avoiding language that stereotypes others based on their sex, race, ethnicity, gender, sexual orientation, or disability.

Sexist language suggests that the two sexes are unequal and that one gender has more status and value and is more capable than the other. For example, in past decades, masculine words were used to include both males and females. But the use of *he* for he or she or *mankind* for the human race in written and spoken discourse excluded women by ignoring them. Today, using gender-neutral pronouns such as "they" in situations where the gender of the person is unknown or when speaking generally helps to diminish the presence of sexist language.

A sexist language practice called **spotlighting** was also used to reinforce the notion that men, not women, set the standard. Though a person was rarely described as a *male physician*, *male lawyer*, or *male physicist*, terms such as *woman doctor* and *female mathematician* were widely used. Today, however, spotlighting is rarer and we are somewhat more apt to substitute gender-inclusive terms, such as *chairperson* and *spokesperson*, and to use language that equalizes rather than highlights the treatment of gender.

Racist language expresses bigoted views about a person or persons from another group, based on a person's ideas of that race. Racist language dehumanizes the members of the group being attacked. It is the deliberate, purposeful, and hurtful use of words intended to oppress someone of a different race.[12]

Ageist language discriminates on the basis of age. U.S. culture tends to disparage the elderly and exalt the youthful. Negative stereotypes such as "She's an old hag," "She's set in her ways," or "He's losing his mind" abound. Ageism is often based on a distaste for and fear of growing older.[13] We need to decategorize individuals and change our expectations to improve our communication effectiveness with persons of all ages.[14]

Keep It Distinctive and Vivid

A distinctive speech grabs your attention. It paints an emotional picture that sears itself into your memory. Speakers accomplish this with vivid language. To speak vividly, you need to be a vivid thinker. You need to see a vivid mental picture in your mind's eye before passing it on. You must hear the cadence of your words and sense the rhythm of your speech's movement before expecting others to do so. To achieve vividness,

- Give yourself the freedom to think imaginatively

- Make a conscious effort to appeal to the senses, using figures of speech and selected sound patterns that add force to your thoughts

Using **figurative language** helps your audience picture your meaning, while the sound and rhythm of certain words help them sense your intensity (see Table 11.4). For instance, were you to deliver a speech on either of these competitive runners, Italy's Lamont Marcell Jacobs, the fastest man alive, or Jamaica's Elaine Thompson-Herah, the fastest woman alive, telling receivers that either runner ran like the wind would be more descriptive than saying they ran fast. Both figurative language and vivid speech will help you gain and sustain the attention of your audience.

TABLE 11.4 ■ Using Figurative Language	
A simile indirectly implies two unlike things are alike.	Her eyes are like daggers.
A metaphor makes a direct comparison between two things usually considered dissimilar.	She scrubbed so hard, her hands turned into steel wool.
Parallelism is the rhythmic repetition of words, phrases, or sentences.	We must act now to stop racism. We must act now to stop sexism. We must act now to stop hate.
Alliteration is repetition of initial consonant sounds in nearby words.	Fighters for freedom made their voices heard in Seneca Falls, Selma, and Stonewall.
Antithesis is one clause set in opposition to another.	Do you choose to go forward or backward, to triumph or fail?
Onomatopoeia is when a word or words imitates natural sounds.	The water whooshed through the pipes.
Hyperbole is deliberate exaggeration.	The acceptance of the policy will be the death of me.
Understatement draws attention to an idea by minimizing its importance.	As I cowered in the closet, it got a bit windy as the tornado passed over us.

Imagery is your partner in keeping your message vivid. Part of your task is to use words to create vivid mental pictures designed to influence how audience members see things, process your message, and share more fully in the speechmaking experience. Colorful and concrete words that appeal to the senses help awaken the imaginations of receivers, shortening the distance to your goal. Notice how civil rights leader Jesse Jackson used the image of a quilt to share an inclusive vision of America:

> America's not a blanket woven from one thread, one color, one cloth. When I was a child growing up in Greenville, South Carolina, and grandmother could not afford a blanket, she didn't complain and we did not freeze. Instead, she took pieces of old cloth—patches, wool, silk, gabardine, crokersack on the patches—barely good enough to wipe off your shoes with. But they didn't stay that way very long. With sturdy hands and a strong cord, she sewed them together into a quilt, a thing of beauty and power and culture.[15]

Jackson then went on to describe for receivers why the people of this country— its farmers, laborers, women, and mothers—needed to work together and pool their resources (their patches) to piece together such a quilt, one that would provide the people of this nation with health care, housing, jobs, and hope.

Use Figures of Speech

Using figures of speech makes ideas vivid. Words that suggest striking mental images add freshness and vitality to a speech.

Among the most commonly used figures of speech are similes and metaphors.[16] A **simile** is an indirect comparison of dissimilar things, usually with the words *like* or *as*.

Chief Seattle, a Native American leader, used effective similes to make his point:

> The white people are many. They are like the grass that covers vast prairies. My people are few. They resemble the scattering trees of a storm-swept plain.[17]

In contrast to a simile that builds an indirect comparison, a **metaphor** builds a direct identification by omitting the words *like* or *as*. In a metaphor, two things not usually considered alike are compared directly, and their relationship is implied. Professional speaker and writer Wayne Dyer used a metaphor when he wrote,

> Your body is nothing more than the garage where you temporarily park your soul.[18]

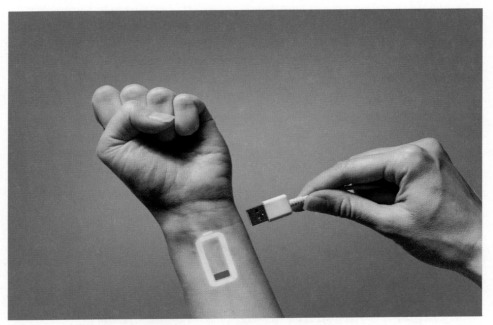

Recharge your batteries. A figure of speech can help an idea stick in your audience's heads.
iStockPhoto.com/Anna Gorbacheva

In this example, the metaphor used helped give concreteness to a more abstract concept. Metaphors enhance the audience's ability to visualize the speaker's message.

Use Sound and Rhythm

Sound and rhythmic patterns can also help improve a speech. Consider using parallelism, alliteration, and antithesis.

Parallelism makes your speech vivid through the repetition of words, phrases, or sentences. In his "I Have a Dream" speech, Martin Luther King Jr. buttressed the forcefulness of his message by adding parallelism and figures of speech to it:

> One hundred years later, we must face the tragic fact that the Negro is still not free. One hundred years later, the life of the Negro is still sadly crippled by the manacles of segregation and the chains of discrimination. One hundred years later, the Negro lives in a lonely island of poverty in the midst of a vast ocean of material prosperity. One hundred years later, the Negro is still languishing in the corners of American society and finds himself in exile in his own land.[19]

Each time King used the phrase "one hundred years later" and evoked an image of the plight faced by African Americans a century after the abolishment of slavery, he was using parallelism.

Alliteration is the repetition of initial consonant sounds in nearby words. For example, the Wizard in the film *The Wizard of Oz* called the Scarecrow a "billowing bale of bovine fodder." In a speech she gave before becoming Vice President of the United States, Kamala Harris used alliteration telling audience members: "When white supremacists march and murder in Charlottesville, or massacre innocent worshippers at a Pittsburgh synagogue, that's not our America."[20]

Read "The Raven." Edgar Allan Poe's famous poem includes alliteration abundantly.

iStockPhoto.com/Schoenfeld

Antithesis, another means of adding vividness to a speech, achieves its objective by presenting opposites within the same or adjoining sentences. By juxtaposing contrasting ideas, the speaker can sharpen the message and clarify a point. Former Urban League spokesperson Whitney M. Young Jr. relied on antithesis to relay this message:

> We seek not to weaken America but to strengthen it; not to decry America but to purify it; not to separate America but to become part of it.[21]

By pointing out opposites, antithesis increases the dramatic impact of a speaker's message.

Onomatopoeia, a word or words imitating natural sounds, also enhances vividness. For instance, in a speech on impending water shortages, one student asked her audience what they would do if the water from their shower was never a splash, but just a slow *drip, drip, drip.*

Hyperbole is the use of extreme exaggeration for effect. One speaker, for example, used hyperbole to indicate the effects of layoffs during the pandemic: "If we fail to provide assistance to employers now," she noted, "every worker in this country will be on unemployment." Although hyperbole can help a speaker to make their point, some believe that because it requires the speaker to exaggerate, the audience may perceive the speaker to be lying. However, when used for emphasis or to spur the imagination of receivers, hyperbole can be effective.

Understatement is hyperbole's opposite, drawing attention to an idea by minimizing its importance. For example, in a speech on how God has been depicted in popular culture, a speaker referred to a scene in the film *Bruce Almighty* in which a room virtually explodes with light when God enters. The film's main character, Bruce, however, describes the room as being only "kinda bright." Bruce's words, spoken upon his meeting God for the first time, are an example of understatement.

When used appropriately, each of these speechmaking devices can make your message more striking, your ideas more intense, and your presentation more vivid. So remember, choose your words carefully and arrange your phrases and sentences creatively, and you will bring your speech to life.

Keep It Personal

Use the personal pronouns *I, us, me, we,* and *you* in your speech. The audience wants to know what you think and what you feel. They want to know you are including them in your thoughts, relating your ideas to them. After all, your speech is for them. Melinda French Gates, the former wife of Bill Gates with whom she partners in the Bill and Melinda Gates Foundation, relied on personalization to connect with the audience in a speech she gave at Duke University:

> Some people assume that Bill and I are too rich to make a connection with someone who's poor, even if our intentions are good. But adjectives like rich and poor don't define who any of us truly are as human beings. And they don't make any one individual less human than the next. The universe is like computer code in that way. Binary. There is life, and there is everything else. Zeroes and ones. I'm a one. You're a one. My friend in the Himalayas is a one.[22]

Despite having great wealth, Melissa Gates succeeded in establishing a personal connection with her audience.

COACHING TIP

"Our language is the reflection of ourselves. A language is an exact reflection of the character and growth of its speakers."

—Cesar Chavez, American civil rights activist

Words, like people, have the power to sway and influence people. Choose your words to help receivers share your vision.

USE ORAL STYLE

11.3   *Adopt an oral style.*

When you create a speech, you create it to be heard and listened to, not read and reread. As a result, you should use an oral rather than a written style. How we speak is very different from how we write. Written and oral styles differ from each other in a number of important ways. Consider the following oral style characteristics:

- **Oral style is more personal than written style.** When delivering a speech, you are able to talk directly to your audience and invite participation in ways a writer cannot. Thus, you want to keep a speech conversational, using everyday language, personal pronouns, and short sentences and descriptive words and phrases that have ear appeal.

- **Oral style is more repetitive than written style.** Listeners cannot rehear what you have said, as they can reread a page of text. They cannot replay your words as they can with a YouTube video. They cannot put you on "pause" to give themselves time to think about what's been said. As a result, use previews, signposts, and transitions to guide the audience, letting your receivers know what's to come. Mix in more repetition and reinforcement. By repeating and restating your ideas, you let listeners know what is important and what they need to remember.

- **Oral style is much *less formal* than written style.** While written discourse often contains abstract ideas, complex phrases, and a sophisticated vocabulary, simpler sentences and shorter words and phrases characterize the oral style. Complex sentence structure and unfamiliar words, while appreciated in written discourse, can confuse receivers when spoken.

- **Oral style is *more adaptive and interactive* than written style.** Since you are looking directly at your listeners, you can get immediate feedback and respond in turn. Like a DJ who revises a playlist based on crowd feedback, should you detect receivers are missing your point, you can adjust by restating or providing another example. The audience influences you as you seek to influence them.

The language of public speaking is less like the language of an essayist and more like the language of a skilled conversationalist. Listeners are better able to retain and recall a speech when it is filled with everyday colloquial expressions, clear transitions, personal pronouns, and questions that invite participation than when it is composed of abstract language, complex sentences, and impersonal references. If you want your audience to remember what you say, make them feel more comfortable by using an oral style. A speech is not mailed to an audience; it is delivered aloud.

SELF-ASSESSMENT 11.1: ARE YOU USING AN ORAL STYLE?

Directions

Use the following questions to evaluate if you can create a speech that is easy for the audience to listen to. Simply respond to each statement.

Questions/Statements	Never	Rarely	Sometimes	Usually	Always
1. I seek to make my message personal, using lots of personal pronouns.	1	2	3	4	5
2. I use easy to understand language.	1	2	3	4	5
3. I keep the sentences in my speech short.	1	2	3	4	5
4. I use repetition and restatement to increase memorability.	1	2	3	4	5
5. I rely on transitions to cue the audience.	1	2	3	4	5
6. I avoid using unfamiliar words.	1	2	3	4	5
7. I rely on feedback from the audience to adapt my message.	1	2	3	4	5
8. I make my speech as conversational as possible.	1	2	3	4	5
9. I use words that appeal to the ear rather than the eye.	1	2	3	4	5
10. I use colloquial expressions in my speech.	1	2	3	4	5

Scoring Method	Add together your scores for each question. _____ Total
Scoring Calculation	The higher your total score, the better your understanding of oral style.
Feedback	What have you discovered about how to keep your speech listener friendly? Although this evaluation is not a scientific instrument, it should give you some indication of what to include in speech introductions and conclusions.

GAME PLAN

Choosing Your Words

- I have researched my topic and reviewed my notes for any words that may cause confusion or misunderstanding among members of my audience.

- I have used plain, unbiased, and respectful language that makes my message clear for my audience to understand.

- I have chosen words that reflect my views of political correctness, but I have also taken into account the need to avoid being sexist, racist, or ageist.

- In choosing my words, I have used figurative language in ways that make my ideas clearer yet more evocative.

- While practicing my speech, I listened for the sound and rhythm of my words, adjusting the wording to use one or more of the following techniques: parallelism, alliteration, antithesis, onomatopoeia, hyperbole, and understatement.

- Finally, while practicing my speech, I paid attention to and developed my own oral style, translating my sentence outline into an extemporaneous one that utilizes repetition and a certain degree of informality.

EXERCISES

Word Matters

Mastering the ability to use words to create speechmaking power plays is integral to your success as a speechmaker.

1. Weave a Word Tapestry

Just as *war, defensive response*, and *massacre* can be words that indicate the same event to different people, consider the 10 words below. Create a figure of speech for each one that evokes fresh images in the minds of different audiences. Decide which choice of word would work best for you and might elicit the response you want from listeners.

1. a distinctive speech
2. immigration
3. a high-school education
4. a dream-job
5. birth
6. marriage
7. racism
8. this text
9. football
10. your speechmaking ability

2. Be Word Wise

You have been asked to give a speech on a popular technology—perhaps Instagram, Snapchat, Periscope, Twitter, or another of your choice. What words would you think appropriate to describe this medium in a speech to your class? How would your word choices change if you were to deliver the speech to an audience of grandparents? What adaptations would be needed, and why?

3. Analyze the Words Used

When giving a speech titled "Campus Sexual Harassment Policies," a student speaker used a number of hypothetical examples. Featured in the examples were two fictional characters the speaker called Dave Stud and Diane Sex Object. Though a number of students laughed when they heard the names, others were offended and objected vocally at the speech's conclusion, noting that the speaker's word choices were sexist.

- Consider your own response. Even if you understand that the speaker didn't mean to offend, would you advise that they cut these words from their next delivery of the speech?

- Is there another way to achieve the same goals of the speech with different words? If so, which words would you choose?

4. Approach the Speaker's Stand

Choose a controversial current event as a subject. Develop two 2-minute speeches that express very different positions—the first containing words and figures of speech that are likely to bias listeners in favor of the subject, the second containing words and figures of speech that are likely to bias them against it.

Deliver both speeches in class. Ask class members which version they find more effective, and why.

RECAP AND REVIEW

11.1 Explain the nature of language, choosing words for your speech that will share meaning and resonate with the audience.

The Triangle of Meaning—a model of the relationships among words, thoughts, and things—depicts how words work. Its primary message is that words and things are only indirectly related to each other through the thoughts of people. Words are symbols. Effective speakers choose words that connect with receivers. Both the message a speaker communicates to an audience and the meaning receivers extract are a result of the words used by the speaker. When words are used effectively, they have the power to unite, evoke fresh images, and encourage a desired response. Public speakers seek to use words that demonstrate their consideration of the audience. Denotative meaning is a word's dictionary meaning. Connotative meaning is subjective and includes the feelings and personal associations that a word stimulates. The meaning we give to words changes due to time and geographical location. Speakers need to be sensitive to how people from different generations and different parts of the world use language.

11.2 Strategically select your words based on understandability, contextual suitability, and tone.

A public speaker accomplishes this by adhering to the following word choice guidelines: keep it simple, keep it concrete, keep it appropriate, and keep it vivid. In addition to facilitating an oral style, these guidelines enable receivers to share the meanings a speaker has in mind.

11.3 Adopt an oral style.

An oral style usually contains short sentences, colloquial expressions, clear transitions, and simpler words than writing. It is also more informal, more inviting of participation, more personal, more concrete, and more repetitive.

KEY TERMS

Ageist language (p. 247)

Alliteration (p. 250)

Antithesis (p. 251)

Connotative meaning (p. 239)

Denotative meaning (p. 239)

Euphemism (p. 245)

Figurative language (p. 247)

Hyperbole (p. 251)

Jargon and technospeak (p. 243)

Metaphor (p. 249)

Onomatopoeia (p. 251)

Political correctness (p. 246)

Racist language (p. 247)

Sexist language (p. 247)

Simile (p. 249)

Spotlighting (p. 247)

Triangle of Meaning (p. 237)

Understatement (p. 251)

istockphoto.com/globalstock

12 DELIVERY MODES AND PRACTICE

UPON COMPLETING THIS CHAPTER, YOU WILL BE ABLE TO

12.1   Distinguish among the following speech delivery modes: impromptu, manuscript, extemporaneous, speaking from memory, and sound bite, describing their impact on a speech.

12.2   Use an effective regimen for preparing and practicing your speech.

12.3   Evaluate your readiness to deliver the speech.

Does delivery make a difference? Yes! A speaker's delivery makes or breaks their speech. Having something to say is only half the battle. The other half is using the right delivery mode to convey a message effectively and with sincerity.[1] Good delivery connects speaker and audience. When you deliver a speech well, it tells your audience that you care about your topic and them. It helps your audience interpret your message appropriately, and it closes whatever gap may exist between you. Because good delivery feels natural and is conversational in tone, it also sounds as if you are talking *with* rather than *at* audience members. In other words, good delivery helps you sound spontaneous, as though you were speaking the words in your presentation for the very first time.[2]

There are a number of delivery options. The five modes we review here are: (1) impromptu, (2) manuscript, (3) extemporaneous, (4) speaking from memory, and (5) sound bite. It is important to understand the rationales for each, set a goal, work on your delivery, and monitor your progress—just as an elite athlete does when preparing for game day.

COACHING TIP

"Public speaking is a perfectly normal act . . . which calls . . . only for an extension and development of that most familiar act, conversation."

—James Albert Winans, one of the founders of the
Speech Association of America

Be natural. Be positive. Be prepared. Be real. Your delivery should not sound phony or stilted. Use a conversational tone, and you will be better able to connect with and relate directly to the members of your audience.

DIFFERENTIATE AMONG DELIVERY MODES

12.1   *Distinguish among the following speech delivery modes: impromptu, manuscript, extemporaneous, speaking from memory, and sound bite, describing their impact on a speech.*

When the option is yours, how do you decide if it will be more appropriate to make a few impromptu remarks, read from a manuscript, speak extemporaneously, deliver a memorized speech, or present a sound bite for media consumption with the hope it will be retweeted and go viral? You base your choice of delivery mode on the nature of the speaking occasion, the speech's purpose, and your speaking strengths and abilities.

Whichever you use or are assigned, you need to adapt to it. The mode of delivery should not call attention to itself. The audience needs to be free to concentrate on your ideas, not your mode of delivery. Each of the styles is appropriate for different occasions, purposes, and speakers (see Table 12.1).

TABLE 12.1 ■ Delivery Modes and Likely Uses	
Delivery Mode	**Likely Use**
Impromptu	When you are asked to speak at a moment's notice
Manuscript	When precise wording is crucial; when you need to avoid being misquoted
Extemporaneous	When you are given sufficient time to prepare, develop a working outline or speaker's notes, and practice
Memorization	When delivering a brief special occasion speech, such as a toast or speech of introduction; when no lengthy quotations or statistical proof are required
Sound bite/Twitter-speak	When you need to provide a quotable, tweetable statement

Impromptu Speaking

Impromptu speaking requires that you be able to think on your feet. While an impromptu speech is delivered at a moment's notice, and usually without any preparation, the humorist Mark Twain is credited with saying, "It usually takes more than three weeks to prepare a good impromptu speech."[3] What Twain likely meant is that it can be challenging to deliver an effective impromptu speech. How did you feel the last time you were put on the spot and asked to say a few words? Perhaps someone asked you to describe yourself in an interview, answer a question in class, or explain your position during a meeting. Were you ready to respond without extensive time to plan, prepare, or practice? You are likely to give at least one, if not many, impromptu speeches daily, and at least some of the public speaking you will do during your business or professional life will probably be unplanned.[4]

All you really have to rely on when delivering an impromptu talk is your knowledge and previous experience. If you are adept at gathering your thoughts quickly and summarizing them succinctly, then you always will be prepared to deliver an impromptu speech. You can apply all the lessons you've learned about delivering planned speeches—the principles of effective structure, support, and delivery—to the impromptu situation. Though unplanned speaking may seem unnatural or awkward to you, it offers you both flexibility and the opportunity to demonstrate your speaking versatility. Perhaps more than any other speechmaking style, delivering an impromptu speech helps you reveal to others who you are, what you are like, and what genuinely concerns you.[5]

Using an acronym can help you stay focused and on message when delivering an impromptu speech. One acronym is **PREP**. P: state your *point*. R: state a *reason* why the point is important.

E: give an *example* to support your point. P: reiterate your *point* or segue to the next one. An alternative acronym is **FAT**. F: express your *feelings* about the subject. A: share a relevant *anecdote*. T: *tie* the story you told back to your subject.

When called on to deliver an impromptu speech, also remember the following guidelines:

- Compose yourself.

- Think about your purpose.

- Relate the subject to what you know and have experienced and receiver interests.

- Organize your talk—connect your ideas to each other, and be certain to use an introduction, body, and conclusion.

- Don't ramble. Keep it brief, covering just two to three points.

- Stay on message.

One advantage of impromptu speaking is that audience expectations are likely to be more realistic. If you follow the directions above and give a strong impromptu speech that builds on your life experience, you should succeed in impressing the audience.

Officially speaking. Formal speaking occasions, such as official proclamations, may require speaking from a manuscript.

iStockPhoto.com/Bet_Noire

Manuscript Reading

When first running for president back in 2016, Donald Trump spent much of his campaign mocking his rivals for their dependence on teleprompters, saying, "If you run for president, you shouldn't be allowed to use teleprompters, because you don't even know if the guy is smart."[6] Ultimately, Trump was forced to use one himself, and was criticized by others for his inability to use the teleprompter effectively. Trump was more at home in impromptu settings. He found it difficult to meet the challenge of more formal speaking demands, often sounding like he was reading his lines, and creating the impression that he was overscripted. Yet if Trump misread a line or went off script, he was accused of being unprepared. Trump's misstatements and off-hand comments would undermine his scripted message, becoming fodder for his critics. For example, let's look at the difference in a Trump scripted response and a subsequent off-the-cuff tweet given after the Stoneman Douglass High School shooting in Florida:[7]

Trump's scripted response, February 15, 2018: "I want to speak now directly to America's children, especially those who feel lost, alone, confused or even scared: I want you to know that you are never alone and you never will be. You have people who care about you, who love you, and who will do anything at all to protect you. If you need help, turn to a teacher, a family member, a local police officer, or a faith leader. Answer hate with love; answer cruelty with kindness."

Trump's tweet, February 17, 2018: "Very sad that the FBI missed all of the many signals sent out by the Florida school shooter. This is not acceptable. They are spending too much time trying to prove Russian collusion with the Trump campaign—there is no collusion. Get back to the basics and make us all proud!"

In general, speakers serving in important political and organizational positions are expected to become very comfortable using the teleprompter as a means of ensuring that they stick to their intended message.

Manuscript reading requires that you write a manuscript in full and deliver it word for word. At the same time, because reading aloud well requires every bit as much skill as mastering a script and delivering it expressively, manuscript reading is not as easy as it sounds. If you do not invest a lot of time practicing reading your manuscript aloud, you could end up *eye-* and *hand-tied* to your manuscript and deprive your audience of meaningful eye contact and gesturing.

Bringing the printed page to life for listeners requires that you take your eyes off the manuscript and close the communicative gap between you and your audience. If you read in a monotone, you will bore receivers. The reading of your speech needs to sound like conversation to your listeners. It needs to sound as though you are speaking rather than reading it, or it will not have the impact you desire. This requires that vocal cues (delivering lines with ease) and physical cues (no poorly timed gestures or inappropriate smiles) also support delivery (see Chapter 13).

Because the manuscript directs the speaker, it affords a speaker less flexibility. Another downside is that the audience also may doubt the speaker's ownership of ideas being shared. A manuscript, however, is beneficial when a speaker needs to be especially careful about the phrasing of a problem or policy. Presidential, foreign policy, and political addresses; official proclamations; and presentations at business, trade, and stockholder meetings—occasions where a slip of the tongue could be disastrous—are appropriate settings for a manuscript speech. In addition, when time is strictly limited, a manuscript speech may be the right choice.

When the demands of the occasion make manuscript delivery necessary, remember the following:

- Write the speech to be listened to; the audience will not be reading along with you.

- Be sure to use a font that is easy to read and large enough to see.

- Mark up the manuscript with delivery cues. Focus on communicating ideas, not words.

- Practice reading it aloud so your words sound fresh.

- Become so familiar with the manuscript that you are able to maintain eye contact and integrate appropriate gestures.

Extemporaneous Speaking

When a speech is prepared and practiced in advance but is neither written out word for word nor memorized, it is most likely an example of **extemporaneous speaking**. Falling between impromptu speaking and manuscript speaking, an extemporaneous speech sounds impromptu but is planned and detailed. It is the kind of speech used most frequently in public speaking classes and by professional speakers. The extemporaneous speaker delivers a speech using only speaker's notes as a reminder. Partly because the speaker selects the exact words virtually at the moment of their delivery, the language seems more natural and spontaneous. When the speech is not memorized, the speaker can exhibit a more conversational quality. When a speech is not read from a script, the speaker can maintain generous eye contact. Extemporaneous speaking facilitates the monitoring of audience reactions and adjusting to the feedback received. As a result, the extemporaneous speaker establishes a more direct connection with audience members.

The emphasis in extemporaneous speaking is on communication, not recitation or memorization. It requires that the speaker be flexible enough to adapt to the audience and demands extensive planning, organization, and practice. An accomplished extemporaneous speaker sounds spontaneous. Because it connects well with audiences and because it builds speaker confidence, extemporaneous speaking is the method preferred by most public speaking teachers and experienced speakers alike.

To prepare a good extemporaneous speech, remember to

- Research the topic thoroughly

- Create an outline and speaker's notes

- Rehearse, familiarizing yourself with the organizational pattern, including the introduction and conclusion

- Speak conversationally

- Become so comfortable with the topic that you are able to adjust your speech, adapting to the audience as needed

Take note. Extemporaneous speeches are delivered conversationally, with the support of speaker's notes.

iStock.com/Bronwyn8

Speaking From Memory

When you write your speech out in full, memorize it, and then recite it word for word for an audience without using a manuscript, outline, or speaker's notes, you are speaking from memory. Speaking from memory, also known as oratory, requires considerable skill and speaking expertise. For one thing, the pressures brought about by the actual presentation could cause you to draw a blank at any point during the speech. Should that occur, instead of listening to you speak, your audience faces a stunning silence as you grope for the words you lost. When you speak from memory, you attempt to deliver your speech word for word, and that makes it even more difficult for you to recover if you make a mistake.

The tension you feel when delivering a memorized speech could affect your delivery in other ways, too. Your delivery could come off as stiff, stilted, and unnatural rather than flexible, friendly, and relaxed. Because you are afraid to deviate from your memorized text for fear of forgetting something, your ability to respond easily to audience feedback might also be inhibited. The danger for some speakers is that they come off sounding mechanical, making this a technique they should not rely on unless absolutely necessary.

Memorizing a speech does, however, offer certain advantages. It is much easier to establish and sustain eye contact with the members of the audience when you don't have to continually look down at a manuscript or notes. Your hands also are freer to gesture and support the meaning of your message.

Although there certainly are a number of speaking occasions that lend themselves to speaking from memory, including toasts and testimonials, acceptance speeches, speeches of introduction, and eulogies, the bulk of your speechmaking experiences will be a composite of the remaining delivery methods. Of course, even when using these, you might find it useful to memorize some sections of your speech, such as the introduction, conclusion, or a particularly effective quotation, but in general, try to avoid having to memorize an entire speech.

When delivering a speech or even a section of a speech from memory, keep these techniques in mind:

- Rehearse sufficiently to sound natural.

- Keep your energy high.

- Use appropriate nonverbal cues to reinforce the spoken words.

Sound Bite Speaking (Twitter-Speak)

Attention spans are shrinking. Contemporary audiences lack the patience to listen to long-winded speakers who, as a result, are going the way of the dinosaurs. Although some instructors caution students to steer clear of sound bite speaking or Twitter-speak in class, you may be involved in some speaking situations that require mastery of this format. Contemporary speakers often are called upon to respond to our "headline society." Rather than offering long-winded, verbose responses, they need to speak to the point and offer a Twitter-friendly statement that has the chance of going viral.

During political conventions or events, after the delivery of speeches by public figures, or in the course of introducing new policies or programs, spokespersons, pundits, and politicians "spin their messages," frequently using sound bites—short, memorable statements that can be tweeted after being delivered aurally. Because audiences today are impatient for information, speakers need to be able to distill their messages effectively. Notice in Table 12.2 how speakers can lose or hold the attention of receivers by the way they package a thought.

TABLE 12.2 ■ Idea Packages

Dull and Forgettable	Interesting and Memorable
The two leading ways to achieve success are improving upon existing technology and diminishing the larger obligation.	The two leading recipes for success are building a better mousetrap and finding a bigger loophole. —Edgar A. Schoaff
To construct an amalgam, you have to be willing to split open its component parts.	To make an omelette, you have to be willing to break a few eggs. —Robert Penn Warren
Capital will not produce great pleasure, but it will remunerate a large research staff to examine the questions proposed for a solution.	Money won't buy happiness, but it will pay the salaries of a large research staff to study the problem. —Bill Vaughan

Keep these techniques in mind when delivering a sound bite or Twitter-speak:

- Develop a sentence or two that captures your subject's essence.

- Make your comments memorable.

- Abbreviate the speech until it is tweet-size—280 characters. You might also create a visually interesting 6- to 15-second video to accompany it, like those featured on TikTok and Twitter, which now carries the Vine archive. Though Vine originally popularized the short-form video, it was replaced by the 6.5-second app Byte. Byte, like Twitter, allows content creators to capture attention and create a following. It has also been called "the Instagram of video."[8]

SELF-ASSESSMENT 12.1: DELIVERY MODE ANALYSIS: WHAT'S YOUR STYLE?

Directions

Use the following continua to evaluate your preference when it comes to impromptu, extemporaneous, manuscript, memorization, and sound bite delivery modes.

Statement	Completely True 5	Mostly True 4	Somewhat True 3	Mostly False 2	Completely False 1
1. I like delivering a speech on the spur of the moment, because it sounds genuine to the audience.					
2. I am up to the challenge of organizing my thoughts quickly when speaking off the cuff.					
3. I find having to think on my feet without any notes or script energizing.					
4. I become a more confident presenter when I have time to prepare a speech, creating and using speaker's notes.					

Statement	Completely True 5	Mostly True 4	Somewhat True 3	Mostly False 2	Completely False 1
5. When using speaker's notes to deliver a speech, I am able to maintain eye contact, speak directly to the audience, and sound spontaneous and conversational.					
6. Having adequate time to prepare a speech is important to me.					
7. When speaking from a manuscript, I do not sound mechanical.					
8. I am most confident when I know in advance the exact words I will be speaking during my presentation.					
9. Neither I nor my audience find my script distracting.					
10. I am up to the challenge of memorizing a speech.					
11. Though it requires extensive practice, and word-for-word memory, I am comfortable speaking without notes or a script.					
12. When speaking from memory, audience members still find me sincere.					
13. I believe the guiding principle of speechmaking should be to keep it short and sweet.					
14. I like to be able to give a one-sentence summary of the idea behind a speech.					
15. A bite-sized idea + a byte-sized video = a viral speech.					

Mode Analysis	Implications
Add together the numbers you chose for each of the following sets of questions.	What do your scores reveal about your speaking style preferences and personal comfort with different kinds of presentations?
To determine your level of comfort speaking impromptu, add together your scores for questions 1–3. Total: _____	To what extent do your preferences and strengths support the kinds of presentations you give in class or at work?
To determine your level of comfort speaking extemporaneously, add together your scores for questions 4–6. Total: _____	
To determine your level of comfort speaking from a manuscript, add together your scores for questions 7–9. Total: _____	
To determine your level of comfort memorizing a script, add together your scores for questions 10–12. Total: _____	
To determine your level of comfort creating a sound bite, add together your scores for questions 13–15. Total: _____	
To determine your overall comfort delivering a speech, add the five scores together. _____ 75 You easily adapt to any mode of delivery. 50–74 You have significant mode flexibility. 24–49 You likely favor one or more styles of delivery over other styles. 1–23 You likely have a favorite speaking style and have not displayed a willingness to master other styles.	

PREPARE AND PRACTICE

> **12.2** *Use an effective regimen for preparing and practicing your speech.*

"If I'm supposed to sound spontaneous and natural, as if I'm giving my speech for the first time, why do I need to rehearse it?" asks the novice speechmaker. This question has several answers. Just as an athlete practices a play until it is second nature, so a speechmaker needs to rehearse their speech until it becomes "one" with them. For athletes, every move matters. Once they know a play cold—so they don't need to think about where they should be on the field— they are free to focus their attention on what the other team does. For speakers and athletes, it is thinking ahead and practicing that get them to this point. The old adage, "Practice makes perfect," also has merit—if you practice correctly. Aspirants to political office know this well.

Prior to the presidential debates, for example, candidates typically spend weeks preparing, including viewing their past performances and engaging in mock debates that are recorded and reviewed.

How often and in what sequence should you practice? As much as it takes to succeed. Although rehearsal is a highly individual matter, we can provide you with some basic practice advice to ensure you practice right.

Practice makes perfect. Like athletes and actors, speakers need to practice regularly to improve performance.

istockphoto.com/HAKINMHAN

Schedule Multiple Early Practices

Don't make time your enemy. Begin practicing at least half a week before you will deliver the speech. Do not wait for the night before. Practicing well ahead of the delivery date lets you master the message.

In early practice sessions, repeatedly read through your manuscript, outline, and/or notes. If you will be delivering a manuscript speech or a speech from memory, rehearse using a triple-spaced manuscript with large and easy-to-read type that you mark up to indicate which words and phrases to stress, when to speed up and slow down, and when to pause. If you will be delivering an extemporaneous speech, after rehearsing initially with your outline, remember to refine that outline into speaker's notes. Begin by reading it over a number of times before you speak it aloud. As you rehearse, develop a list of key words and phrases from that outline and place them on no more than a handful of note cards. Write on one side of the card only. From then on, use the cards to spark your memory. Be sure to print quotations and statistics in large letters on separate cards, but do not reproduce complete paragraphs or the entire speech on these cards. Also, be sure to number the cards to avoid fumbling through them when you are in front of the audience.

Scheduling. Plan your practice times in advance to make sure you don't get stuck memorizing a lot in a little amount of time.

iStockPhoto.com/Bet_Noire

Keep in mind that, though many students use note cards, most professional speakers do not, preferring instead to use a single sheet of paper containing their key words and phrases, quotations, expert testimony, and key statistics, or embedding it on their tablet or smartphone. When used alone or together with any visual aids the speaker plans to use, this page usually suffices.

Verbalize Everything

Practice your delivery of every example and illustration, recite every quotation, and say aloud every statistic you plan to use. Familiarity begets clarity and comfort in public speaking. Without sufficient practice, you won't build the self-confidence you need to deliver an effective presentation.

Practice With Your Visual, Audio, and Memory Aids

If you will be using visual, audio, or memory aids during the speech, work with them during your practice sessions. This will help you work out any kinks, electronic or otherwise, and will make your delivery of the speech smoother and more natural.

Check Your Time

Time your presentation. If it is too long, cut out nonessential information and redundant examples. Tighten your phrasing. You might even need to eliminate one of your key points. If your speech is too short, make it more substantial. You might add another main point or include another illustration or example.

Replicate Actual Speechmaking Conditions

Do your best to mirror the actual conditions and setting you will experience when giving your speech. Although sitting down and running through the speech in your head is useful early in your preparation to increase your familiarity with your speech's content, standing in front of an audience is different. Make sure you practice the speech standing up and hold a realistic dress rehearsal, ideally in a room as much as possible like the one in which you will actually deliver the speech. And run through the entire speech rather than continually stopping.

DECIDE IF YOU'RE READY

> **12.3**   *Evaluate your readiness to deliver the speech.*

Bleep Common Practice Bloopers

Your goal is to feel fully ready to deliver a peak performance. To reach this point, you need to avoid common practice bloopers.

- *Preparing mentally does not replace preparing aurally.* Though thinking through your speech is helpful, it should never replace live practice sessions in which you rehearse your speech aloud.

- *Don't wait to be given feedback.* It's important to seek feedback, not count on others to give it on their own. Ask your mock audience(s) what they think and feel about your speech.

- *Don't skip practice sessions.* Skipping practice is a sign of overconfidence. Telling yourself you have it down when the truth is you need to continue working does a disservice to both you and your audience.

Watch and Listen to Yourself Alone and With Others

It is important to monitor your progress. During your preparation, you should seek feedback before doing your final polishing and running a last dress rehearsal. Get feedback while you still have time to make and master changes.

Video your rehearsal and play it back for self-evaluation. Rehearse in front of friends and family and get feedback from them. Practicing in front of other people has been shown to improve the actual performance.[9]

Give Yourself a Preliminary Evaluation

Pay attention to what works and what needs work. As you review your performance, ask yourself whether you are expressing your ideas as clearly as you would like to. Do you have an attention-getter? Is your language understandable to audience members? Is the support you used adequate? Is the organization easy to follow? Does your conclusion contain both a summary and a psychological appeal? Keep in mind that an organized speech will be easier to remember because it will flow logically.

Refine, Practice, and Refine

In your last stage of practicing, the focus is on refining, not dramatically altering the speech. Practice. Practice. Practice. Make your final rehearsal as realistic as possible.

Attend to Nonverbal Aspects of Delivery

Pay attention to your use of nonverbal cues during your practice sessions. Ask your rehearsal audiences whether you make enough eye contact, employ meaningful gestures, and use your voice and appearance to advantage (techniques we cover in more detail in Chapter 13).

Hold a Mock Q&A Session

While not all speeches are followed with a question-and-answer (Q&A) session, knowing how to handle one can be just as important as preparing yourself to deliver the speech. Though the Q&A has much in common with the impromptu speech, there are things you can do to prepare yourself. You can

- Anticipate some of the questions audience members will ask, and prepare answers to them in advance
- Think about questions you hope audience members won't ask, and prepare answers for them
- Prepare a "Tip Sheet" with points to remember when answering particularly complex questions
- Have someone rehearse you by asking you the potential questions you've brainstormed as well as others designed to unnerve you
- Repeat a question aloud if it is phrased in a neutral manner, before answering it; if necessary, you can rephrase it to remove any venomous or loaded words

- Practice saying, "I don't know," if you don't know. You still have time to find out the answers prior to the delivery day. And if you have to answer a question with an "I don't know" on delivery day, promise to find out the answer and get back to the person who posed the question

- Remember, you don't need to answer more than is asked

(We cover the Q&A session in more depth in Chapter 24.)

GAME PLAN

Refining My Speech Delivery

- After considering my speech topic, the occasion, and my own level of comfort, I have chosen the delivery mode that will enable me to really connect with the audience.

- Given the delivery mode I've chosen to use, my speaking notes are clear, easy to follow, and marked with delivery cues such as "refer to slide," "play video," "slow down for impact," or "stress this word."

- I've practiced my speech several times; at this point, I know the organization and my notes so well that I can adjust to different audience reactions.

- The idea of a question-and-answer session makes me a little nervous, so I held a mock Q&A in which I answered some of the questions I anticipate will be asked.

- To control any anxiety I may experience, I've reviewed some of the confidence-building techniques from Chapter 1.

- I've reviewed video of other accomplished speakers, and through my practice sessions, I have a sense of what will work for me and what won't in reaching my audience.

EXERCISES

Delivery

Prepare and practice so that when you present, you're confident and professional.

1. Get More Comfortable in Front of Others

Prepare a manuscript or notes for a two-minute talk on one of the following topics: A Time My Beliefs Were Challenged; A Space or Environment Where I Felt Out of Place; To Tweet or Not to Tweet; The Best Advice I Have Ever Received; or My Favorite Things About My Hometown.[10] Deliver your talk in three ways: (1) read it word for word, (2) speak from memory, (3) speak using notes. It's okay if it's not perfect; just get a feel for the difference in styles and practice. Remember to refer back to the guidelines for each speaking style.

2. Getting to Know You: Introducing the Q&A

Choose something to "show" that tells others about you—perhaps something personal that you use to distinguish yourself from others, such as your phone's ringtone(s), a favorite pair of shoes, an unusual necklace, a special photo from Facebook or Instagram. Your audience will ask you questions about why you chose the item you did, what your choice means, why you think it distinguishes you, and so on. Be prepared to give impromptu answers.

3. How Talk Show Talents Do It

Compare and contrast the opening monologues of two late-night talk show hosts; for example, you might compare Jimmy Fallon with Jimmy Kimmel. Explain what distinguishes one performer's style from the other.

4. Analyze a Politician's Delivery

View a video of former president Donald Trump's speech given at his inauguration in January 2017 and a video of Joe Biden's speech given at his inauguration in 2021. Then do the following:

1. Identify and evaluate the effectiveness of the style(s) of delivery Trump and Biden used, providing specific examples that speak to their ability to build rapport, make an argument, and forcefully make their case.

2. Compare and contrast Trump's speech with the one given by Biden.
   - Which of the two do you think more quickly established rapport with the audience?
   - Which of the two came across as more natural and personable?
   - Which of the two made you feel as if they were speaking directly to you?
   - Which of the two had better eye contact?
   - Which of the two used their voice more effectively?
   - How did both use gestures to underscore their messages?

3. Discuss the extent to which mode and manner of delivery influence the speaker's ability to personalize a speech and connect with the audience.

5. Approach the Speaker's Stand

First, deliver an impromptu speech on a favorite recreational activity. Once this is done, write out and deliver the speech using a manuscript. Then, revise your notes and deliver the speech extemporaneously.

- How different were these experiences for you? For the audience?
- Which means of delivery do you think had more conversational appeal?
- Which delivery mode was easier for the audience to listen to?

RECAP AND REVIEW

12.1 Distinguish among the following speech delivery modes: impromptu, manuscript, extemporaneous, speaking from memory, and sound bite, describing their impact on a speech.

Speakers who deliver their speeches as if they mean them are better able to connect with their audience. A well-delivered speech helps the audience interpret the message appropriately, closing whatever gap may exist between them and the speaker. When you speak in an impromptu manner, you deliver a speech off the cuff. Manuscript reading requires that you be able to bring the printed page to life, making your words sound like conversation rather than like reading. In contrast, an extemporaneous speech is prepared and delivered in a conversational manner from speaker's notes. When you speak from memory, you attempt to deliver your speech word for word without using a manuscript or notes. Sound bites are brief, packaged thoughts offering simple solutions that appeal to our "headline society" as well as the Twittersphere. The mode you use depends on the nature of the speaking occasion, the purpose of the presentation, and the speaker's strengths and abilities.

12.2 Use an effective regimen for preparing and practicing your speech.

In preparation for delivering your speech, schedule multiple practices; verbalize everything; practice using audio, visual, and memory aids; confirm that the speech fits the time limit; do your best to replicate actual speaking conditions during rehearsal.

12.3 Decide if you're ready to deliver the speech.

Be sure to avoid practice bloopers. View and listen to yourself delivering the speech. Ask others to join you in assessing your readiness. Once this is done, give yourself a preliminary evaluation, polish the nonverbal aspects of your delivery, and gauge your ability to handle the Q&A.

KEY TERMS

Extemporaneous speaking (p. 262)

Impromptu speaking (p. 259)

Manuscript reading (p. 261)

Oratory (p. 263)

Sound bite speaking (p. 264)

Speaking from memory (p. 263)

Twitter-speak (p. 264)

iStock/Oleg Elkov

13 DELIVERING YOUR SPEECH

Nonverbal Messages Matter

UPON COMPLETING THIS CHAPTER, YOU WILL BE ABLE TO

13.1   Describe the general role that nonverbal cues play in public speaking.

13.2   Give voice to a speech, using paralinguistic cues to support speech content.

13.3   Illustrate how to use your body and appearance (kinesics) to communicate with the audience.

13.4   Demonstrate how to use space and distance (proxemics) to enhance the speaker–audience relationship.

Can you name any foreign-born stars who are famous for portraying American characters in film or on stage? Among the many that come to mind are Margot Robbie, Daniel Kaluuya, Freddie Highmore, Nicole Kidman, and Chris Hemsworth. These acting professionals successfully altered their voices, concealing their actual accents and adopting an American accent in its place, to represent the vocal qualities of their American characters. They did this so authentically that unless we already knew the actors were not born in the United States, we never would have been able to tell. Their manner of speaking appeared natural. It did not call attention to itself.

The same principle holds true for how skillful performers, whether born in the United States or not, use their faces and bodies to reflect a character's personality and mood. For example, picture how the superheroes Spider Man, Wasp, Black Widow, Black Panther, or Wolverine move their bodies. Their spoken words, gestures, posture, appearance, and manner of dress send a unified message underscoring their character's confidence, competence, and trustworthiness to those who might question or doubt their abilities. When presenting in public, your goal is to project a similar image of vitality so that you too command attention. Even when you pause or are silent, your appearance, facial expression, eyes, posture, and physical movements will continue communicating to the audience, suggesting to them what you are really thinking and feeling.[1]

The question is, do you have what it takes to be a speech superhero? How effectively will you use your voice, body, and the space around you when it's your turn to come to the front of the room and deliver a speech? In contrast to the superheroes we reference above, however, neither your voice nor your body should call unnecessary attention to you but should reinforce the words you are speaking, helping the audience focus on and respond to your message.

NONVERBAL MESSAGES: BEYOND THE SPEAKER'S WORDS

13.1   *Describe the general role that nonverbal cues play in public speaking.*

Speakers influence audience members, not only by what they say but also by how they look and sound, and how they move and use the space between themselves and their audiences. Like any public figure, your appearance, voice, posture, facial expressions, eye contact, gestures, and distance from the audience either will add to or detract from your presentation.[2]

Have you considered how receivers will respond to the nonverbal messages accompanying your words?[3] Are you skilled at using **paralinguistics** (vocal cues), **kinesics** (body language), and **proxemics** (space and distance) to enhance and promote the acceptance of your spoken message?[4] What vocal, physical, and spatial cues might you use to encourage your audience to respond positively? When audience members are attracted, not distracted, by the sound of your voice and your physical presence, they are better able to concentrate on what you have to say. When listening to an effective presentation, an audience senses a speaker's enthusiasm, feels the force inherent in the speaker's voicing of ideas, and senses the speaker's desire to communicate.

This is a two-way street. Members of the audience also will consciously or unconsciously use nonverbal communication to reveal their reactions to you at the outset, during, and at the end of your presentation. Your ability to adjust your message based on their reactions depends on your picking up a host of nonverbal cues—smiles, frowns, eyes looking at you or away, heads nodding in agreement or shaking in disagreement, rigid or relaxed postures, gasps or laughter. When you respond to these cues appropriately, you build a better speaker–audience relationship.

Researchers maintain that the bulk of a message's personal and connotative meaning is communicated via its nonverbal delivery. According to one study, words carry only some 7 percent of the meaning, with 38 percent of meaning attributed to vocal cues and the remaining 55 percent attributed to the speaker's body language.[5] Audiences tend to trust the nonverbal level of communication. Deliver your speech honestly and effectively, and your audience members are likely to find you more credible and believable.

SELF-ASSESSMENT 13.1: WHAT DO YOU KNOW ABOUT NONVERBAL MESSAGING?

Directions:
For each of the following statements, indicate whether you think the answer is True or False.

Before taking the quiz, predict the grade (from 0–100) you will receive on it. _____

Statement	I Think This Statement Is True	I Think This Statement Is False
1. Widening your eyelids when speaking emphasizes your words.		
2. With a high degree of accuracy most of us are able to recognize a speaker's identity without seeing them because every voice is unique.		

Statement	I Think This Statement Is True	I Think This Statement Is False
3. We are likely to keep greater interaction distance with someone with whom we are unfamiliar than with someone whom we know.		
4. The size of one's pupils influences interpersonal attraction.		
5. Nodding your head rapidly signals the desire for the speaker to finish quickly.		
6. We touch ourselves more when telling the truth than we do when lying.		
7. Blinking suggests physiological arousal.		
8. Men, more than women, pay attention to nonverbal cues they can see when compared with those conveyed by the voice.		
9. Where you sit in class does not influence your participation.		
10. Most observers can tell whether another person's facial expressions are genuine or forced.		
11. When we become socially anxious, we tend to gaze more at the other person during interaction.		
12. When feeling stressed we lower our pitch.		
13. When we become angry, speech rate slows.		

Statement	I Think This Statement Is True	I Think This Statement Is False
14. A person's eyes reveal amusement or enjoyment.		
15. It is possible to estimate another person's age based on the sound of the person's voice.		
16. Men are better than women at reading facial cues.		
17. When angry, most people don't lower their brows.		
18. Interpersonal attraction is not correlated with how close we stand to one another.		
19. Persons who dominate in conversations gaze more when speaking than when listening compared with persons who are less dominant.		
20. We are likely to approach high-and-low-status others more closely than we approach those whose status we perceive to be equal to our own.		

Scoring Method	Score Interpretation
Give yourself 5 points for every correct answer. 1. T; 2. T; 3. T; 4. T; 5. T; 6. F; 7. T; 8. F; 9. T; 10. T; 11. F; 12. F; 13. F; 14. T; 15. T; 16. F; 17. F; 18. F; 19. T; 20. F.	Was your grade expectation confirmed? What does your score suggest about your nonverbal skillfulness? How effective are you at reading nonverbal cues? How can you apply the information contained here?

Source: Adapted from Janelle Rosip and Judith Hall, "Test of Nonverbal Cue Knowledge (TONCK)," *Journal of Nonverbal Behavior 28*, no. 4 (December 2004): 267–286.

TAKE CONTROL OF HOW YOU SOUND

> **13.2**   *Give voice to your speech, using paralinguistic cues to support speech content.*

When used capably, the human voice is an incredible instrument—some even believe it comparable to a full symphony orchestra in its range and flexibility.[6] How would you describe your voice? When you hear it, does it sound pleasant to you? How do others respond to it? What, for example, differentiates a shrill voice from a sweet-sounding one?[7] While we would all like to have a voice that others refer to as "golden," many an effective speaker has a voice that is undistinguished. Consider, for example, that President Abraham Lincoln's voice has been called high pitched and wavering and former British prime minister Margaret Thatcher's shrill and grating.[8] Each of these speakers, however, mastered the art of vocal control.

When you take control of it, your voice is powerfully expressive,[9] playing an important role in your audience's response.[10] Audiences form impressions of speakers based on vocal cues alone, making inferences about the speaker's age, status, ethnicity, and occupation, just to name a few. We stereotype others based on how they sound to us (see Table 13.1).

TABLE 13.1 ■ Vocal Cues and Personality Stereotypes		
Vocal Cues	**Speakers**	**Stereotypes**
Breathiness (a loud whisper)	Males	Young, artistic
	Females	Feminine, pretty, effervescent, high-strung, shallow
Thinness (very delicate)	Males	No effect on listener's image of speaker
	Females	Social, physical, emotional, and mental immaturity; sense of humor and sensitivity
Flatness (emotionless)	Males	Masculine, sluggish, cold, withdrawn
	Females	Masculine, sluggish, cold, withdrawn
Nasality	Males	Wide array of socially undesirable characteristics
	Females	Wide array of socially undesirable characteristics
Tenseness	Males	Old, unyielding, cantankerous
	Females	Young, emotional, feminine, high-strung, less intelligent
Throatiness (guttural)	Males	Old, realistic, mature, sophisticated, well-adjusted
	Females	Less intelligent, masculine, lazy, boorish, unemotional, ugly, sickly, careless, inartistic, humble, uninteresting, neurotic, apathetic
Orotundity (fullness/ richness)	Males	Energetic, healthy, artistic, sophisticated, proud, interesting, enthusiastic
	Females	Lively, gregarious, aesthetically sensitive, proud

Vocal Cues	Speakers	Stereotypes
Increased rate	Males	Animated and extroverted
	Females	Animated and extroverted
Increased pitch variety	Males	Dynamic, feminine, aesthetic
	Females	Dynamic and extroverted

Sources: Based on Dudley Knight, *Speaking With Skill: A Skills Based Approach to Speech Training* (New York: Bloomsbury Publishing, 2012); Kate DeVore, *The Voice Book: Caring for, Protecting, and Improving Your Voice* (Chicago: Chicago Review Press, 2009); and Paul Heinberg, *Voice Training for Speaking and Reading Aloud* (New York: Ronald Press, 1964).

Keeping all this in mind, answer these questions honestly:

- Does my voice help me convey the meaning of my speech clearly?
- If I were in my audience, would I want to listen to me for an extended period of time?
- Does my voice enhance or detract from the impression I make?

Properly Use Pitch, Volume, Rate, Articulation, and Pronunciation

Pitch is the highness or lowness of the voice on a tonal scale. It is the voice's upward or downward inflection. Like a pitcher varies location and speed when throwing a baseball, hoping to make it difficult for the batter to anticipate the coming pitch, we vary our voices to avoid talking in a monotone and to add expressiveness to our words. Audiences judge a speaker who varies their pitch to be livelier, animated, and interesting.

Volume is the loudness or softness of the voice, its intensity. The aim is to speak with enough force that everyone in attendance is able to hear you comfortably, without your voice overwhelming them. Good breath control lets you vary your volume as needed. Breathe deeply from the diaphragm rather than taking shallow, vocal cord-level breaths. Even when speaking at your lowest volume, audience members in the very last row should still be able hear you.

Rate is the speed at which you speak. Most of us speak between 125 and 175 words per minute. Speaking too quickly communicates a desire to get the speech over with in record time, and audience members may find it difficult to keep up. Speaking too slowly communicates tentativeness and lack of confidence and may bore the audience.

Articulation is the way you pronounce individual sounds. Ideally, you speak the sounds of speech sharply and distinctly. While the focus of articulation is on the production of speech sounds, the focus of **pronunciation** is on whether the words themselves are said correctly.

Vary Pitch

Our *habitual pitch,* the level at which we speak most often, may or may not be our *optimal pitch,* which is where our voice functions best and where we have extensive vocal variation up and down the scale. Varying your pitch increases the communicative value of your words. It also helps convey your message's meaning. For example, can you use pitch to change the meaning of these words?

I'm so happy to be here.

Fine-tuning. How can you use the sound of your voice and other vocal cues to impact the meaning of your speech?

iStock.com/FatCamera

With rising and/or falling intonation, you can give that sentence very different meanings, from genuinely expressing happiness, to sarcasm, to disdain. Saying those words in a monotone, for instance, would mean you are not happy. Your pitch also reveals whether you are making a statement or asking a question. It conveys your emotion and can make you sound angry or annoyed, patient or tolerant. Speakers who are able to vary their pitch to reflect the mood they are expressing are more persuasive than those who use a repetitive pitch pattern.[11]

Audiences may stereotype speakers based on their vocal pitch. Lower-pitched voices often are considered more mature, sexier, and stronger than higher-pitched voices, which are frequently associated with helplessness, nervousness, and tension. When we are nervous or scared, the pitch of our voice tends to rise because the muscles around our vocal cords constrict. To keep your pitch natural, review the stress relaxation exercises discussed in Chapter 1.

Adapt Volume to the Situation and Cultural Norms

Regulate your volume to reflect the size and acoustics of the room, the size of the audience, and any competing background noises. Increasing your volume at particular points can help you emphasize specific words and

Volume control. Listen to the room and adjust your volume accordingly.

iStock.com/blueraymac

ideas, add emotional intensity, and energize the room. In contrast, decreasing your volume can also help you gain or sustain audience attention, convey a contrasting emotion, or even add suspense.

Generally, in the United States we consider a voice that is too loud to be intrusive and aggressive and a voice that is too low to be meek, hesitant, and less credible. The volume the members of one culture judge to be appropriate may be unacceptable to and misinterpreted by the members of another culture. In general, Hispanics, Arabs, Israelis, and Italians tend to speak more loudly than Anglo Americans and East Asians.[12] For Arabs, loudness connotes strength and sincerity, whereas speaking too softly implies that one lacks confidence or is timid.[13] For Asians, a gentle, soothing voice is reflective of good manners.[14]

Adjust Rate, Use Silent Pauses, Avoid Fillers

Your rate should vary to reflect any change in the speech's mood: slow when you want to express thoughtfulness, solemnity, concern, or are relaying serious and complex material; quicker when you want to convey excitement, a sense of urgency, eagerness, happiness, or when sharing lighter contents or heading toward a climax.

For example, Martin Luther King Jr. began his "I Have a Dream" speech uttering words at approximately 92 words per minute; he finished it at a rate of approximately 145 words per minute. King's rate of speech quickened as he headed toward his speech's emotional conclusion. Think of rate as the pulse of your speech; it should quicken to convey agitation, excitement, and happiness, and fall to convey seriousness of purpose, serenity, or sadness.

Like a rollercoaster. Build up the rate of your words or slow it down to match what you're trying to convey and take the audience on a ride.

iStock.com/bukharova

To slow the rate of speech . . . *pause*. Pause to emphasize your meaning, underscore the importance of an idea, lend dramatic impact to a statement, give your listeners time to reflect on what you have said, and signal the end of a thought. In fact, according to former *60 Minutes* producer Don Hewitt, "The pauses tell the story. They are as important to us as commas and periods are to the *New York Times*."[15] Pauses help you maintain control. When delivering a speech at the March for Our Lives in 2018, surviving Marjorie Stoneman Douglas High School student–activist Emma Gonzalez fell silent. As the minutes passed, she stared at the audience, her eyes brimming with tears. Her silence was palpable and also a nonverbal reminder of the time it took for the shooter to take the lives of 17 of Gonzalez's peers and instructors. Use the following pause pointers to enhance your effectiveness:

Pause...

- Before starting. Some speakers begin speaking even before getting to the front of the room. This demonstrates a lack of control. Instead, once in position, pause, scan the audience, and then begin.

- After posing a rhetorical question. Give members of the audience time to contemplate the question.

- When you are about to make an important point. Silence signals the significance of what will come next.

Red light. Pauses help signal important points to the audience, and they help slow down the rate of a speech.

iStock.com/SashaFoxWalters

- When transitioning from one part of the speech to another. This gives receivers time to adjust psychologically.

- After delivering your final words. Don't leave your position while still speaking, demonstrating your desire to remove yourself from being the audience's focus. Instead, pause, scan the audience as you did at the outset, and then walk back to your seat at a comfortable pace.

As with other cues, culture intervenes in our perception of the pause. Among European Americans, for example, too extended a pause can cause receivers discomfort, making them feel tense and anxious. In Japan and India, however, long pauses are natural and a sign that one is collecting one's thoughts.

Be sure not to fill a meaningful pause with meaningless sounds and phrases such as *er, uh, um, okay,* or *you know.*[16] Such extraneous vocal fillers disrupt the natural flow of your presentation, diminishing your credibility. Here's an example of how verbal fillers impede effective delivery:

Um . . . I was, uh, hoping, you . . . um, would step up, ah . . . you know, and . . . um, sign this . . . petition, um, because, you know, it is a matter . . . uh, of life, and uh . . . death.

Not very persuasive, is it? Make a conscious effort to notice when you use vocal fillers (ask a friend or family member to point out each use) and focus on eliminating them from your repertoire of spoken sounds.

Er, um. Aim to eliminate verbal fillers that detract from your message.

iStock.com/Deepak Sethi

Attend to Articulation and Pronunciation

When you fail to utter a final sound (a final *t* or *d,* for example); fail to produce the sounds of words properly (substituting or adding a sound where it doesn't belong, like *idear*); or voice a sound in an unclear, imprecise, or incorrect way (*come wimme* instead of *come with me*), then you are guilty of faulty articulation. As a speaker, your responsibility is to say your words so your audience can understand them. If your listeners can't understand you, they can't respond appropriately, and they may simply conclude you either don't know what you are talking about or are an inept speaker.

Have you ever stressed the wrong syllable in a word or pronounced sounds that should stay silent? Among common mispronunciation errors are adding unnecessary sounds, omitting necessary sounds, reversing sounds, or misplacing an accent (see Table 13.2).

TABLE 13.2 ■ Frequently Mispronounced Words		
	Correct	**Incorrect**
athlete	(ATH-leet)	(ATH-a-leet)
Arctic	(ARC-tic)	(AR-tic)
comfortable	(COM-fort-a-ble)	(COMF-ter-ble)
espresso	(ess-PRESS-oh)	(ex-PRESS-oh)
figure	(FIG-yer)	(fig-er)
forte	(FORT)	(for-TAY)—correct only as a music term
lambaste	(lam-BASTE)	(lam-BAST)
menstruation	(men-stroo-A-shun)	(men-STRAY-shun)
nuclear	(NUKE-lee-ar)	(NUKE-yoo-lar)
nuptial	(NUP-shul)	(NUP-shoo-al)
often	(OFF-en)	(OFT-en)
probably	(PROB-ab-ly)	(PRAH-bal-ly, PROB-ly)
realtor	(RE-al-tor)	(REAL-a-tor)
supposedly	(sup-POSE-ed-ly)	(sup-POSE-ab-ly)
taut	(TAUT)	(TAUNT)
toward	(TOW-ward)	(TOR-ward)

Source: Used by permission of Samuel Stoddard, RinkWorks.

To avoid problems with pronunciation, use a dictionary or check a reputable pronunciation guide online to learn how a word should be said. Because mispronouncing a word can cause a loss in credibility, it is something you want to avoid. Don't wait for an audience member to point out an error in pronunciation to you.

Be Aware of Accents, Dialects, and Regionalisms

We all have an accent—no one speaks without one. Yet we often find ourselves commenting on another person's accent—typically when we judge it to be nonnative or nonstandard. This has consequences for the speaker because we are discriminating against them and stereotyping them based on the accent common within our own language group.[17] To combat this, make the effort to guard against such bias.

A **dialect** is a speech pattern characteristic of a group of people from a particular area or of a specific ethnicity. Although there is no one area or group whose dialect is right or wrong, people do have preferences regarding the appropriate use of language and may even stereotype others on the basis of their dialects. For example, people in the South may perceive those in the Northeast as brusque and abrasive, whereas Northeasterners may perceive Southerners as slow and surface sweet. Midwestern speech patterns, in contrast, are frequently held up as a standard to emulate, and they characterize the dialects exhibited by many television news anchors. Most people have grown accustomed to Midwestern speech and prefer to listen either to it or to someone who sounds just like they themselves do.

If you don't have a neutral dialect, this doesn't mean your dialect is "bad" or inferior. Still, ask yourself whether your dialect could prevent understanding in your audience. If the answer is "yes," then you will want to take some action to overcome the prejudices your listeners hold about your dialect. At the same time, each audience member should keep in mind that they should not prejudge a speech based on the speaker's dialect.

Despite this, it may be that audience members will perceive you as more credible if you adapt your dialect, making it more in line with the one they prefer to listen to, which in many cases will be Standard English. Adjusting your dialect (not abandoning it altogether) based on the situation is known as "code switching." Just as you might not use the same words when speaking to a supervisor, professor, or elder as you would when speaking with your friends, so you might use one dialect when interacting with others informally and another when delivering a speech in public.

COACHING TIP

"People trust their ears less than their eyes."

—Herodotus, Greek author

Talk to the audience not just with words but with your body. Your eyes, gestures, and physical demeanor provide audience members clues they can use to assess your sincerity and believability, likeability, and competence. They either underscore or undermine audience judgments of your authenticity and credibility. Make your appearance count, and the audience will count on you.

COORDINATE YOUR BODY LANGUAGE AND SPOKEN WORDS

> **13.3**   *Illustrate how to use your body and appearance (kinesics) to communicate with the audience.*

If what you do with your body is inconsistent with what you say, your listeners will tend to believe your body language more than your words. And they are right to do so because that is probably where the truth lies. Thus, you must use physical cues to make it easier, not harder, for your listeners to believe and listen to you.

In addition, your body movements should be purposeful. Continually pacing like a caged lion, moving randomly or perpetually like a wind-up toy, or standing rigid and expressionless like a statue are attention-distracters; by calling undue attention to your movement (or lack of), you subvert the message.

Gesture Meaningfully

A speaker who gestures meaningfully comes across as natural, relaxed, and in touch with their thoughts, whereas a speaker whose gestures are stiff and unnatural may be perceived as uptight, lacking in enthusiasm, and unsure. The stances and motions identified in Table 13.3 convey these messages.

TABLE 13.3 ■ Gestures Convey Meaning	
If You . . .	**You May Appear to Be . . .**
Clutch one arm with the other or stand in a figleaf pose	Nervous and uptight
Hold your hands stiffly at your sides	Tense and uncomfortable
Cross your arms and legs	Distant and closed off
Place your hands on your hips	Combative and giving orders
Clasp your hands behind your back	Overly confident and too self-assured
Let your arms hang naturally and loosely at your sides	Relaxed and composed

In addition to these, some of us have annoying habits that audience members could find distracting. Gestures like playing with hair, jiggling bracelets or pocket change, cracking knuckles, or tapping a foot interfere with rather than clarify your message. Become aware of whether you have any distracting mannerisms, get feedback and help from others, and work to eliminate them.

Illustrators

Use gestures to reinforce, clarify, describe, and demonstrate the meaning of your words. You can, for example, signal when you're about to hit a main point with one, two, or three fingers.

Such a gesture is called an **illustrator**—it illustrates your content. If you held a finger up vertically over your mouth, that would substitute for saying, "Quiet please." If you shook a finger at receivers while talking about the shame involved in not being an organ donor, that gesture would be emphasizing your message. You should avoid using contradicting gestures—ones that conflict with your words, negating your spoken message—unless you use it purposefully to make a point or a joke. It would not be effective to speak of the death of a hero with a smile on your face.

Emblems

Emblems are nonverbal symbols that have a direct verbal translation and are widely understood by the members of a culture. Be aware that a gesture's meaning may differ across cultures. In Japan and Korea, what Americans know as the "okay" sign symbolizes "money," and among Arabs, when accompanied by a baring of teeth, it signifies extreme hostility.[18]

Vary Gestures

Don't limit yourself to a single, all-purpose gesture. Instead, your movements should flow naturally with your words.[19] Under most conditions, gestures should coincide with, not precede or follow, verbal content.

Ask yourself these questions about your gestures:

- Are my gestures natural and spontaneous rather than exaggerated, too patterned, or uncertain?
- Do they support my words?
- Are they varied appropriately?

OK? If you're going to employ a certain emblem or sign during your speech, make sure it's appropriate for the crowd.

iStock.com/Grandbrothers

Remember, Posture Matters

Posture is the position of your body in space. The posture you display conveys a lot about how you are feeling. Because you will likely stand when giving a speech, we focus on your standing posture. A public speaker who stands tall with shoulders squared sends a message of strength to audiences, whereas a speaker whose shoulders are either raised or stooped sends a message of stress or submissiveness, respectively. A speaker who leans toward an audience is usually perceived more positively than one who leans away or appears to withdraw from the audience.[20] If using a lectern, don't drape yourself over it, slouch, or rock back and forth.

When you are ready to speak, ask yourself these posture-related questions:

- Does my posture convey my command of the speech experience?

- Does it express my interest in the audience?

- Does it demonstrate my comfort with speaking before others?

Good posture. Consider the message that your body position sends to the audience. Imagine this person standing. Would their posture be relaxed?

iStock.com/William Chua

Use Facial Expressions and Eye Contact to Connect

Audience members rely on a speaker's facial cues to reveal what's behind the speaker's words.

Put on Your Game Face

Putting on a game face doesn't mean you are going to act tough or phony; it means you use your face to set the emotional tone for your speech, beginning when the audience sees you for the first time. Then, once you speak, guide your listeners by using facial expressions that match your verbal message. Use the following facial management techniques as needed to intensify, deintensify, neutralize, or mask what you are feeling:

- When you *intensify* an emotion, you exaggerate your facial expressions to reflect the degree of expression you believe audience members expect you to exhibit. For example, you may communicate more excitement than you actually feel in an effort to generate excitement among listeners.

- When you *deintensify* an emotion, you diminish your facial expressions so that audience members will judge your behavior as more acceptable. Thus, you may downplay the rage you feel in an effort to temper audience member reactions.

- When you *neutralize* an emotion, you suppress your real feelings so as to suggest greater inner strength and resilience to listeners. Thus, you attempt to hide any fears, nerves, or sadness.

- And when you *mask* an emotion, you try to replace one emotion with another to which you believe audience members will respond more favorably. You might, for example, choose to conceal feelings of outrage, anger, jealousy, or anxiety if you believe audience members would find them unacceptable.

Inappropriate facial expressions can undermine your efforts. If you smile, for instance, when discussing a serious issue, that behavior contradicts your verbal message and will diminish whatever bond exists between you and your audience. If your face is expressionless, it will also work against you by failing to communicate your interest in your audience and your involvement in your topic.

In preparation for speaking, ask yourself these questions relevant to your facial expressiveness:

- Are my facial expressions conveying the proper emotions?
- Do my facial expressions support my thoughts and feelings?

Maintain Eye Contact

Of all the facial cues you exhibit, none affects your relationship with your audience as much as the presence or absence of eye contact. In general, eye contact should be direct, frequent, and encompassing.

Making effective eye contact early and often with an audience serves a number of important functions:

1. Eye contact signals that the lines of communication are open between speaker and listeners. It is easier for audience members to ignore a speaker who has not established eye contact with them.

2. Eye contact psychologically reduces the distance between speaker and listeners, helping to cement their bond.

3. It allows the speaker to obtain valuable feedback from audience members regarding how the speech is coming across, enabling the speaker to adjust their delivery as needed.

4. It communicates the speaker's confidence, conviction, concern, and interest.

Keep these guidelines in mind when speaking to an audience:

- Begin by looking audience members in the eye.

- Keep your gaze steady and personal as you distribute it evenly about the room or auditorium. In this way, your gaze is encompassing, visually demonstrating your interest in everyone present.

- Do not stare blankly. A blank stare can be mistaken for a hostile glower or a sign of a blank mind.

- Maintain eye contact with your listeners for at least three seconds after you conclude your speech. Let your final words sink in before you leave the lectern.

Look for attention. Audience members are more likely to listen to a speaker who has made eye contact.

iStock.com/Anna Frank

Use Appearance to Support Performance

Eric Adams, the mayor of New York City, pays a lot of attention to what he wears in public. You should, too. According to Adams, "People look at your presentation before they take you seriously. Everything about you must say power."[21] Your clothing and grooming are important in creating a good first impression with your audience members and in influencing their perceptions of your competence and trustworthiness.[22] Because you want audience members to accept and retain your message, you need to present yourself as positively as possible. This means that your appearance, like your gestures, should be unobtrusive and should not isolate you from your receivers. Your words should not have to compete with your appearance for the attention of your listeners. The way you dress will help make both you and your message more appealing to listeners if you keep in mind that your physical appearance needs to reflect both the occasion and the nature of your speech. For instance, if you were giving a speech on surfing, it might be fitting for you to wear shorts or a T-shirt, but a suit would be appropriate when giving a business speech.

Poised for success. Manage your nonverbal communication to build a positive relationship with your audience.

iStock.com/AzmanJaka

Use these questions to assess your appearance:

- Am I well groomed?

- Am I dressed appropriately?

- Does my appearance support both the content and mood of my speech?

- Am I wearing anything that might distract the audience's attention?

MAKE THE MOST OF THE SETTING

> **13.4** *Demonstrate how to use space and distance (proxemics) to enhance the speaker–audience relationship.*

Knowledge of proxemics—the use of space and distance in communication—can also benefit a speaker, helping to improve their relationship with receivers and psychologically reducing the distance between them and the audience.

Aim for Immediacy

Make the space in which you speak work for you and the audience. The amount of space between presenter and receivers can create a sense of immediacy, conveying a connection between the speaker and the audience, or suggest instead that a great distance exists between them. The goal is for you to use space in a way that enhances delivery. For example, compare the demeanor of an orchestra's conductor with an actor appearing in a one-person show. The actor is able to create greater intimacy with the audience simply by approaching the front of the stage—visibly symbolizing a connection to and identification with audience members. In contrast, until the last note sounds in a concert, the conductor looks directly at the orchestra, facing away from the audience— establishing a closer relationship with the orchestra than the audience.

Similarly, the speaker's position in relationship to an audience matters. Stand too close to audience members and they may feel that their personal space is being invaded, but stand too far away, and they could perceive you as uninterested or dispassionate.

Location matters. How can where you're standing and what's around you affect the speech's impact?

iStock.com/SDI Productions

Decide From Where to Speak

It is important to be aware of the space given you. Unless the occasion is a formal or serious one, don't feel stuck to the lectern, which if used ineffectively creates a barrier between you and the audience. Coming out from behind it helps to establish immediacy in much the same way a smile and eye contact do, making you seem more approachable.[23] If comfortable doing so, you could even move among the audience. Whatever your choice, your movement should be purposeful.

Approach the Audience Confidently

A Chinese proverb says, "Let me see you walk, and I'll tell you what you're like." Even as you approach the speaker's stand, you are sending nonverbal messages to your audience. You have not yet spoken a word, yet by your manner of dress, rate of movement, the forcefulness in your step, the way you carry yourself and move your arms, the directness or indirectness of your gaze, your facial expression, and how and where you stand before them, listeners form opinions of you.

On the day you give your speech, be sure to walk deliberately to the front of the room, moving your arms naturally as you do so. Don't make any silly faces or nervous sounds as you approach your speaking location. Once there, pause, and let your eyes address your receivers. Then, building on everything you've learned about giving voice to your message and using eye contact, facial cues, meaningful gestures, and space to enhance nonverbal delivery, begin to speak the speech.

GAME PLAN

Maximizing My Nonverbal Effectiveness

- I have identified my vocal and physical strengths and will ﹍ly on them to support my spoken words.
- I will use pitch, volume, rate, articulation, and pronunciation ﹍ make listening to me easier and to ensure I have sufficient vocal expressiveness.
- I've reviewed video of how other accomplished speakers use vocal ﹍physical cues to connect with the audience.
- I've practiced my speech in front of a full-length mirror more than once t﹍ idea of how well I use posture, gestures, facial expressions, and eye contact to enga﹍ence and if I communicate the right emotions at the right times. ﹍e audi-
- I can envision where in the room I'll be standing in relation to my audience.
- I've picked out an outfit that is comfortable and works with my speech as well as the text in which I'll be presenting.

EXERCISES

Using Your Voice and Body

Mastering the ability to use vocal, physical cues, and space to enhance delivery demonstrates speechmaking acumen. To increase your ability, participate in these activities.

1. Stretch

Take time to conduct an examination of your voice and body in order to expand your comfort using them.

Start by "playing your voice" like an instrument, using different pitches to express your ideas and varying your volume and rate dramatically. If you typically speak softly, now project your words with more force. If you usually speak loudly, lower your volume but still be understandable. Similarly, if you are a "fast talker," deliberately slow the flow of your words, and if you are a "slow talker," speed up without sacrificing clarity.

When speaking in public, your facial expression should match the emotion inherent in your words. Explain your plan for putting your best speech-face forward. For example, you might coach yourself to approach the front of the room confidently and meet the eyes of the members of your audience before beginning to speak.

2. Convey Emotion

First, using the sentence, "I am so happy to be here with you," pair up with a friend and take turns speaking it in a large classroom or empty auditorium, with one of you speaking from the front of the room and the other sitting in the last row. How loud do you need to speak in order to be heard? Aside from being heard, what do you need to do with your voice to make the other person believe you, doubt your sincerity, laugh at the remark, or feel compassion for you?

Next, select an emotion—surprise, happiness, or anger—and take selfies of yourself increasing and decreasing your emotional intensity—say, moving from the slightest indication of the emotion to the most intense and back. Experienced speakers use their faces and bodies to demonstrate such changes. Explain why being able to express such emotional distinctions can benefit you as a speaker.

Finally, vocal and physical delivery distinguish one speaker from another. Using examples found online, compare the vocal and physical speaking styles of a pair of speakers: Elon Musk and Jeff Bezos, Oprah Winfrey and Tiffany Haddish, or another pair of your own choosing. In your comparison, note the following:

- Which speaker engenders more trust, and why
- What you specifically like or dislike about each of the speaker's styles
- Whether the speaker gestures too forcefully or not forcefully enough
- If the speaker's smile comes across as sincere or fake, and why
- When the speaker leans toward and away from the audience
- When the speaker's eye contact is sustained or intermittent

3. Analyze This: The Sound and Look of Speech

First, search for "speeches that inspire" or "speeches by famous people" on YouTube and view two. Choose one delivered by a speaker from your own culture and another by a speaker from a different culture. Take notes on each speaker's use of vocal, physical, and spatial cues, including pitch, volume, rate, articulation, pronunciation, facial expressiveness, gestures, and use of space, listening and looking for differences as well as similarities, and discuss your impressions of their effectiveness.

Then, view the testimony of both Christine Blasey Ford and Judge Brett Kavanaugh durin this now Supreme Court justice's confirmation hearings. Describe how their vocal and physi characteristics contributed to your believing one to be more credible than the other.

4. Approach the Speaker's Stand

Make a video of yourself delivering a one-minute speech on the importance of vocal and cal cues or another topic of your choice. Review the video and evaluate its vocal and ph aspects, being sure to focus on those elements covered in this chapter.

RECAP AND REVIEW

13.1 Describe the general role nonverbal cues play in public speaking.

Researchers maintain that the bulk of a message's personal and connotative mear is communicated via its nonverbal delivery. Speakers skilled in using paralinguistics (vocal cues), kinesics (physical cues), and proxemics (space and distance) have a better chance of having the audience respond appropriately to their presentations.

13.2 Give voice to a speech, using paralinguistic cues to support speech content.

Audiences stereotype speakers based on vocal cues alone, making inferences abou the speaker's age, status, ethnicity, and occupation, just to name a few. Effective speake and audiences are aware of vocal preferences or proclivities influenced by culture, recognizing that the cultural norms of others may differ from their own. By becoming aware of how people from different cultures use their voices, audience members decrease chances for misinterpreting and misjudging a speaker's intentions. Receivers tend to evaluate speakers based on use of pitch (the highness or lowness of the voice on a tonal scale), volume (the loudness or softness of the voice), rate (the speed of speech), articulation (the production of individual speech sounds), and pronunciation (whether the words are correctly said). When these elements of vocal delivery are used effectively, the audience views the speaker more positively.

13.3 Illustrate how to use your body and appearance (kinesics) to communicate with the audience.

What a speaker does when delivering a speech affects the audience's perception of their credibility. By taking time to explore how to use physical cues more effectively, a speaker can work to enhance the understanding and acceptance of ideas by audience members. Physical behavior carries meaning. If a speaker displays effective gestures, body movements, facial expressions, eye contact, and posture, then it is easier to create a good *relationship with receivers.*

13.4 Demonstrate how to use space and distance (proxemics) to enhance the speaker– audience relationship.

How speakers use space and distance influences the audience–speaker relationship. An understanding of proxemics can bridge distance, create a connection, and enhance delivery.

KEY TERMS

Articulation (p. 281)

Dialect (p. 287)

Emblems (p. 289)

Illustrators (p. 289)

Immediacy (p. 294)

Kinesics (p. 277)

Paralinguistics (p. 277)

Pitch (p. 281)

Pronunciation (p. 281)

Proxemics (p. 277)

Rate (p. 281)

Volume (p. 281)

14 USING PRESENTATION AIDS

UPON COMPLETING THIS CHAPTER, YOU WILL BE ABLE TO

14.1   Discuss the strategic use of presentation aids.

14.2   Select, prepare, and use the most relevant presentation aids in your speech.

14.3   Choose appropriate presentation software to get the most from your presentation aids.

What do a sports event, election night results, breaking news, and weather reports have in common? Whenever we view any one of them, we see commentators using presentation aids to augment their reporting. In football, a yellow line indicates the first-down line. During a presidential election, maps are coded red, blue, and sometimes purple to show those states still in contention. Criminal trials feature crime-scene visuals. Visuals help tell each story.

Many of us think of a public speech as filled with words. But words are not always enough. As in broadcast sports, you may discover that **presentation aids**—graphics, a photo or film segment, or maybe dramatic music—can supplement your words and increase receiver engagement. Consider this observation by presidential adviser and communication and media relations specialist Merrie Spaeth:

> When Moses came down from the mountain with clay tablets bearing the Ten Commandments, it was perhaps history's first example of a speaker using props to reinforce his message. It wouldn't have had the same impact if Moses had simply announced: "God just told me 10 things, and I'm going to relay them to you."[1]

Based on this, consider these questions: Why did former president Donald Trump choose to accept his party's nomination for a second term as president standing directly before the South Lawn in front of the White House—effectively using the White House as a visual backdrop?[2] Why at the end of his acceptance speech were fireworks used to highlight the words *Trump 2020* above the Washington Monument?[3] Why did medical artists choose to use a spikey red ball to serve as a visual representation of the COVID-19 virus? Did this visual help to communicate the menacing nature of the disease to the public?[4] The answer? Each of the preceding visuals helped to tell the speaker's story by reinforcing the message each speaker wanted to send.

We are more attuned to messages that have visual appeal than to ones appealing solely to our ears. Because of our immersion in a culture saturated with media and new technology, we expect speakers to stimulate our sight as well as our hearing. Thus, by effectively integrating visual and audio materials into your speech, you can make a significant difference in how your audience responds.

COACHING TIP

"I use many props. The props act as cue cards reminding me of what to say next."

—Tom Ogden, magician

Presentation aids not only prop up your speech, they prop up your memory of what comes next, helping you segue from one important point to another. Because they enable you to speak with greater fluency and confidence and help the audience remember your message, visual and audio evidence help to achieve the goals of your speech.

USE PRESENTATION AIDS STRATEGICALLY

14.1   *Discuss the strategic use of presentation aids.*

Presentation aids are often clearer than speech itself. When audiences see and hear your message, they understand and retain more of it. Keep in mind, however, that the purpose of using presentation aids is to reinforce, not replace, your spoken words. When used to advantage by a speaker, presentation aids fulfill the following functions:

- **Increase comprehension.** Humans process more than 80 percent of all information we receive through our sense of sight.[5]

- **Promote memory and recall.** We remember only 10 percent of what we read, 20 percent of what we hear, and 30 percent of what we see. But we remember more than 50 percent of what we see and hear simultaneously (see Figure 14.1).[6]

- **Facilitate organization.** By displaying main ideas visually, you help your listeners follow your speech's structure and better understand your presentation.

- **Direct attention and control interest.** A dramatic photograph, object, or graph holds a listener's attention more compellingly than words alone.

- **Increase persuasiveness.** Speakers who make visuals an inherent part of their presentations are perceived as better communicators and are 43 percent more likely to persuade their audiences than are speakers who rely exclusively on spoken words.[7]

- **Communicate concisely.** Effective presentation aids help you share information that might otherwise be too complex or take up too much time. An effective chart, for example, can eloquently convey a message.

- **Create an aura of professionalism.** When prepared with care, visual and audio aids demonstrate a professional approach, increasing credibility and your ability to communicate your message.

- **Reduce apprehension.** When using presentation aids, you have something to focus on other than the fear of speaking.

- **Manage time.** Visual aids tied to specific moments in your speech can help you keep on pace and end on time.

FIGURE 14.1 ■ Visual Aids and Retention: When Used in Concert With Speech, Visual Aids Enhance Message Retention		
	RETENTION AFTER THREE HOURS	**RETENTION AFTER THREE DAYS**
Speech Alone	70%	10%
Visual Alone	72%	20%
Speech and Visual	85%	65%

Source: Elena P. Zayas-Baya, "Instructional Media in the Total Language Picture," *International Journal of Instructional Media* 5 (1977–1978): 145–150.

Effective presentation aids make achieving your goal more likely. Media- and technology-savvy audiences are comfortable processing information from multiple sources simultaneously. Adept at reading pictures, they gravitate to the visual.

I can see clearly. There are numerous benefits—both for you and your audience—in using some type of visual aid.

iStock.com/Tempura

Strategy Matters: The Wrong Way to Use Presentation Aids

Imagine going to a presentation on why you should visit national parks and finding yourself seated in the middle of a pitch-black auditorium. The speaker holds up photos of the parks, but you cannot see them well. She then delivers a 10-minute slide show designed to present highlights of each park. The speaker, however, positions herself in front of the screen, leaving you with an obstructed view. As she talks about each slide, she uses a laser pointer, twirling it about randomly when she isn't using it. She spins it so wildly that you actually become dizzy. You fight the urge to leave. The speaker demonstrated the wrong way to use presentation aids.

Strategy Matters: The Right Way to Use Presentation Aids

Speakers who use presentation aids strategically tend to be more successful. Speaking about our national parks, a successful speaker might begin by telling you a story about how she came to visit these national treasures and why you would enjoy visiting them, too. She would not obscure pertinent information with her body but stand out of the way. She would use the laser pointer to guide you through each of the park's highlights but turn it off when not actively using it. And she would ensure that the room had enough ambient light so that you could take notes. The speaker might end by asking you to visualize yourself standing in front of Old Faithful. The last visual you would see would depict the geyser with the following words splashed across the slide: "It's time to experience the spray for yourself."

Visual interest. Compelling visuals and other presentation aids should enhance audience interest in the presentation topic.

iStock.com/shayes17

SELF-ASSESSMENT 14.1: HOW READY ARE YOU TO USE PRESENTATION AIDS?

The purpose of this assessment is for you to consider the extent to which you are comfortable using different kinds of audio and visual aids when delivering a speech.

Use the following questions to evaluate your ability to integrate audio and visual aids into your presentation. Simply respond to each statement.

Questions/ Statements	Never	Rarely	Sometimes	Usually	Always
1. Every presentation aid I use helps to increase my audience's comprehension.	1	2	3	4	5
2. Every presentation aid I use helps to increase audience recall.	1	2	3	4	5
3. The presentation aids I use help me to direct the audience's attention.	1	2	3	4	5
4. The presentation aids I use help me keep my speech concise.	1	2	3	4	5
5. The presentation aids I use enhance my credibility.	1	2	3	4	5
6. The presentation aids I use help me keep my ideas organized.	1	2	3	4	5
7. The presentation aids in my speech interest the audience enhancing their attention.	1	2	3	4	5

Questions/ Statements	Never	Rarely	Sometimes	Usually	Always
8. The presentation aids I use make complex data more understandable.	1	2	3	4	5
9. The presentation aids I use are both informative and persuasive.	1	2	3	4	5
10. In general, the presentation aids I use make my speech more visually or aurally appealing.	1	2	3	4	5

Add together your scores for each question.

_____ Total

The higher your total score, the better your understanding of the purposes presentation aids serve.

What have you discovered about how to keep your speech visually and aurally appealing to the audience?

Although this evaluation is not a scientific instrument, it should give you some indication of what to include in speech introductions and conclusions.

SELECT THE BEST AIDS

> **14.2** *Select, prepare, and integrate the most relevant presentation aids into a speech.*

Presentation aids come in all shapes, sizes, and sounds and include people, models, objects, photographs, graphs, charts, drawings, slides, DVDs, music, and computer-generated materials. When planning on integrating visual or audio aids into a speech, consider these key questions:

1. What can I do to make my presentation more visually and aurally alive for my listeners?

2. Which presentation aids are most appropriate given the situation or setting for my speech? What kinds of presentation aids will the location of the speech allow?

3. Which presentation aids best suit the purpose of my speech?

Real People

A **human visual aid** can be effective if their role is well planned and they are not allowed to distract audience members. A student speaking on self-defense could bring along two people trained in martial arts, but they should not show off their skills until the appropriate moment. When using a human visual aid, follow these coaching pointers:

1. **Be certain your "human visual" is willing and committed to helping you accomplish your objectives.** The human visual should illuminate your speech without distracting the audience.

2. **Be sure to rehearse with this person prior to the big day.** Lack of preparation can be risky and can inhibit the smooth integration of the aide into your presentation.

3. **Any human visual aid is subordinate to your speech.** Do not have the aide share the speaker's area with you until their participation is required. Once the person's role is complete, move them back into the audience or out of sight.

In the effort to bring attention to the Black Lives Matter movement, a number of professional basketball players including LeBron James used themselves as models and wore the Black Lives Matter slogan to protest the shooting in the back of Jacob Blake—a message the protesters sought to share with the public. Do you also think presenters can effectively turn their attire into an integral part of their message?

You, too, may serve as a visual aid. You might demonstrate the proper stance for fencing or model the dress of your native country.

Props and Models

Props and models also can enliven a presentation. When effectively used, both add clarity, interest, and drama to spoken ideas.

Props

A *prop* is an object that has the power to compel listeners to focus their attention on your message and better understand your subject. To be effective, the object should be large enough to be seen but small enough so you can carry it to your presentation and handle it with ease. For example, a tennis racket, a folk costume, a mask, a musical instrument, food, or a toy can show your listeners what you are talking about or demonstrate how to do something. Although they can enhance interest and increase retention, props when misused can also distract the audience. Therefore, the visual aid should remain out of sight until needed. Otherwise, instead of concentrating on you, your listeners may focus on the object, speculating about what it is and what you are going to do with it.

Consider in advance the kinds of problems a prop could create. Animate props must be stored and treated humanely prior to, during, and after the speech. During a speech about how to handle a snake, one student placed the snake on a display table at the front of the room; much to her surprise, as she was turning to make a point, the snake slithered out of her reach and was on its way into the audience when she finally recaptured it. Consider the appropriateness of inanimate objects, as well. During a meeting with constituents, Rep. Ralph Norman spoke to them about guns. As he spoke, he reached into the pocket of his blazer, withdrew his reportedly loaded gun, and placed it on the table before him, leaving it there for a while and inquiring if audience members now felt safer. Some in attendance, however, said they felt intimidated rather than safe.[8] Remember, the visual aid should add credibility and drama to your presentation, not fear or chaos.

Models

If you conclude that your visual aid is too large to bring to your presentation, too small to be seen, or too dangerous, valuable, or fragile to carry around, then you might use a *model* in its place. Effective models can aid in comprehension and retention by increasing the amount of audience engagement and interest. For example, one student who delivered a speech on the human heart used a larger-than-life replica that opened to reveal its chambers. The model helped clarify the information while also keeping the audience's interest.

Prop yourself up. Employed effectively, props can really enhance a speech's message.

iStock.com/studiocasper

Tips to Remember

Keep these coaching pointers in mind when using both props and models:

1. Be sure the prop or model illustrates and reinforces an important point.
2. Be sure it's visible from anywhere in the audience.
3. Keep it hidden until you're ready to use it.
4. Put it away when you've finished using it.
5. Practice so you can use it without difficulty or calling undue attention to yourself.

Photographs

Photographs also make effective visual aids. Rather than delivering the all-too-common apology, "I know you can't see this well, but. . . ," make sure audience members *can* see it well. Select your photos with care and enlarge them sufficiently.

Try not to pass photographs around the room because doing so diverts attention from you. The person waiting to look at the photograph, the person looking at it, and the person who has just looked at it are not with you because they are concentrating on something else.

Whatever the nature of a photo, color pictures are usually more effective than black and white, but it is most important that the photo's central features be clearly visible.[9]

Graphs

Well-designed **graphs** can help speakers communicate statistical information, illustrate trends, and demonstrate patterns. Among the most commonly used are line graphs, bar graphs, pie graphs, and pictographs and infographics.[10]

Line Graphs

Line graphs show trends over time. Figure 14.2 is one such graph a student used in a speech on how to cope with academic anxiety and fear of failure. Referring to the visual, the student said, "This graph is derived from information appearing in the December 19, 2018, issue of *The Wall Street Journal*. It tells us that between the years 2009 and 2018, the share of college graduates reporting that they found college work traumatic and difficult to handle increased dramatically." She then went on to speak about academic stressors and how to address them. The student's visual helped document the seriousness of the problem and showed those students experiencing anxiety that they were not alone. Not only did this line graph reveal a trend over time, it enabled the speaker to make and show important comparisons.

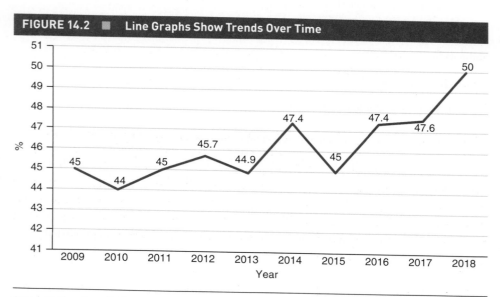

FIGURE 14.2 ■ Line Graphs Show Trends Over Time

Source: Melissa Korn, "Failure 101: Teaching Resilience," *The Wall Street Journal,* December 19, 2018, p. A6.

Were a line graph to feature more than one line, each line in the graph should be color-coded for clarity. When designed well, the line graph is one of the easiest types of visuals for audiences to follow. When designed poorly, it can become confusing, as revealed by the line graph in Figure 14.3, which is complex, poorly color-coded, and difficult for an audience to read easily and quickly.

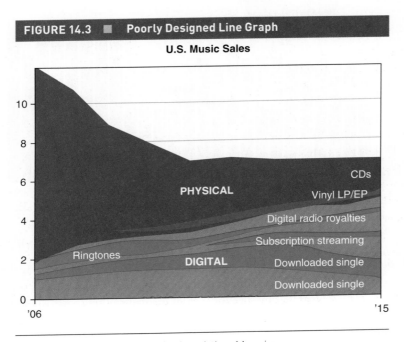

FIGURE 14.3 ■ Poorly Designed Line Graph

U.S. Music Sales

Source: Data from Recording Industry Association of America.

Bar Graphs

Like the line graph, the **bar graph** is useful for comparing or contrasting two or more items or groups. Bar graphs can be either horizontal or vertical. While they vary in length, the bars should be of equal widths. When prepared properly, the bar graph is usually easy for the uninitiated to read and interpret and makes the data more meaningful and dramatic for receivers. A bar graph is used to compare quantities or magnitude. In a speech on the military suicide crisis, a student used the bar graph in Figure 14.4 to represent the increase of suicides occurring among active-duty service members from 2001 through 2018.

Pie Graphs

In contrast to line and bar graphs, **pie graphs** (or circle graphs) illustrate percentages of a whole or distribution patterns. Ideally, pie graphs should contain from two to five clearly

FIGURE 14.4 ■

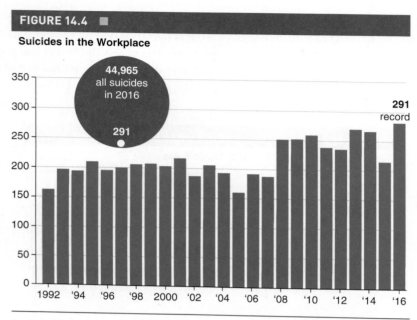

Suicides in the Workplace

Source: *USA Today*, November 11, 2019, p. 7A.

labeled "slices" or divisions. Figure 14.5 shows a pie graph with slices representing the top six sports played by Division I female athletes and a seventh slice representing all other sports these athletes play. A separate tiny slice for each of the many other sports would make the graph too cluttered. Do you see any way the speaker might have reduced the number of slices in Figure 14.5 to five?

Whatever types of graphs you use, keep in mind the following guidelines:

1. Clearly title the graph.

2. Keep the graph as simple as possible. Too many graphs or too much information contributes to information overload.

3. Help receivers with the interpretation process. Don't assume they will read the graph the way you expect them to.

4. Make sure the graph is large enough for the audience to see everything written on it and contains colors that are distinguishable.

Clear graphs facilitate clear speech. See Table 14.1 to review the best uses of each type of graph.

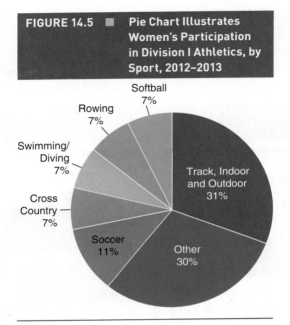

FIGURE 14.5 ■ Pie Chart Illustrates Women's Participation in Division I Athletics, by Sport, 2012–2013

Source: NCAA (National Collegiate Athletic Association), "Sport-by-Sport Participation and Sponsorship Women's Sport 2012–2013 (Division 1)," https://www.ncaa.org/sites/default/files/Participation%20Rates%20Final.pdf.

TABLE 14.1 ■ Best Graph Practices	
Type of Graph	**Function**
Line	To demonstrate trends or changes over time; to reveal how one thing affects another
Bar	To show comparisons and contrasts; to show differences in amount or frequency
Pie	To reveal relationships between parts and the whole; to indicate relative proportions. percentages, or distribution patterns
Infographic	To use pictorial representations to decrease the formality of a graph and enhance its appeal

Infographics

Composites of information, illustration, and design, **infographics** help speakers relay information in more interesting ways. Infographics are particularly useful in helping audience members visualize data.[11] A **pictograph**—a graphic representation of the subject—is a simplified version of an infographic. For example, the graph in Figure 14.6, describing the number of multiple-generation households in the United States, has visual appeal that makes it a little less formal than a bar graph. Figure 14.7 is an example of a more sophisticated infographic that one student used in a speech about robots taking over the jobs of humans.

FIGURE 14.6 ■ Infographics Add Interest and Visual Appeal

Three or more generations in one household

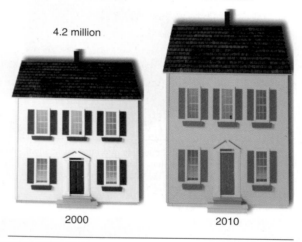

4.2 million

5.1 million

2000

2010

Source: U.S. Census Bureau.

FIGURE 14.7 ■ Will a Robot Replace You?

41% of Americans would be interested in a robot caregiver for themselves or a family member.

PEW RESEARCH CENTER

Source: "Shareable Facts on Americans' Views and Attitudes Toward Automation Technologies," Pew Research Center, Washington, D.C. (October 4, 2017), http://www.pewinternet.org/2017/10/04/shareable-facts-on-americans -views-and-attitudes-toward-automation-technologies/.

Charts, Drawings, and Maps

Charts, drawings, and maps are resources speakers rely on to convey complex information simply and visually.

Charts

Speakers use **charts** to help compress or summarize large amounts of information. By enabling listeners to organize their own thoughts and follow your speech's progress, charts also simplify note-taking and help audiences remember. The most commonly used chart is one that combines descriptions with graphics.

Figure 14.8 illustrates how, with a tenth of a second left to play in a basketball game, a team managed against long odds to inbound the ball and score to win the game. This chart helped a speaker to explain the play and make his point about the importance of not giving up until a game is over.

Charts are particularly useful for speakers who want to discuss a process, channel of communication, or chain of command, as Figure 14.9 demonstrates.

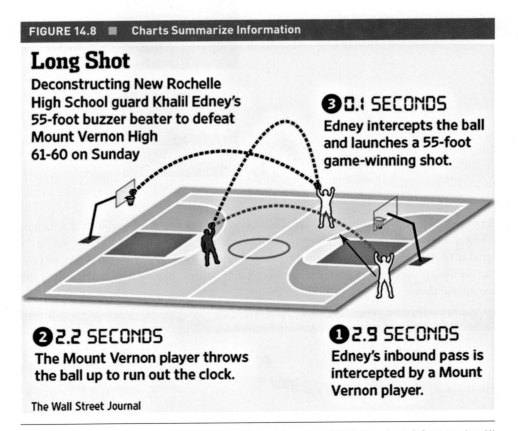

FIGURE 14.8   ■   Charts Summarize Information

Long Shot

Deconstructing New Rochelle High School guard Khalil Edney's 55-foot buzzer beater to defeat Mount Vernon High 61-60 on Sunday

❸ 0.1 SECONDS
Edney intercepts the ball and launches a 55-foot game-winning shot.

❷ 2.2 SECONDS
The Mount Vernon player throws the ball up to run out the clock.

❶ 2.9 SECONDS
Edney's inbound pass is intercepted by a Mount Vernon player.

The Wall Street Journal

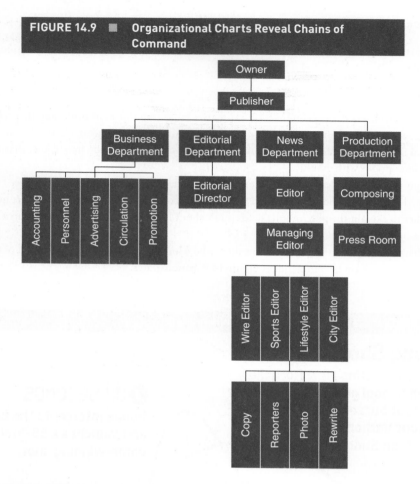

FIGURE 14.9 ■ Organizational Charts Reveal Chains of Command

Owner

Publisher

Business Department | Editorial Department | News Department | Production Department

Accounting | Personnel | Advertising | Circulation | Promotion

Editorial Director

Editor

Composing

Managing Editor

Press Room

Wire Editor | Sports Editor | Lifestyle Editor | City Editor

Copy | Reporters | Photo | Rewrite

Drawings and Maps

Drawings and maps help illustrate key differences, movements, or geographic information. These visuals translate complex information into a format that receivers can grasp readily. A speaker compared different swim strokes using Figure 14.10. As she spoke, she revealed only the portion of the drawing to which she was referring; other sections were covered until she mentioned them.

FIGURE 14.10 ■ Drawings Help Share Meaning

Dorling Kindersley/Thinkstock

Maps also make versatile visual aids. One speaker used the map in Figure 14.11 when delivering a speech on the nature of well-being. As you can see, communities in states scored higher or lower according to where they fell on the Well-Being Index, a measure of health, happiness, job satisfaction, and other factors determining quality of life.

Prepare drawings and maps in advance. Drawing them while your audience is watching consumes valuable speaking time, makes audience members lose patience with you, and produces art that is less suitable for use.

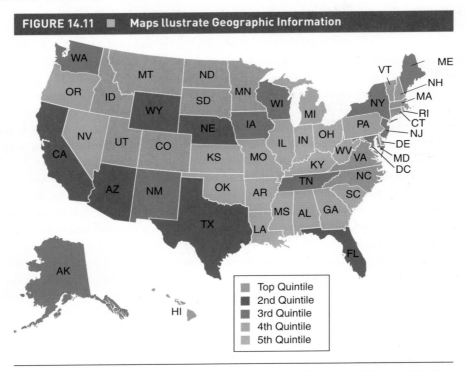

FIGURE 14.11 ■ Maps llustrate Geographic Information

Legend:
■ Top Quintile
■ 2nd Quintile
■ 3rd Quintile
■ 4th Quintile
■ 5th Quintile

Source: Gallup-Healthways Well-Being Index, "State of American Well-Being: 2017 State Well-Being Rankings."

Be sure to properly cite slides or frames used in your presentation by treating them as you would any article included. The following is an example of APA citation for PowerPoint slides:

Author, A. A. (year of publication). Title of presentation [PowerPoint slides]. Retrieved from URL

Park, L. (2011). Effective working teams [PowerPoint slides]. Retrieved from[12]

Audio and Video Clips

Audio and video clips also help make a speech more dynamic, involving, and exciting for receivers. Because they allow a speaker to custom design more sophisticated examples of presentation support, they can be extremely effective tools to use with today's media-savvy audiences.

Though these visual aids require speakers to use technology requiring advance preparation, the vividness they provide is difficult to beat.

Video Clips

Using brief video clips in a speech can establish your credibility as well as increase audiences' interest, memory, and understanding. Imagine speaking about football and the risk of injury and then showing a video of a player being tackled during a game and suffering a concussion. Showing the segment during your speech provides an immediate dramatic impact.

You can find videos at YouTube, Vimeo, MetaCafe.com, and DailyMotion.com, among other sources. To be effective, the clip you use needs to be short—usually consuming no more than 30 seconds of a five-minute speech. Even a six-second video can be useful because you want your audience to remember your words, not just the video. Be sure to cue it up, download it, or have it ready to run prior to starting your presentation. If you will be using your own computer to show the clip, be sure you have compatible files and/or cables to connect to the classroom projector. And remember, double-check that the video will transfer well to a bigger screen. A video that is of low quality or too pixelated will not enhance your presentation. Think carefully about the audience and other constraints before selecting a clip. You don't want to isolate or offend the audience by using a clip that is too violent or generally in poor taste. Whatever you select, be sure to introduce the clip to the audience, preparing them for what they are about to see. Video clips work best when you are able to integrate them smoothly and without interruption into your speech.

A word of caution: During the lead-up to then-president Trump's speech at the 2020 Republican National Convention, a video was shown depicting disturbing images of "Biden's America," with a scene of fire raging in the streets. Unfortunately, the streets shown actually weren't in Biden's America, or even in America at all, but in Barcelona, Spain.[13] A speaker should authenticate the videos they use. Using a video to give the audience a false impression is as harmful as falsifying evidence.

Audio Clips

Though the majority of aids speakers use are visual ones, audio also merits attention. A recording of music, sound, or speech can make your presentation more interesting and memorable. Were you speaking on the purpose of folk music, for example, playing snippets of songs or the recorded words of a musician could help you convey your message.

Audio is readily available and easy to use in your presentation, either by computer or your cell phone. Just be sure to cue it to the precise point at which you want to begin before starting your presentation. And as with video, introduce the audio segment before playing it to orient the audience to what they will be hearing.

Of note is the effectiveness of mixing visual and audio aids together—creating a fully integrated multimedia experience for the audience. Visual clips and computer images when paired with sound and text have the potential to make your speech one the audience will remember.

COACHING TIP

"The power of sound to put an audience in a certain psychological state is vastly undervalued."

—Mike Figgis, film director

Appropriately integrated audio and video clips add drama to your speech. Use them to set, reflect, or amplify a mood. Because they strike a chord with the audience, they will make your words more interesting, involving, and memorable.

BE FAMILIAR WITH PRESENTATION SOFTWARE: YOUR KEY TO USING PRESENTATION AIDS

14.3 *Choose appropriate presentation software to get the most from your presentation aids.*

Because they are professional looking and easy to create, visual slides created using presentation software such as Prezi, Google Docs Presentation, Microsoft PowerPoint, GoAnimate, or SlideRocket can add contemporary flair, drama, professionalism, and credibility to a speech.[14] Using one of these software options also enables you to give visual shape to your arguments. In the words of Harvard psychology professor Steven Pinker, "Language is a linear medium: one word after another. But ideas are multi-dimensional. . . . When properly employed, PowerPoint makes the logical structure of an argument more transparent. Two channels sending the same information are better than one."[15]

Presentation software also makes it easy to include a graph or chart, as most programs provide templates and tutorials explaining how to use them.[16] Every software program has its benefits and drawbacks (see Table 14.2). PowerPoint, for example, is the most widely used presentation software. It is particularly useful for a linear presentation. When creating a PowerPoint presentation, you can choose either a blank presentation, building your slide presentation yourself, or rely on an existing design. You can embed text, visuals, video, audio, and animation into PowerPoint slides. In contrast to PowerPoint, Prezi brags that it enables you to "captivate your audience by zooming through your story." Thus, rather than moving through a series of slides, Prezi lets you zoom in and out across a canvas or interactive surface. Benefits can turn into drawbacks, however. The side effects of zooming and panning with Prezi can be dizzying. In fact, one critic cautioned that Prezi turns presentations into "heavily decorated and animated affairs with excessive motion that distracts from even well-researched content."[17]

Recent versions of presentation software do make it easy for you to create three-dimensional artwork and incorporate sound, music, or video clips into your presentation.

TABLE 14.2 ■ A Guide to Presentation Software		
Software	**Pros**	**Cons**
Microsoft PowerPoint	● The most common presentation software used globally. ● The program is easy to use, particularly for Microsoft Word users. ● PowerPoint comes with multiple slide design options and additional templates can be downloaded directly from Microsoft.	● To utilize this software, students must purchase a license. ● Linear format is not as dynamic for presentations.
Apple Keynote	● Can be accessed from any Mac or iOS compatible device. ● Easy to share presentation files with others. Users can save Keynote documents as PowerPoint files. ● Apple Keynote comes with multiple slide design options and additional templates can be downloaded directly from Apple.	● To utilize this software, students must purchase a license. ● Designed specifically for Mac and iOS devices, so some formatting may be lost when converting Keynote files to PowerPoint to present on a Windows computer. ● Linear format is not as dynamic for presentations.
Prezi	● Users can access the program online; there's no need to have access to a computer with the program installed. ● No fee for basic usage. ● More dynamic and interactive format; presentation is on a single canvas that allows the user to create their own organizational structure.	● Dynamic format not ideal for content-heavy presentations. ● Not all information is spatially related; the canvas format can force a spatial relationship where none exists. ● Rather than being referred to as slides, Prezi images are referred to as frames.
Google Slides	● Free, Web-based presentation program. ● Users can edit presentations when they're offline. ● Collaborative; user can create and edit slides with others in real time. ● Program automatically saves changes.	● Must have access to a Gmail account. ● Not as many customization options as PowerPoint or Keynote.

The ease of using **computer-generated graphics** (see Figure 14.12) is helping transform ordinary presentations into extraordinary speechmaking events, but you need to be selective when deciding whether or not to use presentation software. Once the speech is ready, ask yourself at what points in it will slides help to clarify or vivify an idea. The goal is not to clutter-up a presentation with slides, but to position slides where they will strengthen the message. If your presentation is not prepared with care, the slides may upstage you, overpower your message, or drain your speech of its vitality.[18] Or you may be tempted to use dazzling PowerPoint slides to cover up weak content.[19]

Plan out how to use each of your aids and practice integrating each one. Unless a presentation aid is going to enhance your presentation, don't use it. Just because you can use a glitzy visual doesn't mean you should.

FIGURE 14.12 ■ Sample Slides From a Computer-Generated Graphic

Source: "A Real Search for Alien Life," Sara Seager's presentation for TEDxCambridge 2013, September 25, 2013, http://www.youtube.com/watch?v=NnM4SaGc8R0.

Visuals should be large enough, clear enough, and dramatic enough to enhance the informative and persuasive power of your presentations. Like any other skill, however, selecting, designing, integrating, and using visuals take patience, persistence, and practice.

Devise the Content and Design the Look

Follow these content and design pointers to help craft effective slides. A typical slide features a title or short phrase describing its purpose or theme, a visual, and brief text, often bulleted.

- **Keep it simple.** Each slide should be brief and focus on a single idea.

- **Keep it short.** The fewer words, the better!

- **Use bullets.** Bulleted lists increase readability and help you organize your ideas.

- **Avoid clutter.** Minimize purely decorative design elements that distract viewers from your message.

- **Be direct.** Use active wording and parallel sentence structure.

- **Be design wise.** Keep slides consistent, to avoid distracting the audience with jarring colors or fonts.

- **Use a readable font.** Common fonts are common for a reason: they are the easiest to read. Avoid decorative or handwriting fonts and don't mix more than two font types on a single slide. Use the same fonts on all slides.

- **Use a suitable text size.** Use 36- to 44-point type for main headings, 24 to 36 for subheads, and 18 to 24 for text. Type projected on a screen should never be smaller than 18 point. Use upper and lower case to increase legibility.

- **Be color cautious.** Using the right color enhances readership, receptivity, and retention.[20] But using color requires care. You want the color(s) you use to set the right mood and render your message readable and attractive. Keep the background color consistent. Use no more than two text colors. Differentiate background from text. In general, using a lighter font on a dark background is easier for audience members to read.

- **Be creative.** Rely on images and sounds more than text. Insert tables, art, very brief video clips, and sound directly into your slides.

- **Be in control.** Direct your audience's attention before you start a video. If you're going to talk during the video clip, mute the sound. When not referring to a slide, use a blank slide or cover the lens to bring the focus of the audience back to you.

- **Remember you are a speaker first.** You're delivering a speech, not merely a multimedia presentation. You are not replaceable!

- **Maintain eye contact.** Keep your eyes on the audience, not on the slide. Talk to the audience, not to the screen.

- **Always rehearse.** To make the most of your visual and audio aids and incorporate them seamlessly, rehearse in advance and up to your presentation.

- **Be prepared.** Have a contingency plan in case the equipment fails.

Choose the Right Presentation Aids

How do you choose a presentation aid? Start by considering your topic, your audience, and your options. For example, topics related to health and human services typically include graphs and charts to simplify the communication of complex information. Consider these criteria when deciding whether to use a presentation aid:

1. Is it worth its cost?

   Will the amount of time and effort you expend preparing the aid pay off in audience interest and response?

2. Does it "talk" to receivers?

   Will the visual or audio aid facilitate your task by saving you words? Will your listeners be able to understand and relate to it? Might anyone in your audience find the visuals or sounds you are using inappropriate or distracting?

3. Do I have the skill and technology to use it effectively?

   Is technology on site? Will you have the opportunity to practice using the technology? Unrealistic expectations regarding the time it will take you to master using a program could leave you with too little time to rehearse your speech. Remember, using visual and audio aids well takes practice too.

Finally, when determining the presentation aids to use, keep the objectives of your speech uppermost in your mind and limit each visual to one main point. Simplicity should lead the way. Every visual you use should be clear and concise, large and legible, and simple and straightforward. Don Keough of the Coca-Cola Company said it best: "Some pictures may be worth a thousand words, but a picture of a thousand words isn't worth much."

Integrate the Presentation Aids Into Your Speech

For maximum effectiveness, presentation aids need to be skillfully integrated into your speech and not create awkward moments for you. Here are some tips:

1. Be sure your visual and audio aids are in place before starting.

2. Present and explain each one.

3. Stand to one side of the visual and talk to the audience, making sure everyone can see the visual.

4. Keep physical possession and control of your visual.

5. Put the visual away when you have finished referring to it.

GAME PLAN

Integrating a Presentation Aid Into Your Speech

- I've spoken to my instructor about the equipment I'll need in the classroom for my speech.

- I've made sure that classroom equipment/technology are compatible with my own.

- I've prepared a presentation aid that will be clear to eyes and ears in the front *and* back of the classroom.

- I've rehearsed how I will introduce my presentation aid and I'm comfortable making the transition.

- I have the time to set up any needed equipment prior to giving my speech.

- I have the skills to use the technology needed during my speech.

- After my speech, I can close down and quickly remove my presentation aid to make room for the next presenter's needs.

EXERCISES

Presentation Aids

Mastering the ability to create and use visual and audio aids will enhance your ability to interest and involve audiences. Participating in these activities will build your skills.

1. Visuals and Sound

Suggest visual and sound aids to use in speeches on the following topics:

- Understanding Parkinson's Disease

- The Nature of a Meme

- The Benefits and Drawbacks of Working Remotely

- The Artist Frida Kahlo

2. Props and Models

First, identify a prop or model used in a current television or Internet commercial that is used to grab viewer attention and increase memorability. Reflect on what about the prop or model works well. Then, based on your conclusion, identify a prop or model you could use to attract attention and increase memorability for your own speeches on each of the following topics:

- Medical Training in the United States

- Altruism

- Snowboarding or Surfing
- The Value of Discipline

3. Analyze This: A Speaker's Use of Visual and Audio Aids

One student added both credibility and drama to his speech, titled "Equality," by using four apples as visual aids in the introduction and the body, and then a stone during the conclusion. Selected excerpts of his speech appear below. Read them and then answer the questions that follow:

- In your opinion, to what extent was the speaker's use of visual aids effective? Explain.
- Do you believe audience members would find the visual aids distracting or helpful? Why?
- If you were the speaker, would you have thrown a stone at your audience? Why or why not?
- What audio aids, if any, do you believe the speaker could have used to his advantage?

[From the introduction] *[In turn, the speaker selects and holds up one of four apples for the audience to see]* Four apples—similar by their outer appearance, almost identical by their insides, and yet their flavors are worlds apart. This one right here, it's a sweet one, really sweet. This one right here, it's kind of sour. This one is bitter, and the last is a combination of all. Four apples—two red and two green—similar, but very different.

I'm not just talking about the differences between apples. I'm also talking about the differences between people. Color you may say is only skin-deep, but it is much more than that. Some believe it determines where you come from, what you believe, where your social interests lie, and even whom you fall in love with. Your color helps determine your uniqueness and your individuality. It helps mold you into the person you are and the person you hope to become.

[From the body of the speech] George F. Snyder, author of *Black No More,* imagined a world where everyone was the same color. . . . Could you imagine this world if everyone was the same color? I could, and I would hate it.

The hope some have of a color-blind society brings up the question: If everyone conformed and became the same, which culture would we adapt to? Would the Japanese society of respect and hard work be dominant? Would everyone choose to have the strength and endurance of the African Americans? Would the conquering attitude of the Caucasian American reign supreme? . . .

[Once again picking up an apple] My favorite apple is this green one right here. It is colored but not too colored. It is sweet, yet still sour, but best of all, it is different from every other apple. If someone were to come up with the perfect medium for the taste and color of apples, I would object because I would not have the variety to choose from anymore. I would have to settle for a bland color and a bland taste. I pray this never happens.

A great man once said, "If any of you are without fault, then let him be the first to cast a stone." It is time we stop casting stones and accept people for who they are, color and all. . . .

[From the conclusion] *[The speaker holds up a stone]* Let the man without any fault cast the first stone. During the civil-rights era even police were casting stones at peaceful protesters. I, myself, have been hit with several stones of a color-blind society. For example, there were times when I wanted to speak up as a Black man and not just a human, but I have to forfeit my thoughts, my ideas, and my feelings for you. Equality—that's the solution.

Alexander Kremble, a Black nationalist who spent 20 years as a missionary in Liberia and founded the first organization for African American intellectuals, said the race problem is a moral one, and like all other great battles of humanity, its solution will be fought with weapons of truth. Here it is, the first stone of equality, and I cast it to you. Not because I am without fault, but because I know it is the best solution for both you and me. The solution is equality, and now the solution is no longer in my hands, but yours. So I ask, "What are you going to do with it?"

4. Approach the Speaker's Stand

1. You're giving a speech on one of the following topics:
    - The Electoral College
    - Hang Gliding
    - CPR
    - Careers of the Future
    - The American Foster Care System
    - Copyright Law

    Consider which visual aid applications or approach you would use to prepare your presentation, give your rationale for selecting that one, and share ideas for two to three possible visual and audio aids to include in the speech.

2. Select a speech from YouTube, TED Talks, or *Vital Speeches of the Day,* and brainstorm in class how one or more visual or audio aids either were or could be used to clarify or amplify the speaker's message.

3. Select an interesting news story or op-ed piece on a current issue or event. Create a slide containing a head, a couple of bullet points, a visual to illustrate the article's content, and a citation if needed.

4. Prepare a three- to five-minute presentation in which you use at least two visual aids and one audio aid.

RECAP AND REVIEW

1. **Discuss the strategic use of presentation aids.**

    The right presentation aids increase listener understanding, enhance memory and recall, facilitate message organization, and help the speaker control audience attention and interest. They add impact, reduce speech apprehension, enhance speaker credibility, and increase the persuasiveness of the speaker and message.

2. **Select, prepare, and use the most relevant presentation aids.**

   Human beings, objects, and models focus the audience's attention on the speaker's message. Photographs add realism, drama, and impact to a presentation. Graphs help receivers interpret statistical data and trends. Charts, drawings, and maps summarize large amounts of information. Graphics and sound add contemporary flair, professionalism, and credibility to a speech. Used effectively, all presentation aids add appeal and help illustrate the key points of a speech. A visual or audio aid should strengthen points, connect to audience members, or enhance credibility. Content and design should be simple, straight to the point, and creative. Rehearse introducing the aids with words, and make sure all equipment and cables are in place before approaching the podium. Check the clarity and volume of the visual or audio clip so that all audience members can see and hear the content.

3. **Choose appropriate presentation software to get the most from your presentation aids.**

   Prezi, Google Docs Presentation, Microsoft PowerPoint, and SlideRocket are among the software programs available. Consider the goals of the speech, constraints, and the actual audience before selecting a program.

KEY TERMS

Bar graph (p. 309)
Chart (p. 313)
Computer-generated graphics (p. 318)
Drawings and maps (p. 314)
Graphs (p. 308)
Human visual aid (p. 306)

Infographic (p. 311)
Line graph (p. 308)
Pictograph (p. 312)
Pie graph (p. 309)
Presentation aids (p. 300)

iStock.com/181072565

15 SPEAKING TO INFORM

UPON COMPLETING THIS CHAPTER, YOU WILL BE ABLE TO

15.1   Define informative speaking, explaining its purpose, and the value and nature of information.

15.2   Distinguish among the following types of informative speech: a speech about objects, ideas, or theories; a speech about events or people; and a speech about processes, procedures, or demonstrations.

15.3   Deliver an informative speech that is organized, understandable, and memorable, engaging the audience.

If information is power, how powerful are you? What information do you have that others also would benefit from knowing? What knowledge might you share that could change an audience's world? What do you need to do to develop and deliver an informative speech that achieves these goals? The focus in this chapter is on answering these questions.

While our smart devices afford us access to all the human information in history, they also contribute to our being awash in information, not all of which is valid. In fact, misinformation on Facebook received six times more clicks than factual information did during the 2020 presidential election.[1] The informative speaker's responsibility is to research and harness intellectually stimulating, relevant, and accurate pieces of knowledge. There are an unlimited number of topics about which you can share information and develop understanding. Whether you are an employee, a parent, or a student, speaking informatively is part of daily life. You likely explain, describe, or demonstrate something to others every day. Everyday informing, however, is more informal and less planned than is delivering an informative speech.

THE NATURE AND PURPOSE OF INFORMATIVE SPEAKING

15.1   *Define informative speaking, explaining its purpose, and the value and nature of information.*

The purpose of an informative speech is to convey something new or not fully understood to an audience in the clearest, most accurate, and most compelling way possible. In general, the purpose is to educate, to provide others with a fresh perspective or new and useful knowledge. Audience members should learn from an informative speech, adding to their understanding. Thus, what you choose to speak about depends on the knowledge, experience, and interests of your receivers. In summary, your purpose as an informative speaker is to share information you have with people who lack it but need it, or who possess it but do not yet fully understand it.

What gives information its value? Consider the following formula. The **value of information** (VOI) is the time, effort, or money that a person is willing to invest in order to possess new information prior to rendering a decision or drawing a conclusion.[2] For example, think about a decision that you are about to make. How much time, effort, or money would you expend to have information enabling you to make the best decision possible? Having information of value allows people to make sounder decisions. While it is probable that every piece of information is of value to someone, it is unlikely that individuals actually need to spend money to acquire it. Instead, it is quite likely that if we are willing to do in-depth research and take time to compare different perspectives, we now can uncover any information of value to us for free. Establishing connections to information has been simplified for us.

Figuratively speaking, there is more information available to us right now than there is snow in the Arctic. From an informative speaker's perspective, then, the question is this: Are we able to evaluate the information we find in order to distinguish the most relevant and interesting information from the rest? And this question leads to others: How much information is too much information? Is it possible that we now have the ability to discover and possess too much information? Whereas the amount of information available continues to explode, our individual capacities for absorbing information have not increased. Every day, we face a deluge of new, and often conflicting, data. As a result, we need to be able to filter, process, and edit the information we receive.[3] Here are some questions to consider about information's nature:

1. How much information is it ethically feasible for you to share at one time with an audience?

2. How should you decide when you have gathered sufficient information to bolster your credibility and the credibility of the information you impart? That is, how much and how many sources of information should you reference in your presentation?

3. What can you do to help your audience assess the information and sources you provide as reputable, not questionable?

4. What will you do to avoid over- or underwhelming audience members with data? How will you minimize the effects of both a "data deluge" and "data dearth" when passing information on to receivers?

To be effective, informative speakers also need to conceptualize and break down the information they impart. In fact, while information remains essential, we have moved beyond the information age into the conceptual age. We have transitioned to a time when people with the ability to understand and interpret meaning, think differently, detect patterns, recognize opportunities, and edit and put the pieces together in new ways are in demand, especially in professional sectors. In addition to being able to explain a specific subject clearly, concisely, and correctly as well as ethically, informative speakers need to be concrete, making connections to help the audience synthesize, recall, and retain the knowledge they are sharing.[4] Do you have these skills? Use the information contained in this chapter to develop and/or improve them.

Informative Speakers Avoid Information Overload and Underload

To be able to process, conceptualize, and impart information effectively, speakers need to get a handle on information overload and information anxiety. **Information anxiety** is the psychological stress people experience when information overload confuses them or makes it difficult for them to make sense of the never-ending accumulation of information.[5] Ours is the "big data" age. Vast numbers of workers in the United States and around the world are paid to gather and interpret the morass of information collected. When in the throes of **information overload**, we possess not only an overabundance of information but also so many competing expert opinions that it becomes virtually impossible to apply logical approaches to deliberation and problem-solving. For example, well over 100,000 studies now exist on the topic of depression. How is any doctor or patient even to begin to make sense of all that information and craft a treatment plan? Because of the sheer quantity of information, attempts to draw conclusions often lead to "paralysis by analysis." How much information is too much information? Could endless information, or information overload, result in perpetual argumentation but no conclusion?

While information overload is a challenge, information underload can be just as serious a problem. **Information underload** occurs when speakers have access to information but take the easy way out, acquiring too little of it and underwhelming their receivers. Information underload is made worse when the speaker is unable to provide audience members with the information they deserve. Whether because of a lack of research on the speaker's part, the erroneous belief that receivers will not understand the complexity of the information the speaker presents, or an unwillingness to communicate complex information in a way that makes it understandable and relatable, information underload makes it impossible for a speaker to achieve their goal.

So, while information overload makes it likely that a speaker will try to cram too much information into a presentation, and information underload makes it likely the speaker will provide too little information in a presentation, the speaker who can separate the essential from the nonessential will pass along just the right amount of information to an audience. Are you that speaker?

SELF-ASSESSMENT 15.1: ASSESSING THE EFFECTS OF INFORMATION OVERLOAD

Directions

How overloaded with information do you feel? To find out, score the following statements from 1–5, with 1 representing "never," 2 representing "rarely ever," 3 representing "sometimes," 4 representing "usually," and 5 representing "always."

Statement	1 Never	2 Rarely Ever	3 Sometimes	4 Usually	5 Always
1. My thoughts frequently drift off, making it difficult for me to concentrate on what's before my eyes.					

Statement	1 Never	2 Rarely Ever	3 Sometimes	4 Usually	5 Always
2. I find myself forgetting what I think I should retain.					
3. I feel tired when I think of all the information I have to acquire.					
4. I often put off making a decision because I want to get more information.					
5. After I make a decision, I wonder if I chose the right option because of all the possible choices I had before me.					
6. When I go online, I think about all the other things I have to do.					
7. I check my online networks repeatedly, because I'm concerned that if I don't, I'll miss something important.					
8. I'm distracted by new information, which makes it hard for me to process the information that I already have.					
9. It's hard for me to separate what I need to know from what's interesting and nice to know.					
10. I feel like my texts, emails, and voice messages pile up, causing me to use up too much of my time trying to keep up with them.					

Scoring Method	Total Score Interpretation
Total your score by adding together the numbers of your responses to each question: Total _____	The higher your score, the more difficult it is for you to handle information overload. While many of us experience a normal amount of information overload, for some of us, information obsessiveness becomes debilitating. When it's never enough, that's usually too much to process—and could impede rather than enhance understanding, making it less likely that we will transmit relevant information that enriches knowledge.

Informative Speakers Make Information Relevant

It is especially important that you distinguish and process information that will add to the audience's knowledge. There are things that are known and things that are unknown; in between are doors. When doors are opened and information is turned into knowledge, information confers power. Once speaker and receiver make sense of the *right* information, they can accomplish things they otherwise might not have been able to. Here, the informative speech plays an important role.

Our world is filled with informative messages upon which we depend. Some of these messages are informal, but others are carefully planned, structured, and rehearsed to achieve maximum impact. Some three quarters of the U.S. labor force hold jobs requiring the production, storage, delivery, or interpretation of information. Educators in schools and businesses, sales professionals, medical practitioners, and consultants and managers in a wide array of fields depend on their skill in giving and receiving information for their livelihoods. They all share the need to make their messages clear, relevant, and useful to receivers.

Informative speakers face three primary challenges: (1) to identify information that has importance for others; (2) to put themselves in the position of their receivers and make the information they deliver neither overwhelming nor underwhelming, but understandable; and (3) to communicate and conceptualize information in ways that create interest, enhance learning, and help audience members remember the delivered message.

Informative Speakers Focus on Information, Not Persuasion

The main purpose of an informative speech is to educate, not to advocate. While information is the foundation for persuasion, and some maintain that all information is persuasive, in practice, the two kinds of speaking differ in a significant way, and that difference is the goal of the speaker. The goal of an informative speaker is to discover and share reliable information that is of interest and has value—to help receivers understand a topic better, without advocating for a specific outcome. As a result, informative speakers maintain as much objectivity as possible while persuasive speakers, in contrast, openly display their subjectivity—seeking to sway receivers to accept their point of view or to take action. Thus, while informative speakers may present the pros and cons of a course of action, they conduct their investigation without taking a stand or pushing a position. They maintain neutrality. Think of it this way: whereas the informative speaker presents information without attempting or intending to persuade receivers, the persuasive speaker relies on information presented to sway receivers.

TYPES OF INFORMATIVE PRESENTATIONS

> **15.2**   *Distinguish among the following types of informative speech: a speech about objects, ideas, or theories; a speech about events or people; and a speech about processes, procedures, or demonstrations.*

Being able to convey information and to conceptualize meaning to diverse others are among the most useful skills you can acquire. Here, we consider common kinds of informative speaking and speech development frameworks. For organizational purposes, we divide **informative speech** into three primary categories: speeches about (1) objects and ideas or theories; (2) events and people; and (3) processes, procedures, and demonstrations. Though these categories are far from exhaustive, they represent the most common ways public speakers package information (see Table 15.1). After this, we look at informative speech goals and how to achieve them.

TABLE 15.1 ■ Informative Speech Types and Topics

Speech Type	Sample Topics
Objects/Ideas/Theories	Self-Driving Cars
	Asian American Superheroes
	September 11 Memorial
	The Tomb of Tutankhamun
	Current Threats to Privacy
	Stonehenge
	QAnon Conspiracy Theory
	Sustainable Energy
	Why We Dream
	NFTs (Nonfungible Tokens)
Events/People	The Landing of the *InSight* Spacecraft on Mars
	The Parole of Sirhan Sirhan
	New York ComiCon
	Burning Man
	Harvey Milk
	Ruth Bader Ginsburg
	Kanye West
Processes/Procedures/ Demonstrations	How an Elephant Uses Its Trunk
	How to Speed Read
	How to Prepare for a Job Interview
	How to Stop the Bleeding After an Injury
	What to Do If You're Caught in Your Car in a Flood

COACHING TIP

The main purpose of an informative speech is to educate, not advocate.

Help audience members learn new information, and you help them grow. Knowledge that is applicable to life is power. Power up your audience with information they can understand and use, and you set them on a path unburdened by confusion.

Speeches About Objects and Ideas or Theories

When speaking of an object, animate or inanimate, we usually describe it and tell about its uses. Thus, speeches about objects are rich in description. What objects would you like to describe for others? What about your chosen object and its description would resonate with the audience? When, instead of an object, we speak of an idea or theory, we typically define and explain it. Thus, speeches about ideas or theories rely on explanations and narratives. What narrative might you use to explain global warming? Might you tell about surviving a fire, flood, or hurricane?

Speaking About an Object

An **object speech** can cover anything tangible—a machine, building, structure, place, or phenomenon (see Table 15.1 for examples). The selected object may be living or inanimate, moving or still, visible to the naked eye or beyond its scope. Whatever your object, the goal remains the same: to paint an accurate and information-rich picture.

Once you select an object for your topic, the next step is to create a specific purpose that identifies the particular aspect on which you will focus. The following are sample purpose statements for informative speeches about objects:

- To inform my audience about the ecological features of Florida's Everglades

- To inform my audience about the anatomy of the human brain

Object lesson. Like a tour guide, an informative speaker focuses the audience's attention on what is most important to know about a speech topic.

iStock.com/monkeybusinessimages

- To inform my audience about the design of Roman aqueducts

- To inform my audience about the relationship of black holes to space time

Notice how precise these specific purposes are. They are not overly broad, making them achievable in the time allotted for the speech.

Speaking About an Idea or Theory

What does the word *existentialism* mean? What is *bullying*? How do we clarify the nature of *common law, double jeopardy,* or an *iatrogenic injury*? In a speech about an idea or theory, also known as a **concept or expository speech**, your goal is to explain it in such a way that audience members agree on two things:

1. The idea or theory has relevance and importance for them.

2. They want you to clarify or elaborate on it.

General or abstract ideas generally work best for concept or expository speeches, as they allow for the most creative analysis and interpretation. For example, you might discuss free speech, Buddhism, or inequality (see Table 15.1 for more suggestions).

When we talk about ideas, audience members may have different interpretations of the concepts or words we use—primarily because personal experience influences meaning. This is particularly likely for nontangible topics such as injustice, religion, and responsible citizenship.

Let's look at a few of the general topics we've identified and create some specific purpose statements for each:

- To inform my audience about the meaning of injustice

- To inform my audience about a theory of genius

- To inform my audience about basic tenets of responsible citizenship

Each of these is narrow enough for a speaker to be able to tailor the specific purpose to the time available.

Abstract ideas. What are some concepts you'd be interested in learning or talking about?

Ryan McVay/Photodisc/Thinkstock

Organizational Frameworks for Speaking of Objects, Ideas, or Theories

Speeches about objects, ideas, or theories lend themselves to topical, spatial, and chronological organizational formats. When it comes to an object, a topical format allows you to divide your subject into groups or major categories, as when speaking about volcanoes, for example, focusing first on extinct volcanoes, second on dormant volcanoes, and third on active ones. A spatial or physical framework enables you to discuss one major component of the object at a time, as you might when discussing the entrance, antechamber, and burial chamber of an Egyptian pyramid. And finally, a chronological format is most appropriate if you are going to stress how a design or phenomenon evolved over time (for example, the formation of the Hawaiian Islands). You also can easily develop a speech about an **idea or theory** using a topical order, enumerating and discussing, in turn, key aspects of the idea, for instance explaining the ways racial prejudice affects its victims economically, politically, and socially. Speeches about objects, ideas, or theories also lend themselves to chronological development. When speaking about sexual harassment you might explain how our understanding of the term has changed through the years. See Chapters 8 and 9 for more on organizational formats. Take a look at how a speaker used a topical framework to explain the main features of the QAnon conspiracy theory.

> *Specific Purpose:* To inform my audience about the origins and beliefs of QAnon.
>
> *Central Idea:* QAnon is a big tent conspiracy theory alleging a number of unsubstantiated beliefs.

    I. QAnon alleges there is a battle between good and evil.
    II. QAnon alleges the world is run by a cabal of Satan worshippers.
    III. QAnon alleges the Mueller investigation was a cover story for an investigation into pedophiles.
    IV. QAnon alleges the 2020 election was fraudulent.

Speeches About Events or People

Many of us are interested in the remarkable people and events of our time and history. Events and people make solid, informative speech topics.

Speaking of Events

A speech about an event focuses on something that happens regularly (a holiday, a birthday), or something that happened once (D-Day, the first moon landing), something that marked our lives (graduations, funerals), or something that left us with a lasting impression (the 2021 California fires, the 2018 volcanic eruption of Kilauea in Hawaii). The event you discuss might be one you personally witnessed (a political rally) or one you choose to research (the Constitutional Convention, Rosa Parks's arrest, or the passage of the 19th Amendment, which gave women the vote). Whatever your topic, your goal is to bring the event to life so your audience can visualize and experience it.

Here are three examples of specific purpose statements for informative speeches about events:

- To inform my audience about the experience of competing at the Paralympics.

- To inform my audience about three benefits of Bring Your Child to Work Day.

- To inform my audience about the symptoms of and remedies for seasonal affective disorder.

Speaking of People

If instead of an event you tell about the life of a person—someone famous or someone you know personally, someone living or dead, someone admired by or abhorrent to all—your goal is to make that person come alive for audience members, to enable them to appreciate the person's unique qualities, and to help them understand the impact the individual has had. In other words, you seek to answer this question: Why is this person worthy of our attention?

A speech on Stephen Paddock would become interesting if the speaker used it to explore the mind of a mass murderer. A speech on Amy Schumer or Leslie Jones could develop an understanding of comedic originality. And a speech on Supreme Court Justice Ruth Bader Ginsburg could help audiences comprehend her role in redefining gender discrimination.[6]

Organizational Frameworks for Speaking of Events and People

Speeches on events and people lend themselves to a variety of organizational approaches: chronological, topical, and causal and spatial patterns are especially useful. Look to the purpose of your speech to help you choose. For example, if your speech aims to explain the history of an

Chicken stew. How to cook a certain dish is one of numerous different speeches you could give about processes, procedures, and demonstrations.

iStock.com/jacoblund

event or person—say, Hurricane Ida—you would probably choose a chronological sequence. In contrast, if you want to approach your subject from a different angle and discuss, for instance, the social, economic, and political effects of Hurricane Ida, a topical organization would better suit your needs. And if you want to inform your audience why Hurricane Ida proved so destructive to the states from Louisiana to Massachusetts, you would choose a causal or spatial order.

Speeches About Processes, Procedures, and Demonstrations

How do you do that? Why does this work? Can I make one, too? When we answer questions like these, we share our understanding about processes, procedures, and demonstrations, the third category of informative speeches.

Here are examples of purpose statements about processes, procedures, and demonstrations:

- To inform my audience about how photosynthesis works
- To inform my audience about the workings of the Electoral College
- To inform my audience how to perform the Heimlich Maneuver

If you are delivering a "how" speech, then your primary goal is to increase audience understanding of your subject:

- How the Kidneys Work
- How Colleges Select Students
- How Tornadoes Develop
- How Climate Will Change Us

If, however, you are delivering a "how-to" speech, then your primary goal is to communicate not only information but to demonstrate specific skills so audience members can learn how to do something:

- How to Cut Your Own Hair
- How to Housebreak a Dog
- How to Avoid Online Scams
- How to Lobby Your Legislators

There is virtually no end to the list of processes, procedures, and demonstrations about which you can speak.

Frameworks for Speaking of Processes, Procedures, and Demonstrations

When delivering a speech that focuses on a process, procedure, or demonstration, you will probably find it most useful to arrange your ideas in either chronological or topical order.

Chronological order works well because it naturally reflects the sequence, approach, or series of steps used from start to finish in making or doing something. For instance, in a speech on how scientists may save Earth from collision with a comet, you might detail four key steps in the process, from detecting the comet, determining when contact will occur, sending a spacecraft to intercept it, and lastly, blowing it up. But other times, you might find it more useful to discuss the major principles, techniques, or methods listeners need to understand to master the process or procedure. Then, topical order is your best choice. For instance, you could focus your speech on how scientists prepare for a potential comet on a collision course with Earth, beginning with their researching the effects of past impacts of comets and then describing what they are doing to improve comet-detection technology.

Keep your speech clear and comprehensible. One that contains too many main points or step after step after step with no logical categorization is usually too difficult for receivers to interpret and remember, making it unlikely they will be able to follow what you are sharing. By keeping your main points manageable, you facilitate better understanding of the process or procedure.

Notice that in this outline for a speech on how to escape a car caught in a flood, the speaker used a chronological format.

Specific Purpose: To explain how to survive a flash flood in your car.

Central Idea: Drivers caught in a flash flood follow a series of steps to survive.

I. If you find yourself driving in a flood, listen to the radio to see where the flooding is worst.
II. If the water begins to rise around your car, leave your car.
III. If the water has risen and you can't get out of your car, you still have two options.

Fork in the road. What are the benefits and disadvantages of topical order or chronological development for a speech?

iStock.com/Alex

HOW TO ACHIEVE YOUR INFORMATIVE SPEAKING GOALS

> **15.3**   *Deliver an informative speech that is organized, understandable, and memorable, engaging the audience.*

Sharing information involves transferring an idea or a skill to others, with the hope that you will accomplish at least one of the following two goals:

1. Expand your audience's knowledge

2. Clarify what your audience knows by reducing their confusion or uncertainty or providing a fresh way of perceiving

To accomplish either goal, you need to deliver a speech that:

1. Conveys information that is well organized, clear, and accurate

2. Delivers the right amount of content, avoiding information overload or underload

3. Creates information hunger

4. Is memorable

Be Organized, Clear, and Accurate

A speech is clear if audience members are able to identify its specific purpose and central idea or thesis as well as comprehend, follow, and accept its main points.

Make the Information Easy to Follow

A speaker's message is easier to follow if the presentation has a discernable structure, related facts are grouped together, and oral signposts are used to help receivers follow the progression of ideas. For example, a speaker discussing the nature of secondhand smoke would be more effective if they organized the speech's main ideas around a clear definition and then an examination of the key effects of secondhand smoke than if they confused receivers by intermingling into the speech an analysis of the effects of smoking on health care costs.

Minimize Jargon

To facilitate audience understanding, keep your speech free of unnecessary jargon—special or technical terms used primarily by those who share a profession or trade. Define unfamiliar words and concepts, use everyday language, and compare new information you are trying to convey with information already familiar to them. For example, if you used the word *sabadilla* in a speech on insecticides, you would need to explain that sabadilla is a Mexican plant that chemical companies use to make a variety of insecticides. If you select and explain your words carefully, then others will listen to and learn from you.

Use Concrete Language

When you are concrete, you enhance your message with sufficient specificity and detail for audience members to form clear mental pictures, grounding your ideas in specific references rather than vague abstractions. Avoid using general words like *thing* or *it*. Put your subject directly where it belongs—into receivers' minds.

Be Accurate

Clarity and accuracy go hand in hand. If your message contains inaccurate figures, if your facts are based on rumor or hearsay, and if your ideas are not supported by either primary or secondary research, then your receivers have every right to question your honesty and integrity. Make it your business to do your own fact-checking prior to delivering your message. Take the time you need to verify all the facts and figures you intend to share with receivers; base your message on a solid foundation of well-documented research.

Convey the Right Amount of Information

Ensure you give the audience neither too little nor too much information.

Pace Yourself; It's Not a Race

When you're delivering an informative speech, your job is to communicate your ideas so audience members understand them, not to race to see how much new information you can cram into their brains in five or ten minutes. Develop the main ideas of the speech carefully and clearly. Take enough time to let each point you are making stand out and register with the audience. Integrate supporting information that relates directly, not tangentially, to your main ideas. Reiterate what it is you want receivers to remember. Pace the information you deliver during the speech—being careful to make the information digestible. A challenge is to know not only what to include but what *not* to include, as well.

Don't Take Knowledge for Granted

Work to communicate even the most sophisticated ideas as simply and clearly as possible. The more you assume audience members know, the greater are your chances of being misunderstood. Instead, respect the intelligence of your receivers, but work hard to clarify the complex. Show your audience how you are building on to what they already know. When you relate new information to old and use creative analogies to help receivers make connections, you will make the unfamiliar more familiar. For example, one student compared the pending legalization of recreational marijuana to eating a box of candy, telling receivers that it may be tempting, but hidden dangers await them if they consume too much.

Repeat, but Don't Retreat

Help audience members process new content by using repetition (reusing the exact same words) and restatement (rephrasing an idea in different words to more fully explain it). But you must strike a delicate balance between these and newness so as not to bore your audience.

Create Hunger for Information

How do you motivate your audience to learn a new body of content? You create hunger for information by convincing them that they have a personal need to know what you are about to convey. If your audience believes your speech's content is somehow vital to them, then they are much more likely to listen carefully and act on your recommendation. For example, to create information hunger for a speech on how to lobby a legislator to support school breakfasts for impoverished students, you might ask receivers to imagine how they would feel if they had had neither dinner the night before nor breakfast today before coming to school. What would they be concentrating on—their empty stomachs or learning? Remind them that a relationship exists between filling a stomach and filling a mind.

Pace yourself. Don't cram too much into your speech; strike a balance between new information and clear explanations.
iStock.com/PeopleImages

Capture and Sustain Attention

You must first capture and then sustain the audience's interest so that they want to hear what you will say next throughout your speech. One faculty member created information hunger in a new cohort of first-year college students with these introductory words:

> This event is a formal way of marking the start of the school year, and for you, the start of your college career. Each year, a faculty member shares some ideas with your class. This year, that person is me. And I have these ideas to share with you.

> The first idea is pretty simple: you're screwed. Your generation is screwed.[7]

Adapt to Your Audience

Most subjects become interesting if well adapted to the audience. From the outset, receivers need to believe that your speech will benefit them—that you are about to add to their knowledge, satisfy their curiosity, or show them how what you know can help them enjoy or improve their lives. For example, if you were talking to a group of career women about the management styles of women and men, your speech would probably interest them because of its potential to affect them directly.

Use the material covered in Chapters 4 and 7 to help you adapt to and customize your content for your particular audience.

Be Memorable

Speakers need to use "wake-up and stay tuned" messages to keep the audience on track. In order for your speech to remain with your audience after you have finished speaking, you must convey the enthusiasm you have for your subject to your listeners and make it memorable. To do this, you can

- Let them know what you think is important for them to retain
- Stress those points via verbal and nonverbal means, using repetition, pauses, vocal emphasis, and gestures
- Build in audience participation

By helping the audience use the information you give them during or immediately following your speech—building in audience participation or asking for a behavioral response—you increase the chances of their assimilating and using the information you provide them.

Remember, although your goal may be to share ideas, people are interested in other people. Nothing enhances the communication of information more than the integration of personal anecdotes, examples, and illustrations. The drama of human interest makes a speaker's information memorable by helping it come alive.

GAME PLAN

Preparing an Informative Speech

- I have chosen an organizational framework that works for my topic.
- I have determined the specific purpose of my speech, and it is clearly stated.
- I've reviewed and revised my organization so that main points clearly support the central idea of my speech.
- I've established my topic's importance and relevance in a way that suits my audience.
- I've edited the amount of information I provide so that it is accurate and complete.
- Overall, I believe my speech educates receivers on the topic but does not overwhelm them.

EXERCISES

Informative Speaking

Building on your skills, the following activities help enhance your understanding of informative speaking while providing the extra information savvy needed for you to convey information in interesting and involving ways.

1. Topic Frameworks

Develop a framework that includes a specific purpose, a central idea, and main points for giving an informative speech on one of the following topics:

- The Design of the Pentagon
- Sikhism
- Misinformation
- How AI Works

2. Huh? (Unclear) Versus Aha! (Clear)

Following are a number of highly technical words or phrases that would probably need to be revised using jargon-free words or phrases that audiences readily understand.

Unclear	Clear
Cephalagia	Headache
Agrypnia	Insomnia
Precipitous	Steep
Nil desperandum	"It ain't over till it's over."

Based on your understanding of unclear and clear words, listen to one of the following speeches and locate five examples of words or phrases that you believe need to be simplified in order to enhance clarity or five examples of words or phrases that you believe are perfectly clear.

- Either view the speech or read the transcript of Lauren Pharr's 2017 TED Talk on How Vultures Can Help Solve Crimes on ted.com
- View the speech or read the transcript of Steven D. Allison's 2020 TED Talk on Earth's Original Inhabitants and Their Role in Combating Climate Change on ted.com

3. Analyze the Speech: How American Women Got the Right to Vote

In the speech "How American Women Got the Right to Vote" the speaker begins by acknowledging an important anniversary, using the event to contemporize the topic. After reading the complete transcript of the speech, answer these questions:

1. To what extent did the speech's introduction succeed in getting your attention?

2. To what extent was the speaker successful in achieving closure by tying together the introduction and conclusion?

3. What means did the speaker use to establish and maintain their credibility?

4. Which kinds of information were most useful? Most memorable?

5. Are you now able to understand the significance of the 19th Amendment? If so, what did the speaker do to help you develop such an understanding? If not, what could the speaker have done to promote better understanding?

6. How many different kinds of supporting materials did the speaker use? In what ways, if any, did these supporting materials facilitate your understanding? Your emotional involvement?

7. To what extent, if any, did the speaker integrate the recognition of diversity into their speech, demonstrating their understanding of cultural influences that might resonate with receivers?

8. Focus on the speaker's use of transitions. How effectively did the speaker move from one point to the next? To what extent was it easy to identify the speaker's main points?

9. What did the speaker do to widen receiver appreciation of suffrage issues?

10. What might the speaker change to enhance the speech?

11. Based on this speech transcript, pretend you are the speaker, and develop an outline and speaker's notes to use when delivering the speech.

How American Women Got the Right to Vote[8]

Raise your hand if you were eligible to vote in the last Presidential Election. If you're a woman please put your hand down. Take a moment and imagine what you all would have felt like if only male citizens had been permitted to vote in our last election. How would you have reacted knowing that while men could vote, women remained disenfranchised? This was the actual state of things just over a century ago when only men had the right to vote in the United States. However, it's more than a century later, and just a few years back, on August 26, 2020, we celebrated the centennial anniversary of the 19th amendment—the largest act of enfranchisement in United States history.

SN 1

> *The speaker uses audience involvement, rhetorical questions, and comparison and contrast to introduce the speech. Do you think the speaker succeeded in motivating the audience to listen? Were you speaking on this topic, what other means might you use to win the attention of the audience?*

To find out how the 19th amendment was passed, journey back in time with me. Picture yourself waiting to hear which way the great state of Tennessee would vote—would it or wouldn't it become the 36th state to ratify the 19th amendment giving women the right to vote? According to Elaine Weiss's book The Woman's Hour: The Great Fight to Win the Vote, the status of women in the United States was changed forever when on August 16, 1920, the state of Tennessee, after a great political battle, voted to ratify the 19th amendment to the Constitution granting all women in America the right to vote. The right of women to vote finally was going to be part of our Constitution.

SN 2

> *The speaker sets the scene in time, asking receivers to visualize themselves in another time, citing a reputable source to enhance credibility, and using an anecdote to maintain interest. Do you think the speaker succeeded in stirring the imagination of receivers? Would you have done anything differently?*

But women in this country were not simply given the right to vote. They had to fight for that right. Let's explore the roots of the suffrage movement, the reasons why women fought for the right to vote, what history reveals about what women had to do to win that fight, and how opponents tried to block their progress. Once we understand these four factors, we'll be able to understand why we still celebrate the passage of the 19th amendment as a landmark event.

SN 3

> *The speaker states the thesis of the speech, previewing the speech's contents for the audience. Do you think the central idea offers receivers new information that is worthy of their time? Do you think the central idea for the speech was stated as clearly and precisely as possible?*

How long are the roots of the suffrage movement? Both the Civil War and the fight against slavery had spurred women to consider the state of their own situation. Do you realize that back in the mid-1800s women and men were not yet considered to be equals? While the Seneca Falls Convention of 1848 is believed to be the first gathering of women focused on women's rights and political equality in the United States, women's demands for suffrage actually had begun much earlier than that. In fact, as we will see, the roots of the women's right to vote movement extend back beyond the movement to abolish slavery and involve influences you may not have learned about in school like this one.

According to historian Sally Roesch, the indigenous women of the Haudenosaunee Confederacy, an egalitarian society, initially influenced the suffrage movement. For a thousand years, these indigenous women had had a political voice in the operation of their tribes. The women decided who the chiefs would be, and they advised them. The women also had the ability to remove the chiefs for failing to live up to their responsibilities. They declared any chief who abused a woman or child ineligible to serve. Early suffragists were aware that these indigenous women had rights that they themselves did not possess. They understood that in order to obtain such rights, they would need to fight to gain equality with men. So, the roots of the movement go way back in our nation's history.

SN 4

> *The speaker covers the first main point of the speech, identifying the movement's roots, using an historian for credibility, while comparing the suffragists to indigenous women. Do you think the speaker aided audience understanding by anticipating their interests and needs?*

Next, let's clarify why women wanted to gain such equality. Would you agree that all people are created equal? If your answer is yes, then you'll agree with the other reasons women used to justify the suffrage movement's existence and their fight for the right to vote. Did you know that when the suffrage movement began, in some states married women had to surrender their property to their husbands? Did you know that in a divorce, women had no rights to maintain custody of their children? Did you know that in some states husbands could beat their wives? It gets worse. Did you know that in public meetings, women often weren't permitted to speak? How would you feel if you had little say regarding the political questions that were going to shape your country and determine your life and future? Suffragists had been driven to get the vote for practical reasons. Yet, it would take almost 100 years of activism for three generations of women, working together with their male allies, to ensure women a political voice. It was only with the 19th amendment's passage codifying that right to vote into law, that women gained a say in the country's future and their future.

SN 5

> *The speaker summarizes the first main point, and then using parallel structure, asks a series of questions to motivate receivers to process the second main point of the speech—why women sought voting equality. Do you think the speaker's use of transitions and questions were effective?*

We understand why women fought for the right to vote, but do we realize what they had to do to make their case? The Nineteenth Amendment tells us that the states cannot discriminate at the polls on the basis of sex. While by no means fully comprehensive in its coverage or impact, the passing of this amendment is noteworthy because the right to vote was not simply given to women. No. According to the August 16th, 2020 issue of the New York Times, the battle for suffrage was waged by an army of women, who were white and black, Asian and Latinx, immigrant and indigenous, queer and straight, from big cities and small towns all over this country. Sadly, as noted by Veronica Chambers in Finish the Fight, although they were as committed to the suffrage movement as their white counterparts, the names and backgrounds of minority women such as Frances Ellen Watkins Harper and Mary Church Terrell who were black, queer women like Angelina Weld Grimke, Latina women like Jovita Idar, and Asian American women like Mabel Ping-Hua Lee, often were omitted from the record while the names of a handful of white women like Elizabeth Cady Stanton and Susan B. Anthony were featured as the movement's standard bearers. Yet, women of diverse races and sexual orientations, were instrumental in ensuring the suffrage movement's success. To challenge and overturn the status quo, an army of women protested in public six days a week, arguing that women were more than creatures of the home under the authority and care of men, that women deserved the right to vote instead of having men represent and vote for them. The fight they waged, was neither easy nor certain, and certainly not without its surprises. What kind of surprises you ask? Let me share more about what history reveals.

History is a good teacher. From it, we learn that that we often don't appreciate what we have until we lose it. This maxim certainly applies to women being able to vote! Unbelievable as it may be, according to Casey Cep's July 2019 New Yorker article, though there is little proof that women exercised their right to vote in the colonies, prior to gaining the right to vote, women actually first lost that right. That's right. Some of this country's first suffrage laws stripped women of a right that they already held. For example, early voting laws in New York, Massachusetts and New Hampshire previously had included mention of "he or she" and "his or her ballot" only to have female pronouns struck out, resulting in the dis-enfranchising of women. Somewhere between the years 1777 and 1807 the possibility of women's suffrage was ended. It would be years before the 1848 Seneca Falls Convention suc-ceeded in attracting hundreds to gather in upstate New York to once again address women's rights and the right to vote. The historical record reveals that in January 1866, Congress was presented with the first of hundreds of petitions calling for universal suffrage—voting rights for all citizens, no matter their race or gender. Signed by prominent white suffragists, including Stanton and Anthony, many considered the petition revolutionary. Why is this? Because remember that back then the prevailing belief was that only men should be able to vote. Strengthening this view was the passage of the 14th amendment. Ratified in 1868, it protected the voting rights of male citizens exclusively—including the voting rights of black males born in the U.S. Following on its heels, was the 15th amendment, ratified in 1870, which further strengthened the voting rights of black males—but again made no mention of women, enraging suffragists. In response, led by Stanton and Anthony, the National Woman Suffrage Association refused to back the 15th amendment, going so far as to put forth a fal-lacious argument that because black men were inferior they were less deserving of the vote than were women. Abolitionist Frederick Douglass had advanced a different argument. He said that including women in the 15th amendment would doom it. Opposed to Douglass's stance, Sojourner Truth had argued that black women's rights were equally important to men's rights. According to Brent Staples's New York Times article of February 3, 2019, such disagreements made some conclude that the suffrage movement was splintering. The worry was that middle class white women were selling out the rights of black women by compro-mising with white supremacists.

History, however, shows us that despite their disagreements, women of every race and back-ground pressed ahead, going to the polls and attempting to vote. Each time they were turned back. Some were imprisoned. Then, during the presidential election of 1872, although it was against the law, Susan B. Anthony and hundreds of her supporters attempted to vote once more only to be arrested and fined. Anthony wasn't allowed to testify in her own defense. Can you guess why? That's right. Because she was a woman. Finally, in 1878, the first women's suffrage amendment was introduced in Congress. By 1890, white women had been able to secure the right to vote in four states.

Progress, however, did not follow in a smooth or straight line. While advances were being made in some states, in others there was none. In the face of Jim Crow laws advocating white supremacy, black men who showed up at the polls to vote were being arrested on false charges, or "ballot robbers" simply did not count their votes—effectively rolling back the voting rights that had been secured by African American men. Literacy and educational requirements also were used to prevent both Blacks and immigrants from voting. Sadly, history shows that the leaders of the National American Woman Suffrage Association had allowed the organization's chapters to exclude African American women, leaving African American suffragists to form their own groups. Despite this, women of all races and backgrounds fought together to advance the cause. A broad spectrum of people of all races and backgrounds organized rallies, staged demonstrations, held hunger strikes and boycotts, and carried out acts of civil disobedience in the effort to secure women the right to vote.

SN 6

> *The speaker segues from the speech's second main point (why women sought the vote) to its third main point (what history reveals about what women had to do to prevail). The third main point of the speech has the speaker using numerous examples, illustrations, and questions to interest the audience in following the amendment's progress—including some questionable tactics. Was the progression the speaker used logical and easy for you to follow?*

While history shows us that the movement's supporters may have been portraits of persistence, writing in the New York Times on August 25, 2010, reporter Christine Stansell reminds us that the movement also had plenty of opponents. Opponents of the suffragist movement thought of suffragists as abnormal for desiring equal rights. They sought to sabotage the expansion of voting rights to women—especially black women, by portraying women as threatening national values, the sanctity of the home, and their husbands' masculinity. They also pointed to gender-nonconforming suffragists as evidence of the movement's deviance. Fearing an influx of "unpredictable voters," business interests, religious organizations, political parties and even other women—known as "antis" were among the powerful forces that viewed the idea of women's suffrage as radical and absurd. They sought to block the suffragists from realizing their goal. To combat such attacks, Anna Diamond, author of "Adding a Pen to the Might of the Sword," tells us that the suffragists advanced a narrative prominently featured in articles and cartoons fighting negative stereotypes, stressing their normalcy, and presenting the image of typical suffragists as charming, stylish, and energetic. They downplayed their gender nonconformity, and played instead to the mainstream. According to historian Susan Ware, author of

Why They Marched: Untold Stories of the Women Who Fought for the Right to Vote, and Maya Salam, author of "What Suffrage Owes to Queer Women," this contributed to the invisibility of the movement's many queer suffragists. Thus, the suffrage movement had repeatedly hedged its bets, first by whitewashing the movement, and then by deemphasizing the movement's queering.

Nonetheless, diversity became a hallmark of the suffrage movement. Between 1909 and 1912, a coalition of Black women, queer women, working women, and immigrants joined with white reformers to make a state by state push for the vote, wining suffrage in Oregon, California and Washington with more states following in their footsteps. On February 10, 1919, 39 suffragists were detained in front of the White House—the first group of people ever to stage a protest there, with dozens of them being arrested. Though the "antis" were still at work—doing their part to try and keep men the rulers, such views were now on the wane. They ended with then President Wilson endorsing the constitutional amendment.

SN 7

> *The fourth main point of the speech has the speaker exploring some of the efforts opponents made to block the amendment's passage. Did the speaker make this section understandable? Was the support cited helpful and credibility enhancing?*

Now that we understand the roots of the movement, the reasons women used to justify their fight for equality, and what history tells us about the movement and its opponents, what makes the enfranchisement of women a landmark event that is still worthy of our attention?

SN 8

> *The speaker offers a summary, and then relies on a question to introduce the last main point of the speech. Did you find the summary a help in enhancing your retention of content?*

The passing of the 19th amendment created the greatest infusion of new voters in our nation's history. However, because of Jim Crow regulations, African American women did not benefit from the amendment's passage to the same extent as white women did. Many believed the suffrage movement had favored securing voting rights for white middle class women while viewing black disenfranchisement measures as a race and not a gender problem. In fact, because of voter suppression, large numbers of American women and men did not benefit from true suffrage until the Voting Rights Act of 1965—which finally outlawed racially discriminatory voting practices. Thus, the push for and passage of the 19th amendment was in no way an end, but only another beginning for the push for equality. Once the 19th amendment was ratified, it would be another four years before Native Americans would be considered citizens and eligible for voting rights. For Asian immigrants, also excluded from the enfranchisement of the 19th amendment, it would take even longer. Unfortunately, discrimination at the polls and voter suppression efforts continue to today. Raise your hand if you think voting is a woman's right. Raise your hand if you think it's a human right. As we now see, women winning the right to vote required the efforts of multiple generations of diverse women and men. It required the original suffragists to pass the baton to their children and other supporters so that they could continue the struggle and get the job done. Voting, key in women's drive for equality, turns out, however, not to be just a woman's right but a human right. The 19th Amendment reminds us how precious the right to vote is. Any efforts to prevent any citizen from exercising their right to vote is a blow to suffrage. The struggle against disenfranchisement continues on. The baton is now in our hands.

SN 9

> *The speaker transitions to the conclusion, achieving closure by beginning the conclusion the same way as they introduced the speech. The speaker uses the metaphor of a baton to give receivers something to hold on to. Might you have ended the speech differently? If so, how? Looking back, to what degree, do you consider the information you gained to be of value?*

List of Works Consulted

Casey Cep, "The Imperfect, Unfinished Work of Women's Suffrage," *New Yorker,* July 8 and 15, 2019, https://www.newyorker.com/magazine/2019/07/08/the-imperfect-unfinished-work-of-womens-suffrage.

Veronica Chambers, *Finish the Fight!: The Brave and Revolutionary Women Who Fought for the Right to Vote.* New York: Versify, 2020.

Anna Diamond, "Fighting for the Vote With Cartoons," *New York Times*, August 19, 2020, https://www.nytimes.com/2020/08/14/us/suffrage-cartoons.html.

Jennifer Harlan, "Suffrage at 100: A Visual History," *New York Times,* August 20, 2020, nytimes.com/interactive/2020/08/17/us/suffrage-movement-photos-history.html.

Maya Salam, "How Queer Women Powered the Suffrage Movement," *New York Times,* August 14, 2020, https://www.nytimes.com/2020/08/14/us/queer-lesbian-women-suffrage.html.

Jennifer Schuessler, "The Women Who Fought Against the Vote," *New York Times,* August 14, 2020, https://www.nytimes.com/2020/08/14/us/anti-suffrage-movement-vote.html.

Christine Stansell, "A Forgotten Fight for Suffrage," *New York Times,* August 24, 2010, https://www.nytimes.com/2010/08/25/opinion/25stansell.html.

Brent Staples, "When the Suffrage Movement Sold Out to White Supremacy," *New York Times,* February 2, 2019, https://www.nytimes.com/2019/02/02/opinion/sunday/women-voting-19th-amendment-white-supremacy.html.

Margot Talbot, "Protest Delivered the Nineteenth Amendment," *New Yorker,* July 26, 2020, https://www.newyorker.com/magazine/2020/08/03/protest-delivered-the-nineteenth-amendment.

Sally Roescch Wagner, *We Want Equal Rights: How Suffragists Were Influenced by Haudenosaunee Women.* New York: 7th Generation, 2020.

Susan Ware, *Why They Marched: Untold Stories of Women Who Fought for the Right to Vote.* Cambridge: Harvard University Press, 2019.

Elaine Weiss, *The Woman's Hour: The Great Fight to Win the Vote.* New York: Viking, 2018.

4. Approach the Speaker's Stand

Prepare and deliver a five- to seven-minute informative speech on one of the following topics or another of your own selection: Insomnia, Sickle Cell Disease, Lead Poisoning, the History of Organ Transplants, Diwali, the Witness Protection Program, Bullying, or Birthday Traditions.

In developing your speech, (a) clearly state its specific purpose; (b) identify the central idea of the speech; (c) develop each main point in the speech, integrating research and supporting materials; and (d) use both an organizational format and language that facilitate audience understanding.

Prepare an outline and speaker's notes, and include a bibliography of the sources you consulted.

RECAP AND REVIEW

15.1 Define informative speaking, explaining its purpose, and the value and nature of information.

Informative speaking involves the sharing or transfer of information from speaker to receivers. As a result of an informative speech, the speaker expands or clarifies what receivers know by adding to their knowledge and skills or reducing their confusion. Information has value when it supplies fresh insights enabling its receivers to make better decisions.

15.2 Distinguish among the following informative speech categories: a speech about objects, ideas, or theories; a speech about events or people; and a speech about processes, procedures, or demonstrations.

Speeches about objects cover anything tangible, while speeches about ideas explain concepts or definitions. Speeches about events or people focus on the compelling events or people of our time or history. Process or procedure speeches explore how something is done, works, is made, or why something happens.

15.3 Deliver an informative speech that is organized, understandable, and memorable, engaging the audience.

Like any other good speech, clearly develop the main points of a speech by offering receivers concrete support and using language that is neither overly complex nor vague. A well-crafted, informative speech also avoids over- or underloading the audience with information. Finally, remember to link the ideas of your speech with the interests or goals of receivers, as audience members need to be drawn into and become involved with the speech's main ideas.

KEY TERMS

Abstraction (p. 341)

Concept or expository speech (p. 335)

Concrete (p. 341)

Event/person speech (p. 352)

iStock.com/Carlos Barquero Perez

16 PREPARE TO PERSUADE

UPON COMPLETING THIS CHAPTER, YOU WILL BE ABLE TO

16.1   Define persuasion, differentiating among attitudes, beliefs, and values.

16.2   Identify the persuasive change sought, addressing persuasive resistance.

16.3   Distinguish among persuasive propositions and organizational approaches including Monroe's Motivated Sequence.

Can you imagine yourself speaking in favor of opening U.S. borders to increased numbers of immigrants, or do you see yourself advocating for closing them? Would you speak in support of a woman's right to choose, or are you a proponent of the right to life movement? Would you advocate for expanding voting rights, or do you support the passage of more restrictive voting laws? The positions we take on the issues of our day, including our efforts to convince others of their correctness, can have a real and meaningful impact. The fact is, persuaders *can* advocate to change the world!

In this chapter, we focus on persuasion and its purposes. In the next chapter, Chapter 17, we delve into persuasive speaking techniques. Mastering the contents of these two chapters will make you both a more effective persuader and a more astute consumer of persuasion. No matter if you are a persuasive advocate or target, choice and change are constants of life in the 21st century.[1]

WE ALL PRACTICE PERSUASION

16.1   *Define persuasion, distinguishing among attitudes, beliefs, and values.*

We persuade and are persuaded daily. The following are some examples of persuasion in action: Convincing a friend to wear a mask during the pandemic. Appealing to the boss for a raise. Asking a professor to reconsider a grade. Soliciting volunteers to protest school policies that discriminate against LGBTQAI students. **Persuasion** is the deliberate attempt to change or reinforce attitudes, beliefs, values, or behaviors.[2] Consequently, let's look at attitudes, beliefs, and values and their relationship to persuasion to see how persuaders use them to achieve persuasive goals. Before we do, a word of caution. Persuasion permeates society, but when we engage in it we must do so ethically by refraining from using false information, unsound arguments, engaging in name-calling, deliberate deception, coercion, manipulation, or any of the other questionable tactics unethical persuaders use to try and win at any cost.[3]

Assess Attitudes

An **attitude** is a mental set or predisposition that leads us to respond to or evaluate people, places, things, or events positively or negatively. The attitudes we hold reflect our likes and dislikes. Attitudes are classified along a continuum ranging from positive to negative, with neutrality at the midpoint.

The more you know about audience members' attitudes and why they feel as they do, the better you can tailor your message to speak directly to them.[4] If you and the audience share similar attitudes toward a topic, the task is simplified. Fortunately, audience attitudes tend to cluster at a particular point along the attitude continuum. If you can identify where that point is—that is, what the general audience attitude is—then you can build an approach that takes it into account.

For example, let's assume most people in your audience are neutral toward your topic, perhaps because they know very little about it. Your primary need, in such a case, is to supply them with reasons to care and evidence that substantiates your position. If, however, most audience members oppose your proposition, your task changes. In this case, you need to offer arguments that reduce hostility or negativity and provide information to redirect audience attitudes.

When giving a speech, you have the potential to instill, change, or intensify attitudes. Attitudes differ not only in *direction* (Are they positive or negative?) and *intensity* (How strong is the positive or negative attitude?) but also in *salience* (How important and relevant is the attitude to its holders?). For example, though the audience may have a positive attitude toward paying restitution to the descendants of former slaves and feel strongly about the need to correct previous inequities, if they do not believe it affects them on a personal level, it may not have salience. Among the forces shaping attitudes are family, religion, schooling, social class, and culture. These also shape beliefs, which we look at next.[5]

Build on Beliefs

We measure attitudes along a favorable–unfavorable continuum, and beliefs along a probable–improbable one. Our **beliefs** determine whether we accept something as true or false. Upbringing, past experiences, and evidence work together to convince us of the truth or falsity of statements of belief. Being able to fact-check our beliefs and identify whether one we hold is fake or factual is necessary to control the dissemination of false information.

Attitudes and beliefs work in concert. If you have a positive attitude toward someone or something, you are more likely to believe good things about it and vice versa. For example, if you hold a negative attitude toward young children using screens, you might well believe that watching content on a screen encourages laziness in children, precipitates reading problems in young learners, and contributes to childhood obesity. In contrast, if you started out with a positive attitude toward screens, then you would be more apt to believe such views were either exaggerated or untrue.

Validate Values

Values, sometimes referred to as core beliefs, are enduring and deeply ingrained indicators of what we each feel is good or bad, right or wrong. If we value honesty over deception, for example, we would classify honesty as desirable. Values motivate behavior. They guide conduct by reminding us of what we find most important. They also guide our decisions about what is worth trying to change or influence.

In one Gallup poll, the top five values identified by U.S. citizens were good family, good self-image, being healthy, having a sense of accomplishment, and working for a better America.[6] Researchers note that the members of older and younger generations differ when it comes to the values they consider most important, with younger generations placing more importance on tolerance for others, community involvement, and hard work, and older generations placing more on patriotism, having children, and religion.[7] Speakers can use such findings to show how the ideas they advocate support the values important to audience members.

Tough call. Persuading another person to change their view can be challenging without the right approach.

iStock.com/Tom Kelley Archive

Integrate Attitudes, Beliefs, and Values

When delivering a persuasive speech, consider your own attitudes, beliefs, and values, as well as those of your audience to select your subject. First, identify strong attitudes you hold about five controversial issues. For example, are you for or against granting citizenship to undocumented immigrants currently working in the United States? Next, identify the beliefs you hold that help explain your attitude on each issue—for example, "I believe undocumented immigrants are taking jobs that U.S. citizens would not take," or "I believe that undocumented immigrants are taking jobs away from U.S. citizens." Then, identify the values that support your beliefs—for example, "I value rewarding hard work," or "I value the legal process." Finally, review your list, consider positions held by audience members, and determine which of your strong attitudes, beliefs, or values you could successfully turn into a persuasive speech.

> ## COACHING TIP
>
> *"Keep changing the world, one word at a time."*
>
> Lin-Manuel Miranda, playwright
>
> Lin-Manuel Miranda praised National Youth Poet Laureate Amanda Gorman, telling her that the right words in the right order can change the world. Persuasive speakers also can benefit from following this advice. Put more of yourself into your persuasive message and your words will have a more powerful effect.Seeking Change and Understanding Resistance

SEEKING CHANGE AND UNDERSTANDING RESISTANCE

> **16.2**   *Identify the persuasive change sought, addressing persuasive resistance.*

A speaker may believe that extraterrestrial spacecraft have visited Earth even though most of the audience may not; oppose bilingual education while others support it; or advocate for audience members to become organ donors when audience members feel reluctant to make that commitment. Typically, speakers desire one or both of two general outcomes: (1) They want to convince receivers that something is so (i.e., they want you to change the way you think), and/or (2) They want to cause audience members to take an action (i.e., they want you to change the way you behave). For example, the young environmental activist Greta Thunberg suggested that because world leaders had failed to address the climate crisis, school children should strike for climate change.

Identify the Change You Seek

Whatever the general nature of your persuasive speech, it likely reflects at least one of the following persuasive goals: adoption, discontinuance, deterrence, or continuance.[8] When the goal is *adoption*, the speaker's hope is to persuade the audience to accept a new idea, attitude, belief, or behavior (e.g., that genetically modified food is hazardous to our health or that audience members should march to protest racial injustice). When the goal is *discontinuance*, the speaker's hope is to persuade audience members to stop doing something they currently do (e.g., stop drinking alcohol while pregnant or limit fast-food consumption). When the goal is *deterrence*, as opposed to discontinuance, the speaker's hope is to persuade the audience to avoid an activity or a way of thinking that they do not already engage in and that the speaker does not want them to start engaging in (e.g., "If you believe that every woman has the right to exercise control over her own body, don't vote for candidates who would make abortions illegal"). Finally, if the speaker's goal is *continuance*, then they encourage receivers to continue to think or behave as they now currently do (e.g., keep limiting sun exposure or reaffirm belief in freedom of the press).

Develop a list of things you'd like to persuade others to think, feel, or do. Adoption and discontinuance goals involve asking receivers to alter their ways of thinking or behaving, whereas deterrence and continuance goals involve asking them *not* to alter their thinking or behavior but to reinforce or sustain it. In general, it is easier to accomplish deterrence and continuance objectives than adoption or discontinuance goals. However, if you use a variety of appeals, employ a sound organizational format, and build your credibility, then these goals also are within your reach.

As we noted, the persuasive speaker aims to influence the audience to feel, think, or act differently by the end of their speech than they did before experiencing the speech. To succeed, the persuasive speaker must be able to answer the following two questions:

1. What exactly am I trying to reinforce or change in my receivers?

2. How must the members of my audience alter their attitudes, beliefs, values, or behaviors for them to respond as I desire?

To the extent that you change the ideas and behaviors of one or more of your receivers, obtaining a commitment or eliciting a desired action from them, you are being persuasive, and you are changing the world—presumably for the better. Those who seek to persuade also assume substantial ethical obligations. It is up to you to ensure that any changes you seek are sound and in the best interests of receivers.

For example, which of the following might you want audience members to do?

- *Adopt* a new way of thinking or behaving, such as . . .
  - Donate money to assist wounded veterans
  - March to protest racial injustice
  - Write their legislators to support strict gun control

- *Sustain* or *reinforce* a way of thinking or behaving, such as . . .
  - Reaffirm their belief in freedom of the press
  - Recommit to supporting public education
  - Strengthen their willingness to vote in local and national elections

- *Discontinue* or *extinguish* a way of thinking or behaving, such as . . .
  - Stop sexting
  - Discontinue support for vaping
  - Limit sugar consumption

- *Avoid* a particular way of thinking or behaving, such as . . .
  - Not binge drink
  - Not think of academic cheating as harmless
  - Not exceed the speed limit

Once your persuasive goal is clear—that is, you have decided on the type and direction of the change you seek—you next need to motivate your audience to respond appropriately.

Understand Resistance

How do you react when others try to persuade you to think, feel, or do something? Are their efforts usually successful, or do you resist? And when you do resist, what kinds of rationales do you give for countering their persuasive attempts? The more resistant we are to another's efforts to persuade us, the more difficult their job becomes. The less we resist, the more open we are to weighing alternative viewpoints, and the more willing we are to change our attitudes, beliefs, and behavior.

SELF-ASSESSMENT 16.1: ASSESSING REASONS FOR RESISTING PERSUASION

Directions

To gauge your level of persuasive resistance, read each statement and give yourself 5 points if you strongly agree with it, 4 points if you agree with it, 3 points if you can't decide if you agree or disagree with it, 2 points if you disagree with it, and 1 point if you strongly disagree with it.

Statement	5 Strongly Agree	4 Agree	3 Neither Agree nor Disagree	2 Disagree	1 Strongly Disagree
1. I do my best to resist others' efforts to persuade me.					
2. I don't understand why others are so easily persuaded.					
3. I have a negative opinion of people who are pushy.					
4. My inclination is to resist those who seek to change my mind.					
5. The thought of my caving in and doing what others want me to do, upsets me.					
6. When others urge me to change my mind, I argue back.					

Statement	5 Strongly Agree	4 Agree	3 Neither Agree nor Disagree	2 Disagree	1 Strongly Disagree
7. I don't like it when others try to tell me what to think, feel, or do.					
8. I enjoy playing devil's advocate.					
9. I am wary of those who think they know what's in my best interest.					
10. I am suspicious of others' motives.					

Scoring Method

Total your score by adding together the numbers of each response given to each question:

Total _____

Total Score Interpretation

The higher your score, the more resistant you are to persuasion. When persuasive resistant, you may find that you strengthen the attitudes and beliefs you already hold to defend against changing your perspective.

How might knowing if the members of your audience were persuasive resistant influence your persuasive approach? Keep in mind that the more resistant an audience is, the more likely they are to reject your persuasive message. It's up to you to find ways to ensure that they engage with rather than dismiss you. Understanding your audience helps you design a persuasive message and select the right strategies to use to reach your goal. Usually achieved incrementally, persuasion tends not to be an instant process, but one that occurs gradually over time. According to social judgment theory, an audience will compare your persuasive message to what they already think and believe.[9] We refer to their preexisting opinions as their anchor. Circling their anchor are latitudes of acceptance (messages the audience would not reject; receptive audiences have large latitudes of acceptance), latitudes of rejection (messages the audience would not accept; audiences that are hostile have large latitudes of rejection), and latitudes of noncommitment (messages the audience finds neutral; audiences that do not care strongly or could go either way have large latitudes of noncommitment, and those whose points of view are firmly entrenched have small latitudes of noncommitment). It's better to present the audience with messages that fall within their latitude of noncommitment rather than pushing them too hard by delivering appeals that fall within their latitude of rejection, in which case it becomes likely that they would outright reject your efforts to persuade them.

PROPOSITIONS AND ORGANIZATIONAL APPROACHES

> **16.3**   *Distinguish among persuasive propositions and organizational approaches including Monroe's Motivated Sequence.*

A speaker's goal, referred to as the speech's proposition, indicates the type of change the speaker seeks in audience members. Persuasive speaking is categorized according to whether the proposition focuses on a *question of fact*, a *question of value*, or a *question of policy*. Each kind of proposition requires the use of particular types of evidence, motivational appeals, and methods of organization or approaches to persuasion.

Speak on a Question of Fact

Propositions of fact are statements asserting that something does or does not exist or is or is not true. The following are typical propositions of fact:

- Self-driving cars make driving safer.
- The current U.S. immigration policy is a failure.
- Civility is teachable.
- A Mediterranean diet promotes longevity.
- Sustained exposure to products used in nail salons poses substantial health risks.
- Marijuana is more dangerous than you think.
- The criminal justice system discriminates against racial and ethnic minorities.
- Climate change is a threat to our national security.

Your goal is to persuade receivers of the truth of your proposition with an array of evidence and argument that convinces the audience that your interpretation of a situation is valid, and therefore your assertion is true and accurate, and your conclusion undeniable.

Organizing the Question of Fact Speech

When speaking on a proposition of fact, part of the challenge is to convince the audience that your conclusion is based on objective evidence. At the same time, you need to present the facts as persuasively as possible.

It is common to use a topical organization to organize speeches on questions of fact, with each main point offering listeners a reason they should agree with the speaker.

> **Specific Purpose:** To persuade my audience that the homeless lack the resources to regain a place in American society.

Proposition: Homeless people lack the resources to regain a place in U.S. society.

Main Points:

I.   Homeless people do not have permanent residences, so they are forced to drift from place to place.

II. Homeless people have no place in the economic system.

III. Homeless people suffer from conditions of hunger and physical and mental illness.

However, if you believe that you can best achieve the goals of your persuasive presentation by describing an issue as worsening over time or by describing a subject spatially—for example, how a specific issue under consideration has global implications—then instead of using a topical organizational format, you might choose to use chronological or spatial organization.

Factual. A proposition of fact, such as one about U.S. immigration, requires you to strike a balance between objectiveness and persuasiveness.

iStock.com/mirsad sarajlic

Speak on a Question of Value

A **proposition of value** provides an answer to questions like these: What is bad? What is right? What is moral? A proposition of value represents your assertion of a statement's worth.

When you are speaking on a proposition of value, your task is to justify your belief or opinion so that receivers accept it, too. The following statements are propositions of value:

● Discrimination against transgender people is wrong.

● Adopting a rescue pet is the moral route to pet ownership.

● Advertising drugs directly to consumers is better than marketing them to physicians.

- Universal health care is a human right.

- Solitary confinement is cruel and unusual punishment.

- Beauty pageants treat women unfairly.

- It is unethical to use a cryptocurrency such as bitcoin.

How do you convince your listeners to arrive at the same conclusion as you? By offering information, evidence, and appeals, as well as by establishing standards or criteria that you hope will compel them to agree with your value judgment. In order to analyze a proposition of value, you must do two things:

- Define the object of evaluation and support that definition.

- Provide value criteria for determining what the evaluative term means—that is, how do you define what is "proper," what is "wrong," or what is "immoral"?

In the next example, the speaker explains why she believes it is immoral to fund research to clone human beings. By referring to the work of Father Richard A. McCormick, a professor of Christian ethics at the University of Notre Dame, the speaker hopes to build audience support.

Cloning would tempt people to try to create humans with certain physical or intellectual characteristics. It would elevate mere aspects of human beings above what University of Notre Dame Reverend Richard A. McCormick says is the "beautiful whole that is the human person." But who among us should decide what the desirable traits are, what the acceptable traits are? Might this practice lead to the enslavement of humans by humans?

Organizing the Question of Value Speech

Speeches on propositions of value often use a **reasons approach** to persuasion, a type of topical organization in which each reason in support of the position is presented as a main point. One student used this kind of format to explain why she believes that keeping the detention center at Guantánamo Bay, Cuba, open is contrary to U.S. values.

Note that each reason provides a "because," or justification for the speaker's position.

Specific Purpose: To convince my audience that keeping Guantánamo Bay open is morally wrong because keeping it fails to advance our national security, it runs counter to our values, and it hurts our standing in the world.

Proposition: It is morally wrong to keep the detention center at Guantánamo Bay open.

Main Points:

I. Keeping Guantánamo Bay open fails to advance our national security.

II. Keeping Guantánamo Bay open runs counter to our values.

III. Keeping Guantánamo Bay open hurts our standing in the world.

After hearing that speech, another student was motivated to deliver one supporting an opposing set of values, which calls for a **refutation format**. When arguing against a previously espoused position, you first note the stance being refuted, state your position, support it, and demonstrate why your position undermines the one previously stated. In this case, the student defended the proposition, "It is morally right to keep the detention facility at Guantánamo Bay open."

Speak on a Question of Policy

A **proposition of policy** asks receivers to support a change in policy and/or to take action to remedy an existing situation or solve a perceived problem. You can probably identify countless instances in which you have observed propositions of policy. When a legislator recommends the passage of a mandatory sentencing bill or when a social activist urges the elimination of discriminatory hiring practices, each is petitioning for a particular policy because they believe it is both needed and desirable (hence the traditional inclusion of the word *should* in the proposition).

When speaking on a question of policy, your job is to convince the audience that your stance is right. You accomplish this first with reasons and second by proposing practical action or a solution. Propositions of policy usually build on both propositions of fact and propositions of value. In order for you to persuade your audience that action is merited, you first have to establish a proposition of fact and convince them to accept a proposition of value. Unless you can show a need for a policy, there is no point in arguing for it. Once you demonstrate that a need exists, it is then incumbent on you to suggest a solution and illustrate how that solution would help alleviate the problem.

The following are typical propositions for policy topics:

- To be culturally literate, all college students should study a foreign language.

- COVID-19 vaccination should be mandatory.

- Human cloning should be banned.

- Early childhood (pre-K) education should be compulsory.

- The District of Columbia should be the 51st state.

- The private sale of assault weapons should be banned.

- Voting machines throughout the United States should be standardized.

Organizing the Question of Policy Speech

Individuals may agree about the facts surrounding an issue and even share a similar value orientation. Despite agreeing, however, they may disagree regarding what to do. For example, an entire community may agree that homelessness among children is a serious problem, and they may share the value that holds that we are responsible for all children, not just our own flesh and blood. Yet some might argue that we should place homeless children in foster homes; others might propose spending more money to house the homeless; still others might contend that we should view homelessness as a natural disaster and mount a mammoth effort to rid society of homelessness altogether.

Whatever the nature of the policy disagreement, there are four aspects of any controversy that advocates usually address:

Bare necessities. The burden of proof is on you to establish the need for the proposition of policy before you can argue the solution.

iStock.com/IvelinRadkov

- Is there a problem with the status quo?

- Is it fixable?

- Will the proposed solution work?

- Will the costs of fixing the problem outweigh the benefits of fixing the problem—that is, will the proposed solution help, or will it create new and more serious problems?[10]

Among popular formats for speeches on questions of policy are *problem–causes–solution* and *comparative advantages,* both of which are variants of topical organization covered earlier in this chapter. Often, a proposition of policy speech divides naturally into a *problem–causes–solution* organizational framework. The speech's first main point describes the nature and seriousness of the problem, the second main point explains the problem's causes, and the third main point proposes the solution and describes its practicality and benefits. If your listeners are well informed about the problem you are discussing and convinced of a need for action, you should spend the bulk of your time explaining your plan and its viability. In this case, a *comparative advantages* format works well. This framework is similar but different from refutation in that you adopt a more offensive than defensive approach, using each main point to explain how your plan is better than the alternative. For example, in a speech opposed to online education, your main points might be that in-person classes are more effective learning environments, that they better foster social skills, and that they are more effective at preventing cheating than online classes. The emphasis is on the advantages or benefits of your policy in comparison with others.

Understanding and Using Monroe's Motivated Sequence

As we see, the format speakers use tends to reflect the specific nature of the speaker's question. Thus, speakers are apt to use topical, chronological, and spatial formats when speaking on questions of fact, reasons, or refutation formats when speaking on questions of value, problem–causes–solution, and comparative advantages formats when speaking on questions of policy. However, yet another format favored by speakers on questions of policy is **Monroe's Motivated Sequence**, primarily because they find it particularly effective in motivating receivers to act. Alan Monroe, a professor of speech at Purdue University, developed the framework more than 50 years ago. Based on the psychology of persuasion, Monroe's Motivated Sequence has five phases that move the audience toward accepting and acting on a proposition of policy.

Phase One: Attention. At the speech's outset, you must arouse the interest of your audience, giving them a reason to listen. Once you engage receivers in considering your thesis, build your credibility to speak on the topic, and connect it to the audience, you're ready to preview your main points and transition to the speech's body.

Phase Two: Need. Show receivers that there is a serious problem with a present situation by explicitly stating the need and illustrating it with an array of supporting materials. Demonstrate why it's of concern to them by relating it to their interests and desires.

Phase Three: Satisfaction. After you show your audience that there is a need, you must satisfy their desire for a solution. Present your plan and explain it fully. Help them understand that the solution you advocate to alleviate the problem is reasonable, reflects their concerns, and, by getting behind it, they can help in solving it, too.

Phase Four: Visualization. Show receivers how your proposal will both benefit them and improve the situation. Asking receivers to visualize what the world will be like if they fail to act as you request can also be effective. When you don't have time to emphasize both the positive and negative outcomes, then it's best to focus on the positive if you think the audience is in favor of your position, but wiser to focus on the negative consequences of taking no action if you think they're not yet on board.

Phase Five: Action. Summarize your main points, tell audience members specifically what you would like them to do, and conclude with an appeal that reinforces their commitment.

The following outline illustrates how one speaker used the motivational sequence as a guide when organizing their ideas for a speech on why we should be promoting multiculturalism.

Introduction
Phase One: ATTENTION

I. Hate crimes attributed to ethnocentrism have become too prevalent across the U.S.

II. Racial, ethnic, and religious biases are driving us apart.

III. Today, I would like to explain to you why we should be promoting the acceptance of multiculturalism.

Phase Two: NEED

I. We need to promote multiculturalism in the U.S. so that all who are here feel safer.
    A. The U.S. is home to all the world's races, religions, and ethnic groups.
    B. Learning tolerance and acceptance will make us better people.

Phase Three: SATISFACTION

II. We would alleviate racial, ethnic, and religious tensions by working towards a more pluralistic and less ethnocentric society.
    A. The pluralist approach prepares people to live in a world of competing ideas and values, to be able to live and work with people from different backgrounds, and to learn to examine their own beliefs.
        1. Pluralism teaches us that we are part of a multiracial, multiethnic, multireligious world.
        2. Pluralism teaches that we are all part of a cultural mosaic.
        3. Pluralism stresses critical thinking.
    B. The ethnocentric approach to American culture insists that we must identify only with people who have the same skin color or ethnicity.
        1. Ethnocentrism immerses people in a prideful version of their own race, ethnicity, and religion.
        2. Ethnocentrism teaches people to respect only those who are part of their own group.
        3. Ethnocentrism teaches people not to raise doubts.

Phase Four: VISUALIZATION

III. We must educate the members of all generations to live in a world of differences.
    A. Imagine the history curriculum not as a tool to build ethnic pride but as a subject in which we learn about our society.
    B. Imagine if differences were not grounds for hatred but grounds for respect.

Phase Five: ACTION

IV. Propose programs on multiculturalism to school boards, community centers, and businesses.

   A. Help to ensure their acceptance by attending planning sessions, offering to speak at events, and circulating petitions I will give you after my speech.

   B. If we all support these changes, we can build a more inclusive and accepting society.

Conclusion

V. I urge you to help rid our society of ethnocentrism.

   It is time to demonstrate and teach respect for those who are different.

Using Monroe's Motivated Sequence enables a speaker to anticipate the questions and concerns audience members want addressed as they listen to the speech. Observe how the preceding outline established the topic's relevance, isolated the issue, identified a solution, helped receivers visualize the positive outcomes resulting from the solution, and appealed to them to act accordingly.

GAME PLAN

Using Monroe's Motivated Sequence

- I developed an attention-getter to pique the audience's interest by connecting my topic to their concerns.

- Early in my speech, I showed receivers that there is a serious problem or issue confronting us that we must address.

- I proposed a satisfying solution to the problem or issue, supporting it with appropriate evidence.

- I prompted my audience to visualize how what I'm proposing will improve the situation.

- Finally, I laid out a concrete plan for my audience members, calling on them to take action.

EXERCISES

Persuasion Preparation

Becoming an accomplished persuasive speaker—one who is ethical and a critical thinker—takes practice, as does evaluating the persuasive efforts of others. Use the following persuasive exercises to improve your skills at both.

1. Be a Fact, Value, and Policy Checker

Let's say that you decide to speak about the effects of corporate influence on the foreign policy of the United States, and you have the option of delivering a speech using a proposition of fact, value, or policy. Your propositions for each option might read as follows:

FACT Corporate influence on the foreign policy of the United States is excessive.

VALUE It is wrong for corporations to influence the foreign policy of the United States.

POLICY Congress should act to reduce corporate influence over the foreign policy of the United States.

Now, to enhance your ability to create propositions of fact, value, and policy, choose two controversial topics such as "social media" or "single-payer health care" and write a proposition of fact, value, and policy for each.

2. Incorporate Counterarguments Into Your Speech

In their book *Age of Propaganda,* psychologists Anthony Pratkanis and Elliot Aronson assert that well-informed members of an audience are more likely to be persuaded if a speaker introduces them to opposing arguments that the speaker refutes than they are by a speaker's presentation of a one-sided argument. Why is this? Because the more well-informed audience members are, the greater their awareness of an issue's many sides—including arguments that run counter to the speaker's position. If the speaker ignores these, receivers may assume that the speaker is either unaware of them or unable to refute them.

By contrast, less-informed receivers are easier to persuade while leaving opposing arguments unaddressed. In fact, introducing a counterargument to an uninformed audience could result in confusion.[11]

- Consider this question: When a speaker talking about a controversial topic limits their discussion to just one side of the issue, what judgment is the speaker making about the intelligence of the audience, and how do you feel about that?

- Using one of the propositions you wrote for the previous exercise, brainstorm and jot down some of the opposing arguments that those who have knowledge about the issue might offer.

3. The Motivation Sequence

Identify a television ad or infomercial that illustrates Monroe's Motivated Sequence in action. Draft an outline that explains how the selected commercial fulfills each step in the sequence.

4. Analyze the Speech: The Electoral College Should Have to Uphold the Popular Vote

The speech that follows identifies the speaker's perceived problems with the Electoral College. As you review it, assess the extent to which the speech succeeds in fulfilling its objective.

Respond to these questions:

1. *To what extent, if any, do you find the speech's introduction and conclusion fulfilled their functions?*

2. *Was the proposition of the speech stated clearly? What action was the speaker encouraging the receivers to take?*

3. *What evidence, if any, is there that the speaker considered the attitudes, beliefs, and values of receivers?*

4. *Did the speaker demonstrate that there was a problem with the status quo?*

5. *Was the solution proposed by the speaker to fix the Electoral College problem viable?*

6. *Was the organizational framework of the speech effective?*

The Electoral College Should Have to Uphold the National Popular Vote

How many of you believe that when we cast our vote for president in the last election, that we voted either for Donald J. Trump and Mike Pence or Joseph Biden and Kamala Harris? What if I told you that technically we voted neither for Trump and Pence nor Biden and Harris? Because that's the truth.

> *SN 1*
>
> *The speaker begins asking a series of questions motivating the audience to participate, and involving them in the speech from its outset. Do you find this approach effective? Do you think it was relevant to the audience? How else might the speaker have sparked interest in receivers? Were you giving a persuasive speech on this subject, how would you begin it?*

Writing in Journalists' Resource on October 5, 2020, reporter Clark Merefield reminded us that we Americans never vote directly for our president and vice president. In reality, our votes instead determine which electors will represent our state when the Electoral College cast its votes for president and vice president, which they last did on December 14, 2020, with the votes being counted in a joint session of Congress on January 6, 2021. Prior to that day, on September 8, 2020, in his New York Times article "The Electoral College Will Destroy America," Electoral College expert Jesse Wegman warned us that with every presidential election, because of how it functions, the Electoral College proves that our democracy is neither fair, equal, nor representative. Keeping this warning in mind, I am going to share with you how the Electoral College functions, why it worsens our national divide, the reasons it subverts our democracy, and why we should seek to reform it by changing the way it currently works in favor of awarding all electoral votes to the candidate that wins the national popular vote.

SN 2

The speaker builds credibility in the preview of the speech, referencing reputable sources and segueing to a statement of the speech's thesis or proposition. Do you find the purpose and thesis of the speech clear and worthy of your time? Did it effectively preview what is to follow?

Let's start by looking at the composition and responsibilities of the Electoral College. The Electoral College is composed of 538 electors. In order to become president of the United States, a candidate has to receive a minimum of 270 electoral votes. The number of electors in each state is proportionate to the number of members of Congress that the state has. States get one elector for each Senate member and one elector for each member of the House of Representatives. Usually the candidate winning a state's popular vote, not the country's popular vote, earns all of the state's electoral votes. However, in Maine and Nebraska, two electoral votes are given to the candidate who wins the state's popular vote, and the other votes go to the candidate winning the popular vote in each congressional district. Electors participate in a second vote occurring a month after the presidential election. After this, the votes from each state and the District of Columbia are counted in a joint session of Congress. This is officially when the president is elected, not on Election Day. So, while you may think you have been voting for president when every four years in November you cast your ballot, you actually are not. As New York Times reporter Allyson Walker reminded us in her October 12, 2020, article "The Electoral College Explained," it's the Electoral College, and not the popular vote, that determines who wins the presidency.

SN 3

The speaker transitions into the first main point of the speech, again citing a credible source. The speaker continues to explain the nature of the problem. Do you find the explanation and support adequate?

According to the book Let the People Pick the President: The Case for Abolishing the Electoral College, by Jesse Wegman, having the president voted on by the Electoral College not only is unfair, it deepens our national divide. As things currently stand, even when an election is extremely close, usually all the state's electors are awarded to the candidate earning the most popular votes in the state. States, however, are not "red" or "blue." In every state, votes are cast for more than a single candidate. Thus, rather than being red or blue, states are purple from the East Coast to the West Coast and from North to South. For this reason, a "winner-take-all" practice negates this reality, effectively leaving many voters disenfranchised because their votes did not count. Such a practice is undemocratic. Democracy depends on all votes being treated equally. It also depends on majority rule. Unfortunately, as I will show you, not all our votes count equally, and the candidate receiving most of our votes on Election Day can lose the election. Thus, how the Electoral College functions currently subverts our representative democracy.

SN 4

The speaker focuses on the second main point of the speech, citing an expert source, and using metaphors to demonstrate the divisive nature of "winner-take-all" Electoral College practices. The speaker wants the audience to see the process as unfair. How convincing is the speaker's presentation thus far?

Let me share the five ways that the Electoral College puts our representative democracy at risk. First, while the Electoral College makes it easy to figure out who ultimately wins the election, even when an election is very close, it is possible that electors might not vote as expected. Republican electors are expected to vote for the Republican candidate, and Democratic electors are expected to vote for the Democratic candidate. But sometimes electors, known as "faithless electors," surprise their party and don't vote for their party's choice. Thus, electors can opt to invalidate the will of the electorate, ignoring their responsibility. For example, although Hillary Clinton won the popular vote in Hawaii in the 2016 presidential election, and Hawaii law requires electors to vote for the candidate winning the state popular vote, one elector voted for Bernie Sanders instead. The same thing happened with four electors from Washington and an elector from Minnesota who chose not to vote for Clinton though pledged to do so. While faithless electors have not yet changed the actual result of the Electoral College vote, it remains a possibility that they could do so.

A second way the Electoral College subverts our democracy is by giving some votes more power than others. The sad fact is that citizens living in large states have less influence than citizens living in small states. Consider this: though a little over 39 million people live in California, that state has 55 electoral votes—or one electoral vote for every 714,000 people. In comparison, about 590,000 people live in Wyoming; Wyoming has three electoral votes, or one electoral vote for every 195,000 people. As a result, the vote of one person in Wyoming affects the election results more than does the vote of one living in California. This is patently unfair. Why should votes in some states count more than votes in other states? They should not.

A third way the Electoral College damages our democracy is by affecting where and how the candidates campaign. States with larger populations can significantly influence the election. However, because candidates often assume they'll prevail in states that typically support their political party, they don't campaign in these states as much. Instead, they focus on the "swing or battleground states," in which no party has a clear majority. Candidates similarly overlook states with the lowest populations—those with only three or four electoral votes. These practices are unfair to the people of bigger and smaller states.

A fourth way that the Electoral College harms our democracy is that too many times the winner of the popular vote is not the person winning the Electoral College vote. For example, in 2000, even though 500,000 more people voted for Al Gore than voted for George Bush, George Bush won the electoral vote. In 2016, even though some 3 million more people voted for Hillary Clinton than voted for Donald Trump, Donald Trump became president. Why should the will of a majority of voters be subverted?

A fifth and final way that the Electoral College harms democracy is by limiting the impact of minority voters, and letting a narrow band of supporters determine who becomes president. Primarily, this is because minority voters often live in cities, which tend to grow faster than rural towns. However, because the census determines the number of electors, their number is adjusted only every 10 years. This can make people think their vote doesn't matter and discourage them from voting.

SN 5

> *The speaker transitions into the third main point of the speech, identifying the five ways the Electoral College puts democracy at risk, and using examples and statistics to make each danger to democracy clear. Examine how the speaker explained each of the risk factors. Which, if any, did you find most persuasive?*

Now that we understand the problems with how the Electoral College currently operates, what if we changed the rules? "Can we do that?" you ask. We can, we should, and here's how. Our presidential elections should represent the people's will—our will. For this to happen, we must change the way the Electoral College functions by getting rid of winner-take-all practices and instead have all state electors agree to vote for the winner of the national popular vote rather than for the winner of their statewide vote. This is exactly what the National Popular Vote Interstate Compact mandates. According to Erin Blakemore's article "Here's Why the Electoral College Exists—and How It Could Be Reformed," published October 16, 2020, in National Geographic, by negating the statewide winner-take-all rule, such an agreement among states would let us change the way the Electoral College works without having to pass a constitutional amendment. As of October 2020, this measure has been adopted by 15 states and the District of Columbia. Only an additional 74 electoral votes are needed for it to come into effect. If after trying things this way, a state, for some reason, decides that it no longer wants to be part of the agreement, it would be able to exit the compact, because unlike with an amendment, the National Popular Vote Interstate Compact is not set in stone. In a recent Pew Research Center poll published in March 2020, 58 percent of adults in the U.S. support eliminating the current system in favor of a popular vote. I think it's worth making the change, don't you?

Raise your hand if you agree with the next three statements: (1) Every vote should be relevant. (2) Every vote should have the same influence. (3) Some votes should not count more than other votes. We, the people, should pick the president. The Electoral College should vote in line with our will—the will of the people. The candidate who wins most of our votes should become president of the United States. Once we make the change I'm asking you to support, when you cast your ballot, and I ask you to raise your hand if you believe that you voted for president, you will be to raise your hand high and be right.

SN 6

> *The speaker summarizes why the way the Electoral College functions should be changed, and describes how these changes can be realized, achieving closure in the speech's conclusion by referring back to the speech's introduction. Did you find the speaker's closing appeals effective? Would they have resonated more if the speaker had personalized them, sharing more of their own experiences with the audience? Are you convinced of the concrete benefits of the speaker's proposal?*

List of Works Consulted

Russell Berman, "The Secret to Beating the Electoral College," *The Atlantic,* December 9, 2020, https://www.theatlantic.com/politics/archive/2020/12/electoral-college-biden-trump/617338/.

Erin Blakemore, "Here's Why the Electoral College Exists—and How It Could Be Reformed," *National Geographic,* October 14, 2020, https://www.nationalgeographic.com/history/article/history-electoral-college-could-be-reformed.

Andrew Daniller, "A Majority of Americans Continue to Favor Replacing Electoral College With a National Popular Vote," *Pew Research Center,* March 13, 2020, https://www.pewresearch.org/fact-tank/2020/03/13/a-majority-of-americans-continue-to-favor-replacing-electoral-college-with-a-nationwide-popular-vote/.

Christopher DeMuth, "The Electoral College Saved the Election," *Wall Street Journal,* January 8, 2021, https://www.wsj.com/articles/the-electoral-college-saved-the-election-11610133725.

Clarke Merrefield, "The Electoral College: How America Picks Its President," *Journalist's Resource,* October 5, 2020, https://journalistsresource.org/politics-and-government/electoral-college-how-america-picks-president-2/.

Michael Waldman, "The Briefing: Safe Harbor, Unsafe Democracy," *Brennan Center for Justice,* December 8, 2020.

Allyson Walker, "The Electoral College Explained," *New York Times,* January 5, 2021, https://www.nytimes.com/article/the-electoral-college.html.

Laurel Wamsley, "The Presidency Often Hinges on a Handful of States. Some Have Made a Popular Vote Pact," *NPR.org,* November 6, 2020, https://www.npr.org/2020/11/06/931891674/as-presidency-hinges-on-a-handful-of-states-some-have-made-a-popular-vote-pact.

Jesse Wegman, "The Electoral College Will Destroy America," *New York Times,* September 8, 2020, https://www.nytimes.com/2020/09/08/opinion/electoral-college-trump-biden.html?referringSource=articleShareNationalpopularvote.com/written-explanation

5. Approach the Speaker's Stand

Prepare an outline for a five- to seven-minute persuasive speech on a proposition of fact, value, or policy. Be sure to use an organizational format and integrate supporting materials that help you accomplish your persuasive goal. Include a bibliography of the sources you consulted.

RECAP AND REVIEW

16.1 Define persuasion, distinguishing among attitudes, beliefs, and values.

Persuasion is the attempt to change or reinforce the attitudes, beliefs, values, or behaviors of others. An attitude is a mental set or predisposition to respond to or evaluate stimuli positively or negatively. A belief is that which determines whether you accept something as probable or improbable, true or false. A value is an enduring and deeply ingrained indicator of what we feel is good or bad, right or wrong.

16.2 Identify the persuasive change sought, addressing persuasive resistance.

Among the goals persuasive speakers seek in receivers are for them to adopt a new way of thinking or behaving, sustain or reinforce a way of thinking or behaving, discontinue a way of thinking or behaving, or avoid a particular way of thinking or behaving. Understanding persuasive resistance better enables the speaker to present the audience with appeals falling within their latitude of noncommitment.

16.3 Distinguish among persuasive propositions and organizational approaches including Monroe's Motivated Sequence.

When speaking on a proposition of fact, you argue that something is or is not true. A proposition of value speech focuses on the worth of a given statement. In a proposition of policy speech, you argue for what you believe should be done to solve an existing problem. Monroe's Motivated Sequence contains five key phases designed to move listeners toward accepting and acting on a proposition of policy: attention, need, satisfaction, visualization, and action.

KEY TERMS

Anchor (p. 362)

Attitude (p. 356)

Belief (p. 357)

Latitudes of acceptance (p. 362)

Latitudes of noncommitment (p. 362)

Latitudes of rejection (p. 362)

Monroe's Motivated Sequence (p. 368)

Persuasion (p. 356)

Proposition (p. 364)

Proposition of fact (p. 363)

Proposition of policy (p. 366)

Proposition of value (p. 364)

Reasons approach (p. 365)

Refutation format (p. 366)

Social Judgment Theory (p. 362)

Value (p. 357)

iStock.com/thelefty

17 METHODS OF PERSUASION

UPON COMPLETING THIS CHAPTER, YOU WILL BE ABLE TO
17.1 Build personal credibility and persuasiveness, increasing ethos by tailoring the message to the audience.
17.2 Use logos or sound evidence to develop effective arguments, applying Toulmin's Reasonable Argument Model and different methods of reasoning.
17.3 Develop emotional appeals that speak to the audience, avoiding unethical fallacies.

Which of the political tickets did you find to be the more persuasive in the last presidential election: Donald J. Trump and Mike Pence or Joseph Biden and Kamala Harris? Why? Was it how the candidates presented themselves, the arguments they made, or their appeals to your feelings and emotions that made the difference for you?

What contributes to our finding some individuals more persuasive than others? According to the Greek philosopher Aristotle, three means of persuasion influence our judgments of persuasive effectiveness: **ethos**, the speaker's ability to convince us of their competence, good character, and charisma—their credibility; **logos**, the speaker's ability to use logical proof to demonstrate the reasonableness of their argument(s); and **pathos**, the speaker's ability to develop empathy and passion in others.

Whom have you attempted to persuade recently? Were you successful? What did you say or do that enabled your audience to perceive both you and your message positively? Of course, no one is successful at persuading all people all the time, no matter how high their credibility or skillful their persuasive techniques. We saw this during the COVID-19 pandemic, when more than half of U.S. Americans refused to be vaccinated and vast numbers of people resisted wearing masks. Perhaps you wanted to convince someone—or someone wanted to convince you—to get vaccinated or wear a mask. What worked and didn't work? While identifying the reason for not getting vaccinated or wearing a mask was key, rather than approaching the persuasive effort as a debate, it proved more helpful to approach it as a discussion.[1]

Understanding the positions of others and addressing their concerns, listening and approaching them from a place of empathy as opposed to hostility, yield more productive results. People most effective at convincing others to change their behavior and beliefs recognize the root of their disagreement, and seek to overcome it before trying to change others' minds. The reservations people had about vaccination and mask wearing were logic and emotion based. Both merited attention. Where was their information coming from? Whom did they trust? What did they value? These are questions a persuader needs to be able to answer.

While changing someone's mind is difficult, following the strategies discussed in this chapter will enable you to increase both your credibility and persuasive potential.

COACHING TIP

"Don't raise your voice; improve your argument."

—Desmond Tutu, South African Anglican cleric

Yelling at those who do not share your views rarely succeeds in changing their minds. Use reason and emotion, instead. Convince—don't chastise. Give your audience solid evidence, effective appeals, and reason to trust you, and you'll be on your way to achieving your goal.

Take aim. Tailor your message directly for your target audience.

iStock.com/Marc Dufresne

BUILDING ETHOS OR PERSUASIVE CREDIBILITY

> **17.1** *Build your personal credibility and persuasiveness, increasing ethos by tailoring the message to the audience.*

Consider the following questions related to education: Is a college education worth it? Why are men disappearing from college?[2] Should computerized educational programs replace textbooks? Should teachers receive tenure?[3] When it comes to controversial issues, audience members are not necessarily unified in their thinking. Here, segmenting the audience, understanding the Elaboration Likelihood Model of Persuasion (ELM), and boosting perceptions of credibility can prove helpful.

Focus on the Audience

Although the makeup of the audience matters, so does keeping your persuasive expectations focused and realistic. For example, some members of the audience may hold a position diametrically opposed to yours. With this audience segment, you have little, if any, chance of changing their minds with a single speech.[4] You may, however, be able to move them closer to where you stand. Others in the audience may already accept your stance. For this cohort, you can assume they will stay with you. A third group will be undecided. Provide this segment of the audience with reasons to care, solid evidence, and effective appeals, because they are your *target audience*. It is their needs, their values, their concerns, and their interests that you need to consider most (of course, without ignoring the others) when creating your presentation.

Change, for most of us, does not occur instantaneously; rather, it takes place over time. A speaker needs to prepare an audience to be receptive. According to persuasion expert Robert Cialdini, "What we present first changes the way people respond to what we present to them next."[5] If you strive to create small changes in audience members and do not expect instant conversions, your chances for success increase. Being able to address the same audience members more than once also improves the likelihood you will succeed.

Understanding how receivers approach persuasive messages also impacts the audience's responsiveness and your ability to persuade them. According to the **Elaboration Likelihood Model of Persuasion**, elaboration is the degree to which people will expend energy to think consciously about a message. Audience members typically process persuasive messages in one of two ways, although a combination also is feasible: When highly motivated, receivers use a central route to carefully and thoughtfully weigh the merits of presented information, looking for careful reasoning and credible evidence. When individuals are less motivated, however, they resort to a peripheral route; they are less mindful, focusing instead on a simple cue in the persuasive context such as the attractiveness of the source without scrutinizing the actual merits of the information presented. Receivers relying on a peripheral route seek mental shortcuts instead of working hard. In place of analyzing the message cognitively, they short-circuit it. They don't think as much, giving in to distractions like a celebrity's image, rather than focusing on the reasonableness of the arguments being presented.

Users of the peripheral route are persuaded by factors having nothing to do with the message. Their attention is diverted to the image and likeability factors, instead. As attention is distracted, the effectiveness of carefully prepared arguments is reduced. Yet, according to ELM's originators, Richard Petty and John Cacioppo, the first kind of persuasion, that which travels the central route, is more enduring.[6] When receivers know what's important to them, they invest their efforts in evaluating credible messages. Thus, when receivers perceive the issues to affect them directly, they tend to rely on the central route. When, however, they perceive an issue as inconsequential, they are likely to revert to the peripheral route, instead.

Consequently, for a persuasive speaker to be able to move a thinking audience toward their goal, the audience needs to perceive the speaker's message as relevant to their lives. At the same time, it also helps if those individuals the speaker seeks to persuade perceive the speaker as being likeable and trustworthy. Even though these are peripheral and not central cues, they are positive peripheral cues. Thus, ELM theory shows why it's important to take appearance and delivery into account when delivering a persuasive speech. It's important to harness the power of cues such as dress, open body language, and a confident posture that could contribute to an audience evaluating the presenter positively as opposed to negatively.

Establish Your Persuasive Credibility

An effective persuasive speaker is someone audience members perceive as qualified—as having ethos. We are more likely to be persuaded by a speaker whom we like and respect, trust, and perceive to be an authority. The more credibility receivers feel you have, the more likely they are to believe what you say and think and do as you advocate. Three major factors affect the audience's judgment of your credibility: (1) their perception of your competence; (2) their perception of your personal character, including your trustworthiness and believability; and (3) their opinion of whether you are charismatic and come across as a person of goodwill and personal warmth.

Credibility is not constant; it is fluid. Credibility changes with time, even during the course of giving a three- to five-minute speech. We can divide credibility into its three constituent parts: initial credibility, how receivers perceive you before you speak; derived credibility, how they perceive you while you are speaking; and terminal credibility, how they perceive you after your speech. Having high initial credibility gives a persuasive speaker an advantage, as audience members are more likely to give the speaker's ideas a receptive hearing. But that's just the beginning. Message and delivery style enhance *or* weaken the speaker's initial credibility in receivers' eyes. Thus, the opinion audience members have of you at the end of one speech could also affect their view of you at the beginning of another. You are only as credible as the audience perceives you to be—at the moment. Employ the tenets of persuasion identified below, together with the techniques discussed in the sections that follow, to establish your persuasiveness and build your credibility.

Think Small to Avoid a Big Fall

Persuasion is traditionally a step-by-step process, so keep your expectations realistic. If you try to skip too many steps or if you expect too much from receivers, then you may be disappointed in your results. Receivers will be much more apt to change their way of thinking and/or behaving if the change you request is small.

Use the Desire for Consistency

One way to convince audience members to accept or act on your proposition is to demonstrate for them that a current situation has created an inconsistency in their lives and that you can help them restore their lives to a balanced state. When we feel that what a speaker is asking us to believe, think, or do contradicts our current beliefs, we are unlikely to be persuaded by them. However, if that speaker can show us why what we currently believe, think, or do is out of sync with other attitudes or beliefs we hold or goals we value, then we are more likely to change as requested to restore our comfort or well-being.

Don't Put the Best in the Middle

Use both primacy and recency theories as guides when positioning key persuasive points. Either put your strongest point up front to win audience members to your side early in your presentation, or put your strongest argument last to build momentum as you approach the end of your speech. The middle position is weakest. Your best and strongest argument certainly does not belong there. By positioning your arguments appropriately, you can be perceived as more persuasive.

SELF-ASSESSMENT 17.1: HOW CREDIBLE ARE YOU?

Directions

Use the following questions to evaluate your perception of your credibility as a speaker. Simply respond to each statement.

Statements	Answer Labels				
	Never	Rarely	Sometimes	Usually	Always
1. I use the introduction of my speech to help receivers perceive me as initially credible.	1	2	3	4	5
2. How I deliver the speech increases my credibility.	1	2	3	4	5
3. I give receivers reasons to trust in the contents of my speech.	1	2	3	4	5
4. I use presentation aids to reinforce my credibility.	1	2	3	4	5
5. I build my credibility throughout my presentation.	1	2	3	4	5
6. I take steps to ensure the soundness of the information and evidence I offer.	1	2	3	4	5
7. I use the words of experts to help enhance my personal credibility.	1	2	3	4	5

Statements	Answer Labels				
	Never	Rarely	Sometimes	Usually	Always
8. I only make valid inferences.	1	2	3	4	5
9. I reason logically with the audience.	1	2	3	4	5
10. I avoid fallacious thinking.	1	2	3	4	5
Scoring Method	Add together your scores for each question. _____ Total				
Scoring Calculation	The higher your total score, the better your understanding of how to build credibility.				

What have you discovered about how to help your audience perceive you as credible?

Although this evaluation is not a scientific instrument, it should give you some indication of what to include in speech introductions and conclusions.

USE LOGOS OR SOUND EVIDENCE AND REASONING

> **17.2**   *Use logos, or sound evidence, to develop effective arguments, applying Toulmin's Reasonable Argument Model and different kinds of reasoning.*

Only when you unite credibility with evidence and reasoning, or what Aristotle called *logos,* will you have created a message—an argument—that has believability. Because listeners are skeptical of unsupported generalizations, back your positions with strong **evidence**. Use facts and statistics to lay the groundwork for persuasion and validate the conclusions you are asking receivers to accept. Use detailed examples to create human interest and motivate receivers to respond as you desire. Expert testimony from sources that receivers respect also adds credence to the positions you advocate. When incorporated into a speech, these will change audience judgments of your initial, derived, and terminal credibility.

Review Chapters 6 and 7 for more on research and evidence, as we revisit the key types of evidence and establish guideposts you can use to test the strength and validity of each form of persuasive support.

● **Facts.** A *fact* is a statement that direct observation can prove true or false. Once proven, facts are noncontroversial and readily verifiable. Some common assertions aren't facts because there isn't enough information to support them. For instance, we don't know that cellular phones cause cancer. Still, people may claim that such statements are true. To confirm the validity of the facts you use in support of a persuasive argument, make sure that there is little, if any, controversy regarding whether the statement made is true and that the statement is based on a report by someone who directly observed the situation or event.

Be a sleuth. Track down evidence to support your claims.
iStock.com/aleksle

- **Statistics.** We can often summarize a group of observations with statistics. They are helpful in comparing observed data and in emphasizing and magnifying distinctive patterns and significant differences. Make sure your statistics are recent, unbiased, noncontroversial, and from a reliable source.

- **Examples and illustrations.** Both real and hypothetical examples and illustrations are used to support facts a speaker wants audience members to accept. Longer illustrations add more drama and emotional involvement to a message and help the speaker build a case that encourages audience members to draw desired conclusions. Only use examples that are typical, significant, noncontroversial, and from a reliable source.

- **Testimony.** Speakers use the opinions of respected individuals to add credibility to the conclusions they draw. Testimony should be fair, unbiased, appropriate, and from a recognized expert.

In addition to helping you prove the validity of your proposition, evidence helps "inoculate" receivers against arguments made by those who disagree with you.[7] The most persuasive evidence is that which the audience was not aware of, that makes each listener question their position if it's different from yours, and that anticipates the questions and doubts of receivers and puts them firmly to rest.

Make Valid Inferences

An *inference* is a conclusion we draw *based on a fact*. It connects the dots for your audience, demonstrating how the facts you've presented support your position. But you must assess the validity of your inferences—to ensure they have a high probability of being true.

When Rep. Joe Kennedy III gave the Democratic response to the 2018 State of the Union Address, he contended that though the economy was making stocks soar, investor portfolios bulge, and corporate profits climb, workers were not receiving the rewards due them. He noted that life in America was being turned into a zero-sum game filled with false choices such as

Facts are facts. Research is crucial in preparing your argument and presenting your case.

iStock.com/tomazl

1. In order for one to win, another must lose

2. We can guarantee our safety only if we slash our safety net

3. We can extend health care to Mississippi if we gut it in Massachusetts

4. We can cut taxes for corporations today if we raise them for families tomorrow

5. We can take care of sick kids if we sacrifice Dreamers

Instead, Kennedy argued, the richest, greatest nation in the world shouldn't leave anyone behind, asserting that we need to choose a better deal for all who call this country home.[8]

To confirm the validity of the inferences you use in support of a persuasive argument, apply these two criteria:

1. There is little, if any, controversy regarding whether the statement made is true.

2. The statement is based on a report by someone who directly observed the situation or event.

Apply the Toulmin Model to Argument Development

Cable news hosts are known for taking social or political issues and turning them into arguments with guest commentators. Though this may be entertaining, when we analyze them critically, the arguments often are unsound, lacking logic and sound principles of reasoning.

Effective persuaders reason with their audiences by presenting evidence and arguments that help move audience members closer to the speaker's view. In his book *The Uses of Argument*, Stephen Toulmin shows that effective reasoning has the following components:

1. **A claim.** The basic element of an argument; an assertion of fact, value, or policy; the proposition or thesis you hope to prove—for example, *College football should be banned.*[9]

2. **Data.** Reasons, facts, and evidence for making the claim—for example, *College football should be banned because it has no academic purpose.*

3. **A warrant.** A logical and persuasive relationship that explains how you get to your claim from the data you offer—for example, *The primary purpose of higher education is academics.*

4. **The backing.** Supporting information that answers other questions of concern and strengthens the warrant when it is controversial—for example, *Football is a distraction benefiting alumni and coaches, but not students or players. Coaches make obscene millions while players receive no compensation. The majority of the student body receives no benefit because tuition costs continue to rise while colleges continue to slash budgets.*

5. **The qualifier.** Limitations placed on the connection between the data and the warrant, usually symbolized by words such as *often, rarely,* or *always*—for example, *Colleges often lose money on their football programs.*

6. **Rebuttal**. Potential counterarguments, at times proffered during the initial argument—for example, *The student athlete is a false concept. Any Division I college player will tell you the demands of the game make the student aspect superfluous.*

In diagram form, the **Toulmin Reasonable Argument Model**, shown in Figure 17.1, suggests that if you state your claim clearly and qualify it so as not to overgeneralize an issue, support it with reasons, and connect it to the evidence you offer via the warrant, you improve your chances of persuading others to accept it. You should also anticipate opposing arguments and prepare counterarguments that rebut them.

Use Different Methods of Reasoning

Persuaders rely on four key methods of reasoning to move receivers to affirm or act on their goal: (1) deductive reasoning, (2) inductive reasoning, (3) causal reasoning, and (4) analogical reasoning.[10]

FIGURE 17.1 ■ The Toulmin Reasonable Argument Model

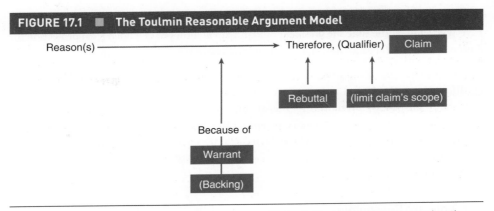

Source: Stephen Toulmin, *The Uses of Argument* (Cambridge, UK: Cambridge University Press, 1958/2003).

Use Deductive Reasoning

When you use **deductive reasoning**, you offer general evidence that leads to a specific conclusion.

Deductive reasons take the form of **syllogisms**, which are patterns to structure arguments. A syllogism has three parts:

1. A major premise—that is, a general statement or truth; for example, *we must condemn speech that precipitates violence.*

2. A minor premise, which is a more specific statement that describes a claim made about a related object; for example, *a speech by the president of the United States precipitated violence at the Capitol.*

3. A conclusion derived from both the major premise and the minor premise; for example, *therefore we must condemn this speech.*

You can evaluate examples of deductive reasoning with these criteria:

● Both the major premise and the minor premise must be true.

● The conclusion must follow logically from the premise.

When you use deductive reasoning, you introduce receivers to your general claim first. One of the potential disadvantages of the deductive approach is that receivers who oppose your claim may tune out and not pay attention to the specifics you offer in the minor premise. Instead of giving you the opportunity to provide them with reasons to accept your conclusion, they may be too busy rebutting your initial contention in their own minds. Of course, if you are addressing an audience that favors your proposal and merely needs reinforcing, then deductive reasoning works well.

In this example from a speech titled "Sacred Rights: Preserving Reproductive Freedom," Faye Wattleton, at the time the president of Planned Parenthood, defended legal protection for reproductive choice. Notice how she uses deductive reasoning to make a point:

> We've already seen some bizarre legal outcomes of this religious definition of human life *[Major Premise]*. Lawsuits have cropped up claiming fetuses as dependents for tax purposes—or claiming "illegal imprisonment" of the fetuses of pregnant inmates—or seeking to reclassify juvenile offenders as adults by tacking an extra nine months onto their age *[Minor Premise]*![11] *[Wattleton's conclusion is that we need to defend legal protection for reproductive choice by avoiding using the religious definition of human life.]*

Use Inductive Reasoning

When you use **inductive reasoning**, you progress from a series of specific observations to a more general claim or conclusion. You offer audience members particular reasons why they should support your generalization. For example,

FACT 1: People who live in poorer countries experience less depression.

FACT 2: Nonmodern countries have the lowest rates of depression.

FACT 3: The Amish have one-tenth the depression of other Americans.

CONCLUSION: Depression is a disease of modernity and affluence.[12]

You can evaluate whether a speaker's use of inductive reasoning is effective by asking and answering these two questions:

- Are enough reasons given to justify the conclusion drawn?

- Are the instances cited typical and representative?

Use Causal Reasoning

When using **causal reasoning**—that is, reasoning that unites two or more events to prove that one or more of them caused the other—a speaker either cites observed causes and infers effects or cites observed effects and infers causes. We use causal reasoning daily. Something takes place and we ask, "Why?" Similarly, we hypothesize about the effects of certain actions. The next series of statements illustrates causal reasoning from effect to cause:

EFFECT: Women are discriminated against in the workplace.

CAUSE 1: Women earn less than men in virtually every occupation.

CAUSE 2: Women are not offered the same training opportunities as men.

CAUSE 3: Society expects women but not men to put family before their jobs.

The next series of statements illustrates causal reasoning from cause to effect:

CAUSE 1: Too much of the food children eat is low in nutritional content but high in sugar, carbohydrates, and fats.

CAUSE 2: Too many of the activities children engage in are sedentary.

EFFECT: Childhood obesity rates are rising.

Make the connection. Explain the linkages between evidence and your argument. How does a caterpillar become a butterfly?

iStock.com/CathyKeifer

Of course, causal reasoning can be problematic. Just because one thing happens and another follows it does not necessarily mean that the first event was the cause. You can evaluate the soundness of causal reasoning by asking:

- Is the cause cited real or actual?

- Is the cause cited an oversimplification?

Remember, causal reasoning associates events that *precede* an occurrence with events that follow. It shows us that antecedents lead to consequences.

Use Reasoning From Analogy

When **reasoning from analogy**, we compare like things and conclude that because they are comparable in a number of ways, they also are comparable in another, new respect. For instance, if you propose that the strategies used to decrease welfare fraud in San Francisco would also work in your city, you would first have to establish that your city was like the other city in a number of important ways—perhaps the number of persons on welfare, the number of social service workers, and the financial resources available. If you can convince audience members that the two cities are alike, except for the fact that your city does not yet have such a system in place, then you would be reasoning from analogy.

Use these two questions to check the validity of an analogy:

1. Are the objects of comparison in the speech alike in essential respects? That is, are they more alike than they are different?

2. Are the differences between them significant?

Like apples and oranges. Use analogies to make new information easier to understand.
iStock.com/Ranta Images

The best speakers combine several kinds of reasoning to justify the positions they are taking. Thus, your reasoning options are open. If you are going to speak ethically, however, you do not have the option of becoming unreasonable—that is, of using an argument that has only the appearance of valid reasoning without the substance.

AROUSE PATHOS OR EMOTION WHILE PRACTICING ETHICAL PERSUASION

> **17.3**   *Develop emotional appeals that speak to the audience, avoiding unethical fallacies.*

We react most strongly when we feel angry, anxious, excited, concerned, or guilty. This also is the point at which we will be tempted to act unethically in order to convince others of the rightness of our position.

The Role of Pathos

Speakers use *pathos*, which Aristotle defines as appeals to the emotions of the audience, to instill the audience with attitudes and beliefs similar to their own and elicit a desired action. The greater your understanding of what members of your audience need, fear, and aspire to achieve, the greater your chances of gaining their attention and persuading them to accept what you are advocating.

Abraham H. Maslow, a psychologist, developed a classic theory to explain human motivation. His theory is now referred to as **Maslow's Hierarchy of Needs.**[13] Maslow depicted motivation as a pyramid, with our most basic needs at the pyramid's base and our most sophisticated needs at its apex (see Figure 17.2). According to Maslow, basic necessities of life are physiological: air, shelter, food, water, and procreation. Next, we need to feel safe and secure and to know that those we care about are protected, as well. Our need for love and belonging is located at the third level of the hierarchy; there also lies our need for social contact and to fit into a group. The fourth tier focuses on esteem needs—our need for self-respect and to feel that others respect and value us. Finally, at the pyramid's apex is our need for self-actualization, defined as our need to realize our full potential and to accomplish everything we are capable of. By focusing on audience members' relevant need levels, speakers have in their possession the keys to unlock audience attention, involvement, and receptivity.

FIGURE 17.2 ■ Maslow's Hierarchy of Needs

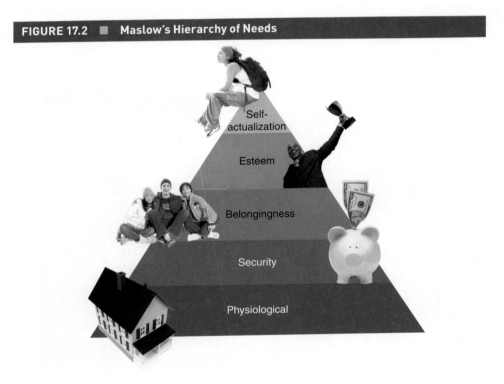

Self-actualization

Esteem

Belongingness

Security

Physiological

Source: Abraham Maslow, *Toward a Psychology of Being* (New York: John Wiley, 1962); images courtesy of Digital Vision/Digital Vision/Thinkstock; George Doyle/Stockbyte/Thinkstock; Thomas Northcut/Photodisc/Thinkstock; Stockbyte/Stockbyte/Thinkstock.

As a persuader, you should realize that unless audience members have their lower-order needs met, you will rarely be able to motivate them by appealing to higher-order needs. For instance, an appeal to esteem needs will likely fail unless the audience's physiological, security, and belonging-ness needs have been met. A speech on the importance of, say, achieving one's goals through higher education is unlikely to be successful if your receiver is homeless or hungry.

You can motivate the members of your audience using both positive and negative appeals. In a positive motivational appeal, you note how your proposal benefits audience members and improves their quality of life. However, a negative motivational appeal, such as a fear appeal, attempts to reach receivers by using the possibility that something dire will happen if they do not support what the speaker advocates.

In order for a fear appeal to work, audience members must believe

- You are a credible source
- The threat you describe is real
- Taking action to remove the threat will restore them to a state of balance[14]

Keep in mind that your message must reveal how receivers can remove the threat. For example, one speaker attempted to persuade receivers that it was only a matter of time before a tsunami hit the United States—an appeal to fear with little if any means for receivers to do something to reduce it.[15] Once you induce fear in audience members, you have an ethical responsibility to explain to them how your proposal will free them of it.

Strategize. Don't bury your most important point in the middle of your speech. Either start your speech with it or bring it out at the very end.

iStock.com/laflor

Persuade Ethically

A logical fallacy is a flawed reason. It is unethical to offer audience members reasoning marred by fallacies. In addition to not using fallacious reasons yourself, you also want to be able to spot them when other speakers use them. Among the kinds of fallacious thinking to avoid are the following:

- **Hasty generalizations.** You make a hasty generalization (in Latin, *dicto simplicito*) when you jump to a conclusion based on too little evidence. To avoid this reasoning defect, you need to review enough typical cases to validate your claim.

- **Post hoc, ergo propter hoc.** This phrase is Latin for "after this; therefore, because of this." Reasoning suffers from this fallacy when you assume that merely because one event preceded another, the first event caused the second event to happen. The sunrise is not caused by a rooster crowing, nor did it rain because you washed your car. Reading scores in a school did not necessarily decline because (or only because) the curriculum was changed.

- **Slippery slope.** You find yourself on a slippery slope when you assert that one action will set in motion a chain of events. Though all choices have consequences, they rarely are as serious as users of slippery-slope reasoning would have you conclude. Because once unwanted things happen, others do not certainly or even probably follow.

- **Red herring.** When you put a red herring in your speech, you lead your audience to consider an irrelevant issue instead of the subject actually under discussion. In an effort to defend the right of individuals to smoke in public places, for example, one speaker tried to deflect his listeners' concerns by focusing instead on the dangers of automobile emissions.

- **False dichotomy.** When you employ a false dichotomy, you require your audience to choose between two options, usually polar extremes, when in reality there are many in between. This polarizes receivers and reduces a complicated issue to a simple choice that all too often obscures other, legitimate options. "America: love it or leave it" and "If you are not part of the solution, you are part of the problem" are examples of the false dichotomy at work.

- **False division.** A false division infers that if something is true of the whole, it is also true of one or more of its parts. For example, just because a boat can float on water doesn't mean its motor can, and an entire organization may not be corrupt simply because one of its members was convicted of embezzlement. What is true of the whole may not be true of its constituent parts.

- **Personal attacks.** When you engage in name-calling, you give an idea, a group, or a person a bad name ("un-American," "neo-Nazi") so that others will condemn your target without thinking critically or examining the evidence.

- **Glittering generalities.** A glittering generality is the opposite of a personal attack. Here, the speaker associates an idea with things that the audience values highly (such as democracy and fairness). Again, however, the aim is to cause audience members to ignore or gloss over the evidence.

- **Ad hominem attacks.** When you present your audience with an **argument ad hominem** (literally, an argument "against the man"), you ask your audience to reject an idea because of a flaw in a person associated with that idea ("she's just a member of the iGeneration"). *An argument ad hominem* places the focus on the person rather than on the veracity of the argument.

- **Bandwagon appeals.** If everyone jumps off a cliff, would you jump off a cliff, too? Also known as the appeal to popular opinion, the **bandwagon appeal** tells receivers that because "everyone is doing it" they should, as well. Just because many believe something, however, does not make it true.

- **Appeal to fear.** A speaker who makes receivers feel overly fearful in order to accomplish their goals often ends up pandering to prejudices or escalating the legitimate fears of receivers. Once receivers find themselves "running scared" because the dangers alluded to by the speaker have been exaggerated beyond what is likely to occur, they are rarely able to think critically and rationally about the issue.

- **Appeal to tradition.** When appealing to tradition, you ask the members of your audience to accept your idea or plan because that is the way it has always been done or to reject a new idea because the old way of doing things is better. But because it was that way before or is that way today does not necessarily make it better or best.

- **Appeal to misplaced authority.** When a speaker asks us to endorse an idea because a well-liked personality who is not an expert on the subject has endorsed it, we should question the request critically. Name recognition does not necessarily equal expertise.

- **Straw man.** When you respond to another's position by distorting, exaggerating, or misrepresenting their argument, you are depending on a "straw man" in an attempt to create the illusion that you refuted the other's stance successfully. Effectively, you misrepresent the other's position to make it easier to attack.

Such fallacies are emotionally charged, dishonest, and undermine reason and rational debate. Because they distort truth, logical fallacies are inherently invalid and, when detected, constitute a major speaker slip-up, causing receivers to question the speaker's ethics.

GAME PLAN

Persuading an Audience

- I've considered my target audience and tailored my arguments to address them.
- I've reviewed the power of Maslow's Hierarchy of Needs and have included appeals to the audience's chief concerns, such as safety, security, and quality of life.

- I've researched and used the most effective forms of evidence, including facts, statistics, examples/illustrations, or testimony.
- I've applied Toulmin's Reasonable Argument Model to test the integrity of my reasoning.
- I've reviewed my speech to be sure I haven't relied on any logical fallacies, and my reasoning is airtight.

EXERCISES

Mastering Methods

Understanding audience positions, building credibility, using solid evidence, and helping the audience feel that the change you call for is necessary are integral to achieving your goals. Completing these exercises will help you accomplish these objectives.

1. Find the Fallacy

Select the transcript of a show from CNN.com, MSNBC.com, FOXNews.com, or Newsmax.com in which the host and one or more guest commentators are arguing about a timely controversial issue. Analyze the claims made, the evidence offered, and the warrants used by each party. To what extent, if any, do you think the arguments made are defensible on the basis of logic and sound principles of reasoning? Support your answer.

2. The Hierarchy of Needs

Use Maslow's Hierarchy of Needs to target the types of needs to which you will appeal in the following situations:

- You want to persuade an audience of high school seniors not to text and drive.
- You want to convince the college community to toughen rules and sanctions for campus-based sexual harassment.
- You want to persuade an audience of college students to get involved in local politics.
- You want to convince the members of your community that using a mask is no different than using a seatbelt.
- You want to convince Congress to pass a law prohibiting former members of Congress from ever becoming lobbyists.

3. Persuade Me if You Can

Work with a partner to develop a persuasive presentation for a new product or app that fulfills a need or solves a problem relevant to the members of your class. Apply the audience analysis skills you've gained and be sure to include appeals to ethos, logic, and emotion to convince receivers of the value of and need for your product or app.

4. Analyze the Speech: When It Comes to Suicide, Let's Talk, Not Stigmatize

The focus of the speech included here is the need to talk about, not stigmatize, suicide. As you read the speech, assess whether it succeeds in sparking your interest in the topic, explains why the subject should concern you, builds confidence in the speaker's credibility, and contains both solid reasoning and arguments designed to win your support.

To help you process it, consider these questions:

1. How would you phrase the speaker's proposition?

2. Is the speech well organized? Is it easy to outline? Do its parts hold together? Were there sufficient transitions? If not, where and what type of transition would you add?

3. At what points in the speech might the speaker have employed a visual or audio aid? What kind of visual or audio aid could the speaker have benefited from using?

4. Which of the speaker's arguments do you find the most and least effective, and why?

5. Did the speaker use ethos, logos, and pathos effectively?

6. What steps did the speaker take to be perceived as credible?

7. If you were the speaker's coach, what advice would you offer to improve the speech?

[The speaker walks to the front of the room holding a cup of coffee. The speaker faces the audience and begins to speak.]

A few years ago, an Oregon therapist named Agnes McKeen lost her son, Harrison, to suicide. Agnes said, "In losing my son Harrison, I lost all direction. Just because Harrison's gone, however, does not mean my love for him went away." Agnes tried to think of ways to memorialize her son. Someone suggested she pass out bracelets at his school. She considered what the bracelets should say, finally settling on "Just talk." She explained that if only Harrison had talked through what was bothering him, things might have turned out differently. [*The speaker puts down the cup of coffee.*] It's time we remove the stigma and talk frankly about suicide. Do you know anyone like Harrison? Harrison was a young person—like you and me. He wasn't famous. Suicide, you know, does not discriminate between the famous and the ordinary. It doesn't discriminate on the basis of color or religion. We all are susceptible. Each of us can play a role in efforts to help save the lives of those who lose all hope and see no other recourse. As G. K. Chesterton wrote, "*The man who kills a man kills a man. The man who kills himself kills all men. As far as he's concerned he wipes out the world.*" Talking about suicide is the best way to find a path to suicide prevention.

SN 1

> *The speaker's opening story is designed to involve the audience while introducing the speech's proposition, establishing the importance of talk, and foreshadowing the speech's end.*

Unfortunately, we don't speak about suicide enough, and when we do bring it up, we often use the wrong words, which creates other problems. The fact is there's a stigma surrounding suicide.

Some believe it's because of how we describe the suicide act itself. Think about it. We are prone to saying something like, "So and so committed suicide." What does that do? It puts the person who took their own life in the same category as someone who commits a crime or a sin. The expression "committed suicide" itself is associated with blame and stigma. Suicide, however, is a death of despair. Someone who is ill does not commit a heart attack any more than someone who dies at their own hand commits suicide. The person who dies at their own hands died by suicide, losing their battle to a disease that now is an epidemic and even being compared to a contagion. How is suicide like a contagion? Whenever a major suicide story breaks, did you know that the suicide rate goes up? In fact, after the celebrities Anthony Bourdain and Kate Spade each died by suicide, the number of calls to suicide hotlines rose 65 percent. After two Parkland High School shooting survivors died by suicide, the father of a Sandy Hook school shooting victim took his own life. After one teenager in Herriman, Utah, killed himself, six more did the same. The impulse to harm oneself after a trauma or the death of a loved one appears to be too common.

SN 2

The speaker identifies the heart of the problem and the reasons for the stigmatization of suicide.

How common is suicide? The CDC notes that suicide is among the leading causes of death for Americans, with suicide rates rising in almost every state. Writing in the March 15, 2019, *New York Times,* columnist David Brooks reported that suicide rates all over are up 30 percent this century and that teenage suicides are rising roughly twice as fast, hitting the youngest Americans hard. Sadly, suicide is the second leading cause of death for those between 10 and 24 years of age. According to Rebecca Dolgin's 2021 *Psycom* article, "The Impact of COVID-19 on Suicide Rates," the COVID-19 pandemic is contributing to more young adults in this country suffering from mental health issues. The fear is that the pandemic could lead to thousands of people dying from deaths by despair with suicide rates rising once the pandemic ends. And, though lower than the civilian rate, suicide is also a leading cause of death for young veterans who served in Afghanistan and the Middle East, with 18 killing themselves every day in 2020. More Vietnam veterans have committed suicide than died in the Vietnam War. For many veterans, their biggest battles often attributed to PTSD (or post-traumatic stress disorder) occur upon their return home. The CrisisTextLine reports that every 28 seconds someone attempts suicide, with approximately 47,000 Americans dying at their own hands every year—that's some 121 daily. Again, however, suicide doesn't discriminate. While more young people attempt suicide, more people aged 45 through 64 succeed. While more women attempt it, more men succeed.

SN 3

The speaker explores the extent of problem.

Why is this suicide epidemic happening now? According to the September 2021 *Journal of Pediatrics,* the COVID-19 pandemic has increased the stress that people feel, contributing to increases in the number of suicides, including among female adolescents experiencing depression. Isolation, attributed to COVID-19, also has worsened the situation, with 2 percent of LGBTQ youth reporting that they considered suicide in the last year. The general suicide rate in the United States is accelerating.

Suicide rarely is the result of a single factor. In fact, according to a CDC publication, *Vital Signs,* a number of factors contribute to suicide. While many suicides are deaths of despair and attributed to depression and mental health disorders, about half of those who die from suicide have no known mental health condition at the time of their deaths. Relationship problems, drug misuse, a family history of suicide, deaths resulting from trauma and mass shootings, access to firearms, and stress attributed to physical health, job, or financial issues increase the suicide risk. Social fragmentation also plays a pivotal role, with more people than ever reporting being lonely. CBS reporter Jericka Duncan noted that researchers now speculate that social media and smartphones are worsening the suicide risk—particularly when cyberbullying and induced feelings of inadequacy are involved. For example, when 12-year-old Mallory Grossman took her own life, her mom believed it was because she was being cyberbullied in texts on Snapchat and on Instagram and made to feel excluded and unpopular. According to the Cyberbullying Research Center, almost 40 percent of teens between the ages of 12 and 17 have been cyberbullied.

SN 4

The speaker explains reasons for the suicide epidemic.

Psychologist Jean Twenge similarly believes that there is a correlation between the popularity of smartphones and increased rates of suicide and depression among young people. This finding is backed up by a recently released Pew Research survey revealing that some 70 percent of teens believe anxiety and depression are critical issues among peers. Rather than relating face-to-face, young people may be spending too much time on electronic devices. According to an article Twenge wrote, "Put That Phone Away—Now," published in the April 1, 2019, issue of *Time,* happiness is highest in teens who spend between only a half-hour to two hours daily using extracurricular digital media. In contrast to this group, heavy users of electronic devices are more unhappy, depressed, or distressed. In fact, Twenge's research reveals that twice as many teens who use their devices five or more hours a day attempt suicide than do those who limit their device time to one hour. With this in mind, Twenge advises limiting the use of electronic devices. Specifically, she suggests the following: First, no phones or tablets in the bedroom at night. Second, no using devices within an hour of bedtime. And third, limit device time to less than two hours of leisure time daily. Teens should not like their phones more than people. As one teen put it, "We don't know how to communicate like normal people and look people in the eye and talk to them."

SN 5

The speaker exposes the relationship between suicide and smartphones and offers some advice.

What can we do? More than 90 percent of people in a suicidal crisis give some kind of warning to those around them. Everyone can help prevent suicide by learning the warning signs and taking time to respond and talk to someone at risk. The aversion we have to discussing mental health problems, admitting our lives aren't perfect, and seeking help from others needs to end. It's the stigma around suicide that quashes discussion. But we have to talk about the hard stuff. Having a genuine conversation is a great starting point. If someone you know expresses self-hate, is having difficulty coping with trauma or loss, has survivor's guilt, jokes with you by saying something like, "Once I'm gone. . . ," offers you or others their prized possessions, talks about death a lot, withdraws from contact, or all of a sudden appears very calm, as if a decision has been made, they may be at risk. Too many take their own lives because at their lowest moment, no person is around, but a gun is around. In fact, because of this finding about guns, the Veterans Administration's policy is to ask veterans being treated for PTSD to lock up or remove any firearms in their homes so that they can't harm themselves should the impulse to do so arise. Brain researchers like Dr. John Mann and Dr. Todd Gould confirm that those prone to suicide feel depression more acutely, are more likely to act on those feelings, see fewer options or solutions, and see individuals around them as more critical and less helpful. Those prone to suicide, however, are not aware of their heightened risk, which can lead them to act before considering the consequences of their actions. If prodded to think about it rather than act compulsively, they might not act. Thus, these researchers assert that more screening and more talking are the best solutions.

SN 6

The speaker dives deeper into the problem's nature while suggesting solutions.

What should we say when we discover someone who is at risk? Words matter. We need to be able to have honest and blunt conversations about suicide. This will help to remove the stigma connected with suicide. When feeling stigmatized, people avoid seeking help. And it's the seeking of help that could be life-saving. When someone brings up suicide, don't argue with them. Don't spout words like, "You have a lot to live for." Don't tell them, "Doing this will devastate the people around you." Those kinds of reactions might shame the person, causing them to withdraw more. Instead, say something like, "I can only imagine what you're feeling right now." Then ask directly, "Are you thinking about ending your life?" or "Are you thinking about suicide or wanting to kill yourself?" To become more skilled at doing this, you can enroll in a one- to two-hour course and learn to use a QPR suicide prevention script. QPR stands for Question, Persuade, and Refer—it's a three-step intervention anyone can use to help save a life from suicide. As a QPR gatekeeper, you learn to recognize the warning signs that someone is contemplating suicide, you learn how to offer hope, and you learn how to get them to let you assist them in getting help. Simply saying "Let me help" can make the difference. Asking someone about the presence of suicidal thoughts and feelings opens up a conversation. Getting a person to open up before a tragedy occurs is key. Listening to them is crucial.

SN 7

The speaker focuses in on the importance of talk as a solution, highlighting an interventional script.

After her son Harrison died, his mom started an organization called "Just Talk"—an informal group that encourages open discussion about suicide. [*The speaker picks up the cup of coffee.*] We need to add suicide to the conversations we have because most people find it difficult to talk about. If you have a broken bone, you seek help. If someone is considering suicide, they should feel it's okay to seek help, too. We need to be able to talk openly about suicide. Some people mistakenly believe that if we talk about suicide, it will plant the idea in the minds of those who are vulnerable. This is untrue. People who contemplate suicide think it's the only way to get out of pain. By being there, helping them bring their feelings into the daylight, and talking with them directly, we can show them that it's okay to seek help and that there are lots of local and national resources available to them that can help take the pain away. Harrison's mom, Agnes McKeen, started a JustTalkSuicidePrevention Facebook page and is setting up a video recording site so that people can tell their stories and maybe help someone else. Remember, notice the warning signs and don't hesitate to ask the tough question of someone who may be in danger of harming themselves. You can change the culture by removing the stigma. Commit to starting the conversation because talking can save a life. Never let yourself be sworn to secrecy. Instead, help those suffering to get help. And most important, make sure they call the National Suicide Prevention Lifeline at 1-800-273-8255. By the way, 8255 spells TALK.

SN 8

The speaker concludes, achieving closure by reiterating the theme begun in the introduction.

Works Consulted

Anne Branigin, "Last Year Was Brutal for Mental Health. For LGBTQ Youth It Was a Crisis," TheLily.com, May 28, 2021, https://www.thelily.com/42-percent-of-lgbtq-youth-said-they-considered-suicide-in-the-last-year-multiple-crises-are-to-blame-experts-say/.

David Brooks, "Fighting Suicide Is a Collective Task," *New York Times,* March 15, 2019, p. A31.

Nancy Cutler, "Why Is Youth Suicide a Crisis, What Can We Do?" *The Record,* May 8, 2019, pp. 1A, 3A.

Michael Gold and Tyler Pager, "Sandy Hook Victim's Father Dies in Apparent Suicide in Newtown," *New York Times.com,* March 25, 2019.

Lindsay Holmes, "Why You Should Stop Saying 'Committed Suicide,'" *Huffington Post,* March 27, 2019.

Ian Lovett, "One Teenager Killed Himself, Then Six More Followed," *The Wall Street Journal,* April 13–14, 2019, pp. A1, A12–13.

Stephanie L. Mayne, et al., "COVID-19 and Adolescent Depression and Suicide Risk Screening Outcomes," *Pediatrics* 148, no. 3 (September 2021), https://pediatrics.aappublications.org/content/148/3/e2021051507.

David Morris, "The Ancient Ways Suicide Continues to Haunt Us," CNN.com, March 27, 2019.

Gerry O'Brien, "Suicide: Start the Conversation," *Herald and News*, March 3, 2019, https://www.heraldandnews.com/news/local_news/suicide-start-the-conversation/article_70ae8420-47d7-5fca-9797-aa83fbea3005.html.

Adam Piore, "Parkland and Sandy Hook Suicides: What Scientists Know About How Brain Scans Can Detect Suicidal Thoughts, Risks," *Newsweek.com,* March 26, 2019.

David Sussman, "How Using QPR Can Prevent Suicides," *Psychology Today,* February 19, 2018, https:// www.psychologytoday.com/us/blog/the-recovery-coach/201802/how-using-qpr-can-prevent-suicides.

Jean M. Twenge, *iGen: Why Today's Super-Connected Kids Are Growing Up Less Rebellious, More Tolerant, Less Happy—and Completely Unprepared for Adulthood—and What That Means for the Rest of Us* (New York: Simon & Schuster, 2018).

Jean M. Twenge, "Put That Phone Away—Now," *Time,* April 1, 2019, pp. 19–20.

"V.A. Releases 2020 National Veteran National Suicide Prevention Annual Report," *Office of Public and Intergovernmental Affairs,* November 12, 2020, https://www.va.gov/opa/pressrel/pressrelease.cfm?id=5565.

Claudia Wallis, "Another Tragic Epidemic: Suicide," *Scientific American,* August 1, 2020, https://www.scientificamerican.com/article/another-tragic-epidemic-suicide/#.

5. Approach the Speaker's Stand

Deliver a five- to seven-minute persuasive speech. Be sure to buttress your presentation with evidence designed to convince your audience that your claim is sensible, as well as with emotional appeals that arouse their desire to respond as you request.

In addition, prepare an outline and include a bibliography of at least five sources you consulted.

RECAP AND REVIEW

17.1 Build personal credibility and persuasiveness, increasing ethos by tailoring the message to the audience.

Audience perceptions of the speaker are dependent on their judgments of the speaker's character and credibility, including their assessments of the speaker's trustworthiness/believability, competence, and charisma or personal warmth and perceived goodwill. Effective persuasive speakers focus on the audience, understand the Elaboration Likelihood Model of Persuasion, and adhere to the following persuasive principles: (1) think small to avoid a big fall; (2) use the desire for consistency; and (3) don't put the best material in the middle.

17.2 Use logos or sound evidence to develop effective arguments, applying Toulmin's Reasonable Argument Model and different kinds of reasoning.

The use of specific facts and statistics, examples and illustrations, and expert testimony increases a speaker's persuasiveness. Toulmin's model divides an argument into three essential parts: a claim, reasons for making the claim, and a warrant that explains how one gets to the claim from the data used. When reasoning deductively, the speaker moves from the general to the specific, whereas if using inductive reasoning, the speaker moves from a series of specific observations to a general conclusion. With causal reasoning, the speaker shows that one event caused another. When reasoning from analogy, the speaker compares like things and concludes that because they are comparable in a number of ways, they are also comparable in another way.

17.3 Develop emotional appeals that speak to the audience, avoiding unethical fallacies.

Speakers use pathos, or appeals to emotion, to arouse our feelings, hoping to motivate us to respond as they desire. They also avoid common logical fallacies or slip-ups.

A logical fallacy is a flawed reason that you should not use and should be able to spot should other speakers violate ethical practices and use one. Speakers who build credibility, use a variety of types of evidence and sound reasoning principles, and avoid logical fallacies are more likely to deliver effective persuasive speeches that demonstrate respect for receivers.

KEY TERMS

Argument ad hominem (p. 396)

Bandwagon appeal (p. 396)

Causal reasoning (p. 390)

Credibility (p. 383)

Deductive reasoning (p. 389)

Derived credibility (p. 383)

Ethos (p. 380)

Elaboration Likelihood Model of Persuasion (p. 382)

Evidence (p. 385)

False dichotomy (p. 395)

False division (p. 395)

Glittering generality (p. 395)

Hasty generalization (p. 395)

Illustrations (p. 386)

Inductive reasoning (p. 390)

Initial credibility (p. 383)

Logical fallacy (p. 395)

Logos (p. 380)

Maslow's Hierarchy of Needs (p. 393)

Pathos (p. 380)

Post hoc, ergo propter hoc (p. 395)

Reasoning from analogy (p. 391)

Red herring (p. 395)

Slippery slope (p. 395)

Syllogism (p. 389)

Terminal credibility (p. 383)

Toulmin's Reasonable Argument Model (p. 388)

18 COMMUNICATING AND PRESENTING IN SMALL GROUPS

UPON COMPLETING THIS CHAPTER, YOU WILL BE ABLE TO

18.1 Define the characteristics of speaking in small groups, identifying how the group's leader(s) and members affect the group's effectiveness.

18.2 Discuss the advantages and disadvantages of group problem-solving, demonstrating how to use reflective thinking and brainstorming to support the problem-solving effort.

18.3 Compare and contrast speaking individually with speaking and presenting as a group, explaining how to assess the group's performance in both cyberspace and in the real world.

Employers seek to hire individuals with problem-solving skills and experience.[1] At school, as well as in your personal and professional life, groups, problem-solving groups in particular, are omnipresent, so much so, that the ability to work in one is among the most important communication skills to master.[2] You may, for example, have chosen to join an improv group, a sports team, or a cappella group. On the other hand, you also may have found yourself assigned to work with others in various classes on group projects. When this happens, how do you characteristically react? Do you voice objections, asserting that you prefer to work independently? Experience has made some of us "group-shy"—at least in part because of the belief that some group members act in ways that undermine the group's functioning. We may have witnessed this personally or experienced it vicariously by viewing programs such as *Big Brother, The Amazing Race, or Survivor*— in which one or more cast members eventually undermines the others in order to win the game. The opposite, of course, is the case with performance or project groups where all need to work interdependently.

Whatever the nature of your group, whether you choose to join it or are assigned to it, its success depends on the ability to work together and coordinate your efforts.[3] During both your college and professional career, it is very likely that you will need to engage in a multitude of group projects, including speaking as part of a panel at an academic conference or completing a task with a small group.

GROUPS AT WORK

18.1 *Define the characteristics of speaking in small groups, identifying how the group's leader(s) and members affect the group's effectiveness.*

A **small group,** whether in the workplace, cyberspace, or class, is composed of a limited number of people who communicate over a period of time to make decisions and accomplish specific goals. Groups comprising five to seven people usually function best because members are able to communicate easily, but it is not uncommon for some to contain as few as three or as many as 15 people. Each individual in a group has the potential to influence the others and is expected to function both as a speaker and a listener. Group members share a common objective. Each person occupies a particular role with respect to the others and works with them, cooperating to achieve a desired end. As they interact, group members develop certain attitudes toward one another and (ideally) a sense of satisfaction from belonging to and participating in the group. Members of a group are expected to adhere to **group norms**—the "do's and don'ts" that groups establish to regulate the behavior of members and make it possible for them to work together to attain the group's goals.

Every group defines its own objectives and establishes its own norms. Ultimately, how members relate to one another, the roles they assume, and how they exchange information and resolve problems determine the effectiveness of the group work. Member interaction—what members say and how they say it—affects both the group's health and its long-term viability.

Healthy groups exhibit five characteristics:

1. Members support one another.

2. Decisions are made together.

3. Members trust one another.

4. Communication is open and candid.

5. The group aims to excel.[4]

Whatever the specific nature of a working group's task, whether it is to develop and present a strategic campaign to a client, develop a policy to recommend to management, or discuss conflicting opinions relative to a complex social issue, knowing how to speak effectively both in the group setting and as a member of the presentation team is vital. Although effective membership and leadership are essential for group success, good leadership often begins with effective membership. All must participate fully and actively in the group. Every member must prepare independently and in concert with others, fulfill roles and responsibilities collaboratively, and recognize how their performance contributes to or detracts from the group attaining its goal.

Preparing Together

To work effectively together, the first thing group members need to do is spend some time sharing their school, work, and extracurricular schedules and getting to know one another. Part of this process is to figure out each member's strengths: Who, for example, is a visual artist? Who is into technology? Who is the most organized? Members also should share their expectations for working together. In other words, members need to decide how to work together to complete their task. They can designate a leader—the person the group determines it can count on to keep members focused and who will work out the logistics of and agendas for their meetings. Sometimes, however, there is no specific leader appointed. In this case, members of effective groups often share the leadership function. Should a group be leaderless, one or more members need to step up or emerge in the leadership role because every group needs leadership. The group can also establish a series of rules for its operation. They might decide, for example, that members must be on time and prepared for meetings and should behave appropriately when another group member is speaking.

Once this initial phase is complete, the task of preparing your group presentation has many of the same steps as any other speech, with the added job of splitting up the work to be done. As ever, you must figure out the audience for your presentation, do research, prepare your outline, and plan what you will say, but you must do all of this in concert with the rest of the group. During the planning period, members should establish how they will conduct their research and pool their findings. Once group members complete the research phase, they then need to spend time outlining the presentation to meet the demands of their assigned or selected delivery format. They also should identify any technologies that might benefit the group's presentation, being certain to develop a means for coordinating templates for presentation slides, including font size, colors, and style. Members also need to work out the order in which group members will speak. And, of course, the group needs to practice its presentation, including the integration of technologies, many times before getting up to present. During the process of working out these details, the group actually moves through a number of stages, which we explore next.

The Dynamics of a Group's Development

According to researchers, the five key stages that a group moves through during its life are forming, storming, norming, performing, and adjourning (see Figure 18.1).[5]

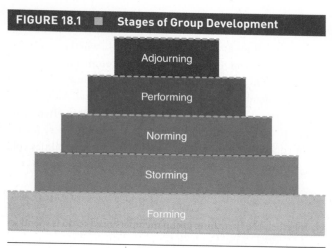

FIGURE 18.1 ■ Stages of Group Development

Adjourning

Performing

Norming

Storming

Forming

Gamble and Gamble, *The Communication Playbook* (SAGE, 2023).

Forming

On joining a new group, we may experience some initial confusion or uncertainty. We're unsure how to behave or interact with others and unclear about the roles that we will have in the group. We need to figure out who's in charge and why we were brought together. Thus, in the *forming stage* of a group, our primary objective is to fit in and be perceived as likeable. We also make an effort to find out about other group members and the group task. Once we feel valued and accepted, we begin to identify with the group.

Storming

Invariably, members experience some conflict as they determine how to work together. Typically, groups experience both task and relational conflicts. During the *storming stage,* the group's members experience tension that results from members' disagreeing and/or struggling to exert leadership as they work to clarify both the goals and the roles members will have in the life of the group. During this stage, rather than being concerned with fitting in, members now focus on expressing their ideas and opinions and securing their place in the group power structure.

Norming

Over time, a clear group structure emerges. Members firm up roles, and a leader or leaders emerge. During the *norming stage,* the group solidifies its behavioral norms, especially those relating to conflict management. In addition, the group forms a sense of identity as member awareness of interdependence and the need to cooperate with each other increases.

Performing

The emphasis of the group next switches to task accomplishment. During the *performing stage,* often considered the most important phase, members combine their skills, knowledge, and abilities to overcome obstacles and realize the group's goals.

Adjourning

Finally, during the *adjourning stage,* members review and reflect on their accomplishments or failures and determine how or whether to end the group and the relationships that have developed during its existence. Ending a group can involve having a celebration or simply saying goodbye to each other, or it can be more complicated and prolonged, with some groups opting to continue working together on a new or different task and some members choosing to continue relationships that developed during the group's life.[6]

How a group develops through each of the preceding stages determines how well it is able to function. The performance of member roles and responsibilities also affects this.

Member Roles and Responsibilities

In every group, members perform similar sets of roles. **Roles** are patterns of behavior. Positive group roles accomplish both task and maintenance functions. That is, they both help meet the group's goal and contribute to the way group members interact with one another. Negative group roles are dysfunctional, limiting the group's abilities to realize the group's goal. When you are a group member, the choice is yours: you can improve task performance and foster a concern for the needs and feelings of group members, or you can inhibit group performance by revealing an overriding concern for self instead of group success.

What kind of group member are you? Consider the assets and liabilities you bring to a group experience by checking off which, if any, of the task-oriented, maintenance-oriented, or self-serving roles identified in Table 18.1 you characteristically perform when in a group. Also consider specific instances of how the roles you checked either contributed to or detracted from the success of your last group.[7]

Do you know your role? What strengths and weaknesses do you bring to groups?

iStock.com/Anchiy

TABLE 18.1 ■ Group Roles		
Role	**Description**	**Example**
TASK-ORIENTED ROLES		
Initiating	You defined a problem; suggested methods, goals, and procedures; and started the group moving along new paths or in different directions by offering a plan.	"Rather than dwelling on problems, let's work on discovering how we can make things better."
Information-seeking	You asked for facts and opinions and sought relevant information about the problem.	"Can you show me what you discovered about why this trend exists?"
Information-giving	You offered ideas, suggestions, personal experiences, and/or factual data.	"The last time we experienced a drop-off in productivity, offering incentives helped."
Clarifying	You elaborated on or paraphrased the ideas of others, offered illustrations, or tried to increase clarity by decreasing confusion.	"So, what I hear you saying is that we need to take a more direct approach. Did I get that right?"
Coordinating	You summarized ideas and tried to draw various contributions together constructively.	"If we combine each of your ideas, I think we can create a win–win situation."
Evaluating	You evaluated the group's decisions or proposed solutions and helped establish criteria that solutions should meet.	"We agreed that whatever solution we select should be comprehensive, fair, and able to stand the test of time."

Role	Description	Example
Consensus-testing	You tested the state of agreement among members to see if the group was approaching a decision.	"Okay. Let's poll the group. In your own words, say what you believe we are agreeing to."
MAINTENANCE-ORIENTED ROLES		
Encouraging	You responded warmly, receptively, and supportively to others and their ideas.	"What a great idea!"
Gatekeeping	You sought to keep channels of communication open by helping reticent members contribute to the group and/or by working to prevent one or two members from dominating.	"Okay. Let's hear how you feel about this, too."
Harmonizing	You mediated differences between members, reconciled disagreements, and sought to reduce tension by injecting humor or other forms of relief at appropriate opportunities.	"Let's agree to disagree for now. We can come back to this later."
Compromising	You exhibited a willingness to compromise to maintain group cohesion; you were willing to modify your stance or admit an error when appropriate.	"Wow. I'll give you that one. I can see how making the change you suggest will put us in a stronger position."
Standard-setting	You assessed the state of member satisfaction with group procedures and indicated the criteria set for evaluating group functioning.	"Let's see how you think we've done today. Did we all come prepared? Are we listening to one another? Are we building on ideas?"
SELF-SERVING ROLES		
Blocking	You were disagreeable and digressed so that nothing was accomplished.	"This is a waste of time. Hey, did you watch the game last night?"
Aggressing	You criticized or blamed others and sought to deflate the egos of other members as a means of enhancing your own status in the group.	"That idea is the worst idea I've ever heard. Can't you think? Can't you be creative? I'm the only one contributing anything worthwhile here."

(Continued)

TABLE 18.1 ■ Group Roles (Continued)

Role	Description	Example
Recognition-seeking	You made yourself the center of attention; you focused attention on yourself rather than the task; you spoke loudly and exhibited unusual or outlandish behavior.	"Am I smart, or what? Did I tell you about the time I won a car?"
Withdrawing	You stopped contributing, appeared indifferent to group efforts, daydreamed, or sulked.	"Whatever you say. I don't care anymore."
Dominating	You insisted on getting your own way; you interrupted others; you sought to impose your ideas and run the group.	"Stop. My solution is the only one worth trying. We don't need to hear any more."
Joking	You engaged in horseplay or exhibited other inappropriate behavior.	"What are you wearing? You look like you just got up. What's with you? Had a late night with Robin?"
Self-confessing	You revealed personal feelings irrelevant to the work of the group.	"I haven't told anyone this. I lied on my job application."
Help-seeking	You played on and tried to elicit the sympathies of other group members.	"Come on. Help me out here. Please also research my part. I'm just overwhelmed right now."

Enacting Leadership

Effective leadership is a defining quality of most successful groups. Effective leaders are versatile. They perform combinations of procedural, task, and maintenance functions designed to move the group closer to its goal. Among the **procedural behaviors** a leader performs are setting the time and place for a meeting, preparing the agenda for the meeting, beginning the meeting, and summarizing the group's progress at the meeting's end. These kinds of activities help to facilitate the conducting of the group's business. **Task leadership behaviors** include giving and soliciting information and opinions, keeping the group on track, and helping the group analyze and evaluate issues and reach a consensus. **Maintenance leadership behaviors** include the expression of agreement and support, the reduction and release of group tensions, the resolution of differences of opinion and group conflicts, and the enhancement of morale and member satisfaction. The leader also must fully comprehend the group's goals and have a clear vision of how to reach them.

As we noted earlier, when we think of a group leader, we usually think of someone who is in an appointed or elected position. However, remember that leadership is not the exclusive possession of any single group member, and a group need not have a designated leader for members to exert leadership. Indeed, groups in which every member feels prepared to share leadership often work best. After all, to lead a group is to influence it. When influence is positive, the group is led toward the realization of its goal.[8]

Leader(s). A group doesn't need a designated leader to succeed; all members can share leadership and still be successful as a group.

iStock.com/nd3000

SOLVING PROBLEMS TOGETHER

> **18.2** *Discuss the advantages and disadvantages of using a group to solve problems, demonstrating how to use reflective thinking and brainstorming to support the problem-solving effort.*

During the COVID-19 pandemic, the medical team at Alaska's largest hospital were called upon to problem-solve; they were tasked with deciding who should get treatment and who should wait, even though waiting meant they might not survive. They never had to do this before.[9] While the decisions you will be required to make in class and on the job may not be as consequential, how you go about solving problems together will affect others. The dynamics of a group's interactions affect the outcomes the group is able to achieve. Although working in groups has both advantages and disadvantages, adhering to a problem-solving framework and engaging in brainstorming facilitate the group's realization of its goal(s).

Advantages of Group Problem-Solving

Working in a group to solve a problem has the following advantages:

- **Group work brings in the ideas and strengths of all members.** Instead of only one contributor, a number of people with different information and contrasting viewpoints are able to contribute to the decision-making process, so an effective solution is more likely to emerge.

- **Groups filter out costly errors before they do any damage.** Because everyone in a group is focused on solving a problem, errors and weaknesses are likely to be detected.

- **A decision made by a group is usually better received than a decision proposed by an individual.** When several people work cooperatively to explore potential solutions, they usually are able to agree on the best.

- **Participating in decision making strengthens individuals' commitment to implement the decision.** Participation and motivation are effective problem-solving partners.

- **Reaching a decision in a group can be more fulfilling and personally reinforcing than reaching a decision alone.** The feeling of belonging makes a difference.

COACHING TIP

"Never doubt that a small group of thoughtful, committed citizens can change the world; indeed, it's the only thing that ever has."

—Margaret Mead, American cultural anthropologist

There is strength in numbers. Working together, you often accomplish more than working on your own. A well-functioning group almost always comes up with better decisions or solutions to problems than an individual working solo.

Disadvantages of Group Problem-Solving

There are potential disadvantages inherent in using a group to solve a problem. Unless the group's norms establish that certain counterproductive behaviors will not be tolerated, they could impede effective group functioning. These behaviors include the following:

Look out. What steps can you take to prevent typical conflicts that occur in group work from impacting your group?

iStock.com/PeopleImages

- **Personal objectives at odds with the group's goals.** As a result, the group's objectives may be sacrificed or sabotaged as we undermine them in an effort to satisfy our personal needs.

- **Too much comfort in numbers.** When we know other people are available to cover for us, we may slack off.

- **More vocal, forceful, or powerful members may dominate the group.** By steamrolling others, we make it harder for all members to participate fully or make their true feelings known.

- **Intransigence of one or more members.** If a member comes to the group unwilling to listen to other points of view or to compromise, the decision-making process may become deadlocked.

- **The group experiences a risky shift.** Groups sometimes make decisions that are riskier than an individual working alone would be comfortable making, a change in behavior known as a risky shift.

- **Slower decision making.** It takes longer for most groups to make a decision than it does individuals.

Whether the potential advantages of working in groups outweigh the potential disadvantages depends on how effectively the group is able to perform its task.

The group's effectiveness also is influenced by how the group make its decisions. Depending on the group and its task, a wide variety of decision-making strategies or approaches may be used. Prime among them are decision by an expert, decision by the leader, decision by a subgroup or minority, decision by the majority, and decision by consensus.[10]

SELF-ASSESSMENT 18.1: DECISIONS, DECISIONS

Directions

Assess your favored means of making a group decision by rank ordering the possibilities identified in the left column from 1 (your first choice) to 8 (your least favored choice) and explaining your reasons for the ranking and the implications of the choice.

Decision-Making Strategy	My Ranking
Ask an expert to decide	
Flip a coin	
Let the majority rule	
Let the group leader decide	

Decision-Making Strategy	My Ranking
Stall until a decision no longer needs to be made	
Let the minority rule because sometimes that's fair	
Determine the average position because this is least likely to be offensive to anyone	
Reach a decision by consensus; that is, be certain all have had input into the discussion, understand the decision, can rephrase it, and will publicly support it	

Ranking Analysis	Ranking Implications
Explain the reason behind each ranking.	Identify the ramifications each choice has for a group's operation and effectiveness.

The greater the involvement of members in the decision-making process, the more effective the group's decision will be. Of course, decisions by a leader, an expert, or a majority or minority vote all take less time than consensus. However, no matter how the decision is made, it is the group that will usually be responsible for implementing the decision. If members disagree with a decision or do not understand it, they may not work very hard to make it succeed. A leader may make routine decisions or be called on to make decisions when little time is available for a real discussion of the issues. Under most circumstances, however, one person cannot be the best resource for all decisions. A drawback of the decision-by-expert method is that it is sometimes difficult to determine who the expert is. Also, decision by an expert, like decision by a leader, fails to involve other group members. Decision by averaging, on the whole, is superior to either decision by a leader or decision by an expert. With averaging, all members can be consulted, individual errors will cancel each other out, and an average position usually will not dissatisfy anyone too much. On the other hand, an average position usually does not satisfy anyone very much. Thus, commitment to the decision tends to be rather low. Under most circumstances, the quality of decision making and the satisfaction of the participants are higher when a group seeks consensus. Consensus puts the resources of the entire group to effective use, permits discussion of all issues and alternatives, and ensures the commitment of all members. It is not the decision alone that is important in group interaction; the reactions and feelings of group members also matter.

Equally important in decision making is the willingness to consider alternative solutions—especially new options not originally brought to the table but that offer potential new paths to a positive outcome.[11] This is best realized by relying on a systematic approach to problem-solving.

Use a Systematic Problem-Solving Framework

A group's success depends on both its leadership and its membership. It also depends on the nature of the decision-making system used by the group. One method that has been known to improve problem-solving is the **Reflective Thinking Framework**, derived from the writings of philosopher and educator John Dewey[12] (see Figure 18.2).

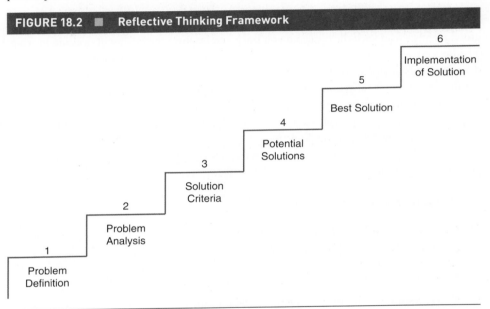

FIGURE 18.2 ■   Reflective Thinking Framework

6 — Implementation of Solution

5 — Best Solution

4 — Potential Solutions

3 — Solution Criteria

2 — Problem Analysis

1 — Problem Definition

Source: Adapted from John Dewey, *How We Think* (Boston: Heath, 1910).

The Reflective Thinking Framework consists of six basic steps and offers a logical system for group discussion. As members work their way through the framework, they must ask and answer a series of questions before advancing to the next stage in the sequence.

- **Step 1. Define the Problem.** Is the problem phrased as a clear and specific question that is not slanted and thus will not arouse defensiveness? Is it phrased so as to allow a wide variety of answers rather than a simple yes or no?

- **Step 2. Analyze the Problem.** What are the facts of the situation? What are its causes? What is its history? How severe is it? Who is affected, and how?

- **Step 3. Establish Criteria for Solutions.** What criteria must an acceptable solution fulfill? By what objective standards should we evaluate a solution? What requirements must a solution meet? How critical is each criterion?

- **Step 4. Generate Potential Solutions.** How will each possible solution remedy the problem? How well does each solution meet the established criteria? What advantages or disadvantages does each solution present?

- **Step 5. Select the Best Solution.** How would you rank each solution? Which solution offers the greatest number of advantages and the fewest disadvantages? How can we combine solutions to produce an even better one?

- **Step 6. Suggest Strategies for Implementation.** How can the solution be implemented? What steps should we take to put the solution into effect?

By systematically working through this framework and suspending judgment as they do so, group members can keep the discussion on track and improve the quality of decision making. The Reflective Thinking Framework helps group members avoid early concurrence—the tendency to conclude discussion prematurely. By requiring members to explore all data and evaluate alternative courses of action methodically and by opening them to new information rather than encouraging them to base decisions on what they know at the moment, the system also helps guard against groupthink—the tendency to let the desire for consensus override careful analysis and reasoned decision making.[13]

In order for the Reflective Thinking Framework to function effectively for your group, ask yourself the following questions as you work your way through it:

- Are the resources of all group members being well used?

- Is the group using its time wisely?

- Is the group emphasizing fact-finding and inquiry?

- Are members listening to and respecting the ideas and feelings of other members?

- Is pressure to conform deemphasized and pressure to search for diverse viewpoints emphasized?

- Is the group's atmosphere supportive, trusting, and cooperative?

Decision-making effectiveness depends on the degree to which group members feel free to speak up, maintain open minds, and exhibit a willingness to search for new information.

Brainstorm While Problem-Solving

Fresh ideas help solve both old and new problems. Fresh ideas come from encouraging new avenues of thought. *Brainstorming,* a system of idea generation devised by Alex Osborn, allows this to happen.[14] During a brainstorming session, all members of a group spontaneously contribute ideas. The group's goal is to collect as many ideas as possible in a short time without interrupting the thought process or stopping to evaluate ideas during the brainstorming process.

Although brainstorming is most frequently incorporated in the solution phase of the Reflective Thinking Framework, it can prompt creative inquiry during any of its stages.

Let it flow. No matter how wild or crazy your ideas may be, get as many on paper as you can with your group, and analyze them later.

iStock.com/andresr

To ensure a successful brainstorming session, follow these guidelines:

- **Suspend judgment.** Brainstorming is not the time to evaluate or criticize ideas.

- **Encourage freewheeling.** Brainstorming is not the time to consider an idea's practicality. You can tame or tone down wild ideas later, if necessary.

- **Aim for quantity.** Brainstorming is not the time to concentrate on idea quality, nor is it the time to censor your contributions. The more ideas you generate, the greater your chances of coming up with a good one.

- **Record all ideas.** Brainstorming is not the time to eliminate possibilities.

- **Evaluate only when brainstorming is concluded.** Only after the brainstorming process is over should you evaluate the ideas you proposed.

COACHING TIP

"There are two kinds of people, those who do the work and those who take the credit. Try to be in the first group; there is less competition there."

—Indira Gandhi, former prime minister of India

Don't expect others to do your work and give you credit for their accomplishments. Slackers need to shape up or risk being the target of other group member complaints, or even being asked to leave the group.

PRESENTING AND ASSESSING THE GROUP'S WORK

> **18.3**   *Compare and contrast speaking individually with speaking and presenting as a group, explaining how to assess the group's performance both in cyberspace and in the real world.*

Your problem-solving group works its way through the Reflective Thinking Framework, including brainstorming, and comes to a decision through a series of private group meetings and without an audience present. The group's next task is likely to report its findings to an audience—to inform them of the group's decision, to advocate for the adoption of the group's proposals, or both. What happens, however, if the group met virtually? What differentiates virtual groups from those that meet in the workplace or class? Whether it meets in the real world or cyberspace, most often, the group presents its findings or recommendations to an audience through an oral report, a panel discussion, a symposium, or a forum. Let us explore each of these possibilities in turn.

The Virtual Group

Technology makes it possible for members to meet and problem-solve in cyberspace.

It has become increasingly common for small groups to meet virtually, relying on technology to facilitate their working together, especially if members are situated in different time zones, cities, or countries, which increasingly is the case. When geographically dispersed, members typically hold asynchronous virtual group meetings—those that do not meet in real time. When meeting asynchronously, members can log on, post, and respond to the messages and posts of team members at any time. Of course, synchronous meetings can also be scheduled so that members can interact in real time in their own voice rather than via text.

During the COVID-19 pandemic, for example, group meetings moved totally online for a while. Getting together to meet synchronously via Zoom (Zoom usage surged from 10 million users before the pandemic to 300 million during the pandemic), WebEx, Skype, or Google Hangouts became a daily ritual.[15] Although, as we noted, groups regularly meet virtually, the pandemic took the virtual team experience to the next level, requiring members to stay connected, committed, and in synch—focused on completing their projects while maintaining a healthy online culture—which was challenging for the following reasons. When meeting online: (1) members report feeling less commitment to the group and express being less happy about working in one; (2) reading the nonverbal reactions of others is more difficult than it would be if group members were physically face to face; and (3) perception of members' belief in their ability to be productive is lower than in face-to-face groups.[16]

There are a number of guidelines to follow to ensure that people participating in video meetings position themselves to overcome the preceding hurdles. These include:

1. Consider the remote meeting room to be a conference room.

2. Show up on time.

3. Show up in-person—an avatar is not a substitute for you.

4. Sit—as if at a conference table—for the meeting. Don't move around or carry your technology from room to room.

5. Develop ground rules for meeting virtually, including establishing the procedure to follow to interact offline, for example, will you text, email, or call?

6. No eating during the meeting.

7. When you have something to add, unmute your sound—this lets others know that you're about to say something.

8. Silence your phone—turning off notifications and Twitter alerts, and keeping it out of sight. Using a cell during a meeting usually is considered rude.

9. Pay close attention to the nonverbal dimension, including the nonverbal cues sent and received; they speak volumes. Smiling and making eye-contact reduce psychological distance.

10. Be sure to allow time for relationship-building and small talk prior to actually getting down to business. Getting to know one another and developing trust in one another facilitates information-sharing.

11. Exhibit enthusiasm for the group's task. Involving everyone and taking steps to ensure that all come to the group prepared and ready to participate will signal interest.

12. Become comfortable exchanging relevant information and encourage others to do the same.

13. If you need to share your screen, take steps to ensure that any personal information, nonbusiness content, or chat windows are not visible. Some platforms, such as Microsoft Teams, have a "Do Not Disturb" or "Presenting" setting that blocks notifications when you are sharing your screen.

14. Close all other windows on your screen, so that you're fully present and mindfully attending to the discussion.[17]

When meeting online, sometimes the best way to solve a problem is to rely on an extensive network. In the online world, the person who provides needed information, advice, or an answer to a problem may be on the periphery of a group, as compared to in the face-to-face world, when group members share extremely strong links and typically know each other better. When online, however, highly creative teams interact via a "pulsing star" pattern, in which they fan out to gather information and then regroup to share what they discover.[18]

The Social Network Paradigm

Individuals and groups in disparate locations link with others using social networks that have woven themselves into the fabric of group life by putting people in touch with one another and giving users access to larger, more interrelated pools of information.[19] In effect, online social networks have migrated group communication into alternative meeting environments.

LinkedIn, in addition to functioning as a job search database, and a network for hiring and getting hired, also transformed itself into a social network for professionals. People from the professional sector join primarily to connect with other professionals whom they use to help them solve daily business problems. One LinkedIn product, Company Groups, automatically gathers all the employees from a company who use LinkedIn into a single, private Web forum. Once in the forum, employees can ask and answer questions, share and discuss information about themselves and their responsibilities, and collaborate on projects. Influencers with specific interests also gravitate to LinkedIn. People talk to one another in LinkedIn much like they do in their respective offices. Since it fosters worker connectivity, LinkedIn also facilitates worker productivity.[20]

Similar to LinkedIn are TownSquare and SharePoint, each of which enable a company's employees to follow one another's activities.[21] Connectbeam is a consultancy that sets up secure social networks for the corporate Internets of Fortune 500 companies that do not want workers putting information on social networking sites such as Facebook, which use servers beyond the company's control. Some companies use Yammer, a system similar to Twitter but open only to employees. Yammer lets people brag, share information, and learn about what others are doing in the company, facilitating their collaboration.[22] Thousands of workplace teams also use Slack, an internal messaging and archiving program, to encourage communication among members.

Other companies bring workers together by having them meet in sites such as Second Life, a virtual reality operation with 900,000 active users. Their avatars—alter egos of the employees—meet in the company's own virtual workspace. During the pandemic, for example, Second Life attracted companies to use its site to run immersive business meetings.[23] Many organizations use Second Life to hold meetings.[24]

Benefits of Online Groups

Group members who use virtual sites report feeling more comfortable talking and expressing ideas or calling others' views into question. They may not display such behavior in real-world meetings because of feelings of intimidation. Social networking gets employees talking, brainstorming, and cooperating across the organization, fostering the sharing of information and the collection of ideas. To make the most of virtual collaboration, companies also tap into the wisdom of a crowd—a practice known as crowdsourcing—in which they invite, either publicly or semipublicly, a community to provide input, effectively enlarging their brainstorming efforts.[25]

Drawbacks of Online Groups

On the flip side, using technology and social media in the workplace also can have negative effects for both employees and employers. It may blur the lines between personal and professional identities. Because of heavy social media use, employees worry that everyone has access to the information they place online. At the same time, employers worry that employees are misusing social media, spending valuable meeting time tweeting or game-playing when they should be working.[26]

Social media can encourage other bad habits besides distraction. Participants in virtual meetings sometimes behave as if they have less accountability than people meeting face to face. People need to show up physically and mentally for a face-to-face meeting. When a meeting is held online, attendees are not always as prepared and willing to participate actively, preferring to have side conversations or check sports scores.[27]

Virtual meetings also disrupt some of the communication channels we rely on in-person. It becomes more difficult to read nonverbal cues, making it more likely for misunderstandings to occur. When you can't tell if someone is confused or uneasy, agreeing or disagreeing, it becomes more difficult to be certain you're interpreting the words being exchanged correctly. The increasing sophistication of videoconferencing technology removes some of these obstacles. Telepresence systems enable members who are not actually present to appear virtually, often via life-sized video screens. The high-definition system simulates face-to-face meetings by allowing group members to make eye contact and observe body language.[28]

Generally, it is important to keep in mind that what works face to face may not translate to the virtual world. The members of virtual teams may not share the same culture or make the same effort to see things from colleagues' points of view. Thus, although social media offers a relatively inexpensive way for colleagues around the world to connect, it also presents new and considerable challenges.

COACHING TIP

"i suggest that you try as an experiment to capitalize those whom You address while leaving yourselves in the lowercase. It may be a humbling experience."

Caroline Winter, writer, scholar, and author of "Is the Vertical Pronoun Really Such a Capital Idea?"[2]

To remind yourself about the importance of teamwork, when referring to yourself, use the work "i" instead of I. When referring to others, use words like "You" and "We" instead of you and we. Because English is the language that capitalizes the word I, visualizing a small i in its place might diminish the impact that individualistic tendencies have for working effectively in groups.

Artificial Intelligence (AI) and Group Work

About 60 percent of occupations have some 30 percent of activities that could be automated or taken over by a machine, freeing up the worker to be more productive.[30] Among the challenges people can now delegate to AI are the actual scheduling and contents of meetings. Instead, AI-powered personal assistants can now take care of meeting scheduling, rescheduling, and cancellations. They also can compile and distribute meeting notes. AISense, for example, available as part of Zoom, can provide transcriptions of meetings to attendees for their records. Freeing team members from mindless tasks, AI gives them more time to solve problems and exercise their creativity, improving their collaboration.[31] Because it is less susceptible to automation, the ability to work in a team becomes an even more valuable asset.[32] The group presentations that follow here may be presented virtually or when all are physically present. Each format is readily adaptable to either setting.

The Oral Group Report

Approach the group's oral report of its work as you would any other speech. Your report should contain an introduction, body, and conclusion. Consider your audience and your goal when deciding whether one or more group member or all members of the group should participate in delivering the oral report, perhaps dividing it up by topic or section. If more than one member speaks, make sure you incorporate transitions, not just between sections of the speech, but also between speakers. Like any speech, in addition to being well organized, an oral report must be adapted to reflect the needs, concerns, and interests of the people you are addressing; contain an array of supporting materials and evidence (including visual aids, if appropriate); use language that accurately and effectively communicates its content; and, of course, be well rehearsed. All group members should be prepared to respond to questions from those receiving the report.

The Round Table

When engaged in a round table discussion, group members typically arrange themselves in a semicircle. They work together to share information or solve a problem. Who speaks is not pre-determined. Instead, members contribute when they have something to offer. A leader or moderator may help facilitate the group's work by keeping the discussion on topic and encouraging participation from all members.

The Panel Discussion

A panel discussion requires group members to be "experts" as they talk through an issue in front of an audience. The positive and negative aspects are debated, usually without the direct involvement of the audience.

In effect, the group replays in public the problem-solving discussion it had in private. While neither memorized nor scripted, the panel discussion is carefully planned so that all important points are made and all group members are able to participate.

Most panel discussions also include a moderator whose role is to introduce the topic and panelists and to ensure that the topic is explored adequately. Panel discussions are held on controversial topics, where panelists may disagree.

The Symposium

A symposium is a discussion in which a number of individuals present individual speeches of approximately the same length on a central subject before an audience. Because a symposium's speakers address members of the audience directly, there usually is little, if any, interaction among the speakers during their presentations; however, participants may discuss their reactions with each other afterward, as well as field questions from the audience.

Symposia are designed to (1) shed light on or explore different aspects of a problem, (2) provide material for subsequent discussion, or (3) review different steps covered during a group's problem-solving experience. Ideally, each speaker is aware of what others will present, so there is little, if any, duplication of information. Speakers are typically not in opposition to each other but rather frame their contributions based on their focus and interests.

The Forum Presentation

The purpose of a forum is to provide a medium for an open and interactive discussion between the group and an audience. Unlike the other formats, a forum is a discussion requiring full audience participation. After a moderator and/or each speaker make a brief opening statement, audience members then are free to question the participants, who answer their queries with brief, impromptu responses. A town meeting is one example of the forum in action.

A forum works best when there is a moderator to introduce the program and the speakers, as well as to clarify and summarize the program's progress as needed. It also helps when group members are aware of which issues will be discussed during the forum and are knowledgeable about the subject because they can then prepare themselves to respond to questions quickly and thoroughly.

Evaluating the Group's Performance

After every group project, it's important to look back at how group members worked together. Whether the group operated in cyberspace or in the real world, it's necessary to assess if members were fully engaged, lived up to their responsibilities, performed helpful roles, supported others' efforts, used systematic problem-solving and brainstorming, managed any conflicts, and overall, were able to contribute positively to the group's performance and outcomes. By honestly looking back at your own and the group's strengths and weaknesses, identifying the nature of the roles you and other members performed in the group and the dynamics of the group's leadership, reviewing the challenges you had to overcome in order to achieve a positive result, and summarizing how you might work together differently to produce an even better outcome if given another opportunity, you foster personal growth and an enhanced appreciation of the benefits of planning and presenting in groups.

GAME PLAN

Presenting in Groups

- I understand our group will pass through five different stages during its tenure. I will evaluate how we do in each stage and what we can do better.
- While we may have designated one of our members as the leader who will coordinate the order in which we speak, we are all prepared to exert leadership.
- I understand the goal of our presentation, and I understand my own role within the group.
- I know who will speak before and after me, and I am prepared to transition from and to those individuals.
- Our group will tackle our topic using the Reflective Thinking Framework and brainstorming.
- Our group is equally adept to prepare and present online or in a shared physical space.

EXERCISES

Communicating and Presenting in a Group

Planning and presenting in a group poses unique challenges. By participating in the following activities, you can further develop the skills and understandings needed to succeed as both group member and leader.

1. Getting to Know You

Building on this opening line, "Once upon a time, there was a group of college students who decided to get to know each other better by sharing their work habits and strengths," reveal something about yourself that others in your group should know in order for you to perform your best when working with them.

2. Assessing Group Interaction in the Media

Mediated forms of group discourse have grown in popularity over the years. The increasing number of hours devoted to talk radio programs, as well as to opinion and interview shows, testifies to this. But instead of engaging in reasoned debate, hosts and guests on some programs engage in uncivil wars characterized by escalating levels of conflict. What lessons can we learn from such programs? How can we use them to help us develop into more effective discussion group members?

   Just as you need to evaluate the effectiveness of your own fact-finding and decision-making groups, so also do you need to evaluate mediated discussion groups as a receiver by assessing both their methods and their conclusions. Using any mediated discussion offering of your choice, answer the following questions:

1. Was the program's topic well analyzed by participants?

2. Were both host and guests free to share ideas and feelings?

3. Did host or guests monopolize discussion?

4. Did host or guests become aggressive or abusive?

5. What did the program's host and guests do to handle any conflicts that developed?

6. Were claims made by the host or guests supported by evidence?

7. What norms appeared to govern the discussion?

8. What were the program's outcomes? Did a consensus emerge?

9. What was learned?

10. What recommendations would you make to the show's host and guests regarding their on-air behavior? What communication skills would both host and guests need to possess in order to put your recommendations into practice?

3. Brainstorming Your Way to Consensus

First, read the research findings summarized in the paragraph that follows these instructions. Then, brainstorm possible rationales for the statistics presented. Attempt to reach consensus as to which rationale is most likely. Once discussion is over, appoint a member to present the group's conclusions to the class:

> Despite commonly held belief, chivalry does not appear to rule at sea. According to a recent study, in at least 16 maritime shipwrecks dating back from today to 1852, two times as many men have survived the disasters as women. What is more, 18.7 percent more crew survived than passengers.[33] Why do you think this is?

Use the following checklist to analyze how effective your group was in discussing its task.

- Did the group define the problem?
- Did the group thoroughly analyze the problem?
- Did the group brainstorm to generate a wide range of possible rationales in support of the statistical findings?
- Did the group evaluate each rationale carefully?
- Did the group succeed in reaching a consensus with regard to the most likely rationale?

4. Analyze a Group Presentation

Attend a panel discussion, symposium, or forum conducted on campus, in the community, or in cyberspace. Evaluate how well the moderator and group participants fulfilled their respective functions.

5. Approach the Speaker's Stand

Your instructor will divide you into small groups. Your assignment is to identify and formulate a question of fact, value, or policy for your group to discuss. Then, using the Reflective Thinking Framework, conduct a group discussion on your chosen question. Be sure to outline exactly what you hope to accomplish during each stage of the sequence.

After you complete your discussion, prepare a brief paper explaining your group's accomplishments and identifying obstacles to overcome while completing your task. Also analyze the quality of leadership, membership, and decision making displayed by your group.

Finally, your instructor will ask you to use one or more of the following formats to present your findings to the class: a panel discussion, an oral report, a symposium, or a forum presentation.

RECAP AND REVIEW

18.1 Define the characteristics of speaking in small groups, identifying how the group's leader(s) and members affect the group's effectiveness.

A small group contains a limited number of people who communicate with each other over a period of time, usually face to face, to make decisions and accomplish specific goals. All members of a group have the potential to influence all other members and are expected to function as both speaker and receiver. Every group defines its own objectives, norms, and operating climate. More successful groups have a number of major attributes that distinguish them. In particular, these are effective leadership, effective membership, and effective implementation of a decision-making system.

18.2 Discuss the advantages and disadvantages of group problem-solving, demonstrating how to use reflective thinking and brainstorming to support the problem-solving effort.

Working collaboratively enables the group to weed out errors and increase commitment to a decision. Groups have to be careful not to let more powerful members dominate or take too many risks. The Reflective Thinking Framework involves six steps: (1) problem definition, (2) problem analysis, (3) the establishment of solution criteria, (4) the generation of solutions, (5) the selection of the best solution, and (6) strategies for implementation. Brainstorming is an idea generation system during which group members suspend judgment, encourage freewheeling, aim for quantity of ideas, and record all ideas. Group members evaluate ideas produced during brainstorming after the brainstorming session concludes.

18.3 Compare and contrast speaking individually with speaking and presenting as a group, explaining how to assess the group's performance in both cyberspace and in the real world.

In contrast to an individual speech in which the audience is focused on a solo speaker, a group presentation involves interaction among multiple speakers and listeners; these occur in both real-world and online settings. When a part of a group, members need to organize themselves and their information to present their findings to an audience. In many instances, after a group reaches a decision or solves a problem, the group presents its findings to others through an oral report, a panel discussion, a symposium, or a forum. Generally, it is important to keep in mind that what works face to face may not translate to the virtual world, and vice versa. Following guidelines facilitating the maintenance of a healthy group culture, whether meeting and presenting online or in the real world, is key.

KEY TERMS

Decision-making group (p. 426)

Early concurrence (p. 418)

Fact-finding group (p. 426)

Groupthink (p. 418)

Healthy group (p. 407)

Maintenance leadership behaviors (p. 412)

Norms (p. 407)

Procedural behaviors (p. 412)

Reflective Thinking Framework (p. 417)

Risky shift (p. 415)

Roles (p. 409)

Small group (p. 406)

Task leadership behaviors (p. 412)

iStock.com/gchutka

19 SPECIAL OCCASION SPEECHES

UPON COMPLETING THIS CHAPTER, YOU WILL BE ABLE TO

19.1 Describe the nature and purpose of special occasion speeches, distinguishing among speeches of celebration, speeches of inspiration, speeches to entertain, and speeches to commemorate.

19.2 Demonstrate the characteristics of celebratory speeches, including the introduction, the award presentation, the acceptance, and the toast.

19.3 Illustrate the functions of inspirational speeches as revealed in commencement and keynote speeches.

19.4 Define the goals of the speech to entertain, focusing on the roast and after-dinner speech.

19.5 Identify key characteristics of commemorative speeches exemplified in the tribute speech and eulogy.

On September 11, 2021, the United States observed the 20th anniversary of 9/11. The nation commemorated the terrible day when terrorists hijacked four U.S. airplanes, flying two of them into the Twin Towers of the World Trade Center in New York City, and a third into the Pentagon. The fourth plane, which many said had been destined to hit the Capitol in Washington, D.C., crashed instead into a field in Shanksville, Pennsylvania, the result of the plane's passengers fighting back against the hijackers in a heroic attempt to regain control of the weaponized plane. To commemorate 9/11, speeches were given in all crash sites, with former president George W. Bush, who was president on 9/11, delivering the commemorative address in Shanksville. We will look at that speech a little later in this chapter.

Nearly a century and a half before 9/11, in 1863, another commemorative address was given by another president. "Four score and seven years ago" begins one of the most famous special occasion speeches ever delivered in the history of the United States. Abraham Lincoln's address at the dedication of the national cemetery at Gettysburg was designed to reflect the needs of a very special occasion. When delivering that speech, now referred to as the "Gettysburg Address," Lincoln's purpose was not only to pay tribute to those who died during the Civil War but also to help bring the nation together. As a special occasion speaker, you too may be called on to celebrate an individual, inspire or entertain an audience, or join with the audience in commemorating a person, group, or event.

GOALS AND FUNCTIONS OF SPECIAL OCCASION SPEECHES

19.1 *Describe the nature and purpose of special occasion speeches, distinguishing among speeches of celebration, speeches of inspiration, speeches to entertain, and speeches to commemorate.*

The speeches we deliver to recognize life's special moments distinguish themselves from other kinds of speeches. Though special occasion speeches may also inform or persuade, this is rarely their primary function. Instead, their goal is to mark the special occasion that brings the audience together. Although a speaker always considers the nature of the occasion when delivering any speech, with speeches of special occasion, the occasion itself *is* the speaker's primary purpose for speaking. The occasion sets the audience's expectations.

The Nature of Special Occasion Speeches

When preparing a special occasion speech, the speaker focuses on the reason behind the occasion. Special occasion speeches serve two functions. First, they help magnify the significance of the event or person being honored; and second, they help unify the audience by affirming the common values exhibited through the celebration of this person or event. To accomplish these objectives, the speaker must fully understand both the nature of the special occasion and the role speaker and audience play in it. For example, commencement speakers frequently reinforce the value of education and try to spur graduates on to achieve greatness. Whatever the context, it is the speaker's obligation to deliver a speech to mark the day, which likely is exceptional in one or more ways. Audiences approach such events with particular expectations, and the success of the speaker depends on their ability to conform to established norms when working to meet an audience's expectations (see Table 19.1).

TABLE 19.1 ■ Types of Special Occasion (Ceremonial) Speeches

Type	Purpose
Celebratory Speeches	Speech of introduction: To introduce a featured speaker to the audience
	Speech of presentation: To present an award or special recognition
	Speech of acceptance: To accept an award or special recognition
	Toast: To recognize a celebrant at a special occasion, such as a wedding, a graduation party, a birth or birthday, or an anniversary
Inspirational Speeches	Commencement address: To praise and congratulate a graduating class
	Keynote address: To motivate and inspire an audience at a meeting or special event
Speeches to Entertain	Roast: To entertain the audience by poking good-natured fun at the person being honored
	After-dinner speech: To entertain an audience with a sometimes humorous, whimsical, or mildly satirical look at a topic of interest and relevance
Commemorative Speeches	Tribute speech: To honor or praise a person or event
	Eulogy: To pay tribute to a person who has died

SELF-ASSESSMENT 19.1: CREATING SPEECHES FOR CEREMONIES

Directions

Circle the numbers that most accurately reflect your level of comfort delivering the following kinds of special event speeches: 1 = Not at all prepared; 2 = somewhat prepared; 3 = prepared; 4 = very prepared; 5 = fully prepared.

	1	2	3	4	5
Introducing a Speaker					
Presenting an Award					
Accepting an Award					
Delivering a Toast					
Commencement Speech					
Keynote Speech					
Roast					
After-Dinner Speech					
Tribute Speech					
Eulogy					

Scoring Method

Total the numbers you circled to arrive at your comfort level with ceremonial speaking in general.

Total _____

Total Score Interpretation

Your scores indicate how prepared you think you are to present each kind of ceremonial speech. For which kinds of speeches do you feel most and least prepared? How prepared do you feel in general? For example, if you accumulated 45 to 50 points, in general, you feel fully ready to present; if you scored 35 to 44 points, you feel just about ready; if you scored 20 to 34 points, you feel that you're on your way; if you scored 11 to 20 points, you know you have a way to go; if you scored 10 points or less, you have a lot of work to do.

Categorizing Ceremonial Speech

In the years ahead, you will be part of a number of special occasions that may require you to engage in ceremonial speaking and deliver a special occasion or **ceremonial speech**, one marking the contributions and significance of a person or event. Some, like toasts, you either may have time to plan or be expected to deliver impromptu. They are not always prepared and structured prior to your being asked to speak. You may, for example, be at a wedding and handed the mic to speak on behalf of the happy couple's attendants. Others will be more formal and require significant time and definite preparation on your part.

Among the kinds of special occasion/ceremonial speeches you will most likely give are: *speeches of celebration*—speeches celebrating a person, group, institution, or event; *speeches of inspiration*—speeches that encourage, motivate, and stimulate the audience; *speeches to entertain*—speeches that are designed to amuse and entertain; and s*peeches to commemorate*—speeches that honor and remember. Whatever the occasion precipitating the speech, it remains important to analyze the audience, their expectations, and the details of the event. In general, most ceremonial speeches have the following commonalities:

Context and Content Matter

The occasion determines the speech. The context, including the physical setting, the temporal setting, and the sociocultural aspects of the event, guides what is said, as well as delivery. Like every speech, the special occasion speech contains an introduction, body, and conclusion—with the parts condensed and the majority of the available time devoted to developing the body.

It's Likely Invitational

The speaker and attendees usually are invited to participate. Their involvement aligns with the purpose for the special occasion.

The Speech Is Brief, Sincere, and Positive

Special occasion speeches are traditionally brief, genuine expressions of appreciation that display respect and admiration for the person, group, or event being celebrated.

It's Special

On days throughout our lives, these speeches recognize the extraordinary. The special occasion speech, like every speech, deserves to be crafted creatively.

COACHING TIP

"The more you praise and celebrate your life, the more there is in life to celebrate."

—Oprah Winfrey, media mogul

Life itself is a special occasion. When giving a special occasion speech, be sure to affirm that. Speak the right words, and you bind those listening together. Acknowledge the events that mark our lives. Make the experience powerful!

Be kind. It's a wedding toast, not a roast!

iStock.com/pixdeluxe

SPEECHES OF CELEBRATION

> **19.2**   *Demonstrate the characteristics of celebratory speeches, including the introduction, the award presentation, the acceptance, and the toast.*

Celebratory speeches include speeches of introduction, award presentations and acceptances, and toasts. The general purpose of a celebratory speech is to recognize someone of note, someone who has made a difference, or someone who is experiencing a special milestone.

Speech of Introduction

When delivering a **speech of introduction**, the task is to create a desire among audience members to listen to the person being introduced: the featured speaker. By serving as a "warm-up" for the main speaker, you pave the way and psychologically prepare receivers for that speaker's presentation. During your brief introductory remarks, your goal is to

- Identify why the speaker is to speak
- Enhance the speaker's credibility with receivers
- Stress the importance and timeliness of the speech

Though your speech of introduction should be short, lasting no more than two to three minutes, your job is to tell receivers who will be addressing them, what the subject of that person's speech will be, and why they should pay careful attention to it. Your role, though limited in scope (after all, you are not presenting the featured speech yourself), is nonetheless very important. The way you introduce the speaker will affect the reception given them.

Be sure your remarks are in keeping with the tone the main speaker will set. Focus a spotlight on the speaker, but avoid creating expectations they will be unable to fulfill. The more renowned the featured speaker is, the briefer the introduction that will be needed. For example, the president of a country is usually introduced with, "Ladies and gentlemen, the president of. . . ." And though brief remarks suffice to introduce well-known people such as Mark Zuckerberg, the founder of Meta (formerly Facebook), longer introductions could be required to build excitement when presenting individuals of lesser stature.

Sample Speech of Introduction

The following speech of introduction was given at the beginning of a scholarship award program and used by a student to introduce Russel Taylor, the founder of the Taylor Study Abroad Scholarship at the College of New Rochelle.

SN 1

The introduction is short while providing needed background.

Over the course of his teaching career at the college, a career that spans more than 35 years, Dr. Russel Taylor has had a significant impact on the study abroad program. In addition to serving as an unofficial advisor to aspiring entrepreneurs, Dr. Taylor also spearheaded the study abroad program—generously donating and raising funds to ensure that each year students like yourselves are able to secure the financial resources needed to spend a semester or a summer studying in another country. Because of Dr. Taylor's efforts, a number of you here tonight will also be able to live that dream.

Formerly a CEO and then a professor of business, Dr. Taylor is now a devoted mentor who makes it his mission to raise awareness about our need to be "global citizens," individuals armed with the cultural experiences and knowledge we will need to connect with others, not only in business, but in life.

SN 2

The introduction ends on a warm note.

I am very pleased to present to you the originator of the Taylor Study Abroad Scholarship, Dr. Russel Taylor, my mentor and friend.

Speech of Presentation

The **speech of presentation** is another common form of ceremonial speaking. The occasion for this kind of speech is the presentation of an award such as the Nobel Prize or a teaching award at your school. Like the speech of introduction, the speech of presentation is usually brief, but it often contains somewhat more formal praise for its subject.

Your Responsibilities as a Presenter

When delivering a speech of presentation, you are not just recognizing an individual, you are also honoring an ideal. You have three goals to achieve:

1. To summarize the purpose of the award or gift, including its history, its sponsor, the ideals it represents, and the criteria used to select the recipient.

2. To discuss the accomplishments of the person being honored, including what the individual specifically did to achieve the award.

3. To introduce and present the award winner to the audience. When possible, leave identifying the recipient to the very end; it adds drama to the announcement.

As with the speech of introduction, the speaker is not the star of the occasion; the audience did not come to celebrate the speaker but to celebrate the winner.

Avoid overpraising the recipient. Instead, express sincere appreciation for their accomplishments and highlight the behavior, values, and ideals that led to their receiving the award. After listening to your speech, there should be no question among audience members that the individual being honored deserves the award.

Sample Speech of Presentation

Peter Hero, president of the Community Foundation of Silicon Valley, presented Bill Gates, then the chair of Microsoft, with the foundation's 50th anniversary Spirit of Philanthropy Award. Notice how by focusing on the special contributions Gates made, Hero explains the reasons for bestowing him the honor. While most recognize Bill Gates for his global business acumen, it's his passion for philanthropy that has touched lives throughout the world. The Bill & Melinda Gates Foundation has awarded more than $4 billion—that's billion with a *b*—since it was created in 2000.

SN 1

The speaker discusses the generosity of the honoree.

The Gates Foundation efforts in education, its libraries initiatives, and its efforts to eradicate disease in our world's poorest nations are innovative and bold. . . .

Last year alone Microsoft contributed more than $79 million in cash and $367 million in software to nearly 5,000 schools and nonprofit organizations. . . .

I first met Bill Gates in 1999 when he stopped in San Francisco and met with a group of us responding to a call from one of our board members, . . . Steve Kirsch. . . . Steve had sent out an email urging high-tech CEOs to join him in each giving $1 million to help resolve the unexpected $11 million shortfall at our United Way in Silicon Valley. Bill Gates and the Gates

Foundation responded with a $5 million gift, more than any of our local donors. This visit gave me a preview of the generosity of both Microsoft and the Gates Foundation, and for this we want to recognize and honor Bill Gates today.

SN 2

The speaker summarizes the purpose of the award and presents the award winner to the audience.

So Bill, on behalf of the board of directors, the advisory council, the entire Community Foundation of Silicon Valley, I'm honored to present you with our 50th anniversary Spirit of Philanthropy Award.

Speech of Acceptance

The speech of acceptance is given in response to a speech of presentation. It is usually brief and gives the person being recognized the opportunity to formally accept the award or praise being given to them.

Your Responsibilities Giving an Acceptance Speech

In an acceptance speech, the recipient thanks, recognizes, and gives credit to both those who bestowed the honor and those who helped them attain it; reflects on the values represented by the award; explains, in particular, what the award means to them; and graciously accepts it. Speeches of acceptance, though usually brief, are often inspirational in tone, and when well done leave no doubt in the minds of audience members that the award was given to the right person.

Sample Acceptance Speech

In the following acceptance speech excerpts, notice how the late Elie Wiesel, Holocaust survivor and human rights activist, upon receiving the Nobel Peace Prize, helped receivers understand the meaning of the award and the ideals it honors. By pledging to continue his efforts and by using language in keeping with the dignity of the occasion, Wiesel also communicated the deeper meaning inherent in the award.

Elie Wiesel Accepts Award

SN 1

The speaker accepts the award.

It is with a profound sense of humility that I accept the honor you have chosen to bestow upon me. I know: your choice transcends me. This both frightens and pleases me.

SN 2

The speaker credits those who helped him attain the award and through an extended narrative reflects on the values the award represents.

It frightens me because I wonder: Do I have the right to represent the multitudes who have perished? Do I have the right to accept this great honor on their behalf? I do not. That would be presumptuous. No one may speak for the dead, no one may interpret their mutilated dreams and visions.

It pleases me because I may say that this honor belongs to all the survivors and their children, and through us, to the Jewish people with whose destiny I have always identified.

SN 3

The speaker explains the personal meaning the award has for him.

I remember: It happened yesterday or eternities ago. A young Jewish boy discovered the kingdom of the night. I remember his bewilderment. I remember his anguish. It all happened so fast. The ghetto. The deportation. The sealed cattle car. The fiery altar upon which the history of our people and the future of mankind were meant to be sacrificed.

I remember: He asked his father, "Can this be true? This is the 20th century, not the Middle Ages. Who would allow such crimes to be committed? How could the world remain silent?"

And now the boy is turning to me: "Tell me," he asks, "what have you done with my future? What have you done with your life?"

And I tell him that I have tried. That I have tried to keep memory alive, that I have tried to fight those who would forget. Because if we forget, we are guilty, we are accomplices. . . .

And that is why I swore never to be silent whenever and wherever human beings endure suffering and humiliation. We must always take sides. . . . There is so much injustice and suffering crying out for our attention: victims of hunger, or racism and political persecution, writers and poets, prisoners in so many lands governed by the left and by the right. Human rights are being violated on every continent. More people are oppressed than are free. . . . One person—a Raoul Wallenberg, an Albert Schweitzer, one person of integrity, can make a difference, a difference of life and death. . . .

This is what I say to the young Jewish boy wondering what I have done with his years. It is in his name that I speak to you and that I express to you my deepest gratitude. No one is as capable of gratitude as one who has emerged from the kingdom of the night.

SN 4

The speaker accepts the award graciously and with humility.

We know that every moment is a moment of grace, every hour an offering; not to share them would mean to betray them. Our lives no longer belong to us alone; they belong to all those who need us desperately.

Thank you Chairman Aarvik. Thank you members of the Nobel Committee. Thank you, people of Norway, for declaring on this singular occasion that our survival has a meaning for mankind.[1]

The Toast

A toast is given to celebrate an event such as New Year's Eve, a friend or relative's wedding, anniversary, baby's birth or a birthday, graduation, the success of a business venture, or retirement. It is composed of a few, brief sentences that are positive and gracious in nature, appreciative and congratulatory in content, and range from solemn to humorous (but should not be embarrassing) in tone. A toast is not a roast. Rather, it is a very abbreviated tribute, often associated with raising a glass and taking a drink.

Your Responsibilities When Delivering a Toast

When you offer or specifically are requested to deliver a toast, it is likely because you know the subject very well and will be able to share your insights with those present. Thus, while the nature of your celebratory remarks should be brief, they also need to come across as sincere and personal and be focused on one or two characteristics of the person and occasion being celebrated that you reveal through a story. Let your knowledge of those in attendance also guide you in deciding what to say to mark the event. If given the opportunity to prepare, don't choose to wing it. Think about what you want to say. Then, write it down and rehearse it in front of a mirror. Be sure to stand when delivering your toast. Tailor your remarks to reflect the attitudes, beliefs, and values of the honoree as you offer your praise and compliments. A toast is often accompanied by the clinking of glasses and sip of wine, champagne, or other beverage, so after speaking, raise your glass and ask the guests to raise theirs. Finish with heartfelt congratulations.

Sample Toast

The following toast was offered at our daughter's post–law school graduation and admission to the New York State Bar party by her brother:

> Tonight, I'd like to offer a toast to a new lawyer whom I love, admire, and respect. Just remember, I supported you before you were admitted to the New York State Bar. I supported you when we went to the bar. But seriously, Lindsay, I know how hard you worked for this. And tonight, we celebrate your achievement. Let's raise a glass of champagne: To Lindsay—my attorney and soon to be your attorney too. Congratulations!

COACHING TIP

"May you have warm words on a cold evening, a full moon on a dark night, and a road downhill all the way to your door."

—Irish blessing

Should you not know the person or event being celebrated all that well, it becomes acceptable to use a more generic kind of toast, such as the Irish blessing featured here.

SPEECHES OF INSPIRATION

> **19.3**   *Illustrate the functions of inspirational speeches as revealed in commencement and keynote speeches.*

Inspirational speech is emotionally uplifting speech. Speeches of inspiration are designed to inspire the audience, congratulating them and raising their spirits, their expectations for their future, and their beliefs in what they can accomplish.

The Commencement Speech

The **commencement address** speaker praises and congratulates a graduating class. All sorts of people deliver commencement addresses, including politicians, distinguished alumni, actors, educators, notable citizens, and students.

Your Responsibilities as a Commencement Speaker

Because the commencement audience is predominantly composed of the families and friends of the graduates, commencement speakers usually acknowledge how both the graduates and the members of the audience contributed to the success being recognized that day.

Most commencement addresses do not stop with celebrating the recent achievements of graduates, however; they also challenge the graduates to focus on the future and the roles they will play in the months and years ahead. Commencement addresses that avoid clichés while emphasizing the accomplishments and promise of the graduates are the most effective.

Sample Commencement Speech

Jimmy Fallon delivered the following speech during his 2018 commencement address to the graduates of Marjory Stoneman Douglas High School in Parkland, Florida, to honor the inspiring work of students at the school following the mass shooting that occurred there on February 14 of the same year. During his remarks, Fallon lauded the activism of the students and the impact they were having on bringing attention to the issue of gun and school safety.[2]

   SN 1

   The speaker recognizes and honors all those in attendance.

Thank you very much. Thank you, Principal Thompson, the faculty and staff, parents and friends, and most of all, thank you to Marjory Stoneman Douglas High School Class of 2018. It's an honor to be here today.

   SN 2

   The speaker uses humor to build a relationship with the students.

When you think of commencement speakers, you think of people who are inspirational, people who are eloquent, people who change the world. When you think of high school students, you think of people who are a little immature, slightly awkward, still learning to be an adult. Welcome to opposite day.

Today you're graduating from high school. You should feel incredibly proud of yourselves. That doesn't mean you should rest on your laurels—or your yannys. Some of you will grow up to hear Yanny. Some of you will grow up to hear Laurel. But the most important thing to know is that neither of these things will matter by the end of the summer.

Here's what will matter: You, the Class of 2018, will have graduated, and you won't be classmates anymore. You'll be adults who Facebook search each other at two in the morning for the next ten years. But more important than that, you'll be out in the real world. So before you go I want to share a few thoughts with you—not advice necessarily—just a few things I've learned that helped me along the way.

The first thing is this: When something feels hard, remember that it gets better. Choose to move forward. Don't let anything stop you. I met many of you earlier this year at the March For Our Lives in Washington, D.C., and it was an amazing day. Thank you for your courage and your bravery and for giving amazing speeches that I could never possibly live up to.

My wife and I brought our two little girls because we wanted them to see what hope and light looks like, and as we were standing there watching you guys in awe, I was lucky enough to stand with a lot of your teachers. And let me tell you something, your teachers are so proud of you. Really. They were like, *I taught him! I taught her! I taught them history!* And now, you're making history. It's pretty cool. And that's just a few of you I was able to meet. I can only imagine what the rest of this class is accomplishing and will be able to accomplish. And your teachers—everyone—they're all so proud of you.

My teachers weren't really proud of me like that. I wasn't really the best student. I wouldn't say I was dumb, I just had "other strengths." I didn't always feel like studying so I had to go to summer school. And my mom and dad were like, *look at you, Mr. Smart Guy. Now you have to go to summer school. How's that make you feel? Huh? You've ruined your whole summer now.* It made me feel awful, and I went to my bed and I cried.

But here's the thing—I got up one morning and went to summer school, and I met 15 versions of myself. Everyone was funny and slightly dumb—I loved it. I loved summer school. It was fantastic. I met my people!

SN 3

The speaker identifies the challenges that the graduates have overcome.

My point is every bad experience can have something good that comes out. Sometimes things that seem like setbacks can take our lives in a totally new direction that can change us in ways we don't expect. They make us better and stronger. You guys have already proved that to everyone. You took something horrific and instead of letting it stop you, you started a movement, not just here in Florida, not just in America, but throughout the whole world. The whole world has heard your voice and that was you making a choice. That was you choosing to take something awful and using it to create change. That was you choosing hope over fear.

Another thing I want to say is keep making good choices. I'm not saying that I think you need to learn it, I'm saying it because you've already taught it to all of us. I can't promise you that life will be easy, but if you make good choices and keep moving forward, I can promise you that it will get better in ways we haven't even thought yet.

SN 4

The speaker asks graduates to focus on the future.

We have no idea what the future holds and that's okay. Don't get too hung up on that. My advice to you is don't think about what you want to do, think about why you want to do it, and the rest will figure itself out. I love what I do. I get to tell jokes and make people laugh and it's awesome. People often ask me, *what's the best part of your job?* I say, *I get to make people happy.* I'll give you an example. About six or seven months ago, I ran into this girl on the street, and she came up to me and said, *I just want to let you know that I was going through a tough time, I was very depressed, and you got me through my depression. I watched all your clips on YouTube and I just want to thank you so much for getting me through such a tough time.* We talked for about twenty minutes and then she goes, *Can I get a selfie?* I go, *Yeah, of course.* We take a selfie and she goes, *Can we get one more for Snapchat?* And I go, *Yeah, of course,* so we take another one. Then I say goodbye to her, and as she's leaving, she said out loud, *Oh my god, I just met Jimmy Kimmel!* The point is, I love my job and I know I'd clearly make her laugh if she knew who I was.

SN 5

The speaker reviews the graduates' experiences and their preparation for meeting challenges head-on.

A question people ask me a lot is, *what would you tell your younger self?* And there's so many things that I'd say. But the first would be lay off the carbs. The second I would say is listen. Listen to everyone around you. Hear other voices. There are so many different voices in the world, and we're all different voices, different flavors, different colors, but we're all in the same rainbow. And we need red just as much as we need yellow, and purple, and orange, and blue, and green, and burgundy. There's good in everyone, so find what's good in people. If we listen to each other, we can find it.

Another thing I'd tell my younger self is work hard for everything. Put one foot in front of the other and keep going—day by day, moment by moment. You always have the chance to be building something, working on something, pushing something up the hill, practicing every day, rain or shine, in the mood or not. It's not easy, but you have to keep trying and keep failing and having goals and pushing them ahead every day.

I'd also say take good care of yourself. Check in with yourself every day. Put your phone down and be silent for a moment or two. And be kind, and think ahead, and have courage. Try new things. Remember the past but don't stay there. Honor your fellow humans. Keep laughing. Celebrate anything you can as often as you can because it's fun. Write letters and send them with a stamp in the mailbox. Try that. Say hello to people. Smile more often. Be kind to people who wait on your table, bag your groceries, move your furniture. And when you dance, dance from the inside.

SN 6

The speaker ends by reminding the graduates that the future is in their capable hands.

If I could give you one last piece of advice, it would be this: Don't ever get off your parents' wireless plan. Ride that train as long as possible. You don't know how expensive data is.

On our show we write out thank you notes every Friday—for the most part, they're funnier, or at least they try to be. But today, I want to say a real thank you. I want to thank you guys personally for showing us what it looks like to have integrity and courage and bravery in the face of terrible tragedy. Thank you for showing me and the whole world that there is hope.

Source: Commencement address of Jimmy Fallon delivered at Marjory Stoneman Douglas High School in 2018, June 4, 2018, http://time.com/5300396/jimmy-fallon-speech-stoneman-douglas-graduation/.

The Keynote Speech

The purpose of the **keynote address** is to get a meeting or conference off to a good start by establishing the right tone or mood. The keynote underscores the meeting's purpose and themes. The speaker offers specific examples to which the audience can relate in the effort to motivate them to work harder.

Your Responsibilities as a Keynote Speaker

The functions of the keynoter vary. Some keynote speeches challenge receivers to act or achieve a goal, while others outline a problem or series of problems for them to solve. Some keynote speeches are designed to generate enthusiasm and commitment for the agenda of an industry, corporate enterprise, or political group, while others are designed to demonstrate the importance of a theme or outcome.

The best keynote speakers are adept at focusing audience attention on common goals, communicating the central focus of those gathered, and setting a tone that arouses interest and encourages commitment.

Sample Keynote Speech

The functions of the keynote speech are illustrated in excerpts from this keynote address delivered by Tim Cook, the CEO of Apple, at a conference of European privacy commissioners in Brussels in 2018.[3]

SN 1

The speaker establishes the purpose of the occasion and speech.

It is an honor to be here with you today in this grand hall . . . a room that represents what is possible when people of different backgrounds, histories, and philosophies come together to build something bigger than themselves. . . .

Now Italy has produced more than its share of great leaders and public servants. Machiavelli taught us how leaders can get away with evil deeds. . . . And Dante showed us what happens when they get caught. . . .

We need you to keep making progress—now more than ever. Because these are transformative times. Around the world, from Copenhagen to Chennai to Cupertino, new technologies are driving breakthroughs in humanity's greatest common projects. From preventing and fighting disease . . . To curbing the effects of climate change . . . To ensuring every person has access to information and economic opportunity.

At the same time, we see vividly—painfully—how technology can harm rather than help. Platforms and algorithms that promised to improve our lives can actually magnify our worst human tendencies. Rogue actors and even governments have taken advantage of user trust to deepen divisions, incite violence, and even undermine our shared sense of what is true and what is false. This crisis is real. It is not imagined, or exaggerated, or "crazy." And those of us who believe in technology's potential for good must not shrink from this moment.

SN 2

The speaker focuses audience attention on the problems they need to face.

Now, more than ever—as leaders of governments, as decision-makers in business, and as citizens—we must ask ourselves a fundamental question: What kind of world do we want to live in?

I'm here today because we hope to work with you as partners in answering this question.

At Apple, we are optimistic about technology's awesome potential for good. But we know that it won't happen on its own. Every day, we work to infuse the devices we make with the humanity that makes us. As I've said before, "Technology is capable of doing great things. But it doesn't want to do great things. It doesn't want anything. That part takes all of us. . . .".

We at Apple believe that privacy is a fundamental human right. But we also recognize that not everyone sees things as we do. In a way, the desire to put profits over privacy is nothing new. As far back as 1890, future Supreme Court Justice Louis Brandeis published an article in the *Harvard Law Review*, making the case for a "Right to Privacy" in the United States.

He warned: "Gossip is no longer the resource of the idle and of the vicious, but has become a trade." Today that trade has exploded into a data industrial complex. Our own information, from the everyday to the deeply personal, is being weaponized against us with military efficiency. Every day, billions of dollars change hands, and countless decisions are made, on the basis of our likes and dislikes, our friends and families, Our relationships and conversations . . . Our wishes and fears . . . Our hopes and dreams.

These scraps of data . . . each one harmless enough on its own . . . are carefully assembled, synthesized, traded, and sold. Taken to its extreme, this process creates an enduring digital profile and lets companies know you better than you may know yourself. Your profile is then run through algorithms that can serve up increasingly extreme content, pounding our harmless preferences into hardened convictions. If green is your favorite color, you may find yourself reading a lot of articles—or watching a lot of videos—about the insidious threat from people who like orange. In the news, almost every day, we bear witness to the harmful, even deadly, effects of these narrowed world views. We shouldn't sugarcoat the consequences. This is surveillance. And these stockpiles of personal data serve only to enrich the companies that collect them. This should make us very uncomfortable. It should unsettle us. And it illustrates the importance of our shared work and the challenges still ahead of us. . . .

SN 3

The speaker's inspirational tone reminds audience members of the importance of taking action.

We at Apple are in full support of a comprehensive federal privacy law in the United States. There, and everywhere, it should be rooted in four essential rights: First, the right to have personal data minimized. Companies should challenge themselves to de-identify customer data—or not to collect it in the first place. Second, the right to knowledge. Users should always know what data is being collected and what it is being collected for. This is the only way to empower users to decide what collection is legitimate and what isn't. Anything less is a sham. Third, the right to access. Companies should recognize that data belongs to users, and we should all make it easy for users to get a copy of . . . correct . . . and delete their personal data. And fourth, the right to security. Security is foundational to trust and all other privacy rights. . . .

Technology's potential is, and always must be, rooted in the faith people have in it . . . In the optimism and creativity that it stirs in the hearts of individuals . . . In its promise and capacity to make the world a better place. It's time to face facts. We will never achieve technology's true potential without the full faith and confidence of the people who use it. At Apple, respect for privacy—and a healthy suspicion of authority—have always been in our bloodstream. Our first computers were built by misfits, tinkerers, and rebels—not in a laboratory or a board room, but in a suburban garage. We introduced the Macintosh with a famous TV ad channeling George Orwell's 1984—a warning of what can happen when technology becomes a tool of power and loses touch with humanity. And way back in 2010, Steve Jobs said in no uncertain terms: "Privacy means people know what they're signing up for, in plain language, and repeatedly." It's worth remembering the foresight and courage it took to make that statement. When we designed this device, we knew it could put more personal data in your pocket than most of us keep in our homes. And there was enormous pressure on Steve and Apple to bend our values and to freely share this information. But we refused to compromise. In fact, we've only deepened our commitment in the decade since . . . we always try to return to that simple question: What kind of world do we want to live in? . . .

In the mid-19th Century, the great American writer Henry David Thoreau found himself so fed up with the pace and change of Industrial society that he moved to a cabin in the woods by Walden Pond. Call it the first digital cleanse. Yet even there, where he hoped to find a bit of peace, he could hear a distant clatter and whistle of a steam engine passing by. "We do not ride on the railroad," he said. "It rides upon us."

SN 4

The speaker appeals to the audience, attempting to generate enthusiasm in them to join the effort in making technology safe.

Those of us who are fortunate enough to work in technology have an enormous responsibility. It is not to please every grumpy Thoreau out there. That's an unreasonable standard, and we'll never meet it. We are responsible, however, for recognizing that the devices we make and the platforms we build have real . . . lasting . . . even permanent effects on the individuals and communities who use them. We must never stop asking ourselves . . . What kind of world do we want to live in? The answer to that question must not be an afterthought, it should be our primary concern. We at Apple can—and do—provide the very best to our users while treating their most personal data like the precious cargo that it is. And if we can do it, then everyone can do it. Fortunately, we have your example before us.

Thank you for your work . . . For your commitment to the possibility of human-centered technology . . . And for your firm belief that our best days are still ahead of us.

Thank you very much.[4]

SPEECHES TO ENTERTAIN

> **19.4**   *Define the goals of a speech to entertain, focusing on the roast and after-dinner speech.*

What do you imagine is the general purpose of the speech to entertain? Yup! To entertain! The speaker's role is to amuse the audience by sharing a lighthearted, easy on the brain, but relevant presentation. Usually delivered before, during, or after a meal, at meetings, or at special events, this type of speech is meant to be upbeat, and may contain funny information that is meant to be enjoyed. Yet the **speech to entertain** also should be inoffensive and in good taste, clear, and tailored to meet the occasion. Roasts and after-dinner speeches are both forms of speech designed to amuse.

The Roast

In a **roast**, humor is the key ingredient, with a series of speakers delivering remarks that poke good-natured fun at an honoree. The honoree might be a coach, professor, entertainer, or public figure. Akin to a stand-up comedy routine, some roast participants err on the side of insulting and embarrassing the honoree, so it's important to strike the right tone when part of a roast. Since you will be one of a number of speakers, be brief. End on a high note, by expressing your admiration and respect for the individual being roasted. When it comes to speeches that entertain, an after-dinner speech is more frequently delivered than a roast.

The After-Dinner Speech

Generally designed to be entertaining, the **after-dinner speech** is a common form of public address. Neither overly technical nor filled with ponderous details or complex information, the after-dinner speech is usually upbeat and takes a good-natured, sometimes humorous, whimsical, or mildly satirical look at a topic of interest and relevance to the audience.

Your Responsibilities Delivering an After-Dinner Speech

If you are asked to give an after-dinner speech, you'll probably want to choose a lighthearted topic that allows you to inject humor into your presentation. Humor, when used appropriately, helps relieve tension and relax receivers. It also helps receivers remember your presentation.[5] However, humor should be functional, not forced, and help you make a point.

The after-dinner speech depends on your ability to make a point while maintaining a sense of decorum and good taste. Remember, after-dinner speeches are usually delivered when audience members are in a mood for entertainment; therefore, they must be easy to digest—like dessert.

Sample After-Dinner Speech

The following are excerpts from an after-dinner speech, titled "Artificial Intelligence," that was delivered by Massachusetts Institute of Technology professor Marvin Minsky at a personal computer forum.

SN 1

The speaker sets a light tone.

I've heard people explaining from time to time that there really wasn't any such thing, that artificial intelligence was just programs. And they were right, of course, because everything is just programs. That's called "nothing buttery." A program is nothing but a sequence of instructions, and a living thing is nothing but a bunch of atoms with various chemical bonds, and a machine is nothing but parts, and so forth. And that's a very important idea. People who don't believe that eventually get into very serious trouble, because then they end up believing that something comes from nowhere. . . .

SN 2

The speaker's good nature and appropriately humorous examples help receivers process the content.

Have you ever had lunch with a writer and asked them how they write? They're always fidgety and embarrassed. Isaac Asimov is the master of this. He says that you sit in front of the typewriter and move your fingers. He's willing to face the whole mystery of that in its completeness and not pretend to know what to do. . . .

You see, you can be skeptical of artificial intelligence because it doesn't write Beethoven quartets. But the real reason to be skeptical of artificial intelligence is that it doesn't know how to eat with a fork or chopsticks, or dress itself, or walk across the room. . . . Nobody has the foggiest idea, really, of how that stuff is programmed. . . .

The number of pieces of brain that actually do anything like move your finger is very small. You'd be surprised at the number of people who think that the gift of playing the piano is in your hands. That's a joke. The hands are just I/O devices, and there's no difference between the nerves and muscles of a pianist and anyone else, except that pianists are stronger, you can believe. Never get into a fight with a pianist. They have terribly powerful arms.[6]

Source: Marvin Minsky, http://zhurnaly.com/cgi-bin/wiki/MarvinMinskySpeaks.

SPEECHES TO COMMEMORATE

> **19.5**   *Identify the key characteristics of commemorative speeches exemplified in the tribute speech and eulogy.*

We introduced this chapter by referring to the 20th anniversary of 9/11. We will close this chapter by asking you to think about why the country schedules ceremonies to commemorate this day. September 11 has become a day for remembering and reflecting on how the events of 9/11 forever changed the United States and the world. One this day, each speaker delivers a **commemorative speech**, commemorating the lives lost, praising the first responders, and celebrating and honoring the values that the terrorists attacked.

The Speech of Tribute

The **speech of tribute** is a form of commemorative speaking. Whether delivered to honor a living or dead person, a group, or an event, its purpose is to acknowledge and praise the honoree(s). A tribute speech may be concluded with a toast.

Your Responsibilities Giving a Speech of Tribute

The tribute speaker's job is to inform the audience of the accomplishments of a person or the importance of an event, but it is also to heighten the audience's awareness of and appreciation for the contributions or values of the honoree.

To achieve this, the tribute speaker needs to involve the audience members by making those contributions relevant to their lives. They also need to clearly explain why the individual or event is being celebrated or recognized, telling stories that show why the honor is merited, and memorializing the occasion.

Success in delivering a tribute speech depends on using the right words to convey the thoughts and emotions inherent in the occasion. Sincerity and knowledge are key. The tribute speaker's focus is on creating vivid, specific images of accomplishments that demonstrate the influence and importance of the honoree.

Three main features characterize the speech of tribute:

1. A section describing what makes the subject of the speech worthy of special recognition

2. A section explaining in more depth what was accomplished

3. A section urging the audience to be inspired by the accomplishments, so that they will seek new and greater goals

Sample Speech of Tribute

On September 11, 2021, standing in the same field in Shanksville, Pennsylvania, where passengers had fought back against the terrorist hijackers, President Bush paid tribute to both the day and the group of heroes on the plane.[7]

SN 1

The speaker thanks those in attendance, acknowledging the event's purpose.

Thank you very much. Laura and I are honored to be with you. Madam Vice President, Vice President Cheney. Governor Wolf, Secretary Haaland, and distinguished guests:

Twenty years ago, we all found—in different ways, in different places, but all at the same moment—that our lives would be changed forever. The world was loud with carnage and sirens, and then quiet with missing voices that would never be heard again. These lives remain precious to our country, and infinitely precious to many of you. Today we remember your loss, we share your sorrow, and we honor the men and women you have loved so long and so well.

SN 2

The speaker pays attention to the needs of the audience, providing background and honoring the memories of those who made the ultimate sacrifice.

For those too young to recall that clear September day, it is hard to describe the mix of feelings we experienced. There was horror at the scale—there was horror at the scale of destruction, and awe at the bravery and kindness that rose to meet it. There was shock at the audacity—audacity of evil—and gratitude for the heroism and decency that opposed it. In the sacrifice of the first responders, in the mutual aid of strangers, in the solidarity of grief and grace, the actions of an enemy revealed the spirit of a people. And we were proud of our wounded nation. In these memories, the passengers and crew of Flight 93 must always have an honored place. Here the intended targets became the instruments of rescue. And many who are now alive owe a vast, unconscious debt to the defiance displayed in the skies above this field.

SN 3

The speaker is specific in recalling the feelings and recounting the core lessons of 9/11.

It would be a mistake to idealize the experience of those terrible events. All that many people could initially see was the brute randomness of death. All that many could feel was unearned suffering. All that many could hear was God's terrible silence. There are many who still struggle with a lonely pain that cuts deep within. In those fateful hours, we learned other lessons as well. We saw that Americans were vulnerable, but not fragile—that they possess a core of strength that survives the worst that life can bring. We learned that bravery is more common than we imagined, emerging with sudden splendor in the face of death. We vividly felt how every hour with our loved ones was a temporary and holy gift. And we found that even the longest days end.

SN 4

The speaker stresses the struggles and adjustments of survivors.

Many of us have tried to make spiritual sense of these events. There is no simple explanation for the mix of providence and human will that sets the direction of our lives. But comfort can come from a different sort of knowledge. After wandering long and lost in the dark, many have found they were actually walking, step by step, toward grace.

As a nation, our adjustments have been profound. Many Americans struggled to understand why an enemy would hate us with such zeal. The security measures incorporated into our lives are both sources of comfort and reminders of our vulnerability. And we have seen growing evidence that the dangers to our country can come not only across borders, but from violence that gathers within. There is little cultural overlap between violent extremists abroad and violent extremists at home. But in their disdain for pluralism, in their disregard for human life, in their determination to defile national symbols, they are children of the same foul spirit. And it is our continuing duty to confront them.

SN 5

The speaker praises those who served in the footsteps of those who perished.

After 9/11, millions of brave Americans stepped forward and volunteered to serve in the Armed Forces. The military measures taken over the last 20 years to pursue dangers at their source have led to debate. But one thing is certain: We owe an assurance to all who have fought our nation's most recent battles. Let me speak directly to veterans and people in uniform: The cause you pursued at the call of duty is the noblest America has to offer. You have shielded your fellow citizens from danger. You have defended the beliefs of your country and advanced the rights of the downtrodden. You have been the face of hope and mercy in dark places. You have been a force for good in the world. Nothing that has followed—nothing—can tarnish your honor or diminish your accomplishments. To you, and to the honored dead, our country is forever grateful.

SN 6

The speaker demonstrates the differences between the weeks and months following the attack and today, showing the audience what they can learn from the past, including how the nation had welcomed immigrants.

In the weeks and months following the 9/11 attacks, I was proud to lead an amazing, resilient, united people. When it comes to the unity of America, those days seem distant from our own. A malign force seems at work in our common life that turns every disagreement into an argument, and every argument into a clash of cultures. So much of our politics has become a naked appeal to anger, fear, and resentment. That leaves us worried about our nation and our future together.

I come without explanations or solutions. I can only tell you what I have seen.

On America's day of trial and grief, I saw millions of people instinctively grab for a neighbor's hand and rally to the cause of one another. That is the America I know.

At a time when religious bigotry might have flowed freely, I saw Americans reject prejudice and embrace people of Muslim faith. That is the nation I know.

At a time when nativism could have stirred hatred and violence against people perceived as outsiders, I saw Americans reaffirm their welcome to immigrants and refugees. That is the nation I know.

At a time when some viewed the rising generation as individualistic and decadent, I saw young people embrace an ethic of service and rise to selfless action. That is the nation I know.

This is not mere nostalgia; it is the truest version of ourselves. It is what we have been—and what we can be again.

SN 7

The speaker reminds the audience of the legacy left by the displays of courage in the face of adversity, reminding them that their strength of character lives on in Americans today.

Twenty years ago, terrorists chose a random group of Americans, on a routine flight, to be collateral damage in a spectacular act of terror. The 33 passengers and 7 crew of Flight 93 could have been any group of citizens selected by fate. In a sense, they stood in for us all.

The terrorists soon discovered that a random group of Americans is an exceptional group of people. Facing an impossible circumstance, they comforted their loved ones by phone, braced each other for action, and defeated the designs of evil.

These Americans were brave, strong, and united in ways that shocked the terrorists—but should not surprise any of us. This is the nation we know. And whenever we need hope and inspiration, we can look to the skies and remember. God bless.

https://abcnews.go.com/US/full-transcript-president-george-bush-speaks-911-memorial/story?id=79959676

Although a tribute speech may commemorate an event, group, or figure that is well known, persons and events being singled out for special recognition do not need to be famous. In fact, each of us probably can think of one or more individuals who are neither famous nor public figures or events but who still deserve special praise.

The Eulogy

A special form of tribute speech is the **eulogy**. When delivering a eulogy, the speaker pays tribute to a person who has died. A eulogy is usually presented graveside or at a memorial service. Though some are very brief, lasting only a minute or two, others are longer, lasting 10 or 20 minutes.

Your Responsibilities Delivering a Eulogy

When delivering a eulogy, your goal is to comfort the members of your audience without letting your own grief overwhelm you. This sometimes becomes difficult because of the emotional nature of the speech and occasion. The following qualities characterize the eulogy:

1. The speaker begins by acknowledging the special loss suffered by the family of the deceased and/or society.

2. The speaker celebrates the life of the deceased by acknowledging the legacy of the individual.

3. The speaker emphasizes the uniqueness or essence of the subject with honest emotion, anecdotes, personal recollections, and quotations from others. They bring the group together to share and ease their sense of loss by concentrating instead on how fortunate they were to have known the deceased and what they have learned from that person's life.

Sample Eulogy

Former president Barack Obama penned this eulogy for the late world champion boxer and humanitarian, Muhammad Ali.

Muhammad Ali was The Greatest. Period. If you just asked him, he'd tell you. He'd tell you he was the double greatest; that he'd "handcuffed lightning, thrown thunder into jail."

SN 1

President Obama begins by acknowledging the loss of the subject and the legacy he left.
But what made The Champ the greatest—what truly separated him from everyone else—is that everyone else would tell you pretty much the same thing.

Like everyone else on the planet, Michelle and I mourn his passing. But we're also grateful to God for how fortunate we are to have known him, if just for a while; for how fortunate we all are that The Greatest chose to grace our time.

In my private study, just off the Oval Office, I keep a pair of his gloves on display, just under that iconic photograph of him—the young champ, just 22 years old, roaring like a lion over a fallen Sonny Liston. I was too young when it was taken to understand who he was—still Cassius Clay, already an Olympic Gold Medal winner, yet to set out on a spiritual journey that would lead him to his Muslim faith, exile him at the peak of his power, and set the stage for his return to greatness with a name as familiar to the downtrodden in the slums of Southeast Asia and the villages of Africa as it was to cheering crowds in Madison Square Garden.

"I am America," he once declared. "I am the part you won't recognize. But get used to me— black, confident, cocky; my name, not yours; my religion, not yours; my goals, my own. Get used to me."

SN 2

The president celebrates the subject's life and talents, identifying the qualities that made him special.

That's the Ali I came to know as I came of age—not just as skilled a poet on the mic as he was a fighter in the ring, but a man who fought for what was right. A man who fought for us. He stood with King and Mandela; stood up when it was hard; spoke out when others wouldn't. His fight outside the ring would cost him his title and his public standing. It would earn him enemies on the left and the right, make him reviled, and nearly send him to jail. But Ali stood his ground. And his victory helped us get used to the America we recognize today.

SN 3

The president describes for us the subject's legacy.

He wasn't perfect, of course. For all his magic in the ring, he could be careless with his words, and full of contradictions as his faith evolved. But his wonderful, infectious, even innocent spirit ultimately won him more fans than foes—maybe because in him, we hoped to see something of ourselves. Later, as his physical powers ebbed, he became an even more powerful force for peace and reconciliation around the world. We saw a man who said he was so mean he'd make medicine sick reveal a soft spot, visiting children with illness and disability around the world, telling them they, too, could become the greatest. We watched a hero light a torch, and fight his greatest fight of all on the world stage once again; a battle against the disease that ravaged his body, but couldn't take the spark from his eyes.

SN 4

The president directly addresses those in mourning, reiterating what is to be learned from the subject's life.

Muhammad Ali shook up the world. And the world is better for it. We are all better for it. Michelle and I send our deepest condolences to his family, and we pray that the greatest fighter of them all finally rests in peace.[8]

Source: Barack Obama, "Statement from President Barack Obama and First Lady Michelle Obama on the Passing of Muhammad Ali," The White House, June 4, 2016, https://www.whitehouse.gov/the-press-office/2016/06/04/statement-president-barack-obama-and-first-lady-michelle-obama-passing.

GAME PLAN

Giving a Special Occasion Speech

- I understand the occasion for my speech, my speech's purpose, and the audience attending my speech.
- I have considered and fulfilled the responsibilities and goals of the speech.
- I have crafted a creative and unique approach to the topic.
- Based on what I've learned in previous chapters of the playbook, I have prepared for and practiced my speech.

EXERCISES

Speaking on Special Occasions

By developing the skills necessary to fulfill the responsibilities of a special occasion speaker, you prepare yourself to speak effectively throughout your life span. Participating in the following activities will help hone your understandings and abilities.

1. Family Introductions

Introduce a family member by specifying two of their defining characteristics and explain why the relationship you share is meaningful.

2. And the Award Goes to . . .

Select a historical figure, artist, author, athlete, or coach. Your selected person is to receive an award (silly or serious) that you create specifically for them.

1. Name the award and its purpose.

2. Outline the accomplishments of the person as they relate to the award.

3. Paying Tribute

Imagine being given the opportunity to compose a tribute speech for someone you believe instrumental in helping you grow as a person. What words would you use to celebrate that person to let others understand the role they have played in your life? Try your hand at writing such a speech.

4. Approach the Speaker's Stand: Let's Toast

You are giving a toast to celebrate a special occasion such as a birthday, a housewarming, or a wedding anniversary. What steps will you take to ensure the tone of your toast reflects the person(s) or event being celebrated? Specifically, think about the following:

1. What factors do you need to consider as you prepare the toast?

2. What will you do to build rapport with your audience?

3. What will you speak about?

4. What effect do you hope your toast has?

RECAP AND REVIEW

19.1 Describe the nature and purpose of special occasion speeches, distinguishing among speeches of celebration, speeches of inspiration, speeches to entertain, and speeches to commemorate.

Special occasion speeches help punctuate the high-water marks of our lives. They are part of the rituals that draw us together. Speeches of celebration are designed to reflect the nature and needs of the occasions that prompted their delivery.

19.2 Demonstrate the characteristics of celebratory speeches, including the introduction, the presentation, the acceptance, and the toast.

A speech of introduction functions as a "warm-up" for a featured speaker, whereas presenting an award to a recipient usually includes more formal accolades. An acceptance speech is given in response to a speech of presentation, affording the honoree the opportunity to describe how much receiving such an award means. A toast is an abbreviated celebratory speech.

19.3 Illustrate the functions of inspirational speeches as revealed in the commencement address and a keynote address.

Like a coach, the commencement speech praises and congratulates a graduating class for their accomplishments. The keynote speech gets a meeting off to a good start, establishing an appropriate mood and helping attendees focus on the challenges ahead of them.

19.4 Define the goals of a speech to entertain, focusing on the roast and after-dinner speech.

A roast is a humorous acknowledgment of or tribute to a person by a series of speakers. The after-dinner speech is a speech that usually is lighthearted and takes a humorous or satirical look at a topic of interest.

19.5 Identify the key characteristics of commemorative speeches exemplified in the tribute speech and eulogy.

A speech of tribute is given to acknowledge and praise a living or dead honoree. A eulogy, a special form of tribute, pays homage to a person who has died.

KEY TERMS

After-dinner speech (p. 449)

Celebratory speech (p. 436)

Ceremonial speaking (p. 435)

Commemorative speech (p. 450)

Commencement address (p. 442)

Eulogy (p. 454)

Inspirational speech (p. 442)

Keynote address (p. 445)

Roast (p. 448)

Speech of acceptance (p. 439)

Speech of introduction (p. 436)

Speech of presentation (p. 437)

Speech to entertain (p. 448)

Speech of tribute (p. 450)

20 BUSINESS AND PROFESSIONAL SPEAKING

UPON COMPLETING THIS CHAPTER, YOU WILL BE ABLE TO
20.1 Prepare proactively for employment interviews and performance reviews.
20.2 Interact effectively in a meeting.
20.3 Present a pitch.
20.4 Deliver a briefing and a report.
20.5 Conduct a training session.

What does speaking have to do with your workplace and career success? Everything! In fact, when it comes to the kinds of skills that job recruiters look for, communication skills top the list.[1] Speaking ability influences whether you get the job you want, hold onto the position, and advance in your field. Much of your work life also hinges upon how effectively you construct your professional image and build relationships. Career success depends on knowing how to present yourself and your ideas to others—whether when interviewing for a position, participating in a meeting, pitching an idea, presenting a briefing or report, or holding a training session. It's also necessary to know how to adjust your presentation and message when speaking to those in authority, your peers, and those who report to you.

FIRST, GET THE JOB. THEN, KEEP IT: HOW TO HANDLE JOB INTERVIEWS AND PERFORMANCE REVIEWS

20.1 *Prepare proactively for employment interviews and performance reviews.*

An interview with the hiring manager often is a key part of landing a job. Think of the answers you give to questions during the interview as a series of impromptu speeches. Do the work to prepare and set yourself up for success.

Research the Job and the Position: Submitting a Cover Letter and Résumé

It's your responsibility to know as much as possible about the firm you are interviewing with, the job you are interviewing for, and the skills required to succeed in the organization and position. If you know someone within the organization, speak with them. Search the Internet for the specifics of the job you seek, including typical employee responsibilities, assignments, advancement opportunities, and average salaries. Read what has been written about the company. Acquaint yourself with its successes and failures, products, and opportunities.

Compile a list of potential questions the interviewer might ask you and rehearse your answers. Possible questions include the following:

- Why are you interested in working with us?

- How would you describe your greatest strength and weakness?

- How has your background prepared you for this job?

- Provide an example of when you convinced your supervisor to implement your idea. What was the outcome?

- Describe a time when you had to balance multiple assignments. How did you do?

Of course, in addition to preparing for potential questions, you need to prepare yourself for the fact that you likely will be asked some questions that you have not anticipated. It is also likely that the interviewer will ask you if you have any questions for them. Thus, your role is not only to be able to respond seemingly spontaneously to questions you are asked, but also to come prepared to ask questions. Before arriving, compile a list of questions you want to ask the interviewer. The following are among the questions you might ask:

- What qualities are you seeking in the candidate you hire?

- How do you gauge an employee's value?

- What do you like best about the organization's culture?

- What are three things that I can contribute in the first 100 days to make you feel great about hiring me?[2]

Finally, be sure to review your application, including two key documents, your cover letter and your résumé, updating each as needed. Your task is to ensure that both are well written, register a positive impression, and provide the interviewer with a preview of who you are and why you are qualified for the open position.

Prepare the Cover Letter

The cover letter introduces you to the interviewer. One career coach advises that it even be as short as 120 words because your average reader reads approximately six words per second and will give your letter about 20 seconds, providing it looks good to begin with.[3] The well-written cover letter reveals your purpose and whether you are replying to a posting, following up on a referral, or writing an unsolicited introduction. Whatever type of cover letter you write, it should fulfill the following six criteria: (1) it expresses your interest in a position, (2) it tells how you learned of the position, (3) it reviews your primary skills and accomplishments, (4) it explains why these qualify you for the job, (5) it highlights any items of special interest about you that are relevant to your ability to perform on the job, and (6) it contains a request for an interview. Although a résumé is always included with a cover letter, your cover letter needs to make a compelling statement about the value you will bring to the firm. The cover letter should not merely reiterate information contained in your résumé. Rather, it should expand on that information and connect it to the role you hope to perform, demonstrating why you're a great fit for the position.[4]

Prepare Your Résumé

A variety of online resources and computer programs exist to help you prepare your résumé electronically. Many provide you with templates that you can complete or customize. You can also post your résumé online at a number of job listing sites. Electronic résumés require standard formats. Line breaks and block letters may be used, but no boldface type, underlining, or bullets. The text is all that matters. Once the résumé is added to the company's tracking system, when a job becomes available, the employer can efficiently search the résumés contained in the database by the keywords that describe a candidate qualified for the position. In cases such as these, you may also be asked to submit a résumé in the PDF file format, which can be formatted more attractively.

To facilitate the initial résumé screening, which probably will be done by a bias-free computer or bot rather than a human, it's vitally important that the receiving system can read your résumé. Some systems, for example, read a PDF as a single image, so Microsoft Word may be a safer option. You definitely want to optimize your résumé for digital eyes. To get through the bot: (1) be sure to use Word docs; (2) stick to common words; (3) use the same keywords in your résumé that appeared in the ad for the job; and (4) be sure the format is simple and appealing.[5] Take the time to enumerate your skills clearly up top in your résumé. Be specific. Generalized language won't appeal to the "machine parsers"; keywords will.

Remember, the résumé summarizes your abilities and accomplishments. It details what you have to contribute that will meet the company's needs and help solve the employer's problems. It is a reflection of you and should showcase your passion for a position.[6] Be sure your résumé emphasizes your skills. Although formats differ, the résumé typically includes the following, in order:

1. Contact information—your name, address, telephone number, and email address

2. Job objective—a phrase or a sentence or two that focuses on your area of expertise

3. Employment history—your job experience, both paid and unpaid, beginning with the most recent

4. Education—schools attended, degree(s) completed or expected, dates of completion, college major (if you have not yet completed the degree) and a review of courses that relate directly to your ability to perform the job

5. Relevant professional certifications and affiliations

6. Community service and involvement in extracurricular activities

7. Special skills and interests you possess that are relevant to the job

8. References—people who agree to elaborate on your work history, abilities, and character; state only that references are available on request unless you are asked to provide specific references at the time you submit your résumé.

Because the average résumé gets about five seconds of the reader's time, crafting an effective one is essential.[7] Although sending a video résumé may intrigue you, check out if the company you're interested in accepts them. In the COVID-19 era, a video résumé may help you get hired. Video résumés are becoming attention-getting media—a way for job candidates to share their passions and personalities. A video résumé can represent you as a person, as a worker, and as a content creator.[8]

Job seekers can also create their own home pages, featuring both their résumé and business card.[9] By posting your résumé on a home page, you increase the likelihood that an employer looking for someone with your background and qualifications will access your résumé and contact you directly. It also is possible to create a multipage, online portfolio that contains samples of your work, a page of references, and testimonials. Be sure to check with the company or its Human Resources site to identify which format they will accept. When posting your résumé online, you may want to be more private. You might, for example, not include your home address but feature an email address. Some people use a Google Voice phone number that keeps their actual phone number private.

Handle Common Concerns

How do you feel about interviewing for a job? What concerns you most? For example: How worried are you about being asked questions you won't be able to answer? Dressing inappropriately? Coming off as unprofessional? Appearing nervous? Being cross-examined? Talking too much or too little? Not being able to establish rapport with the interviewer? Under- or overselling yourself? Not asking the interviewer the right questions? Not getting the job?

SELF-ASSESSMENT 20.1: THOUGHTS ABOUT THE JOB INTERVIEW

Directions:

Circle the numbers that most accurately reflect your level of interview apprehension: 1 = completely unconcerned; 2 = unconcerned; 3 = neutral; 4 = concerned; 5 = a nervous wreck.

Statement	1 Completely Unconcerned	2 Unconcerned	3 Neutral	4 Concerned	5 A nervous wreck
1. I will be asked questions I cannot answer.					

Statement	1 Completely Unconcerned	2 Unconcerned	3 Neutral	4 Concerned	5 A nervous wreck
2. I will be inappropriately dressed for the interview.					
3. I will appear to be nervous.					
4. I will appear to be incompetent.					
5. The interviewer will cross-examine me.					
6. I will talk too much or too little.					
7. I will have poor rapport with the interviewer.					
8. I will undersell or oversell myself.					
9. I won't know what questions to ask.					
10. I won't be hired.					

Scoring Method	Total Score Interpretation
Total the numbers you circled to arrive at your "interviewee anxiety" score. Total _____	Your scores indicate how frightened you are of assuming the role of interviewee. If you accumulated 45 to 50 points, you are extremely nervous; if you scored 35 to 44 points, you are very frightened; if you scored 20 to 34 points, you are somewhat apprehensive; if you scored 11 to 20 points, you are too casual; if you scored 10 points or less, you are not at all concerned—that is, you simply do not care.

Thinking that the interviewer will be looking at you as if you were mounted on a slide and placed under a glass microscope may cause you to feel vulnerable and exposed.[10] Contrary to what you might assume, however, not being concerned at all about participating in an interview is just as much of a problem as being a nervous wreck, and being too casual can do as much damage as being too frightened. An interviewee should be apprehensive to a degree. If you are not concerned about what will happen during the interview, then you will not care about making a good impression and, as a result, you will not perform as effectively as you otherwise would.

Preparation for an interview is key. That includes using social networking appropriately. If not misused or relied on exclusively, social networks can enhance your job search. Social networks such as Facebook, Twitter, and LinkedIn are effective ways to build your contact network by making it easy for you to reach out to former associates and classmates, as well as to industry professionals and alumni. A 2020 Jobvite survey revealed that most companies use social networking sites to fill job openings, with the following the most used: LinkedIn, Facebook, Twitter, Instagram, Glassdoor, and YouTube.[11] You can also use LinkedIn to check out your interviewer's profile. Be sure you keep all your information on LinkedIn up to date and that you've requested references to post recommendations on your behalf. You can be sure your interviewer will use it to check you out, as well.[12] Additionally, social networking sites such as TikTok contain abundant videos offering job seekers interview advice from HR professionals and others on how to put their best foot forward in an interview.[13] While social networks are key, keep in mind that what you reveal on your social networking sites also can eliminate you from consideration. According to Careerbuilder.com, companies regularly remove applicants from consideration because of their social networking mistakes such as posting provocative or inappropriate photographs and information, or revealing a lack of interpersonal or communication skills.[14] Here is a rule to follow: if you wouldn't want your grandparent to see it, keep it offline!

Plan the Conversation

The conversation during an **interview** distinguishes itself from casual conversation in that it is planned and designed to achieve specific objectives. In an interview, you and your interviewer have opportunities to share information. Based on what is said, each of you is then left to decide whether continued association will be positive and productive.

Just as with a speech, to succeed in an interview you need to prepare, gain control of any nerves, establish rapport, communicate your confidence and competence, inform about yourself, and answer questions asked forthrightly. It is assumed that how you behave during an interview reveals how you behave in general. Potential employers rely on a number of interview formats, whether they conduct the interview in-person or online. They may interview you using the traditional one-on-one format, have a panel of interviewers question you, or place you in a simulation, giving you the opportunity to demonstrate your skills.

Well-planned interviews are structured, divided into stages. The interview's opening is an orientation to the interview process. It is also the stage during which rapport is built, figuratively breaking the ice between interviewer and interviewee. The middle or interview body is the longest interview segment. During this stage, participants get down to business. They discuss the interviewee's educational and work experiences, seeking to establish the applicant's strengths, weaknesses, accomplishments, and goals. The interview's close finds the parties reviewing the main points covered, offering final statements, and taking leave of one another.

Let's get down to business. Like any speech, planning ahead is the key to interview success.
iStock.com/1178451455

COACHING TIP

"Before a job interview, I think, what color tie best represents me as a person this company would be interested in?"

—Jarod Kintz, author

Professional image is critical. Work on yours! Knowing how to present yourself and your ideas is a ticket to success. Relationship-building begins with the first impression others form of you. Make yours a good one!

Get to the Heart of the Questions

Remember, questions are key in gathering the information needed to make a decision. Most interviews contain different kinds of questions (see Figure 20.1). **Closed questions** can be answered with a few words. The following are closed questions: Where do you live? What was your major area of interest? What are your compensation expectations?

Open questions are broader, offering more freedom in answering them: Would you tell me about yourself?[15] How has your background prepared you for this position? What would you like to know about our firm? Can you please describe your greatest success and failure? Open questions like these foster the expression of feelings, attitudes, and values.

FIGURE 20.1 ■ The Communication Process in Action
Tell me a little about yourself.
Why did you apply for this position?
What makes you qualified for this position? Why should we hire you?
What are your strengths? What are your weaknesses?
What would your former employer (professor, friend) say about you?
What are three words that describe you?
What are your short-term goals? What are your long-term goals?
Do you have any questions for us?

Source: Kelly M. Quintanilla and Shawn T. Wahl, *Business and Professional Communication: KEYS for Workplace Excellence*, 3rd ed. (Thousand Oaks, CA: SAGE, 2016).

Open and closed questions can be either primary or secondary. **Primary questions** introduce a topic or area for exploration. **Secondary questions**, also known as probing questions, follow up on primary questions. Thus, the following is a primary question: What is your favorite assignment? And these are secondary questions used to follow up: What specifically did you like about that assignment? What does that mean? Can you give me an example?

Once the interviewer begins asking questions, use the following acronym to guide you in answering: **S.T.A.R.** (situation, task, action, result).[16] For example, let's say that the interviewer asks you what others would say when asked what it's like to work with you. Using the S.T.A.R. system, you would answer the question by revealing a *situation* you faced when working with another person ("My coworker fell behind in completing an assigned project"), how you assessed the *task* needing to be completed ("I realized that if he didn't complete the project on time, the promotion he had recently been promised could be in jeopardy"), the *action* you took ("I'm a team player, so I stepped up and did some of the research myself, which enabled him to complete his analysis"), and the *results* you achieved ("When he was promoted to regional director, he asked me to be his assistant; he knew he could count on me"). "So I think if asked what it's like to work with me, others would say I always have their back. I do whatever I can to help."

What if the Interviewer Asks an Illegal Question?

We have seen that interview questions may be tough and probing. As long as they are legal, that's to be expected. However, questions that concern age, race, marital status, and other personal characteristics protected under antidiscrimination statutes are illegal for the interviewer to ask. Despite this, surveys reveal that half of all Americans report being asked questions that could be used to discriminate against a protected class.[17] The Equal Employment Opportunity Commission (EEOC) is the arm of the federal government responsible for monitoring discriminatory practices in hiring decisions. The guidelines are updated periodically, and the laws of the EEOC apply in all 50 states and the District of Columbia.

According to the EEOC, criteria that are legally irrelevant to job qualifications are discriminatory. Interviewees are protected from answering questions about race, color, national origin, marital status, age, sex (including gender identity, sexual orientation, and pregnancy), genetic information (including family medical history), and disability. Some states have additional protected categories. It is important for both interviewers and interviewees to realize which questions are legally impermissible in employment interviews. Both parties to the interview have to be well versed in their rights to be able to protect them. The determining factor in whether a question is lawful is simple: Is the information sought relevant to your ability to perform the job? The following are among the most commonly asked illegal questions:

- Are you physically disabled?
- How old are you?
- Are you married?
- What gender do you identify with?
- What is your sexual orientation?
- Have you ever had transition treatments or surgery?
- Do you have or are you planning to have a family?
- What political party do you belong to?
- Is English your native language?
- What is your religion?
- Will you need to live near a mosque?
- Is it hard for you to find child care?
- Are you a United States citizen?
- Where were your parents born?
- Who lives with you?
- When did you graduate from college?
- What was the date of your last physical exam?
- To what clubs or social organizations do you belong?
- Have you had any recent or past illnesses or operations?
- How is your family's health?
- If you have been in the military, were you honorably discharged?
- What's your current or most recent salary?

Taking past salary into account when setting starting pay at a new job often disadvantages women and those whose pay disparity otherwise would follow them from one job to another.[18] When it comes to questions regarding salary expectations, it is best to respond that you'll be happy to discuss salary once there's an offer, or that your answer will depend on what your precise role will be. Suggest that, for now, you'd like to focus on what you bring to the company, while acknowledging that you'd like to hear what they think when you do get to that stage.[19]

On the other hand, it is legal to ask the following questions:

- Are you authorized to work in the United States?

- What languages do you read or speak fluently (if relevant to the job)?

- Are you over 18?

- Would you relocate?

- Would you be willing to travel as needed?

- Would you be able and willing to work overtime as necessary?

- Do you belong to any groups that are relevant to your ability to perform this job?

- What education do you have?

- Have you ever been convicted of a crime?

- In what branch of the armed forces did you serve?[20]

If you are asked an illegal question you can object diplomatically and remind the interviewer that the question is inappropriate. Doing so, however, can make the interviewer defensive and less willing to select you for the job. Another option is to respond to the illegal question with only information that the interviewer legally could have sought from you. That is, you handle the question by answering the part you do not object to without providing any information you do not wish to offer. For example, if the interviewer asks whether English is your native language, you can respond, "I am fluent in English." If they ask whether you belong to a political group, you can respond, "The only groups with which I affiliate that are relevant to this job are the Public Relations Society of America and the American Society for Training and Development."

Be an Active Interview Participant

During the interview, you seek to present yourself well and answer questions clearly, providing the interviewer with sufficient information to determine whether you are the right person for the job. But you also need to ask questions that will help you decide whether to accept the job should an offer of employment be made.[21] Asking, not just answering, questions demonstrates your enthusiasm for the job. In addition to asking the questions you prepared in advance, make sure that you ask secondary questions to follow up on what the interviewer says, which shows interest and engagement.

Interestingly, successful job applicants speak for some 55 percent of the total time allotted for the interview and initiate 56 percent of the comments made, in comparison with unsuccessful applicants, who initiate only 37 percent of the comments made and speak for only 37 percent of the time.

Make a Positive Impression

Whether the interview is conducted online or in-person, there are steps you can take to help others view you as professional. Even prior to the COVID-19 pandemic, companies sought to save time and money by using video-chat software such as Skype, Zoom, Microsoft Teams, or GoToMeeting as their tool of choice when conducting preliminary screenings of job candidates in the effort to narrow the field. The pandemic made this option even more popular. While such long-distance interviews may not be as effective as meeting face to face, they tend to be better than phone calls.

Follow these six guidelines if the interview is online:

1. **Set the stage.** Clean up the area so the interviewer isn't looking at a messy room. Consider setting up in front of a curtain; hanging a clean, solid-color sheet behind you; or choosing another, appropriate background. If you can, feature some memorabilia that showcases your personality during the interview.

2. **Quiet please.** Be sure the space where you will be speaking is quiet—no barking dogs or loud music allowed. Make sure there's no bright light behind you, as this will darken your face. Be sure to adjust the microphone settings. Do your best to ensure your wi-fi connection is strong and reliable.

3. **The camera is your friend.** Make sure the camera angle and lighting are right and help you come off as professional. If possible, light yourself with sunshine coming from a window facing you or a lamp bouncing light off a wall that reflects softly. You can also use computer screen clip-on lights. The computer's camera should be eye-level or slightly above eye-level and facing down. If needed, use a stack of books to raise the computer up. Be sure nothing in the background will distract the interviewer.

4. **Think about and practice your posture.** Pull your shoulders back to communicate confidence. Your ability to express your adaptability and flexibility, the fact that you are a self-starter and adept at working independently, is even more important if you'll not only be interviewing remotely, but potentially working remotely. So be sure to talk about how you conducted yourself as a student during the pandemic. Remember, each party to the interview has questions—both you and the employer. Each of your tasks is to find out the answers to those questions.

5. **Dress appropriately.** A CareerBuilder survey revealed that the color of your clothing conveys distinct impressions influencing the reactions of hiring managers and human resource professionals.[22] The following colors are recommended: blue because it suggests you're a team-player, black because it sends a message of leadership potential,

gray because it suggests you're logical and analytical, red because it reveals a flair for power, and brown because it suggests you're organized. A color to avoid is orange because it conveys a message of unprofessionalness.[23] Even though you are not meeting the interviewer in-person, you are meeting visually, so dress as if you were in the same room as the person interviewing you. In addition to considering color choices, refrain from wearing bold patterns, as they can be distracting, or white, which is noticed on a screen first.

6. **Be videogenic.** Repeatedly remind yourself that the interviewer is able to see your facial expressions and read your body language. Remember to sit tall but not lean too close to the webcam, as this offers the interviewer a close-up of your nose. Decide on a flattering angle. Try swiveling your chair toward the corner of your screen. Look at the interviewer's image when they talk, but when you answer, look at the camera so you make virtual eye contact with them. To look good on video, you need to look at the video lens. To sound good, you need to use your voice to communicate your enthusiasm for the opportunity being given you.[24] Just like when speaking in public, you need to rehearse aloud and via video prior to "showing up" for the actual virtual interview.

Applicants can endure multiple rounds of interviews and assessments before ever encountering a human face to face. More and more frequently, candidates for a job are being asked to play a set of online games and submit videos of themselves responding to questions about how they would tackle challenges of the job. These games have been designed to assess skills such as ability to concentrate under pressure and short-term memory. Algorithms then are used to sort the candidates. If there ever will be a person-to-person interview, it usually is the last step in the interviewing process.[25] Getting a job today has much in common with reality-show contests. Hundreds of job candidates compete, but there will be just one winner. You want to be awarded the rose!

The point is that when you give a formal speech, you must consider not just what you will say but how you will present yourself. The same is true in a job interview conducted online or face to face. Assuming you want the job, one of your goals is to help an interviewer perceive you in a positive light.[26] Looking, sounding, and acting professionally throughout the interview facilitate this. If you can answer each of the following questions with a "yes," you are on track:

- Am I dressed appropriately for the interview?
- Am I familiar with the company, its competition, and industry trends?
- Am I conveying enthusiasm and energy?
- Am I communicating my happiness at being interviewed?
- Does my nonverbal behavior send the right messages, underscoring my confidence, competence, and trustworthiness?

In contrast, the following interviewee behaviors turn off interviewers:

- Arrogance
- Lack of enthusiasm
- Immaturity
- Poor communication
- Unclear goals
- Unwillingness to travel or relocate
- Deficient preparation
- Unprofessional appearance[27]

To communicate professionalism, never inquire about vacation, personal days, or benefits on your first interview. Always end the interview affirming your interest in the position. Always follow up sending a thank-you note to each person with whom you interviewed.[28]

The Performance Review/Coaching Session

After you ace the interview and land the job you seek, performance reviews are likely to occur. They are the means employers use to summarize feedback given to you, share assessments of your strengths and accomplishments, and identify areas in need of improvement. They also work with you to outline a plan for further skill development. You are a participant in the performance review. Listen and comment mindfully rather than emotionally. Communicate your appreciation for positive feedback, your confidence in what you can accomplish, and your intention to continue to grow. The purpose of the performance review is to inspire you to improve. Sadly, only 14 percent of employees say that it fulfills that function.[29] If not approached correctly, performance reviews actually can harm performance. To ensure that doesn't happen, ask for more frequent, maybe even weekly, reviews of your work. Such meetings may be more akin to coaching sessions that create a learning environment and are more motivating and engaging. This will enable you to have meaningful conversations with a supervisor about what you can do to be more successful and what your future with the organization looks like.

SPEAKING IN A MEETING

20.2   *Interact effectively in a meeting.*

Meetings are commonplace at work and in most professional arenas. Whether you will be the meeting leader or a participant, meeting in-person or online (see Chapter 18 for meeting online guidelines), adequate preparation is essential. So, too, are understanding the meeting's purpose, reviewing its agenda, engaging actively in the exchanging of information, and ensuring the meeting does not veer off topic.

Again, how you come across counts. As with other kinds of communication at work, how you present during a meeting, including what you say and how you act, affects others' impressions of you and builds, maintains, or detracts from your professional image. Ability to relate to others interpersonally in big and small groups, large and small meetings, is essential for your professional growth.

Participating in the Meeting

Every participant shares responsibility for a meeting with the meeting's leader. When participating in a meeting, be sure to follow these guidelines:

- Review the reasons for meeting ahead of time and suggest items for the agenda if requested.

- Give yourself time to prepare by reading the agenda as much in advance of the meeting as possible and considering the concerns and questions you have regarding each agenda item.

- Participate enthusiastically but be certain to avoid interrupting when others speak and refrain from denigrating others' input.

- Praise others' comments when appropriate.

- Keep your contributions relevant by building on and responding to others' ideas.

- Solicit feedback, ask questions, and keep track of accomplishments and responsibilities.

When a meeting is effective, just as when people work in groups (see Chapter 18), members seamlessly perform task and maintenance roles but avoid performing self-serving roles—those roles focused exclusively on an individual's needs but not helpful to or in the best interests of others in the meeting. In contrast to selfish, self-centered roles, task roles facilitate the meeting and the realization of its goal. Maintenance roles facilitate interaction between members.

Meetings tend to be most effective when their working atmosphere is informal, comfortable, and relaxed; there is time for ample discussion with all members participating, listening to one another, and expressing ideas and feelings freely; disagreement is not suppressed; decisions are reached by consensus; no one is personally attacked; and neither the leader nor any single member dominates.

Leading the Meeting

Although at this stage in your work life you most likely will be a meeting participant, preparing yourself to lead a meeting can be a career builder. When leading a meeting, taking the following steps will help ensure it is a positive and productive experience:

- Formulate and share the meeting's purpose in advance with those who will be attending. When called to a meeting with no clear goal, employees worry that their time will be wasted.

- Develop an agenda and circulate it in advance.

- Arrive early to ask and answer questions, chat and/or talk off topic with others (saves doing it during the meeting), and build rapport to help others feel comfortable.

- Turn off your cell phone; have others do the same.

- Introduce any guests or new attendees.

- Provide a meeting orientation—referring to the agenda and your goals.

- Maintain control of the meeting. Seek to engage all present. Take steps to ensure that no one member monopolizes discussion. Focus on covering agenda items.

- Summarize results, reviewing what was covered, reminding members of their responsibilities, and affirming accomplishments or goals met.

- Answer any questions.

- Thank members for their attendance and input, and if needed, schedule the next meeting date.

Team leader. When leading a meeting, make sure it has defined goals and objectives so as not to waste time.

iStock.com/Ridofranz

An effective leader facilitates a meeting's start and contributes to its ultimate success. The leader sets the meeting's tone, which when constructive encourages everyone to participate, precipitating high-quality interaction and a positive and productive outcome.

PITCHING AN IDEA

> **20.3**   *Present a pitch.*

Some years back, Workman Publishing, an independent publishing house, held a "Pitchapalooza" session during which a few dozen aspiring authors were given one minute each to describe their book idea before a panel of publishing professionals.[30] This kind of brief, highly prepared persuasive presentation of a new idea or product is known as a **pitch**. Many workplaces provide similar opportunities for you to sell your ideas to higher-ups on a regular basis.

When pitching, your goal is to convince the people holding the power that what you propose is worthy of their money, time, or energy. Promotional pitches are usually made in-person or increasingly via video or video conferencing. Formulating an effective pitch is difficult work.

A pitch is a persuasive presentation in a business setting. Some pitches are very brief—we call them "**elevator pitches**"—and basically depend on you distilling your idea into a few words that can be conveyed to an audience within five to 10 seconds. If given the luxury of 30 seconds, you can also speak to the benefits of your proposal. If given five minutes to pitch, you have time to present your idea, the problem it solves, its benefits, supporting evidence, the challenges you face, and the resources you require to make it happen. Elevator pitches also are used to introduce yourself to someone of importance in the organization. In the brief time available (the length of a ride up or down an elevator), you let the person know who you are, what you do including your qualifications, and what you're seeking or hope to achieve.

Whether your pitch is five seconds, 30 seconds, or five minutes, you need to do your homework if your words are going to excite those listening. You will need to decide how to involve your audience, connect your pitch with the organization's mission, and get receivers to imagine the possibilities. A five-minute formal pitch presentation is enough time to use technology—PowerPoint or Prezi and presentation aids—that transforms your proposal into an "aha" moment.

Down the middle. Make your pitches clear and easy to understand for your audience so they don't get overwhelmed, bored, or forget them.

iStock.com/Pixel_Pig

The following are typical pitch components:

- Identify a need or opportunity.

- State your proposal simply and clearly; tell what you do.

- Explain your rationale (the needs and benefits fulfilled) and strategy.

- Communicate your USP (unique selling proposition)—reveal what makes your idea unique.

- Engage with your audience; make it easy for them to respond affirmatively.

- Review the timeline, costs, and challenges.

- Integrate presentation aids to make your vision come alive.

- End by reiterating the benefits of your proposal, linking it again with the goals of decision makers, and appealing in your close for them to give you the go-ahead.

Sometimes it is better to pitch with a partner or a team. When presenting with others, prepare a detailed outline specifying each person's role and responsibilities. Be sure to hold one another accountable as you work to coordinate the presentation's parts. You are aiming for a coherent whole, not several individual little speeches.

As when preparing a speech, research thoroughly, know your audience, and rehearse, rehearse, rehearse! Anticipate possible questions and practice responses. Remember, you need to make it easy for those making the decision to say yes.

DELIVERING A BRIEFING OR REPORT

> **20.4**   *Deliver a briefing and a report.*

Briefings and reports are informative presentations commonly delivered in organizations. A **briefing** is a brief talk that provides information needed to complete a task or make a decision. Briefings may focus on the past to bring others up to date, letting them know what was accomplished in their absence or since their last briefing. Briefings can also be future oriented, focusing on client interests and needs. Whatever their purpose, briefings have the following in common:

- They are short, typically one to three minutes in length.

- They are simply organized, usually topically or chronologically.

- They concisely summarize what has been done and/or what needs to be done.

- They may utilize simple presentation aids.

- They are delivered conversationally.

A **report** provides a summary of what you have learned or accomplished. Status reports, feasibility studies, and investigative reports are presented regularly in organizations. Each of these reports informs decision makers or team members on goals that have been reached and remaining obstacles. Such information may be communicated to your boss, a project team, other committees or boards, clients, and the general public. An organization's culture influences the nature of the reports, including whether they are formal or informal, include presentation aids or not, and allow for question-and-answer (Q&A) follow-ups. The following guidelines will serve you in preparing and delivering a report:

- Begin by providing an overview or summary of the project's purpose.

- Describe the current status of the project, providing a brief summation of progress made relative to each of the project's goals.

- Be open and forthright, explaining hurdles overcome, reasons for any delays, detailing what is yet to be accomplished, and requesting assistance, if needed.

- Conclude by sharing a realistic assessment of the project's future.

- Ask for and answer questions, being careful not to become defensive.

- Thank those listening for their attention.

Like pitches, reports can be presented with a team, requiring that members divide up responsibilities, agree on a timeline, and coordinate the preparation, rehearsal, and delivery of information. Members of a successful team formulate the report's purpose, craft its outline, and collaborate to answer the following questions:

- How do we introduce the information so those in attendance will listen attentively?

- What are the report's main points?

- How should we present its central message?

- At what point are transitions most appropriate?

- How do we conclude so that all aspects are summarized and the presentation ends on a high note?

- What presentation aids should we use?

- How should we prepare for the Q&A that follows?

- How do we approach and learn from the rehearsal period?

After the presentation, the group holds a debriefing session to assess its effectiveness. Keep in mind that when reporting, you are building on skills and knowledge gained in preparing other kinds of speeches.

RUNNING A TRAINING SESSION

> **20.5**   *Conduct a training session.*

Building on informative speech strategies, trainers teach their audience members how to do something. Although the content of a training session is similar to a "how-to" speech, both the purpose and method of delivery are substantially different.

Trainers give live and online workshops on virtually any subject: how to develop sales or interpersonal skills, how to avoid a lawsuit, how to handle cultural diversity, or how to run a meeting. Sometimes training is conducted informally and involves relatively direct advice—such as appropriate business-casual dress or what to wear on casual Fridays. Other times, training is highly sophisticated and coordinated. For example, the Disney organization has an entire training institute devoted to running courses related to custom business solutions and professional development.

Although what follows is a prescription for adult learning, it applies to college students and others, as well:

- Demonstrate the relevance of the training to those in attendance. Help them understand and be able to explain how they will use the material.

- Plan activities to ensure attendees are actively involved in the session. Avoid the lecture format. The session you lead should involve active learning so that those in it are given ample opportunities to apply and practice skills, experiencing for themselves the session's content.

Hands-on. Training should differ from any other speech because it should have interactive elements allowing staff members to practice their skills.

iStock.com/Chaay_Tee

- Understand what attendees do and do not know. Aim the session "where they are," not above or below their knowledge level.

- Pace the session appropriately. Spaced learning tends to work—learn, apply, learn, apply.

GAME PLAN

Preparing for an Interview

- I know when the interview is scheduled, so I can give myself adequate time to prepare. I will arrive or log on to the interview on time.

- I will dress appropriately, choosing clothes that do not distract from the professional impression I hope to make.

- I've practiced my greeting before a mirror or with another person.

- I've thoroughly researched the company as well as the position I seek.

- I've prepared a professional-looking résumé and considered what aspects about my experience the interviewer will likely question me.

- I've practiced answering both common and challenging questions. I'm prepared to ask the interviewer questions.

EXERCISES

Speaking on the Job

Mastering the ability to prepare and deliver different kinds of work-related presentations is a professional image enhancer. Participating in these activities will help you increase the value you bring to your employer.

1. Research the Employer and Position You Want

First, review the careers page on the website of a company or an organization where you would like to work. Based on your research, answer these questions:

- What values does the company promote?

- What is the company looking for in an employee?

- What benefits does the company offer in return?

- Do you imagine you would be happy working for this company? Why?

Next, peruse the company's job postings and select one that particularly interests you. Identify a minimum of three personal traits you possess that you believe an interviewer at that company would value. Identify a minimum of three specific skills you have that will enable you to succeed in the sought position.

2. Practice Your Response

Review the following interview questions. Then pair up and practice answering them:

- Why do you want this job?

- How would you describe yourself?

- Would you tell me about a past experience that reveals you can handle pressure and are resilient?

- What was your greatest success in college?

- This job requires creativity. What have you done that demonstrates your creativity?

- What do you think would be your greatest challenge were we to hire you?

- If I were to Google you, what would I find out that we haven't discussed?

- What questions do you have for me?

3. Plan It

Develop a plan to interview for an on-campus position and brief your professor on progress, or develop a pitch to persuade the dean of students to grant club status and funding to a group you create.

4. Analyze the Pitch

Watch an episode of *Shark Tank*, a television show in which wealthy venture capitalists—the "sharks"—interview aspiring entrepreneurs who each deliver a pitch designed to persuade the sharks to invest in them and their business. Analyze the effectiveness of each entrepreneur's pitch and evaluate the extent to which the individuals seeking funding effectively answered the questions posed by the sharks.

5. Approach the Speaker's Stand

1. **The Pitch.** Develop and deliver a pitch to persuade a loan officer at a bank in your community to lend you money for one of the following: a proposed business venture, to travel abroad, or to go to graduate school.

2. **The S.T.A.R.** You are being interviewed. The interviewer asks, "What do you think others would say if I asked them if you were dependable?" Answer the question using the S (situation); T (task); A (action); R (result) strategy.

RECAP AND REVIEW

20.1 Prepare proactively for employment interviews and performance reviews.

You need to prepare yourself to interview. Research the company, anticipate questions, answer questions knowledgeably and honestly, and present yourself as professionally as possible. Once you have the job, participating mindfully in performance reviews and coaching sessions will increase the value you bring to the organization.

20.2 Interact effectively in a meeting.

Leaders and members work collaboratively to ensure the success of a meeting. Both need to prepare for the meeting, review its agenda, and participate enthusiastically.

20.3 Present a pitch.

Pitches are persuasive in nature and are planned to convince others that an investment in what is being asked for promotes the organization's mission and is worth the time, money, and energy that needs to be expended.

20.4 Deliver a briefing and a report.

Briefings, though very short, make sure everyone is on the same page, reviewing or previewing what has or needs to be done. A report summarizes the status of a project or other undertaking, letting others know what you have accomplished, what remains to be completed, and what it means for the organization.

20.5 Conduct a training session.

Training sessions are held on a wide range of topics related to the specific needs and goals of an organization and the specific audiences addressed.

KEY TERMS

Briefing (p. 476)
Closed question (p. 466)
Elevator pitch (p. 475)
Interview (p. 465)
Open question (p. 466)

Pitch (p. 475)
Primary question (p. 467)
Report (p. 477)
Secondary question (p. 467)
S.T.A.R. (p. 467)

21 STORYTELLING

UPON COMPLETING THIS CHAPTER, YOU WILL BE ABLE TO
21.1   Explain ingredients integral to a story, identifying narratives from your life and the lives of others to involve and motivate an audience.
21.2   Demonstrate ability in using a variety of language tools to tell stories.
21.3   Use storytelling techniques that increase audience engagement.

If we weren't already so, social media has made us all storytellers. One post at a time, on Facebook, Instagram, and Twitter, we reveal episodes of our personal story daily. We use our point of view to shape a visual narrative about ourselves. Stories are not just visual, however. They also are oral. *Storycorps* is an organization that collects the stories of ordinary people that the U.S. Library of Congress then archives. It is a treasure trove, an amazing collection of human voices representing the wisdom of humanity. Prompts such as "What was your proudest moment?" or "Can you tell me about someone who influenced your life?" help to guide the storyteller in relaying a life story that educates, clarifies, or inspires. The point is, everyone has a story. A speaker's job is to find the story and tell it. Storytelling is both an ancient art form and a valued communication skill. Storytelling is undergoing a renaissance, of sorts, in part because of the popularity of all kinds of podcasts, some of which compel audience members to debate oodles of questions. A good narrative commands audience attention and involvement.[1]

In this chapter, we explore how to tell stories that invite audiences into your world. Whether a story is told during a business presentation, a sales call, or a public speech, preparing yourself to pass on personal narrations helps communicate who you are and what you stand for. A well-told story reveals your thoughts and dreams, bridges barriers, takes hold of others, engenders positive feelings, brings receivers psychologically closer, and helps them adapt and engage with you. Stories are a fundamental part of learning and persuasion. Telling a story strengthens your speaking skills.[2] Amid information clutter, stories stand out.

COACHING TIP

"Those who tell the stories rule society."

—Plato, philosopher

Tell a story and change the world. Good stories embody powerful messages. Tell one at the right time and you build a connection that will last.

DISCOVER YOUR INNER STORYTELLER

21.1   *Explain ingredients integral to a story, identifying narratives from your life and the lives of others to involve and motivate an audience.*

Effective speechmakers tell a wide range of stories, some based on difficult experiences, others on formative ones. Your goal is to reframe your experiences, learn how to embody and perform them, and then create stories, articulating powerful messages that surmount boredom, inspiring and guiding others, fostering their participation. The more personal and authentic your stories, the easier it becomes for others to identify with and latch onto their themes and the more likely they are to identify with you, gain insight, and take the action you advocate. It's time to meet your inner storyteller.

SELF-ASSESSMENT 21.1: YOUR INNER STORYTELLER

Directions:

Circle the numbers that most accurately reflect your assessment of the extent to which you rely on each of the storytelling factors identified below: 1 = never; 2 = rarely; 3 = sometimes; 4 = usually; 5 = always.

Statement	1 Never	2 Rarely	3 Sometimes	4 Usually	5 Always
1. I speak to build connections with others.					
2. I tell a story to help make my point.					
3. Others respond positively when I tell a story.					
4. I find it easy to speak in metaphorical language.					
5. I reach others on an emotional level.					
6. My words are an apt reflection of me.					
7. Others remember my words.					
8. Others find my words motivating.					
9. I repeat what I think is important.					
10. When presenting ideas, I invite audience interaction.					

Scoring Method	Total Score Interpretation
Total the numbers you circled to arrive at your inner storytelling score. Total _____ The more points you award yourself on each item, the more proficient you believe your storytelling skill to be. What do your scores suggest about your readiness to use words to inspire and lead others to a new understanding?	Your scores indicate the extent to which you have internalized the qualities of a storyteller. If you accumulated 45 to 50 points, you have what it takes to be a great storyteller; if you scored 35 to 44 points, you're on your way to being a great storyteller; if you scored 20 to 34 points, you have potential but have more to learn; if you scored 11 to 20 points, think about why you're missing out on the benefits that being a storyteller can provide; if you scored 10 points or less, buckle down and reflect honestly on why learning to be a storyteller could improve life outcomes.

Find Your Voice

What is your authentic voice? It is the voice you use when you are being genuine and true to yourself. To discover our authentic voice, we first figure out who we are and what of our life story can be shared with others. Our potential to affect and influence others emerges from this act. In fact, as the author John Barth noted, "The story of your life is not your life. It is your story."[3] Football great Tom Brady knows this. A quarterback and team captain, Brady is a motivator. Brady's task is to make his teammates believe they can win. The team speeches and the many public appearance speeches that Brady delivers have gone viral on TikTok and other social media. How does Brady use stories? Brady tells his audiences stories about overcoming personal challenges, tying the message of the speech to something bigger than himself. In 2020, for example, Brady gave a virtual commencement speech to the graduating class of a Connecticut high school for students with learning disabilities.[4] Brady's theme in this speech was learning from adversity.

Brady began the speech by looking back at his own high school graduation 25 years earlier. Despite his passion to play football in college, he was not a highly desirable recruit. "I was the seventh quarterback on [Michigan's] depth chart. Number seven, if you can imagine that. I never thought I'd get an opportunity to play," Brady said. Brady didn't play in his first year. When he finally got the opportunity to take the field in the fourth quarter of a game in his second year, he threw an interception, which a defensive lineman ran 45 yards to score a touchdown. In his third year, Brady hit another obstacle. He "fought really hard" to become the starting quarterback, but failed. He played backup, instead. This is the point where Brady connected the story to the class. Instead of feeling sorry for himself, Brady learned from others around him. His coaches taught him how to be a great leader and to earn the trust of his teammates. Brady told the class, "Your future is going to be what you make of it because you're not going to be able to rely on people to do things for you." Anyone who wants to achieve something great, he added, will face obstacles and challenges, but, ultimately, they are responsible for what they achieve. By sharing his story, including his disappointments and setbacks, Brady inspired the audience, turning the lesson he learned into one with appeal for the wider audience.

To be an effective storyteller, you need to be adept at using words to tell stories that demonstrate goals. To make an impression that lasts, you'll want to share the history and motivations of your life because you convey your identity and beliefs as you do so.[5] Because one of the speaker's tasks is to instill, describe, and communicate a vision, your success depends upon your ability to tell stories that capture your essence, create meanings, and shape others' expectations—motivating their positive response. If you can use words and narration that resonate with receivers, helping them to imagine new perspectives, then you have a valuable tool in facilitating your personal connection with others.[6]

Give Voice to Your Goals

Whether our goal is to share knowledge, inspire, remind others of the past or prepare them for the future, build credibility, or enhance brand recognition, the stories we tell help determine our success.

Storytelling is perhaps the most significant act anyone hoping to influence others can perform. Being able to translate thoughts and ideas into words that others understand and respond to is an essential speaking skill. Through the stories you tell, receivers reflect on experiences designed to capture their hearts and minds, or as executive coaches Richard Maxell and Robert Dickman assert, "A story is a fact, wrapped in an emotion that compels us to take an action that transforms our world."[7] Stories engage and inspire audiences. They help you shape the reality you seek others to imagine.

For example, if your goal were to convince your audience to take action against bullying, you might consider sharing with them the tragic story of two girls, ages 12 and 14, who were charged with a felony—aggravated stalking—for relentlessly bullying another 12-year-old girl with tragic results. The target of their bullying, Rebecca Sedwick, ultimately committed suicide by jumping off a tower.[8]

Use a Narrative to Frame Your Goals

A *narrative* describes what people are doing, and why. It is an organized story of a sequence of events, characters or agents, a thesis or theme, and an outcome. Narratives enable you to personalize your speech's message, provide it with a frame, and reveal an outcome that offers a lesson we can learn from. Such stories reveal your perspective. We all present events in a way that suits our personal interests.

To influence others with a story, first reflect on the purpose(s) you want your story to serve and when to use it. Consider how to reach and tap into the experiences of those whom you seek to influence, how you can build connections that impart information, facilitate learning, and spark the insights you desire.

Five key elements give a story its legs:

1. A good story reflects your passion or a sense of purpose, rallying others to participate with you in creating a better future.

2. A good story supplies a source of conflict—something (or someone) that everyone is able to agree threatens the future.

3. A good story offers up a hero or protagonist who will conquer the villain or offer a solution to the problem.

4. A good story creates an awakening in the hero and audience—an "aha" moment—one that, once taken to heart, will make the world a better place.

5. And a good story reveals a need for change or an opportunity for transformation.

Let's try it. Pick one of the following story starters, and use it to tell a story from your experience that will teach others a lesson you learned. Tell us who the hero and villain are, describe them and the situation they face, explain the conflict, and reveal the solution or "aha" moment and its impact.

Grandma's house. Stories can help personalize your speech and make it more memorable for your audience.

iStock.com/Kombinerki

- Once upon a time . . .

- I'll never forget the first time . . .

- It was the scariest day of my life . . .

- It was the best day of my life . . .

- When I was growing up, my (grandma, grandpa, mom, dad, sister, brother, best friend) told me . . .

- What if . . . ?[9]

After telling your story and actively listening to the stories of others, reflect on how doing so enhances your awareness and understanding of the human experience. According to Peter Senge, when people understand one another, it is easier for a commonality of direction to emerge.[10] By sharing stories, we are able to see through each other's eyes.

COACHING TIP

"What unites people?" Tyrion asked. "Armies? Gold? Flags?" "Stories," he continued. "There's nothing in the world more powerful than a good story. Nothing can stop it. No enemy can defeat it."[11]

—*Game of Thrones* (last episode)

In a nutshell, stories mean more than anything else. The essence of speechmaking is effective storytelling.

Stories have a beginning, a middle, and an end. The beginning presents things as they are and proceeds to describe how they could be, establishing a connection with the audience. The middle reflects on the contrast between the present and the future, helping receivers to perceive the future as more appealing. The end is a call to respond—a motivational demonstration of how the ideas contained in the story benefit the audience.

Remember That Timing Matters

When telling a story, timing matters. When you tell the right story at the right time, it's as though your words and actions are magical, causing others to respond to and follow you, taking your words to heart. If communicated properly, stories are capable of changing how we look at the world. A speaker can shape behavior by building an idea inside the minds of receivers. Two examples come to mind:

First, picture this. In May 2019, Kendrick Castillo was just days away from graduating from STEM School Highlands Ranch in Colorado when two teenaged shooters entered his classroom. Kendrick's father, John, told the story of his son's heroism, saying that it came as no surprise to him and his wife that Kendrick had acted to disarm one of the shooters. He said he knew Kendrick was a hero even before he died saving others. "We can all be like Kenrick," his father noted. "There is risk in love. He knew that. A fellow student echoed the sentiments of Kendrick's father, saying, "He died for us. Now it's time for us to live for him." At Kendrick's memorial service, 600 Jeeps formed a procession and an honor guard of robots lined the walkway to pay respects to Kendrick, a member of the Robotics team. The images and stories told at Kendrick's memorial represented the right stories at the right time, depicting a protagonist who offered his life to save the lives of his classmates.[12]

Next, try and visualize that which occurred during former president Donald Trump's term in office when protesters stormed the Capitol on January 6, 2021, to protest the results of the presidential election and disrupt the certification of the Electoral College vote. Trump widely praised those who were part of the insurrection, repeatedly using the word *love* to describe the event's tone and referring to those involved as patriots and Ashli Babbitt, who was killed by Capitol police, as a great hero, an incredible woman, a military woman.[13] His rhetoric echoed remarks he made years earlier after Heather Heyer, a counterprotester at a white nationalist demonstration in Charlottesville, was killed by a white nationalist supporter who hit her with his car. In responding back then, President Trump expressed sympathy for the demonstration against the removal of a statue of General Robert E. Lee, defending the white nationalists and noting that counterprotesters deserved at least some of the blame for the resulting violence. The president observed, "You also had some very good people on both sides." Trump invoked an explicit comparison between Robert E. Lee and the Founding Fathers, saying, "This week it's Robert E. Lee. And I notice that Stonewall Jackson is coming down. I wonder, is it George Washington next? And is it Thomas Jefferson the week after that? You know, you have to ask yourself, where does it stop?"[14] Dozens of statues of Washington, Jefferson, and others have come down or been defaced in the past couple of years.

When a speaker tells the wrong story, or tells a story at the wrong time, it causes us to pause, question the speaker's performance, and look elsewhere for inspiration.[15]

Lead With Stories

Because humans are wired to listen to stories, a story makes a particularly effective presentation frame. Many of the most effective talks rely on a narrative structure similar to that on which detective stories are based. The speaker starts with a problem, describes the search for a solution, and moves toward an "aha" moment during which the audience's perspective evolves meaningfully as they realize how the idea being shared will benefit them.[16] What kinds of stories do effective speakers tell? According to Stephen Denning, stories can spark action, reveal who the speaker is, transmit ideas, communicate the nature of the speaker's cause, share knowledge, and lead the audience into the future. For example, if your goal is to spark action, you might tell a story describing a successful change yet leave room for the listener to imagine. You might even say, "Just imagine . . ." or "What if. . . ?" If your objective is to share knowledge, your story might focus on a mistake made, how it was corrected, and why the solution was effective. Those listening to you will benefit from thinking, "We'd better look out for that, too."[17]

By using and telling stories others identify with, and that will benefit them, you engage receivers, inspiring them to accept your message, follow your lead, and act. Effective speakers use stories not to emotionally manipulate audiences, but to give a meaningful idea life in the minds of others. Whatever story is told should meet the following criteria:

1. It needs to reflect your purpose. It should illustrate the key idea of your speech.

2. It needs to fit the audience. It should have relevance for them.

3. It needs to have a narrative structure (that beginning, middle, and ending we delineated). It should identify a challenge, describe a struggle, and offer a resolution.

USE LANGUAGE TO CONNECT

> **21.2** *Demonstrate ability in using a variety of language tools to tell stories.*

When worded effectively, stories cement the speaker–audience connection. When worded ineffectively, however, they precipitate questions and concerns threatening to sever the ties. Should this occur, you are left to clean up the mess made with words.

To be effective and enhance your ability to inspire, heighten your sensitivity to language. Choose words that (1) add vividness and force to ideas, (2) steer others toward your goal, and (3) strengthen a positive image among audience members. Language should function as a credibility enhancer. Your words can help others perceive you as confident and trustworthy or cause them to question your competence and confidence. Though there is no set formula that will ensure your storytelling success—we can't tell you to add two similes, one metaphor, a moving illustration, and a startling example to a presentation to get others to accept your ideas—we can review some of the language tools at your disposal and how to use them in the stories you tell.

Short and sweet. Don't complicate your message with complex, intricate, and confusing language.

iStock.com/franckreporter

Develop Language Sensitivity

Avoid using words or expressions that insult, anger, demean, or devalue others. Calling others derogatory names, intimidating them, or using profanity typically produces negative outcomes. For example, calling environmentalists "tree huggers" or labeling people with conservative social and political values "religious nuts and rednecks" could reflect badly on a speaker among those who disagree with their assessment.

You would also be wise to avoid using clichés—words or phrases that at one time were effective but due to overuse have now lost their impact. For example, asking others to "think outside of the box" has now become cliché; it would be better to ask receivers to view the situation from an alternative perspective.

Keep It Simple

When insecure, speakers fall back on complex language. The most effective ones, however, forsake "word armor," or speech that cloaks thought or appeals to narrow audiences. Clear speakers use focused and jargon-free language and short sentences.

Strategize About Word Choices

Remember that audience members are not walking dictionaries. Avoid using words that confuse and alienate. Most will respond to the connotative or subjective meanings of words, not their denotative or dictionary meanings. So recognize the feelings and personal associations that your words might stimulate in others. This enables you to control the perceptions, conceptions, and reflections of receivers so you can steer them toward the response you desire.

Use Word Pictures

Visionary stories—stories that paint a compelling picture of what things will look and feel like in the future—are powerful and motivating. You can harness visionary language by using metaphors. According to **framing theory**, when we compare two unlike things in a figure of speech, the comparison influences us on an unconscious level. The metaphor causes us to make an association. Change the metaphor and you change how others think about the subject.[18] Complex metaphors form the basis for narratives or stories. For example, one student compared Twitter to a tracking device when speaking about the hidden dangers of the service:

Worth a thousand words. Invoking visionary language through metaphors will help your audience make strong connections.

iStock.com/GOCMEN

Using Twitter is an easy way to share information and thoughts. Sounds harmless, doesn't it? I don't think it is harmless. Like GPS, Twitter is one big tracking device. Hit the tweet button on websites, and Twitter knows what websites you visit. Tweet a link or share what you like via Twitter, and Twitter knows who you follow, your location, and what you usually tweet about.

ENGAGE THE AUDIENCE

21.3	*Use storytelling techniques that increase audience engagement.*

It's the storyteller's responsibility to engage the audience, while being sure they understand the story's point and respond as anticipated.

Repeat/Repeat/Repeat

Ideas fight for attention. They rarely get through the first time. They rely on restatement and repetition. The more you repeat an idea, the more receivers remember it. One of the most famous examples of successful use of repetition is the speech Martin Luther King Jr. delivered in 1963 at the Lincoln Memorial:

> I say to you today, my friends, so even though we face the difficulties of today and tomorrow, I still have a dream. It is a dream deeply rooted in the American dream. I have a dream that one day this nation will rise up, live out the true meaning of its creed: "We hold these truths to be self-evident: that all men are created equal. . .".
>
> I have a dream that my four little children will one day live in a nation where they will not be judged by the color of their skin but by the content of their character. I have a dream today. . . .
>
> I have a dream that one day every valley shall be exalted, and every hill and mountain shall be made low, the rough places shall be made plain, and the crooked places shall be made straight, and the glory of the Lord will be revealed, and all flesh shall see it together.[19]

Because of the repetition of "I have a dream," the speech has a rhythm that enhanced its memorability and staying power.

Speak of "I" and "We"

"I" language finds you taking responsibility for or ownership of your story. You assume responsibility for your thoughts, feelings, and actions. "We" language indicates shared responsibility.

For example, one student speaking about how to respond when you see someone being bullied told the story of freshman goalie Daniel Cui, who was publicly bullied on Facebook after allowing the winning goal in a soccer game. But Cui's teammates rallied behind him, posting a photo of him making a winning save in another game. The student told the audience, "We can make the difference. We can't be bystanders to another's bullying. We need to fight back. We can't let the bullies have the last word."

By using "we" language, you build a collaborative climate—a kind of "We're in this together" story. When receivers feel this sentiment, they won't forget it.

Generate Involvement and Participation

A speaker who creates an emotionally charged event captures our interest. Inviting participation accomplishes this. When you connect with audience members, they are more likely to become involved. When you also ask them to do something during your presentation, their engagement increases.

For example, here's how one student used audience participation to demonstrate the prevalence of lying:

> How important is honesty to you? Let's conduct a class survey to find out. I'd like to start with everyone on his or her feet, so please stand up. I'm going to ask some questions now. If you answer "yes" to any question, please sit down and remain seated.
>
> Have you ever had to lie or cheat?
>
> According to an NBC poll on lying, some 39 percent of those surveyed reported that they never had to lie or cheat. I wonder if they were telling the truth.
>
> Have you lied to anyone in the past week?
>
> According to the NBC poll, only 25 percent of those surveyed admitted having told at least one lie in the past week. I wonder if they understood the question.
>
> Do you think that you can ever justify lying to another person?
>
> According to the NBC poll, 52 percent of those surveyed believe that lying can never be justified.
>
> Have you ever lied to someone to avoid hurting his or her feelings?
>
> The NBC poll reveals that 65 percent of those surveyed have done just that.
>
> Look around. How many members of our class are still standing?[20] What does that tell us about the role lying really plays in our lives?

The speaker drew receivers in by asking them questions that physically involved them in the speech. The speaker's visual depiction of the prevalence of lying added impact to the speaker's message.

Thus, a story can serve as a presentation's core—its central message. Like a mental movie filled with images that paint pictures and provide movement by revealing personal understanding, growth, and perhaps transformation, a story engages the senses. Besides helping to build tension and heighten emotion, most of all, a story communicates about you, often providing a satisfying experience or conclusion that is memorable and has staying power.

GAME PLAN

I Know a Story Is a Good One When . . .

- It is delivered in simple language and is easy to understand.
- It contains rich visual imagery.
- The goal of the speech is easy to discern.
- The goal of the speech is delivered in compelling language.
- The speech engages listeners and encourages them to be involved and participate.

EXERCISES

Storytelling

Though we have told stories to our families, friends, and teachers all our lives, we can become better at telling them to members of different audiences—especially those we hope will follow our lead. The following activities prepare you to do that.

1. Your Day

Pair up with a partner and prepare a short outline that describes a day in your life. Instead of merely listing your schedule of events, tell a story about them. Using the guidelines from this chapter, describe in detail what you had hoped to accomplish, whom you worked with, what you did to motivate or energize yourself and them, and how you felt about the results achieved at day's end.

2. Unifying Metaphors

Suppose you had to give a speech on what it means to think globally. First, identify the specific points you would make in your talk. Next, identify a unifying metaphor, explaining how you will use it to relate to the audience. Last, choose three additional language tools and describe how you will integrate them into the five ingredients of a story.

3. Analyze the Speech: What Separates Us From Chimpanzees

View Jane Goodall's speech, "What Separates Us From Chimpanzees," on TED Talks. Focus on Goodall's use of props, sound effects, and stories in the speech.

1. How did Goodall establish a connection with the audience?

2. What purpose do you think that Goodall's imitation of a chimpanzee's voice served?

3. To what extent, if any, did Goodall's integration of stories influence your reaction to the speech?

4. Approach the Speaker's Stand

According to Marshall Ganz, an expert on public policy at Harvard's John F. Kennedy School of Government, a social movement emerges as a result of the efforts of purposeful actors who assert new public values, form new relationships rooted in those values, and mobilize followers to translate the values into action by telling a new story.[21]

For example, in 1962 Rachel Carson published *Silent Spring,* a book that is widely acknowledged to have launched the American environmental movement. Craft a speech that focuses on a story about a movement of your choice in one of the following ways:

- Make your story a story of *self:* a moment when you or someone else faced a challenge

- A story of *us:* a story that expresses shared values

- A story of *now:* a story articulating an urgent challenge that demands immediate action

RECAP AND REVIEW

21.1 Explain ingredients integral to a story, identifying narratives from your life and the lives of others to involve and motivate an audience.

Finding your authentic voice and sharing stories that motivate others to join you in seeking a goal will make you a more effective speaker and help you bring about the transformations you seek. Stories reflect the speaker's passion or sense of purpose. They supply antagonists or villains that threaten the future. They offer up heroes or protagonists who offer solutions. They create an awakening or "aha" moment. They reveal a need for change or a transformation opportunity.

21.2 Demonstrate ability in using a variety of language tools to tell stories.

Effective storytellers have language sensitivity. They make strategic word choices, keep their language clear, and use word pictures or figures of speech to bring their stories alive.

21.3 Use storytelling techniques that increase audience engagement.

Storytellers understand the value of repetition and restatement, employ both "I" and "we" language, and work to realize audience buy-in. Stories make words memorable. They challenge the audience to make the speaker's dream of the future a reality.

KEY TERMS

Framing theory (p. 492)

"I" language (p. 493)

Storytelling (p. 487)

"We" language (p. 493)

iStock.com/ferrantraite

22

PRESENTING IN CLASSES BEYOND THE PUBLIC SPEAKING COURSE

> ## UPON COMPLETING THIS CHAPTER, YOU WILL BE ABLE TO
>
> **22.1**   Discuss dimensions of presenting orally in courses across the college curriculum.
>
> **22.2**   Adapt oral presentations to specific educational contexts and audiences, including preparing and delivering a report on a professional or scholarly article, a poster presentation, and a service learning or internship report.
>
> **22.3**   Prepare to present position presentations or debates on subjects relevant to any field.

How many presentations would you estimate that you give in all your classes combined over the course of a semester? The classroom speaking context is one you likely deal with regularly. With the emphasis educators now place on the flipped classroom, with instructional content being delivered outside of the classroom and applied activities constituting the focus of what happens in the classroom, it's likely that the number of presentations you will be asked to deliver will continue to rise.[1] Your public speaking course will prepare you for this change.

The skills needed to speak in a public speaking course share much in common with the skills needed to speak before any college class. In a broad array of courses, you may be given assignments in which you must develop a topic and communicate findings to your instructors and fellow students. In every class in which an oral presentation is assigned, you will need to define for yourself the assignment's purpose, the professor's expectations, and your fellow students' needs. Not much different from giving a speech in speech class, is it?

COACHING TIP

"There is no such thing as presentation talent; it is called presentation skills."

—David JP Phillips, international speaker and coach

This book gives you the skills you need to speak well and purposefully in every course, not just speech class. Use these skills to your advantage. Apply your skills across the curriculum, and you expand your reach. Presentation skills make a difference.

PRESENTING ACROSS COLLEGE COURSES

> **22.1**   *Discuss dimensions of presenting orally in courses across the college curriculum.*

Your public speaking class offers you numerous opportunities to practice presenting to an audience. However, such a course probably is not the only college course in which you are called upon to give oral presentations.

SELF-ASSESSMENT 22.1: PRESENTING ACROSS THE CURRICULUM

Directions:

Indicate how ready you feel to deliver such a presentation where 1 represents not at all ready, 2 represents not terribly ready, 3 represents somewhat ready, 4 represents ready, and 5 represents absolutely ready.

Type of Presentation	Course (Identify courses requiring the presentation listed)	Readiness Level
Informative Talk or Oral Report		
Group Presentation or Panel		
Problem-Solving Discussion		
Virtual Presentation		
Q&A Session		
Interview		
Persuasive Presentation		
Poster Presentation		
Other: Identify any other types of oral presentations required		

Analysis of Results	Ranking Implications
Describe the kinds of presentations most frequently required in the different courses you take	Identify the ramifications each kind of presentation has to your success in the course.

Communicate Your Ideas to Others

Oral presentations are a staple in many courses across the college curriculum. Engineering students are expected to present their designs. Art students are expected to explain their approaches to a piece and critique the work of others. No matter your major or area of concentration, it is important for you to be adept at communicating your ideas to your peers and professors. Imagine how good it will be to appear more confident when sharing your ideas to others in all of your courses that require you to present a talk. For each course, consider how others see and hear you, how you respond to questions, and how you present.

Pay Attention to Context

Class presentations strike a happy balance. They tend to be less formal than public speeches but more formal than daily conversations. Class audiences tend to be more homogeneous than public audiences because receivers usually have a knowledge base similar to that of the presenter. It is probably safe to assume that your classmates have retained the information covered in the course to date, but beyond that, it is still wise to double-check your receivers' level of understanding. Some members of the audience will match your expertise, others will surpass it or not measure up, and still others will have no special expertise at all.

Although you will speak less formally before an audience of your peers than to a general audience, demonstrating your respect for everyone present remains essential.

You cannot hide. No matter your field, communicating with others and presenting your ideas well are essential skills to develop.

iStock.com/sanjeri

Apply Knowledge and Skills Gained

When the time comes to prepare and deliver a presentation in another class, you have an advantage. You can build on what you've learned and apply what you know about preparing and delivering a public speech to preparing and delivering whatever speaking assignments are given you in other courses.

Center on the Audience

Ask yourself how the audience you will present to in another class differs from the audience you presented to in your public speaking course. Take the unique characteristics and concerns of the present audience into consideration when preparing your talk so that you're sure to connect with them. Be sure to review Chapter 4.

Be Confident, Capable, and Creative

Review how to control nervousness, demonstrate credibility, and use creativity to distinguish your presentation and yourself. Know as much about the topic of your talk as possible, use language the audience understands, and be imaginative and resourceful in your approach. Work through your content logically and thoroughly. Choose interesting supporting materials and remember to cite sources orally. Be sure to review Chapters 5 and 6.

Be Organized

Include an introduction that engages and introduces your presentation, an appropriate body of content, and a conclusion that summarizes what you've covered and leaves the audience thinking about what you've shared. Be sure to review Chapters 7, 8, and 9.

Demonstrate Your Presentation Technique

Review delivery options in Chapter 12. There likely will be no need to memorize or read from a manuscript. Your presentation will probably be extemporaneous in style. You also should be prepared to integrate visual and audio aids if they will add to your presentation (review Chapter 14). You know how much practice matters, so be sure to give yourself ample time to rehearse.

SUBJECT-ORIENTED SPEAKING ASSIGNMENTS

> **22.2** *Adapt oral presentations to specific educational contexts and audiences, including preparing and delivering a report on a professional or scholarly article, a poster presentation, and service learning or internship report.*

The nature of the applied assignments and presentations assigned to you in courses other than speech class may involve alternative topics and formats, such as reviewing a scholarly or professional article, delivering a poster presentation, or reporting on a service learning or internship experience. Each of these speaking opportunities calls on you to apply the generic speaking skills you gained in speech classes to different kinds of presentations that highlight your mastery of specific subject matter while reinforcing or supplementing specific course content. For each of these, you need to understand the instructor's purpose and assignment guidelines.

Review a Scholarly or Professional Article

Part of the learning process in any college course is to become conversant in the scholarly and professional literature of the field. Sometimes, an instructor will assign a student to read and review an article in class. To do so, follow this outline:

- Introduce the article by identifying its author(s), title, the issue, date, and pages of the journal in which it appeared. Next, summarize its purpose, the thesis, or hypothesis it advanced, and your understanding of the author's theoretical perspective.

- Describe the research methods the author(s) used, identifying subjects, instruments, and procedures.

- Discuss findings, specifying what the author(s) concluded and the implications of the conclusions drawn.

- Evaluate the article, summarizing its weaknesses, strengths, and significance.

- Discuss the author's credibility based on the work completed, sources consulted, and validity or reliability of the study.

- Explain how you and others can apply the article to your own lives.

- Offer suggestions for further research.

Twenty percent of your grade. While perhaps a little less formal, a class presentation still necessitates following the other rules of speaking.

iStock.com/Marcus Chung

Deliver a Poster Presentation

A **poster presentation** is a graphical approach to presenting information. A poster shows and tells a story on virtually any subject.

When preparing a poster, simplicity is key. In poster text sections, headings should be bold and the body kept brief, with any text block typically not exceeding 50 words. Those looking at your poster should be able to read it from a distance of five feet. Thus, lettering should be at least 24 points, with heads a minimum of 36 points. Use bold visuals to augment the text with two or three colors. Both the poster's text sections and visuals should be given titles.

The poster's layout should be visually creative. Open layouts help maintain interest. The poster should pull the viewer from its top to the bottom and from left to right. Text and visuals should be balanced, with white (empty) space defining the information flow. Sample layouts appear in Figure 22.1.

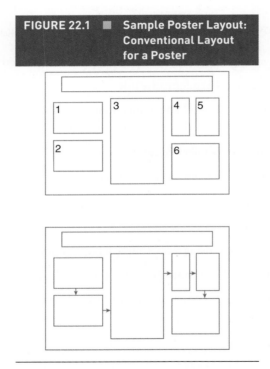

FIGURE 22.1 ■ Sample Poster Layout: Conventional Layout for a Poster

Note: Long panel at top center is title/author banner. Individual panels can be connected by numbers and arrows. Also, note the use of space between panels to achieve visual appeal.

Source: Carol Waite Connor, "The Poster Session: A Guide for Preparation" (U.S. Geological Survey Open-File Report, 88–667), 1992.

Offer a short abstract to orient the poster viewer. On the poster, summarize your message clearly. Design the poster to cut through jargon and get at the heart of a topic—its central message. Objectives and main points should be crystal clear and well organized, with graphs and images doing much of the work. The goal is to engage others in conversation about the poster. While you may have prepared a brief oral summary of your work, as others ask you questions about your poster, you may find yourself delivering what are actually a series of brief, impromptu speeches. In fact, as you prepare the poster, it is good practice to anticipate the questions others might ask you.

When well prepared and presented, a poster fulfills one or more of the following objectives:

- It is a source of information.

- It begins a conversation.

- It advertises your work.

- It summarizes your work.

Use the following suggestions to guide you in creating and presenting a poster:

- Consider the message you want your poster to communicate before starting it.

- Give the poster a short but informative title.

- Keep the message focused and simple, identifying what the audience should come away knowing.

- Use a logical and easy-to-follow layout.

- Use headings to orient viewers and establish main points.

- Edit text judiciously.

- Emphasize graphics.

- Use appropriate color and font sizes to make it easy to read.

- Prepare to discuss and answer questions about the poster by rehearsing.

- When presenting, explain your work succinctly, speaking clearly and establishing eye contact with receivers.

Report on a Service Learning or Internship Experience

Reporting on a service learning project or internship requires that you reflect on what you gained from participating in the experience.

When first engaged in **service learning**—a project that addresses a nonprofit community or public agency need—or an internship, keep a weekly timetable and daily log of your experiences. Keep notes on the meetings you attended, conversations you had, challenges you faced, and any relevant interactions and relationships you made. In addition to applying curricular concepts to both the service learning and internship experiences, you also serve a local organization.

Begin by providing the audience with background information on the organization, agency, or group you served and your specific department or assignment in it. Then, share your expectations going into the experience. Review the kinds of tasks you performed, telling stories about the nature of particular days, as appropriate. Describe how the tasks affected you, explaining what you learned both personally and professionally and reflecting on how your work contributed to the organization. End by sharing whether your expectations were fulfilled; identifying how you will apply new skills, qualifications, and understandings you were able to acquire during the experience; and offering your recommendations for future service learning volunteers or interns at the same site.

Because both service learning and internships are learning experiences, reflection and analysis play integral parts in your report for either.

DEBATE OR ADVOCATE FOR POSITIONS OF RELEVANCE TO A FIELD

> **22.3** *Prepare to present position presentations or debates on subjects relevant to any field.*

Position presentations and debates are also used across a variety of disciplines as well as in civic settings. Both call upon you to use your persuasive skills to argue an issue.

When giving a **position presentation**, you deliver a persuasive argument on a controversial issue, much like you do in a persuasive speech. In this case, you take an arguable position on an issue of concern to the particular field. You might, for example, express a viewpoint, or argue for a specific policy. The goal is to convince the audience that the stance you are advocating for is valid, and that they should support it. To accomplish this, you need to ensure your position is well substantiated, and that you anticipate and defuse counterclaims, demonstrating that you are informed on all sides of the issue. When presenting a position presentation, as in all presentations, introduce the subject, explain why it's important, and assert and defend your thesis. Address potential counterpositions, refute them, and give evidence in support of the argument you are making. When concluding, summarize your argument, restate it, and recommend a plan of action.

In a **debate**, two sides take turns presenting pro and con positions, with each side competing to win over the audience. The "pro" side of a debate is called the **affirmative side**. The role of the affirmative side is to support a resolution calling for change, such as "Resolved: Congress should increase the inheritance tax." In contrast, the "con" or **negative side** seeks to convince the judges and/or members of the audience that change is not needed, working to defeat the resolution and maintain the status quo.

Whether you are debating solo or as part of a team, your role is to develop and present arguments to support your stance. Throughout the course of a debate, you will have the opportunity to refute the arguments the opposing side presents. This phase—known as *refutation*—involves pointing out the flaws of the other side's arguments and rebuilding the arguments you presented yourself. This may require you to point out their errors in reasoning, demonstrate their use of weak evidence, and offer new evidence in support of your claims.

En garde. Be ready both to defend your side and attack the other in a debate.

iStock.com/gorodenkoff

Think of a debate like a fencing match: you need to attack the other side while defending your own arguments and position. If you ignore an argument or error made by the other side, you weaken your ability to win. Thus, it is important to keep track of everything the other side says and every argument they put forth, being certain to effectively refute or weaken them.

To prevail in a debate, be sure to

- Present an organized speech

- Communicate your passion for your position

- Identify and present credible and convincing evidence in support of your side's position

- Either tell the judges and receivers what they should decide or, if your position is an unpopular one, ask them to suspend judgment until hearing both sides' arguments

- Stress your side's strong points

- Emphasize the opposing side's weaknesses

- Think quickly and creatively

GAME PLAN

Debating

- Whether or not I personally believe in the pro/con stance I've been asked to take, I've prepared to deliver an argument that is passionate in defending my assigned position.

- As part of my research, I have examined and read up on both sides of the issue. Doing so helps me prepare refutations.

- I've researched the opposing side's arguments to find flaws that expose their weaknesses.
- I've practiced delivering a defense of the strongest points of my position.
- I've practiced my opening and closing statements.

EXERCISES

Speaking Across College Courses

Good presentations, whatever the course, can be informative, persuasive, and entertaining. Every presentation helps the audience think and learn. Participating in the following activities will help you develop the skills needed to present in different classes and before different audiences.

1. The List

Opportunities for oral assignments, group or individual, include more than podium speeches, especially in courses other than speech class. Identify courses you are currently taking in which you can apply the skills learned in this chapter. Be specific in detailing the skills learned that benefited you the most.

2. Student Observation

Observe a student delivering an oral presentation in a course other than speech. Note the following:

1. What was the course? What was the assignment?
2. How did the speaker approach the assignment?

Then, depending on the type of presentation the speaker completed, explain the extent to which the speaker succeeded in doing one or more of the following:

- Effectively provided the background of the scholarly article
- Presented a clear poster presentation
- Convinced or left you undecided by the debate
- Demonstrated the meaningfulness of the service learning or internship experience

3. Analyze the Speech

In a debate on the following question: "Should states repeal felon disenfranchisement laws?" a speaker taking the affirmative position offered an argument explaining why they should.

Included below are excerpts from the affirmative debater's speech. As you read the speech excerpts, consider these two questions:

1. To what extent, if any, do you find the argument presented effective?

2. How do you imagine the negative side refuted the argument?

States should repeal felon disenfranchisement laws because having a right to vote is essential to the functioning of our democracy. Despite this, more than six million of our fellow American citizens have had that right taken away—many of them forever—because they have been found guilty of committing crimes and put in prison.

SN 1

The speaker states the affirmative position.

In some states, more than 7 percent of the state's adult citizens have been disenfranchised in this manner—with a disproportionate number of them minorities. When Florida repealed its disenfranchisement law in 2018, voting rights were returned to some 1.4 million Floridians who had already served their sentences, many of them African American. Yet to date, in Kentucky and Virginia, 20 percent of African Americans still cannot vote because of having formerly been convicted of a crime. And in Kentucky and Iowa, lifetime disenfranchisement is imposed for all with felony convictions. At least 10 states permanently restrict certain convicted felons from voting.

SN 2

The speaker uses statistics to explain the problem's magnitude.

According to Eric Holder Jr., attorney general of the United States, this system of disenfranchisement is both outdated and counterproductive. Here's why.

SN 3

The speaker references a credible source.

Once a convicted felon serves out a sentence, that person should be considered rehabilitated. Instead, in states with disenfranchisement policies, former convicts are stigmatized and isolated, which only increases the probability of their committing crimes in the future.

SN 4

The speaker explains the dangers of not supporting the affirmative position.

Additionally, disenfranchisement may be affecting the outcome of elections. Remember, presidential elections can end up being decided by one state's voters. For example, when George

W. Bush won the state of Florida by 537 votes in 2000, some attribute it to the fact that more than 800,000 Floridians who had criminal records were not allowed to vote at the time. At the time of the 2016 presidential election, the number of disenfranchised Floridians had risen to 1.5 million. At least in Florida in 2020, that won't happen again.

In order to not undermine the citizenship of those who have paid their debt to society and to preserve the integrity of our democracy, we need to make it easier for former convicts to regain the right to vote.

SN 5

The speaker closes the argument's presentation by affirming what is to be gained if receivers support it.

4. Approach the Speaker's Stand

Select and deliver a position statement on one of the following belief statements or one of your own choosing:

- Anyone in the United States can make it if they work hard.
- Shakespeare is the most influential writer of all time.
- Actors are role models whether they want to be or not.
- A parliamentary system is a superior form of government.

RECAP AND REVIEW

22.1 Discuss dimensions of presenting orally in courses across the college curriculum.

Although oral presentations differ from class to class, you can apply the skills you have acquired in planning and preparing public speeches to presentations assigned in other classes. Every audience is different, requiring different information and the application of a different skill set. Although some audiences you address will share your knowledge level, others will match it, surpass it, or not measure up.

22.2 Adapt oral presentations to specific educational contexts and audiences, including preparing and delivering a report on a professional or scholarly article, a poster presentation, and service learning or internship report.

Each of these speaking opportunities calls on you to apply the generic speaking skills you gained in speech classes to different kinds of presentations that highlight your mastery of specific subject matter while reinforcing or supplementing specific course content. Reviews need to be thorough, posters need to tell a cogent story, and in a service learning or internship report you need to demonstrate what you have accomplished and how you have profited from the experience.

22.3 Prepare to present position presentations or debates on subjects relevant to any field.

Position presentations and debates are of value across a variety of disciplines as well as in civic settings. Each form of speech calls upon you to demonstrate your persuasive skills as you argue an issue.

KEY TERMS

Affirmative side (p. 505)

Debate (p. 505)

Negative side (p. 505)

Position presentation (p. 505)

Poster presentation (p. 503)

Service learning (p. 504)

iStock.com/SDI Productions

23 PRESENTING ONLINE

UPON COMPLETING THIS CHAPTER, YOU WILL BE ABLE TO
23.1 Compare and contrast presenting online and offline.
23.2 Differentiate online formats and presentation styles.
23.3 Distinguish among online platforms, identifying guidelines for presenting.

Are you used to being onscreen? Most of us are. Do you frequently log on to video-conferencing apps such as Zoom or FaceTime? Most of us do. The COVID-19 pandemic contributed to our relying on these communication platforms more than we were accustomed to in our pre-pandemic days. In fact, the COVID-19 pandemic precipitated a Zoom revolution.[1] Just as we connect digitally with friends, family members, and coworkers near and far, so today's speakers depend on technology to help them establish ties and connect with audiences locally and globally. We are "at home" logging on to virtual meeting rooms to give online presentations or to serve as a member of online audiences. We do it so regularly that it's now commonplace. Delivering online presentations extends both our options for presenting and the life of the presentations we create. At the same time, online presentations increase our flexibility by disconnecting our presentations from time, place, and audience constraints. Additionally, online presentations have the potential to reach much wider and larger audiences. Whether used during webinars, voice or video Internet conferences, or streamed events, online presentations both live (synchronous) and recorded (asynchronous) play prominent roles in the digital and real world.

THE TECHNOLOGICAL DIFFERENCE

23.1 *Compare and contrast presenting online and offline.*

You need to plan, prepare, and deliver your online presentation just as you would prepare to deliver your presentation face to face, in person. However, despite their similarities (online presentations have you doing everything you do when delivering a face-to-face speech), the online format actually calls on you to imagine and do more. It also is distinct in several ways. Unlike when you deliver a presentation and share the same physical space with the audience, with an online presentation, speaker and receivers inhabit distinctly different locations and therefore share a different relationship. Rather than being able to look one another in the eye and respond quickly to one another's feedback, when presenting virtually, feedback may be delayed and reading nonverbal cues is more difficult.

Technology-Dependent Delivery

Although face-to-face presentations may use technology to support the speaker's delivery, online presentations are totally dependent on technology for their delivery. The speaker and the members of the audience must think and plan ahead for things to go smoothly. The speaker needs to be adept at using the technology and setting things up. Audience members require Internet connectivity and the skills to view and respond online. Sometimes, as became evident in the disparity in use among students compelled to receive their education remotely during the COVID-19 pandemic, the **digital divide** (the social and/or economic inequality of access to communication technologies) distinguishes those who are included from those who find themselves excluded. One of the major challenges is to equalize access and participation.

The items on the following list constitute the equipment essential for creating online presentations. Both presenters and users must be proficient in understanding the technology and its requirements.

- A computer with sufficient memory/bandwidth
- A hard drive with sufficient space
- Recording and editing software
- Webcam, high-quality smartphone, or video camera
- A microphone
- A broadband Internet connection

Whatever software program you use, it's important to familiarize yourself with it. There are numerous tutorials you can find online for Zoom and WebEx, for example. Some programs allow you to switch easily between focusing on yourself to integrating relevant visuals by clicking "share screen." You can revert back by clicking "Stop Sharing Screen."

Presentation Cues and Miscues for Online Speeches

Video accentuates facial features and cues. As a result, the speaker transitioning from communicating face to face to online needs to adjust as an actor might when transitioning from stage to television. Though live theater calls for larger gestures and exaggerated facial expressions, mediated screens call for much more nuanced nonverbal expressions and require speakers to tone down their gestures and face work. To be considered genuine, body language in the virtual world should connect presenter and receiver without seeming forced or unnatural.

What other adjustments should online presenters prepare for? The visual and aural environment, including the lighting and sound limitations of the room, need to be taken into consideration. If your computer screen and camera face a window, for example, the lighting could make it difficult for those viewing you on their computers to see your face. If you neglect to clean the area within range of the camera, or if you dress inappropriately, the audience will be privy to your clutter and lack of attention to detail. Because you are presenting online does not mean you can forget all that you have learned about giving a speech when situated in the same room as the audience. In fact, when presenting online, you face all the challenges that live speakers face—plus a few extra ones. Other people or animals, for example, can enter the room and distract you. There may be log-on issues (some receivers may log on late), or the computer connection

Loud and clear. Having a firm grasp on technology is obviously essential for an online presentation but also for many other types of speeches.

iStock.com/gorodenkoff

may drop. Audience members may decide to check their messages, email, online shop, or text friends. These kinds of distractions, aside from causing receivers to disengage, can also leave the speaker fumbling for attention.

No matter the means used to present a speech, the speaker's task is to keep the audience engaged. Speakers do this by building interaction into their presentations. When delivering a speech virtually, you also engage receivers by looking directly at the webcam rather than into the computer screen or trying to make eye contact with receivers. If you need to, raise your computer to a more appropriate height by placing your laptop on a stand or a stack of books so that the webcam is tilted slightly downward at your face and is easy for you to look into. Aside from this angle being more flattering, it also will help you seem more approachable to receivers. To foster more engagement, ask questions; use polling; use summarizing slides and/or a whiteboard; use your voice and word pictures to draw receivers in while working to eliminate random or jerky movements on your part; and be certain to begin and end on time.[2]

SELF-ASSESSMENT 23.1: VIRTUAL PRESENTATIONS

Directions:

Assess your favored means of presenting virtually by first indicating the degree to which you prefer presentations that are synchronous or asynchronous (where 1 represents don't like at all and 5 means really like), and then rank ordering the six listed possibilities identified in the left column from 1 (your first choice) to 6 (your least-favored choice). Explain your reasons for your ranking and the implications of your preferences for the role virtual presentations have in your future.

Decision-Making Strategy	My Ranking
Synchronous presentation	
Asynchronous presentation	
TED-like Talk	
Discussion	
Interview	
Portfolio/PowerPoint/Graphical Presentation/Digital Story	
Webinar	
Podcast	

Ranking Analysis	Ranking Implications
Explain the reason behind each ranking.	Identify how you see yourself engaging in virtual presentations in the future.

FORMATS FOR ONLINE PRESENTATIONS

23.2 *Differentiate online formats and presentation styles.*

Like live presenters, online presenters have an array of formats (synchronous or asynchronous) and presentation styles to choose from, including but not limited to the single-speaker presentation (interactive or not), the panel presentation (moderated or not), the interview, and the digital story. No matter the format or style, you will need to practice until you own the material and the technology.

Choose a Synchronous or Asynchronous Format

Online presentations can be presented live and viewed in real time on the Internet or recorded, streamed, and presented at a later time, like a TED Talk. Presentations delivered in real time are synchronous. Presentations recorded and played back or viewed at another time are asynchronous.

A synchronous webinar, like a face-to-face presentation, for example, allows for audience participation and questions, is conversational in tone, and precipitates more of a connection between speaker(s) and receiver(s). As a result, synchronous online speakers are able to interact with and receive more immediate feedback from their audiences, which can be a significant advantage. But there are also disadvantages. For example, the synchronous speaker has just one chance to achieve their goals. Once the webinar begins, the speaker cannot start over without adversely affecting their credibility with members of the audience.

In addition, since a synchronous presentation is given at a set time, some members of the audience can be unavailable simply because the presentation begins very late or very early in their time zones.

In comparison to the synchronous online presentation, a talk delivered asynchronously, whether initially delivered before a live audience or not, also offers benefits and challenges. One benefit is that audiences can view asynchronous presentations as many times as they want and whenever it is convenient for them to do so. For this reason, speeches first delivered synchronously are sometimes saved and posted online. Another advantage is that the speaker has the ability to refine the final performance before it is released to the audience. The speaker can stop and start over as many times as needed to produce a polished final product without adversely affecting the speaker's credibility. Recording too many times, however, may result in the speaker appearing less natural to the audience. Similarly, the lack of immediate feedback and the loss of direct interaction between the speaker and audience are additional challenges associated with asynchronous presentations.

Whether a presentation is synchronous or asynchronous also affects the nature of your eye contact. For example, in a synchronous presentation you speak and look directly into the webcam rather than at your computer screen. In an asynchronous presentation, however, when an audience is present, you establish contact with the in-person audience rather than with the computer camera. Remember to position the computer at the right height. The computer should be placed at a level so that the webcam is aimed slightly down toward your face rather than up at it. A low angle shot is more kind to you than a high angle shot.

Concerned with delivery? Like most speeches, you get one chance with a synchronous presentation, while an asynchronous one gives you multiple chances to nail your delivery.
iStock.com/Chaay_Tee

When It's Just You

Like public presentations, online presentations may rely on a single speaker communicating content. A big difference is the speaker and the audience don't occupy the same space. When the camera is focused on a single person, it is essential to offer a compelling visual that won't distract your audience. Get ready for your close-up, and attend to these reminders:

- **Make sure you have good lighting.** If the audience can't see you, they're less likely to absorb your message. Check that the light is bright and even. It is often the case that the light in your room is sufficient. Should you need to adjust the lighting, setting up three-point lighting can help achieve a more professional effect. To accomplish this on your own, you can position a floor lamp as a backlight (position the light behind you), a smaller table lamp as a fill light (position this light beside you), and position either a flashlight or other light source that you secure in front of and directly on you as your key light (the primary light aimed most directly on you).

- **Test the microphone for clarity.** If possible, wear a headset with a built-in mic or use an external mic if the microphone on your laptop is not of high enough quality.

- **Check your Internet speed to ensure your bandwidth and service are sufficient.** Speeds under 20 megabits could cause the image to look pixelated and lead to audio delays.[3]

- **Present in front of a neat background.** Consider what's behind and above you. A simple background is best. The background should not compete with you.[4]

- **Wear colors, clothing, and jewelry that are technology friendly.** Avoid loud clothing patterns. Blue is a safe color for the screen, while green can be tricky. Pastels and shades of brown are generally acceptable, but consider the color of your background, so you don't blend in. Avoid wearing jewelry that moves (like long earrings) or makes noise (such as bangle bracelets) to minimize distractions.

- **Keep your energy up.** Demonstrate your enthusiasm, but be sure to modulate your voice, pausing for emphasis.

- **Refrain from fidgeting.** Unnecessary movement can be distracting. If your whole body is on camera, gesture naturally. If you are sitting, gesture sparingly. If the chair you are seated in swivels, avoid spinning, or switch to a chair that is stationary.

- **Know where to look.** Don't look up at the ceiling or down at your notes for more than a couple of seconds. Your eyes should not wander aimlessly. Look at the camera as if it is a person. When presenting online, the camera is your substitute audience.

- **Avoid slideshow speak.** Use photos, graphics, and video clips to capture and maintain interest, but don't read slides aloud. You should remain the key source of information.

- **Be sure to rehearse, rehearse, rehearse.** Just as when presenting face to face, when presenting online, practice and preparation are your keys to an effective performance.

Where's Waldo? Make sure that what the viewer sees online is clear and not distracting.

iStock.com/francescoch

Most single-person online presentations are kept brief because of the tendency of the audience to become bored if the speaker delivers a monologue lacking in dynamism. As with face-to-face presentations, delivery matters.

When It's You With Others

Some topics benefit from having multiple speakers involved. Panel presentations find you and usually three to four others discussing a subject, with a moderator also present to ensure that you stay on topic and that no one member monopolizes the discussion. The moderator plays an important role. It's their responsibility to guide the conversation—not to outshine the participants. The best moderators have a good sense of pacing, making sure that no one panelist talks too long on any one aspect, redirecting the conversation should a panelist stray off topic, weaving questions from the audience seamlessly into the conversation, and following up when appropriate by asking a more probing question.

The advantage of a panel is that different views are shared and commented upon. As with the single-speaker presentation, a panel presentation can be interactive and media rich or not. Synchronous online panels mirror their face-to-face counterparts. Software programs such as Adobe Presenter allow members of the audience to interact with the panelists by asking questions or providing commentary during or after each presentation. If the panel discussion will be recorded and shared, panels may request that the asynchronous audience email comments and questions to the presenters or moderator.

As with a solo online speech, consider the visual aspect of the presentation. Make sure the participants' apparel and manner, as well as the physical space, do not distract from the message.

When It's an Interview

Sometimes the delivery of information is made more interesting if one person questions or interviews another person about a preselected subject. Just as with face-to-face interviews, the online interview format works best when the interviewee is a credible source and the interviewer is well prepared. During interactive, synchronous interviews, audience members are sometimes able to submit questions they would like the interviewer to ask, often via email, Twitter, or text. Interviews conducted in a conversational manner usually appeal more to audience members than strictly Q&A interviews, and remember not to distract your audience from your message with your apparel or setting.

Video chat. Interviews online can be just as effective as in-person, and multiple people can usually submit questions.

iStock.com/Prostock-Studio

When It's a Digital Story

As revealed in Chapter 22, you have great stories in you that are worth sharing with others. What's more, storytelling is a powerful promotional tool. With technology, speakers can integrate audio, video, verbal content, and narration to create story-based presentations. Digital storytelling can highlight the importance of an event or communicate the essence of a particular individual. Featuring such a presentation on YouTube, LinkedIn, or a personal website increases its reach.

To prepare a digital story, first outline the story's components, describing its plot, characters, setting, and theme or moral. Then, prepare a storyboard or structured presentation blueprint detailing the audio, video, and any other illustrative support to be included to enhance dramatic interest. Consider using narrative infographics, which convey more information than typical stylized data presentations because they take full advantage of the capabilities of the visual medium, including its capacity for animation.[5]

A special kind of digital story is a *digital portfolio*. A digital portfolio is designed to showcase or market you, demonstrating your skills and highlighting what you can do. It is particularly helpful in interviewing and other competitive situations. Among the contents of your digital portfolio might be a discussion of who you are, what you hope to accomplish professionally, successes you have experienced, the best thing about working with you, sample reports you are proud of, a training session you designed and/or conducted, and sample letters or testimonials of recognition or praise—all reinforcing and building your personal brand.

COACHING TIP

"Whether speaking online or face-to-face, the best way to sound like you know what you're talking about is to know what you're talking about."

—Author unknown

Prepare yourself! Though presenting a speech online doesn't change the basics of speech-making, you now also need to adapt to the demands of whatever technology platform you use. Choose your platform based on its ability to support your presentation goals and keep your audience engaged.

ONLINE PRESENTATION PLATFORMS: SCREENS AND SOUND

> **23.3** *Distinguish among online platforms, identifying guidelines for presenting.*

Among the online platforms you should be familiar with are video, podcasts, webinars, and PowerPoint or other graphical presentation software. Let us look at each in turn.

Video

A well-made or well-chosen video adds impact to a presentation. A site like YouTube is populated with a plethora of presentations, including how-to speeches, political statements, civic appeals, and tributes, ranging from amateur videos produced using webcams or cell phones to professionally produced presentations created using high-definition digital video equipment. Both unsophisticated and sophisticated videos can go viral and spread rapidly across the Internet.

As we have discussed, video can be used successfully for presentations involving any number of people. The greater the number of people involved, however, the more complex the shoot. Users may record directly from a video camera or webcam or use programs such as Vimeo and Panopto, which can record the presentation directly from a computer or other device that has a video camera. Such programs are designed to capture the user as well as what appears on a computer screen, making it easy to incorporate video and other visuals or provide voiceover. Once the recording has been completed, the user can save the file and upload it to YouTube or another distribution platform to share with others.

Podcast

Online presenter(s) may rely solely on audio for message delivery. A highly popular audio format is the **podcast**, a digital audio recording that is made accessible online. Podcasts can be accessed on demand. They can be listened to when you're on the go. Name it, and there's a podcast about it. You can sign up to receive a podcast on a regular basis over an RSS (really simple syndication) feed, listen to it via the podcast's website, or download it onto your smartphone via a podcast app. Effectively, a podcast is an audio file of one or more people talking that you download. As of 2021, there were over 2 million podcasts, 48 million podcast episodes. Six in 10 U.S. consumers over the age of 12 have listened to a podcast.[6] The Library of Congress, iTunes, and Stitcher are three of many podcast repositories. Podcasts can feature a single speaker, two speakers—perhaps using the interview format—or a panel. Most news organizations, such as National Public Radio, offer podcast versions of their programs as well as original podcasts for download. Following this model, you might create a podcast that the members of your class can download. Speakers presenting via podcasts can use a script or speak extemporaneously. As we saw in Chapter 21, we all have stories inside us that others want to hear. Podcasts make a great platform for those stories. In addition to functioning as curators of podcasts, student consumers of podcasts can become podcast creators. Student-produced podcasts call on you to showcase project-based learning, storytelling, and digital media skills as you teach something new or explore a topic of interest to you and your peers.

Podcasts are relatively easy to create, requiring only a quiet room, a computer with a built-in or plugged-in decent microphone, headphones, free audio-recording software such as Alitu (easiest to use), Audacity or GarageBand, a portable audio recorder (optional), and a website from which it can be downloaded. One of the most popular podcasting microphones is the Audio-Technica ATR2100x-USB. It is both a USB microphone and has an XLR connection, which lets you upgrade your recording equipment without needing a new mic.[7] A portable audio XLR recorder lets you record anywhere on multiple tracks. Each mic will record a separate audio file, and the machine will record these tracks onto a memory card that you can easily transfer to your computer.[8]

In addition to creating your own podcast, you might consider making the podcast part of your rehearsal regimen. Simply record one of your rehearsal sessions, send it to a few friends and family members, and solicit their feedback. Any subject is ripe for a podcast, including board games, political discourse, tips on organic farming, and scandals.

Webinar

A **webinar** is a conference held online that is viewable by invited guests with a Web connection. Though initially delivered synchronously or streamed, webinars can also be saved for later viewing. Webinars can present a single speaker, panel, or group collaborating in real time across time zones. They are especially useful for training seminars when participants are geographically dispersed. An advantage of a webinar is that the facilitator or presenter can obtain feedback from participants, respond to questions, and adjust the webinar content and presentation during the session.

For your presentation, you need access to a webinar hosting platform such as GoToMeeting, WebEx, or Zoom, which will provide a Web link or phone number for audience members to use to access the event. Most webinar software also allows you to show slides, incorporate videos, and moderate audience participation. Creating a chat window for participants or encouraging participants to share, tweet, or blog reactions during the online event fosters engagement. Periodically integrating polls, chats, and instant feedback increases interactivity while also letting you gauge the pulse of the remote audience.

Come together. Webinars are a great way to hold classes online for people spread far apart.

iStock.com/Edwin Tan

PowerPoint/Graphical Presentations

Wisely used, slides help to control a presentation's momentum and facilitate the speaker moving through points smoothly. Online presenters often use more visual aids than live presenters in an effort to keep participants fully engaged. PowerPoint presentations can be synchronous or asynchronous. You can record a voiceover to accompany the slides that are saved and given to an audience. Speakers can also use PowerPoint live during the online presentation.

Though PowerPoint has become a presentation staple (sometimes overused in face-to-face presentations), it also may stand alone as a graphic-rich online presentation—with or without audio or video enhancements. Prezi (prezi.com), another Web-based resource for creating dramatic online graphic presentations, offers a free basic version that is easy to use. So does Google Slides, which enables you to work independently or collaborate with others to create a new presentation and edit it using your computer, phone, or tablet. Many graphical platforms offer user tutorials.

Text overload. When using PowerPoint or a similar program, be sure not to overwhelm your audience with heavy text paragraphs on your slides.

iStock.com/PeopleImages

GAME PLAN

Preparing for a Webinar Presentation

- I've identified the format for my webinar.
- I've organized my information to fit the time constraints.
- I've planned for interactivity and a means by which audience members can ask questions or respond to a poll.
- I've prepared visuals to integrate into the webinar.
- I've prepared an introduction for myself and any other presenters.
- I've prepared an explanation of how a webinar works, its interactive nature, and how the audience can participate by asking questions.
- I've rehearsed and held dry runs prior to holding the webinar.
- I've made a plan to record the webinar to make it available for those unable to participate in real time.

EXERCISES

Presenting Online

Developing your understanding of online presentations and the skills needed to present online will increase your breadth and depth as a speaker.

1. Know What You Need

Using the equipment list in Section 23.1, review the technology available to you. Explore the equipment in your classroom and the media center. Does your classroom feature a Smart Board? If not, might it still rely on a projector and screen and DVD player? Are you able to easily stream video? Do you have whatever cables are required, or do you need to have them delivered from the media center?

Troubleshoot technology well before you present. Try to anticipate anything that can go wrong during your presentation. The goal is to solve a potential problem before it presents itself.

2. Know Your Options

Explore and discuss the merits of various media platforms or software for the following formats:

- Podcasting: SoundCloud versus iTunes
- Video sharing: YouTube versus Vimeo
- Webinars: GoToMeeting versus WebEx

3. Analyze This

View an online presentation of your choosing, such as a how-to video on YouTube, a TED Talk, or a training video for software. As an alternative, listen to a podcast. Using a 10-point scale ranging from 1 (totally ineffective) to 10 (totally effective) and the following criteria, evaluate the selected speech or presentation:

1. Adaptation of content for online platform_____
2. Adaptation of speaker to online platform_____
3. Speaker's ability to sustain interest_____
4. Organization of presentation_____
5. Language_____
6. Timeliness of content_____
7. Integration of audio, and/or video and graphical support_____
8. Speaker's vocal and/or visual delivery_____

9. Quality of recording_____

10. Overall effectiveness_____

4. Approach the Speaker's Stand

Prepare and post online a how-to speech on a technology topic such as "How to Prepare a Podcast" or "How to Post a Video Online." Each speech should include the following steps:

1. Identification of equipment required

2. Review of software and platform used

3. Clear instructions on preparation and presentation

4. Anything more you believe is necessary

RECAP AND REVIEW

23.1 Compare and contrast presenting online and offline.

Online presentations have fewer time, place, and audience constraints than face-to-face speeches, as well as the potential to reach a global audience. An online speech is dependent on technology, and the speaker must be aware of their facial and body language cues.

23.2 Differentiate online formats and presentation styles.

Among popular online formats are the single presenter, the panel of presenters, the interview, and digital storytelling. Online speeches can be presented live or be prerecorded.

23.3 Distinguish among online platforms identifying guidelines for presenting.

The most popular online platforms regularly used for presentations include video, podcasts, and webinars. Online presentations require many of the same skills, abilities, and preparation as presentations made before live audiences. However, the online presenter must also be versed in the demands and requirements of the technology being used.

KEY TERMS

Asynchronous presentation (p. 515)   Synchronous presentation (p. 515)
Digital Divide (p. 513)   Webinar (p. 521)
Podcast (p. 521)

24 ANSWERING QUESTIONS

Preparing for and Managing the Q&A

UPON COMPLETING THIS CHAPTER, YOU WILL BE ABLE TO

24.1   Explain the purpose and content of the question-and-answer (Q&A) session, determining how best to run one.

24.2   Follow guidelines to handle all questions asked in the Q&A session.

24.3   Demonstrate composure when fielding all questions asked in the Q&A session.

The question-and-answer (**Q&A**) session plays an integral role in most presentations, especially business and professional ones. Enjoyable, as well as challenging, the Q&A gives audience members a voice, affording them opportunities to ask speakers questions about their remarks and to share reactions. From both a speaker's and an audience's perspective, these are real benefits. The Q&A also gives speakers one last crack at winning over an audience and gives the audience another opportunity to assess the speaker's preparedness, credibility, and expertise. For example, if a speaker's answers leave the audience confused or unconvinced, the speaker may lose ground. Speakers need to be able to voice skillful responses to the questions audience members ask.

COACHING TIP

"Questions are great, but only if you know the answers."

—Laurell K. Hamilton, American writer

Be a mind reader! Anticipate the questions audience members will ask you after listening to your speech. Answer questions clearly and competently and receivers will conclude you were prepared, knowledgeable, and confident. Take control of the Q&A session. Keep your focus on the question asked you. Relate every question asked to your goal.

THE PURPOSE, CONTENT, AND TIMING OF THE Q&A SESSION

24.1   *Explain the purpose and content of the question-and-answer (Q&A) session, determining how best to run one.*

Each of President Biden's press secretaries, first Jen Psaki and then her replacement, Karine Jean-Pierre, carried a giant briefing book to most press conferences. That way they could wield off facts and statistics when queried by the press about administration policies.[1] Like Jean-Pierre and Psaki, every speaker should prepare for questions that the audience might ask. How the question-and-answer session goes directly affects a presentation's outcome, including whether it's considered a success. The purpose of the Q&A is for audience members to ask speaker the questions they have relative to the speaker's presentation. A lively Q&A means presenta- tion was engaging and thought-provoking. It also gives the prepared speaker anoth ance to demonstrate their competence, credibility, and ability to handle themselves before a nce. How prepared do you feel to ask questions of a speaker? How prepared do you feel to a Q&A when you are the speaker?

SELF-ASSESSMENT 24.1: Q&A

Directions:

Use the following statements and evaluation scales to determine your readiness to handle questions about your presentation.

Statement	Absolutely True	Mostly True	Somewhat True	Hardly at All True	Not at All True
1. I feel comfortable anticipating the questions audience members will ask.					
2. I am able to engage the audience in asking questions.					
3. I formulate answers to possible questions in advance.					
4. I let the question be asked without interrupting the questioner.					
5. I know how to keep questions on track.					
6. I can keep myself from becoming defensive.					

...ement	Absolutely True	Mostly True	Somewhat True	Hardly at All True	Not at All True
. I am comfortable admitting when I don't know an answer to a question.					
8. I practice before a Q&A session.					
9. I approach every Q&A with a positive mindset.					
10. I know how to bring the Q&A session to a close.					

Scoring Method	Analysis
Scoring Calculation Identify the statements to which you responded fully, mostly, somewhat, hardly at all, or not at all.	Explain specifically what you need to do regarding your preparation and management of a Q&A to be able to respond "absolutely" to each statement.

What kinds of questions are audience members likely to ask a speaker? When the speaker, have you found audience members eager to ask questions? Audience members may be reluctant to raise their hand to ask a question, if only because they struggle to formulate a good question. In preparation for asking questions of a speaker, here are some possibilities to consider. You might ask the speaker to expand on something they said, perhaps a concept or phrase they mentioned that you believe merits more information. You might ask the speaker to summarize an argument they made because you need further clarification. You might challenge something the speaker said, offering an alternative perspective. You might ask the speaker to offer additional support or evidence, perhaps to supply you with additional sources you could use to dig deeper into their topic. You might ask the speaker what they would have included had they had more time to prepare.

At what point(s) during your talk should audience members ask you questions, and at what point(s) in the talk might you answer the questions they asked? Should they be asked before, during, or after the presentation? Should they be separate from or part of the presentation itself? The answer to each of these questions is, it depends.

In preparation for fielding questions during the Q&A, and in the effort to integrate technology, you can ask the audience to email you questions by creating a unique email address for your speech, or you might set up a Twitter hashtag for the audience to tweet questions about your presentation.

Before Presenting

Sometimes, a speaker solicits questions from the audience in advance, perhaps passing out note cards and asking potential receivers to jot down and submit questions they would like answered. Doing this prior to speaking lets the speaker adapt the talk so it covers the key concerns of receivers.

Other times, to demonstrate their expertise and confidence, speakers solicit questions personally from the audience at the outset of a presentation. If the speaker has prepared effectively, many of the questions asked will be ones the speaker anticipated, and they can assure receivers that all their questions will soon be answered.

Raise your hand. Getting questions from the audience prior to your speech can be an effective way to tailor the speech to the crowd's needs.

iStock.com/jeffbergen

While Presenting

A speaker can also allow questions during a presentation. If you are giving a business presentation, for example, your boss may interrupt with a question at any point—and you likely have no choice but to stop and answer it. Although such questions may disrupt your presentation's flow, you can respond immediately to any concerns, which can keep receivers focused on your message instead of fixating on their objection. However, audience members may ask questions prematurely about points you intend to cover later. When this happens, you have a choice: you can answer the question, or you can tell the audience that you will answer it shortly if they will just be patient for a few moments. For example, you might respond, "Great question. In fact, I'm going to cover that in just a minute."

What if during your talk a listener raises an irrelevant question—one that could throw your presentation off track? When this happens, you need to take control by reframing the question to focus on your goal. For example, if you were asked about the effects of diet on childhood diabetes during a speech on Type II diabetes, you could reframe the question by noting, "Childhood diabetes is Type 1 diabetes; diet, however, is also consequential for Type II diabetes."

After Presenting

Questions can also be held until the presentation's end. This has a number of benefits:

- You control how and when you share your presentation's content.

- You avoid being distracted by poorly timed or irrelevant queries.

- You avoid the objection-finder or rude questioner whose goal is to demonstrate how much they know and focus attention on themselves.

- It helps ensure you will complete your talk on time.

- It helps audience members to focus on what you are saying, instead of being preoccupied with formulating questions while you speak—thereby missing key content.

This is not to suggest that saving questions to the end does not also have its drawbacks. Sometimes, for example, if a question occurs to you as an audience member, you find it difficult to maintain your concentration on what the speaker is saying. Another drawback has to do with how receivers remember—or what we have referred to as the **primacy–recency factor**. We tend to remember what we hear first and last—losing much of the middle over time. Thus, saving questions to the end makes it more likely receivers will remember how you answered a question rather than the points you made during your talk.

MASTER CONTENT TO MANAGE THE Q&A

> **24.2** *Follow guidelines to manage questions in the Q&A session.*

Whenever questions are asked, they can pose challenges for you. Some questions may attack your position. Others may be stated so poorly that you have difficulty understanding them. And others may be completely off topic. Whatever their nature, preparing yourself to field questions that you could be asked equips you to handle them in the Q&A.

Anticipate Questions—Especially Hard Ones

Empathy is a speaker's ally. Being able to put yourself in the shoes of audience members will enable you to look at your presentation through their eyes and anticipate questions they will likely ask. For example, what aspects of your remarks might they find confusing? Which might they find objectionable? Which of your points might they like to know more about? Preparing your responses to potential questions is just as important as preparing the presentation itself.

Understand Every Question Asked

Rather than multiply confusion, **paraphrase** each question asked you to confirm you understand it. "What I hear you asking is. . . . Am I correct?" In addition to uncovering if you "get the question," or heard it correctly, restating a question in your own words helps you provide a frame or context for the question that makes it easier for you to answer and for the audience to understand.

Don't Pontificate

Every question deserves an answer that demonstrates your respect for the questioner. An answer should never be a put-down. If you belittle or embarrass a questioner, even if the question they posed was demeaning, hostile, or has an answer obvious to many in the audience, you lose. Instead of pontificating and attempting to one-up the questioner, work to build support by taking the question seriously and answering politely. You might even offer the questioner a compliment: "I understand why you find this point troublesome. We did, too. However, the more we researched, the more evidence we uncovered that told us we were on the right track. Let me share some of that evidence with you."

MASTER DELIVERY TO MANAGE THE Q&A

> **24.3** *Demonstrate composure when fielding all questions asked in the Q&A session.*

How you present yourself when addressing audience members during the Q&A can make all the difference. By giving questioners your full attention while they are speaking and following these guidelines, you will be able to handle yourself with poise.

Give Audience Members the Green Light

Adhere to protocol when fielding questions: the first hand up or first question submitted should be the first you answer. But be prepared. Audience members sometimes hesitate to ask questions, fearing asking a question that you or others might consider stupid. Let receivers know that there is no such thing as a stupid question. Help them understand that you hope they will ask questions because your goal is to ensure their understanding. If they still hesitate, ask yourself a question you believe they might want answered, saying something such as, "A question you probably have is. . . ." Receivers will be pleased you opened the channel.

Stay on Course

When off track, a question can sidetrack you and your talk, defeating your purpose for speaking. Instead of being drawn off target, respond to every question in a way reflective and supportive of your ultimate goal. You might say, "Let me approach the question this way. . . ." If the questioner objects, agree either to meet with them later to discuss the issue or promise to send information clarifying your position.

Think Through Your Answer

Use caution; pause before answering a question, especially one you find particularly challenging. First, repeat or paraphrase the question asked and then ask the questioner how they might answer the question themselves. If needed, you might also defer to another audience member prior to responding yourself. If you don't know or can't come up with a good answer, don't bluff or say, "No comment." Simply respond, "That's a question I would like to look into. Let me have your contact information, and I will get back to you."

Control the traffic. What methods can you use to manage hostile and inappropriate questions while maintaining a healthy dialogue?

iStock.com/monticelllo

Keep Defensiveness at Bay

Some members of the audience may ask you questions that you don't like. If this happens and you are asked a hostile question, don't be put off or get defensive. Maintain your composure, expressing your respect for the questioner, rephrasing the question more appropriately, and responding politely. This will earn you the respect of the audience.

Address Answers to Both the Questioner and the Audience

Though a specific individual asked you a question, address your answer to the entire audience. Make initial eye contact with the questioner, but then widen your gaze to encompass everyone in the room. This will connect you to the audience, keep everyone interested and involved, and make it less likely that the person asking the question will become hostile if they do not like your answer. It will also decrease the likelihood of the questioner trying to engage you in a one-on-one debate.

Gracefully Bring the Q&A Session to a Close

A Q&A session should not terminate without warning. Rather than ending abruptly, tell the audience when the Q&A session is about to end. You might say, "I will take two more questions, and then we will have to call it a day." Take the two questions, closing with a statement that reinforces your message: "It has been a pleasure spending time with you today. I'm glad for the opportunity to answer your questions. I appreciate your willingness to share your thoughts with me."

Graceful finish. Smoothly transition toward the end of the Q&A, and let the audience know you're coming to a close.

iStock.com/Artur Didyk

GAME PLAN

Prepping for a Q&A Session

- While preparing for and researching my speech, I kept a running list of my own questions, taking note of the ones that were left unanswered.

- I've reviewed my speech for potentially confusing language.

- I've reviewed all of my research and notes (even material that did not make it into my final draft) so I would have the information needed to answer potential questions.

- I've reviewed the guidelines in this chapter and have reserved enough time to conduct a Q&A session, confident in my ability to come up with reliable answers to questions asked.

EXERCISES

The Question-and-Answer Session

Developing skill in handling the question-and-answer session helps build a speaker's comfort, expertise, and overall credibility. Maintaining composure while handling challenges and clearing up confusion helps receivers view you as confident, competent, and trustworthy. Completing these exercises will pave the way to a more productive Q&A.

1. Vital Questions

Select a recent TED Talk at www.ted.com. Imagine you are a member of the audience. What questions would you want to ask the speaker? Were you the speaker, how would you answer the questions you posed?

2. Anticipate and Prepare

The topic you have been assigned is "The Hidden Meaning of *Monopoly for Cheaters*." A recent edition of *Monopoly* known as *Monopoly for Cheaters*[2] contains cheat cards allowing any player to shortchange those playing the game with them. If you are successful at conning another player—that is, you are able to get away with cheating them—you're given a pat on the back, but if you're caught cheating, you're chained to the board with pretend handcuffs until someone else goes to jail. Research *Monopoly for Cheaters*, and develop a list of five questions to ask about it. After creating your five questions, prepare an information sheet containing details you can consult if asked any one of those questions.

3. Analyze the Speech: The Interview

Search for a prerecorded interview with a person you admire—a scholar, politician, musician, artist, writer, or actor. Write down the names of the interviewer and interviewee and assess the effectiveness of the questions asked by the interviewer and the responses given by the interviewee. To what extent did the interviewee do the following?

1. Have facts needed to answer the questions asked

2. Answer questions courteously

3. Display goodwill

4. Exhibit a lack of defensiveness

5. Acknowledge respect for the interviewer

6. Avoid answering impulsively

7. Communicate credibly

4. Approach the Speaker's Stand

Attend a presentation at your school. After listening to the speaker(s) present, ask at least one question plus a follow-up question. Using the questions in the previous exercise, critique the speaker's response to your questions. In a report to the class, share your evaluation, explaining your expectations about how the speaker ought to have answered. Role-play how you would have responded to one of the questions you posed.

RECAP AND REVIEW

24.1 Explain the purpose and content of the question-and-answer (Q&A) session, determining how best to run one.

The purpose of the question-and-answer session is to clear up any confusion or misperceptions on the part of members of the audience. It is the also the speaker's final opportunity to demonstrate topic mastery and credibility. Though usually held at the end of a presentation, the speaker may also field questions prior to or during a speech.

24.2 Follow guidelines to handle all questions asked in the Q&A session.

Practice and preparation are key. Effective speakers anticipate tough questions, take steps to ensure they understand every question asked, and don't pontificate when responding.

24.3 Demonstrate composure when fielding all questions asked in the Q&A session.

To competently manage the Q&A, speakers call on questioners in the order that hands were raised or questions were submitted, and they don't shy away from answering difficult questions. Good speakers demonstrate their respect for questions. They think through questions to avoid inappropriate responses and keep defensiveness in check. They address answers to the questioner and the audience as a whole. Finally, they gracefully close the Q&A session.

KEY TERMS

Paraphrase (p. 533)
Primacy–recency factor (p. 532)
Q&A (p. 528)

GLOSSARY

Abstraction. Something that is vague; language that is neither concrete nor specific

Accumulative experiences. The sum of all our experiences

Active listening. listening that improves mutual understanding; fully concentrating on what is said rather than merely hearing the message

Affirmative side. The pro side in a debate; the side speaking in support of a resolution calling for change

After-dinner speech. A speech that is relevant to the occasion and designed to entertain by taking a good-natured, sometimes humorous, whimsical, or mildly satirical look at a topic of interest

Ageist language. Language that discriminates on the basis of age

Alliteration. Repetition of the initial consonant sounds in nearby words

Anchor. Preexisting opinions

Antithesis. The presence of opposites within the same or adjoining sentences; the juxtaposition of opposing ideas

Argument ad hominem. Name-calling; the use of offensive and insulting words to win an argument

Articulation. The act of producing individual sounds

Asynchronous presentation. An online presentation that is recorded and then viewed at another time

Attending. The listening stage during which an individual selects to pay attention to one or more specific aural stimuli

Attitude. A mental set or predisposition to respond to something favorably or unfavorably; a readiness to respond positively or negatively

Attitude. A mental set or predisposition to respond to something favorably or unfavorably; a readiness to respond positively or negatively

Audience analysis. The systematic identification of the demographic and psychographic characteristics of an audience to determine member interests and motivation

Audience-centered. a speaking style that is not self-centered but is motivated by an understanding of receivers.

Bandwagon appeal. An appeal to popular opinion

Bar graph. A type of graph used to compare or contrast two or more items or groups

Behavioral objective. A desired specific speech outcome; a desired observable and measurable audience response

Belief. That which one holds to be true or false, probable or improbable

Belief. That which one holds to be true or false, probable or improbable

Accumulative experiences. The sum of all our experiences

Body of the speech. That portion of the speech made up of and elaborated by the speech's main points

Brainstorming. A system of idea generation devised by Alex Osborne

Briefing. A short talk providing those with a stake in the outcome a summary of what has been done or still needs to be done to complete a project

Causal reasoning. Reasoning that unites two or more events to prove that one or more of them caused the other

Causal transitions. Transitions that help show the cause-and-effect relationships between ideas

Cause-and-effect order. An organizational pattern in which information is categorized according to whether it is related to a problem's causes or effects

Celebratory speech. A speech to introduce, present or accept an award, or toast a celebrant

Centering. The directing of thoughts internally via a deep or centering breath

Centering breath. A deep breath followed by a strong exhalation

Central idea. The topic statement of a speech

Ceremonial speaking. Special occasion speaking

Channel. A pathway through which a message passes

Chart. A visual aid used to compress or summarize a large amount of information

Chronological order. An organizational format based around time or the order in which things happen

Chronological transitions. Transitions that help in understanding the time relationship between ideas

Claim. An assertion made in arguing; a debatable conclusion

Closed-ended questions. Highly structured questions requiring only that the respondent indicate which of the provided responses most accurately reflects his or her answer to a question

Closed question. A highly structured question seeking a short and precise answer such as yes or no

Closure. A technique designed to achieve psychological symmetry or balance; the speaker refers in the conclusion of a speech to the same ideas explored during the speech's beginning

Co-culture. A group of people who share a culture outside of the dominant culture

Cognitive restructuring. A technique designed to redirect thinking away from body sensations and irrational beliefs to beliefs that promote growth

Commemorative speech. A speech that honors or pays tribute

Commencement address. A speech of inspiration praising and congratulating a graduating class

Common ground. The concerns and interests shared by the speaker and the audience

Communication. A process that involves the attempted sharing of information; the means by which people generate meaning

Complementary transitions. Transitions that help the speaker add one idea to the next

Computer-generated graphics. The use of technology in creating graphics

Concept or expository speech. A speech given to explain or define something intangible or abstract

Conclusion. The ending of a speech; designed to reinforce the central idea or thesis, motivate an appropriate audience response, and achieve closure

Concrete. A description attributed to words that evoke precise meaning; language that is free of jargon

Configural formats. Listener-responsible organizational formats in which examples and stories carry the crux of a message

Connotative meaning. Personal meaning; meaning that is subjective and variable

Contrasting transitions. Transitions that show how the idea that follows differs from the ones that precede it

Coordinate points. Points in an outline that are of equal weight or substance

Coordination. The principle establishing that main points should be relatively equal in importance

Covert lie. An unspoken lie; a lie designed to conceal sensitive information that needs to be said but isn't

Credibility. Audience judgments of a speaker's competence, character, and charisma

Critical thinking. The process of arriving at a judgment only after an honest evaluation of alternatives; the exhibiting of careful and deliberate evaluation of a claim

Cultural diversity. The recognition and valuing of difference

Cultural identity. The internalization of culturally appropriate beliefs, values, and roles acquired through interacting with members of a cultural group; a product of group membership

Culture. The system of knowledge, beliefs, values,

attitudes, behavior, and artifacts that the members of a society learn, accept, and use in daily life

Debate. A form of argument in which two sides take turns presenting pro and con positions, with each side competing to win adherents

Decision-making group. A group whose members seek a consensus regarding what the group should or should not do to solve a problem

Deductive reasoning. Reasoning that takes a known idea or principle and applies it to a situation; reasoning that moves from the general to the specific

Deferred-thesis pattern. A kind of configural format in which the main points of a speech gradually build to the speaker's thesis

Definitions. Statements used to clarify the meaning of words and concepts

Demographic profile. A composite of audience characteristics including age; gender; educational level; racial, ethnic, or cultural ties; group affiliations; and socioeconomic background

Denotative meaning. The dictionary meaning of a word

Derived credibility. Audience perception of a speaker's credibility during the giving of a speech

Descriptions. Words that evoke fresh imagery or sensory response

Dialect. A speech pattern characteristic of a group of people from a particular area or of a specific ethnicity

Digital Divide. The social and/or economic inequality of access to communication technologies

Disinformation. The deliberate spread of false or inaccurate information with the intention of influencing public opinion

Drawings and maps. Visual aids used to illustrate differences, movements, or geographic information

Early concurrence. The tendency to conclude discussion prematurely

Effects of communication. Communication outcomes

Elaboration Likelihood Model of Persuasion. A model predicting the degree to which people will expend energy to think consciously about a message

Elevator pitch. A brief, persuasive message

Emblems. Nonverbal symbols with direct translations that are culturally learned

Empathy. Derived from the Greek word *empatheia*, meaning "feeling into"; the ability to suspend one's own point of view, internalizing or feeling into the cultural values, beliefs, and perspectives of others, in this case the audience

Ethical communication. Communication that presents ideas fairly; the revealing of information receivers need to assess both the message and speaker critically

Ethical speechmaking. Speech that involves the responsible handling of information and an awareness of the outcomes or consequences of a speech

Ethics. An exploration of how values distinguish actions; a society's notions about the rightness and wrongness of behavior

Ethnocentricity. A belief that one's culture is better than others

Ethnocentrism. Judging another culture solely by the standards of your own culture

Ethnocentrism. Judging another culture solely by the standards of your own culture

Ethos. The ability to convince the audience of your good character or credibility

Eulogy. A special form of tribute speech that pays tribute to a deceased person, usually given at a gravesite or at a memorial service

Euphemism. An indirect expression that makes it easier to handle unpleasant subjects

Evaluating. The process of using critical thinking skills to weigh a message's worth

Event/person speech. A speech designed around a remarkable person or compelling event

Evidence. Material used to validate a claim

Expert testimony. Testimony provided by sources recognized as authorities on the topic

Explanations. Clarifying words

Extemporaneous (or presentation) outline. An outline containing brief notes, also known as speakers notes, to remind the speaker of key parts of the speech and references

Extemporaneous speaking. Speaking that is planned and rehearsed but delivered using only a few notes

Fact-finding group. A group whose members share thoughts and information to enhance understanding and learning

Facts. Statements that are verifiably true

False dichotomy. A proposition that requires the audience to choose between two options when in reality there are many

False division. A false statement suggesting that if something is true of the whole, it is also true of one or more of the parts

Feedback. Information received in response to a sent message

Field of experience. The sum of all experiences; the attitudes, values, and lessons one brings to a situation

Figurative analogy. An analogy comparing two things that are distinctively dissimilar

Figurative language. Words that facilitate the picturing of meaning

Framing theory. A theory focusing on the shaping of experience to promote an interpretation

General purpose. The overall purpose of a speech, such as to inform, persuade, or entertain

General purpose. The overall purpose of a speech, such

as to inform, persuade, or entertain

Glittering generality. The use of positive association designed to encourage idea acceptance

Graphs. Visual aids that are designed to communicate statistical information, illustrate trends, and/or demonstrate patterns

Groupthink. The tendency to let a desire for consensus override careful analysis and reasoned decision making

Hasty generalization. The act of being too quick to draw an inference; jumping to a conclusion on the basis of too little evidence

Healthy group. A group in which members support one another, make decisions together, trust one another, have open communication, and aim to excel

Hearing. An involuntary physiological process

Heterogeneous audience. An audience whose members possess dissimilar characteristics, rich in age, attitude, value, and knowledge diversity

High-context communication. Communication that avoids confrontation; communication that relies on indirect messages

Homogeneous audience. An audience whose members possess similar characteristics, such as age, attitude, value, and knowledge similarity

Human visual aid. The use of a real person as a visual or audio aid

Hyperbole. Extreme exaggeration

Hypothetical examples. Examples that have not actually occurred but might

Idea or theory. A speech given to explain or define something intangible or abstract

"I" language. Language of responsibility and ownership

Illustrations. Extended examples or narratives

Illustrators. Gestures to reinforce, clarify, describe, and demonstrate the meaning of your words

Immediacy. A sense of closeness

Impromptu speaking. Speaking that is "off the cuff" and accomplished with little or no notice

Inclusion. The opposite of exclusion and marginalization; the effort to ensure that everyone has an equal opportunity to belong, influence, and be heard

Inductive reasoning. Reasoning that relies on observation and specific instances to build an argument; reasoning progressing from specific observations to a conclusion

Infographic. A composite of information, illustration, and design

Information anxiety. The psychological stress people experience when information overload confuses them or makes it difficult for them to make sense of the never-ending accumulation of information

Information overload. Being given too much information to process or handle

Information underload. Being given too little information; underestimating the amount of information needed

Informative speech. A speech designed to impart new information, a new skill, or a fresh way of thinking about something

Initial credibility. The receiver's perception of a speaker's credibility prior to their speaking

Inspirational speech. Emotionally uplifting speech designed to praise and congratulate such as a commencement speech or a speech to motivate and inspire such as a keynote speech

Internal preview. A speech segment that helps the speaker hold a speech together, by indicating what to look for as a speech progresses

Internal summary. A speech segment that helps the speaker clarify or emphasize what was said

Interpreting. A listening stage during which the focus is on meaning and the decoding of the speaker's message

Interview. A meeting during which questions are asked and answered by both interviewer and interviewee

Introduction. The opening of a speech; designed to capture the audience's attention, build credibility, and orient receivers to what is to follow

Invention. The rhetorical process of discovering what you're going to say and speak about

Jargon and technospeak. Types of specialized language clear only to people with specific knowledge

Keynote address. A speech designed to get a meeting or conference off to a good start by establishing the right tone or mood

Kinesics. The study of body language or human body motion, including gestures, body movements, facial expressions, eye behavior, and posture

Latitudes of acceptance. Messages an audience would not reject

Latitudes of noncommitment. Messages the audience finds neutral

Latitudes of rejection. Messages an audience would not accept

Lay testimony. Peer testimony, the opinions of "ordinary people"

Linear formats. Speech formats by which the main points relate to the topic sentence

Line graph. A graph that shows trends over time

Listening. A voluntary mental process occurring in stages

Literal analogy. An analogy comparing two things from similar classes

Logical fallacy. A flawed reason

Logos. Logical proof demonstrating the reasonableness of argument(s)

Low-context communication. Communication that is direct and addresses issues head-on

Main points. The central themes of a speech; the key ideas that serve as the outline's framework; the subtopics directly supporting the thesis

Main points. The central themes of a speech; the key ideas that serve as the outline's framework; the subtopics directly supporting the thesis

Maintenance leadership behaviors. Roles focused on maintaining the group, including expressing agreement and support

Manuscript reading. A speech in which the speaker delivers a written manuscript word for word

Marginalized group. A group whose members feel like outsiders

Maslow's Hierarchy of Needs. A pyramid progressing from the most basic to the most sophisticated human needs

Message. The content of communication

Metaphor. A direct comparison between two things or ideas

Mindful listening. Staying attentive, maintaining focus, not letting electronic devices serve as distractions, displaying sufficient mental energy to engage fully in the speech-moment including thinking of good questions and providing feedback

Monroe's Motivated Sequence. An organizational framework particularly effective in moving receivers toward accepting and acting on a proposition of policy

Narrative. An extended example or illustration; a story describing what people are doing and why

Narrative pattern. A configural format in which the speaker tells a story or series of stories without stating a thesis or identifying main points

Negative side. The side in a debate seeking to maintain the status quo

Noise. Anything that interferes with the ability to send or receive a message

Norms. The "do's and don'ts" that groups establish to regulate the behavior of members and make it possible for them to work together to attain the group's goals

Object speech. A speech about something tangible

One-sided presentation. A presentation offering only a single perspective on an issue

Onomatopoeia. A word or words that imitate natural sounds

Open-ended questions. Questions allowing a respondent to answer fully and in his or her own words

Open question. A question offering freedom in answering by calling for more than a one-word response

Oral citations. Verbal references

Oratory. Speaking from memory

Outline. A speech skeleton on which main ideas and support are hung

Overt lie. A deliberate lie; a distortion of the facts

Paralinguistics. The study of messages sent using vocal cues

Parallelism. Words, phrases, or sentences that parallel or balance each other; repetition of words, phrases, or sentences

Paraphrase. Restating material in your own words

Pathos. The ability to develop empathy and passion in others

Peer testimony. Testimony provided by lay or ordinary people who possess firsthand experience on a subject

Performance anxiety. A variant of communication anxiety; fear of presenting a speech

Persuasion. The deliberate attempt to change or reinforce attitudes, beliefs, values, or behavior

Pictograph. A simplified infographic; a pictorial representation of a graph's subject

Pie graph. A graph used to illustrate percentages of a whole or distribution patterns

Pitch. The highness or lowness of the voice on a tonal scale; a voice's upward or downward inflection

Pitch. A kind of persuasive or sales presentation during which the speaker attempts to obtain an endorsement for a proposal

Plagiarism. The deliberate or accidental claiming of another's words or ideas as one's own

Playbook. A gameplan for continuous improvement

Podcast. A digital audio recording accessible to Web user

Political correctness. The act of using words that are polite and convey respect for the needs and interests of different groups

Position presentation. A presentation in which the speaker delivers a persuasive argument on a controversial issue

Poster presentation. A graphically based approach to presenting information or research

Post hoc, ergo propter hoc. A logical fallacy asserting that because one event preceded another, it caused it

Presentation aids. Audio and visual stimuli that support and enhance speech content

Primacy-recency effect. The tendency to remember information that is placed at the beginning and end of a speech better than the information that is placed in the middle of the speech

Primacy–recency factor. The tendency to remember what we hear first and last more readily than the content between

Primary question. A question that introduces a topic or area for exploration

Primary research. Original research involving the collection of firsthand data

Probing question. A question that seeks more information

Problem–solution order. An organizational format that divides information into two main parts, the problem and its solution

Procedural behaviors. Activities a leader performs that help facilitate conducting the group's business

Process/procedure and demonstration speech. A speech designed to convey how something works or how to do something

Process anxiety. Fear of preparing a speech

Pronunciation. The accepted way to sound a word; identifying whether the production of the individual sounds used to form a word is correct

Proposition. The relationship the speaker wishes to establish between accepted facts and the speaker's desired conclusions

Proposition of fact. An assertion that something does or does not exist, is or is not true, or is or is not of value; an effort to prove something factual

Proposition of policy. A recommendation for change or no change; a type of persuasive speech focusing on what the speaker thinks should be done

Proposition of value. An assertion of a statement's worth; a type of persuasive speech rendering a judgment about something

Proxemics. The study of space and distance in communication

Psychographics. A description of values, beliefs, and interests, including how members of an audience see themselves, their attitudes, and motives

Public speaking. The act of preparing, staging, and delivering a presentation to an audience

Public speaking. The act of preparing, staging, and delivering a presentation to an audience

Public speaking anxiety. A variant of communication anxiety, made up of process and performance anxiety

Q&A. A question-and-answer session

Racist language. Language discriminatory toward the members of a race; words that express bigoted views

Rate. The speed at which words are spoken

Reasoning from analogy. The process of comparing like things and concluding that because they are comparable in a number of ways, they also are comparable in another, new respect

Reasons approach. The presentation of reasons to justify a speech's goal

Receiver. The recipient of a message; a party to communication

Red herring. A distraction; the process of leading the audience to consider an irrelevant issue

Reflective Thinking Framework. A problem-solving system advanced by John Dewey

Refutation format. The style of debate when one side points out the flaws in the other side's arguments and offers new evidence to support its own claim

Remembering. The mental saving of a message for further use

Repetition. Restatement of the exact same words

Report. A summary of what you have learned or accomplished

Responding. The process of replying and providing feedback

Restatement. Rephrasing an idea in different words to more fully explain it

Rhetorical questions. Questions requiring no overt answer or response

Risky shift. A group phenomenon in which a group makes a decision that is riskier than an individual would make if working alone

Roast. A speech to entertain the audience by poking good-natured fun at an honoree

Roles. Patterns of behavior

S.T.A.R. An acronym for answering interview questions; the letters in S.T.A.R. stand for situation, task, action, and result

Scaled questions. Questions enabling respondents to indicate their views along a continuum or scale

Secondary question. A probing question; a question following up on a primary question

Secondary research. Research carried out with existing data, such as published statistics, texts, and articles by experts, together with media and personal documents

Self-talk. Internal communication; intrapersonal communication

Service learning. A learning project addressing a community or public agency need

Sexist language. Language that suggests the sexes are unequal and that one gender has more status and value and is more capable than another

Signposts. Signaling cues designed to help focus the attention of receivers

Simile. An indirect comparison of dissimilar things, usually with the words *like* or *as*

Situational/cultural context. The setting for communication; the communication environment

Slippery slope. An erroneous assertion that one action will set in motion a chain of events

Small group. A limited number of people who communicate over time to make decisions and accomplish goals

Social Judgment Theory. The claim that an individual's position on an issue depends on their anchor or preferred position on the issue; alternatives classified as acceptable, rejectable, and neutral; and ego-involvement

Sound bite speaking. A short clip of speech promoting or spinning a perspective

Source. The message originator

Spatial order. An organizational framework that uses space as the means of arrangement

Speaker's notes. An extemporaneous or presentation outline

Speaking from memory. Making a speech that is committed to memory and then spoken without using any notes

Specific purpose. A single sentence or infinitive phrase identifying the speaker's goal

Specific purpose. A single sentence or infinitive phrase identifying the speaker's goal

Speech of acceptance. A speech given in response to a speech of presentation

Speech of introduction. A speech designed to create a desire among audience members to listen to a featured speaker

Speech of presentation. A speech presenting an award

Speech of tribute. A form of commemorative speaking honoring a living or dead person or an event

Speech–thought differential. The difference between speaking speed and thinking speed

Speech to entertain. A speech such as a roast or after-dinner speech that may be humorous, whimsical, or mildly satirical that looks at a topic or subject of interest and relevance

Spotlighting. A sexist language practice used to reinforce inequality

Statistics. Numbers summarizing a group of observations

Storytelling. A means of communicating a complex idea clearly and powerfully through words and images

Subordinate points. Information supportive of the main points in a speech; the foundation on which larger ideas are constructed

Subordination. The support underlying an outline's main points

Syllogism. A form of deductive reasoning containing a major premise, minor premise, and claim

Synchronous presentation. An online presentation delivered in real time

Task leadership behaviors. Roles that advance the group's completion of its task

Terminal credibility. The audience's perception of a speaker's credibility after listening to their speech

Testimony. The use of opinions of others to support positions the speaker is taking or to reinforce claims the speaker is making

Thesis. A clear statement or claim about a topic; a means of dividing a speech into its major components

Thesis statement. The expression of a speech's central idea; the claim or core idea of a speech

Thought stopping. A technique designed to control speech anxiety; an example of cognitive restructuring

Topical order. An organizational pattern composed of a series of topics related to the subject

Toulmin's Reasonable Argument Model. A model describing the parts of an argument

Transitions. Words that bridge ideas

Triangle of Meaning. The model depicting the relationship that exists among words, things, and thoughts

Twitter-speak. A sound bite containing no more than 140 characters

Two-sided presentation. A presentation containing two alternative perspectives

Understanding. A stage in listening

Understatement. Drawing attention to an idea by minimizing its importance

Value. Core beliefs; the standards we use to judge that which is good and bad, worthwhile and worthless, ethical and unethical, right and wrong

Value of information. The time, effort, or money that a person is willing to invest in order to possess new information prior to rendering a decision or drawing a conclusion

Values. Core beliefs; the standards we use to judge that which is good and bad, worthwhile and worthless,

ethical and unethical, right and wrong

Verbal references. An oral citation revealing the source

Volume. The loudness or softness of the voice; vocal intensity

Webinar. An online conference

Web pattern. A configural format in which threads of thought refer back to the speaker's central purpose

"We" language. Language indicating shared responsibility

Wiki. A collaborative website whose content is composed and edited by members of the public

NOTES

CHAPTER 1

1. John Wooden and Jay Carty, *Coach Wooden's Pyramid of Success Playbook* (New York: Regal Publishers, 2005): 11; and Nancy Bach, "Why Playbooks are a Must for Successful Continuous Improvement," *Eon*, July 10, 2018, https://www.eonsolutions.io/blog/why-playbooks-are-a-must-for-successful-continuous-improvement.

2. See Chris Anderson, *TED Talks: The Official TED Guide to Public Speaking* (New York: Houghton Mifflin, 2016); and "Speaking About the TED Effect," CBS News, February 7, 2016.

3. See, for example, "Occupational Employment and Wage Statistics," *U.S. Bureau of Labor Statistics*, May 2020, https://www.bls.gov/oes/current/area_emp_chart/area_emp_chart.htm.

4. Chris Anderson, curator of TED Talks, as stated in "How to Overcome Fear and Make Your Voice Heard in 2019," *Financial Times*, December 31, 2018, 8.

5. See, for example, *Job Outlook, 2018*, National Association of Colleges and Employers, https://www.naceweb.org/about-us/press/2017/the-key-attributes-employers-seek-on-students-resumes/ and Hart Research Associates, *Fulfilling the American Dream: Liberal Education and the Future of Work.* ihttps://www.aacu.org/sites/default/files/files/LEAP/2018EmployerResearchReport.pdf, 2018.

6. "Job Outlook," a survey conducted by the National Association of Colleges and Employers (2018). See also "Employers responding to the 2018 Job Outlook survey said problem-solving skills and teamwork ability— beyond a strong GPA—are what they most want to see on students' resumes. Goo,.gl/ztcM7r https://twitter.com/naceorg/status/948242538212872192?lang=en.

7. See, for example, UN/DESA Policy Brief #61: COVID-19: Embracing Digital Government during the Pandemic and Beyond," April 14, 2020, https://www.un.org/development/desa/dpad/publication/un-desa-policy-brief-61-covid-19-embracing-digital-government-during-the-pandemic-and-beyond/.

8. Cathy Cassata, "How President Joe Biden Is Giving Hope to Millions Who Stutter," *Healthline*, January 28, 2021, https://www.healthline.com/health-news/how-president-joe-biden-is-giving-hope-to-millions-who-stutter.

9. See, for example, A. Ville and J. Biggs, *Grace Under Pressure* (United Kingdom: Lulu Press, 2004); and David Angeron, *The Mental Training Guide for Elite Athletes.* (New Orleans, LA: John Melvin Publishing, 2020).

10. Richard H. Cox, *Sport Psychology: Concepts and Applications*, 7th ed. (New York: McGraw-Hill, 2012).

11. "How to Overcome Fear and Make Your Voice Heard in 2019," *Financial Times*, December 31, 2018, 8.

12. David Wallechinsky, Irving Wallace, and Amy Wallace, *The Book of Lists.* (New York: Morrow, 1977), 469. See also K. K. Dwyer and M. M. Davidson, "Is Public Speaking Really More Feared Than

Death?" *Communication Research Reports*, 29 (April-June 2012): 99–107 and Christopher Ingraham, "America's Top Fears: Public Speaking, Heights and Bugs," *Washington Post*, October 30, 2014, https://www.washingtonpost.com/news/wonk/wp/2014/10/30/clowns-are-twice-as-scary-to-democrats-as-they-are-to-republicans/.

13. See, for example, Rosemary Black, "Glossophobia (Fear of Public Speaking): Are You Glossophic?" *PsyCom*, September 12, 2019, https://www.psycom.net/glossophobia-fear-of-public-speaking#:~:text=Glossophobia%2C%20or%20a%20fear%20of,full%2Don%20panic%20and%20fear; and Nathan Heller, "Tips for Public Speakers," *The New Yorker*, February 8, 2021, 25.

14. See, for example, Ralph R. Behnke, Amber N. Finn, and Chris R. Sawyer, "Audience Perceived Anxiety Patterns of Public Speakers," *Communication Quarterly* 51, no. 4 (2003): 470–81; Roper Starch, "How Americans Communicate," a poll commissioned by the National Communication Association (1999), "Anxious about Public Speaking? Your Smart Speaker Could Help," *Science Daily*, April 25, 2020, https://www.sciencedaily.com/releases/2020/04/200425094114.htm; and Farhan Raja, "Anxiety Level in Students of Public Speaking: Causes and Remedies," *Journal of Education and Educational Development 4:1*, June 2017, 94–110. https://files.eric.ed.gov/fulltext/EJ1161521.pdf.

15. Amy M. Bippus and John A. Daly, "What Do People Think Causes Stage Fright? Native Attributions About the Reasons for Public Speaking Anxiety," *Communication Education* 48 (April 1999): 63–72; Carmine Gallo, "How Adele is Managing Stage Fright," *Forbes.com*, December 5, 2015, https://www.forbes.com/sites/carminegallo/2015/12/05/how-adele-is-managing-stage-fright/?sh=c0865267faf0; and Sara Tijou, "Adele Should Read Read This Advice on Stage Fright," BBC News, March 27, 2017, https://www.bbc.com/news/newsbeat-39404666.

16. David Wallechinsky, "Irving Wallace, and Amy Wallace," 469.

17. L. LeFebvre, L.E. LeFebvre, and M. Allen, "Training the Butterflies to Fly in Formation: Cataloguing Student Fears About Public Speaking," *Communication Education 67, no. 3* (2018): 348–62.

18. Joe Ayres, "Perception of Speaking Ability: An Explanation for Speech Fright," *Communication Education*, July 1986, 275–87; and Theo Tsaousides, "Why Are We Scared of Public Speaking?" *Psychology Today*, November 27, 2017, https://www.psychologytoday.com/us/blog/smashing-the-brainblocks/201711/why-are-we-scared-public-speaking.

19. See, e.g., Bernardo J. Carducci with Phillip G. Zimbardo, "Are You Shy?" *Psychology Today*, November/December 1995, 34-41, 64–70, 78–82; and Sarah Keating, "The Science Behind Why Some of Us Are Shy," *BBC*, June 5, 2019, https://www.bbc.com/future/article/20190604-the-science-behind-why-some-of-us-are-shy.

20. Apprehension has long been addressed by communication scholars and practitioners. See, for example, D. W. Klopf, "Cross Cultural Apprehension Research: A Summary of Pacific Basin Studies," in J. A. Daly and J. A. McCroskey, eds., *Avoiding Communication: Shyness, Reticence, and Communication Apprehension.* (Beverly Hills, CA: Sage, 1984), 157–69; D. W. Klopf and R. E. Cambra, "Communication Apprehension Among College Students in America, Australia, Japan, and Korea," *Journal of Psychology* 102 (1979): 27–31; S. M.

Ralston, R. Ambler, and J. N. Scudder, "Reconsidering the Impact of Racial Differences in the College Public Speaking Classroom on Minority Student Communication Anxiety," *Communication Reports*, 4 (1991): 43–50, and Stephen M. Croucher et al., "A Cross Cultural Analysis of Communication Apprehension: A Comparison of Three European Nations," *Journal of Intercultural Communication 38*, July 2015, https://www.researchgate.net/publication/280776063_A_Cross-Cultural_Analysis_of_Communication_Apprehension_A_Comparison_of_Three_European_Nations.

21. Virginia P. Richmond and James P. McCroskey, *Communication: Apprehension, Avoidance, and Effectiveness*, 3rd ed. (Scottsdale, AZ: Gorsuch Scarisbrick, 1992); and Farhan Raja, "Anxiety Level in Students of Public Speaking," 94–110. https://files.eric.ed.gov/fulltext/EJ1161521.pdf.

22. See Sue Shellenbarger, "Strike a Powerful Pose," *Wall Street Journal*, August 21, 2013, D1, D2.

23. See Hattie C. Cooper, *Thriving With Social Anxiety: Daily Strategies for Overcoming Anxiety and Building Self Confidence* (Berkeley, CA: Althea Press, 2014); Ian Robertson, *The Stress Test: How Pressure Can Make You Stronger and Sharper*

(New York: Bloomsbury, 2016); and Mary Marcel, "Communication Apprehension Across the Career Span," *International Journal of Business Communication*, June 22, 2019, https://journals.sagepub.com/doi/abs/10.1177/2329488419856803.

24. See, for example, Scott Jeffrey, "How to Find Your Center," https://scottjeffrey.com/center-yourself/; K. Haddad and P. Tremayne, "The Effects of Centering on the Free-Throw Shooting Performance of Young Athletes," *Sport Psychologist* 23 (2009): 118–136.

25. See, for example, Karin Nordin and Melissa A. Broeckelman-Post, "Can I Get Better? Exploring Mindset Theory in the Introductory Communication Course," *Communication Education* 68, no. 1 (January 2019): 44–60.

26. See, for example, L. Kelly, "Social Skills Training as a Mode of Treatment for Social Communication Problems," in *Avoiding Communication: Shyness, Reticence, and Communication Apprehension*, eds. J. A. Daly and J. C. McCroskey (Beverly Hills, CA: Sage, 1984), 189–207; and G. M. Phillips, "Rhetoritherapy Versus the Medical Model: Dealing With Reticence," *Communication Education* 26 (1977): 34–43; and Karla

M. Hunter, Joshua N. Westwick, and Laurie L. Haleta, "Assessing Success: The Impacts of a Fundamentals of Speech Course on Decreasing Public Speaking Anxiety," *Communication Education 63* (2014): 124–35.

27. Eric Finzi, *Face of Emotion: How Botox Affects Our Mood and Relationships* (New York: Palgrave Macmillan, 2013).

28. Karen Weintraub, "Turning a Frown Upside-Down May Help Lessen Depression," *USA Today*, January 29, 2013, 6D.

29. Theodore Clevenger Jr., "A Synthesis of Experimental Research in Stage Fright," *Quarterly Journal of Speech* 45 (April 1959): 136.

30. J. A. Daly et al., "Pre-Performance Concerns Associated With Public Speaking Anxiety," *Communication Quarterly* 37 (1989): 39–53; and Marcel Takac, et. al. "Public Speaking Anxiety Decreases With Repeated Virtual Reality Training Sessions," *PLoS One*, 14, no. 5 (2019). https://www.ncbi.nlm.nih.gov/pmc/articles/PMC6544213/.

31. Azi Paybarah, "Louisville May Become Latest City to Declare Racism a Public Health Crisis," *New York Times*, July 30, 2020.

32. Developed as part of an exercise in a public speaking class at

the New York Institute of Technology. Students examined an online site, "Welcome to Lily's Hometown: Shanghai, China," h ttp://linguistlist.or g/fund-drive/2008/ hometown-tour/lily/ index.htm, and were then asked to create a speech as if Shanghai was their hometown. New York Institute of Technology offered degrees in New York, China, and the Middle East.

CHAPTER 2

1. Janet Barow, "14 Cultural Faux Pas Around the World," *ALTA*, June 20, 2019, https:/ /www.altalang.com/ beyond-words/14-cultural-faux-pas-around-the-world/.

2. Melissa Hahn and Andy Molinsky, "How to Recover From a Cultural Faux-Pas," *Harvard Business Review*, June 12, 2018, https://hbr. org/2018/04/how-to-recover-from-a-cultural-faux-pas.

3. See, for example, Gaby Hinsliff, "How to Be Heard: The Art of Public Speaking," *The Guardian*, October 21, 2018, https:// www.theguardian.com/l ifeandstyle/2018/oct/21/ art-of-speaking-up-for-yourself; and Gail L. Thompson, "Teachers' Cultural Ignorance Imperils Student

Success," *USA Today*, May 29, 2002, 13A.

4. William H. Fry, "The Nation Is Diversifying Even Quicker Than Predicted According to New Census Data," *Brookings*, July 1, 2020, https://www .brookings.edu/research /new-census-data-shows-the-nation-is-diversifying-even -faster-than-predicted /; and Tara Bahrampour and Ted Mellnik, "Census Data Shows Widening Diversity; Number of White People Falls for the First Time," *Washington Post*, August 12, 2021, https://www.washingto npost.com/dc-md-va/2 021/08/12/census-data -race-ethnicity-neighbo rhoods/.

5. Bahrampour and Mellnik; and Paul Overberg and John McCormick, "Census Data Show America's White Population Shrank for the First Time," *Wall Street Journal*, August 12, 2021, https://www.wsj.com/ articles/census-race-population-redistricting-changes-11628714807.

6. "New Census Bureau Report Analyzes U.S. Population Projections," March 3, 2015, https://w ww.census.gov/newsro om/press-releases/201 5/cb15-tps16.html; and William H. Frey, "Less Than Half of Children Under 15 are White," *Brookings*, June 24, 2019, https://www.brookings. edu/research/less-than

-half-of-us-children -under-15-are-white -census-shows/.

7. Wendy Griswold, *Cultures and Societies in a Changing World* (Thousand Oaks, CA: Pine Forge Press, 1994): 1; see also "Nine Tips for High Impact Presentations Across Cultures," *GlobeSmart*, https://w ww.globesmart.com /blog/9-tips-for-high -impact-presentations -across-cultures/.

8. Ibid.

9. See Larry A. Samovar et al., *Communication Between Cultures*, 9th ed. (Boston, MA: Wadsworth, 2017), 220–230.

10. Robert R. Harris and Robert T. Moran, *Managing Cultural Differences*, 3rd ed. (Houston, TX: Gulf, 1991).

11. D. Tannen, *You Just Don't Understand: Women and Men in Conversation* (New York: Morrow, 1990).

12. Susan Goldberg, "A Note From Our Editor: Six Words About Race," *National Geographic*, June 6, 2021.

13. Anna Marie Chavez, "Why Girls Matter," *Vital Speeches of the Day*, March 2016, 85–87.

14. Sarah Maslin Nir, "In Diverse City, Audiences Where Every Joke Translates," *New York Times*, March 5, 2013, A20, A22.

15. Louis A. Day, *Ethics in Media Communications: Cases and Controversies*,

2nd ed. (Belmont, CA: Wadsworth, 1991), 2. See also the 5th ed. (2006).

16. Melissa Korn, "Does an 'A' in Ethics Have Any Value?" *Wall Street Journal,* February 7, 2013, B4.

17. See Sissela Bok, *Lying* (New York: Pantheon, 1978); Sissela Bok, *Secrets* (New York: Random House, 1989); Paul Ekman, *Telling Lies: Clues to Deceit in the Marketplace, Politics, and Marriage* (New York: W. W. Norton, 2009); Stephen M. Cahn and Peter Markie, *Ethics: History, Theory and Contemporary Issues* (New York: Oxford University Press, 2015); and Daniel J. Levitin, *A Field Guide to Lies* (New York: Dutton, 2016).

18. See, for example, Ira Hyman, "Why Disinformation Campaigns Are Dangerous," *Psychology Today,* January 15, 2021, https://www.psychologytoday.com/us/blog/mental-mishaps/2021 01/why-disinformation -campaigns-are-dangerous.

19. Adetokunbo F. Knowles-Borishade, "Paradigm for Classical African Orature," in *Diversity in Public Communication: A Reader,* eds. Christine Kelly et al. (Dubuque, IA: Kendall-Hunt, 1995), 100.

20. Larry A. Samovar et al., *Communication Between Cultures* 220–230.

21. See, for example, Albert Rutherford, *The Art of Thinking Critically: Ask Great Questions, Spot Illogical Reasoning, and Make Sharp Arguments* (New York: Kindle, 2020); Vincent Ryan Ruggiero, *Thinking Critically About Ethical Issues,* 7th ed. (New York: McGraw-Hill), 2008.

22. Marie Hattingh et al., "The Use of Critical Thinking to Identify Fake News: A Systematic Literature Review," *Responsible Design, Implementation and Use of Information and Communication Technology,* March 10, 2020, https://www.ncbi.nlm.nih.gov/pmc/articles/PMC713 4234/.

23. Donald Hatcher, "Critical Thinking: A New Definition and Defense," *Inquiry* 20, no. 1 (June 28, 2000): 3–8; and W. James Potter, *Media Literacy* (Los Angeles, Sage: 2019).

24. Holger Kluge, "Reflections on Diversity," *Vital Speeches of the Day,* January 1997, 171.

CHAPTER 3

1. Joanna Nikas, "No More Small Talk," *The New York Times,* September 28, 2017, D6.

2. Daniel Ames, Lily Benjamin Maissen, and Joel Brockner, "The Role of Listening in Interpersonal Influence," *Journal of Research in Personality* 46 (2012): 345–49; and Kate Murphy, "Listening During a Pandemic," *New York Times,* May 5, 2020, https://www.nytimes.com/2020/05/05/well/family/listening-coronavirus.html?referringSource=a rticleShare.

3. See, for example, Virginia Q. Tilley and Kevin C. Dunn, "Hobart and William Smith Professors Give Powell's Speech a Failing Grade," Hobart and William Smith Colleges, February 15–17, 2003; and Alexander Cockburn, "Colin Powell and the Great 'Intelligence Fraud,'" *The Nation,* March 3, 2003, http://www.counter punch.org/2003/02/15/colin-powell-and-the-great-quot-intelligence-fraud-quot/.

4. Jancee Dunn, "Become a Better Listener. Your Family Will Thank You," *New York Times,* October 19, 2020, https://www.nytimes.com/2020/10/19/parenting/active-listening-communication-advice.html?referringSource=a rticleShare.

5. Judi Brownell, *Listening: Attitudes, Principles, and Skills,* 3rd ed. (Boston: Allyn & Bacon, 2006); and Nixaly Leonardo, *Active Listening Techniques* (Emeryville, CA: Rockridge Press, 2020).

6. Daniela Hernandez, "Trick of the Ear: 'Yanny' or 'Laurel,'" *The Wall Street Journal,* May 18, 2018, A3; Jefferson Graham and Brett Molina,

"First It Was 'The Dress,' Now This: Do You Hear 'Laurel' or 'Yanny'"? *USA Today*, May 17, 2018, 3B.

7. William B. Gudykunst, *Bridging Differences*, 14th ed. (Thousand Oaks, CA: Sage, 2004), 196–97.

8. See Richard Paul, Critical Thinking: What Every Person Needs to Survive in a Rapidly Changing World (Rohnert Park, CA: Center for Critical Thinking, 1990).

9. See, for example, R. Emanuel et al., "How College Students Spend Their Time Communicating," *International Journal of Listening* 22 (2008): 13–28; William Pauk, *How to Study in College* (Boston: Houghton Mifflin, 1989), 121–33.

10. Kevin Roose, "Preparing for a World of Lies and Half-Truths," *The New York Times*, December 18, 2018, B1, B5.

11. Markham Heid, "Is Listening to Music Good for Your Health?" *Time*, May 14, 2018, 23.

12. See also Chapter 4. For additional insight into empathic listening, also see Judi Brownell, *Listening: Attitudes and Skills*, 5th ed. (New York: Routledge, 2012).

13. Ralph G. Nichols and Leonard A. Stevens, *Are You Listening?* (New York: McGraw-Hill, 1957).

14. Ryan W. Miller, "Cold Offices Could Make Women Less Productive at Work, Study Finds,"

USA Today, May 23, 2019, https://www.usatoday.com/story/news/health/2019/05/23/cold-offices-may-hurting-womens-productivity-study-says/1204020001/.

15. See, for example, David Glenn, "Divided Attention: In an Age of Classroom Multitasking, Scholars Probe the Nature of Learning and Memory," *Chronicle of Higher Education*, February 28, 2010, http://chronicle.com/article/Scholars-Turn-Their-Attention/63746; Faith Brynie, "The Madness of Multitasking," *Psychology Today*, Brain Sense blog, August 24, 2009, https://www.psychologytoday.com/blog/brain-sense/200908/the-madness-multitasking; Travis Bradbury, "Multitasking Damages Your Brain and Career New Studies Suggest," *Forbes*, October 8, 2014, https://www.forbes.com/sites/travisbradberry/2014/10/08/multitasking-damages-your-brain-and-career-new-studies-suggest/#6774266e56ee; and Mehruz Kamal, Stephen Kevlin, and Yangyan Dong, "Investigating Multitasking With Technology in Academic Settings," (SAIS 2016 Proceedings 16), https://aisel.aisnet.org/sais2016/16.

16. For more information on the relationship between

note-taking and listening, see Robert Bostrom and Bruce Searle, "Encoding Media, Affect and Gender," in *Listening Behavior: Measurement and Application*, ed. Robert Bostrom (New York: Guilford, 1990), 28–30; and Florence L. Wolff et al., *Perceptive Listening* (Englewood Cliffs, NJ: Prentice Hall, 1983), 88–97.

17. See, for example, Elizabeth Harper, "The Best Way to Take Notes," May 31, 2018, https://www.techlicious.com/tip/best-note-taking-apps-and-devices/.

18. See also Ariana Huffington, "Give Compassionate Feedback While Still Being Constructive," *New York Times*, February 24, 2020, https://www.nytimes.com/2020/02/24/smarter-living/how-to-give-helpful-feedback.html?referringSource=articleShare.

CHAPTER 4

1. Lane Cooper, *The Rhetoric of Aristotle: An Expanded Translation With Supplementary Examples for Students of Composition and Public Speaking* (New York: Appleton-Century-Crofts, 1960), 136.

2. See, for example, A. Finlayson, J. Martin, and K. Phillips, *Rhetorical Audience Studies and Reception of Rhetoric* (Norway:

Palgrave Macmillan, 2018).

3. Peggy Noonan, *What I Saw at the Revolution* (New York: Ivy Books, 1990), 70–72.

4. Ellen DeGeneres, Tulane commencement speech (2009), https://www.goodnet.org/articles/1087.

5. *Stanford News,* "2021 Commencement Address by Dr. Atul Gawande," June 12, 2021, https://news.stanford.edu/2021/06/12/2021-commencement-address-dr-atul-gawande/.

6. Lynne C. Lancaster and David Stillman, *When Generations Collide* (New York: Harper, 2002), 1–32.

7. See Pew Research Center, "Millennials. Confident. Connected. Open to Change," *Executive Summary,* http://www.pewsocialtrends.org/2010/02/24/millennials-confident-connected-open-to-change.

8. See, for example, Jeanne Twenge, *iGen: Why Today's Super Connected Kids Are Growing Up Less Rebellious, More Tolerant, Less Happy—and Completely Unprepared for Adulthood—and What That Means for the Rest of Us* (New York: Simon & Schuster, 2017); and Kristin Bialic and Richard Fry, "Millennial Life: How Young Adulthood Today Compares With Prior Generations," *Pew Research,* January 30, 2019, https://www.pewresearch.org/social-trends/2019/02/14/millennial-life-how-young-adulthood-today-compares-with-prior-generations-2/.

9. Deep Patel, "8 Ways Generation Z Will Differ From Millennials in the Workplace," *Fortune,* September 21, 2017, https://www.forbes.com/sites/deeppatel/2017/09/21/8-ways-generation-z-will-differ-from-millennials-in-the-work-place/#db2e49976e5e.

10. Joe Pinsker, Oh No, They've Come Up With Another Generation," *The Atlantic,* February 21, 2020, https://apple.news/AGyXy4z3C-QvSZQ36Krkd6Ng.

11. Deborah Tannen, *You Just Don't Understand* (New York: Ballantine, 1992), 42.

12. See Carl Iver Hovland, Irving Lester Janis, and Harold H. Kelley, *Communication and Persuasion* (New Haven, CT: Yale University Press, 1961), 183.

13. See William J. McGuire, "Persuasion, Resistance and Attitude Change," in *Handbook of Communication,* eds. I. Pool et al. (Skokie, IL: Rand McNally, 1973), 216–252.

14. Alfred Joyner, "Who Is Ali Stoker? 'Oklahoma Actress Becomes First Wheelchair User to Win Tony Award," *Newsweek,* June 10, 2019, https://www.newsweek.com/who-ali-stroker-oklahoma-actress-becomes-first-wheelchair-user-win-tony-award-1443066.

15. Richard D. Lewis, *When Cultures Collide: Leading Across Cultures,* 3rd ed. (Boston: Intercultural Press, 2005); and Teri Kwal Gamble and Michael W. Gamble, *The Intercultural Communication Playbook* (Thousand Oaks, CA: SAGE. 2023).

CHAPTER 5

1. Robbie Duschinsky, "Tabula Rasa and Human Nature," *Philosophy* 87, no. 04 (October 2012): 509–529, https://www.researchgate.net/publication/259425824_Tabula_Rasa_and_Human_Nature.

2. See, for example, Aaron K. Chatterji and Michael W. Toffel, "The New CEO Activists," *Harvard Business Review,* January/February, 2018, https://hbr.org/2018/01/the-new-ceo-activists; Andrew Dugan, "The Secret of Choosing Successful Speech Topics," *Six Minutes: Speaking and Presentation Skills,* October 25, 2010, http://sixminutes.dlugan.com/speech-topics/. For an analysis of topics used in

speeches by leaders of the largest corporations in the United States, see Robert J. Meyers and Martha Stout Kessler, "Business Speeches: A Study of the Themes in Speeches by America's Corporate Leaders," *Journal of Business Communication* 17, no. 3 (1980): 5–17.

3. See, for example, Nathan Crick, *Rhetorical Public Speaking: Civic Engagement in the Digital Age*, 3rd ed. (New York: Routledge, 2017).

4. For a discussion on brainstorming by a key developer of the process, see Alex F. Osborn, *Applied Imagination* (New York: Scribner, 1962); see also Lonnie Pacelli, *The Perfect Brainstorm: Getting the Most Out of Brainstorming Sessions* (New York: Pacelli Publishing, 2010).

5. James Endrst, "'On Looking' Peers Into Our Attention-Deficient Lives," *USA Today,* January 29, 2013, 2D; and Ben Healy, "Attention, Please: The Highs and Lows of Chronic Distraction," *The Atlantic*, December 2018, 17.

6. For a variation on this technique, see R. R. Allen and Ray E. McKerron, *The Pragmatics of Public Communication*, 3rd ed. (Dubuque, IA: Kendall-Hunt, 1985), 42–44.

7. Motoko Rich, "Tokyo Olympics Open to a Sea of Empty Seats," *New York Times,* July 23, 2021, https://www.nytimes.com/2021/07/23/world/asia/tokyo-olympics-opening-ceremony.html.

8. David Livermore, *Leading With Cultural Intelligence* (New York: AMACOM, 2010); and Vanessa Elle, "10 Things That Are Normal in North America, That Are Rude in Other Cultures," *The Travel,* September 19, 2019, https://www.thetravel.com/things-normal-in-north-america-and-rude-in-other-cultures/.

9. See also Richard D. Lewis, *When Cultures Collide* (London: Nicholas Brealey, 1996).

10. See, for example, "The Best Brainstorming Tools for 2019," *Lifewire,* https://www.lifewire.com/best-brainstorming-tools-4157812; B. Kirchner, "MindMap Your Way to an Idea: Here Is One Approach to Rooting Out Workable Topics That Move You," *Writer* 122, no. 3 (2009): 28–29.

CHAPTER 6

1. We thank the reference librarians at both the College of New Rochelle and the New York Institute of Technology for their invaluable input for this section.

2. Radoslav Ch, "How Many Websites Are There? How Many Are Active in 2022?" *Hosting Tribunal*, April 6, 2022, https://webtribunal.net/blog/how-many-websites/#gref

3. H. Fleshler, J. Ilardo, and J. Demorectsky, "The Influence of Field Dependence, Speaker Credibility Set, and Message Documentation on Evaluations of Speaker and Message Credibility," *Southern Speech Communication Journal* 39 (Summer 1974): 389–402.

4. Dethia Ricks and Roni Rabin, "Panel's Ties to Drugmakers Not Cited in New Cholesterol Guidelines," *Newsday.com*, July 15, 2004.

5. "Inaugural Address by President Joseph R. Biden," *The White House,* January 20, 2021, https://www.whitehouse.gov/briefing-room/speeches-remarks/2021/01/20/inaugural-address-by-president-joseph-r-biden-jr/.

6. See Gordon Pennycook and David Rand, "Why Do People Fall for Fake News?" *New York Times,* January 20, 2019, SR12.

7. To learn more about citation formats, see the *Publication Manual of the American Psychological Association*, 7th ed. (Washington, DC: APA, 2020), and *The MLA Handbook for Writers of Research Papers*, 9th ed. (New York: Modern Language Association, 2021).

CHAPTER 7

1. Nancy Duarte, *Resonate: Present Visual Stories That Transform Audiences* (New York: Wiley, 2010).

2. In part, the student based the examples on information appearing in Rachel Feinzeig, "The Lies We Tell During Job Interviews," *Wall Street Journal*, January 10, 2021, https://www.wsj.com/articles/the-lies-we-tell-during-job-interviews-11610326800.

3. Barack Obama, excerpted from his speech before the Democratic National Convention, July 27, 2004, Boston, MA.

4. Ron Reagan, excerpt from his speech before the Democratic National Convention, July 27, 2004, Boston, MA.

5. See Kara Yorio, "Everyone Can Benefit From Understanding Tourette's," *The Record*, May 26, 2015, BL 1–2.

6. Bernie Sanders, "What Foreign Policy Is," *Vital Speeches of the Day*, November 2017, 316.

7. See Amy, McKeever, "What Is a Derecho, and Why Is It So Destructive?" *National Geographic.com*, August 12, 2020, https://www.nationalgeographic.com/environment/natural-disasters/what-is-a-derecho-and-why-is-it-so-destructive/.

8. Andrea S. Libresco, "We Are All Public Officials," *Vital Speeches of the Day*, November 2012, 350.

9. Reuters, "Confirmed Corona Virus May Force Americans to Avoid Crowds and Cancel Cruises; U.S. Cases Near 550," March 9, 2020, https://www.cnbc.com/2020/03/09/confirmed-coronavirus-may-force-americans-to-avoid-crowds-and-cancel-cruises-us-cases-near-550.html.

10. See Hans Hoeken and Lettica Hustinx, "When Is Statistical Evidence Superior to Anecdotal Evidence in Supporting Probability Claims? The Role of Argument Type," *Human Communication Research* 35 (2009): 491–510; Neil J. Salkind, *Statistics for People Who (Think They) Hate Statistics*, 4th ed. (Thousand Oaks, CA: SAGE, 2011).

11. "The State of America's Children 2020," https://www.childrensdefense.org/policy/resources/soac-2020-gun-violence/.

12. See, for example, Cynthia Crossen, *Tainted Truth: The Manipulation of Fact in America* (New York: Simon & Schuster, 1994).

13. See Cancer Facts and Figures 2021, https://www.cancer.org/research/cancer-facts-statistics/all-cancer-facts-figures/cancer-facts-figures-2021.html.

14. Kelly Leigh Cooper, "The Deadly Problem With U.S. College Fraternities," *BBC News*, November 17, 2017, https://www.bbc.com/news/world-us-canada-42014128.

15. Lauran Neergaard and Hannah Fingerhut, "Poll: Most in U.S. Who Remain Unvaccinated Need Convincing," *Associated Press*, May 11, 2021, https://apnews.com/article/coronavirus-pandemic-health-0f0b89c8060da6dcce74057d2324dc44.

16. Becky McKay, "Homeless Children: A National Crisis," in *Winning Orations, 1990* (Mankato, MN: Interstate Oratorical Association, 1990), 42.

CHAPTER 8

1. To increase understanding of how the arrangement of information affects message reception, see Dacia Charlesworth, "Re-presenting Subversive Songs: Applying Strategies for Invention and Arrangement to Nontraditional Speech Texts," *Communication Teacher* 24, no. 3 (July 2010): 122–26; and Jens E. Kjeldsen, "Audience Analysis and Reception Studies of Rhetoric," in *Rhetorical Audience Studies and Reception of Rhetoric*, ed.

Kjeldsen J (Cham, Rhetoric, Politics and Society. Palgrave Macmillan, 2018). https://doi.org/10.1007/978-3-319-61618-6_1.

2. Ernest C. Thompson, "An Experimental Investigation of the Relative Effectiveness of Organizational Structure in Oral Communication," *Southern Speech Journal* 26 (1960): 59–69. Though conducted more than a half- century ago, this study is still relevant. See also S. J. E. Langeslag, "Effects of Organization and Disorganization on Pleasantness, Calmness, and the Frontal Negativity in the Event-related Potential," *PLoS ONE* 13, no. 8 (2018) Article e0202726. https://doi.org/10.1371/journal.pone.0202726.

3. Christopher Spicer and Ronald Bassett, "The Effect of Organization Learning From an Informative Message," *Southern Speech Communication Journal* 41 (Spring 1976): 290–99; for a scholarly discussion of what we can learn about organization from an orderly universe, see Margaret J. Wheatley, *Leadership and the New Science* (San Francisco: Berrett-Koehler, 1994).

4. See, for example, Sumi Yoon, "Is Korean Really a Listener-Responsible Language Like Japanese? A Contrastive Analysis of Discourse in Apologies Between Korean and Japanese," *Acta Linguistica Asiatica*, 1, no. 3 (January 2011): 73–94. https://www.researchgate.net/publication/276031300_Is_Korean_Really_a_Listener-Responsible_Language_like_Japanese_A_Contrastive_Analysis_of_Discourse_in_Apologies_between_Korean_and_Japanese.

5. See, for example, J. Hinds, "Reader Versus Writer Responsibility: A New Typology," in *Writing Across Languages: Analysis of 1.2 Written Text*, eds. Ulla Connor and Robert B. Kapan (Reading, MA: Addison- Wesley, 1986), 141–52.

6. See, for example, Arran Gare, "Narratives and Culture: The Role of Stories in Self-Creation," *Telos* (Winter 2002); Jessica Lee Shumake, "Reconceptualizing Communication and Rhetoric From a Feminist Perspective," *Guidance & Counseling* (Summer 2002); and Lani Peterson, "The Science Behind the Art of Storytelling," *Harvard Business Review*, November 14, 2017, https://www.harvardbusiness.org/the-science-behind-the-art-of-storytelling/.

7. Richard Nisbett, *The Geography of Thought: How Asians and Westerners Think Differently... and Why* (New York: Free Press, 2003).

8. National Public Radio, "Analysis: Geography of Thought," *Talk of the Nation* broadcast of interview of Richard Nisbett by Neal Conan, March 3, 2003.

9. Ibid.

CHAPTER 9

1. Alternative approaches to outlining abound. For alternatives, see Christina G. Paxman, "Map Your Way to Speech Success! Employing Mind Mapping as a Speech Preparation Technique," *Communication Teacher 25*, no. 1 (January 2011): 7–11; and "The Mad-Lib From Hell: Three Alternatives to Traditional Outlining," January 21, 2019, http://ucwbling.chicagolandwritingcenters.org/the-mad-lib-from-hell-three-alternatives-to-traditional-outlining/.

2. "Housing Discrimination: Last Week Tonight With John Oliver—Transcript," *Scraps From the Loft*, July 26, 2021, https://scrapsfromtheloft.com/2021/07/26/housing-discrimination-last-week-tonight-with-john-oliver-transcript/.

CHAPTER 10

1. For an update on this, see Saeed Shaflee Sabet, Carsten Griwodz, and

Sebasian Miller, "Influence of Primacy, Recency and Peak Effects on the Game Experience Questionnaire," *Proceedings of the 11th ACM Workshop in Immersive Mixed and Virtual Environment Systems,* June 2018, 22–27, https://doi.org/10.1145/3304113.3326113.

2. William M. Jennings, "The Story of the Lost Corpse," *Vital Speeches of the Day,* November 2012, 359.

3. See, for example, Steven D. Cohen, "The Art of Public Narrative: Teaching Students How to Construct Memorable Anecdotes," *Communication Teacher* 25, no. 4 (October 2011): 197–204.

4. The speaker cited this article: Sarah E. Needleman, "Videogame Skills Score With Employers," *The Wall Street Journal,* March 7, 2019, B6.

5. Barack Obama, "Anti-Semitism Is on the Rise. We Cannot Deny It," *Vital Speeches of the Day,* March 2016, 87–89.

6. See Charles R. Gruner, "Advice to the Beginning Speaker on Using Humor—What the Research Tells Us," *Communication Education* 34 (April 1988): 142–47.

7. Conan O'Brien, commencement address at Dartmouth, https://www.dartmouth.edu/~commence/news/speeches/2011/obrien-speech.html.

8. Ann Marie Ursini, "Subtitle Nation," *Winning Orations* (Mankato, MN: Interstate Oratorical Association, 2003).

9. John M. Murphy, "Inventing Authority: Bill Clinton, Martin Luther King Jr., and the Orchestration of Rhetorical Traditions," *Quarterly Journal of Speech* 83 (1997): 71–89.

10. William J. Clinton, "Remarks to the Eighth Annual Holy Convocation of the Church of God in Christ," in *Selected Speeches of President William Jefferson Clinton* (Washington, DC: President of the United States, 1991), 21.

11. Ibid.

12. Alicia Croshal, "Gossip: It's Worth Talking About," in *Winning Orations, 1991* (Mankato, MN: Interstate Oratorical Association, 1991), 1.

13. See Daniel Rose, "Message, Messenger Audience," *Vital Speeches of the Day,* December 2012, 392.

14. From a speech developed by students in 2018 during a workshop in the basic course at the New York Institute of Technology.

15. Romaine Seguin, "Becoming Visible: Insights for Working Women From the Women of Hidden Figures," *Vital Speeches of the Day,* October 2017, 306.

16. Ronald Berenbeim, "Ethical Leadership—Winning With Integrity," *Vital Speeches of the Day,* January 2017, 25.

17. Denalie Silha, "Rediscovering a Lost Resource," in *Winning Orations, 1991* (Mankato, MN: Interstate Oratorical Association, 1991), 81.

18. See Margaret Sullivan, "By Bearing Witness—and Hitting 'Record'—17-Year-Old Darnella Frazier May Have Changed the World," *Washington Post,* April 20, 2021, https://www.washingtonpost.com/lifestyle/media/darnella-frazier-george-floyd-trial/2021/04/20/9e261cc6-a1e2-11eb-a774-7b47ce-b36ee8_story.html.

CHAPTER 11

1. See Teri Kwal Gamble and Michael Gamble, *The Communication Playbook* (Thousand Oaks, CA: SAGE, 2020).

2. See John McCrone, *The Ape That Spoke: Language and the Evolution of the Human Mind* (New York: Marroni, 1991).

3. See, for example, "12 Words That Have Taken on Completely Different Meanings Thanks to the Internet," *The Huffington Post,* December 6, 2017, https://www.huffingtonpost.com/2014/12/01/

words-with-new-meanings-internet_n_5804736.html.

4. Richard Breslin and Tomoko Yoshida, *Intercultural Communication Training: An Introduction* (Thousand Oaks, CA: SAGE, 1994).

5. Larry A. Samovar, Richard E. Porter, and Edwin R. McDaniel, *Communication Between Cultures*, 7th ed. (Boston, MA: Wadsworth, 2010).

6. Larry A. Samovar and Richard E. Porter, *Communication Between Cultures*, 1st ed. (Belmont, CA: Wordsworth, 1991), 152.

7. See, for example, R. S. Zaharna, "Bridging Cultural Differences: American Public Relations Practices and Arab Communication Patterns," *Public Relations Review* 21 (1995): 241–255.

8. Christopher Engholm, *When Business East Meets Business West* (New York: Wiley, 1991), 106.

9. See, for example, R. L. De Mente, *Japan Unmasked: The Character and Culture of the Japanese* (Tokyo: Tuttle, 2005), 179.

10. M. Hecht, M. S. Collier, and S. Ribeau, *African American Communication: Ethnic Identity and Cultural Interpretation* (Thousand Oaks, CA: SAGE, 1993).

11. Sandra E. Garcia, "Brokaw Apologizes for Comments About Hispanics," *New York Times*, January 29, 2019, B3.

12. See, for example, David Schuman and Dick Olufs, *Diversity on Campus* (Boston: Allyn & Bacon, 1995).

13. For a discussion of age discrimination in the workplace, see Marianne Lavelle, "On the Edge of Age Discrimination," *New York Times Magazine*, March 9, 1997, 66–69.

14. William B. Gudykunst, *Bridging Differences*, 4th ed. (Thousand Oaks, CA: SAGE, 2004).

15. Jesse Jackson, "Common Ground and Common Sense," *Vital Speeches of the Day*, August 1988, 649–653.

16. See James Geary, *I Is an Other: The Secret Life of Metaphor and How It Shapes the Way We See the World* (New York: Harper, 2011).

17. Chief Seattle, "The Indian's Night Promises to Be Dark," in *Indian Oratory: Famous Speeches by Noted Indian Chieftains*, ed. W. C. Vanderwerth (Norman: University of Oklahoma Press, 1971).

18. Wayne Dyer, *Everyday Wisdom*, rev. ed. (New York: Hay House, 2005).

19. Reprinted by arrangement with the heirs to the estate of Martin Luther King Jr., c/o Writers House as agent for the proprietor, New York, NY.

20. Kamala Harris, speech delivered in Oakland, CA., "I'm Running to Be President of the People, by the People, and for the People," January 27, 2019, http://www.4president.org/speeches/2020/kamala-harris2020announcement.htm.

21. W. J. Banach, "In Search of an Eloquent Thank You," *Vital Speeches of the Day*, October 1991, 63.

22. See "Melinda Gates: Creating a Brotherhood," *Duke Today*, May 12, 2013, http://today.duke.edu/2013/05/ gatestalk.

CHAPTER 12

1. R. Jay Magill Jr., *Sincerity* (New York: Norton, 2012); and Carmine Gallo, *Talk Like Ted: The Nine Public Speaking Secrets of the World's Top Minds* (New York: St. Martin's Press, 2016).

2. See, for example, Rebecca K. Ivic and Robert J. Green, "Developing Charismatic Delivery Through Transformational Presentations: Modeling the Persona of Steve Jobs," *Communication Teacher* 26, no. 2 (April 2012): 65–68.

3. Joseph Guarino, "Top 20 Speaking Quotes," *Institute of Public Speaking*, https://www.instituteofpublicspeaking.com/top-20-public-speaking-quotes/.

4. See "The Public Course: Is It Preparing Students

With Work Related Skills?" *Communication Education* 36 (1987): 131–137; and Andril Sedniev, *The Magic of Impromptu Speaking* (New York: Amazon, 2016).

5. Daniel Akst, "Say It as If You Mean It," *Wall Street Journal,* July 9, 2012, A12; and Armani Talks, "The Art of Impromptu Speaking," January 2, 2021, https://armanitalks.com/the-art-of-impromptu-speaking/.

6. David Smith, Paul Lewis, Josh Holder, and Frank Hulley-Jones, "The Teleprompter Test: Why Trump's Populism Is Not His Own," *The Guardian,* March 6, 2019, https://www.theguardian.com/world/ng-interactive/2019/mar/07/the-teleprompter-test-why-trumps-populism-is-often-scripted.

7. Chuck Todd and Carrie Dann, "Trump's Teleprompter Temperament Isn't the Message—What Comes Next Is," *NBC News,* August 6, 2019, https://www.nbcnews.com/politics/meet-the-press/trump-s-teleprompter-temperament-isn-t-message-what-comes-next-n1039551.

8. John Brandon, "Because 15 Second Videos Are Way Too Long: Byte App Reaches a Massive Audience," *Forbes,* February 4, 2020, https://www.forbes.com/sites/johnbbrandon/2020/02/04/because-15-second-videos-are-way-too-long-byte-app-reaches-a-massive-audience/?sh=11ede217672d.

9. T. E. Smith and A. B. Frymier, "Get 'Real': Does Practicing Speeches Before an Audience Improve Performance?" *Communication Quarterly* 54 (2006): 111–125.

10. These topics appeared in Michael Smerconish, "College Essay Questions Make for Spirited Conversations," *The Record,* December 25, 2013, A23.

CHAPTER 13

1. See, for example, M. Bowden, *Winning Body Language: Control the Conversation, Command Attention, and Convey the Right Message Without Saying a Word* (New York: McGraw-Hill, 2011).

2. Bert Decker, *You've Got to Be Believed to Be Heard* (New York: St. Martin's Press, 1992), 31; and Teri Gamble and Michael Gamble, *Nonverbal Messages Tell More: A Practical Guide to Nonverbal Communication* (New York: Routledge, 2017).

3. See Vernon B. Harper, "Walking the Walk: Understanding Nonverbal Communication Through Walking," *Communication Teacher* 18, no. 1 (January 2004): 17–19.

4. See Garr Reynolds, *The Naked Presenter* (Berkeley, CA: New Riders, 2011). For a more scholarly discussion of what happens when a speaker's body language is inconsistent with their words, see James B. Stiff and Gerald R. Miller, "Come to Think of It . . . Interrogative Probes, Deceptive Communication and Deception Detection," *Human Communication Research* 12 (1986): 339–357.

5. See, for example, Robert Rivlin and Karen Gravelle, *Deciphering the Senses: The Expanding World of Human Perception* (New York: Simon & Schuster, 1998), 98; A. Warfield, "Do You Speak Body Language?" *Training and Development* 55, no. 4 (2001): 60; Ray Birdwhistell, *Kinesics and Context* (Philadelphia: University of Pennsylvania Press, 1970); and Albert Mehrabian, *Silent Messages* (Belmont, CA: Wadsworth, 1971).

6. Burkhard Bilger, "Extreme Range: The Vocal Experiments of Roomful of Teeth," *The New Yorker,* February 8, 2019, 44–53.

7. Eugenia Cheng, "What Makes One Voice Shrill, Another Sweet?" *The*

Wall Street Journal, April 14–15, 2018, C2.

8. See, for example, Megan Gambino, "Ask an Expert: What Did Abraham Lincoln's Voice Sound Like?" *Smithsonian.com,* http://www.smithsonianmag.com/history/ask-an-expert-what-did-abraham-lincolns-voice-sound-like-13446201/.

9. Bert Decker, *You've Got to Be Believed to Be Heard* (New York: St. Martin's Press, 1992), 31.

10. For an interesting discussion of nonverbal cues, lying, and judgments of speaker credibility, see Paul Ekman, *Telling Lies* (New York: Norton, 1992).

11. Judith A. Hall, "Voice Tone and Persuasiveness," *Journal of Personality and Social Psychology* 38 (1980): 924–934.

12. Rosita Daskel Albert and Gayle L. Nelson, "Hispanic/Anglo-American Differences in Attributions to Paralinguistic Behavior," *International Journal of Intercultural Relations* 17 (1993): 19–40.

13. Larry A. Samovar, Richard E. Porter, Edwin R. McDaniel, and Carolyn S. Roy, *Communication Between Cultures,* 9th ed. (Boston: Cengage, 2017), 321.

14. Ibid.

15. Leon Fletcher, "Polishing Your Silent Languages," *The Toastmaster,* March 1990, 15.

16. Julie Beck, "The Secret Life of 'Um'" *The Atlantic,* December 10, 2017, https://www.theatlantic.com/science/archive/2017/12/the-secret-life-of-um/547961/.

17. Roberto Rey Agudo, "Everyone Has an Accent," *New York Times,* July 15, 2018, SR2.

18. Robert G. Harper, Arthur N. Wiens, and Joseph D. Matarazzo, *Nonverbal Communication: The State of the Art* (New York: Wiley, 1978), 164.

19. See A. Melinger and W. M. Levelt, "Gesture and the Communicative Intention of the Speaker," *Gesture* 4 (2004): 119–41, and James McGregor and Shelly Tan, "What to Do With Your Hands When Speaking in Public," *Washington Post,* November 17, 2015, https://www.washingtonpost.com/news/on-leader-ship/wp/2015/11/17/what-to-do-with-your-hands-when-speaking-in-public/?utm_term=.6b1a0a6e33d5.

20. See Nancy Henley, *Body Politics* (Englewood Cliffs, NJ: Prentice Hall, 1977).

21. Vanessa Friedman, "'Everything About You Must Say Power,'" *New York Times,* November 3, 2021, https://www.nytimes.com/2021/11/03/style/eric-adams-style.html?referringSource=articleShare.

22. Shelly Chiden, "Communication of Physical Attractiveness and Persuasion," *Journal of Personality and Social Psychology* 37 (1979): 1387–1397.

23. See Virginia P. Richmond, Derek R. Lange, and James C. McCroskey, "Teacher Immediacy and the Teacher–Student Relationship," In *Handbook of Instructional Communication: Rhetorical and Relational Perspectives,* eds. Timothy P. Mottet, Virginia P. Richmond, and James C. McCroskey (Boston: Allyn & Bacon, 2006), 167–193.

CHAPTER 14

1. Merrie Spaeth, "'Prop' Up Your Speaking Skills," *The Wall Street Journal,* July 1, 1996, A14.

2. Libby Cathey, Lauren King, and Stephanie Ebbs, "RNC 2020 Day Four: Trump Accepts Nomination From White House," ABC News, August 18, 2020, https://abcnews.go.com/Politics/rnc-2020-day-trump-accept-nomination-white-house/story?id=72577769.

3. Sophia Ankel, "The RNC Ended With Firework Display Over the

Washington Monument Spelling Out Trump," *Business Insider,* August 28, 2020, https://www.businessinsider.com/last-night-rnc-ends-with-trump-fireworks-over-washington-monument-2020-8.

4. Cara Giaimo, "The Spiky Blob Seen Round the World," *New York Times,* April 1, 2020, https://www.nytimes.com/2020/04/01/health/coronavirus-illustration-cdc.html.

5. See Richard E. Mayer, ed., *Multimedia Learning* (New York: Cambridge University Press, 2009); Dale Cyphert, "Power-Point and the Evolution of Electronic Evidence From the Contemporary Business Presentation," *American Communication Journal* 11, no. 2 (Summer 2009): 1–20; Dale Cyphert, "Presentation Technology in the Age of Electronic Eloquence: From Visual Aid to Visual Rhetoric," *Communication Education* 56, no. 2 (2007): 168–192; Alan L. Brown, *Power Pitches* (Chicago: Irwin, 1997); Virginia Johnson, "Picture-Perfect Presentations," *Training and Development Journal* 43 (1989): 45; Yukiko Inoue-Smith and Shuyan Wang (reviewing ed.), "College-Based Case Studies in Using PowerPoint Effectively," *Cogent Education* 3, no. 1 (2016), doi:10.1080/2331186X.2015.1127745,

https://www.tandfonline.com/doi/full/10.1080/2331186X.2015.1127745; "Pros and Cons of Digital Slide Presentations," https://edge.sagepub.com/sites/default/files/presentation_section_03_module01.pdf; and Nancy Duarte, *Data Story: Explain Data and Inspire Action Through Story* (Ideapress Publishing, 2019). Also see Amy Balliett, *Killer Visual Strategies* (New York: Wiley, 2020).

6. See Elena P. Zayas-Baya, "Instructional Media in the Total Language Picture," *International Journal of Instructional Media* 5 (1977–1978): 145–150.

7. See Garr Reyonds, *Presentation Zen,* 2nd ed. (Berkeley, CA: New Riders, 2012); "Presenting Effective Presentations With Visual Aids," United States Department of Labor, Occupational Safety and Health Administration (May 1996), http://www.rufwork.com/110/mats/oshaVisualAids.html; "Thriving in Academe: A Rationale for Visual Communication," National Education Association Advocate Online (December 2001); Donald R. Vogel, Gary W. Dickson, and John A. Lehman, "Persuasion and the Role of Visual Presentation Support: The UM/3M Study," commissioned by Visual Systems Division of 3M (1986).

8. Matt Stevens and Christina Caron, "Congressman Draws a (Loaded) Visual Aid, in Defense of Guns," *New York Times,* April 9, 2018, A11.

9. Todd T. Holm, "A Cheap and Easy Way to Mount Visual Aids," *The Forensic of Pi Kappa Delta* 96 (Summer 2011): 21–24.

10. See Tom Mucciolo, "Driving Data With Charts," *Speechwriter's Newsletter,* January 1, 1997, 6.

11. See, for example, Drew Skau, "11 Infographics About Infographics," February 18, 2013, http://www.scribblelive.com/blog/2013/02/18/11-infographics-about-infographics/; and Jennifer J. Otten, Karen Cheng, and Adam Drewnowski, "Infographics and Public Policy: Using Data Visualization to Convey Complex Information," *HealthAffairs* 34 (November 2015): 11, https://www.healthaffairs.org/doi/full/10.1377/hlthaff.2015.0642.

12. Taken from "APA Citation for PowerPoint Slides, https://library.purdueglobal.edu/writingcenter/apacitationforpowerpointslide.

13. Nicholas Kristof, "The Lawbreakers Trump Loves," *New York Times,* August 30, 2020, SR9.

14. See Kiera Abbomonte, "The Best Presentation Software in 2021,"

Zapier, April 29, 2021, https://zapier.com/blog/best-powerpoint-alternatives/. For background, also see R. Larson, "Enhancing the Recall of Presented Material," *Computers and Education* 53, no. 4 (2009): 1278–1284; Nancy Duarte, *Slideology: The Art and Science of Creating Great Presentations* (Sebastopol, CA: O'Reilly, 2008); and Tom Mucciolo and Rich Mucciolo, *Purpose, Movement, Color: A Strategy for Effective Presentations* (New York: MediaNet, 1994).

15. Pinker is quoted in Ian Parker, "Absolute PowerPoint," *The New Yorker:* May 20, 2001, https://www.newyorker.com/magazine/2001/05/28/absolute-powerpoint.

16. See, for example, D. D. Booher, *Speak With Confidence: Powerful Presentations That Inform, Inspire, and Persuade* (New York: McGraw-Hill, 2003); and Samuel T. Moulton, Selen Turkay, and Stephen M. Kosslyn, "Does a Presentation's Medium Affect Its Message? PowerPoint, Prezi and Oral Presentations," *PLOS/One,* July 5, 2017, https://journals.plos.org/plosone/article?id=10.1371/journal.pone.0178774.

17. Garr Reynolds, *Presentation Zen: Simple Ideas on Presentation and Delivery,* 2nd ed. (Berkeley, CA: Riders Press, 2012).

18. L. Zuckerman, "Words Go Right to the Brain, but Can They Stir the Heart?" *New York Times,* April 17, 1999, A17–A19.

19. See Dale Cypert, "The Problem of PowerPoint: Visual Aid or Visual Rhetoric?" *Business Communication Quarterly* (March 2004): 80–84; June Kronholz, "PowerPoint Goes to School," *The Wall Street Journal,* November 12, 2002, B1, B6; and Rodney M. Schmaltz and Richard Enstrom, "Death to Weak PowerPoint: Strategies to Create Effective Visual Presentations," *Frontiers in Psychology* 5 (2014): 1138.

20. See Virginia Johnson, "Picture Perfect Presentations," *The Toastmaster,* February 1990, 7; Gabrielle Reed, "The Scientific Use of Color in Presentation Design," *Ethos3,* August 1, 2016, https://www.ethos3.com/2016/08/the-scientific-use-of-color-in-presentation-design/.

CHAPTER 15

1. Elizabeth Dwoskin, "Misinformation on Facebook Got Six Times More Clicks Than Factual News During the 2020 Election, Study Says," *Washington Post,* September 4, 2021, https://www.washingtonpost.com/technology/2021/09/03/facebook-misinformation-nyu-study/.

2. "14 Point Criteria for Defining the Value of Information," *IndraStra,* July 26, 2017, https://medium.com/indrastra/14-point-criteria-for-defining-the-value-of-information-voi-5d26bfbfa74f; Asha Saxena, "What Is Data Value, and Should It Be Viewed as a Corporate Asset?" *Dataversity,* March 18, 2019, https://www.dataversity.net/what-is-data-value-and-should-it-be-viewed-as-a-corporate-asset/.

3. See Francis Cairncross, "The Roots of Revolution and the Trendspotter's Guide to New Communications," in Erik P. Bucy, *Living in the Information Age: A New Media Reader* (Stamford, CT: Wadsworth/Thomson Learning, 2002), 3–10.

4. Daniel Pink, *A Whole New Mind: Moving From the Information Age to the Conceptual Age* (New York: Riverhead Books, 2005); Garr Reynolds, *Presentation Zen* (New York: New Ridges Press, 2008); and Ben Walker and Hilary Rasmussen, ". . . and Finally Examining Some Implications": Misuse of Evidence in Informative Speaking," *National Forensic Journal* 33, no. 1 (Summer 2015): 5–13, http://www.nationalforensicjournal.org/

uploads/9/1/9/3/91938460/nfj_volume_33_issue_1_summer_2015.pdf.

5. Richard Saul Wurman, *Information Anxiety 2.* Indianapolis: Que, 2000; and Peter Landau, "Save Yourself: 7 Ways to Prevent Information Overload," July 3, 2019, https://www.project-manager.com/blog/prevent-information-overload.

6. The 2018 film *On the Basis of Sex* provides an overview of Ginsburg's role in bringing a groundbreaking case before the U.S. Court of Appeals that began the process of overturning a century of gender discrimination.

7. Jeffrey Bosworth, "Hunting for Hope in Modern America," *Vital Speeches of the Day,* October 2013, 332.

8. This speech was developed as a group activity in a required speech class at the New York Institute of Technology in 2021.

CHAPTER 16

1. Robert B. Cialdini, *Influence, New and Expanded: The Psychology of Persuasion* (New York: Harper Business, 2021).

2. See, for example, Gerald R. Miller, "On Being Persuaded: Some Basic Distinctions," in *The Persuasive Handbook: Developments in Theory and Practice,* eds. James Price Dillard and Michael Pfau (Thousand Oaks, CA: SAGE, 2002), 3–16; and P. Brinol, D. D. Rucker, and R. E. Petty, "Naïve Theories About Persuasion: Implications for Information Processing and Consumer Attitude Change," *International Journal of Advertising: The Review of Marketing Communications* 34 (2015): 85–105.

3. See R. Wilson, "Fury Fuels the Modern Climate in US," *The Hill,* January 15, 2019, http://thehill.com/homenews/state-watch/351432-fury-fuels-the-modern-political-climate-in-us, and Herbert W. Simons and Jean G. Jones, *Persuasion in Society,* 2nd ed. (New York: Routledge, 2011); Jennifer Mercieca, "A Field Guide to Trump's Dangerous Rhetoric," *The Conversation,* June 19, 2020, https://theconversation.com/a-field-guide-to-trumps-dangerous-rhetoric-139531; and Daniel L. Byman, "How Hateful Rhetoric Connects to Real World Violence," *Brookings,* April 9, 2021, https://www.brookings.edu/blog/order-from-chaos/2021/04/09/how-hateful-rhetoric-connects-to-real-world-violence/.

4. See, for example, Richard M. Perloff, *The Dynamics of Persuasion: Communication and Attitudes in the 21st Century,* 4th ed. (New York: Routledge, 2010); and Robert Cialdini, *Pre-suasion: A Revolutionary Way to Influence and Persuade* (New York: Simon & Schuster, 2018).

5. A framework for understanding both attitudes and beliefs is offered by Martin Fishbein and Icek Ajzen, *Belief, Attitude, Intention and Behavior: An Introduction to Theory and Research* (Reading, MA: Addison-Wesley, 1975).

6. See, for example, "Most in U.S. Say Americans Are Divided on Important Values," Gallup.com, December 14, 2012, http://www.gallup.com/poll/159257/say-americans-divided-important-values.aspx; and "Social Values: Public Values Intangible Assets More Than Material Possessions," *Gallup Report* (March/April 1989): 35–44.

7. Chad Day, "Americans Have Shifted Dramatically on What Values Matter Most," *Wall Street Journal,* https://www.wsj.com/articles/americans-have-shifted-dramatically-on-what-values-matter-most-11566738001, August 25, 2019.

8. See Wallace Folderingham, *Perspectives on Persuasion* (Boston: Allyn & Bacon, 1966), p. 33; and James Price Dillard,

"Persuasion Past and Present: Attitudes Aren't What They Used to Be," *Communication Monographs*, 60, no. 1 (March 1993): 90–97.

9. See, for example, M. Sherif, C. Sherif, and R. Nebergall, *Attitude and Attitude Change: The Social Judgment-Involvement Approach* (Philadelphia: Saunders, 1965); and S. W. Littlejohn and K. A. Foss, *Theories of Human Communication* (Long Grove, IL: Waveland Press, 2017).

10. See Martha Cooper, *Analyzing Public Discourse* (Prospect Heights, IL: Waveland, 1989), 46; and Douglas Walton, *Burden of Proof, Presumption and Argumentation* (New York: Cambridge University Press, 2014).

11. Anthony Pratkanis and Elliot Aronson, *Age of Propaganda* (New York: Holt, 2001); and Joel E. Dismdale, *Dark Persuasion: A History of Brainwashing From Pavlov to Social Media* (New Haven: Yale University Press, 2021).

CHAPTER 17

1. Jessica Roy, "How to Convince Someone to Get the Vaccine," *Los Angeles Times*, May 17, 2021, https://www.latimes.com/science/story/2021-05-17/tips-how-to-convince-someone-to-get-vaccinated.

2. Jon Marcus, "The Pandemic Is Speeding Up the Mass Disappearance of Men From College," *The Hechinger Report*, January 19, 2021, https://hechingerreport.org/the-pandemic-is-speeding-up-the-mass-disappearance-of-men-from-college/.

3. See ProCon.Org: Understand the Issues, Understand Each Other, https://www.procon.org/debate-topics.php.

4. See, for example, John A. Banas and Stephen A. Rains, "A Meta-Analysis of Research on Inoculation Theory," *Communication Monographs* 77 (2010): 282–311.

5. Robert Cialdini, *Pre-Suasion: A Revolutionary Way to Influence and Persuade* (New York: Simon & Schuster, 2016), 4.

6. See R. E. Petty and J. Cacioppo, "The Elaboration Likelihood Model of Persuasion," in L. Berkowitz, ed., *Advances in Experimental Social Psychology* 19 (New York: Academic Press, 1986), 123–205; R. E. Petty and J. Cacioppo, "The Effects of Involvement on Responses to Argument Quantity and Quality: Central and Peripheral Routes to Persuasion," *Journal of Personality and Social Psychology* 46 (1984): 69–81; R. E. Petty and J. Cacioppo, *Communication and Persuasion: Central and Peripheral Routes to Attitude Change* (New York: Springer-Verlag, 1986); and J. Cooper, S. F. Blackman, and K. T. Keller, *The Science of Attitudes* (New York: Routledge, 2016).

7. See John C. Reinard, "The Empirical Study of the Persuasive Effects of Evidence: The Status After Fifty Years of Research," *Human Communication Research* 15 (1988): 3–59.

8. See Joe Kennedy II, U.S. Representative (D-MA), "We Choose Both. We Fight for Both," *Vital Speeches of the Day*, no. 3 (March 2018): 68–69.

9. See Buzz Bissinger, "Why College Football Should Be Banned," *Wall Street Journal*, May 5–6, 2012, C3.

10. See, for example, Nancy M. Cavender and Howard Kahane, *Logic and Contemporary Rhetoric: The Use of Reason in Everyday Life*, 11th ed. (Belmont, CA: Wadsworth, 2010).

11. Faye Wattleton, "Sacred Rights: Preserving Reproductive Freedom for Women," in *Contemporary American Speeches*, 7th ed., eds. Richard L. Johannesen, R. R. Allen, and Wil A. Linkugel (Dubuque, IA: Kendall Hunt, 1992), 269–273.

12. See Andrew Weil, "Don't Let Chaos Get You Down,"

Newsweek, November 7 and 14, 2011, 9.

13. See Abraham H. Maslow, *Motivation and Personality,* 2nd ed. (New York: Harper & Row, 1970).

14. See F. J. Boster and P. Mongeau, "Fear Arousing Persuasive Messages," in *Communication Yearbook,* ed. R. N. Bostrom (Beverly Hills, CA: SAGE, 1984), 330–375; and Shoba Screenavasin and Linda E. Weinberger, "Fear Appeals: An Approach to Change Our Attitudes and Behavior," *Psychology Today,* September 18, 2018, https://www.psychologytoday.com/us/blog/emotional-nourishment/201809/fear-appeals.

15. See, for example, Frank Rich, "Decision 2004: Fear Fatigue vs. Sheer Fatigue," *New York Times,* October 31, 2004, sec. 2, 1, 34.

CHAPTER 18

1. See, for example, Ryan Luke, "How to Show Off Problem Solving Skills in an Interview," *Ladders,* July 11, 2021, https://www.theladders.com/career-advice/how-to-show-off-problem-solving-skills-in-an-interview.

2. D. Johnson and F. Johnson, *Joining Together: Group Theory and Group Skills,* 12th ed. (Boston: Pearson, 2016).

3. See, for example, Gloria J. Galanes and Katherine Adams, *Effective Group Discussion: Theory and Practice,* 15th ed. (New York: McGraw-Hill, 2019).

4. Charles Redding, *Communication Within the Organization* (New York: Industrial Communication Council, 1972).

5. See B. Tuchman, "Developmental Sequence in Small Groups," *Psychological Bulletin* 63 (1965): 384–399; and S. A. Wheelen and J. M. Hockberger, "Validation Studies of the Group Development Questionnaire," *Small Group Research* 27, no. 1 (1996): 143–170.

6. See, for example, J. Keyton, "Group Termination: Completing the Study of Group Development," *Small Group Research* 24 (1999): 84–100.

7. See Kenneth Benne and Paul Sheats, "Functional Roles of Group Members," *Journal of Social Issues* 4 (1948): 41–49.

8. See Teri Gamble and Michael Gamble, *Leading With Communication* (Thousand Oaks, CA: SAGE, 2013); Craig E. Johnson and Michael Z. Hackman, *Leadership: A Communication Perspective,* 7th ed. (Long Grove, IL: Waveland, 2018); and Kevin Barge, "Leadership as Medium: A Leaderless Group Discussion Model," *Communication*

Quarterly 37, no. 4 (Fall 1989): 237–247.

9. Dan Frosh and Melanie Evans, "Overwhelmed by Covid-19 Patients, Alaska's Doctors Make Life and Death Decisions," *Wall Street Journal,* October 3, 2021.

10. For example, see Chris Westfall, "4 Leadership Strategies for Making Better Decisions in Your Career," *Forbes,* September 10, 2019, https://www.forbes.com/sites/chriswestfall/2019/09/10/4-leadership-strategies-making-better-decisions-career-decision-making/?sh=66f11aab77ab.

11. Johnson and Johnson, *Joining Together* (2016).

12. See John Dewey, *How We Think* (Boston: MA: Heath, 1910).

13. See Irving Janis, *Victims of Groupthink: A Psychological Study of Foreign Policy Decisions and Fiascos* (Boston: Houghton Mifflin, 1972).

14. Alex Osborn, *Applied Imagination* (New York: Scribner, 1957).

15. See Dain Evans, "How Zoom Became So Popular During Social Distancing," *CNBC.com,* April 4, 2020, https://www.cnbc.com/2020/04/03/how-zoom-rose-to-the-top-during-the-coronavirus-pandemic.html.

16. See S. K. Johnson, K. Bettenhausen, and E. Gibbons, "Realities of Working in Virtual Teams: Affective and Attitudinal Outcomes of Using Computer-Mediated Communication," *Small Group Research* 40 (2009): 623–649; and A. M Harding, M. S. Fuller, and R. M. Davison, "I Know I Can, but Can We? Culture and Efficiency Beliefs in Global Virtual Teams," *Small Group Research* 38 (2007): 130–155.

17. Betty Morris, "Seven Rules of Zoom Meeting Etiquette From the Pros," *Wall Street Journal,* July 12, 2020, https://www.wsj.com/articles/seven-rules-of-zoom-meeting-etiquette-from-the-pros-11594551601.

18. Clive Thompson, "Close Encounters," *Wired,* August 2008.

19. Laurie J. Flynn, "MySpace Mind-Set Finally Shows Up at the Office," *New York Times,* April 9, 2008, p. 7.

20. John Herrman, "Why Aren't We Talking About LinkedIn?" *New York Times,* August 8, 2019, https://www.nytimes.com/2019/08/08/style/linkedin-social-media.html.

21. Brad Stone, "At Social Site, Only the Business-like Need Apply," *New York Times,* June 18, pp. C1, C2.

22. Adam Bryant, "Views From the Top," *Wall Street Journal,* April 21, 2011, p. A11.

23. Matthew Parsons, "Second Life Targets Corporate Sector as TravelLockdown Bites," *Skift,* March 23, 2020, https://skift.com/2020/03/23/second-life-targets-corporate-sector-as-travel-lockdown-bites/.

24. Mark Tuton, "Going to the Virtual Office in Second Life," CNN.com. See also Matt Weinberger, "This Company Was 13 Years Early to Virtual Reality and It's Getting Ready to Try Again," http://www.businessinsider.com/second-life-is-still-around-and-getting-ready-to-conquer-virtual-reality-2015-3; and Jolene Buscemi, "Second Life Still Has Dedicated Users in 2020," *Mic,* February 16, 2020, https://www.mic.com/p/second-life-still-has-dedicated-users-in-2020-heres-what-keeps-them-sticking-around-18693758.

25. Laura Rich, "Tapping the Wisdom of the Crowd," *New York Times,* August 5, 2012, p. B8; and Pete Cardon and Bryan Marshall, "The Hype and Reality of Social Media Use for Work Collaboration and Teamwork," *International Journal of Business Communication* 52, no. 3 (May 2014): 273–293, https://www.researchgate.net/publication/277882285_The_Hype_and_Reality_of_Social_Media_Use_for_Work_Collaboration_and_Team_Communication.

26. David Gelles, "The Personal at Work Can Be a Disruptive Mix," *Financial Times,* April 20, 2011, p. 2.

27. Eileen Zimmerman, "Staying Professional in Virtual Meetings," *New York Times,* September 26, 2010, p. BU9; and J. Stepper, *Working Out Loud: For a Better Career and Life* (Farnborough, NH: Ikigai Press, 2015).

28. Joanne Lublin, "Video Comes to Board Meetings," *Wall Street Journal,* April 25, 2011, p. B6.

29. Caroline Winter, "Is the Vertical Pronoun Really Such a Capital Idea?" *New York Times Magazine,* August 3, 2008.

30. Andy Cotgreave, "Working With Artificial Intelligence—Teamwork Is Dreamwork," *Technology Magazine,* July 23, 2020, https://www.atspoke.com/blog/support/how-ai-is-transforming-workplace/.

31. Jessica Greene, 21 Ways AI Is Transforming the Workplace in 2019," *atspoke,* https://www.atspoke.com/blog/support/how-ai-is-transforming-workplace/; and Blair Pleasant, "The Future of Meetings—Using AI to Improve Team

Collaboration," *Business Insights and Ideas*, April 1, 2019, https://www.microsoft.com/en-us/microsoft-365/business-insights-ideas/resources/the-future-of-meetings-using-ai-to-improve-team-collaboration.

32. Chester S. Spell, "Artificial Intelligence and Teamwork," *Psychology Today*, March 20, 2019, https://www.psychologytoday.com/us/blog/team-spirit/201903/artificial-intelligence-and-teamwork.

33. Christopher Shea, "Altruism: Every Man for Himself," *Wall Street Journal*, Saturday/Sunday, May 19–20, 2012, C4.

CHAPTER 19

1. Elie Wiesel acceptance of the 1986 Nobel Peace Prize, *New York Times*, December 11, 1986, p. 8.

2. Commencement address of Jimmy Fallon delivered at Marjory Stoneman Douglas High School, June 4, 2018, http://time.com/5300396/jimmy-fallon-speech-stoneman-douglas-graduation/.

3. Keynote speech by Tim Cook, October 24, 2018, https://www.computerworld.com/article/3315623/complete-transcript-video-of-apple-ceo-tim-cooks-eu-privacy-speech.html.

4. https://www.computerworld.com/article/3315623/complete-transcript-video-of-apple-ceo-tim-cooks-eu-privacy-speech.html

5. Robert M. Kaplan and Gregory C. Pascoe, "Humorous Lectures and Humorous Examples: Some Effects Upon Comprehension and Retention," *Journal of Educational Psychology* 69 (1977): 61–65.

6. "Marvin Minsky Speaks," http://zhurnaly.com/cgi-bin/wiki/MarvinMinskySpeaks.

7. George W. Bush, 9/11 Commemorative Speech Delivered on September 11, 2021, https://www.cnn.com/2021/09/11/politics/transcript-george-w-bush-speech-09-11-2021/index.html.

8. Remarks penned by President Barack Obama to mark the passing of Muhammad Ali. See Arnie Seipel, "READ: President Obama's Remembrance of Muhammad Ali," *NPR Politics Newsletter*, June 4, 2016, https://www.npr.org/2016/06/04/480743833/read-president-obamas-remembrance-of-muhammad-ali.

CHAPTER 20

1. Eli Amdur, "How Workers Should Prepare for the World in 2050," *The Record*, May 23, 2008, pp. J1–J2; see also "Employers Still Seek Communication Skills in New Hires," *mba.com*, July 30, 2020, https://www.mba.com/information-and-news/research-and-data/employers-seek-communications-skills.

2. Mark Cenedella, *Ladders*, https://www.theladders.com/career-advice/29-questions-you-must-ask-in-2021-job-interviews, "29 Questions You Must Ask in 2021 Interviews," February 22, 2021.

3. Eli Amdur, "The Great All-American Cover Letter Challenge," *The Record*, September 12, 2010, pp. J1–J2.

4. See, for example, Alison Green, "How to Write a Great Cover Letter," *Ask a Manager.org*, May 20, 2018, https://www.askamanager.org/2018/05/how-to-write-a-great-cover-letter.html; and Lisa Vaas and Ladders Staff, "How to Write a Good Cover Letter," *Ladders*, October 20, 2020, https://www.theladders.com/career-advice/how-to-write-cover-letter.

5. Samantha Hawrylack, "Resumes Aren't Read by Humans. Here's How to Get Past the Bots," *Ladders*, April 9, 2021, https://www.theladders.com/career-advice/

resumes-arent-read-by-humans-heres-how-to-get-past-the-bots.

6. Allison Pohle, "How to Prep for Your First Job Search: A Two-Day Boot Camp," *The Wall Street Journal*, April 30, 2021, https://www.wsj.com/articles/how-to-prep-for-your-first-job-search-a-two-day-boot-camp-11619798399.

7. Eli Amdur, "On a Résumé, There's Nothing Like a Good Opening," *The Record*, January 27, 2008, pp. J1, J2. See also "How to Write an Opening Statement for Your Résumé," www.getting-hired.com, January 26, 2012.

8. Alex Janin, "How a Video Resume Can Get You Hired in the Covid-19 Job Market," *The Wall Street Journal*, August 20, 2021, https://www.wsj.com/articles/how-a-video-resume-can-get-you-hired-in-the-covid-19-job-market-11629457200.

9. For a discussion of online search techniques, see Cynthia Leshin, *Internet Investigations in Business Communication* (Saddle River, NJ: Prentice Hall, 1997); for more on personal websites and résumé effectiveness, also see "20 Personal Website Examples to Inspire Job Seekers," *Deputy*, August 29, 2018, https://www.deputy.com/blog/20-personal-website-examples-

to-inspire-job-seekers; and Kristi DePaul, "How to Get Your Resume Noticed (and Out of the Trash Bin)," *Harvard Business Review*, September 7, 2020, https://hbr.org/2020/09/how-to-get-your-resume-noticed-and-out-of-the-trash-bin.

10. Bryan Clark, "How to Answer Common Difficult Interview Questions," *New York Times*, March 13, 2020, https://www.nytimes.com/2020/03/13/smarter-living/how-to-answer-common-difficult-interview-questions.html?referringSource=articleShare.

11. "2020 Recruiter Nation Survey," https://www.jobvite.com/wp-content/uploads/2020/10/Jobvite-Recruiter-Nation-Report-Final.pdf.

12. Julie Weed, "How to Ace an Online Job Interview," *New York Times*, August 3, 2020, https://www.nytimes.com/2020/08/03/business/online-job-interview-tips.html?referringSource=articleShare.

13. Katherine Dill, "Gen Z Gets Career Advice, One TikTok at a Time," *The Wall Street Journal*, May 20, 2021, https://www.wsj.com/articles/gen-z-gets-career-advice-one-tiktok-at-a-time-11621526403.

14. Ibid.; and Matthew Tarpey, "Not Getting

Job Offers? Your Social Media Could Be the Reason," *CareerBuilder*, August 9, 2018, https://www.careerbuilder.com/advice/not-getting-job-offers-your-social-media-could-be-the-reason.

15. Arlene Hirsch, "Tell Me About Yourself Doesn't Mean 'Tell It All,'" *The Record*, November 28, 2004, pp. J1, J2; and Anthony DePalma, "Preparing for 'Tell Us About Yourself,'" *New York Times*, July 27, 2003, p. NJ1. See also Jen Doll, "Lessons Learned From 7 Botched Interviews," *New York Times*, December 7, 2018, p. B9.

16. Eli Amdur, "Train Yourself to Be a S.T.A.R. During the Job Interview," *The Record*, September 4, 2005, p. J1.

17. Sarah Skidore Sell, "Poll: Interview Questions Often Improper," *The Record*, November 3, 2017, p. 7L.

18. Paul Davidson, "'What's Your Salary?' A No-No in Interviews," *The Record*, May 1, 2017, p. 5A.

19. Monica Torres, "How to Answer the Salary Expectation Questions in a Job Interview," *HuffPost*, December 23, 2019, https://www.huffpost.com/entry/salary-expectations-question-job-interview_l_5dfa4ec2e4b0969b618ee923.

20. From David Kirby, "Selling Yourself: There Are Questions You Shouldn't

Answer," adapted from *New York Times*, January 30, 2001; see also Maddie Lloyd, "9 Illegal Interview Questions and How to Handle Them," *Zippia*, February 21, 2021, https://www.zippia.com/advice/illegal-interview-questions/.

21. Eli Amdur, "An Interview Is a Two-Way Deal, so Ask Questions," *The Record*, April 17, 2005, pp. J1, J2. See also Alison Green, "10 Impressive Questions to Ask in a Job Interview," *The Cut*, November 6, 2018, https://www.thecut.com/article/questions-to-ask-in-a-job-interview.html.

22. See *PR Newswire*, "New CareerBuilder Survey Looks at Best and Worst Colors to Wear to a Job Interview," November 21, 2013, https://press.careerbuilder.com/2013-11-20-New-CareerBuilder-Study-Looks-at-Best-and-Worst-Colors-to-Wear-in-a-Job-Interview; and Jennifer Calfas, "You Should Never Wear This Color to a Job Interview According to 2,000 Hiring Managers," *Money*, December 27, 2018, https://money.com/never-wear-color-job-interview/.

23. Shana Liebowitz, "21 Psychological Tricks That Will Help You Ace a Job Interview," *Ladders*, November 16, 2018, https://www.theladders.com/career-advice/21-

psychological-tricks-that-will-help-you-ace-a-job-interview.

24. Barbara Kiviat, "Résumé? Check. Nice Suit? Check. Webcam," *Time*, November 9, 2009, pp. 89–90; Jonnelle Marte, "Nailing the Interview," *The Wall Street Journal*, March 14, 2010, p. B4; and A-J Aronstein, "I Have Read Thousands of Resumes and I Have Some Advice," *New York Times*, April 17, 2021, https://www.nytimes.com/2021/04/17/opinion/resume-advice.html?referringSource=articleShare.

25. Ibid.

26. Eli Amdur, "Be the Person Companies Will Want to Hire," *The Record*, October 24, 2004, pp. J1, J2; "Initial Minutes of Job Interview Are Critical," *USA Today*, January 1, 2000, 8.

27. See, for example, Malcolm Gladwell, "What Do Job Interviews Really Tell Us?" *New Yorker*, May 29, 2000, 84. See also Susannah Snyder, "How to Ace a Job Interview: What to Wear, What to Bring and Other Tips," *U.S. News*, January 16, 2019, https://money.usnews.com/money/careers/interviewing/articles/how-to-ace-a-job-interview.

28. See Allison Doyle, "How to Write an Interview Thank You Letter," thebalance.com, updated May 16, 2016, http://

jobsearch.about.com/b/2013/07/31/thank-you-letter-after-interview.htm; and Joann S. Lublin, "Notes to Interviewers Should Go Beyond a Simple Thank You," *The Wall Street Journal*, February 5, 2008, p. B1.

29. Robert Sutton and Ben Wigert, "More Harm Than Good: The Truth About Performance Reviews," *Gallup.com*, May 6, 2019, https://www.gallup.com/workplace/249332/harm-good-truth-performance-reviews.aspx.

30. David Shapiro Jr., "Finding Niches for Authors' Pitches," *The Wall Street Journal*, July 1, 2013, p. A21.

CHAPTER 21

1. Rob Biesenbach, *Unleash the Power of Storytelling: Win Hearts, Change Minds, Get Results* (Evanston, IL: Eastlawn Media, 2018).

2. T. T. Barker and K. Gower, "Strategic Application of Storytelling in Organizations," *Journal of Business Communication* 4, no. 73 (2010): 295–312. See also Erika Frye, "Why Storytelling Became the Hot New Skill in Business," *Fortune*, October 2, 1018, http://fortune.com/2018/10/01/storytelling-skill-business/.

3. See Bill George, Peter Sims, Andrew N. McLean, and Diana Mayer, "Discovering Your Authentic Leadership," *Harvard Business Review,* February 2007, www.HBR.org; Kimberly A. Whitler, "Three Reasons Why Storytelling Should Be a Priority for Marketers," *Forbes,* July 14, 2018, https://www.forbes.com/sites/kimberlywhitler/2018/07/14/3-reasons-why-storytelling-should-be-a-priority-for-marketers/#4e60c1856758.

4. Carmine Gallo, "Tom Brady's Speeches Are Going Viral. Here's What They Can Teach You About Public Speaking," Inc.com, February 11, 2021, https://www.inc.com/carmine-gallo/tom-bradys-speeches-are-going-viral-heres-what-they-can-teach-you-about-public-speaking.html,

5. K. B. Boal and P. I. Schultz, "Storytelling, Time, and Evolution: The Role of Strategic Leadership in Complex Adaptive Systems," *Leadership Quarterly* 18, no. 4 (2007): 411–428; and "The Art of Storytelling: Researchers Explore Why We Relate to Characters," *ScienceDaily,* September 13, 2018, www.sciencedaily.com/releases/2018/09/180913113822.htm.

6. T. Mohan, H. McGregor, S. Saunders, and R. Archee, *Communicating as Professionals* (Melbourne: Thomson, 2008).

7. Richard Maxell and Robert Dickman, *The Elements of Persuasion* (New York: HarperCollins, 2007), 5.

8. See, for example, "Today's Debate: Digital Harassment," *USA Today,* October 24, 2013, 8A.

9. C. M. Phoel, "Leading Words: How to Use Stories to Change Minds and Ignite Action," *Harvard Management Communication Letter* 3, no. 2 (Spring 2006): 3–5.

10. M. K. Smith, "Peter Senge and the Learning Organization," *Encyclopedia of Informal Education* (2001), http://infed.org/mobi/petersenge-and-the-learning-organization/.

11. Hank Stuever, "The 'Game of Thrones' Finale, While Lacking, Goes Out on an Important Note: Stories Matter," *Washington Post,* May 20, 2019, https://www.washingtonpost.com/entertainment/tv/the-game-of-thrones-finale-while-lacking-goes-out-on-an-important-note-.

12. Kelly Ragan, "Thousands Gather at Memorial for Colorado School Shooting Victim Kendrick Castillo," *Colorodian,* May 15, 2019, https://www.coloradoan.

com/story/news/education/2019/05/15/thousands-gather-memorial-colorado-school-shooting-victim-kendrick-castillo-stem-school/3686827002/.

13. David Cohen, "Trump on January 6th Insurrection: These Were Great People," *Politico,* July 11, 2021, https://www.politico.com/news/2021/07/11/trump-jan-6-insurrection-these-were-great-people-499165.

14. Rosie Gray, "Trump Defends White Nationalist Protestors: 'Some Very Fine People on Both Sides,'" *The Atlantic,* August 15, 2017, https://www.theatlantic.com/politics/archive/2017/08/trump-defends-white-nationalist-protesters-some-very-fine-people-on-both-sides/537012/.

15. Steven Pinker, *The Stuff of Thought: Language as a Window Into Human Nature* (New York: Viking, 2007).

16. See, for example, Chris Anderson, "How to Give a Killer Presentation," *Harvard Business Review,* June 2013, https://hbr.org/2013/06/how-to-give-a-killer-presentation.

17. Stephen Denning, *The Secret Language of Leadership* (San Francisco: Jossey-Bass, 2007); also see Stephen Denning,

The Leader's Guide to Storytelling: Mastering the Art and Discipline of Business Narrative (San Francisco: Jossey-Bass, 2011).

18. See, for example, G. Lakoff, "Framing the Dems," *American Prospect,* August 1, 2003; and G. Lakoff and M. Johnson, *Metaphors We Live By* (Chicago: University of Chicago Press, 1980).

19. Martin Luther King Jr., "I Have a Dream," presented at Lincoln Memorial in Washington, DC, August 28, 1963. Reprinted by arrangement with the Heirs to the Estate of Martin Luther King Jr., c/o Writers House as agent for the proprietor New York, NY.

20. NBC News, "Lying Survey Results at a Glance," updated July 11, 2006, https://www.nbcnews.com/id/13819955/ns/us_news-life/t/lying-survey-results-glance/.

21. Marshall Ganz, "Leading Change: Leadership, Organization, and Social Movements, in *Handbook of Leadership Theory and Practice,* eds. Nitin Nohria and Rakesh Khurana (Boston: Harvard Business Press, 2010), 527–568.

CHAPTER 22

1. See Jean Dimeo, "Study: Students Learn More in Flipped Classroom,"

Inside Higher Ed, September 27, 2017, https://www.insidehighered.com/digital-learning/insights/2017/09/27/study-students-learn-more-flipped-classroom.

CHAPTER 23

1. Jennifer Nason, "The Zoom Revolution Empowers Women to Speak Up," *The Wall Street Journal,* July 2, 2021, https://www.wsj.com/articles/the-zoom-revolution-empowers-women-to-speak-up-11625260956.

2. Matt Abrahams, "10 Tips for Giving Effective Virtual Presentations," *Stamford Business,* September 26, 2016, https://www.gsb.stanford.edu/insights/10-tips-giving-effective-virtual-presentations.

3. Brian X. Chen, "The Dos and Don'ts of Online Video Meetings," *New York Times,* March 25, 2020, https://www.nytimes.com/2020/03/25/technology/personaltech/online-video-meetings-etiquette-virus.html?referringSource=articleShare.

4. Janine Barchas, "How to Curate Your Zoom Backdrop and Why You Should," *The Chronicle of Higher Education,* August 12, 2020, https://www.chronicle.com/article/how-to-curate-your-

zoom-backdrop-and-why-you-should?cid=gen_sign_in.

5. For more information on narrative infographics, see "Teaching Storytelling Through Narrative Infographics," on Bovee and Thill's Business Communication blog, http://blog.business-communicationnetwork.com/.

6. "2021 Podcast Stats and Facts," April 2021, https://www.podcastinsights.com/podcast-statistics/.

7. "Learn How to Start a Podcast," *Podcast Insights,* August 26, 2021, https://www.podcastinsights.com/start-a-podcast/.

8. See Kristen Meinzer, *So You Want to Start a Podcast* (New York: William Morrow, 2019); and Glen Weldon, *NPR's Podcast Start Up Guide* (New York: Ten Speed Press, 2021).

CHAPTER 24

1. Lizzie Widdicombe, "Press Secretary Jen Psaki is Good at Mending Fences. Just Don't Call Her Nice," *Vogue,* August 9, 2021, https://www.vogue.com/article/press-secretary-jen-psaki-is-good-at-mending-fences.

2. Jim Beckerman, "Monopoly for Cheaters," *The Record*, March 24, 2019, pp. 1BL, 2BL.

INDEX